HOW BRIEF
A CANDLE

HOW BRIEF A CANDLE

MODERN MAN IN THE INSISTENT DIALECTIC

by

Fr. John P. Coony

*"If you continue in my word, you shall
be my disciples indeed. You shall know the
truth and the truth shall make you free."*
—John 8:31-32

PRO FRATRIBUS PRESS
Cochiti Lake, New Mexico 87041

PRO FRATRIBUS PRESS
P.O. Box 158
Cochiti Lake, New Mexico 87041

1987

DEDICATION

Dedicated to Our Lady of Victories and to her loving daughter Frances, my partner in many adventures.

ABOUT THE COVER

The original artwork for the cover was done by Nora Botzaki of Athens, Greece. It depicts symbolically the concept of the insistent dialectic—the cleavage between man's animality and his spirituality. The earthly man is attracted primarily to the physical aspects of life, which tend toward gratification of our passions. He is represented by the somewhat brutal face turned away from the light.

The spiritual man is shown as a shadow of man's being—a recognition that man has aspirations as part of his less obvious drives. This shadow is turned always toward the light to counteract the material drives and to bring man into the fullness of his humanity. It is the urging of man's soul and his conscience, the fruit of a true maturity.

In the words of St. Augustine, "Late have I loved You, O Beauty ever ancient. Late have I loved You. You were within me, but I was outside and it was there that I searched for You."

—*Confessions* of Saint Augustine

TABLE OF CONTENTS

vii

Tables

Figures

PREFACE

We live in a fascinating period of history—one of those zones which comes along every five centuries or so in which a severe change in direction seems about to be forced upon the world's people. Everything comes into question. Decisions of great importance seem to be held in abeyance in a suspense of uncertainty. There is an all-pervading air of tension and disquiet embracing morals, religion, economics, politics and, literally, fates of empires. They are periods foreshadowing great upheavals in social structure and relationships.

Friedrich Nietzsche was one of the earliest to foresee the crisis in civilization of this transitional period coming about in the closing decades of the twentieth century. With his dictum of the "Death of God," he also projected the rise of nihilism which would eventually surge into the tremendous vacuum left by the gradual but general acceptance of the death of God by the mass of the people in the West. He said in his notes written about 1890, from which the posthumous *The Will to Power* was produced:

> What I relate is the history of the next two centuries. I describe what is coming, what can no longer come differently: the advent of nihilism . . .our whole European culture is moving for some time now with a tortured tension that is growing from decade to decade as toward a catastrophe; restlessly, violently, headlong, like a river that wants to reach its end, that no longer reflects and is afraid to reflect.

Nietzsche's words were intented to be, and are, prophetic in application to our own times although we are not yet half way to the ultimate term of his prediction. For it is the whole cultural system in the West which seems to be rushing headlong, "wanting to come to its end, no longer reflecting, afraid to reflect." One wonders particularly at the observation "afraid to reflect." How could Nietzsche have sensed that aspect of our current troubled times and our turbulent world so potentially rich and fruitful in human development which seems deliberately tearing itself to pieces, afraid to pause and to reflect as though driven by some mad, lemming-like impulse to self-destruction.

Why the fear? Is it a type of guilt fixation leading to a universal death wish—if God is dead, how can we live? An anxiety complex—is God dead, or is God alive as always—and we merely dead to Him, and He to us, because of our fears and rejection? Are we locked into a pattern that we can't bear to break, yet fear the certain outcome? Are we in a worldwide situation much like C. P. Snow saw for the British in his essay *Two Cultures and the Scientific Revolution?*

> A good many of them [the Venetians] were tough-minded, realistic, patriotic men. They knew, just as clearly as we know, that the current of history had begun to flow past them. Many of them gave their minds to working out ways to keep going. It would have meant breaking the pattern into which they had crystallized. They were fond of the pattern, just as we are fond of ours. They never found the will to break it.

But there are other scenarios. The one which this writer chooses to focus on as an alternative possibility has also been predicted. The script writer this time is the distinguished British historian, the late Arnold J. Toynbee. Toynbee, in his approach to history, has consistently rejected giving the decisive role to the materialistic, the pragmatic, or the coldly calculating in establishing the course of history. He saw the decisive role in the esprit of the peoples themselves, in a psychic force which determines their ability to rise to challenges presented by the environment including changes in cultural modes of life. In 1952, in an address at the University of Edinburgh, he consigned the twentieth century to technology but assigned the twenty-first to religion. Earlier, in 1947, in his work *Encounter Between Civilizations,* he had written:

> In our air age the locus of the center of gravity of human affairs may be determined not by physical but by human geography; not by the lay-out of oceans and seas, steppes and deserts, rivers and mountain ranges, passes and straits, but by the distribution of human numbers, energy, ability, skill and character. And among these human factors, the weight of numbers, may eventually come to count for more than

its influence in the past...A tiny sophisticated ruling minority perched on the back of a neolithic peasantry, as Sinbad the sailor was ridden by the old man
of the sea. The neolithic peasantry is the last and
mightiest sleeper, before herself, who the West has
waked.

The rousing of this passively industrious mass of
humanity has been a slow business. Athens and Florence each flashed her brief candle in the sleeper's
drowsy eyes, but each time he just turned onto his
side and sank to sleep again. It was left for modern
England to urbanize the peasantry with sufficient
energy on a large enough scale to set the movement
traveling round the circumference of the earth...
Their wakening is now only a matter of time, and,
when it has been accomplished, numbers will begin
to tell.

The brief candles of Athens and Florence—the ideas of individuals concerning individual human dignity in these cultures
in Toynbee's view did not involve enough illumination in proportion to the world's problems to carry through the ensuing darkness. With the maturing of the Industrial Revolution throughout
the world, Toynbee saw the opportunity to spread the ideas
of the dignity of man among the masses of men. He saw a
new era of recognition of man's interdependence and mutual
responsibility. From that recognition, Toynbee saw emerging a
world community of free men developing the resources of the
earth. In the fruitful decade following World War II these ideas
seemed clearly attainable. Since then, the vision grows dim—
the individual flames flicker fitfully.

Nietzsche's and Toynbee's views are antithetical in their final
outcome although they are not necessarily so at this transitional
stage of history. Yet, the transition period is critical as to which
way the course of history will flow. Which peoples and which
principles or values, will catch fire and flame in the oncoming
age. The chief fascination of living in a transition period in
the Toynbee scenario, is the uncertainty, even amid the awareness that it is the attitudes, and resoluteness in these attitudes,
of individuals themselves—the lights of individual candles—
which will largely govern the outcome.

The fundamental purpose of this book is to develop a base
for a sociology of morals using the current world picture as
the frame of reference. Any sociologist who wanders off into

the realm of the sociology of morals is treading on ground which few have ventured into deliberately, and on which fewer have found firm footing. There is a distinct lack of enthusiasm to probe deeply into what has to be the central issue: Is there a legitimate body of moral obligation binding on individuals and society, which defines norms by which they must be guided? And if so, how is it legitimatized? It is a proper field of sociological investigation. The insistent dialectic centers on that issue. If man is the self-sufficient, independent being of Nietzsche, there is, as Nietzsche said, in the person of Zarathustra, "No being above him to which he owes anything" and all he owes himself is his own satisfaction as he sees it. If that answer is correct, there can be no legitimate basis for any code of morality binding on individuals generally, though a base can be temporarily imposed by force—Nietzsche's ultimate solution—the supermen.

The difficulty with the concept of a sociology of morality in terms of the value-free approach so prized by scientists, is that the subject matter is totally value-oriented. Further, certain concessions must be made in advance concerning the nature of that unique being, man; for instance, that he is incurably normative which is to say he insists on establishing standards for everything, including himself. In spite of the tireless efforts of the behaviorists to convince him he is only a biologic form which should respond to sense stimuli like any other well behaved and predictable animal, he insists he is different. He insists that his self-consciousness of himself requires him to live so that he can tolerate the image of himself as he sees it. While there are variations in the pattern, there is a general agreement in a substantial core area as to how a human being ought to live to be fully human.

Morality, then, is not, nor can ever be, a neatly bound body of observed behavioral response to sense stimuli or a scientifically established code. Morality is a complex matrix of value judgments concerning what constitutes the good, the beautiful, the dignified, the sacred, the lovable; all inter-tied with ideas of the deity, the infinite, the all-holy, the all-knowing, the compassionate and yielding ideas of justice, responsibility, duty, generosity, heroism, happiness and immortality. These, in turn, are contrasted with, and evaluated by, each man under stress of the drives of the passions, with selfishness, pain, ugliness and the recognized existence of evil in the world. The conflict which arises because of man's relative independence and freedom of choice among all these value judgments and under the guidance of his emotions and intellect, provides a matrix of almost infinite complexity in variations on each theme. That matrix comprises the subject matter which must be assessed. It is as futile to approach it, as value-free as to approach statistics from the viewpoint of love. A posture of scientific distance from the object of investigation cannot be maintained. The subject matter is value laden and the investigator necessarily views this field from a point within the matrix.

The mass of the moral matrix revolves about the polar question of the deity. The historic source of morality and its support throughout the centuries has been that somehow, somewhere, but inevitably, there is retribution and recompense for evil and good. The denial of that source has been of short duration. In terms of human history, man in the modern world is a brief candle having about the same time span as Athens and Florence, but the problems demanding illumination are far more numerous and opaque. The closing decades of this century are presenting moral problems of unprecedented complexity and intensity at the individual, family, community, national and worldwide levels which must be solved within the framework of modern technology but without sacrificing the values which authentic humanity demands.

Can we not look at both Nietzsche's and Toynbee's views as mere hyperbole and pursue an agnostic course—"It doesn't really matter which viewpoint one takes"—as the late American journalist, Walter Lippman, the interpreter for the middle scene, had suggested "Just strive to follow what the heart desires without transgressing what is right . . . it is the only possible hygiene of the soul for men whose selves have become disjointed by the loss of their central certainties, because it counsels them to draw the sting of possessiveness out of their passions, and thus, by removing anxiety to render them harmonious and serene." Soothing words are given to a complacent age. Ignore the pathology and attack the symptom, the gnawing anxiety. That is precisely what Nietzsche suggests we will do. It is poor advice to an emerging passionate age; a yearning, searching, anxious, demanding age which says, "Give us the truth and we will live with it."

Are there truly no remaining central certainties? Why do we not first look for the answer to the most obvious of all questions from the viewpoint of morality: Does God exist or not? Where does the weight of evidence lie? If God exists, then the legitimatization of morality should be sought there. On the other hand, if He does not exist, and there is no middle ground, all is absurd. Pretense to a rational morality is all an illusion on man's part and so much the worse for him. Without an ultimate intending ego to which man must respond there can be no ultimate purposefulness or rationality in the universe, much less a basis for a stable morality. Is there a personal God or not? That is the key question facing this age as it has faced no other.

If Toynbee's overall philosophy of history is correct, the outcome of the present crisis in civilization will depend on the dominant spirit of the peoples concerned as individuals in their various roles. The conflict in the world today, and it is indeed a world in ideational conflict in the decisive stages, reflects the early end-game position within a true dialectic—the dialectic choice presented in the allegory of the fall in Genesis, the choice given man between the tree of knowledge of good and evil and the tree of life.

The two scenarios which we will contrast develop the history and project the end game from the strategic position of the present. Whereas, in the middle game, the engagement now approaching criticality was predominately ideological and nationalistic in motivation and political in execution. The final stages will be moral and cultural in motivation and sociologic in execution. Nietzsche's forces dominated the middle game but the competing ideologies are becoming indistinguishable on the issue of the concept of man which is crucial to the final outcome for mankind in general. One ideology is, traditionally at least, theistic and the other atheistic philosophically, if not practically. Both are materialistic in basic viewpoint.

The Communist World is pragmatic and dogmatic: the Free World is hedonistic and permissive. There are enclaves in each camp, and quite large enclaves, which are theistic in orientation. But the dominant collective attitude in practice is agnostic or atheistic. The sociologic interaction within, and between, the ideological complexes in this ancient dialectic which will determine the final outcome will be in the nature of large-scale social movements. The prototypes were Marxism in its early pre-political, pre-military stages in various countries, and Christianity in the pre-Constantine Roman empire. The Third World, Toynbee's mass humanity, wherever located, will make itself felt in this sociology-dominated arena.

Man has always been caught in the tension between the two opposing concepts of his nature. In stable periods of history the synthesis arising from the continuous insistent dialectic has been a position more or less balanced between the end points so that the average individual considered himself as reasonably self-sufficient; yet, as owing a good measure of his well-being to divine providence, however he visualized it. The position which has been developing for several centuries, and is approaching culmination, places man in a polar position close to the image represented by alienated man. He finds himself independent of any creator, yet, in spite of spectacular technological and scientific advances, far from self-sufficient. It is an unfamiliar and uncomfortable position. Like Adam and Eve in Genesis, men find themselves naked and absurd.

This book has been chiefly one of exploring, comparing and contrasting ideas, and thus the completed product is largely the assembly of thoughts and words of other people far more competent than the author. It has been said, somewhat cynically, but not entirely untruthfully, that the researcher in the literature of any field differs from the plagiarist only in that he steals the ideas and words of many rather than just one. I have tried to be honest where practicable, recognizing all the while that, in a larger sense, almost every idea in this work has been borrowed from someone. In the bibliography prefatory note, acknowledgement is made of those sources to which I am particularly indebted.

HOW BRIEF
A CANDLE

PART I

INTRODUCTION

Chapter 1

ONE VIEW OF REALITY

Section 1 - The Crisis in Sociology

In formulating a viable scenario for the next half century or so in the continuously changing image of man as he looks at himself—and that is, in essence, what philosophy is all about and much of history too—I have selected two opposed forecasts to provide what might be called envelopes of, or boundaries of, a likely or probable real situation which will unfold.

The nihilism projected by Friedrich Nietzsche reflects the views of an atheistic, existentialistic philosopher who saw the western-based cultural and value system completely disintegrating with the recognition, and inevitable acceptance of, the "Death of God" by the mass of the people. Eventually, according to him, a new cultural and value system would arise based on an intellectual and physical elitist aristocracy but not until the present system had been destroyed.

The resurgent religious projection of Arnold Toynbee, on the other hand, reflects the views of a historian who has always stressed the importance of the spiritual aspects of man in historical developments, as opposed to the animalistic forces. Toynbee's forecast, moreover, was not based on the outcome of the ideologic, sociologic and philosophic contest in the West, but on the dominance of the worldwide spiritual role of mankind and with some emphasis on the influence of the traditional spiritual bias of the East. The conflict, as Toynbee saw it, would thus end in a victory of eastern and western spiritual forces over western-derived materialism, and not in a victory of western individualistic ideology.

On our time horizon at the beginning of the last decade of the twentieth century, about ninety years after Nietzsche's projection and forty years after Toynbee's, western materialism has made substantial inroads in the East and has proceeded at an accelerating rate in the West. A certain obvious stuttering of

1

the advance is apparent in the West in very recent years.

The term, "The West," as used by this writer refers far more to an attitude toward humanity than it does to a geographical area. It is that attitude which evolved from the Hellenistic philosophies modified by the concept of human dignity and ethics in the Judeo-Christian tradition. It includes the adherents of Islam as well as those ethnic groups originally within the ancient Byzantine Empire, wherever located. In addition, it includes those acculturated by these philosophies which spread from the western European base during the colonial period. (These peoples have a substantial cultural and philosophical heritage in common, despite great differences in local adaptation over the centuries). It is a cultural tradition in which the dialectical, yet filial, relationship between the infinite, unchangeable one and the finite changeable many has always been recognized regardless of the particularities of the situation. It has been a highly individualistic attitude until late in this century. "The West" is a term of convenience, although its shortcomings in accuracy are recognized and its use here is of wider application than Toynbee's.

In spite of the time lapse, and somewhat differing staging, the Nietzsche and Toynbee viewpoints still pretty well represent the limiting alternative positions. To place the situation in military terms for a moment, the initiative up to the present has been with the Nietzschean forces and, in some cases, the withdrawal of the Toynbee forces has not been too orderly. There has been, however, a certain "religious" driving spirit toward social ends on the part of militant materialistic forces which would, in fact, reflect Toynbee's general thesis. In the long run this spirit works toward the defeat of a nihilistic outcome which, of its nature, is devoid of directed motivation. Such a sociologically generated *esprit* is always subject to diversion to other vehicles which appear to offer greater promise.

It is the objective of this book to stay rather close to Toynbee's thought and project the future on his thesis that, in the last analysis, the decisive energy within the spirit of man will be directed by that force which captures man's imagination and holds it. That force, in all cases, must be the one which man perceives as reflecting his rightful place in the world, his image of himself. While that image has changed from time to time through history, as we will review in some depth, it has never been that of a pure beast or a lump of protoplasm that incidentally talks. At the minimum, man always sees himself as possessing a certain dignity by reason of his humanity, a dignity which, of its nature, demands the respect of and for his fellow man. His collective imagination cannot be captured by anything offering less than that minimum, though the promise of pleasure may distract him temporarily or he may also be temporarily tyrannized into subjugation and slavery. Hope, which denotes a generally optimistic view of the future, is closely connected with the image man has of himself, the image of that which he is capable of becoming, that which represents him in his authenticity. Man cannot survive without something to which he can look forward, even if it is only the atheist existentialist's grim code of living and dying in a courageous rebellion against the absurdity of fate.

Let us look at the dialectic which man has formulated for himself and, in fact, always placed himself in: man, the self-sufficient individual, versus man, the dependent creature. In order to follow the Toynbee script, we must take a position between these two poles and perhaps somewhat closer to the second rather than the first. Nietzsche's script ultimately places man at the first pole by denial of the existence of the second. For Nietzsche, the second polar position was an artificial construction which events have rendered obsolete and void. His prediction stems from his denial of the dialectic—his assertion that God does not exist—and his confidence that the situation will be factually recognized by man. Following that assumption, the predicted outcome is inevitable.

As we review Nietzsche's life and philosophic position in Part II, it remains somewhat uncertain that he was personally convinced of the "death of God," but that is unimportant if the mass of the people believed it. There is really no way to demonstrate that anything "non-exists," although it is clearly possible to demonstrate logically that God does not both exist and non-exist. These concepts being mutually exclusive, only one can be correct, and one must necessarily be correct. Therefore, for Nietzsche's prediction to come to pass, there are two possible sets of preconditions, one of which must be met: First, God does not exist and people recognize the fact; or second, God does exist but people fail to recognize that fact. It is the people's judgment that God does not exist that is essential, assuming no intervention by God, in the latter set.

Under Toynbee's position the situation is the reverse. It is the people's judgment that God does exist which is an essential ingredient. However, here there is one more essential. The people must believe that there is a meaningful and important relationship between God and man, in a filial relationship more intimate than just Creator and creature. In other words, the people must believe that there is a basis for a true religious belief and a hope arising from that belief.

It is thus easier from the standpoint of intellectual effort to follow the Nietzschean script. An inactive, indifferent, even inert, attitude on the part of the mass population is sufficient to assure a victory by default.

Toynbee's outcome, on the other hand, requires a positive recognition on the part of the mass of the people that there is a dependency on, and an accompanying commitment to, a providential Deity. A dedicated commitment to an objective is also an essential requirement for any social movement which is to command and direct the spiritual energies of man. Thus the required ingredient of the Toynbee thesis for historical dominance is also required *per se* for a theistic viewpoint of mankind generally. The problem, therefore, for a scenario writer is to bring the two aspects together. That involves demonstrating the feasibility of convincing the mass of the people that God, in fact, does exist, and that effort in His service is required for man to achieve his authentic aspirations.

Both Christianity and Islam historically have been active expansionist movements, whereas the oriental religions and Judaism have tended to be more self-containing and self-limiting. Christianity in particular has had to bear the brunt of the materialistic counter-movement stemming from conjunction of the heady novelties of the scientific and industrial revolutions. Both events promised, particularly in combination, the early resolution of all man's problems. Self-sufficient man incarnate was there ready to step to the altar to be worshipped. The impact fell when the forces of Christianity were in greatest disarray, with internal quarreling sapping most of the spiritual energy.

Antoine Marquis de Condorcet (1743-1794), French revolutionary and mathematician, in his unfinished *Sketch for a Historical Picture of the Progress of the Human Mind,* captured the spirit which generated the social movement represented by the French Revolution.

If man can, with almost complete assurance, predict phenomena when he knows their laws, . . .why, then, should it be regarded as a fantastic undertaking to sketch, with some pretence to truth, the future destiny of man on the basis of his history? The sole foundation for belief in the natural sciences is this idea, that the general laws directing the phenomena of the universe, known or unknown, are necessary and constant. Why should this principle be any less true for the development of the intellectual and moral faculties of man than for the other operations of nature?. . .

Our hopes for the future condition of the human race can be subsumed under three important heads: the abolition of inequality between nations, the progress of equality within each nation, and the true perfection of mankind. . .

The time will therefore come when the sun will shine only on free men who know no other master but their reason; when tyrants and slaves, priests and their stupid or hypocritical instruments will exist only in works of history and on the stage; and when we shall think of them only. . .to learn how to recognize and so destroy, by force of reason, the first seeds of tyranny and superstition, should they ever dare to reappear amongst us. . . .

How consoling for the philosopher who laments the errors, the crimes, the injustices which still pollute the earth and of which he is often the victim is this view of the human race, emancipated from its shackles, released from the empire of fate and from that of the enemies of its progress, advancing with a firm and sure step along the path of truth, virtue and happiness!

The current situation in the West seems to reflect a disillusionment with Condorcet's rosily promised gifts of science and technology. Reason itself is being questioned. The current, frantic, sex-driven hedonism has all the aspects of the last-gasp effort of the aging human organism seeking to extract the final exquisite pleasure before old age claims it. It is not the expression of a young, exuberant, vital movement claiming the world as its oyster but of a senescent, satiated, last-ditch binge, an era coming to its close.

The current scene, however, is not one to provide undue optimism for Toynbee's prediction. If the age is one of jaded scientific enthusiasm, it is also one of general scientific sophistication. At least, in the West, a movement which can capture the modern man's imagination must have in itself an authenticity which can stand close-up rational scrutiny. If self-sufficient man is to step down from his somewhat disordered dais and admit that his is not the greatest and the last word, and that he needs outside help, he will insist on the credibility of the help he seeks.

The major part of this work is one of evaluating the evidence for a theistic rationale of life from all of the disciplines bearing on the subject at present levels of knowledge. The writer does not believe that such concepts as Kant's "Moral Imperative" or Kierkegaard's "Leap of Faith" will be, in themselves, sufficiently compelling evidence, although there is value in both viewpoints and both viewpoints will be examined. A much firmer rational base is needed. If the existence of a personal beneficent God is supported by the evidence from all sources, at a very high level of confidence, approaching certitude, and if likewise, largely as a corollary, it can be established that man does have an immortal vector in his being—a personal survival after death—Nietzsche's premise is destroyed. A strong case for Toynbee's scenario flows rather easily from that point. All that remains is a methodology to energize men with the idea of the dignity of the individual in brotherhood as a worldwide human community, not as an insectile collectivity.

The two motivating elements in the world today which can capture the imagination of mass humanity remain about what they always have been. One element is the religious, and the other the humanitarian as expressed in never-ending hope for improvement of the human condition based on man's control over his physical environment. These are by no means mutually exclusive motivations. When we speak of the imagination of mass humanity, here is, indeed, an example where a term which has two dimensions may be applied to society *qua* society. There is not only a condition of "averaging out," a statistical polling and integration of the collective mental attitude (the attribute which Emile Durkheim claimed to entitle society to be treated as an object of science in its own right), but there is also reinforcement of the individual elan, an emotional "lift," provided by the interaction with others both as comrades and opponents. A social group united in a cause is synergistic.

A "cause" is inevitably both for something and against something. In fact, the modern Spanish philosopher, Jose Ortega y Gasset, proposes the thesis that every philosophy must have an adversary as an essential ingredient. For example, Kant's Idealism and the Positivists' and Marxists' materialisms, though highly different in their basic grounding, chose metaphysics as the adversary position. In the world today it is apparent that the bourgeoisie vision of the self-sufficient free individual, in the ascendency for seven centuries, is rapidly giving way to the collectivist vision of man self-sufficient in society. Even in the most staunchly capitalistic countries, socialist principles of the welfare state dominate political action. Individualism here has been focused on as the general adversary as capitalism is becoming more and more just another aspect of collectivism. And yet, capitalistic principles of competition have been adapted even in the most communistic countries to stimulate production. From an economic viewpoint, the two ideologies are rapidly converging. What about the role of man as an individual human being?

It appears to me that the next phase of the contest is centered precisely on that question, and its outcome in the last analysis will depend upon whether man sees his image best fulfilled as man dependent upon the beneficence of the state or as man the dependent, yet free, individual creature of God united in a free community.

The idea of man the self-sufficient as an individual seems to have lost its credibility and with it, its energy. George Orwell exploited and displayed the opposed first thesis, the absolute collectivity, quite well. It depicts Nietzsche's finally emerged society of the elite Superman ruling class and its following herd very adequately. The "spiritual" force which Nietzsche saw as finally pulling man out of his dark night of nihilism is the irrepressible "will to power" possessed by each man but to greatest extent by the "superior" individual. The concept of the will to power has indeed been present throughout history as a strong personal motivation. But it is largely personal in appeal, and the individual is little stimulated by another's will to power as it appears in that form. Toynbee, along with Max Weber, would be quick to point out that this personal drive was effective in history only in situations in which it could be translated by the "charisma" of the leader into a social movement or by a willingness of the followers as individuals to identify themselves with the particular charismatic "great man" in making his goals their goals, his ultimate concern their ultimate concern. This is true whether the leader was religious, political or military. There was in every case a "faith" that the leader knew where he was leading, that the goal was desirable and that the leader was capable of bringing the followers to that desirable terminus. A wavering of faith by the followers was fatal.

It thus appears that the answers are to be sought in the sociologic area, in the theory of social movements, their motivation, their principles of development and growth and their interaction. The outcome will depend upon which side of the insistent dialectic at this period in history can mobilize and command the social forces which, when focused, energize social movements. What is the current condition of sociology and what positive and predictive guidance can sociologists offer?

In looking at his profession critically in what he believes to be an era of approaching crisis, Allen Gouldner in his *Coming Crisis in Sociology* (Gouldner 1970), accuses sociology of viewing man from too isolated a position; as though sociology were somehow separate from the everyday concerns of human beings, as though working with scientific detachment, and cold and dispassionate analysis, sociologists are able to discern the pure distillate and elemental essence of social relationships. As a result, man in sociology is "disembodied" and unreal, an intellectual construct with little or no validity in the real world.

The social sciences generally, and anthropology and sociology particularly, occupy especially sensitive positions in the academic world. As with the physical sciences there are several modes in which they operate. These are principally, theoretical research—to extend the knowledge in the discipline; educative—to disseminate the accumulated findings to the world at large, and applied—to put to use the findings of the science toward the betterment of mankind. In the first mode, the attitude which Dr. Gouldner criticizes in sociology may be justified in the interest of assuring the "repeatability" of the various research endeavors. But even here, the very subject matter of the social sciences—man himself in his various relationships with his fellowmen—tends to greatly limit the areas where such methodologies can be applied. However, in the last two modes—and in the social sciences these modes are closely related to the broader philosophical aspects of man in a way far beyond that of the physical sciences—there is almost no place for such an attitude of value-free orientation. For better or for worse, and in spite of himself, the social scientist interprets and passes to the world at large a philosophy of life. The life scene variously portrayed is a society with great internal stability inherent in its structure and function, or it is a world where progress comes only from conflict, or it is a world following evolutionary deterministic dialectic paths to the perfect society. Man in all cases is a rather atomistic creature having little control of his destiny. The sociologist is in an incredibly difficult position. While he tries, or should try, to be the scientist in his theorizing, his rational models are frequently seized upon as reality, as the way things in fact are. If the individual is treated as a statistic in a research study, that is what he becomes for many readers and, too frequently, for the scientist himself. Then what was only a pure hypothesis becomes a scientifically established fact of life. A mere reflection of a personal philosophic viewpoint becomes almost a tenet of dogmatic belief which is indiscriminately spread to the world at large. Unfortunately, the dehumanized version of man, of the intelligent animal responding as a predictable statistic in a collective, leaves little room for the concept of the dignity of man as an individual.

This writer's criticism therefore would follow close to the same path as Dr. Gouldner's but would conclude differently that the sociologist's man has become a dispirited non-entity, scarcely more than a showroom mannequin, dressed up to demonstrate the particular style or fashion on sale that week. In either case, the complaint is similar, that man is not being studied and displayed as he is, in his total humanity. And, hence, the resulting academic picture of society and all the complexities connoted by that collective are largely constructs, useful in the immediate environment in which they are examined, but lacking in applicability toward analysis of the profound problems that reach to the very soul of modern man. Gouldner concludes, as I do, that if sociology and the social sciences in general are to be useful in any large context, and not merely erudite intellectual exercises for their own sake, a change must take place. The drawing room atmosphere of the early nineteenth century in which these ideas were conceived, incubated and nurtured in the spirit of Condorcet must be replaced by the less sanitized but more stimulating air in which the real human beings, including social scientists, live.

In fact, Gouldner seems to direct his thematic quotation from Nietzsche, "Here are the priests and although they are my enemies. . .my blood is related to theirs" at the early founding fathers of sociology in the period of scientific adoration following the "enlightenment." That is to say that those who, accepting Condorcet's view, saw in the emerging physical sciences a model for a science of man in which the laws governing man's belief and behavior could be ascertained with equal certitude and applied with the same predictive accuracy. They foresaw a perfect, harmonious society with mankind guided by the beneficent priesthood of the social scientists. For sociology was to serve as a religion, and oddly enough, while Comte and his coterie of disciples had utterly cast aside the theologically oriented metaphysics of the medieval period and renaissance, they espoused a metaphysics, regardless of how they wished to disguise it, of human dimension. For them the deity was science and it was absolute; matter was the first and last principle.

On this point, Gouldner says, "Outlandish as this priestly conception of the sociologist may now seem, it gave an answer to the question of who the sociologist is that is probably far more serious and certainly more interesting than the one sociologists now conventionally give."

The thing which contributed most to the demise of positivism—a philosophy dedicated to the scientistic position— as a viable philosophy was precisely that, within its framework of rigor in empirical verificability, it could only look at those human problems which were in some way visible to the senses, and those fade into triviality when contrasted with the problems rising from the essential spirit of man. Since positivism as a philosophy and sociology as a science had a common father in August Comte, the genetics of the two are clearly related. Sociologists should, therefore, look at the fate of positivism and ponder the future outlook of sociology if it does not broaden its base of relevancy. Now, society as a collective (with all due regard for Emile Durkheim's genius) can speak only for the statistical man who is, in fact, a dispirited non-entity. If sociologic interest goes no deeper than the impersonal level in a modern world of stress and turmoil, it fails man miserably. What is being discussed is not the abdication of sociology as a science but a change in its scientific posture such as the physical sciences have undergone. The crisis in sociology, and many sociologists are beginning to recognize the problem, thus boils down to a few simple questions: Does sociology as it has been constituted provide modern man with any information, any theoretical guidelines which would assist in readjusting society, or man in society, to the tremendous social changes which have occurred and will continue to occur? Has sociology been relevant to man in society? If all it can provide is data on the effects of patterns of social behavior noncommittally, that is, where certain patterns exist certain, sociological outcomes can be expected—with no suggestions as to basic causes of the patterns; if, in fact, many of the patterns and their effects are demoralizing, what value has the sociologist's work? Are social disorder and social order of equal status in sociology? That is, are these conditions examples of mere phenomena, perhaps more intellectually titillating in the case of disorder?

Academic sociology has been accused by its "conflict" wing of supporting the "establishment" and of being hostile to change.

To the extent it can consider only the theoretical man, both parts of the accusation appear ridiculous. It literally cannot support, or be hostile to, any position. It can only be indifferent. Conditions only exist. They are neither good nor bad. That is a situation made to order for the nihilistic outcome. If sociology could consider a vector of man which is spiritual—the truly human man with values—it could not remain indifferent. A community of people living in harmony with each other without excessive crime, having respect for each other's rights as human beings and not, solely as legal entities, is certainly superior in human values to a community whose people live at arm's length, hostile and suspicious, victimizing each other at every opportunity. Encouragement would be appropriate for the first behavior pattern and corrective measures appropriate for the second behavior pattern. In a thoroughly unbiased report, change would be supported for the second pattern, so that it might approach the first. Yet many communities within the United States come closer to the second paradigm than to the first. Most sociologists would agree, probably even professionally, with the conclusion. Yet, they would probably not agree that, as sociologists, they are competent to support educational and political policies which are designed to bring about a morally oriented attitude in individuals comprising the community. That action would require a moral judgment and, even though evidence was available linking educational and political policies to the contrasting community conditions, they would be unwilling to say something *ought* to be done because it would tend to produce better communities.

A physicist, botanist or astronomer seldom if ever is faced with a professional moral judgment. The subjects of their science are impersonal by their nature. The sociologist is not in that happy position unless he never considers man as a human being when he is a member of society and, in that case, he can be of little use to man.

In fact, had the social scientists followed more closely the physical sciences or, as will be seen, the modern philosophies they would have discerned that the physical universe, as viewed by the physical sciences, had greatly changed from that of the positivists and the materialists of the late nineteenth century. The physical scientists, early in the twentieth century between the world wars, far from considering themselves priests to a deified science, began to see themselves as adventurers and humble seekers of knowledge in a world of profound mystery. As early as 1931, Robert Millikan, Nobel prize winner in physics, in an article in the *Literary Digest* (January 24, 1931), described his work in seeking the source of the cosmic ray "as the finger printing of God." In an address to the American Association for the Advancement of Science, delivered before some 5,000 members on the occasion of his retirement as president of the organization, he advanced that theory, adding that it demonstrated "A creator constantly on the job."

Albert Einstein, in an address at Oxford in 1933, said:

> To the sphere of religion belongs the faith that the regulations valid for the world of existence are rational, that is, comprehensible to reason. I cannot conceive of a genuine scientist without that profound faith. The situation may be expressed by an image. Science without religion is lame, religion without science is blind. (Frank, 1963, page 286)

And later in an address to a conference group in New York in 1940, he said:

> The most beautiful emotion we can experience is the mystical. It is the source of all true art and science. He to whom this emotion is a stranger, who can no longer wonder and stand rapt in awe is as good as dead. To know what is impenetrable to us really exists, manifesting itself as the highest wisdom and the most radiant beauty which our dull faculties can comprehend only in their most primitive forms, this knowledge, this feeling is at the center of true religiousness. In this sense, and in this sense only, I belong to the ranks of the devoutly religious men. (Frank, 1963, page 284)

I am not trying to portray Millikan or Einstein as evangelists. They were not, but there was none of the arrogant, omniscient attitude in any of their work. They considered themselves as searchers for reality in an arena of numbing vastness. In many ways, the arena of man is far more vast, for it is literally dimensionless when the intellect becomes the area of study. If modesty befits the physical scientist, how much more so should it befit the sociologist or the anthropologist. For every man, while he is constrained by the physical laws, by the mores and folkways and traditions of his time, culture and society, and thus is to an extent predictable, nonetheless is intensely individual, and hence, unpredictable in a way that an atom or a galaxy cannot possibly be. And this individuating characteristic lies not chiefly in his biologic background, but in that which tells him, "I am not a statistic, I am me. I am the one who is anxious, fearful, joyous, exuberant. I am me. I am the one who loves, hates, ponders my future, dwells on my past. It is all very well to talk about mankind in general and immortality of the species, the upward thrust of civilization through time, the unconquerability of the spirit of liberty, but how about me, my life, my liberty? What happens to me? What does my life mean?"

Every man asks these questions as an individual, and he deserves answers as an individual and as a member of society. He deserves the best answer that can be given him by all the resources available to his intellectual insights. Primitive man received answers from his tribal leaders, and the answers, in simple terms, were also simple. In many ways his total life supplied his answer. Virtually everything had a religious significance. Religion was his reality. These answers do not satisfy us because our lives are not simple, our mental processes are not simple, nor is there any hope or reason to wish that they should be simple. But that does not mean that there are not pervasive concepts which of their very simplicity cut through the nexus of social problems in modern civilization as only detail in a far broader pattern. For example, in the Einsteinian physics, it was just such a breakthrough with a few simple but sophisticated concepts which permitted the pattern of the universe to unfold in breathtaking simplicity in spite of its complex infrastructure.

The problems within the social matrices will remain to be individually solved, but the solutions should flow from concepts which can supply the great energy required. For the past 100 years the problems have been building far faster than the solutions have been provided. Many of the solutions, in fact, have provided even more vexatious confrontations. In many cases the solutions have come from philosophic attitude and axiom very close to the biologic motivations used by the Calaveras frog jockey. True, man is more complex than the frog. He will not continue to swallow shot by reflex until he cannot jump. Eventually he grasps that he is being led astray, and so new theoretical approaches have to be devised, but always with the constraint, Man is only a gifted animal. He must be treated as a gifted animal, and if something has to go, let it be the dubious fact that he is gifted. Eventually, as the tangle of problems resulting from this approach becomes impenetrable, people lose faith in their leaders and educators as blind guides, and the crisis is at hand.

Reflecting the emphasis on the biologic and materialistic themes which characterize American sociology a comment on the same trend from another source may be pertinent to indicate how widespread it is. Professor Duncan Williams in his book *Trousered Apes* (Williams, 1973) views the current literature, an index of cultural quality, as in a state of poverty unequaled in history, perhaps at a point of less than zero. He says:

"If it [Western Society] proceeds on its present course—a course which has produced a society recently described as one consisting of technological giants and moral pygmies—then the seemingly inevitable end will be the extermination of the species, probably with a whimper rather than a bang. Man does, however, differ from other creatures which have become extinct in that he possesses the conceptual ability (if he will only exercise it) to realize where he stands in relation to his past and to his problematical future.

"What we are in danger of forgetting, however, is that no valid discussion of such a hypothetical future can, in the last analysis, ignore the question of human value. If a man is induced to regard himself as merely a trousered ape, or 'a walking bag of sea water' as certain scientists choose to see him, or a complex but predictable collection of reactions to various stimuli as Dr. B. F. Skinner and other behaviorists assert, then he is simply an exceptionally extravagent, predatory and messy mammal, and apart from a natural but sentimental loyalty to one's own species his disappearance from the scene would ecologically be no disaster.

"Man is more than a physical animal. He needs, above all, hope to endure. The destruction of such hope and dissemination of nihilism appear to be the message of the new impuritanism, which is not simply the old puritanism 'writ large' but which springs from a barely concealed cultural, social and individual death wish."

If one takes Professor Williams' analysis seriously, and I do, the time to quit playing the sociological game is past. If the sociologists want to contribute to restoration of viable human values, their devout adherence to value-free orientation had best be questioned seriously and quickly, lest sociology become totally valueless.

To the inquiry as to what values, I merely suggest that we take a holistic view of man as he is. If the high probabilities are that man has a transcendent nature, one with a surviving spiritual vector; if morality is not just a matter of a label attached by a dominant class in a particular society for its own benefit; if our lives should be guided by principles having absolute value because transcendent—frankly, if there is a God in the picture to which man has ultimate reference—why should the values represented by these concepts be denied?

One need not question or publicize the obvious fact that man is an animal. If, however, he is any more than this—if he is also a creature having a transcendent aspect—that viewpoint also should be provided and projected with greater emphasis, if for no other reason than its lack of visibility. Yet that view is not only ignored, it is publicly ridiculed. And the consequences to society of continued stress on exclusive biologic existence are far-reaching, and becoming self-evident.

At root, we go back to the question Hobbes raised in the seventeenth century, which is, in essence: If man is nothing but a gifted animal, how is society possible? What rational deterrents are there to a completely pragmatic opportunism by each individual leading to early species annihilation? And, if he is only a gifted animal, as Professor Williams says, really, who cares? Hobbes did not, at least openly, consider the fact that the society he was addressing was far from one of men viewing themselves as gifted animals. Western civilization and its dominant cultures grew from a value system based on man as a transcendent being and have survived in that concept. Hobbes' question, while perhaps academic in his day, is very real and very cogent when man, in fact, sees himself only as a trousered ape.

The urgency today stems from the fact that a culture's value system in most cases directs behavior and morality, and conversely culturally-approved behavior and morality reflect back on the value system. While anthropologists can show that mores and traditional habits and customs of culture die hard, their persistence is a consequence of the normal, fairly slow process of indoctrination geared to the generational cycle. Today's situation, which is characterized by indoctrination through mass media external to the generational units, guarantees no such continuity of western culture or values; quite the contrary, it almost guarantees their extinction. An indication of the present situation and trends is given by a nationwide opinion survey conducted in the United States for the John D. Rockefeller III Foundation and others (by Daniel Yankelovich Inc.). The purpose of the survey was to develop a picture of value trends among the young. A sampling was taken in 1969 and then again five years later in 1974. The total sample in 1974 was of 3,522 individuals between the ages of 16 and 25, of whom 1,006 were college students; the rest were employed at various jobs, but not unemployed. The earlier sample was similar in scale. A partial summary of results is given in the following tabulation.

Table 1

Trend in Value Orientation

Sample Population Age 16 to 25 Inclusive

	Percent Affirmative Response			
Question	Non-College		College	
	1969	1974	1969	1974
Is religion an important value?	64	42	38	28
Is living a clean moral life an important value?	77	57	45	34
Does hard work pay off?	79	56	56	44

The results scarcely need any editorializing as to the trend and absolute value in stature among the young given to what has been the traditional image of western man. Likewise, attention scarcely needs to be drawn to the correlation between loss of the value of religion and hence of a transcendent viewpoint of man as a value and the following two questions—not that there are not other or rather mutual causative elements. Of significance to the future is that this same age group is also among the largest in the population distribution profile and will grow in importance in the positions of national control and policy guidance over the next 25 years. They will be dominant in the year 2000.

I get the distinct impression from hundreds of articles, essays, and books, that for a writer in the behavioral sciences to raise the subject of a God-related morality in a serious paper would be professionally fatal. Yet, according to Gouldner's survey conducted in 1964, over two-thirds of the sociologists responding had some religious affiliation. (Gouldner, 1970, page 259).

These data indicate that a high percentage believe in man's transcendent nature, but are so afraid of mixing professional and private attitudes that they, in effect, deny it.

In light of the cynicism and attitude of amused condescension which greet papers addressing the idea of a supreme being or having human transcendent overtones in the behavioral sciences, one would have to search hard among them for an expression of an eternal, purposeful causality as clear as that in the purely technical article "Energy in the Universe" prepared by Freeman J. Dyson of the Institute of Advanced Studies for the Special Energy and Power Edition of *Scientific American* (September 1971, pages 51-59). For instance, Dyson says "It would not be surprising if it should turn out that the origin and destiny of the energy of the universe cannot be completely understood in isolation from the phenomena of life and consciousness." Again, "As we look out into the universe and identify the many incidents of physics and astronomy that have worked together to our benefit, it almost seems as if the universe must in some sense have known that we were coming." And in Dyson's closing paragraph he says:

> "Ko Fung was one of the great natural philosophers of ancient China. In the Fourth Century, he wrote 'As for belief, there are things that are as clear as the sky, yet men prefer to sit under an upturned barrel.' I hope that this article may have persuaded a few people to come out from under the barrel and to look to the stars with hopeful eyes. I began with an article from Blake. Let me close now with another from him, this time echoing the thought of Ko Fung, ' "If the door of perception were cleansed, everything would appear to man as it is, infinite. For man has closed himself up till he sees all things through narrow chinks of his cavern." '

Dyson's initial thematic quotation from Blake opens with "Man has no body distinct from his soul, for that body is a portion of soul." This is an absolute reverse of the modern materialism.

Why cannot sociologists and anthropologists be at least as affirmative of values as the physical scientists? Dyson's statement as well as Einstein's and Millikan's given earlier do so suggest values above the material. Unless and until sociologists also become open to their subject matter on this issue they are in fact advancing the cause of nihilism. As we have seen, paradoxically, it is impossible to be neutral without taking that side. No one wants sociologists or anthropologists teaching religion, but likewise no one should want them teaching non-religion either. Yet how can the subject of religion be avoided, if as is widely admitted all men ask themselves: What is man? What is life? What is death? Can such universally asked questions be ignored as irrelevant to sociology? And if responded to under constraint of biologism the answer is: He is a trousered ape. A life is a complex chemical reaction. Death is the result of a non-correctable malfunction of the process mechanism.

Typical of current anthropological texts, primitive man is referred to as an imaginative myth-making animal who builds answers to those questions by wishful-thinking. Can the anthropologist not say, that: The form and forces in the primitive world manifested the divine reality, and the myths were offspring of that reality, that the myth was the reflection of reality as perceived in terms of a primitive world? Can he not conclude that if it was wishful-thinking, both the wish and the thought had a basis in observation? For in truth it is likely that the primitive people did far more than imagine, unless the mental processes are all reduced to imagination. They looked about them and discerned and discussed how things were, concluding that there had to be answers to these questions which lay at a level above them. They were using the same raw materials as Einstein, and came to about the same conclusions. They displayed more intelligence in approaching reality than do many sociologists and anthropologists, at least in their professional lives.

Section 2—God and Transcendent Man— A Matter of Analysis

Friedrich Nietzsche's projection of the advent of nihilism sprang from his view that philosophy should be prophetic in its role of defining and clarifying existence. He arrived on the scene at a crossroads in philosophy which saw a three-way confrontation of the fundamentally-theistic Kantian and Hegelian thought; the then swiftly rising empirical and positivistic thought of Hume, Mill and Comte seeking to establish the scientific method as the only route to knowledge and the emerging atheistic, dialectical materialism of Marx and Engels. All of these were displayed against a background of centuries of a Christian western culture. Nietzsche's projection, therefore, had a deep historically oriented basis. He visualized a struggle to the death in which the historic and now decadent value system of European culture, exemplified by the educated middle-class of Germany of the late nineteenth century, would go down to defeat. But it could not be replaced by a culture brought into existence by the surviving schools of thought which had no viable value system in themselves. Nietzsche distinguished sharply between philosophy and science in the nineteenth century version and did not see a humanly-sensitive value system, or culture, emerging from the latter. Since cultures and value systems are symbiotic concepts, mutually supportive, the collapse of the older theistic philosophy and demise of its value system and, with it, European culture, would leave the gap of nihilism. What Nietzsche was postulating, therefore, in the death of God was the death and destruction of the basis of European culture. And his death of God, in practical application, was brought about by the undermining of the prevalent theistic philosophic system by the materialistic and scientistic theories and their application to life. Nietzsche's dictum was based on no detailed analysis but on intuition. He was an irrationalist in his approach to almost every problem, but he had an unequaled skill in grasping the "feel" of a situation and sensing its conclusions.

For the last century, the Nietzschean script has been followed almost to the letter and, unless that reflection which Nietzsche postulated we would be afraid to undertake is undertaken, the trend will likely go on to its dismal conclusion and the age of nihilism will have its tortured reign. Nietzsche saw an unreflecting people, fearing to reflect, and, as it were, in a trance, marching steadily toward disaster. Why should we not reflect? Even more urgently, why should we be afraid to reflect? Why should we behave like the youngster at a horror movie catching only brief glimpses through his spread fingers, then quickly closing off the scene because he can't stand it? The psychology is much the same. Man lives in a tension between hope and despair—but he can't live in despair, so he snatches glimpses of reality to sustain hope but is sometimes afraid to reflect on what he sees because it might confirm his despair. Might it not far more likely confirm his hope? Why should not the bright promise of man's scientific and technological potential be fulfilled in a joyous rebirth of a life of spiritual and cultural richness? Nietzsche did not say explicitly what it was we would not reflect on because of our fears. No doubt it was the matter which he saw as causing the downfall of civilization. Men would not look at the question of the existence of God maturely and honestly. They would prefer to see their value system, their culture, their civilization erode away in ever-increasing doubt than subject the question to careful scrutiny—fearful that, in fact, that scrutiny would verify the awful reality of God's non-existence. Better that the horror movie should go to its conclusion without looking at it. Things usually come out right in the end. This situation, however, will not, unless the trend is changed, and that demands that the doubts be cast aside, to be replaced by confidence, and the matter put at rest so that reconstruction of values can begin.

Recognizing that human society cannot survive with nihilism, Nietzsche foresaw the eventual reestablishment of a value system which he somehow tied to a superior elite breed of intellectual who would rule with a coldly disciplined eye to the well-being of humanity, especially themselves. Continuing in his preface to *The Will to Power* he writes,

> Why has the advent of nihilism become necessary? Because the values we have had hitherto thus draw their final consequence; because nihilism represents the ultimate conclusion of our great values and ideals—because we must experience nihilism before we can find out what value these "values" really had—we require, at some time new values.

Mature reflection should proceed on a mature basis. In complex problems, such as this most certainly is, that means that all of the aspects of a problem must be studied in context with all related subject matter. It suggests the approach of systems analysis. Webster's New World Dictionary defines systems analysis as "An engineering technique that breaks down complex technical, social, biological, and other problems into basic elements and subsystems where interrelations are evaluated and programmed . . . into a complete and integrated system." It is as good a definition as any. The emphasis is on the integration of all the diverse elements in the final solution—the many becoming one. No area of thought is off-limits if its relevance to the problem can be shown, and similarly no methods of analysis or illumination are off-limits. The term "brainstorming" was popularly given the preliminary pre-analytic steps to frame the problem, establish its boundaries and suggest its possible solutions. The more sophisticated the problem, generally, the more "intuitive insights" must be critically examined intellectually and rationally, before they can be accepted or eliminated as a sound approach. They are never laughed off as subjective unscientific nonsense. In fact, it could be said the development in illumination of the analysis proceeds from the highly imaginative toward the sharply mathematical ends of the spectrum.

Habitually, sociologists write for other sociologists, historians for historians, philosophers for philosophers, theologians for theologians, and scientists for other scientists. Relatively little is done to promote idea transfer across disciplinary lines. An exception in this regard is the engineer, where professional life depends, not so much on discourse with his colleagues, as on the conveyance of ideas to a wide interdisciplinary group. What is to be fabricated or constructed must be set forth explicitly to those who have any concern in the final product, from owner to craftsman. The systems engineer responsible for integration of complex undertakings must seek to optimize the total assembly by compromise of competing functions in time, space and resources. Functional adequacy is sought rather than an idealization of each sector. The concept of systems analysis contains both of these engineering characteristics—explicitness and functional adequacy in process analysis and synthesis.

The sociologist, philosopher, historian, theologian or scientist may be less than satisfied with the rigor of definition given these segments of this study; but if the fundamental ideas have been evaluated and presented adequately to the understanding of non-professionals in these highly technical disciplines, the objective has been achieved. Systems analysis is only a modern name for an approach to problem solving which is as old as man. But the techniques used are new, made necessary by the complexity of many modern problems such as development of a major weapon system or providing an optimum solution to a geopolitical dilemma. It is a method for forcing or coercing a solution by closing in on an optimum answer in an ever tightening spiral through iteration and elimination. In mathematical logic, it is much like arriving at an answer through a solution of simultaneous equations. All equations must be satisfied. The answers obtained to other than purely numerical problems are, for the most part, in terms of confidence levels, not certitudes. For problems involving multiple numerical data sets, the answers can usually be given in terms of probabilities of error or of failure rates. For our problem the answer can be given only in terms of what could be called derived probability as distinguished from statistical probability. Let us take an example from the old shell game. In an honest game, probability of the pea being under any one of the three shells in one-third. If, to keep the game honest, one identifies two of the shells and says it is not under them and demonstrates it, is he then justified in saying with 100 percent probability—certitude—that the pea is under the third shell without lifting it to examine the facts? Obviously in the real game the effective answer is "yes" because the operator must admit that it is, or be run out of town. There is a working level of confidence, if not philosophical certitude. But, depending upon the operator's honesty, the pea might or might not be there—and that is an imponderable to which no probability could be assigned. Still, of the three alternatives all but one-third has been eliminated and the gambler's confidence level is much higher than when he started—not so much of where the pea is, but of where it is not. If now one has played the game several times and won and *lost* in a normal percentage of cases, he has a far higher level of confidence. It is still not certitude and still not a statistical probability that the pea is under that third shell because there remains that non-numerical vector—an imponderable—that perhaps this time the operator is dishonest. It is an alternative which cannot be statistically evaluated, but one can play the game with increasing confidence. If we examine many sets of alternatives and eliminate all but one in each set, we have increased confidence that the pea is in fact under the remaining shell although there may be alternatives of which we have no knowledge. If, additionally, we have, in all appropriate cases, examined the remaining shell and found that the pea is there, obviously, we have even greater confidence in the honesty of the game.

The writer uses that basic methodology combined with a further analytical technique of bringing discussions to a series of logic gates through which the reader must pass before moving to the next phase. If the reader agrees with the logic to that point, the gate is closed behind him. Theoretically if he does not pass the gate—that is, disagrees or remains in doubt—a new cycle of discussions is entered and the alternatives are re-examined. That activity has to be left to the reader. If the writer has done his homework, it should not be a too frequent occurrence.

Let us begin with a quotation from Plato's *Republic* (Jowett, 1942), specifically in his well-known parable of the cave. In the person of Socrates speaking to his companion, Glaucon, Plato sees mankind as prisoners in a cave, chained, so that they must perpetually look away from the light and see nothing but moving images of themselves and their worldly possessions, cast by a fire upon the cavern wall, and thus not see their own vital reality. A conversation between Glaucon and Socrates proceeds, beginning with Glaucon:

"You have shown me a strange image, and they are strange prisoners."

"Like ourselves," I replied; "and they see only their own shadows or the shadows of one another, which the fire throws on the opposite wall of the cave?"

"True," he said; "how could they see anything but the shadows if they were never allowed to move their heads?"

"And of the objects which are being carried in like manner they would only see the shadows?"

"Yes," he said.

"And if they were able to converse with one another, would they not suppose that they were naming what was actually before them?"

"Very true."

"And suppose further that the prison had an echo which came from the other side, would they not be sure to fancy when one of the passers-by spoke that the voice which they heard came from the passing shadow?"

"No question," he replied.

"To them," I said, "the truth would be literally nothing but the shadows of the images."

"That is certain."

"And now look again, and see what will naturally follow if the prisoners are released and disabused of their error. At first, when any of them is liberated and compelled suddenly to stand up and turn his neck round and walk and look towards the light, he will suffer sharp pains; the glare will distress him, and he will be unable to see the realities of which in his former state he had seen the shadows; and then conceive someone saying to him that what he saw before was an illusion, but that now, when he is approaching nearer to being and his eye is turned towards more real existence, he has a clearer vision—what will be his reply? And you may further imagine that his instructor is pointing to the objects as they pass and requiring him to name them—will he not be perplexed? Will he not fancy that the shadows which he formerly saw are truer than the objects which are now shown to him?"

"Far truer."

Plato's parable is singularly applicable to our world today. We are, many of us, literally cave dwellers in urban canyons, and much of our perception of reality is formed by images cast by the illumination of an electron beam on a television screen. This, and the mass of publications and literature buffet us with a repetitive thematic monotony of striving for happiness in our possessions. The reflected images are construed as reality and where there is a conflict between reality and the image, as with Plato's prisoners, we tend to select the image. It is this aspect of late modern times which truly creates a crisis of civilization and the urgency of doing something to restore a measure of reality to a world of men bemused by distorted images of themselves, their lives and their relationships.

Not to stray too far from Plato's theme, the question inevitably arises: What is reality? Is there any such thing? Or is reality, as alleged for beauty, only in the eye of the beholder? Is it only a subjective construct? Philosophers have labored for centuries, even millenia, on the question. Two aspects of reality are sometimes identified and inaccurately designated as objective and subjective reality? Subjective reality is a viewing purely as interpreted by the individual, a personal idea of the thing viewed, having different aspects depending on the point of view. Objective reality designates the thing as it in fact is—truth. Like the mathematical concept of an asymptote it is forever approached, but never attained by men. In many ways, it is impossible for us ever to escape permanently from Plato's cave and a measure of indirect viewing. About the most we can hope to do is to escape occasionally, to refresh our vision and thus, in general, to improve our idea of the image on the cavern wall.

A model by which I propose to explicate objective and subjective truth as I will use the terms is an ellipsoid of revolution, an idealized transparent egg, in which the energy source representing "objective" truth or reality is at one of the conjugate foci, and its image representing its interpretation by man, the only thing he comprehends, is therefore automatically formed at the other focus. If we would imagine the "egg shell" being made of various segments representing the different viewpoints of knowledge, each one of varying reflectivity, the image formed will also vary depending upon the strength of impinging illumination and level of reflectivity of the individual segments. If we divide the continuum, we will see that the image projected still represents some aspect of truth and reality, but never the complete truth until all the segments are perfectly illuminated and absolutely reflected.

The model is in considerable contrast to the views which have been developed from the time of Descartes and which have tended to split our acquisition of knowledge in relation to reality into two highly differentiated elements. This dualism reached solidity, oddly enough, in the idealistic philosophy of Immanuel Kant. Kant did not agree with Descartes entirely, however. Descartes had seen a difference between that knowledge which is gained by internal mental processes within man himself, and that knowledge of the external world which he gains through the senses. Moreover, he postulated a degree of "innateness" to certain ideas which conferred a "predisposition" to the emergence of related concepts, the existence of God for instance, when the question was proposed to the thinking mind. Kant denied any innateness of ideas but set up certain categories of mental processes which are, *a priori*, a part of our mental equipment. But they apply only to processing of data received through the senses. Any other "knowledge" he denied as knowledge, though there was a sort of awareness of such things as a moral imperative which implied God, again, for instance. But it was not knowledge. He called this function the operation of the "practical reason" which, in a sense, proposed concepts we were forced to accept on faith. However, these concepts were totally different from those representing the outside material world, and the concepts themselves were subjective interpretations of a thing "unknowable" in itself. Man's knowledge was severely limited and man's mental processes compartmentalized.

My model proposes that there is no such compartmentalization in man's knowledge acquisition process, nor are there innate ideas. Artificial rules to force philosophy into such a segmented posture are self-defeating of the primary purpose of philosophizing. The splintering up of the thought processes as a function of data input classification seems a totally unnecessary fiction introduced to permit the separate handling and privileged status which the empiricists claimed for the sensed data.

The task of the intellect in every situation is one of analytical evaluation and judgment. If I am traveling in the desert and observe a shimmering body of blue water in the distance, I must decide whether it is real or imaginary; I can open and shut my eyes and take a thousand individual impressions and be no nearer a conclusion than at first sight. The sensing only provides a data input, not a final process. It is only when I compare the sense input with other data which I have stored in my memory banks from previous travel here, or from what others have told me, or from a map of the vicinity, or just from pondering the likelihood of water in such a place on logical grounds, that I can come to a conclusion; it would be a conclusion having greater or lesser probability of correctness based on my stored data and intellectual acuity. Now, the fact that

I can go there and verify empirically that water is or is not there does not alter the mental activity which has been carried out, although it does provide the satisfaction of certitude (assuming that one agrees reality is an existent) rather than various levels of probability. And if tomorrow I repeat the trip and see the body of water, I will relate what I see to stored memory data and evaluate again, perhaps unconsciously, whether it is or is not a mirage, and feel no need to verify the conclusion. I am satisfied with a probability: if water was or was not there yesterday, probably water is or is not there today. The verification was not an essential process of intellection. It provides only a different level of assurance. Why should there be a categorization of the process by data source or verification?

The normal human reasoning process accepts input data from any of many sources, compares the new data against stored data from many other sources, and comes to a balanced or biased conclusion based on its total accumulated resources. The answer is subjective in the sense used in our model. One such source of ideas, called intuition, is the free readout in the mind of stored information on a particular subject. It provides a background of data against which a particular intellected subject or idea is displayed. Out of this action comes an impression or judgment as to the true nature of the subject. It is an insight in the truest possible sense, and it is subjective as before. The difference between this and the externally received impulse is that the data input calling for the analysis did not come immediately from sense data as a question requiring an answer, but was from an internally intellected question requiring an answer.

The result of mental processing of an inquiry originating either directly from sense or pure idea is equally subjective in its form of answer. It is true that sense data questions are usually simple while ideational data questions are usually complex, but this does not change the nature of the process, only its range of search. Furthermore, the human reasoning mechanism is preprogrammed for just such activity. It is in the preprogrammed handling that the simple analogy to the computer must cease. The human mental evaluation, as it proceeds to its conclusion, permits value judgments to be made, and on all classes of data inputs. The evaluation transcends the indicative positive—negative yes/no, and provides answers in terms of the subjunctive mood such as ought, could, should, and would, as well as in gradations of the indicative mood such as: this is good, this is bad, this is better, this is worse, this is best, this is worst.

A particular difficulty of looking at "abstract" ideas has been raised in a denial of the validity of the concept of universals. Is "human nature" for instance, a proper objective of intellectual activity capable of yielding knowledge? The problem goes back to Plato. We will not stop to review the history now but later. It is sufficient now to say, that for me, "human nature" is a collective idea of the common attributes of man of which we are perfectly well aware. Obviously, however, no such composite being exists.

Another related, and currently very popular, concept which pervades all of modern thinking from theology to sociology is that of relativism. That is, the total absence of any absolutes. It is the idea that truth is always and only the truth in a particular environment in its highly specific space-time reference. Accordingly, much stress has been laid on the impossibility of grasping the ideas of the ancients from their writings concerning God or man himself, for that matter, because of the totally different circumstances of their lives and ours. Man is a credible historic being only in the context of his "lived-in" experiences. There is no way for us to literally crawl into the ancients' skins; therefore we cannot understand them with any assurance. We have already noted a degree of agreement with this idea, that there are differences in viewpoint no one can deny. However, the idea that the differences are so great as to render the results of thought processes, at different periods, totally untranslatable is a fanciful distortion. Men today are constituted and think and react far more like than unlike their historic confreres. Placed in its historic stage setting, there can be little doubt that *Antigone* or *Hamlet* convey the impression desired by their authors. This was true with respect to the contemporary audiences and to us. Those plays reflect human emotional and intellectual conflicts that are readily appreciated in the twentieth century. What is necessary, however, is to be aware of the historical circumstances under which the works were written, and to avoid anachronisms in our interpretation of them. In other words, it is necessary not to let detail destroy the insights contained in those plays. The world of science, for Plato and Aristotle, was not much like our world. We cannot criticize their work in terms of our scientific knowledge of things today, but we can criticize their works in the light of our knowledge of their world which, in many respects, is better than their contemporary knowledge because of the advantage of our broader geographic and historic perspective.

Our goal should not be that of subjective reality. There is

but one reality, our concept of which will always remain imperfect and more or less subjective. But our image of this reality or truth is always best when all the forces of our powers of inquiry are directed toward its illumination from all viewpoints. We should strive to look at all facets with maximum illumination. What should be sought is a comprehensive understanding from every viewpoint, and then to note what viewpoints produce resonance in our understanding. Objectivity, in the sense of freedom from all human prejudgments or bias, is an impossibility.

Our responses to sense data and our internal thought processes are conditioned by our experiences. We are the summation of our experiences in many ways. It has been said jokingly that the individual's bias index is directly proportional to his disclaimer of bias, ie., those who think they are unbiased are the most biased. The solution is not to attempt to completely damp out those personal frequencies or to become inert but to so stimulate the real resonant frequencies as to make those respond as the key elements in our evaluation.

While much of this book is devoted to the intellectual assessment of the nature of man and the existence of God, the fact is that while rational philosophic answers are necessary, they are not sufficient in a sophisticated age. Philosophy must stop at the generalized level of principles. Answers which would be classed as religious, for instance, are needed to complete the picture. Conviction and persuasion are of different genres. Man is not exclusively nor even primarily intellectual; he is also aesthetic, emotional and intuitive. It is principally the latter group of characteristics, in fact, which energizes social movements. But it remains true that, since most of the knowledge critical to our development as authentic human beings cannot be subjected to laboratory analyses, the need for intellectual analyses across the spectrum becomes more important, more enriching, more fulfilling.

If we now consider the concept of man—essential human nature—in our model, the images we see reflected from the various viewpoints of science, reason, tradition, faith, intuition, and art are but aspects of that human nature, and the best image would be that of a balanced reflection with maximum intensity of source illumination. Man cannot achieve a perfect image because his intellectual tools are imperfect, and so, from time to time, in attempts to improve the image, he has altered it, as first one aspect of man and then another predominates.

Looking at man in this model, we can trace, in general terms, the predominating reflection for each period from ancient times to the present. Each image will contain an element of truth but none complete truth. The reflection will differ from place to place and from time to time.

In this study, we will examine man as represented in the philosophic thought from its ancient beginning, but with emphasis on the last 800 years in the West. The dominant viewpoint of man in the 12th and 13th centuries was that of the traditional Christian faith in the dignity of man chiefly in his transcendent nature as the well-loved child of God destined for an eternal life of happiness after a test period in this life. At that time, the material aspects were almost completely subordinated. From that vantage point, we will trace developments to an early period in our present century which manifested a dominant, hard line materialism of man as the gifted animal almost directly opposite to the position of the late Middle Ages. The concept of man in this last period is vastly different. Man is less exalted. His dignity is largely a question of his power over other men.

Of critical concern is the direction of the next shift in emphasis. Using the model as a projection stage, it is difficult to see any further shift toward the materialistic end except to utter bestiality, to a position in the model of no illumination that is recognizable as human. Such a shift would be, to the "Nietzsche" scenario, one of nihilism and convergence of the image into a distortion so narrow and dark that it scarcely represents any aspect of substantive truth. I propose greatly increased emphasis on the illumination from the spiritual segment as the best way to restore a balanced image, an image more in accord with the "Toynbee" scenario. Such a shift would enhance the illumination of the intermediate segments as well. As will be seen, such a shift can be noted in philosophic thought in the past fifty years, but the general population has yet to feel the impact. The lag is a historic, and in this case, unfortunate tendency.

The essential point to be borne in mind is that it is the truth, as reflected by the transcendent viewpoint, which must be projected, not of any extreme band at the other side, of erotic, wild imagination which would as badly distort the truth as does narrow materialism. One of the hazards of a true civilization crisis is that all momentum has gone out of the system. It is like an aircraft at the stall point. If energy from some positive source is not forthcoming, all control is lost and disaster is unavoidable; there is no lift left to counter the irrational and violent. If no energy is provided by a constructive philosophy, it will be provided by other sources. People cannot live without answers.

That there is currently such a danger (though not in that context) is affirmed by Leslie A. Fiedler in his historical analysis of literature entitled *"Waiting for the End."* In reviewing philosophic approaches to literary efforts of the early 1960's he discusses the popular novel in its relationship to the theory of consciousness modification as follows (Fiedler, 1964, pages 167-168):

> But at the end of the nineteenth century, various revolutionary philosophers, most notably Karl Marx, had begun to insist that the point was to change the world, not to understand it. No matter how clearly seen, such thinkers argued, poverty was an offence, man's alienation from his work a scandal, and only action rather than consciousness was capable of mitigating the offense and the scandal. Even religious credulity and superstition, the Marxists argued, had survived the onslaught of reason because they were sustained by a social system which the rationalist philosophers had not challenged at all. However, we have now lived through more than a century of attempts to change the world by assaulting the social structure and have only learned what some from the first tried to tell us, namely, that the more it changes, the more it is the same—*so long as a particular way of perceiving and understanding, bred by science out of scholasticism, persists.*
>
> In Russia and America alike, the alterationists would plead, men study physics and build the bomb, worship the ego and fear their own bodies, ban heroin and drink alcohol, so what is there to choose? The world apparently cannot be changed by fiat or force of arms, by understanding or revolution, but what can be altered is the range of our perception and its mode. We can see a different world without firing a shot or framing a syllogism, merely by altering our consciousness; and the ways to alter it are at hand: drugs, on the one hand: the techniques of oriental adepts on the other. To be sure, at the very moment some voices in the West cry out in favor of hashish and yoga, heroin and Zen, the East has opted for

the principle: science and work, and the conversion of id into ego.

No matter. There is a weariness in the West which undercuts the struggle between socialism and capitalism, democracy and autocracy; a weariness with humanism itself which underlies all the movements of our world, a weariness with the striving to be men. It is the end of man which the school of Burroughs [a contemporary author] foretells, not in terms of doom but of triumph. Let the experiment be over; let the focused consciousness blur into the cosmic night; let the hallucinatory monsters bred of fragmented consciousness prowl that night again; let the perilously sustained absurdity of the 'soul' be abandoned; yet let the demons who once trafficked in souls thrive anew."

The literary situation has not improved with the intervening decades since Fiedler wrote. The image being projected by much of the popular literature remains that of the erotic and irrational. The "weariness in the West" persists and deepens. The absorption and re-projection by any substantial population of the sub-human, even sub-animalistic image, (described by Fiedler in specific works), could constitute a danger of the highest order.

The sentence which Fiedler placed in italics and his following two paragraphs are strongly reminiscent of the words of the existentialist philosopher Albert Camus in *La vie Intellectuale:* "Contemporary disbelief no longer relies on science as it did at the end of the last century. It denies both science and religion. It is no longer a skeptical reaction to miracles, it is passionate disbelief." As H. A. Hodges said in his work, *The Crisis of Philosophy* (Hodges, 1947), ". . .What we are dealing with is not a contention which might be answered by a counter-contention but a deep-seated attitude of the will, a despair or at least a shifting of the focus of hope; an abandonment of intellectual aims and standards which have been determinative in our culture since the time of Thales."

Even as we saw how the concept of man could be viewed in our model from any or all of many facets, so any other entity having objective reality can be visualized, each projection being, to some extent, a subjective reflection. The wider the band reflected and the more intense the illumination, the closer the image will be to objective reality.

If a Supreme Being exists and thus has objective reality, and the transcendent viewpoint of man has no validity without that concept, so He too can be, and certainly has been, viewed differently at many times and places. Each positive viewpoint has a measure of truth, and the attainment of an image having absolute objective reality is here a double impossibility because of the inherent unknowableness, to a finite intellect, of the intrinsic nature of an infinite being, and also because of our own human intellectual deficiencies.

The primitive man saw the Supreme Being in the light of primitive knowledge, and we see Him individually in the light of our cultural background and intelligence. The great mystics saw Him with far greater illumination but, even there, the image could be skewed and incomplete as their individual situations provided a less than perfectly reflective background. Probably, as to this concept, the mystic stands at one end of the continuum of illumination and the atheistic materialist at the other.

In Part II, we will try to capture the concept of God and His relationship with man as it has been viewed generally in the pattern of thought of intellectuals of high historical import through the series of ages from about 1200 A.D. until the present, and to see how this image has been reflected in the changing times. Man's concept of the deity—including his denial—are intimately tied to man's view of himself. In no age have concepts developed out of a void. Each age either accepted, rejected or modified concepts handed down to it. Individual thinkers modified concepts to fit what they considered to be a closer approach to reality usually. The writer believes that, almost universally, these were honestly held conceptions.

This historical tracing is not performed for its intrinsic interest only, but to provide the essential background for an understanding of the intolerable intellectual tension to which man now finds himself subjected. The review of philosophic history is to show the diverse paths men have taken, many in retrogression, to arrive at this present state of precarious balance on the edge of nihilism.

The burden of the next four parts of this book is to establish at levels of high credibility, from all sources of knowledge, that God, in fact, exists; that the ultimate measure of the dignity of man lies in recognition of God's existence and our close relationship to Him; and that, this being so, the social forces in the world discussed in the last part, "The Extrapolation," will, in all probability, bring about a situation in the next century much as Toynbee's scenario suggests. Nietzsche's reign of nihilism is not likely to occur, at least in this coming era of history. The study seeks to establish, in realistic intellectual grounds, that man is not just a biologic specimen, but has a transcendent vector which survives after death. It seeks to show that the hope of a future life is not just a diversionary fiction for the simple-minded, but is supported with a degree of probability approaching certitude by clear evidence from the physical sciences and mathematics as well as from philosophic and religious insights.

The primary objective of the book, which is to identify the only firm basis of a sociology of morals, has certain correlative objectives. Chief among these is to provide the confidence and conviction needed to live authentically in an age largely stripped of religious meaning. Through this means it is hoped in some small way to encourage a massive return to a total life style centered in the concept of man's individual worth as a free creature of a loving and provident God. This means a life style which recognizes every man's innate value and his own individual responsibility to God and to his fellowman. It means individual recognition of a morality based on authentic moral sanctions.

In this sophisticated age, unless the traditional moral viewpoint has a deeply sensed validity, a solid rational foundation and acknowledged credibility of the highest order, it will not be accepted as a basis for conduct in personal and public life. The "morality" of the soft life is far more appealing in the absence of such conviction. Few will pass up a present pleasure for a future dream.

This book, then, within the overall methodology of systems analysis, first reviews the historical development of the concept of man in detail beginning with the emerging universities of the twelfth century, to provide the intellectual basis for the later analyses. The roots of the present controversy on man's nature go back to the conflicting concepts of the ancient Greeks and to the first medieval confrontation of Platonic and Aristotelian thought at the beginnings of modern philosophy. It is important to know the origin of an idea and the history of its development to deal with it intelligently. Second, following the historical development, the study analyzes the concepts of man as seen in contemporary philosophy and sociology, the latter largely through the responses provided to the "Hobbesian" question by the various sociologic theories and models now in general use. Part II, through review of the philosophical thought, seeks to demonstrate the accessibility of the concept of God and human immortality to the human reason. The accessibility, in turn, leads to the development, largely from analysis of the fact of being, of a high confidence level that God exists and that man's destiny is fulfilled in relationship with God.

In Part III, by resort to current mathematical and scientific thought, the study seeks to demonstrate, at very high confidence levels of derived probability, that the universe is the product of an intelligent, purposeful Creator. In Part IV, through use of empirical evidence involving identifiable physical anomalies of religious significance, the study provides support to a high probability that man has a transcendent nature and also that he is the object of concern and guidance by a Creator not only infinitely powerful, intelligent, and purposeful but, at the same time, intimately personal. In Part V, the study reviews current theologic and religious thought in the light of the emerging crisis and discusses problems of the relationship between God and men which have been found hard to accept by the modern mind. It attempts an analysis in depth of the concept of morality and of the validity of that concept. Lastly, in Part VI, the study extrapolates from the analytical foundations laid in the previous sections to follow the Nietzsche and Toynbee scenarios through the current world geopolitical-political scene as a model for the future. It projects in this model major sociological movements based on competing moral theories. Finally, the study pulls together all of the areas explored into a personal and sociological *modus vivendi* along the lines suggested in the Toynbee prediction. This life style promises a future of great social fruitfulness and personal satisfaction if people are willing to act as the true human beings within the insistent dialectic, which the studies have shown them to be.

PART II

MAN LOOKS AT MAN

Chapter 2

ARISTOTLE CONTESTS PLATO

In Part II, I will review the concept of man in the West as it has been visualized from late medieval times into the 20th century. This period, in my view, represents an epoch between two points of thought convergence on the idea of man, and in many ways of an entire way of life as well.

At the beginning of the epoch, about the year 1200, the fate of feudalism as a viable political institution had already been sealed although it would linger on for another three centuries. It was the victim of its own structural fragmentation and its heavy hierarchic overburden, secular and religious. The creative energy was leaving the system, probably sapped in great measure by the exhausting and futile tragedy of the Crusades which had already lasted 100 years, and which in one form or another would continue intermittently for another 500 years. In addition, interminable internal bickering and bloody strife for individual and dynastic control had destroyed all but the outward appearances of unity in the Holy Roman Empire. The peace of Christ did not appear imminent, and though much had changed during this period which can be identified as being progressive, the intellectual life had become monolithic, centering on theology and largely confined to the monastic institutions.

Although the "modern" period is vastly more complex than the above epoch, its end is similar, and also represents a convergence point in intellectual life, but on the different theme of materialism. Likewise, the energy seems to have gone out of this system, exhausted by two major wars, almost incessant localized conflict, and again a weariness, a sense of surfeit with the life which the prevalent philosophy promised but seems unable to fulfill.

In narrowly oriented slices of history, such as this study involves, the focus must be intense and the skeletal frame carefully delineated to avoid interesting but irrelevant byways. The skeleton I use is that chain of events which leads through the prevailing major systems of learning and hence primarily of the broad philosophies which were taught during those periods and by which the systems were dominated. For, in most periods of history, the philosophic system of thought is the leading edge of the sociological system which eventuates in a social behavior pattern extending down to the personal and up to the political. The educational system inevitably lies between the two. This skeleton will be fleshed out with political, economic, military, cultural, sociologic and religious details as they are relevant and necessary to an understanding of the main thread. Principally the work will be a discussion of individuals whose importance in thought has stood the test of survival in history, although it by no means follows the "Great Man" theory.

The concept of man, as man has viewed it, in succeeding generations is inextricably tied to his answers to those questions he inevitably poses to himself about the meaning of his life, its significance in relation to all that he sees about him, its origins, its purpose, its final end. It has been said that philosophy in any given age is a reflection of those things which men of that period hold to be most important. Each age has its own hierarchy of values, intellectual, spiritual, cultural and material. In every age, of course, there is a mixture of all of these aspects and the composition is highly varied.

Philosophers themselves attempt to look into the mists of the future and prophesy what man will become when he fully realizes that *this* value is the highest reality, *this* is the truth about himself. But philosophers are also men in history and do reflect the times and circumstances through which and in which they live. Their reflection may be either a reaction against the prevailing value system or a concurrence in it. But regardless of the viewpoint taken, philosophy, which does not address these fundamental questions in one way or another, can scarcely be said to be relevant to the people of its age although it may be intellectually stimulating within its own esoteric circle. True philosophy is not a game of wits, but an honest intellectual search for the truth by a "lover of wisdom." The term itself unites two aspects of man's life—the elements of passion and of learning. Hence, the correct position of the philosopher is not one of cold intellection but of a deeply felt, sincere but humble desire to approach the unattainable, perfect truth.

The early 13th century was at the edge of great change and also at a point where events could pause to take a breath. The Third Crusade, (1189-1192) led by Holy Roman Emperor Frederic

I, Philip II of France, and Richard I, Coeur de Lion, of England, while failing to capture Jerusalem, succeeded in establishing free access of Christians to the Eastern Mediterranean and the Holy Sepulcher. The abortive Fourth Crusade, (1202-1204) which became a Venetian political venture, succeeded only in further hardening differences between the Latin and Byzantine Christian forces to the benefit of Islam, but did not disrupt the reopening of the Eastern Mediterranean. It was a period when Frederic II of Aragon, Holy Roman Emperor, controlled in fair fealty from Germany to Sicily and was at peace with the church through the pact of San Germano. In fact, the defeat of the Emperor Otto, predecessor of Frederic II, and John of England, by Philip II of France, at the Battle of Bouvines in 1214, marked the real end of the dominant, feudal hierarchic system and a break point to a new era.

The Moors, while still controlling the Spanish Kingdom of Granada and, in overall terms, possessing the military initiative, had been defeated at Los Naves in 1212. And Frederic II, between 1228 and 1229, in what is called the Sixth Crusade, but what was really a tour de force for negotiation, broadened the rights of free access to the holy places and sea routes in the Mediterranean. It was a period when the forces of Islam essentially Arabic in leadership were also looking for a detente. The Nomads of Turkistan in Central Asia, migrating into the Middle East, were to revivify the Islamic drive in the fourteen, fifteenth and sixteenth centuries. But in the thirteenth, both Christians and Moslems were tired, though intermittent flare ups continued which eventually saw the Christian forces completely driven from Palestine in 1291.

The Crusades resulted in intellectual changes to Western Europe more extensive than the military changes. At the end of the eleventh century when the Crusades were initiated, Europe was Christendom and Christendom was Europe. For the people of Europe, of all levels, the world was defined largely by Christendom. The intellectual life of Monastic schools was rooted in the teaching of Saint Augustine, which in turn had been formed on Neo-Platonic and Platonic schools of philosophy. The universe, which was large in comparison with man, was nevertheless limited, and man had his place in it in his relationship to God. Time also had its base point. The birth of Christ was central; everything before it was prelude, everything afterwards, a denouement. History attained meaning from this transcendent event, the impingement of eternity on time.

The Middle Ages were built upon a base of solidified religion which underpinned every facet of life. Learning started with the concept of God, the Almighty Father, and flowed from that to everything that touched His children. Everything in life drew meaning from its relationship with the central fact. Morality, literature, music, architecture, art, the seasons of the year, birth and death, all the critical events between—pain, sickness, joy, sorrows. Everywhere man went, he saw the symbolism which constantly brought his mind into the deeply sensed relationship of his dignity as a child of God. Every village and town was centered around its church and monastery. Yet, life was not all an emotional creation. There was a deep seeking for knowledge. It was not accomplished by empiricism, but by seeking deeper insights into the works of the Fathers of the Church and the Scriptures. It was a learning based on authority, not experimentation. In philosophy, largely interwoven with theology, it was Plato, filtered in Latin scholarship primarily through Plotinus and Augustine. Although the logic of Aristotle was known and used by the monastic schools, the empiricism of Aristotle in natural science was not. And Platonism of itself was not well known except as it had been intellectually massaged through the centuries.

The advance of Islam and the Crusades brought a change to the monolith and a spreading from this point of sharp convergence. It became apparent that the world was not limited to the Holy Roman Empire which Charlemagne had hacked into existence four centuries before. Beyond the Danube, the Tartars, foreign forces, were pressing into the flanks of Eastern Christendom. The Middle East was being changed from a sister Christian Byzantine-Roman Empire into a Moslem Empire under constant pressure of Islam. Extreme southwestern Europe had been successfully assaulted in the eighth century, and a firm beachhead of Islam established in Iberia. Manifestly, the world of man was not a monolith. The Europeans had become increasingly conscious that the Christian faith touched only a segment of humanity, and beyond its boundaries extended a world of many peoples of utterly foreign thought.

But beyond this, by exchange with both Byzantine and Islamic forces, other philosophies began to invade the West. In 1226, Louis IX of France, St. Louis, began his long reign with his mother, Queen Blanche of Castile, as regent. Though his reign involved many foreign military adventures, ending in his death of the plague in Tunis in 1270 while embarking on yet another Crusade, his reign in France was one of peace, progress, and prosperity. Most of the great Gothic cathedrals in

France were built during his reign. He essentially stopped feudal quarreling, equalized taxation and strengthened legal right of appeal to the crown.

Closer to our own interest, during his reign the Sorbonne opened in 1257, the first endowed college in the University of Paris. It was founded by Louis's chaplain, Robert Sorbon. The University gained precedence by the excellence of its academic reputation over the earlier colleges of Paris which had existed in one form or another since the time of Charlemagne.

Concerning the creation of the University of Paris and its relationship to the city, as viewed in the 13th century, Thomas of Ireland wrote, with some bias no doubt:

> "Like Athens, the city of Paris is divided into three parts. One is that of the merchants, the laborers, and the common people; it is called the Town at large (magna villa). Another is that of the noblemen in which are located the king's court and the cathedral church; it is called the City. The third is that of the students and of the colleges; it is called the University. Studies were first transferred from Greece to Rome, then from Rome to Paris during Charlemagne's time, around the year 800, and the school had four founders: Rhabanus, Claudius Alcuin, master of King Charles, and John surnamed the Scott who, however, was born in Ireland, Ireland being greater Scotland."

During the succeeding 600 years, the scholarship of Paris dominated the philosophic theme, even though for geographic and military reasons the larger cultural renaissance began elsewhere. The University had achieved such excellence of reputation earlier, in fact, that in 1169 Henry II of England had offered to submit his quarrel with Thomas a Becket to the assembled masters of Paris for resolution. (Chenu, 1964, page 23).

The University was cosmopolitan, its leadership at different times during the period being under Alexander of Hales, an Englishman; Albert the Great, a German; and Italians, Bonaventure and Aquinas. Within fifty years to either side of the year 1200, colleges or universities independent of the monastic system were organized to a large extent on the Paris model in Bologna, Oxford (University College, 1249), Cambridge, Cologne, Padua, Naples, Toulouse, Siena and Piacenza, and these were followed rapidly by many others.

This conjunction of the newly established city universities

and influx of the philosophies of Aristotle and Arabic and Eastern schools started a process of ferment, which not only stimulated the Renaissance, but also the eventual rise to supremacy of the scientism of the modern age. For with the advance of Islam, Byzantine scholars fled the front areas and moved into Sicily and the port cities of southern Europe itself, bringing their libraries with them. Further, the Arabic forces in Spain, by then established for several centuries, included many scholars. Toledo became a major exchange point from the middle of the eleventh century when, as an independent kingdom, it was a center of Moorish, Christian and Jewish cultures.

The character of the new universities was entirely different from the monastic institutions of the earlier centuries, and the population settling the new centers and communes in the cities was different from that of the older, true feudal towns.

As so often seems to happen in history, an idea and the circumstances permitting fruition of the idea, coincided. The social and economic revolution accompanying the self-demolition of feudalism caused a concentration of the displaced rural population in the urban centers. The reopening of the Mediterranean to shipping, the increased emphasis on shipping and commerce, the influx of displaced scholars and new ideas from the near east and a rapidly increasing overall population all conspired to shift the educational center of gravity from the old conservative baronial monastic schools, which were largely feudal in their basic orientation, to the rapidly growing centers.

A new class of people had arisen—the future bourgeoisie. People who, having won freedom from the feudal agrarian system, started to envision themselves as individual free agents. Labor was seen as an economic commodity in the market place freed of the stigma of serfdom. Skilled workmen were at a premium. A man could improve his position economically, and that was being seen as perhaps as rewarding a goal as social distinction in the aristocracy. The idea that an education was the key to achievement in the commercial world gained ground. The universities filled with students from that city class of ambitious independent-thinking citizens and even included some commercially-oriented subjects in the curricula.

The impact of this combination of circumstances on medieval scholarship is hard to overemphasize. It opened up questions of methodology; i.e., of rationalistic experimentation versus authoritative sources in determining values. The former methodology was completely foreign to that of the contemplative seeking after truth, which had been followed for over 600 years.

For while the Aristotelian and the Platonic and Neo-Platonic schools had a common origin in Plato, the basic approach in their search for truth was divergent, and increasingly more so as subsequent generations of commentaries accumulated. Both Plato and Aristotle believed in a Supreme Being. For Plato, it was a Supreme Good, almost goodness personified; for Aristotle, the first cause without a cause, the Prime Mover of all things.

Perhaps it is wise to look very briefly at the philosophic history which led to Plato's and Aristotle's viewpoints. There never seems to be a completely satisfactory time at which to begin a review of the historic concept of man. For while there are crisis points in man's view of himself like the one facing medieval man in the thirteenth century and modern man again in the twentieth, the roots always go farther back. However, there is a convenient place to begin the history of the philosophic concept of man— that of the birth of western philosophy itself.

It is no coincidence that philosophy began in a period of a declining predominate religious system. For, if the traditional gods were no longer to be honored or sacred, there was a need for some other explanation of nature and guidance for man's relationship to it, and to each other, as a basis of co-existence. The intellect seeks a unifying principle, something which gives the appropriate stable background against which to display the motion and change of phenomena. Even at the time of Homer, about 750 B.C., the ancient beliefs were not accepted by the intellectuals except as symbolic of the observable constantly changing forces of nature. The symbolic gods were in fact an evolution from a primitive animism tied directly to nature. About the time of Homer, other religious forces were beginning to be felt in Greece. By the year 600 the Dionysian religion, of some remote Thracian derivation, and the oracular religions, particularly of Delphi, were attracting the attention of the ruling class, but had not yet replaced the older religion.

In the brief quotation cited earlier, H. A. Hodges credited Thales with the beginning of the rational approach to knowledge. Thales appears to have been born in the early seventh century B.C. in Miletus on the Ionian coast of Asia Minor, today's Turkey. An eclipse of the sun mentioned by Herodotus as marking the conclusion of the war between the Lydians and Medes was reputedly predicted by Thales. This eclipse has been calculated in modern times as that of May 28, 585 B.C. so that Thales was a grown man before that date. He was perhaps best known as an astronomer but also was recognized as a sage who used mathematical relationships as a guide to reason. He started the long search for a solution to the perennial philosophic problem of the "One and the Many" which, as we will see, still eludes discovery.

For more practical purposes, the development of philosophy as a discursive science is usually given as originating in the dialectical positions taken by Heraclitus and Parmenides, both born about 520 B.C. Since Parmenides was an actual commentator on Heraclitus, it is assumed he was somewhat his junior. They were active in opposite ends of the Greek world as well as being poles apart in their philosophies. Heraclitus was active in Ephesus in present day Turkey and Parmenides in Elea, in what is now southern Italy. For our purposes, their positions on the concept of man is most important.

Heraclitus was an aloof man who looked on his fellow-men as grasping, sensual, and unconcerned with matters of the intellect. If we can use anticipatory language, the common man was "Hobbesian" in his instincts and outlook. Heraclitus was a descendant of one of the founding families of Ephesus but gave up this birthright because he wished to live his own life-style. Life in authenticity was an important concept to him. The surviving works of Heraclitus are largely in the nature of "wisdom literature"—proverbs and maxims—having an oracular, semi-poetic tone resonant of the Sibylline and Delphic oracles. As we saw, he lived in a period, as did Parmenides, when the dying ancient religion was observed only by the common people, though it was encouraged by the leaders to foster a sense of patriotism and order. The oracular religions were taking their place.

In spite of his oracular style of writing, Heraclitus was hostile to both the traditional and oracular religions. He was pantheistic in his basic orientation, and that was reflected in his resolution of the problem of the "One and the Many" as "unity in diversity." The many are absorbed in the one; they are one and in the one. Heraclitus wrote, "Men do not know how what is at variance agrees with itself. It is an attunement of opposite tensions like that of the bow and the lyre." And he says, "It is wise to hearken, not to me, but to my Word, and to confess that all things are one." "Further, all things, the many, are only aspects of the one."

But to Heraclitus, God was the one and the all-knowing and made himself known, "The sibyl who in a delirium utters things unjokingly, unadorned and unperfumed, reaches milleniums with her voice for she is divinely inspired." "The wise is one only, both willing and unwilling to be called by the name of 'Zeus'." God, for Heraclitus, is the universal "Logos", reason itself, so men should strive to live by reason. The law of reason is unalterable, realizing the unity of all things, and the truth is given not in directive or fiat but by suggestion of reason and is everywhere apparent in its signs. "The lord to whom the oracle of Delphi belongs neither affirms nor conceals but suggests," and reason and consciousness in man are the only things of value. When that "fiery element" leaves man in death, the rest is worthless. "Corpses are more fit to be cast out than dung." Yet the God of Heraclitus was not inert, and in Him all tensions and differences are resolved. "Man is called a baby by God even as a child is by man" and "To God all things are fair and good and right, but men hold some things wrong and some right."

To Heraclitus, man in spite of his faculty of reason, is blind to reality and sees only that which is change. "All things are in a state of flux." "All things are in motion, nothing is steadfast." Of his teaching of the "One existing in the many" the "Identity in Difference," he says, "Men are as unable to understand it when they hear it the first time as before they heard it at all."

Heraclitus's God was still somehow material, associated with fire, as was all of the intellectual element. It is not possible to ascertain what Heraclitus saw in the relationship of God to man or of the destiny of man's intellectual power and consciousness. It can be inferred perhaps that he believed, as Aristotle appears to have later, in a reabsorption into the eternal intellect. For Heraclitus, man's dignity lay solely in his intellectual powers to some extent related to the one.

Parmenides took the opposite tack in his solution of the problem of the "One and the Many." Only the one is—the many are but an illusion. Where Heraclitus accepted change as real and evident, Parmenides denied it. He wrote in verse, and about all that remains of his work directly consists in fragments of a poem, or poems, which were collected and titled, *On Nature* by a physician, Sextus Empiricus, in the second century A.D., and some fragments of his thought are contained in commentaries of Simplicus in the sixth century A.D. Parmenides's poetry was symbolic, using the imagery of the ancient religious mythology. In many ways, his symbology was not unlike the effort by Nietzsche some 2,500 years later in his *Thus Spake Zarathustra* to convey difficult ideas by image. Parmenides was an intellectual descendant, though in opposition, of the Pythagoreans who had moved from Ionia to Kroton in south Italy in the late sixth century B.C.

Pythagoras, himself of Samos, founded a religious colony or a "school of philosophy" in Kroton. It is not possible to distinguish truth from fantasy in the origin of the colony or of the life of Pythagoras himself, but the philosophical roots of the Pythagoreans are tied to astronomy and physics in a manner reminiscent of Thales and so, likely have actual basis in Thalian thought. If so, Parmenides and Heraclitus had similar philosophical genetics.

In modern terminology, Parmenides rejected, as illusion, the idea of "Becoming" and stressed "Being." He is perhaps the first to emphasize the crucial view that nothingness is absolutely and totally unproductive of anything. "Out of nothing comes nothing"—a subject which I will defer in discussion until considering Scheler's philosophy in modern times. Parmenides' thought—and Heidegger in modern times had admitted he was attracted to it—was centered on, almost obsessed by, the apparent dialectic, "Being versus non-being." After showing the impossibility of a condition of non-being as real, he developed his thesis that change was impossible. Parmenides said, "One path only is left us to speak of, namely that *it is*. In this path are many tokens that what is, is uncreated and indestructible for it is complete, immovable and without end."

It flows from this emphasis that Parmenides introduced a tension between that which is sense knowledge and that which is arrived at through reason and also between being and becoming. If all sense knowledge, revealer of the many, is only illusion and the only real being is the One, it follows that the "ideal" is also the only reality or the only "being." However, this is not the much later Kantian concept, for to Parmenides the "One," being was tied to the material "Many," perhaps something like Kant's "thing-in-itself." Parmenides has been called both the father of idealism and a monistic materialist. The latter seems more appropriate.

What can we say of Parmenides' view of man? Parmenides himself was an aristocrat and maintained, according to later writers, an air of authority and dignity of his position as a philosopher. He wrote in mystical language-forms, but was at the same time almost coldly rational in his approach to his problems. Parmenides, like Heraclitus, was opposed to the extant religious forms. Heraclitus was opposed on the general grounds that his own pantheism was superior, while Parmenides seems to have been opposed on the more rigorous grounds that the religions were both irrational. There is really little further to go on in the fragments of his work. The Pythagoreans, of course, held the idea of transmigration of souls between men and animals which implies a kind of "immortality," and Parmenides' emphasis on reason certainly says that man's excellence derives from his intellectual achievements. There is no evidence, however, in Parmenides' residual work that he saw any real immortality of the soul. We do know that Socrates, and through him Plato, was influenced by Parmenides' work—his quasi-idealism. Socrates, as a young man, in fact, met Parmenides and had discussions with him about 450 B.C. when Parmenides must have been an old man.

It is unnecessary to review Socrates' (c.470-399 B.C.) tremendous contribution to philosophy before turning to Plato because what we know of Socrates' thought is principally that which Plato presents us in his dialogues, for Socrates himself did not write. That was not his teaching methodology, and the story of his life is so well known it needs no repetition here.

In his various works Plato and, by implication, Socrates through him devoted much energy to explication of three major metaphysical questions: Where and how can man know truth? What is the essense of the natural world in which man lives? Why was man created and, in this light, what was the proper goal of life? Plato was convinced that the senses alone are dubious routes to truth, being too easily led astray. Common opinion is shallow. Only through reason, applied to the totality of information supplied, can we arrive at real knowledge. In such a synthesis we can pick up the pattern, invisible but real, behind all permanent values. Plato leaned heavily on the deductive approach—logic in its broadest context. The persistent application of reason to generalized observation would lead to the truth. "By means of reason, the many particulars of the senses become unity." Although inductive processes are involved, they are not detailed.

Aristotle was more hardheaded, though far from being a materialist in any modern sense; he was at heart, an empiricist. One of Aristotle's basic premises like Parmenides' was the "immortality of matter," which said that something can never be produced from nothingness. Since matter and form are now observed in continuous motion and existence, so must they have always been. Time, too, was without an origin (Book 12, Chapter 8, *Metaphysics*). This concept is also remarkably like that of the physical universe as held by positivistic philosophers of the nineteenth and early twentieth centuries.

Nevertheless, and here the similarity with the modern empiricists ceases, there must be a first cause of all this activity, and something which keeps it in motion. This something must be itself immutable, motionless, eternal, unaffected by external events, immaterial. It must be pure form, pure intelligence. Man relates to this being: "The actuality of thought is life and God is that actuality. And God's essential actuality is life most good and everlasting. We may say then that God is a living being, eternal and most good, so that life and duration, unbroken and eternal existence are God's, for this is God." (*Metaphysics*, Book 12, Chapter 8).

Aristotle's Supreme Being is then different from Plato's, but the difference is not really qualitative—it is principally in the manner of its approach. For Aristotle, material being eternal, the "Creator" is only the activator, though Himself not acted upon in the material world. Once He activates the world, then He is indifferent to it. Plato's Creator, or, at least detailed organizer of the universe, in addition to His creativity, is also a model of goodness toward which man must aspire as life's goal. Man is immortal; in fact, his soul preceded in existence the formation of the body, which became ensouled. In the *Phaedrus,* Plato describes the soul as: "real existence, colorless, formless and intangible, visible only to the intelligence," and which seeks "absolute justice and absolute temperance and absolute science; not such as they appear in creation, nor under a variety of forms but as in real and essential being." For Plato, man's body was a sort of incubus, a thing of little importance in comparison with the soul.

While to the casual reader the difference between Plato and Aristotle seems somewhat secondary (Aristotle's thought is often seen as an evolution out of Plato, his outgrown teacher) there are several points which have consistently divided philosophers down to the present. Looking first at our basic dichotomy: Man, the self-sufficient, versus Man, the dependent creature. Aristotle took the first position, Plato the second. Plato saw the world of sense data as only a shadow of reality which was the universal ideal contained in the mind of God. Plato's "Parable of the Cave" is largely directed to this point. Aristotle saw the real world as real; there were no divine exemplars. He did not deny, as some did later, that there were no universals, but universals were concepts in the mind of man—mental abstractions of the essential qualities or properties of things. On the question of the "One and the Many," Plato, as could be anticipated from his emphasis on the ideal, saw the One as God, and the ultimate ideal exemplars which exist in his mind are the synthesized *Many.* The world of change and motion of the senses which comprises the Many is figuratively dismissed as of little consequence. Like our shadow, it has no reality apart from that which it images, its idealistic cause. But, since Plato does not—

literally can not (much like Kant centuries later)—dismiss the evidence of the senses, his thought forces a dualism of the ideal and the sensible world, and the solution to the problem of the One and the Many then results in another dualism equally unsatisfying intellectually. The problem is not solved. Since Aristotle held that the material which constitutes the world of the senses is uncreated, he did not attempt a synthesis between the outside world and the One, the prime mover. But by establishing the prime mover as the energizer and ordering agency he subordinated the Many to the One and provided stability to the intellectual picture.

Both Aristotle and Plato were primarily philosophers of being, ontologists in modern terminology. Aristotle was more inquisitive into the methods of knowledge, but his approach was in response to the question, "How do we know?" rather than to the "Can we know?" of the modern epistemology. Offhand it may appear that the difference between the two terms is purely academic, but on the contrary, the difference is crucial to the concept of man. The question, "How do we know?" presupposes that, in fact, man is capable of knowing and all we are interested in is the methodology. It is a clinical question, so to speak. It satisfies a scientific curiosity as to a question of procedure. "Can we know?" on the other hand, presupposes a doubt as to man as a rational being. If we cannot know, then the term rational, which has always been used to distinguish man from the beasts, has no meaning. Aristotle would never have raised that question.

Plato's work was also strongly mathematical in approach, following close to the Pythagoreans in the idea of the pervasiveness of numbers in all aspects of nature; whereas Aristotle clearly felt that mathematical analysis was mechanical and inferior. Thus, where Aristotle was oriented to the empirical approach to nature, Plato preferred the mathematical and rational or logical. Although Aristotle was a geometer, he had no great respect for mathematics in philosophy. He commented pejoratively in the *Metaphysics:* "Mathematics has come to be the whole of philosophy for modern thinkers, though they say that it should be studied for the sake of other things." In large measure, the differences between Plato and Aristotle were in viewpoint and emphasis; Plato's view the richer, the deeper in spiritual implications but Aristotle's the more insistent that man as a being in this world was of prime importance. Aristotle was a dedicated humanist.

In a medieval world, in which goodness and the imitation

of God were the apex of all symbolic structures of religion, the difference between Plato and Aristotle was severe. The original impact was in the area of methodology. Aristotle was the prototype of the natural scientist, experimenting as widely as he could. He started systematic exploration in many areas previously untouched and drew conclusions from his observations to advance knowledge. He placed inductive theorizing based on observed data in the highest category of men's means toward scientific advancement. Theory, in the realm of his physics, unsupported by observed facts and experience, could only be presumptive and tentative. Yet, he warned quite properly of the dangers involved in stretching conclusions too far from the supporting data, and deductive logic was essential in drawing appropriate inferences from the data. The developing universities of the twelfth century eagerly seized on Aristotle's techniques as the best way to gain an understanding of the world.

One more thing must be said. The original works of Plato, which were available to the early scholars, were largely textually complete in their Latin translations. Plato wrote them, not as a basis of lectures to students, but for the sophisticated adult Athenian, citizenry. They are literally masterpieces in the true sense, in addition to their compelling philosophic content. In the Neo-Platonic phase, Plotinus spiritualized Plato in an almost Christian sense. In turn, these works had been interpreted and commented on by St. Augustine, who was undoubtedly one of the world's great literary geniuses, a true artist, as well as a brilliant theologian. The resulting works were so sweeping and powerful, so eloquent in their affective as well as cognitive approach to God, and man's relationship to God, as to be overwhelming to the sensitive Germanic people who had had no previous long history of abstract thought.

This was the philosophic appeal which caught the imagination of all the Germanic tribes at the collapse of the Western Roman Empire and converted it into the theologic monolith that it was at the entrance to the twelfth century. The contrast between the soaring Western Gothic architecture and the classic Greek, formal Roman and Sybaritic Byzantine, reveals this upward thrusting, aspiring toward God which in many ways reflects that Platonic-Augustinian theme. While the religion was a montage of Roman, Greek, Hebrew and Germanic thought, it was the people of Western Europe who gave it the characteristic flavor distinct from the Byzantine church which, while virtually identical in dogma, was Greek and Semitic in tradition and culture.

Unlike Plato's, the writings of Aristotle were fragmentary, being largely lecture notes for students. The greater portion of his major works corresponding to Plato's dialogues were lost in the dissolution of the Alexandrian Empire. The remainder were fragments which were pieced together and hence lost the continuity of theme which characterized Plato's works. Roman, Greek and Arabic scholars reworked these fragments to the point that, when they were reintroduced to the West in the twelfth and thirteenth centuries, there was some confusion as to which were Aristotle and which were works of scholars interpreting and commenting on Aristotle.

This was the general situation when Thomas Aquinas, whose works began the divergent phase, appeared on the scene. But before going ahead with Aquinas, what was the philosophy which had served so well over the centuries—that thought of Plato and Plotinus as seen through the eyes of Augustine? Who was Augustine and what was his philosophy?

Aurelius Augustinus was born November 13, 354, at Tragaste in Numidia, North Africa of a family of fairly limited means. His father, Patricius, was a pagan, and his mother, Monica, the real strength of the family, a Christian.

Augustine studied rhetoric in Carthage and later taught the subject in Rome and Milan. He was influenced in philosophic thought first by the Manichean sect which taught a duality of good and evil forces, then by skepticism and finally Neoplatonism. He was in his mid-thirties when he found moral and intellectual peace and received baptism largely through the influence of St. Ambrose. He returned to Africa where he established numerous monasteries, and became a priest in 391. Although he preferred a solitary existence, he was forced to leave that life when he was named Bishop of Hippo in 395. He died in 430 even as the city was being sacked by the Vandals.

Augustine led a dissolute life from his adolescence until the time of his conversion. During that period he was plagued with a conscience which, while not deterring him, constantly reprimanded him for his evil ways. Before his conversion, while still in his early teens, he read a now non-extant book *Hortensius,* written by Cicero. The book inflamed his imagination. The effect of this work on Augustine clearly shows that even in his formative years he sought knowledge in deep spiritual intuition rather than in the intellectualism of the philosopher. His concept of metaphysics can be best gleaned from his own words reflected in this experience as he wrote them in his *Confessions:*

"But the one thing that delighted me in Cicero's exhortation was that I should love, and seek, and win, and hold, and embrace not this or that philosophical school but Wisdom itself, whatever it might be. The book excited and inflamed me; in my ardour the only thing I found lacking was that the name of Christ was not there. For with my mother's milk my infant heart had drunk in, and still held deep down in it, that name according to Your mercy, O Lord, the name of Your Son, My Saviour; and whatever lacked that name, no matter how learned and excellently written and true, could not win me wholly.''

Later reflecting on his life as a rhetorician, he again returns to this theme of God as the ultimate source of all good in existence and of happiness, the futility of this worldly life and his near despair of rising above it. He says,

"At the time my soul was in misery, and You pricked the soreness of its wound, that leaving all things it might turn to You, who are over all and without whom all would return to nothing, that it might turn to You and be healed. I was in utter misery and there was one day especially on which You acted to bring home to me the realization of my misery. I was preparing an oration in praise of the Emperor in which I was to utter any number of lies to win the applause of people who knew they were lies . . . I was passing along a certain street in Milan when I noticed a beggar. He was jesting and laughing and, I imagine, more than a little drunk. I fell into gloom and spoke to the friends who were with me about the endless sorrows that our own insanity brings us: for here was I striving away, dragging the load of my unhappiness under the spurring of my desires, and making it worse by dragging it: and with all our striving, our one aim was to arrive at some sort of happiness without care: the beggar had reached the same goal before us, and we might quite well never reach it at all."

But finally after many years of vacillation the light burst through on his consciousness and the theologic base which underlay all of his work in interpreting and extending Plato and Plotinus is clearly revealed. He wrote:

"Being admonished by all this to return to myself, I entered into my own depths, with You as guide;

and I was able to do it because You were my helper. I entered, and with the eye of my soul, such as it was, I saw Your unchangeable Light shining over that same eye of my soul, over my mind. It was not the light of every day that the eye of flesh can see, nor some greater light of the same order, such as might be if the brightness of our daily light should be seen shining with a more intense brightness and filling all things with its greatness. Your Light was not that, but other, than all such lights. Nor was it above my mind as oil above the water it floats on, nor as the sky is above the earth; it was above because it made me, and I was below because made by it. He who knows the truth knows that Light, and he that knows the Light knows eternity. Charity knows it. O eternal truth and true love and beloved eternity! Thou art my God, I sigh to Thee by day and by night. When first I knew Thee, Thou didst lift me up so that I might see that there was something to see, but that I was not yet the man to see it. And Thou didst beat back the weakness of my gaze, blazing upon me too strongly, and I was shaken with love and with dread. And I knew that I was far from Thee in the region of unlikeness, as if I heard Thy voice from on high: 'I am the food of grown men; grow and you shall eat Me. And you shall not change Me into yourself as bodily food, but into Me you shall be changed.' And I learned that Thou hast corrected man for iniquity and Thou didst make my soul shrivel up like a moth. And I said 'Is truth then nothing at all, since it is not extended either through finite spaces or infinite?' And Thou didst cry to me from afar: 'I am who am.' And I heard Thee, as one hears in the heart; and there was from that moment no ground of doubt in me: I would more easily have doubted my own life than have doubted that truth is: which is clearly seen being understood by the things that are made." (Augustine 1943 III-4).

While the more strictly philosophic works of Augustine, and none were purely philosophic, did not have the religious intensity revealed in these excerpts from his *Confessions,* the deeply internalized charisma came through clearly. The body was Plato and Plotinus, but the spirit was Augustine. St. Augustine was the dominant figure in the formation of a scholastic philosophy which St. Thomas Aquinas reorganized and modified in the Aristotelian logical form.

While Augustine gave theology the leading place in his writings, he nevertheless organized his philosophy in the order of: first, to things, then to self and finally to God. These three aspects bring into focus what in modern terms could be considered a dialectic approach, or interplay of opposing forces, in a general existential energy field of divine illumination. Thus, judgments between competing concepts of knowledge need a poetic illumination and in morals an illumination of basic principles of behavior. Every being is illuminated ontologically by number, form, unity and order. A thing has identifiable reality insofar as it is flooded by light in these component aspects. The laws of thought are of divine origin, but the forms or ideas of all things actually existing in the world are experienced as they are. Things are not imaginary. Things are real, and we learn about them by experiencing them. Yet they also exist in the divine mind, and the divine mind through its illuminations enables us to establish the truth concerning them. Man of himself is insufficient. Augustine's philosophy, essentially then, was one pervaded by God's paternal care and love for man and his eagerness to provide the insights to those who turn to him in filial love.

The great protagonist of Augustinian philosophy at the time of St. Thomas was St. Bonaventure who, in fact, died the same year as St. Thomas. However, Bonaventure, who studied at the University of Paris under Alexander of Hales and taught theology there for seven years, made some modifications to Augustine's thought to accommodate certain of Aristotle's ideas. But in the main, the doctrines of a certain divine exemplarism, the stressing of the psychological importance of the will and, above all, the illumination theory were typically St. Augustine. Bonaventure was truly in the Augustinian tradition and made no attempt to separate philosophy as a science from theology. The distinction did not seem important, and in those times it probably was not. It was, and remained after Thomas, the philosophy which, at root, saw the bond of love between God and man as the source and end to which all men's lives must be oriented.

Thomas Aquinas was born either in late 1224 or early 1225 at Roccasecca, Italy, the youngest son of Landulf of Aquino, a nobleman who was personally involved in political struggles of the Holy Roman Empire. Thomas was educated at the Benedictine Abbey of Monte Cassino and then the University of Naples in the faculty of Arts. He spent five years there and then went to the Universities of Paris and Cologne. He received his license to teach as a master at Paris in 1256. His teaching career brought him to several schools in Italy and then back to Paris in 1268. He early espoused Aristotelianism while in Paris in 1252.

The greater part of Aquinas' life was devoted to reconciling Aristotle with the basic position of the church which was firmly anchored in Platonism. He did not reject Plato, and he had almost a passionate affection for Augustine, but he felt that science, as organized knowledge, should be approached along Aristotelian lines. Along with other scholars of his time, Aquinas had a serious problem in gleaning Aristotelian themes from the intermingled works of commentators. A number of works were circulated in the twelfth and thirteenth centuries in the name of Aristotle which were completely spurious. Of particular concern to Thomas was the work of Averroes, (Mohammed ibn Roshd) a man of genius, and a Toledan Moor, born at Cordova in 1126, who had superimposed some Islamic interpretation of Aristotle into his texts. He was probably doing for Islam what Aquinas was doing for the Christian philosophy. Averroes was accepted, at least superficially, as Aristotle by some of the Christian writers of the time, and followers of Averroes' text and commentary became important in the Christian community. The most influential group was represented by Siger of Brabant who had introduced Averroes' text at the University of Paris in Thomas' absence. A great deal of Thomas' time during his late years was taken up in disputations of the question with that group.

The key point involved was the individual nature of the human soul. Aristotle appears to have shown a "preference" for the concept that there was one universal intellect and after death the human soul was reintegrated with that intellect and lost its identity. It is at least arguable that this was Aristotle's view. Although contrary to Islamic thought, Averroes taught this as the true Aristotelian position. Siger of Brabant and the "Latin Averroists" followed in accepting this concept as the philosophical truth. To reconcile this idea to the Christian teaching of individual salvation, they held that the latter was true from the theological viewpoint because God could intervene in a miraculous way and make it true, but that was a matter of faith, not reason, the two need not coincide. This duality, the viewpoint of separating reason and faith, has persisted in one form or another down to the present as of course has the pure monopsychistic theory also. As we shall see, Spinoza for one, the

pantheists in general and some philosophers in the splintering
of Idealism following Kant, continued in that theory. St. Thomas,
of course, held that objective truth was one for both faith and
reason, though faith went beyond but never contrary to reason
in the light of revelation. It has been held by some commentators that Siger changed his opinion later, but it is uncertain from
his writings. His life was cut short as he was murdered by his
secretary in 1282 when he was but 48 years old.

St. Thomas insisted on establishing man at the center of
philosophical thought. In that sense he was the father of modern humanism. Man and the universe were stable realities and
of major importance. Thomas opposed the thirteenth century
Augustinian view of man's incapacity to learn for himself and,
thus to denigration of man's natural ability in the natural order,
to obtain true knowledge and make true judgments. Thomas
used to good advantage the fact that the Greeks and the Ara-
bians had both succeeded in arriving at substantial truth by their
natural talents alone, implying that the Christians had done little better with the illumination postulated by Augustine. What
man needed to do was to develop a methodology of true thinking and Aristotle was the better guide in that field than Plato,
according to St. Thomas.

Probably it was the divisiveness between reason and faith to
which Averroes gave support which bothered Aquinas the most,
for the two-tiered approach to truth, in fact, denied that the
human mind can attain any knowledge of God through its own
resources. Still, for Thomas, there were no innate ideas of God
in men, only innate capacity to comprehend the ideas. Men
learned through the senses alone.

Aquinas was adamant that there were at least five ways in
which man's unaided intellect could approach God from the
observable universe. Aristotle had, in fact, arrived at his concept of and through the efficient causal succession to a final
cause in all things itself uncaused. Thomas extended this by
adding that, as a corollary of the observable dependence of
all things on other things for their existence, the contingency
of all observable things pointed to a necessary something which
was in itself independent and upon which all else depended.
Further, the fact that there is observable motion and change
implies that which is in itself immovable—a prime mover. The
order and harmony observable in the universe, its following
of a natural law, pointed to a lawmaker. Laws are not chance
occurrences. Finally, the gradations in excellence posited a standard of excellence, an optimum, which gave this particular level

of excellence a meaning—a relative goodness implies a supreme good. For Aquinas, the fact of the existence of Being and man's ability to reason from observations of aspects of Being is the basis of all.

St. Thomas was a stickler for a basis in sensed observation to support the intellect. He refused to accept the ontological proof of the existence of God which had been advanced by St. Anselm (1033-1109) two centuries before, because it relied on an implicit recognition that the concept "God" carries with it necessarily the fact of His existence. . .even in denying God, the atheist admits His existence by recognizing the concept. Strangely, this "proof" appears to be the one that has bothered the modern analytical philosophers the most, as we shall see a bit further on.

On morality Thomas had written, "A man who acts of his own accord acts freely, but one who is impelled by another is not free. He who avoids evil, not because it is evil, but because a precept of the Lord forbids it is not free. On the other hand, he who avoids evil because it is evil is free. Now, it is precisely this the Holy Spirit accomplishes, by inwardly equipping the soul with an inner dynamism. The result is that a man refrains from evil out of love, as though the divine law were commanding him. He is free, not because he is not subject to the divine law but because his inner dynamism enables him to do freely out of love what the divine law requires." Among the moral virtues, Thomas gives first rank to prudence under the guidance of charity. The prudent man evaluates each case individually and then responds in love, first of God, then of fellow and self. All of Thomas' moral theology is centered in God: Division I of Part II of the *Summa* contains Thomas' views on the precedence of the will in moral decisions and on man's last end being keyed to his moral life—the end, the Beatific view of God; the means, love of God applied in our lives.

Obviously, the world of the thirteenth century was not the same as that of which Aristotle wrote. Many concepts had changed, but while the concepts had changed, the basic principles of reasoning on which they were developed had not. The problem in adaptation was one of updating the concepts while maintaining the basic principles and methodology intact. This was the procedure to which Thomas set himself. He had manifest difficulties. The chief theologic problems with Aristotle were: first, he did not mention a Creator; second, his world was eternal, subject only to deterministic forces; third, he provided a God who, while supplying energy to the system, was wholly indifferent to man's problems; fourth, man was only matter and religious values did not enter into the concept of moral perfection. Finally as noted above, man was on his own, and individually his intelligence did not continue to exist after his death.

Thomas' opponents were principally those who believed that the only proper source of all philosophy was Plato and his followers, especially St. Augustine. Plato, particularly in the concept of the Creator, the loving model of Goodness, remained in Thomas' *Summa Theologica,* but this was not enough for the strict Platonists.

The dispute with Siger of Brabant in many ways marked and marred the end of Thomas Aquinas' productive years, although he demolished Siger, "Behold our refutation of the error. It is not based on documents of faith, but on the reasons and statements of the philosophers themselves. If then anyone. . .wishes to challenge what we have written, let him not do it in some corner nor before children who are powerless to decide on such difficult matters. Let him reply openly if he dare. He shall find me there confronting him, not only my negligible self [all 250 pounds of him], but also many another whose study is truth. We shall do battle with his errors or bring a cure to his ignorance." Aquinas knew and taught that there was but *one* truth, attainable, however, by different paths, two of which were faith and science. Despite his rousing refutation of Siger, Thomas was brought the first time to realize the misconstruction which the others could place on his work. Others, after Siger, could twist the statements to the effect that there were two levels of truth reached by the two parts, two completely incompatible truths, in fact, as Kant would hold five hundred years later. Shortly before his death, Thomas Aquinas is reported to have said to his associates, "Everything I have written is as so much straw compared with the realities." He did not complete his *Summa.*

The details of the conflict between individuals involved in the Platonic and Aristotelian approach are not important here. It is sufficient to say that by the time of Thomas' death in 1274, Aristotle still had not been solidly accepted in scholastic philosophy. St. Thomas Aquinas' work was condemned by the Church in 1277, and his work dismissed. But the groundwork had been laid. The University of Paris as far back as 1252, with Thomas' first teaching assignment, had already been turned toward Aristotle with the introduction of *De Anima* as a text. By 1255, the whole body of Aristotelian works had been placed on the curriculum of the faculty of Arts, oddly in the department of the English nation. Aristotle was not denied his place.

For a time, both Plato and Aristotle shared the stage and then Plato was to be eclipsed for awhile. The road via Aristotle led straight forward to rationalism as the basis of learning and to all of the diverse paths which started from there. Certainly, Aristotle would have been introduced without Thomas. The age was one of change and Thomas but its instrument. The work of Thomas provided the intellectual toughness lacking in Augustinian Platonism to maintain a strong God-oriented scholastic philosophy down through the ages. It is one of the strong viable philosophies reemerging in the twentieth century. This toughness was badly needed to combat the materialistic philosophies which were to follow in the secular Aristotelian chain and in revivified scientistic Platonism.

It is perhaps a good idea to take a look at that scholasticism which had been the wellspring of medieval learning. In the first place, it was the philosophy of a *Christian society.* It thus was differentiated from the earlier philosophies which had been either of whole peoples, tied to a regional culture, for instance, or to a very limited philosophy of a single outstanding individual and a small band of disciples. It is also differentiated from the modern philosophic systems which tend to concentrate on a single theme developed by an outstanding individual, but which may be worldwide as one "school" of philosophy among many others.

In the early periods, the term scholasticism was applied to the entire system of pedagogy in the monastic schools and was not limited to philosophy only. As a philosophy it was subordinated to theology to which it played a supporting or elucidative role. Philosophy was to assist theology and not the other way around. The themes which predominated the philosophic effort were thus, in the early days, selected largely from theology. As we have seen, the early Christians, particularly from Augustine on, seized the "ready built" Greek philosophies, principally Plato, Plotinus and Aristotle, but they included ideas even out of pre-Socratic philosophic thought. This amalgam was wedded to a largely "ready built" theologic system in the Judeo-Christian tradition. Justin Martyr, writing in the second century, had said: "Whatever things were rightly said among all men are the property of us Christians." (*Second Apology,* Chapter XIII). Hence a characteristic of the scholastic philosophies, and the plural is justified, including those of the present is that they do bring in other philosophic methodologies where useful to update the system. Scholasticism has thus been labeled a "perennial" philosophy since it does tend to grow in phase with other learning.

The chief characteristics since Aquinas of the system and method, and it is both, are its devotion to systematic thought, to realism and logic, and emphasis on the natural ability of the human mind to arrive at the truth through the processes of reasoning, deductive and inductive. The latter is generally subordinate to the former. The syllogistic form of argumentation has, perhaps, become its hallmark.

During the period between Augustine and Aquinas there were many different variations on the Platonic theme which the several monastic schools developed and played in a slow-paced obligato to a theologic chorale. There were periods of greater and lesser excellence, as would be expected in an 800 year rendition conducted amid incessant feudal wars. Two philosophers' works will be reviewed briefly because of their subsequent importance to the continuing history and not because of their contemporaneous status. The first philosophical work is by St. Anselm of Canterbury. His studies have already been mentioned in connection with his ontological "proof" of the existence of God.

Anselm was born in 1033 at Aosta in the Italian Piedmont and, hence, while generally associated with England, was an Italian educated chiefly in France. He lived during the intellectual decline following the Carolingian Renaissance and before the twelfth century rebirth in the university movement so that his genius perhaps is all the more outstanding. He became Archbishop of Canterbury in 1093 and died there in 1109. His theme throughout his philosophy was that of Augustine, *Credo ut intelligam*—"I believe, that I may understand." He did not pursue philosophy in order that he might have faith. Rather, it was his faith that permitted him to develop his understanding of reality. One should attempt to understand what one believes. Two of his works are of prime importance and, for our purposes, should be considered as one. *The Monologium* is devoted to the "proof" of the existence of God from observation—levels of beauty, of perfection, of goodness imply a gradation to an ultimate beauty, perfection and goodness. Following that chain, the undeniable existence of being—any being—and the observable gradation of being contradict—any possible condition of non-existence or non-being. There is therefore, a necessary condition of being-in-itself which must, following the gradation theory, exceed in excellence and greatness any and all observed being.

In Anselm's *Proslogium* he developed his highly persistent ontological argument which we will look at in some detail in current philosophic viewpoints. It should be considered in relationship to the last argument in the *Monologium* which established—if the reader agrees—that there must be a "being in itself," since being is and is a necessary condition in contradiction to any postulated non-being. It will be recalled that this was also Parmenides' argument for the eternity and infinity of the "One." In the *Proslogium,* Anselm says, in effect, any being having existence is greater than the same being in concept only—a real horse is greater than an imaginary horse—but, by definition, God is that being beyond which no greater can be conceived. If He exists, that is what He is. But if God exists in concept only—is only imaginary—He is not the greatest we can conceive. Any real being is greater than any imaginary being. Therefore the existence of the greatest conceivable being must be an intrinsic quality of its being as it is conceived. The very idea demands the being's existence. The argument, as contained in the *Proslogium,* has been used by Descartes. As we have seen, it was denied by Aquinas and was denied by Kant in the eighteenth century, but raises its head again late in the twentieth century. As combined with the argument in the *Monologium,* which *a posteriori* develops that there is a greatest Being, Anselm's purely ontological argument is given much greater strength.

The other philosopher of importance to this work from the period just prior to Aquinas, is Robert Grosseteste. He was born in Suffolk, England about 1170. Grosseteste can be said to have been the originator of an empirical tradition at Oxford which has characterized English philosophy down to the present. Grosseteste came up with the remarkably modern concept that light is the essential substance—the first "corporeal form." Light unites with Aristotelian prime matter, which is not necessarily material, to form a simple substance without dimensions. From that, all other things of nature are derived. It is also the principle of motion. But God is light—pure light in its essential form. Grosseteste sees the intellectual illumination postulated by Augustine as this very light. Roger Bacon (1214-1294), the titular forerunner of the empirical trend in England, in writing about Grosseteste, whom he followed at Oxford, mentioned Grosseteste's wide interest not only in following Augustine and Aristotle but also in relying greatly on his own experience and observations.

Chapter 3

The Humanists

At the close of the thirteenth century, on the threshold of the Renaissance, there was a single concept of man in the West, which saw him having transcendent dignity as a child of an almighty, eternal and loving Father and whose place in the world was secure because his place in eternity was secure. Man was at home with himself and within himself. God was with him and within him. Regardless of the vicissitudes of life, he knew who he was and why he was here. The route ahead, however, would change. The theologic monolith was laboring badly in its contests with bourgeoning commercial enterprises. Essentially agricultural in its orientation, it found difficulty with the rising urban affluence and attractiveness. A new age, and not only a renaissance, was coming into being. Medieval man was willing to look at Aristotle's work in the light of a constructive methodologic tool in expression of natural truth and to develop it on that basis. Renaissance man would use it as a knife to cut away tradition and authority as a source of guidance.

As mentioned earlier, the Renaissance did not appear full-blown in the fourteenth century, but rather evolved from conditions principally theologic, philosophic and commercial in thrust which had been established during the twelfth and thirteenth centuries. At the close of the thirteenth century, Aristotle had been established as the source of a viable basic intellectual complex, from the most lofty metaphysics to the lowliest natural science and in many areas superseded Plato almost completely. Plato's approach was essentially that of deductive logic from broad principles. The approach was not easily modified to fit a new world outlook which saw progress in change. On the other hand, the Aristotelian emphasis on the empirical source of knowledge was readily adaptable. Plato began with God and worked down, but Aristotle began at the ground and worked up, and that approach better suited the rising moods. In his empirical approach Aristotle would regard an earthworm with as great attention as he would an eagle, but he would dismiss an angel.

Now, entering the fourteenth century, the philosophic concept of humanism initiated by St. Thomas began to emerge and to occupy center stage. In the theoretical interest of giving greater prominence to man in the universe, the effect, in practice, was to drive a wedge between man and the God-centered monolith of the past centuries. Aristotle's inquisitive rationalism ultimately provided the leading edge. The humanistic movement began in Italy in the first half of the fourteenth century and combined the rediscovered ancient secular classics with the sense-oriented philosophy of Aristotle to propound its ideas.

The humanists drew upon the intellectuals being turned out by the universities in the fourteenth and fifteenth centuries. By this time virtually every major city had a university. The alumni were appearing more and more as public officials, as counselors in high office, and they formed among themselves a separate intellectual community active in correspondence and publication.

While printing had not yet come upon the scene in the fourteenth century, one of its necessary antecedents, cheaper manuscript material, a literary medium easier to work with, came about with the introduction of true paper. While the Arabs in Damascus had used a paper with a cotton base as early as the eighth century, it was not until the thirteenth century that a cheap variety using Spanish hemp and flax entered much of Europe from Toledo and other points in Spain. This linen paper permitted books to be copied cheaper, easier and faster, and was naturally an incentive to later development of printing techniques. Thus, even before printing came about some 100 years later, reproduction of classics and other secular literary works and private correspondence was being facilitated.

Although not properly classed as a "humanist," William of Ockham was a transition figure of tremendous importance to philosophic thought—particularly in the scientific view from his time to the present. He was born in England and, judging from his surname, probably in Surrey toward the end of the thirteenth century. He studied at Oxford and became a Franciscan. While at Avignon he became involved in state-church disputes as a result of which he fled in 1328 to Munich for refuge under Ludwig of Bavaria, who appears to have been a particular patron to the dissidents of that period. However, 20 years later Ludwig died and Ockham applied for reconciliation to the church. Ockham himself died of the Black Death in 1349 before that action was completed.

During the years of his exile he had been tremendously busy in producing theologic and philosophic literary polemics—works ranging from what would now be called essays to fully developed books. He was basically Aristotelian in approach, but also in many ways an independent thinker. It is a legitimate inference that his empiricism and his independence in thought stemmed from the Oxford tradition. His chief break with the tradition of Aquinas was in his attitude toward reality and the capability of the human intellect to approach it. To some extent, in his rejection of the view that the unaided intellect can come to a demonstrative knowledge of God or personal immortality of the soul, he echoes back to the Latin Averroists and the two-tiered theory of truth. In his *Summa Totius Logicae* he developed a comprehensive theory of logic for which he is considered the model in scientific theorizing. "Ockham's Razor" is a term applied to this approach. It states, in effect, that a hypothesis must be stripped of all but its essential elements. The simplest, most economical hypothesis explaining all associated observable phenomena has the greatest probability of being correct and should be the first examined. Like Aristotle, he rejected the idea of universals formed in a class.

Thus, the class, "horse" has no independent reality. This is what Aquinas also taught. For Aristotle and Aquinas, contrary to Plato, who thought the form of the universal existed in actuality, held that while the universal did not exist as a substantial thing, it had real objectivity in itself as a concept. But Ockham extended the idea. The term of a universal for Ockham has subjective value only and has no significance in philosophy outside of a proposition in argument or general discourse, and then only as an image. Thus "human nature" has no meaning in itself except in individual observable human beings. It is improper to say that men by their nature are curious: only individual men are curious as individuals. That does not sound too drastic, but the question goes to the root of one's ability to acquire knowledge and to generalize or deduce from general principles or universals. If none such are real, no such argument has any validity. "A" may cause "B" observably, but to say nothing comes into existence without a cause is a generalization not sustainable in logic, even though no exceptions are known. And ultimately it follows that no theological doctrine of God's existence or of immortality of the soul can come from intellectual processes. All religious tenets and doctrines must depend solely on faith, with no support from scientific sources.

Oddly the driving force for Ockham's argument was his profound conviction that attempts to arrive at theological truths via a rational approach were a usurpation of God's independence and restricted His liberty and omnipotence. It is almost a foreshadowing of Kant's viewpoint and Kant's motivation to remove the idea of God, immortality of the soul and human freedom from scientific attack. Both approaches, of course, eventually backfired from their advocates' deeply felt intentions in the interests of theism. Ockham's philosophy minus his theological works could well be used as a model for the logical positivists of the early twentieth century. We will follow this development among others. Aquinas would have viewed Ockhamism as a reaction against humanism, since it would have reduced man's inherent independence in his intellectual life. Yet, of course, in the actual effect, by reducing philosophical emphasis on the metaphysical aspect of humanism, it stimulated or made available more effort for application toward the physical, the biological aspect of humanism. Ockham's personal view of man's dignity lay in his relationship as a humble creature of God entirely dependent on the free gift of supernatural faith. From that viewpoint he was a true intellectual progenitor of Martin Luther two hundred years later. By the end of the fourteenth century Ockhamism or Nominalism, the *"via moderna,"* was strongly represented in the universities of central Europe such as Vienna, Leipzig, Cracow, Heidelburg, Erfurt and in the fifteenth century at Paris and Oxford.

The difficulty about the argument on universals for those who held that the "recognized universals" constituted legitimate general principles is that if they attempt to "prove" them they are faced with inductive rather than deductive argumentation at root, and an impossible induction at that, though seemingly self-evident as to require no "proof." Is "human nature" a valid concept so that we universally say that some trait or set of traits is human? For instance, can we say all men are mortal per se, or all men are curious? The way we know people are curious is that everyone we know exhibits the quality to some extent. That is equally true of mortality—but in a more absolute sense—there is no gradation. Likewise, since everything we know which has come into existence has a cause, does that justify the conclusion that every such thing has a cause of its existence? We may believe so, but short of an impossible polling of everything existent, or possibly existent, and the observation of things coming into existence, we cannot prove it rigorously.

Ockham held that when two things are distinct and separate there is no necessary connection between them. There are "fathers" and "sons" and one does not have to postulate the relationship of "paternity." Ockham was not so simple-minded that he denied there were in actuality such relationships in specific cases, only that there is no *a priori* argument which is adequate to demand the relationship, and further it is an unnecessary complication to an understanding of nature. There are only two sources of knowledge—empirical determination and revelation—and these two sources are completely separate and adequate. It never occurred to Ockham that at some future time revelation might be denied as a source of knowledge.

Of the six topic questions, What? When? Where? Who? Why? and How, the last three seeking purpose and the intending ego are chiefly affected by this restriction on universals. They are peculiarly human questions. Practically all of the species of fauna can at least in some dim way raise the first three questions and through instinct in some dim way seek answers—they are oriented to matter. The relationship that is sought by the others is precisely that which Ockham discounts. How did the universe come into existence? Why did the universe come into existence? Who is the intending ego which provides the answer to why and how the universe came into existence? "Why" implies a relationship of intention. "How" implies a relationship of method. And "Who" implies a relationship of personality in intention and method. Does the spider, the beaver or the bird consciously intend the web, the dam and the nest respectively, and deliberately select a methodology? Is there behind the manifest purposefulness of the instinctive acts at some remote remove an intending ego that responds to the "Who," "How" and "Why" that purposefulness implies? For Ockham, the question is "off limits." We will look at his question when reviewing the work of Merleau-Ponty in the twentieth century.

What about the classes oxygen and hydrogen? Do they exist as legitimate class identities so that we may generalize, or must we examine each atom as an individual? One can assert, at a fairly high confidence level, that all men are mortal, and similarly one can say with a high level of confidence that nothing comes into existence without a cause. Or, we can say with a high confidence level that all men are curious and that oxygen and hydrogen have specific natures on which we can rely so that one can use it as a working principle. This is one reason in most practical fields one settles for a "confidence level" even where the level seems adequate to use the expression "with certitude." Let the skeptic have his doubt in the remote and uncalculable decimal positions of certitude. As the late Jacques Maritain said on the matter of human nature in an essay of human rights prepared as an address to the United Nations:

"Since I have not time here to discuss nonsense (we can always find very intelligent philosophers, not to name Mr. Bertrand Russell, who defends it most brilliantly) I take it for granted that we admit that there is a human nature."

There were others who had raised the question before Ockham, Boethius in the sixth century and Roscellinus in the twelfth, but Ockham was the first to establish it as a basic element in a system of thought and Ockhamism can be said to have initiated the systematic questioning of modern epistemology along the lines, "Can we know?" Once one starts chopping off man's essential rational powers where does one stop?

The works of Ockham and the true early humanists such as Petrarch, Boccaccio and Pico della Mirandola, which we will look at shortly, were widely disseminated from and between university focal points. These works caused an almost explosive outburst of this critical aspect of speculative thought and of polished editions of the Roman and Greek classics, submerging the more pedestrian medieval scholars.

The humanists dismissed as virtually worthless some 1,000 years of history. They assumed an intellectual gap between Cicero and Petrarch. Man's reason, his acts and his innate human capability, rather than his status as a child of God destined for eternity, gave him dignity. The man to be glorified was the man of genius in the human arts. The educational system was modified from the more formal philosophical orientation of logic and intellectualism toward that of literary development through study of the secular classics. It was directed to development of the personality.

The first and leading exponent of this scheme was Francesco Petrarch, who was born in Italian Tuscany in 1304. His early life was in the papal service, where he received his background in the Italian classics. Thereafter he spent his entire life in literary pursuits, both in study and writing to revive the spirit of antiquity. He openly rejected the works in the medieval style and turned to the literary classics, particularly those of the Ciceronean period, for the subject matter of his works. He used the classical style even in his vernacular works extolling the spirit of the classics and the new humanism and was an enormous influence on the development of humanism. The great volume of works in epistles or essays and poems in classical Latin testified to his vast interest and dedication. He was called "The Scholar." Kings and popes heaped honors and wealth, too, upon him. The University of Paris received him in honor. The City of Rome crowned him with laurel in 1341, and Venice gave him the "key to the City."

The great pity for the people of the Renaissance period was that during the Middle Ages the national vernacular languages had produced great, even eloquent literature in terms of true dramatic appeal in prose and poetry. These literary masterpieces in German, English, Provencal, Castilian, Portuguese, Slavic and, above all, in Italian, were virtually lost to the classicist flavor of humanism which, viewing it from a point five centuries later, was artificial and formal and not suited to the masses of the peoples of the times. Ironically, while Petrarch was chiefly proud of his Latin epic, *Africa,* which had all the contrived imagery of the classics suited to Cicero's time, it is the Italian popular poems and the larger Italian *Trionfi,* that he wrote as a sideline for which he is best known. His Latin classics are secondary and virtually unread in the original Latin of which he was so proud.

Neither Petrarch nor Boccaccio (1313-1375), his close friend, who is also ranked as a leading early humanist, had broadly developed philosophic backgrounds, though they dealt with philosophic themes. Their genius was literary. Both rejected Aristotelian viewpoints as pedestrian. Their important contribution to the humanist movement lay in the supply of literary nutrient which was fed to the developing organism even after their deaths. It is interesting to contrast these two with Florentine Dante Alighiere (1265-1321) who preceded them by roughly half a century and who was much more a philosopher than they. Dante's works were typically medieval in theme and execution, even though he produced some works in Latin and has been considered a humanist because of them. Today, the works of Dante are far better known than the works of the other two and he has a tremendous literary impact, but little or no impact on the trend of the concept of man. At most, he served as a transitional figure between the high Middle Ages and the Renaissance.

If Petrarch and Boccaccio provided the nutrient to the early humanist organism, Pico della Mirandola supplied the spirit. He was born in 1463 and was a member of the Florentine Academy of Cosimo de Medici, which, ironically from the standpoint of humanism, was Platonic in basic orientation. The academy was a model in structure for the later general movement in the next two centuries throughout Europe. Cosimo de Medici had brought in George Plethon, who had been a scholar in Byzantinum but who, in flight from Islam, came to Italy in 1438. He was an ardent Platonist, and under his tutelage a revival of Platonism developed centered in the academy. Plethon bitterly attacked all forms of Aristotelianism, and the academy followed his viewpoint.

Pico della Mirandola was not a literary genius like Petrarch and Boccaccio, but rather, a philosopher, well-trained in all theoretical and methodological aspects of the medieval and the ancient schools. He possessed a command of both Greek and Hebrew, and he attempted to unify Greek and Hebrew viewpoints of God and man. He was linked closely with the humanist movement which had originated about a hundred years earlier with the emergence of the strong literary trend toward glorifying the classics and therefore man, but his Platonism gave it a different twist.

Pico shared with the early humanists a deep-felt concern for man and his place in the universe. He evolved a position from the Platonic metaphysical idea that man stood somewhere in the hierarchy of existence between animal and the pure spirit, which of itself fitted well into the Christian concept, of course. Pico's derivation did not. His oration, the *Dignity of Man,* was condemned by Pope Innocent VIII, and was not published by Pico, but by his nephew after his death in 1492. It gained wide circulation. By this time the printing press had been developed, and the universities were eager for new and controversial material.

In substance, Pico held that man's ultimate position in the hierarchy of existence depended on man himself. He had no defined position, and depending on how he utilized his talents, he might (figuratively) become as low as a plant, or unified with God Himself. Man must strive to elevate himself by human means to achieve the higher levels. Pico found man's dignity specifically in man's freedom of choice. In this freedom man shared with God the ability to unite all things. The difference between God and man was largely quantitative. God contains all because He is the first cause of all, and man, being the center of all, likewise combines all. Pico considered that God created man so that there would be an earthly creature who could appreciate the world and admire and love its beauty and magnificence of scale. He says, "Therefore, all things having been already completed (as Moses and Timaeus testify) He took thought finally to produce man." Pico's overall thought was Christian in context, for he held it is through Christ in the Incarnation that the way for men to approach God has been opened. The "unchristian" idea of the perfectibility of man as an individual through his own efforts alone contained in

Pico's concept has been expanded in recent times into the theme of perfectibility of man as a species. Again, the difference is quantitative.

In addition to the main line Aristotelian humanist position which was gaining importance, there were divisive offshoots from the older scholastic philosophy, which by now largely was that patterned after Thomas Aquinas. These offshoots merged with the humanist movement, and the most prominent of these deviationists during the early Renaissance was Pietro Pomponazzi, born in 1462. Trained at the University of Padua, he taught there and also later at the University of Bologna. He had a background of solid scholasticism and was familiar with all of the Thomistic methodology and Aristotelian logic and natural science. Pietro insisted, however, in applying strict Aristotelian thought in his concept of the soul of man, which denied that individual man survived death in any sensible way. When the union between intellect and body dissolved, that was it, as far as the individual was concerned. On this point Aristotle had said (*Aristotle,* 1943, pages 97-98):

> We may safely then define a happy man as one who is active in accord with perfect virtue and adequately furnished with external goods, not for some chance period of time but for his whole lifetime. But perhaps we ought to add that he should always live so and die as he has lived. It is not given us to foresee the future, but we take happiness as an end, altogether final and complete; and, this being so, we shall call people happy during their lifetime if they possess and continue to possess these characteristics—yet happy only so far as men are happy. . .
>
> A serious doubt has been raised as to the participation of the dead in any good or evil. It is probable that if anything, whether good or evil, reaches the dead at all, it is feeble and insignificant, both in itself and in relation to them. If not, it is at least of no such magnitude and character as to be capable of making happy those who are not happy or of depriving of their felicity those who are.

Therefore, said Pomponazzi, perhaps exaggerating Aristotle, and more after Alexander of Aphrodisias than Averroes, the application of moral virtue in this life produces happiness in and of itself. Virtue is its own reward. And this in turn is nobler than working here and being virtuous in order to achieve a reward in an afterlife. Man's intrinsic dignity, therefore, consists in lifting himself, by himself, to excellence and thereby to rule himself, his passions and his intellect and to improve the lot of his fellowman. Human life here has its own intrinsic value and dignity when man lives it like a whole man. Pomponazzi appealed, as had Aristotle, to empirical evidence to support his view, though in a different way. Since all knowledge arises from sense perception, the human person is therefore completely dependent on matter for his knowledge and existence; and since there is no empirical evidence that there is anything in man which could exist without matter, there is no basis for holding to the immortality of the soul in any form. In the last analysis, Pomponazzi was probably more of an agnostic than a pure atheistic humanist in the sense that all activity should be directed to man, in man and for man here, with no hereafter to be considered. He did not close the door to the possibility of a soul or immortality, merely saying along with Aristotle, "I can't prove it. Therefore, I have my serious doubts it survives as an entity. And if it does, the facts are unknowable on any rational grounds." Nevertheless, the philosophy was strictly "unchristian" and materialistic to the core and foreshadowed the empirical and epistemological turn in philosophy several centuries later.

At the beginning of the sixteenth century there were four discernible distinct philosophic paths among the intellectual leadership, each with a different concept of man. The old Platonic-Augustinian or traditional concept saw the apex of man's dignity in that state of sanctity achievable through mystical union with God in a life of intense contemplation. Man's individual dignity depended upon his own freely-willed response to God. Authority and revelation were the primary guides; reason was supporting. Man's dignity rested in his relationship to God. This was a continuation of the old monastic ideal and it was a quiet philosophy in the fifteenth century.

A second path was that of Thomas' main line scholastics, who agreed fundamentally with the first, but placed greater emphasis on the ability of man to achieve true knowledge and on the value of intellectual, rather than emotional or intuitive, motivation in approach to God. They gave about equal weight to reason, authority and revelation as sources of knowledge of God—though in case of conflict revelation and authority would control. This group logically includes those who followed William of Ockham, the Nominalists, who were probably the most active in the scientific movement of the early Renaissance.

A third path was that of the "basic" humanists who saw the dignity of man in the glorification of the human essence, the developing of genius in all forms, and in the maximizing of man's capabilities to live a full human life. Morality was one facet of this full life, primarily because it was ascertainable through reason as superior, but still man's free choice, and secondarily because it was a revealed requirement. God was important, but subdued. Man's dignity lay in his freedom to develop his genius and to freely choose right over wrong. This group was subdivided between Platonists and Aristotelians, the Aristotelians probably having numerical superiority, the Platonists advancing in the scientific arena because of stronger orientation to mathematics.

The fourth path was that of the rationalistic humanists who saw the dignity of man much as did the other humanists, but who saw any requirement of morality as basically human or natural in origin, to be followed for its own sake if at all. "Satisfaction is better than sacrifice, and self-gratification, than self-denial." (Hayes, 1932, page 203). This group was a development largely of the Averroes and Alexandrean wings of Aristotle and was in itself involved in deep dispute. The debates raged among the intellectuals, while the great bulk of Renaissance common people continued to live as they had for centuries, following the same basic Christian morality.

Now, though, four great changes in the educational environment set the stage for intellectual changes as never before in history. First, the advance of Islam, culminating in the fall of Constantinople in 1453, had vastly enlarged the reservoir of Greek, Arabic and Byzantine scholarship and libraries in the West. Second, the great spread of the university system and relative freedom of movement between schools formed a highly efficient communication network for dissemination of new ideas throughout Europe. Third, the development of printing and a cheap medium in paper greatly facilitated the reproduction and distribution of uniformly indexed books and pamphlets, free of individual copyist errors. And, fourth, the renewed emphasis on Latin in all the universities with a greatly expanded technical vocabulary led to a cohesiveness of learning throughout Europe. The detailed academically-oriented Latin of the universities of the late fifteenth century would have been as strange to Cicero in relative terms, as a late twentieth century technical dictionary to a person of the nineteenth century.

The Renaissance developed differently in the various areas of Europe. Its first impact was in Italy, and the characteristics which most people think about when the idea of the Renaissance era is mentioned are of the display and ornamentation which is still in evidence in cities such as Florence and Venice. In the north the spirit was greatly subdued. For one thing, the Byzantine influence tended to remain in the south, and the severity of northern climates tended to discourage the outward manifestations. But, for another, there was an intellectual sobriety about the responses in the north. The chief impact in the north indeed seems to be in the sphere of morality and philosophy and a deepening of skepticism along with serious scientific advance. Had a period called the Renaissance not been established it would scarcely have been noticed in England, where it arrived still later and coalesced with the Elizabethan period in literature, from which it is almost indistinguishable.

One aspect of the Renaissance which I have not touched on previously but which had an influence on later thought and should be mentioned is the rise of a naturalistic movement in philosophy differentiated from the other themes.

Nicholas Krebs was born at Cusa on the Moselle in 1401, was educated at Heidelberg, and received his doctorate at Padua in canon law. He was ordained priest in 1426 and assigned at Coblenz. His general philosophy was tied to the ancient problem of the One and the Many, and he conceived the solution as a unity which was a harmonious synthesis of differences. Nature was theocentric. Of interest to us, principally, is the idea that everything partakes of the nature of everything else, though all things are different, and all things achieve perfection in relation to the divine nature in God. While God remains separate and distinct, the Motivator and Sustainer of all the externalia, which persist only because they are participants in the essential nature, nature is to some extent a growing organism unfolding and developing in its course through history in the experiences of all creatures. It seems almost as though Krebs would like to have had a "Demiurge" in the Platonic tradition which would be nature, but his theologic background would not permit it. Krebs held that if nature is the growing developing manifestation of God we should investigate its operation and its essential properties with all the greater emphasis.

Following Nicholas Krebs, came speculative physician Theophrastus Bombast von Hohenheim (for obvious reasons better known as Paracelsus, 1493-1541), Giordano Bruno (1548-1600) and scientist Van Helmont. They and other speculative philosophers began an emphasis leading toward the philosophies of life of our present time. Nicholas of Cusa's speculations were a direct influence on Leonardo da Vinci in his nature-orientated work. But the scene shifted in following centuries from Italy to northern Europe. Spinoza's ideas which we will look at later were philosophically similar, though conditioned by different backgrounds.

At the opening of the sixteenth century, the Renaissance, particularly in Italy—Toynbee's Florentine brief candle—was in full maturity, and the diversity and brilliance of thought, if not richness in depth, attained a high plateau which would continue for three centuries, gradually changing in character throughout Europe from a philosophic to a scientific orientation. At the same time, there was a reawakening of the national literatures which had, in effect, been suspended for more than a century by the early humanists.

A new form of intellectual community was coming into being, perhaps foreshadowed by the Academy of Cosimo de Medici of Florence. In fact this development culminated in the various national academies of science of the seventeenth century, continuing into our own time. Originally these were privately organized, voluntary associations of intellectuals, centered in a particular city or community to foster learning outside the university. The subject matter was diverse but dedicated to the "humanities," a modified use of the old formal Ciceronian designation for a curriculum heavy in literary and philosophic themes. As with learning generally, the academies changed gradually from a literary to a scientific tone. The most significant aspect of these academies was the far greater base they gave to the publication of scholarly work and dissemination of thought. Their effect was greatest among those in the ruling class and in political and economic leadership. They were a force from which the "Age of Enlightenment" would spring. Carleton Hayes, the historian, expresses well the restlessness and change of the new period and the alterations in viewpoint taking place, exemplified especially in the attitude toward the church:

> By the sixteenth century the situation was greatly altered. Civil rulers were repressing feudalism. Political ambition was increasing among laymen. Local pride was being expanded into national patriotism. Strong states were emerging in western Europe, and elsewhere the popular demands for national states was growing. National monarchs and would-be national monarchs were reading authors like Machiavelli and were aspiring to an absolutism and despotism

for which the Middle Ages furnished no precedent. National sovereignty was rapidly being established in fact as well as in theory, and the one thing still needed to complete it was to bring religion under national control. National monarchs were anxious to enlist the wealth and influence of the Church in their behalf. They coveted her lands, her taxes, and her courts. Patriots in countries which still lacked national states were prone to perceive in the political power of the church the principal obstacle to the attainment of their national desires.

In these circumstances, kings and princes and patriots of the sixteenth century were not likely to resist encroachments on the historic rights of the Church. Indeed, if they were not saints—and saints among sixteenth-century monarchs were almost as rare as hens' teeth—they would welcome any opportunity to revolutionize the Church in their own favor. A goodly number of them, like many prelates of the age, were really hostile to any religious reformation which might radically purify the Church and gravely restrict their personal pleasures and political ambitions; and yet, with an unscrupulousness never surpassed, they stood ready to put themselves at the head of movements for ecclesiastical reform, or even rebellion, if thereby they could serve their own ends.

Economic circumstances of the time were similar. The same capitalistic spirit, the same eagerness for money and profits, which was immensely aggravating the financial abuses in the Church particularly among the higher clergy, was possessing the minds of innumerable laymen. Manufacturers, merchants, and landlords were becoming capitalistic and were coveting the accumulated wealth, the princely revenues, and the large landed estates of ostentatious bishops and abbots. They were arguing that the riches of the Church should be put to productive and profitable uses, and many of them, with a fine show of disinterested sympathy for religious reform, were quite willing to cooperate with kings and princes in confiscating Church property, provided, of course, that they got a liberal share of it for themselves. In this way, men of means contributed to the religious and social unrest which characterized the beginning of the sixteenth century and to the eventual upheaval which brought forth not only religious rebellion and reformation but also social revolution. This social revolution, while temporarily exalting lay monarchs at the expense of popes, was permanently to transfer economic influence from theologians to capitalists. It was at once a result and a cause of the rise of modern capitalism. (Hayes, 1932, pages 149-150).

Intellectual thought now filled the full continuum from the meditations of the great Spanish mystic and doctor of the church, Saint Teresa of Avila (1515-1582) to the philosophies tending toward agnosticism and dualism following largely from the ideas of Pompanozzi, which were to lead to the idealism of Kant two centuries later. There were skeptical wings developing in humanism. But a materialistic atheism had not yet come into being. The explosiveness of intellectualism can be measured by the sheer number of people who were of importance in shaping the current ideas.

Whereas, before it had been relatively easy to pick two or three outstanding individuals and discuss the prevailing concepts of man in general terms around their thought, it was, in the sixteenth century, very difficult or impossible. Faced with an extensive group from which to choose, I have selected three individuals who represent the mainstream of thought and have extracted from them some ideas on the prevailing concepts of man. They are Erasmus, Luther and Montaigne.

Undoubtedly in terms of the changing concept of man, the religious upheaval between Catholic and Protestant forces which took place principally in the sixteenth century was the outstanding historical development of the period.

No commentary of the sixteenth century renaissance, regardless of how narrow its scope, can avoid at least brief mention of Nicolo Machiavelli (1465-1527). His name is synonomous with the cynical, political pragmatism of the Renaissance in Italy which, in turn, is almost synonymous with the popular picture of intrigue of that romantic but bloody period.

However, Machiavelli, in 1513, when he addressed *The Prince* to Lorenzo Duke of Urbino, was providing a coldly rational as well as cold-blooded appraisal of sound political strategy for the contemporary situation. He was providing expert advice as a professional consultant to a client—no doubt for a fee, at least in patronage. It is unfortunate that this advice has been so well adapted to much of history since that time, and likely before.

Machiavelli, in fact, expressed his admiration for the civic virtues which as a good humanist he saw everywhere in the ancient pagan world. But in a society of villains only the most villainous survives and prospers. Looking at the fragmented, unruly collection of quasi-states that comprised Italy in 1500, and as the sincere patriot which he appeared to be, he saw unity and eventual tranquility coming about only through consolidation in the hands of one strong man, and Lorenzo might just as well be that man if he had the temper and stomach for it. Machiavelli says, "This is to be taken as a general rule; that it happens rarely, or not at all, that any republic or kingdom is either well-ordered at the beginning or completely reformed in regard to its old institutions, if this is not done by one man. The prince must always display, in outward appearance, that he is the very soul of good faith and reliability. It is a good thing publicly to appear upright, kindly, courteous, religious, and it is a good thing to be that way in actual personal life." As the prince, however, one cannot carry such views into the political and military arena and survive. "A prudent ruler ought not to keep faith when by so doing it would be against his interest, and when the reasons which made him bind himself no longer exist. . . . If men were all good, this precept would not be a good one; but as they are all bad, and would not observe their faith with you, so you are not bound to keep faith with them." Charity not only begins at home, but had best remain inside with the doors locked.

The Church in its papal states was ever an integral part—if one could use that term—of the Italian political scene. There is little doubt that in the centuries immediately preceding the sixteenth at least in top ecclesiastical circles, the original apostolic spirit of Christianity had been submerged in politics, politics narrowly construed, politics openly pursuing the secular interests of the great dynastic families. These were notoriously dirty politics as conducted at the courts of the individual princes and heads of widespread commercial interests typified by the Medicis.

Blinded by the concerns of his own temporal affairs and those proper to the Papal See, Pope Leo X (1513-21), Giovanni di Medici, from the beginning of his reign refused to recognize either the need of internal reform or the seriousness of the schism developing in Germany and elsewhere. Following the short interim reign of Adrian IV (1521-1523), Clement VII (1523-1534), nephew of Leo X, headed the church. He, too, still acted more as an Italian prince than as the head of a worldwide church.

There had been earnest efforts during the fifteenth century to bring about reform, but it was impossible to get these ideas across in the midst of all the dynamics of the exploding renaissance. The attitude in the Church was one of complacent, almost absent-minded, unconcern with the rising sense of anger and distrust being reflected in the major urban centers throughout Europe. Now in the sixteenth century, as the fabric of a united western Christendom was being torn to shreds, many still sought to carry out constructive, internal reform. Meanwhile, in the midst of the internecine strife which occupied the time and efforts of the best Christian-oriented philosophic intellects of the time, the developing countervailing philosophies of rationalistic humanism continued in their quiet way to reap a harvest of support among the disgusted and disenchanted in the bloody affray.

One who sought in a non-violent way to repair the old garment that had provided warmth and protection for so many centuries was Desiderius Erasmus, who typifies those valiant, almost desperate efforts. Erasmus was born on October 28, 1466. His name was of his own choosing. He said of himself, not modestly, but probably correctly, "Behold me, Desiderius Erasmus of Rotterdam, the most renowned scholar of the age, who yet began his career as the unknown son of an obscure father." (Erasmus, 1942, page 28). He was, as he said, the most renowned scholar of the age.

Most of his life was spent outside of Rotterdam. He was a man of all Europe. At one time he presided over the new College of France, established as one of the academies for intellectual advancement. He was educated first by the Christian Brothers at Deventer, then at the Augustinian school at Steyn near Gouda. Erasmus became an Augustinian monk in 1492. Two years later, apparently of his own choice, he was appointed Secretary to the Bishop of Cambrais near Paris, so that he would be near that university, as he wished to complete his education in the humanities. He entered the University of Paris at the College of Montaigu. There he began a habit of correspondence (at first to solicit funds) which lasted throughout his life. His letters reached not only every scholar of any status, but also kings, popes and ministers of state.

Eventually Erasmus got his Ph.D in Turin in 1506 and during his lifetime visited, in one position or another, most of the important universities of Europe. In 1509 he went to England as the guest of Thomas More, and there he wrote his *Praise of Folly*. Apart from the religious context, Erasmus is best known for his role as counselor and teacher to Charles I of Spain, who became Charles V, Holy Roman Emperor. In this position, Erasmus enjoyed the king's complete trust in a way similar to that of the relationship between Thomas More and Henry VIII of England, although Erasmus' had a more happy ending. Out of this relationship arose many political implications in the progress of the reformation in Germany.

Erasmus' chief tools were his sharp wit, his biting satire and his sarcasm which he used to assail the hair-splitting theologians and the pretentiousness of his times. The Church was his particular target, and by his criticism he earnestly sought to prod the Church to reform within its own structure. After about 1525 Erasmus became a foe of Luther, although they had many complaints against the Church in common, and initially Erasmus had been sympathetic to Luther. Erasmus had written, "If, as we deduce from the mighty advance of Luther's cause, God desires all this, and perhaps requires just such a rough physician as Luther to cure the decay of these times, then it is not for me to resist him." But Erasmus saw in the destruction of the unity of the Church the end of what was left of a unified cultural humanity and a fair-minded scholarship. While he was accused of damaging the Church with his sharp barbs by some later clerics lacking in subtlety, for the most part his work did serve its purpose and, along with other similar efforts, provoked the belated Council of Trent (1545-1563), which was an attempt to correct the abuses. But it was too little and too late to avoid the break. Rome fiddled while the Church burned.

Although the *Praise of Folly* was recognized generally as a satirical poking of fun at all the pretentiousness and posturings of secular and religious life of the times, its last sections were stripped of all the humanistic classical imagery of the majority of the work. Erasmus, at the conclusion, brought into focus the true intent of his work in a deadly-serious expression of his view of man's real goals in an honest approach to God. Erasmus, speaking in the character of Dame Folly, says (Erasmus, 1942 pages 246-252),

> "Agen, if this happens upon the score of Religion, though perhaps it may not be the same kind of madness, yet 'tis near it that a great many men would judge it no better, especially when a few inconsiderable people shall differ from the rest of the world in the whole course of their life. And therefore it fares with them, as, according to the Fiction of Plato,

happens to those that being coopt up in a cave standing gaping with admiration at the shadows of things; and that fugitive who, having broke from 'em and returning to 'em again, told 'em he had seen things truly as they were, and that they were the most mistaken in believing there was nothing but pitiful shadows. For as this wise man pitty'd and bewail'd their palpable madness that were possest with so grosse an error, so they in return laught at him as a doating fool, and cast him out of their company.

In like manner the common sort of men chiefly admire those things that are most corporeal, and almost believe there is nothing beyond 'em. Whereas on the contrary, these devout persons, by how much the nearer anything concerns the body, and by so much the more they neglect it, and are wholly hurry'd away with the contemplation of things invisible. For the one give the first place to riches, the next to their corporal pleasures, leaving the last place to their soul; which yet most of 'em do scarce believe, because they can't see it with their eyes. On the contrary, the others first rely wholly on God, the most unchangeable of all things; and next him, yet on this that comes nearest him, they bestow the second on their soul; and lastly, for their body, they neglect that care, and contemn and fly monies as superfluity that may be well spar'd; or if they are forc't to meddle with any of these things, they do it carelessly and much against their wills, having as if they had it not, and possessing as if they possessed it not. . . .

"And this happiness though 'tis only then perfected when souls being joyn'd to their former bodies shall be made immortal, yet forasmuch as the life of holy men is nothing but a continu'd meditation and, as it were, shadow of that life, it so happens that at length they have some taste or relish of it; which, though it be but as the smallest drop in comparison of the fountain of eternal happiness, yet it far surpasses all worldly delight, though all the pleasures of all mankind were all joyn'd together. So much better are things spiritual than things corporal, and things invisible than things visible; which doubtless is that which the Prophet promiseth: 'The eye hath not seen, nor the ear heard, nor has it entred into the heart of man to consider what God has provided for them that love Him.' And this is that Mary's better part, which is not taken away by change of life, but perfected.''

Erasmus' viewpoint of man, as seen in the quotation from the *Praise of Folly,* gave emphasis to the spiritual, even mystical values. But his life, generally, is in the mainline of humanism. He was a sincerely pious man as revealed by his writings, and he was an honest man of principles. In his view, the dignity of man lay not only in the image of his own genius, but also as a being with preeminent value as an image of the transcendent God.

As a side comment on the great advance of printing and dissemination of information, Erasmus lived to see more than 40 editions of the *Praise of Folly* in Latin, and many in French, which first appeared in 1517. Translations in German, Dutch, Flemish, English, Swedish, Danish, Polish, Russian, Czech and Greek followed after his death in 1536.

Martin Luther, contemporary of Erasmus and his bitter opponent, was born to a poor family in Eisleben, Germany, in 1483. He started studies in law at the University of Erfurt, but changed to theology and the humanities and in 1507 became an Augustinian monk. During this period he was introduced to the work of Gabriel Biel (d. 1495), from which he adopted in part the Nominalist ideas of William of Ockham on the inadequacy of reason of itself to apprehend any theologic doctrines and the need, therefore, to rely completely on faith. In 1508, he was assigned to Wittenberg to teach at the University and was shortly thereafter named professor of theology. Luther, noted for being a powerful speaker and headstrong to the point of intemperance, was a man of great intellectual talents. He was overwhelmingly concerned with his eternal salvation. This is perhaps an odd comment when that obviously should be a matter of no little interest to a monk. Among monks, however, he was outstanding for this trait.

Luther felt that as a result of "Original Sin" man had fallen to so low a level of depravity that he was utterly incapable of any good works. Therefore, salvation must result from faith alone, and not from all the sacramentals and prayers and paraphernalia of the church. Whether Luther arrived at this idea via the Ockham nominalism is uncertain. Ockham's teaching did not relate the incapacity of reason to "Original Sin," though the two ideas have the same effect of emphasizing the absolute dependence on faith. But Luther was no friend of scholasticism in any form, not even Ockham's. Until 1517, while perhaps having personal misgivings, Luther entertained no idea of rebellion. However, in that year, he became distraught at the methods of Tetzel, a priest who had been given the task by the Archbishop of Mainz of raising money for the construction of the Basilica of St. Peter and incidentally, for the archbishop. Tetzel's method was aggressive and of dubious ecclesiastical antecedent, and it outraged Luther, since he himself believed indulgences and the like to be completely valueless toward salvation. The result was, of course, the ninety-five theses on indulgences, posted on the Castle Church door according to ill-founded legend. The Church glossed over the episode. But in 1519, at Leipzig, Luther openly questioned the authority of the Church in debate with theologian John Eck, and the issue was joined. Luther left the Church in 1520 and began a program of teaching his own doctrine of salvation through faith alone, a much more attractive proposition than that need of a lifetime spent in good works.

In view of the state of the Church hierarchy, whose lives provided few examples of good works in practice, the program was successful from the start. He achieved in a short time what John Huss had tried to do a century earlier in Prague and had been burned to death for. But times had changed. So after a life marked by verbal conflict and fury, Luther died of natural causes at Eisleben in 1546.

Aside from the religious view of Luther's life, he was important as a literary figure. His translation of the Bible into German, published in 1522, while not the first (the first had been printed in 1466), is considered a classic in the history of German literature. His impact on the history of Western Europe and, individually on the concept of man is tremendous.

Luther's position on the concept of man flowed from his view of man as a creature innately depraved by the Fall, but nevertheless a child of God and an object of His love. Any dignity man had would derive from that relationship. In many ways Luther started a new thread of thought, although among the pessimists of the old Augustine-Platonic school there was the same element of man's worthlessness in himself. This attitude, like that of William Ockham before him, obviously did not lie in the Aristotelian or Thomistic humanist line which stressed the dignity of man as an intellectual being. While Luther himself did not hew to the humanist line, his chief disciple and collaborator, Philip Melanchthon (1497-1560), did. Melanchthon did not become acquainted with Luther until his own philosophical humanistic viewpoints, modelled on those of Erasmus, had been solidified. After his conversion by Luther, Melanchthon for awhile rejected these viewpoints, but later resumed them, and he became the leader in the Protestant wing of humanism in the north. To some extent, he had a companion status to Erasmus, though obviously greatly different in view of Luther's concept of man. Melanchthon believed that the key to moral development lay in the classical studies, and he was of basic Aristotelian orientation though, contrary to Aristotle, he had little interest in metaphysics. He believed man possessed innate ideas of God and of morality flowing from God. Though man might be innately depraved, he also had innate capacity to come to the knowledge of God in a cognitive way.

In spite of the great differences between Luther and Erasmus—differences in temperament, ideas, and motivations—Erasmus's writings were directed to the same points that Luther thundered forth. John Eck said that "Erasmus laid the egg that Luther hatched," and that either "Erasmus was Lutheran or Luther, Erasmusan."

Notwithstanding Luther's deep sense of the great evil which sin is, there is the still deeper sense that no matter what, given faith, salvation awaits us. In a letter to Jerome Weller, one of his faithful followers who was suffering from guilt feelings, Luther wrote in 1530, "What does it matter, then, if we commit a sin.... On occasion a man has to drink deep, gamble, jest, must indeed sin to defy the devil so as to leave him no scope to let us become conscious struck over petty affairs." And to Melanchthon, "Nothing will separate us from the forgiving Lamb of God even if we fornicate and murder a thousand times a day." The twentieth century idea of the "Mystique of Sin" contains the same sense—only after the experience of evil can we appreciate the good. Thus good somehow comes out of evil.

It appears that some of Luther's inherents took him too literally, for in his later years he frequently lamented the low level of morality in his followers, "Since the pure doctrine of the Gospel has been illuminated by our message, the world has become each day a worse place...disunity, usury, greed, tyranny, lust and unchastity are to be seen overwhelming us like the flood, so that things will never be righted—not with ten councils and twenty *Reichstags*."

Luther had no deep involvement in the humanist movement. His idea of the natural depravity of man and lack of free will made man a low creature of little responsibility in his actions. Yet Luther saw himself as a participant in that broad movement and adopted the humanistic signature form, "Eleuthesius," even before his break with Rome. As we have seen, Luther profited from the literary works of humanists, particularly Erasmus, but none of his own works is in the humanist tradition.

Following Luther, many other religious reformers were to project the same viewpoint of man's depravity, and the Jansenists in the late seventeenth century started a similar movement within the Catholic Church. The movement was condemned by Clement XI. Oddly enough, the Jansenists' remedy to the depravity was a life of intense moral rectitude. They emphasized works to offset depravity. The Pietists and Puritans of a later period gave Luther a similar twist. In addition to the principal cleavage of Protestant and Catholic forms, there were other splinter groups caught in between, among them the Unitarians, illustrated by the unfortunate Michael Servetus (1511-1553) who was condemned by the Catholics and then burned at the stake by the Calvinists in Geneva.

The explosiveness of the sixteenth century Protestant Reformation in Germany cannot be understood other than against the background of the climactic philosophical, political, economic, sociologic and moral pressures which had been building for some two hundred years. The pressure reflected the transitional dynamism involved in the change from the largely agrarian, feudal, theocentric culture of the Middle Ages based on Platonism which existed in the thirteenth century, to the embryonic nationalistic, urban, humanistic culture based in Aristolelian empiricism which was to emerge in the seventeeth century. The pressure gradient was severe. The Church, as the dominant organizing element of Western Europe in the fifteenth century, was the tendon subject to the greatest strain. Theology was not a major consideration at first, it was only the excuse. Germany, a melange of competing duchies, was caught between the competing nations of England, France and Spain in the west and a consolidating Poland in the east. The emergence of German national consciousness was inevitable and coincided with, or was even triggered by, the Reformation. The papacy was looked on as an Italian institution and a foreign political power. Further, the century-long exploitation of the Catholic Church in Germany by the series of French popes at Avignon, while a hundred years past, remained a rankling memory.

By 1535 the die was cast. The chance of a reconciliation through a council urged by Charles V, but resisted by both sides for quite different reasons, had passed. Things had gone too far. Protestantism had split up into many groups of seemingly all possible variations from the most peace-loving, morality seeking to the most aggressive and morally irresponsible.

In addition to the extremes, there were the truly Erasmian elements who held to a strict moralism (and hence rejection of the notion of justification by faith alone), and to the denial of free will because both of these views tended to discourage moral effort. Their extreme love of peace, their non-dogmatic inclinations toward toleration and a certain mysticism indicate that there were indeed elements within undoubted reformation forces which retained Erasmianism to a marked degree.

Michael de Montaigne, "the wisest Frenchman who ever lived," was born February 1533, of well-to-do parents in the Dordogne Valley near Bordeaux in Southwestern France. His father had served two years as mayor of Bordeaux, a position which Michael also held from 1581 to 1585. Montaigne's parentage was important to his later dedication to a tolerant view in religious matters. His father was Catholic, and his mother was by descent a Spanish Jewess who became a Protestant later. Two of their eight children were raised as Protestants, Michael and five brothers and sisters as Catholics. Thus he grew up in a family of mixed religious background which developed in him his skeptical attitude and a general sense of ease in controversy in a period when such an attitude was extremely rare. Montaigne's father had classical humanist leanings. Latin was the language Michael learned to speak exclusively until he was six. He studied law at the University of Toulouse and practiced as counselor at law at the Cout des Aides at Perigeueux, from which position he became a magistrate at Bordeaux. As was obvious from consideration of the lives of Erasmus and Luther, the period was one of religious upheaval and of turmoil in the very basic concepts of human existence. Montaigne's own family was badly split in support of the dynastic rivalries in France which emerged primarily from the breakdown of religious unity.

Montaigne apparently had no real taste for the law and retired from practice in 1571. Thereafter, except for brief periods, he lived and wrote at his estate in the Dordogne Valley. His chief literary form was the essay, a style which he is considered to have originated. He published his first two books of essays in 1580. These were classic works influenced by Seneca, Plutarch and to some extent by the ancient skeptics and stoics. The classic ancient literature, together with his family background, really formed the theme of his writing, although his works were also

affected by his travels. He made a pleasure trip to Rome following publication of his first essays and was honored there as a
citizen of the city and had the opportunity of meeting with
some of the literary and philosophical thinkers of early post-
Renaissance Italy.

The trip was shortened because he was elected mayor of Bordeaux in absentia. He declined the position, but on personal
request from King Henry IV, he finally accepted. He served until
the plague which swept France in 1585 struck his family, whereupon he resigned on a plea of urgent family necessity. He then
resumed work on his essays and published his third book. It
is from these later essays that his literary reputation and his
impact on the future course of intellectual thought chiefly flows.
Of particular importance are essays *Of Vanity*, which spoke of
freedom from confirmed doubt and man's faith in experience
and common sense; *Of Experience*, which fostered suspicion
of moral codes; and *Of Repentance*, which emphasized the right
and duty of individuals to find their own way.

Montaigne died September 13, 1592 as a Catholic. His life
had been one of personal doubts, but far more importantly of
finding ways of expressing and understanding doubts and finally of rising above them.

Montaigne thought and wrote almost exclusively on the complex of ideas arising from the question of what man is and
how he should live. His answer seemed to be that man's existence was his only sure knowledge, and that he should live
to enjoy that existence as best he could. He could best accomplish this by responding to the exigencies as they developed
and proceeding in accord with his best judgment from experience. Honest individuality was Montaigne's keynote.

Montaigne saw only a quantitative rather than a qualitative
difference in the intellectual powers of men as related to the
other animals. Man's concept of the moral life, of happiness,
of religion, of politics are all disputable because man's intellect
is imperfect: "Unless God lends His help by divine revelation,
we must remain forever ignorant." Again this Ockhamistic approach seems like an absolute retreat from the humanism which
had been developing earlier. Its emphasis now is more biologic
than intellectual. But, says Montaigne, "It's all we have and we
must do the best with it. We can enjoy life; we can learn about
ourselves; we can learn how to live if only we study ourselves
in our relationships to other men. For all men are very much
alike, just as are sheep or cattle. Each man bears the entire form
of human nature." This is a view which by inversion expresses

the Nominalists' position: The universal is the individual multi-plied, but in the end there is only the individual. Each man is the center of his own universe. For Montaigne, living was not a science but an art, which each man in his own way must cultivate. Our success depends on us—we must become ourselves by knowing ourselves. We are creatures of God, but He wishes us to be ourselves as He made us, not as others would modify us. We must be at home with our own souls, and it is in this that we obtain the key to wiser, happier living.

> Our good and our ill depend on ourselves alone...The poverty of goods is easily cured; the poverty of the soul is incurable...It is the enjoyment, not the possessing, that makes us happy... There is no use our mounting on stilts, for on stilts we must still walk with our legs. And on the loftiest throne in the world we are still sitting only on our own rear. . . . Our Great and glorious masterpiece is to live appropriately. (Montaigne, 1943).

Montaigne's attitude, in addition to its humanism, seems to foreshadow the rise of existentialism some 400 years later, for it was the authentic life, the life well-lived for itself at the moment, which seemed to be his "ultimate concern." Yet his view of man as just one of the creatures of nature also foreshadowed the rise of naturalism, a concept dear to the enlightenment and already being groomed by an incipient naturalistic movement, primarily in Germany. But Montaigne, though a skeptic concerning man's intellectual powers, was quite conservative in his religious and political viewpoints. He chose to go with the prevailing thought rather than oppose it since he was certain about very little. His viewpoint was akin to the stoic in that regard.

Montaigne, though a conservative, was truly the fountainhead of the activist philosophy which guided intellectual thought, at least in France, through the next two epochal centuries. His concept of man was primarily that of rationalistic humanism from which the dominant, materialistic philosophy of the late nineteenth and early twentieth centuries is phylogenically descended.

Before leaving the sixteenth century, some mention must be made of collateral developments. The Americas had been discovered just prior to the beginning of the century, and exploration was under way. The first printing press in the New World had been placed in operation in Mexico City in 1534, and there were already some ten million Christians in Mexico by 1550. Vasco da Gama (1460 - 1524) had made his trip to India via the passage of Cape of Good Hope, and, in Portugal, a romantic literary epic, *The Lusiads* by Camoens (1524 - 1580) had spread the story. There had been wide-ranging voyages of discovery by all of the seafaring nations. European man's picture of the world had changed dramatically once more, and with that change came an attendant alteration of his picture of the heavens and earth's place in those heavens. Initially, this took place through the works of Copernicus (1473 - 1543), a Polish priest who extended his heavenly mission into the physical realm as well.

The theory centering the universe on the earth had been held throughout Christendom since the times of Claudius Ptolemaeus, a Graeco-Egyptian astronomer of the second century A.D. Among the classics which had reached Europe from the Byzantine world were those of the ancient Pythagorean astronomers who saw the "solar system" as sun-centered. Copernicus, as a consequence of private studies in mathematics and astronomy while he was officially studying canon law and medicine at various schools in Italy, came across these ancient works, became convinced of their truth, and studied the theory extensively. The year he died (1543) he published his book, *On the Revolution of the Celestial Bodies*. He commented that he delayed publishing because he did not wish "to be laughed at and hissed off the stage" by his fellow scientists.

Obviously, the work was contrary to anthropocentric thought among all philosophers from humanists to Augustinian-Platonists, and it got widespread attention at first chiefly from those who opposed it. One who sought experimental corroboration was Tycho Brahe, born in 1546, whose main thrust was to reconcile the Copernican and Ptolemaic theories. He persuaded Frederick II of Denmark to establish an astronomical laboratory on an island in the Baltic Sea. He, of course, did not succeed in reconciling the two theories, but he gathered a great deal of useful data and manufactured some first-class optical instruments. As a consequence of his ill-temper and vanity he was dismissed from Denmark and ended his days in Prague in 1601. After Brahe's death, John Kepler (1571 - 1630), who had been his assistant, published his own work in which he essentially established the theory in three volumes issued in 1609, 1618 and 1619. Brahe had opposed Kepler's position, but it was the carefully recorded precise data on the movements of the planets among the stars under Brahe's direction which permitted the demonstrations to be made.

The first really solid corroboration of the Copernican theory was thus from a German, Kepler, and then by an Italian, Galileo (1564-1642), at the beginning of the seventeenth century. The evils that befell Galileo as a consequence are, of course, well known. His troubles started when he demanded a reinterpretation of Scripture which had a contrary connotation such as Joshua 10:12-13 commanding the sun to stop in its orbit. But the Copernican theory had been established; man was a rather small being in a large world, but on a relatively minor planet.

There were other less earth-shattering, but just as significant, advances made in mechanics and physics by Galileo leading into the Newtonian concepts. In mathematics, scholars working from advanced Arabic texts clarified mathematical concepts and developed organized symbolism. Notable progress was made in medicine, zoology and botany. And in metallurgy, one work of great importance described for the first time the techniques of manufacturing steel by the puddling process. This was only one, though the most important of innovative works contained in the *Twelve Books on Metals* by Georg Agricola (1490 - 1555), a German physician and scientist. It constituted a huge advance for the rapidly growing metals industry.

A new field of study was also opening up in what might be called a first venturing into the social sciences. Geography had entered into a new phase with the works of Gerhard Kremer (Mercator) (1512 - 1594), at Louvain University, where he studied and where he also started a geographical laboratory that developed scientific mapping techniques. Machiavelli and Bodin were looking at politics as a subject of scientific investigation and were theorizing upon the nature of government. Even economics and history were being looked at critically—economics in the sense of the idea of wealth of nations, and history in close review and cross-checking of source materials.

At the close of the century the humanists appear to have clearly established predominance. Man's image was now chiefly man-oriented, though some believed he was innately depraved fundamentally, and Montaigne himself severely limited his powers of reason, yet man's dignity was perceived in his own free accomplishments. Montaigne probably represented the central thrust of humanism among the secular intellectuals and among those of the ecclesiastical world as well, the latter with perhaps a God-related bias. Further, most Catholics and Protestants were in agreement with Montaigne's form of humanism.

In the fourteenth and fifteenth centuries scholasticism had become increasingly splintered in viewpoint even while maintaining its essential methodology. As we have seen, under the influence of William of Ockham the earlier Nominalism of the twelfth century was resuscitated. It severely restricted the realm of reason and introduced a deep skepticism not before present. Whereas the other branches of scholasticism were stagnant, this wing was highly active. But now in the sixteenth century the basic Thomistic-Aristotelian scholasticism, with a good deal of the flavor of a theistic humanism in the tradition of Erasmus, was being regenerated in these circles dominated by the Society of Jesus, the Jesuits. This new religious order was founded in 1539 by Ignatius Loyola, a Spanish ex-soldier and mystic, theologian and philosopher. From the beginning, the Jesuits had a strong scientific bent which they blended with their philosophy and theology. They were a highly important force in the internal reform of the Catholic Church and in general education of the laity.

As has been seen, the emerging dominant humanism arose in the dialectic between the late medieval Aristotelian scholasticism and the Platonic-oriented scientific development of the late Renaissance. The synthesized humanism was a curious blend of Aristotelian and Platonic thought, rejecting the Aristotelian physics but accepting its ethics. The scientific wing, typified by Copernicus and Galileo, preferred the approach of Plato (and of the Pythagoreans) because of the strong emphasis on mathematics and deductive logic, areas in which Aristotle was notoriously weak. But the naturalism and inductive empiricism of Aristotle, modified to avoid Aristotelian dogmatics, held out in the areas of scientific learning less mathematical and more minutely observational in character, such as botany, zoology, biology and the embryonic social sciences.

There was another change of deep significance in philosophy taking place at the end of the sixteenth century. The preceding four centuries had been preoccupied with the ontological aspects of philosophy—What was the nature of being—Who and what was man in relationship with the world and with God? What were the realities which determined these relationships? Now suddenly we see the matter of epistemology coming to the forefront. What was the nature and what were the limits of man's knowledge? This would be the principal theme through the next three centuries. The skepticism concerning man's power of reasoning introduced by Nominalism was but the first symptom of a spreading critical dissatisfaction of man with man's picture of himself as a being of great potential somehow set apart in a privileged position in the universe, in the contemplation of his loving Father. Man was behaving like a rebellious adolescent. The dissatisfaction came from the implication that man was, by the very nature of this concept, limited in his liberty. He could not be completely the captain of his soul. Better he should be one with the other animals. There had been questioning before of man's capacity to know; Erasmus with his allusion to Plato's cave conceived that most men were living in a dream world, not recognizing true reality which consisted in those things of eternal value. But along with Plato, Erasmus was convinced that man could understand such values if he came out of his cave. And Aristotle had said, "For as the eyes of bats are to the brightness of daylight, so is the reason in our soul to the things that by nature are clearest of all." The problem, as with Plato and Aristotle, was ontological still, but the solutions being considered were to be controlled by epistemology. In a sense, the contest between Plato and Aristotle was one between rationalism and empiricism, but on a relative, not radical, basis. Epistemology was a factor, but a minor one. But now the question was being raised in qualitive epistemological terms, an either/or confrontation—a dialectic situation which would deepen in the next century. And the concentration would be on the mechanism of man's perception. How does man assimilate the sense data of the experiential outside world into his self-conscious intellect? And in the light of that answer, what is the nature of self-consciousness? The ontological would be approached via the epistemological, a reversal of the earlier order. This air of philosophical uncertainty at basic informational levels was the stage-setting at the onset of the Age of Enlightenment.

Chapter 4

THE ACADEMIES AND THE ENLIGHTENMENT

At the close of the sixteenth century Spain was still the dominant European power. Upon the death of Philip II, (1527-1598) however, new tides began to run. Spain had literally bled itself to death in continuous wars both in Europe and in its far flung empire. In 1598 a peace was concluded with France at Vervins which did two things: It gave Spain a short and insufficient breathing spell in which to try to consolidate its empire, and it gave France, which had also been continuously in turmoil, a chance to recover internal control. Domestically the scene in France, at least superficially, was worse than in Spain since the fighting had been on French soil, while in Spain it had been chiefly elsewhere, from the Netherlands to the Philippines to the Americas. If Spain was bled white, France was a shambles. The following quotation indicates the conditions there. (Hayes, 1932, page 278).

> Sorry, indeed, was the plight of France which Henry IV set out to remedy. A century of civil and foreign war had produced most unfortunate consequences for the French state and for the French people. The state was nearly bankrupt. Country districts lay largely uncultivated. Towns were burned or abandoned. Roads were rough and neglected, and bridges in ruins. Many of the discharged soldiers turned highwaymen, pillaged farm houses, and robbed travellers. Trade was at a standstill and the artisans of the cities were out of work. During the wars, moreover, great noblemen had taken many rights into their own hands and had acquired a habit of not obeying the king. The French crown seemed to be in danger of losing what power it had gained in the fifteenth century.

Moving to the seventeenth century the accession of a strong king, Henry IV, in 1589 and, counteracting subsequent weakness at the throne, a succession of strong ministers of state, Sully (1560-1641), Richelieu (1585-1642), and Mazarin (1601-1661), restored the domestic strength in France. These leaders instituted sound financial management, fostered agriculture and commerce and made sagacious, even crafty foreign alliances which, at the expense of Spain, brought France back to the place of prominence she had held under Louis XII.

The peace for Spain was not to last as a result, initially, of internal dynastic politics of the Hapsburgs. Philip IV of Spain, at the behest of the Hapsburgs of Austria, caused Spain to resume war on the side of Austria in the Thirty Years' War, (1618-1648). The war soon became a religious conflict of continental proportions. In the end it was disastrous for Spain and very beneficial to France. It was apparent that Cardinal Richelieu was more devoted to France than to the Hapsburg Catholicism. On this point Hayes says, (Hayes, page 270.).

> "What wrecked the peace of Prague was not so much the disinclination of the Protestant princes of Germany to accept its terms as the policy of Cardinal Richelieu of France. Richelieu was convinced more than ever that French greatness depended upon Hapsburg defeat. He would not suffer the princes to make peace with the emperor until the latter was soundly trounced and all Germany devastated. Instead of supplying the Swedes and the German Protestants with assistance from behind the scenes, he would now come boldly upon the stage and engage the emperor and the king of Spain in open combat.
>
> "The final, or French, period of the Thirty Years' War lasted from 1635 to 1648—almost as long as the other three periods put together. Richelieu wished to humble the Austrian Hapsburgs and, if possible to wrest Alsace from the Holy Roman Empire. But his major designs were against Austria's close ally, Philip IV of Spain. The wily French cardinal could count upon the Swedes and many of the German princes to keep up the fighting in Germany against the Hapsburg emperor, while French armies attacked the encircling dominions of the Hapsburg king of Spain."

In fact, Richelieu successfully prevented peace from being made until after his death in 1642. The war was finally ended after a series of treaties by the Peace of Westphalia in 1648. Of the impact, Hayes says: (Hayes, pages 273-274).

"The era of the Thirty Years' War and of the peace of Westphalia is highly important in the history of modern Europe. The Thirty Years' War itself was the worst, but the last, of the so-called religious wars. While it began as a fight between Protestants and Catholics, its chief stakes were ever economic and political, and it closed in a major conflict between Hapsburg and Bourbon dynasties, both nominally Catholic, but both chiefly concerned with statecraft. That a Protestant prince of Brandenburg should give assistance to the Catholic emperor and that a cardinal of the Roman Church should incite Catholic France to aid German Protestants were clear signs of a noteworthy transfer of interest, in the first half of the seventeenth century, from religious fanaticism to secular ambition. The Thirty Years' War paved a rocky road toward the eventual dawn of religious liberty."

The Thirty Years' War also established the base from which the modern nation states of Europe emerged and developed their own sovereignty. That was impossible so long as dynastic linkages with super states, the Holy Roman Empire, or independent dynastic empires, such as the Hapsburgs, continued to be superior to any combination of national states. By the end of the century, France was again the dominant European power.

The Humanist trend continued to advance as it had in the sixteenth century, and the academies which had emerged more than 100 years earlier, primarily fostering the humanities, now began to expand with the advancement of scientific knowledge of the sixteenth century. At Rome, a group of scientists and supporters of science formed the Academy of Lynxes in 1603. This was followed by others in the major urban centers of Italy and Germany. The chief advance in Germany, however, was somewhat delayed and followed the "enlightenment" efforts of Frederick the Great (1712-1786). In 1662, Charles II of England chartered the Royal Society and in 1666 France revised and expanded its earlier Academy of sciences. There were also academies started in some of the new colonial areas, such as Massachusetts in 1683. The seventeenth century was a time of explosive scientific advance following the works of Galileo which opened up many new mathematical-scientific linkages. Several individuals made outstanding contributions, including Englishmen Isaac Newton (1642-1727), Boyle (1627-1691), Halley (1656-1742) and Harvey (1578-1657). Frenchman Rene

Descartes (1596-1650); Dutchmen Huygens (1629-1695) and Van Helmont (1577-1644); and Italian Torricelli (1608-1647). The most important aspect of science during this period, from the standpoint of the concept of man, was its popularization. Science appealed to the imagination from the heads of state right down to the clerks in the rising commercial cities. What theology was in the thirteenth century, natural science was becoming in the seventeenth. Even the classics had to take second billing.

Again, perhaps increasingly so, the selection of a few seventeenth century individuals who could give a feel for the concept of man is difficult. In the sixteenth century, ecclesiastical matters were most important and decided the issue. In the seventeenth century, it was the attitude toward natural science, including political science, which played the leading role. Biographical sketches of Rene Descartes, Baruch Spinoza, Thomas Hobbes and John Locke indicate this change in emphasis.

Rene Descartes was born March 31, 1596, at La Haye, Tourraine, France. He was educated at the Jesuit school at La Fleche and later at the University of Poitiers. He was a man of tremendous energy with an omnivorous and voracious appetite for knowledge. His interests, and more importantly, his achievements in mathematics, physics, biology, psychology, physiology, astronomy, philosophy and theology, had incalculable impact on the world. During the period of the Thirty Years' War, he served in the Netherlands, Hungary and Bavaria in the army of Maurice of Nassau in the war of independence from Spain. After the war he settled in Holland, and there he did most of his work. Two of his works, *Discourse on Method,* published in 1637, and *Principals of Philosophy,* in 1644, established methodology which shaped the approach to scientific investigation up to modern times. He originated analytical geometry, which wedded algebra to the graphic model in the Cartesian system of coordinates and was a necessary forerunner to development of the calculus which followed soon after, arrived at independently by Leibnitz and Newton. In many ways, his approach to physics anticipated that of Einstein in the twentieth century because he relied on rationalization, logic and mathematics rather than on experiment. On the other hand, in the field of biology, he used dissection. He is said to have told one visitor who inquired about his library, "Here are my books," as he pointed to a basketful of rabbits. He rejected tradition absolutely. He made significant advances in the theory of optics, principally reflection and refraction of light, and in the physical and mathematical aspects of astronomy.

Of even greater significance to this work in following trends in the concept of man were Descartes' philosophic studies which portended the trend to epistemology in philosophy generally. In his *Discourse on Method,* he attempted to apply mathematical methods to philosophy. He had been trained in scholastic philosophy and largely discarded its authoritarian assumptions but not its logic. His system was called that of universal doubt, emphasizing the drive to establish a legitimate base for knowledge. Two things alone cannot be doubted: doubt itself and the fact of one's own existence. His famous answer, not completely original, in proof of the latter doubt-free reality was *Cogito, ergo sum*—I think, therefore I am. From that base Descartes developed his entire philosophy after first establishing the existence of God via a version of St. Anselm's ontological proof which does not require an empirical base. Anticipating Einstein's words, Descartes believed that, "God does not play at dice with the world. God does not deceive us. What He presents to us in nature is real—God was the guarantor of that reality." The ontological fact of one's being is predicated on the epistemological certainty that one does think about oneself, and that one is conscious that one thinks about oneself and external things. Descartes developed a complex theory of man's knowledge. He held that there was a quasi-innateness of certain ideas—a virtual innateness in the sense of a natural predilection of man's reason to accept certain metaphysical ideas when presented.

The question concerning Descartes "innateness' goes to the matter of the primacy of being. First there is "being." Descartes took the fact of his thinking as coercively evidential of his existence. A thought is not possible without a being who thinks. But if there is no external object about which to think, is it possible to have a thought? Is our consciousness of thinking, and therefore of existence, an innate bit of knowledge, or does it depend entirely upon the experience of thinking—we know we think because we have thought about some external object? Does the faculty of intelligence exist independently of the world of objects? Obviously there is no possible empirical demonstration—is there a logically unassailable position *a priori* to support the view that intelligence inheres in a thinking being before the object is presented to it?

Descartes held, in the limiting case, that the self would be the object without which the thought could not exist. Aristotle's concept—God as the "self-thinking thought" implies that in essence the thought and the self are conterminous—that a self is always an intrinsic element of thought. Man's primary self-knowledge is virtually innate. While he learns "facts" about himself experientially, he differentiates between the contingency of those facts as self-related and the self to which they relate.

The facts are adjectival—are descriptive only—of the noun which comprises the free-standing self—the individual. Man accepts and takes for granted his selfness as a basic platform from which intent is directed. That platform and that self are identified in thought. Subject and object are one in the limiting case of introspective thought—an activity limited to man in the natural order. Although the presentation of the object of thought and direction of intent of the thinking are simultaneous events, the actual thought is a primary function of the directed intent and only secondarily a function of the presented object. The dependency sequence of thought is thinking subject, directed intent, apprehended object, thought. The direction of intent is an act of will by the subject which must precede the intellectual acquisition of data concerning the object. Until the object is apprehended by the subject as object, there is no thought. It appears conclusive, as Descartes held, that the capacity of thought as a capability exists totally independently of the external object to which that capability is exposed.

Descartes was among the first to attempt a physiological analysis of the way sense perception is acquired by the brain and transmitted to the intellect. But ultimately he admitted that "It is the soul that sees and not the eyes." That which is finally assembled in the brain as sense impression is integrated by the reason and reflected as the conceptual image in the soul. That is what we are conscious of as the thing perceived in its relation to us and to all else in space and time.

One can almost picture Descartes deciding he would establish a mathematically sure philosophy. The one "certainty" he had was his consciousness of self. Now he places himself as a fully developed consciousness in the total void and in a completely blank state. No knowledge had yet been impressed on that consciousness. He was not even able to consider his own body—no sensations whatsoever—a free floating self-consciousness. Now he asks himself, "Can I even say 'I think therefore I am?' " Each word must correspond to an intrinsic element of pure self-consciousness and here, in this state, he is a subject with absolutely no objects except self-consciousness, "I am me." He can make no other declarative statements *ab initio,* but he can question in the topical modes. Of the six topic questions, he could only ask himself "How" and "Why" at first. Neither of these questions presupposes a consideration of any "other" or of an "out there"—and they are undifferentiated as to self, or other, or time, or place. In asking of "How" and "Why" he is yet limited. If he asked, "How am I?" he could only respond, "I came to be self-aware." To ask "how" and "why" were his only functions. He might then ask, "How did I come to be aware that my purpose was to be self-aware?" He then could answer, "I intended to become aware that my purpose was to be self-aware. I directed myself at myself in inquiry. I determined to find out how I came to be self-aware." He now can even suggest to himself, "I am an intending self-awareness." As the phenomenologists would say, the first identity he could establish is that he is an "intending ego" even though the only object he has is himself. He could then ask once more, "Why did I come to be an intending self-awareness?" He can respond, but with an added identity, "I came to be an intending self-awareness because that is what I am intended to be—that is *what* and *who* I can be."

The next questions would follow, "Did I self-intend to be an intending self-awareness? Did I direct myself to come to be and how did I self-intend to come to be an intending self-awareness?" These questions immediately raise another. "If I did not intend myself to become, is there an 'other' which did intend me to become me?" He could conjecture, "If there is a me, it is certainly possible there is an other far more likely than—there be no other, and that while yet self-unaware I directed myself to become to be aware." Further, the other also would be seen as no peer but a superior who could call him into self-awareness, for he would be aware he had no such power. It seems thus obvious why Descartes next, before venturing into the world of others, sought to prove the existence of God and seized on St. Anselm's "ontological proof" to establish *a priori* a God who could become the guarantor, the authenticator of all others. While he would be conscious of the sequence of his thinking events and of time in that context, he could not yet ask When or Where in space and time terms. He would have no coordinate system. He could ask "Who" at this point, having become aware of a personal identity. But it would have been almost the end of the line for Descartes' alter ego suspended in the void. Having established a minimum identity as the "intending ego" and the existence of a superior other which had intended him to become an intending self-awareness, he had almost exhausted his resources except perhaps to speculate on the coming to be of other intending egos like himself. But if some communication had come to him asking in St. Anselm's language, "Does that 'other' than which no greater can be conceived, exist?" he would have said "Yes." That other than which no greater can be conceived would have been that other through whose intention he had come to be an intending self-awareness. He could conceive of no greater other and certainly he existed. One can thus see why Descartes had expanded his *cogito* to "I exist, therefore God exists."

Descartes appears to have remained a practicing Catholic throughout his life, and in his philosophic studies he attempted to redefine or refine the scholastic arguments for the existence of God which were those of St. Thomas Aquinas. These arguments are still valid philosophically, though perhaps not as coercively as St. Thomas would have contended. Descartes could be said to have weakened the arguments. Descartes held that God constituted, in himself, a linkage between the physical world of the senses and the rational world of the mind and that hence in opposition to Ockhamism it was possible to have a direct mental apprehension of God from observation of the physical universe. As a point of fact, Descartes' position was very close to that of St. Thomas in his argument from the observed harmony in existence. Descartes can also be said to have started the philosophic fashion of dichotomy which was to develop in various forms through the succeeding centuries. He conceived a sharp distinction between soul and body, mind and matter. He argued that whatever he was clearly conscious of as having essential existence from observation and experience was real and true. Therefore, God and man's soul and mind had real existence. Nevertheless, the essential nature of this real but intangible existence was completely different from the material phenomenon, including the body, which is observed in nature by the senses. These primal intangible existences can be derived logically from observation of nature and effects on nature, but not sensed directly. Descartes is thus considered the father of dualism in the ontological separation of the subject-thinking ego and the external extended world outside, which to some extent reflected the earlier dualism between intelligible and sensible worlds held by Plato.

Some have claimed that Descartes denied any possible intraction of the supernatural on the natural, but that did not seem to flow from his other arguments. Rightly, it could be claimed that, in the normal observation of physical phenomena, Descartes held that direct supernatural intervention can be disregarded as affecting the outcome.

Descartes' position on the concept of man was quite compatible with the older Thomists, except that he believed that everything directly observable was completely material; no difference between form and substance. Overall, however, Descartes qualified as a humanist. For him, the chief dignity of man lay in the free development of his capabilities, not in his relationship to God. Descartes died in Sweden while embarking on a project for Queen Christina. The severity of Swedish winters and the equal severity of Christina's regimen of rising at five in the morning and insisting on a discussion of philosophy, when Descartes was used to lying abed in the morning thinking, was too much. He contracted a fever and died January 11, 1650.

Thomas Hobbes was born at Westport, Wiltshire, England, April 5, 1588, the son of the Anglican vicar of Westport. His father abandoned his church and family shortly thereafter, and Thomas was raised by an uncle in Malmsburg. He graduated from Magdalen Hall, Oxford in 1608 and became a tutor of William, later second Earl of Devonshire, and his long and fruitful association with the Cavandish family began at that point. Shortly after this employment, and largely as a result of a trip to Italy and France with his young charge, Hobbes decided to become a classicist. It was a fairly short-term romantically inspired avocation.

Hobbes gradually turned his interests toward the Pythagorean philosophies, probably because of the importance of the then emerging Copernican astronomy, and embarked on his final career field in philosophy and an embryonic political science. When he returned to England from another trip on the continent in 1636, during which he had met Galileo in Florence, and later members of the French scientific circle, he was convinced that everything was explainable in terms of matter in motion, and he has been dubbed the forerunner of the materialistic empiricist wing in England. While he disputed Descartes, there was no denying that he was also attracted to Descartes' principles, particularly as they applied to the mathematics of philosophy. Hobbes' greatest importance for our purposes rests not in his view of the philosophy of matter or of metaphysics, however, but in his view of man as a social being.

For Hobbes, as expressed in his major work, *Leviathan*, published in 1651, man's behavior in a civilized world must be traced to what man was in a state of nature before being subjected to all artificiality and constraints of civilization. As he viewed it, in the state of nature men were so equal in their abilities that they must also have been equal in their anticipated rewards and equal in their desire of obtaining them. But in a world of limited rewards, competition must have resulted, each would have sought to outdo the other to obtain the benefits. Men would have completely distrusted each other and have schemed in every possible way to gain the upper hand and to achieve power over each other. It comprised a pack of super-intelligent dogs with too few bones to go around. The result would be violence and utter disorder and discord. So Hobbes asked the question: "This being so, how did mankind survive? His answer was the social contract. Whereas irrational beasts are controlled by instinct, in *Leviathan,* Hobbes says: "That control of men is by Covenant only, which is artificial: and therefore, it is no wonder if there be somewhat else required besides Covenant to make their agreement constant and lasting; which is Common Power, to keep them in awe, and to direct their actions to the Common Benefit." Men, being intelligent and aware that unless they controlled themselves they would not survive, agreed to a leadership of some sort and to a method of settling disputes. Thus, governments, in the most primitive fashion, came into being. Unless men had a common power of which they were in awe, they would remain in a constant state of war, every man against every other man, and in "constant fear and danger of violent death; and the life of man, solitary, poor, nasty, brutish, and short." Therefore, concluded Hobbes, strong governments were essential.

Hobbes felt that the government should also control religion, otherwise it had no control; but "if it was necessary to choose between temporal and eternal things," man should choose the eternal. The contrary was foolishness. Hobbes has been called an atheist, but he obviously was not, though he left God out of consideration in his social aspect to note that "This is the Generation of the great Leviathan, or rather, (to speak more reverently), of that MORTAL GOD to which we owe, under the Immortal God, our peace and defense." (Emphasis Hobbes'). Although he was not a religious man, he had a rather vague idea that God was the Creator and first cause, and Christ was the Saviour.

Hobbes' political philosophy was a reaction to the Puritan revolution, the execution of Charles I of England, and the civil war which ensued. Patently, his ideas were not received kindly by Cromwell, and they were not liked by the Royalists either because of their irreligious character. Over time, however, but largely after his death in 1679, his views had an overall positive impact on the English system through their insistence on a strong central government.

Hobbes' image of man was that of an innately selfish being, but one gifted with intelligence sufficient to see that he had to be controlled if he was to be secure. His dignity lay in his freedom to choose and in his election to surrender his personal sovereignty to the common good. Apparently, in a dim way also, Hobbes, though he held resolutely that God, being immaterial cannot be a subject of philosophy, perceived man in spite of himself and his selfishness and his material nature as an object of concern of a loving God.

Hobbes had said in fact: "That it is impossible to make any profound inquiry into natural causes without being inclined thereby to believe there is a God eternal; though they (men) cannot have any idea of Him in their mind, answerable to His nature."

Benedictus (Baruch) de Spinoza was born in Amsterdam November 24, 1632 of prosperous Jewish parentage and attended the Jewish schools. Fairly early though, he appears to have left Jewish orthodoxy and was a logical intellectual descendant of Maimonides (1135-1204) rather than of rabbinical thought. Spinoza was put out of the local Jewish community against his wishes for his radical ideas, though he was probably being more disputatious than earnest. For instance, he argued that the Bible contains no proof that God had no body. Certainly he did not hold that God did have a body in any physical sense, for at the time he was on the verge of skepticism of all orthodoxy, although not of the idea of God. Spinoza was banished from Amsterdam when the Jewish community disavowed any responsibility for him.

Spinoza was attracted to the philosophy of Descartes and new scholasticism as proposed by ex-Jesuit, Francis Van den Enden. Possessing no formal, advanced education, Spinoza developed a broad education in philosophy, science and mathematics through his own efforts and through a wide acquaintanceship with a great variety of scholars. Meanwhile, he learned the trade of lens grinder and supported himself that way, rather than through an academic career. He organized a circle of intellectuals in religious and philosophical thought, and his early writings reflect the interchange of that period. He withdrew in 1660 to Rijnsburg, a small village near Lieden, where the same intellectual pattern of friendship developed.

Spinoza, particularly attracted to the mathematical basis of Descartes' methods, was only thirty when he began drafting his first important work, the *Ethica Ordini Geometrica Demonstrada,* which basically followed Cartesian thought. The first part of this work, *De Deo,* was published in 1663. The entire content of his *Ethica,* as he planned it, was to embrace the concepts of God, the highest happiness of man, and the rational soul. *Ethica* was not published until 1675, and then it was held to a close circle of friends because of the unfavorable atmosphere of the time and the hostility which Spinoza had already experienced sufficiently. He died at The Hague February 20, 1677 and most of his voluminous writings were published posthumously.

From Spinoza's point of view, a satisfactory system of metaphysics must be intelligible and must be mathematically coherent and consistent. It must follow some plan which is ordered to a consistent view of the physical world, Cartesian or otherwise—especially in fields of human life—but embracing ideas of truth and morality. It must provide, in the Supreme Being and the resulting metaphysical complex, a total plan worthy of devout belief and worship. For Spinoza to the last remained a man of sincere religious feeling. His idea of the totality of God's relationship with all existence was to some extent pantheistic although he did not hold that there was no reality outside the intellect or being of God. In some manner the world of things was absorbed by or, perhaps better, structured by the being of God. Spinoza emphasized the objects, the things of nature ahead of the subject, the ego, the thinking absolute. His God, if He was worthy of love, was Himself unloving and impersonal. Again, somewhat in accord with the Aristotelian disinterested prime mover, the self-thinking thought.

Spinoza believed in some sort of immortality, but gave no indication of belief in individual survival. He saw, rather, a reabsorption of the human intelligence into the infinite intellect. Traditionally, he was respected more by the Romanticists and philosophers of nature and life who were attracted to the idea of a conjunction of nature and the Deity. It is likely that his thought had more influence on the development of Deism in the next century and on the ideas of the Romanticists in the nineteenth century than it did on those of the intellectuals of his own period.

Spinoza was acquainted with John Locke, and while he seemed to share Hobbes' unfavorable view of mankind, he preferred Locke's version of the social contract rather than Hobbes'. Spinoza's concept of man was complex since he held that everything was both body and spirit, which idea may have sparked his early conflict with the Jewish community. He held both were manifestations of the same phenomenon, with different space and thought environments. Thus, he was not as materialistic as Hobbes, who considered that matter and motion determined everything. While Hobbes somehow believed in an individual immortality, Spinoza did not. The dignity of man thus had no stake in any future existence. Human life and its dignity were strictly a matter of living in this world as a decent, rationally responsible individual. To Spinoza, man was not a transcendent being in any knowable sense.

John Locke was born at Warington, England in 1632, the son of a rural attorney. He attended Christ Church College at Oxford where he received BA and MA degrees and in 1660 was named lecturer in Greek and later Censor of Moral Philosophy at Christ Church College. Though Hobbes preceded him in time by a few years, Locke is rated as the first great empiricist of England, though he was not as materialistic as Hobbes. In fact, if Descartes' interest in the empirical approach which was strictly subordinated to his logic is discounted, Locke is the first truly dedicated modern empiricist philosopher. Locke was greatly influenced by Descartes, though he was never a Cartesian other than in methodology. He was personally acquainted with Sir Robert Boyle and his scientific circle at Oxford and from them became interested in chemistry, physics and the scientific method, generally. He eventually (1674) received his medical degree and license to practice, though he never did so except in a very private way with close friends. Locke was aware of the empirical work of Francis Bacon (1561 - 1624) who, while rejecting Aristotelian and scholastic philosophies, accepted Aristotle's empirical approach in the physical sciences. The extent of Bacon's influence on Locke cannot be assessed, but both were in the English empirical-trending tradition.

Locke's greatest influence historically was in political science but, as distinguished from Hobbes for our purposes, his clear break with speculative philosophic tradition generally was the most important thing in the continuing march of man's concept of man. Locke denied any innateness in man's thinking, in contrast to Descartes and Liebnitz, who had fostered different versions of innateness on the continent, though, for both, the innateness was virtual rather than actual. Locke's denial excluded the possibility of any in-built concepts of moral principles. When man was born his mind was a clean slate; its whole content develops only with the continuing sense experience as manipulated in the mental processes through life. This was nothing new, since Aquinas had held very close to the same thing, but the application of the concept was new. Locke, in a further contraction on the Ockham theme, severely limited the extent of real knowledge. And while Locke agreed there is the demonstrative knowledge of God, which Ockham denied in favor of revelation, that is as far as it goes. All other universal principles are merely superficial images or reflections possessing no inherent reality. While we can develop abstract notions such as cause and effect, power, substance, identity and infinity, these notions are really confessions of our ignorance concerning the nature of those things in which the qualities inhere. The only way to expand our knowledge of these things is through experienced observation and limited extrapolation from the sensed data through the rational operations of introspection as to the meaning of the sensed data. Thus, while he was an empiricist beyond the point Ockham had been— Ockham's being more in theory than in practice—Locke was not yet quite a Nominalist. He gave the mind greater scope than did Ockham but reduced further its sources of knowledge.

Locke did not exclude metaphysics from his philosophy. He was of the view that all opinions and beliefs of every nature should be brought before the "tribunal of reason" with emotion and sentiment excluded. What could stand under those conditions regardless of their nature was acceptable as proper knowledge. Locke did not deny spiritual reality, or the supernatural order, but he placed these things at a level generally above reason, and he held that while they were not contrary to reason, they were also only vaguely understandable. He was a religious man, but he was opposed to all forms of fanaticism. In fact, he was pedestrian in most of his opinions, never farfetched in his viewpoints, never polemic in his words. He would not have made the Sunday supplements, yet in his quiet way he started a trend both politically and philosophically which had a tremendous impact on the concept of man in the future. He started the modern age emphasis on sense knowledge and the precedence of epistemology in philosophy, generally.

Locke's social contract or compact was derived with that of Hobbes firmly in mind and in frank opposition to Hobbes. Like Hobbes, he began with a state of nature, but men were not merely advanced brutes—they were rational beings with a social nature. They would have lived together according to reason and there is a moral law discoverable by reason out of experience, not innate, but discoverable. The unlimited competition visualized by Hobbes would have represented unreason—a state of war: "Men living together according to reason, without a common superior on earth with authority to judge between them is properly the state of nature." The fundamental difference between Hobbes and Locke is that Locke presupposes an "unearthly entity" discoverable by reason of whom "men stand in awe," whereas Hobbes had to manufacture his entity. In a sense, both agreed that an external judging agency beyond the individual was necessary. In any event, the social compact of Locke is a freely entered agreement having no overtones of coercion but rather recognizing the inherent advantages which will accrue to man through cooperation.

Locke's concept of man was of a free individual with rights and privileges which must be respected but not of a being of unlimited possibilities. He was yet and foremost a creature under the jurisdiction of God. Locke was not fully "enlightened" and though the philosophers of the enlightenment regarded him as the "prophet of reason," at his death in 1704 empiricism had not achieved the commanding place in the epistemological hierarchy that it was to attain in the late eighteenth century in the full bloom of the enlightenment.

The blossoming of research in the natural sciences of the seventeenth century produced fruit in the philosophy of the enlightenment of the eighteenth century. That philosophy, while it did not abolish the idea of a supreme being, certainly depersonalized him. It saw a substitution of the new metaphysics of the natural for the old metaphysics of the supernatural, which had held center stage, at least during the centuries of the Christian era. The trend had been developed for better than a century, at least from the time of Montaigne, but, as we have seen, its roots were in the Renaissance, and now it was central to the evolving concept of man as a being in total command of his own destiny. The practice of this philosophy was not by any means limited to professionally trained philosophers. On the contrary, anyone who was anybody, from King to bookseller, was a philosopher. And in addition, scientists were philosophical and philosophers were scientific. It was a heady period. Man was on the threshold of bringing all the forces of nature to heel. Thomas More's Utopia was a place of drudgery compared with what was in store for the human race with all of nature's vast storehouse ready to be unlocked by man's scientific knowledge. The intellectual atmosphere was one having all of the aspects of a child's delighted enthusiasm with a new toy.

While France's dominant military and economic position in

Europe was declining from its eminence under Louis XIV in the late seventeenth and early eighteenth centuries, the main force of the Enlightenment nevertheless settled in Paris and its environs, even though the central military and political stage had been taken by the rising of England and Prussia. Colbert (1619 - 1683), who was Louis XIV's principal minister, greatly strengthened the French Academy of Sciences which he renamed the Institute of France. Colbert built a great astronomical laboratory at Paris, and through highly attractive financial arrangements brought many foreign artists and scholars to France. For intellectual depth, the great resource of the University of Paris was available, though the university itself was overwhelmed in intellectual appeal by the Institute of France and its non-professional membership. France indeed remained the intellectual center of the West. On the character of the Enlightenment, historian Hayes says, (pages 511-512):

The roots of the new "enlightenment" lay in the sixteenth and seventeenth centuries, but its greatest spread and most obvious fruitage were so characteristic of the eighteenth century that it is this century which is known as the age of the "enlightenment." To the majority of eighteenth-century thinkers, the development of natural science was associated with a new metaphysics which, as interpreted to common folks, involved four major concepts: (1) It involved the substitution of the natural for the supernatural, of science for theology, and the assumption that the whole universe of matter and mind is guided and controlled by ineluctable natural law. (2) It exalted and almost deified human reason, which could and, according to the rational moral sense should be, utilized by the individual to discover the laws of nature and to enable him to conform his life to them. (3) Assuming that man would use his reason and obey the natural law, it promised the speedy progress and ultimate perfectibility of the human race. (4) It included a tender regard for the natural rights of the individual and a predilection for the social blessings of an enlightened humanitarianism.

In the light of these metaphysical concepts, a good deal of criticism was indulged in, much of it destructive and some of it constructive. Institutions and practices which through the ages had acquired any degree of popular veneration in the domains of religion, politics, and society were ruthlessly dissected by the "enlightened" in order to discover: if they were rational, if they were in harmony with natural law, if they promoted human progress, guaranteed individual rights, and conferred immediate benefits on the world. It was this acutely critical spirit which somewhat paradoxically combined with a lively faith in the new metaphysical concepts to produce the most notable features of the Intellectual Revolution.

Looking back upon the Enlightenment from the comfortable distance of a couple of centuries, several driving forces which shaped its philosophical outlook can be discerned. The tremendous impact of the successes in the field of the physical sciences during the seventeenth century exalted the place of science and the methodology of science in the minds of people of all walks of life. It literally inflamed the imaginations as to the future potential progress in that field. In stark contrast, the murderous religious wars of the sixteenth and seventeenth centuries and the enmities and prejudices which had sprung from those conflicts thoroughly discredited religion in the role of the ultimate friend of man and path for his advance toward peace and prosperity. Though as we have seen, those wars were fought largely over political and economic issues and, in fact, crossed religious lines rather than being along religious lines, the emotive fuel which was used was the religious issue. That was what remained uppermost in people's minds. The philosophical view on all religious fronts was the ontologically oriented viewpoint. That philosophical viewpoint, along with organized religion in general, was discredited by association with the religious wars. Finally, those same religious wars which were, in fact, interdynastic feuds had clearly shown that the aspirations of individual nations or of people were expendable and available for sacrifice to suit the dynastic aims. On the other hand, the national academies of science were oriented toward their specific region and peoples and were nationalistic. Independent national sovereignty therefore was a philosophic and scientific issue having quasi-religious emotional support. In the minds of many scientists and philosophers therefore, the organized religions, which tended to be extra-territorial in influence, were also considered enemies in the fight for national sovereignty. Given this array of bias-producing influences the attitude of the Enlightenment could hardly have been otherwise than scientific in preference to the speculative. And, given the scientific or fundamentally epistemologically oriented dominance, that empirical aspect of philosophy would also be the major aspect in the succeeding period.

In addition to the Enlightenment's effects on the general intellectual atmosphere, it also had a deep effect on the nature of religious thought and promoted the creation of splinter groups from the main formal Protestant movement. The Pietists somewhat as a reaction to Luther, stressed the need for pious feelings and behavior. The Pietists tended to be a personal rather than institutionalized religion and were thus differentiated from the Methodists and the Quakers who held similar views. There was a reemergence of the ancient doctrine of pantheism, augured by Spinoza both under the old form of all reality as an emanation integral with God and also under a modified form, as proposed by Bishop Berkeley (1684 - 1753). The latter's philosophy is perhaps closer to a pure idealism and has been called pluralistic idealism. Berkeley accepted Newtonian physics and the rest of the material world of science, but held, nevertheless, that it was only man's senses that made it real, and outside of men's minds there was no material universe. Reality was in the realm of thought alone. He did not, however, go the next step which would have had all thought and all being, as only emanations from a central intelligence—God. Some current philosophers believe that Berkeley did not hold with pantheism at all, or idealism for that matter, but took this far-out position to counteract the growing materialism in the strongest possible way. Paradoxically, Berkeley's philosophy did not lead into the idealism of Immanuel Kant and Fichte but into the empiricism of David Hume. Berkeley is considered among the empiricists in the English tradition.

All in all, however, and for obvious reasons, religion was in eclipse during the main Enlightenment period. Philosophy in broadest terms dominated the scene. Only Immanuel Kant among philosophers of religious orientation is considered to be of sufficient stature to justify selection because of his tremendous impact in later periods. The other representatives selected are David Hume, Jacques Rousseau and Francois de Voltaire.

David Hume was born at Edinburgh in 1711 of middle class parents. His father wished him to become a lawyer, but David seemed to have a natural inclination to the liberal arts, particularly literature and philosophy, and in 1734 left Scotland for France. He felt he could make a living while still pursuing his preferred field of interest in France. It was there during the next three years that he composed his work *Treatise of Human Nature,* which as originally organized was financially unsuccessful. He returned to Scotland where he published his first successful work, *Essays, Moral and Political.* He subsequently reworked the *Treatise of Human Nature* and issued it in separate sections. Following this, he turned to history and did not return to any major philosophical work except incidentally for *Political Discourses,* published in 1752, though he consorted with philosophers in France and England, among them Jacques Rousseau whom he brought to England in 1766. The two quarrelled bitterly shortly thereafter and Rousseau returned to France.

Hume died in 1776, his *Dialogues Concerning Natural Religion,* being published posthumously in 1779, though it had been written in 1752. His importance in philosophy stems from his concept of man's apprehension of knowledge solely through the senses. Hume finds the source of cognition in impressions of sensation and their reflection in the mind. All simple ideas are derived from, and are copies of, simple impressions. Complex ideas are merely physical composites of simple impressions—"bundles of impressions"—made in the organic sensory neuro-psychological complex.

By pulling together ideas from Berkeley, Descartes and Locke, Hume assumes that all intellection is merely the result of a stimulation of the extended sensory system. There is no continuous self or ego, only a succession of impressions. Each separately reacted to, but like the phenomena of persistence of vision, there is an overlap of impressions which gives us a sense of continuity and of an integrating personality which endures through our life. Thus, empiricism is the sole source and basis of our knowledge. Deductive logic has no basis for its premises other than in sensed data and then only in very limited application.

The arguments which Hume developed to "prove" that no logically necessary connection between causes and effects can be demonstrated deeply affected Kant's idealistic philosophy and apparently caused him to develop a two-tiered level of man's apprehension of truth. The empirically-sensed phenomena being the only true informational source—all other cognition must be a judgmental modulation and not properly considered knowledge, though it might represent the real. And no causal connection can possibly be established between the two areas. As we had noted earlier, the Latin Averroists had resorted to a similar but by no means identical dual concept of our apprehension of theological as distinguished from philosophical truth.

Hume believed that because there are no logically coercive arguments for moral and religious propositions—all metaphysical in origin and non-sensory concepts—such propositions must find their justifications in terms of: mental habits, observable human customs, self-interest, and a sensed altruistic need. They are purely a matter of sentiment. Needless to say his views on religion and the nature of the Deity are tenuous indeed. God is unknowable—but may, as a concept, be necessary to make life livable. He may even be real. What a denouement for Berkeley's religiously motivated ideal construct—because Hume credited Berkeley for providing the psychological basis for the imaginative role in converting sensed data to phantasms or mental impressions in the brain!

Hume's philosophic concept of man was, thus, not a very exalted one. Life was merely a photographic sequence, like a movie film, and all the aesthetic appreciation of art, the passions, the affections and ecstacies were mere fabrications from organic manipulation of sensed data. Not a very inspiring viewpoint to say the least.

Hume's ideas, though long since abandoned as they were rather crudely formulated, nevertheless clearly established the empiricist's viewpoint in philosophy for those who sought to reduce everything to the world of sensed data, a viewpoint which has remained prominent up to the present. And through the impact of Kant's idealism, Hume also helped establish the source-biased duality of knowledge which still persists in some current philosophic systems.

However, Hume did not try to live by his philosophic construction. He agreed, somewhat inaccurately, that "It is universally allowed that nothing exists without a cause of its existence." He seems almost to be playing a game, and uninterested in discovering whether there are causal relationships or not but in defining what it means to state that there are causal relationships. He stated, for instance, that "The experienced train of events is the great standard by which we all regulate our conduct. Nothing else can be appealed to in the field or in the senate. Nothing else ought ever to be heard of in the school or in the closet." Our lives are dominated by custom and belief and in the assured realities of our personalities. In fact, we could not live otherwise, but that does not mean that is the way it is. In his *Enquiry Concerning Human Understanding*, a reissue of a part of the Treatise, he says in the preamble, "Be a philosopher but, amidst of your philosophy, be still a man."

Hume was not an atheist, only a thorough-going professional

skeptic; nor was he a fanatic in his skepticism—far from it—he said, "I dine, I play a game of backgammon, I converse and am merry with my friends; and when after three or four hours amusement, I would return to these speculations, they appear so cold and strained and ridiculous that I can't find it in my heart to enter into them any further." Truly, he was a professional devotee of the Enlightenment.

Francois de Voltaire was born in Paris, November 21, 1694 and registered as Francois Arouet. He disavowed the records, saying that he was the son of a song writer, Rochebrune. He was to be educated in accordance with his official father's desires as a lawyer. Arouet was a notary who later became an accountant at the *Cout des Comptes* and desired his son to follow in the government service. Francois disliked the law and had no use for his father, his elder brother, Armand, or for their way of life. His godfather, Abbe de Chateuneuf, a free-thinker and epicurean at heart, had a major part in his upbringing. Voltaire's main education was by the Jesuits at the College of Louis le Grand in Paris. He was good at rhetoric but poor at religion, being a skeptic from the first. He left college in 1711, concluding his formal schooling at the age of seventeen, and was employed by the French embassy at The Hague.

He always had a remarkable facility at writing, but his mind was far more clever than it was profound. Nevertheless, during the Enlightenment, the important thing for a rising young man was to impress important people. Voltaire succeeded in doing this, although not always in the ways he wished. He enjoyed showing his wittiness in the equivalent of our "jet set" society. In one of his rhymes, he poked fun at the stupidity of the Prince Regent of France, the Duc de Orleans, who was in fact, not particularly stupid. That episode resulted in one year in the Bastille in 1717.

In 1718, his first work, *Oedipus,* was published successfully and at that Francois Arouet took the name Voltaire. However, he still had not learned from his previous experience and continued his practice of barbed criticism which cost him another tour in the Bastille and exile to England for three years (1726 - 1729). While in exile Voltaire made friends with like-minded Englishmen and acquired a tremendous regard for England and the English constitutional form of government. During this period, he wrote his *Letters on the English,* which carried the thrust of his religious beliefs. Even before his exile Voltaire had been attracted to the ideas of Pierre Bayle (1647 - 1706), a Frenchman, who was the leading genius in the spread of deism.

Deism was a naturalistic form of religion, or irreligion, which drew its philosophic support from Descartes but added a deeper skepticism of revelation of its own. The creed of deism was simple and to some extent based on the Aristotelian concept of the prime mover, certainly more so than Plato's supreme goodness though there were overtones of Plato's Demiurge.

The god of deism was the god of nature, who, having started things and established the natural law, abandoned creation to those laws which applied alike to man, beast and the stars. Prayers and any form of worship were utterly useless as well as irrational. Voltaire took this theme as a part of his life, mingling it generously with the prodigious volume of this literary works. Most of his life was lived at Cirey in Lorraine. This included a laboratory for his own "dabbling" in science. Voltaire actually had little formal education in the sciences. He enjoyed puncturing "existing balloons" and putting up his own. He was an iconoclast while building his own self-image. Hayes says of him in this regard (pages 523-524):

> Voltaire was at once a product and a popularizer of the Enlightenment—its interest in natural science, its belief in natural law, in natural rights, in human reason, and in human perfectibility—and his significance lay in his use of the philosophy of the Enlightenment as the foil for the sharp rapier which he repeatedly thrust at the "irrational" ideas and institutions of the eighteenth century. Usually his criticism was more destructive than constructive. It was doubtless easier to poke fun at existing abuses than to suggest practical means of remedying them. He wittily criticized manners and morals, society and government, professing admiration for English liberties, but never explaining just how the "liberties" of England were to be transplanted into France.
>
> Against ecclesiastical Christianity, Voltaire made peculiarly sharp thrusts. "The infamous thing" ("*l'infame*"), he repeatedly called it. He had no patience with organized Christianity, whether Protestant or Catholic; the only Christian body for which he expressed any sympathy was the Quakers. To him all priests were imposters, all miracles were illusions, and all revelations were human inventions. Christian churches might remain for a time to solace the ignorant and keep the lower classes in order, but for

intelligent men Voltaire was sure that deism—the true
religion of Nature—was sufficient. He was certain that
the God of Nature who had made the myriad stars
of the firmament and had promulgated eternal laws
for the universe could have no concern for the petty
and, perhaps, imaginary souls of human beings.

Voltaire always had a penchant for enraging people. He was
invited to Prussia to brighten up the Court of Frederick the
Great but had to leave in haste to escape the king's vengeance
over some irritating comment. He made a fortune in speculation fairly early. This left him free of financial worries and also
free to tweak people's sensitivities to his heart's content. He
learned early that a barb, at the proper location, in high places
makes one man mad, but delights a thousand.

His important works include an outstanding history of France
during the period of Louis XIV, published in 1751. Another work,
primarily on the cultural and economic history of his time, was
published in 1752. Probably *Candide,* published in 1757, and
some of his other philosophical short novels are currently best
known. Voltaire died in Paris, in 1778, at the age of 84. He
died immediately following a tumultuous, triumphant return to
the city. He enjoyed every moment of his hectic career right
up to that last flavorsome moment of acclaim, serving as the
arbiter of Europe to the very end.

Voltaire earned the doubtful honor, in history, of being named
the principal intellectual motivator of the French Revolution.
It certainly was not intentional; subtle sarcasm, satire and clever
ridicule were his weapons. The thought of setting off a bloody
civil war was unthinkable to him. As Hayes said, he preferred
the rapier. The bludgeon was not in his style.

Voltaire's place in establishing the image of man as a completely independent creature, having no responsibility other than
to himself, is unexceeded to the present. He had a vague consideration for a social humanity yet always in terms of individual
liberties. His views induced many of the present similar attitudes on man's complete independence from external control.
Still, Voltaire was no atheist nor did he deny man's transcendent nature. As a proper skeptic and deist, he said that if man
had such a nature, God could not care less about what he did
with it.

Jean Jacque Rousseau was born in Geneva on June 28, 1712.
His father was a watchmaker and Jean was apprenticed as an
engraver. After a few years he ran away and became the protege

of Baronne de Warens. As with Voltaire, Rousseau had little formal education but was broadly self-educated and for a number of years served as a private tutor. In many ways, he ignored the main theme of the Enlightenment, that of deifying natural science. For Rousseau, it was enough just to deify nature. In some ways he was born a century too soon, for the Romanticism of the Brownings, Goethe, Carlyle, Bryant and other nineteenth century poets, essayists, novelists and dramatists borrowed much from his theme of nature as a bountiful mother. Yet, he was a man with tremendous impact on the emerging political scene with his idea of the Natural Man. Rousseau's concept of the natural morality of man influenced Kant in his theme of idealism disseminated in Germany. Rousseau was not a rationalist. However, he along with Hobbes and Locke and fellow thinkers, understood that government should be systematized based on a knowledge of society and should serve the interest of society. Government should be independent of religion or authority other than that vested in the people themselves. To that extent, politics should be a science.

Rousseau visualized "man" idyllically as a naturally trustful and virtuous being, without the poisonous artificiality of civilization. This picture was far removed from the Hobbesian concept of the savage brute who would destroy everything unless controlled by some form of imposed and inforced enlightened self-interest.

Rousseau's first major work published in 1750 was *Discourse on Arts and Sciences* for which he won a prize at Dijon and in which he drew his totally imaginary picture of natural man. He theorized that if civilization could be eliminated, all man's ills would be cured. The work was highly successful, an unusual circumstance for Rousseau who till then had been a failure in everything else he had attempted. In his second essay, *Origin of Inequality Among Men,* published in 1858, he blamed the beginnings of the social problems on the rights of private property which gave rise to greed and to fencing out neighbors. The stronger man was naturally able to make off with the larger and better share of property. In 1761 or 1762 he published a pamphlet, *Social Contact,* patterned largely after Locke's effort of the same name seventy years before. But whereas Locke's effort was largely ignored except by professional students of politics, Rousseau's was instantly received with fervor and with predictably polarized sentiment. Supporters of popular sovereignty acclaimed it; opponents denounced it. The opening words of the work, "Man is born free but everywhere he is in chains" sets the problem as Rousseau saw it. Man, as he was constituted naturally, must "obey only himself." Rousseau's solution was thus different than either Locke's or Hobbes'. Rousseau introduced the concept of the "general will," a voluntary recognition (almost of a naturally arrived-at consensus) of how men should conduct their relations, and this consensus formed the basis of his "contract." By this contract, under the "general will," man arrives at a liberty even greater than under nature. Each man can realize himself more fully. Instead of "a stupid and unimaginative animal," he becomes "an intelligent being and a man." Once the "general will" was established, men were obliged to comply with it. It was represented by the national sovereignty. Because of the work, Rousseau had to flee France for Switzerland and from there to Berlin and, as we have seen, from there to England with David Hume in 1766.

He was named the father, legitimate or illegitimate, depending upon the viewpoint, of republicanism and modern democracy. He was denounced by Voltaire and acclaimed by Thomas Paine. Even royalty was impressed by his view of nature. Marie Antoinette and her ladies in waiting played the parts of dairy maids at the *Petit Trianon*. Rousseau's plea for the rights of man as an individual, as enunciated in his Liberty, Equality, Fraternity, were soon echoed through the alleys of Paris in the Reign of Terror. This was far from what the romantic, half-demented, paranoid Rousseau, could have foreseen or desired. Rousseau was totally sincere, if hopelessly romantic. His *Confessions,* an autobiographical work, expressed an intense sentimentality and deep affection for nature. He wrote two novels, *The New Heloise,* published in 1761, and *Emile,* published in 1762. Both have strong social connotations and both contributed to his persecution and his fame.

Rousseau's personal life was one of contrast with the ideals of his work. His family life was a disaster. He was a wanderer, with no real attachments to any place. He lived at various times in Geneva, Paris, Berlin, Turin, Vienna and London. He found a permanent residence in none, and died in 1778, before the real impact of his work could be felt.

Rousseau's view, clear from his work, was that of man naturally noble, but corruptible and corrupted. Rousseau believed in a God who "had given the land to all." But by and large man was a victim of his own greed. If man had dignity, it was in direct proportion to the extent that he surpassed his natural condition by recognizing and giving his true support to the "general will." God remained an enigma for Rousseau. Although he had espoused both Catholicism and Protestantism, his associations with Hume as well as the enlightened French philosophers convinced him that the Deist's God was the best solution for man in freedom. Feeling and sentiment were all that pointed to God, reason did not. Still, the idea of a personal God was attractive to Rousseau.

Immanual Kant was born on April 22, 1724 at Koenigsberg in East Prussia. He was the grandson of a Scottish immigrant to Prussia, and his father was a master saddler of little means. He was educated at the Collegium Fredericianum and then later at the University of Koenigsberg, where he became a professor of logic and metaphysics. Strangely, he was an admirer of both Voltaire and Rousseau whose viewpoints were so divergent. His philosophy was greatly affected by his other major contemporary, David Hume. Kant had a life-long interest in natural science to the extent that he was, in an age when everyone dabbled in a science, truly competent in physics, geophysics and physical geography. He wrote authoritatively on such subjects as the nature and cause of earthquakes, volcanology and astronomy, but it was as a philosopher that he was of greatest, even commanding, importance.

Today Kant is rated as one of the greatest figures in the history of philosophy, and as contrasted with many others of his day, he spoke from a real background in science as well. He labored earnestly to reconcile his own deep sense of morality, and man's responsibility for his actions, with what he saw as a deterministic world which the physical sciences revealed in the forces of nature, as interpreted by Newton and, in turn, adjusted by Hume's empiricism. He tried to reconcile the dual aspects of metaphysics; to bring the realities of natural science into concord with those of revealed religion. His greatest works, all produced after he was 57 years of age, are *Critique of Pure Reason* (1781), *Foundations of Metaphysics of Ethics,* and *Critique of Practical Reason* in 1788, *The Critique of Judgement* (1790) and *Religion Within the Boundaries of Pure Reason* (1794). His works are difficult, if not impossible, to analyze in any brief way. Fortunately we are interested here only in the slender, though highly important sector of his philosophy that influenced man's changing concept of man. His main theme was that of Idealism, sometimes called critical transcendent idealism. Influenced largely by Hume, Kant came to the opinion that while the existence of God cannot be known from unaided reason, his existence is compellingly demostrated by man's almost instinctual moral sense. Conjoined with that apprehended awareness of God is the recognition of the transcendent nature of the human essence the immortality of the soul and the freedom of man's will.

Kant's basic training in philosophy was in the scholastic tradition via Christian Wolff (1679-1754) and of Gottfried Leibnitz (1646-1716), via Wolff. Leibnitz himself was of course a great scientist and mathematician as well as a philosopher. Like Descartes, Leibnitz had postulated that man had certain "virtually innate" ideas which permitted him to apprehend the spiritual and moral realities as well as directly sensed knowledge. Kant early rejected the concept of Leibnitz' innateness but held a "predisposition" to such ideas. In cybernetic language, Kant held that there was a sort of an *a priori* preprogramming of the intellect to accept such ideas and properly handle them when they were presented in the course of speculative thinking. This idea was later abandoned and is only remotely related to his later *a priori* intuitive judgments. Kant did not accept Hume's entire thesis, but he agreed with Hume's emphasis on the senses as the only sources of cognitive knowledge. He said of Hume's work that it "awoke him from his dogmatic slumbers."

When, as he said, he roused from his slumber, Kant modified his ideas to reconcile the two concepts of the spiritual and the material and accordingly severely separated the two aspects of man's intellectual life. By 1765, he believed the only source of true knowledge was the senses responding to the physical world. The response was as a passing of ideational essence through a membrane that was impermeable to the sense data directly. Kant restricted intuition to the immediate and sensuous. The discursive or purely intellectual had no similar source of knowledge.

Throughout his early life, probably until age 40, he had accepted the metaphysics in the tradition of Aristotle and the scholastics generally. After that time, he drastically reversed opinions and denied that the rational intellect would form a true metaphysics by transcending from the material milieu to the spiritual. Kant says that attempts in metaphysics had been colossal failures, and were even fated to be such, since there is no way the ascent can be made through pure reason. This appears to be the conclusion he reached from Hume's premises. Human knowledge, thus, has a composite source. The first source is the faculty of the intellect to receive or acquire the sense data by intuition—an intuition which is incapable of thinking—and the second source is the "data processing" via the understanding which relativizes the sensations and forms concepts. The "data processing" through the understanding is blind without the intuitive faculty and the intuition is ignorant and unknowing without the understanding. Both processes have their individual sets of laws which govern their operations.

In his *Critique of Judgement* he establishes three cognitive powers within the reason. "Reason" is here used in Kant's broadest use of that term. First there is the judgment, then the understanding as noted above and finally the reason in a narrow sense. Kant assigns the faculty, Judgment, the role of mediator between the understanding and the "narrow" practical reason. The understanding establishes order and law *a priori* to the apprehended reality so that we can appreciate the truth of the external world of nature. The practical reason selects the "good" in contradistinction to the "true." The judgment mediates therefore between the concepts of the true and the good and permits us to universalize from the particular in this limited application.

Essentially the only bridge between the world of the senses, or phenomena, and the world of the spirit, or noumena, is the morally desirable. The morally desirable is defined by human judgment, and this is based on the concept of *a priori* determination. Proofs are impossible, but human judgmental conclusions are clearly available chiefly from moral confidence. Kant in his own mind had established a stronger position for morality, for man's freedom of will, for the existence of God and for the immortality of the soul than had the metaphysicists he opposed. He believed he had placed these judgmental imperatives beyond the reach of science and had, as it were, disarmed the opposition. But to a critical reader, it seems more like a retreat out of fear than an advance out of confidence. God, for instance, seems to become an ambiguity, only an idea useful for the preservation of happiness and moral virtue. God is not clearly established as *Being* at its quintessence but as an idealization of the *Summum bonum*. Doubtless, with Kant's strongly developed moral sense, the existence and being of God were real to him. However, to one without such a sense, the arguments appear weak and inadequate, not to say unconvincing.

It seems clear in retrospect that Kant needlessly curtailed the capacity of the human reason in his philosophy. He retreated to a position even less humanistic than the Augustinians at the time of Aquinas who saw the intellect "illumined so that it could reason logically to the metaphysical truths." Kant abandoned the field to the tender mercies of the "enlightened" who would, and did, laugh at his treasured categorical moral imperatives and the insights of the "practical reason." If the leader among the theistic philosophers declared so strongly that the reason could not approach any of the first principles, pretty obviously they need not take the matter too seriously.

Kant believed that he had achieved for philosophy, what Copernicus had done for astronomy in moving from an earth-centered to a sun-centered system. His "Copernican Revolution" was an ordering of the objects of perception to fit the mind rather than of the mind conforming to the perceived object. What man achieved by his intuition was a representation of the "thing in itself" which was forced to fit the subject's own intuitive space-time concept. Kant would have said that we can have no knowledge of the "thing in itself," all we have is the effect it conveys. "Thing in itself" is noumena beyond our reach. The ancient problem of the one and the many becomes lost in the incapacity of the human reason to approach either side of the dilemma.

Thus in his works, Kant carefully distinguished the noumena of all types, *including* the "thing in itself," from that of the intuitively sensed, and thus perceived, natural phenomena which can be rationally examined as to their specific nature. These latter ideas, though subjective and ideational, he placed in several categories, chiefly in accordance with coherence and substantiality. Kant's dichotomies, forced by this duality, involved deliberate statements on principles logically incompatible—statements such as demonstrations—that time and space existed yet did not exist—were finite yet also infinite—that God existed yet did not exist. The apparent incompatibility was resolved in what amounts to the two-tiered level of apprehended truth—the phenomenal and the noumenal. With Kant, the logical, ethical, aesthetic subjective were as far as human knowledge could take us toward the spiritual. Beyond that, knowledge as such was unobtainable. Subjective truth based on the moral consciousness became the basis for meaning in spiritual experience. While the "noumena" are felt judgmentally, and hence cannot be known cognitively, ethics and aesthetics must be based on their real existence. Moral conduct rests upon the categorical imperative which may be stated: "Man must act *as if* the maxims from which he acts were to become, through his will, a universal law of nature. Men must so act as to treat humanity, whether in their own person [sic] or that of another, in every case, as an end in itself, never as a means" (emphasis added). But Kant also says, perhaps echoing Rousseau, "A person is subject to no laws other than those which he (either alone or jointly with others) gives to himself."

Kant was the first to propound, in philosophical terms, the now widely held view that metaphysical truth, if you can even use the term, is subjective. Even physical reality in a broad sense is subjective depending on the judgmental application of the *a priori* categorization. In matters of "metaphysics" there is no higher basis of decision than man's self-consciousness of truth. Recalling the model given earlier in Part I for truth and reality, "objective" and "subjective," Kant would partition off the elipsoid on a longitudinal plane through the vertical axis and look at his object only from one side. The side selected would depend on the nature of the object. The spiritual segments would be eliminated in one, the material in the other. He would say that it was impossible to get any larger spectrum than the individual's own subjective projection for the noumena. Kant implied that for the noumena there was no objective truth at all in a humanly attainable way. His was a viewpoint also that a consensus was no better than an individual perception. Whatever piece of the spectrum was perceived, that was truth for the individual. Faith based on a judgmental apprehension, the categorical moral imperative, therefore, not knowledge, justified belief in God, immortality and freedom of the will.

On a hard and quick analysis, which cannot do full justice to the value of his works, Kant's final philosophy leads to the conclusion that one cannot even know himself as the intending ego under scrutiny because when in examining himself as an object he is as limited to his sense perception as he is in examining anything else as object. One cannot know—in any real way—oneself, God or any possible spiritual realities. Neither can one know anything of the outside material world as "it is in itself," as "thing in itself," because these are all noumena and hidden from knowledge. All one can know is the fictionalized version of material reality including oneself in the representation which, through apperceptive integration of reason, one's senses provided. It is a totally never-never land. Kant's duality in separating intellectual knowledge and the intelligible world further from sensitive knowledge and the world of observation increasingly subdivided man as a rational being. In Kant's strange world, intellectual knowledge, that is knowledge of the *intelligibilia* or those things such as the "thing in itself" or spiritual things which the senses cannot reveal directly, must remain outside that realm of scientific knowledge which can rely on the intuition provided by sense data for its validity. Kant says, "An intuition of intelligible objects is not given man, but only a symbolic knowledge." Maritain would have been quick to point out that a symbol is meaningless unless the perceptor has in mind that which is symbolized. Since one can gain no information on the intelligibilia which includes the total area of metaphysics, Kant adds, "But in pure philosophy, such as in metaphysics, in which the use of the intellect concerning principles is *real* (that is, has no sense data), that is where primitive concepts of things and relations and the very axioms are originally provided by the pure intellect itself, and where, since there are no intuitions, we are not immune from error. Method precedes all science, and whatever is undertaken before the precepts of this method have been duly worked out and firmly established, seems to be rashly conceived and fit to be rejected as a vain and ridiculous activity of the mind." (Italics Kant's) Further, there was no remedy available to man to work out the approved methodology of intelligibilia.

Kant's entire structure of philosophy rests upon the rather fragile base of his epistemological representational theory of perception. The weak point, later expertly isolated and displayed by Fichte, is the "thing in itself" which according to Kant was noumenon. That is, completely unknowable by sense perception. Yet it was this "thing in itself" which undergirded all of "phenomena;" that is, that permitted sense perception or that which was the cause of sense data. That which is perceived, which is sensed, is the construction which the human mind makes of the "things in themselves." We really cannot know what the "thing in itself" is like. Fichte merely said in effect, "forget it, there is nothing there, it is all a mental construct, or pure idea." Friedrich Jacobi (1743-1819), in criticizing Kant says that the only reason Kant uses "thing in itself" is the causal principle. There must be a "something" which causes the sense perception to form as an effect. But Kant elsewhere holds that the causal principle cannot be extended to the noumena so that in the "thing in itself" he denies his own philosophy. If there is no reality but only a mental image formed *ex nihilo* one is led either to solipsism or to a conclusion of a universal mind as the source of all ideas, which is Fichte's proposal—a metaphysics of pure speculation—just what Kant set out to dispose of! But on the other hand, if the "thing in itself" is in fact there, it is the only ontological reality and the sense perception is only a fictionalized version and Kant is worse off than with Fichte's solution—pure fantasy.

Kant is not unaware, though perhaps somewhat unappreciative, of the scope of his dilemma. He says that, in a sense, the "thing in itself" can be considered a boundary situation, presumably halfway between phenomena and noumena. But this does not get him off the horns of his dilemma. He can't have it both ways or, in fact, either way. If the noumena, "things in themselves," are real but unknowable and sense perception an ideational concept only—not a reproduction of reality but pure subjective construct—to that extent, the objects of sense "knowledge" are fictitious and unreal. Science and empirical knowledge are farcical. Or, if the noumena, the "things in themselves" are not real but merely a limiting concept, the function of which is "to curb the pretensions of sensibility," then Fichte is right and pure idealism is the only answer. Kant's concept falls either way. To say that the "thing in itself" is partly real and partly ideational is a speculative monstrosity.

Kant's "Copernican Revolution" gets him into more entanglements than using the basic "common sense" view of the metaphysical realists or of Einstein, that what we perceive is substantially what "is out there." In the main, it is true that the mind must conform itself to the object and not the reverse. Though we can still be deceived, we can reduce the deception by further closer examination. By Ockham's razor, Kant's epistemological theory should be rejected preemptorily and with the epistemology there goes the entire system. Kant's concept of God as noumenon, like his concept of the "thing in itself," is treated ambiguously. Sometimes God is discussed as an ontological reality while at other times He is discussed as a purely regulatory mechanism useful to help man live, but in any event unknowable—except by faith.

Kant, probably taking his cue from Rousseau, was among the early philosophers to personalize "nature" as an expression reflecting the workings of God in the world. It was a popular theme during the romantic period of philosophy immediately ahead. He had written:

> In her (Nature's) mechanical course we see that her aim is to produce a harmony among men, against their will and indeed through their discord. As a necessity working according to laws we do not know, we call it destiny. But, considering its design in world history, we call it "providence," inasmuch as we discern in it the profound wisdom of a higher cause which predetermines the course of nature and directs it to the objective final end of the human race.
>
> The use of the word "nature" is more fitting to the limits of human reason and more modest than

an expression indicating a providence unknown to us. This is especially true when we are dealing with questions of theory and not of religion, as at present, for human reason in questions of the relation of effects to their causes must remain with the limits of possible experience.

Kant typically undersells the capacity of human reason and typically also slides off the issue of recognizing the obvious "higher cause" as God. A century later, John Dewey would totally remove the idea of "providence" from the concept of "nature."

Kant, for all his wide ranging field of interest, never traveled, and lived all of his eighty years in the immediate vicinity of Koenigsburg. He died in Koenigsburg on February 12, 1804. So far as is known, he never left Prussia. He was recognized as a systematic, kindhearted, high-minded, and above all, truthful man, a man who had internalized deeply his idealistic attitudes and high standards of morality. He was also a man who permitted little sense of humor or sentiment to show through his writings, though reputedly, his lectures were spiced with humorous anecdotes.

Johann Gottfried Herder (1744-1803), a contemporary of Kant, and to some extent a disciple, did not share Kant's philosophical reluctance to identify nature with God. He called God the "Omni-potent Goodness." He belongs to the continuing naturalistic thread of philosophy, carrying the thought into the period of romanticism. His views concerning man's position are well summed up in the following excerpt from his *Ideas on the Philosophy of the History of Humanity*.

Everything in nature is connected: one state pushes forward and prepares another. If then man be the last and highest link, closing the chain of terrestrial organization, he must begin the chain of a higher order of creatures as its lowest link, and is probably, therefore, the middle ring between two adjoining systems of creation.

The earth is an inn for travelers; a planet, on which birds of passage rest themselves, and from which they hasten away. The brute lives out his life; and, if his years be too few to attain higher ends, his inmost purpose is accomplished: his capacities exist, and he is what he was intended to be. Man alone is in contradiction with himself, and with the earth: for, being the most perfect of creatures, his capacities are the farthest from being perfected, even when he attains the longest term of life before he quits the world. But the reason is evident: his state, being the last upon this earth, is the first in another sphere of existence, with respect to which he appears here as a child making his first essays. Thus he is the representative of two worlds at once; and hence the apparent duplicity of his essence. It is the same with man here below: his defects are perplexing to an earthly mind: but a superior spirit that inspects the internal structure, and sees more links of the chain, may indeed pity, but cannot despise him. He perceives why man must quit the world in so many different states, young and old, wise and foolish, grown gray in second childhood, or an embryo yet unborn. Omnipotent goodness embraces madness and deformity, all the degrees of cultivation, and all the errors of man, and wants not balsams to heal the wounds that death alone could mitigate. Since probably the future state springs out of the present, as our organization from inferior ones, its business is no doubt more closely connected with our existence here than we imagine. The garden above blooms only with plants, of which the seeds have been sown here, and put forth their first germs from a coarser husk.

If, then, as we have seen, sociality, friendship, or active participation in the pains and pleasures of others, be the principal end, to which humanity is directed, this finest flower of human life must necessarily there attain the vivifying form, the overshadowing height, for which our heart thirsts in vain in any earthly situation. Our brethren above, therefore, assuredly love us with more warmth and purity of affection than we can bear to them: for they see our state more clearly, to them the moment of time is no more, all discrepancies are harmonized, and in us they are educating, unseen, partners of their happiness and companions of their labors. But one step farther, and the opposed spirit can breathe more freely, and the wounded heart recovers: They see the passenger approach and stay his sliding feet with a powerful hand.

Herder's views are strongly suggestive of a view of man which will be explored in some depth in Parts III and V, that man, the "discontented animal," is in fact "over-qualified" intellectually for his present environment. "The overshadowing height for which our heart thirsts in vain in any earthly situation" which Herder sees as man's principal end is indeed "other worldly."

The last half of the eighteenth century, as is clear from these brief summaries, was one of great change in basic human concepts. For purposes of this work the philosophic and moral implications are paramount and those would be reflected chiefly in the following century. Deism had gained a dominant position among the intellectuals and this would not change as the move into the Idealism and Romanticism of the early nineteenth century unfolded. Skepticism, the offspring of rationalistic humanism, had taken over the field of play. Man was literally a doubting creature of doubtful value. Even the idea of the dignity of man through individual free development of genius had begun to give way to that of man's mediocrity. The idea of the common man, sturdy, self-reliant, making his own free choice of political leadership, was probably the mass ideal rather than the individual of genius. It should be noted that, of those considered in detail, only Kant was a university professor and professional philosopher.

In the agricultural areas away from the major cities, the viewpoint still was one of man's dignity, seen more dimly now in his relationship with a loving God and father. Paul Henri Thiry, Baron de Holbach (1723-1789), a native of the German Palatinate, who had moved to Paris as a youth, openly advocated the cause of atheism for the first time. In a series of works, *Christianity Unveiled* (1767), and in his *Systems of Nature* (1770), in which he collaborated with Diderot (1713-1784), he maintained that there was no God, not even the god of nature. He saw the universe as "spontaneous matter in motion." He made an unexplained as well as unsupported assumption, and with a single stroke eliminated Aristotle's "prime mover." The enlightened skeptics found no trouble with that assumption or its conclusion. For Holbach, self-enjoyment was the sole object of mankind. Man was innately moral but perverted, principally, by education. Thus, by the end of the eighteenth century, atheism was contending with deism, as deism was with Christianity and Judaism. Humanism in one form or another was now in command. The academies, the stronger force in the intellectual milieu of the period, were largely dedicated to humanism and its central theme of the dignity of man in development of his own genius. But now even humanism was being divided in several ways. The ideas of liberty, equality and fraternity were not completely in harmony with the idea of the man of genius. The equalitarian attitude espoused the dignity of man in his political freedom, secure from any form of dominance of superiority, intellectual or otherwise. The untrammeled man of nature was also an ideal. There was, therefore, a horizontal cultural and political split in humanism as well as a vertical split into two wings. First, the traditional theistic humanism now reflecting a deistic influence, and, second, a new naturalistic humanism springing from the atheistic influence.

Kant's detailed and highly technical treatment of the crucial role of empirically based perception in controlling total knowledge formation appeared to give technical philosophical authority to the atheistic-tending rationalists and empiricists, though that was the opposite of Kant's intent. Kant abandoned reason to the positivists, consigned the total source of knowledge to the empiricists, and set the scenes for the emergence of a broad spectrum of fantastic idealistic systems.

The importance of the last half of the eighteenth century on the trend in man's concept of man can hardly be overemphasized. It was almost as if events conspired to bring about the rise of positivism and materialism to be the dominant philosophical position one hundred years later. The effects of the philosophies of Hume, Kant, Voltaire and Rousseau provided a positive thrust to the materialistic trend. Simultaneously, the suppression of the Jesuits, by far the largest and most influential teaching organization in the world at the time, effectively eliminated the countervailing theistic scholastic philosophers. The order was first suppressed in Portugal in 1759, France in 1764, Spain and its worldwide territories in 1767 and finally, Clement XIV was forced, by pressure from Catholic sources, to dissolve the order in 1773. Frederick the Great in Prussia and Czarina Catherine the Great of Russia both refused to comply with the papal order because they considered the directive an infringement of their sovereignty and not because they were overly devoted to the Jesuits. Elsewhere, the organization was disbanded, not to be reactivated until 1814. The intervening half century saw not only destruction of the primary scholastic educational base but also almost no effective philosophical work from a theistic standpoint with the exception of Kant. However, his work, as we have seen by the denial of the power of reason to approach the transcendent ideas as knowledge, was really a surrender of the heights and an attempt to defend the valleys.

At the close of the eighteenth century, the epistemological situation which existed was far different than that at the end of the seventeenth century. Reason was now deified. It was nevertheless a reason limited to the physical senses. It was a very narrow range of the possible zone of intellection, far narrower than that which Descartes, Spinoza and Hobbes, or even Locke, would have taken. Knowledge, while viewed as virtually limitless by Voltaire and others of the enlightenment, could only be obtained by the senses; largely by some second remove from the physical object itself. Prior to this time the world of physics and metaphysics, after the Aristotelian usage, had been considered as two completely complementary areas of study within the overall grasp of knowledge. Only metaphysics could bring one to the knowledge of first principles.

The very term, "epistemology," as the philosophical theory of knowledge and as the investigative methodology of knowledge, was not used until the nineteenth century in philosophical literature. The term was "invented" because the dominant place that methodology had taken in the study of knowledge was introducing confusion into the concepts of understanding. A separate branch of philosophy was created to handle it.

One point probably should be made here. The relationship of cause and effect was organic to the thought of Aristotle and indeed has been the heart of the physical sciences up to the present day. It is the relationship which permits the world to be considered intelligible and susceptible to the development of physical "laws" of nature.

Now Ockham, and following closely to his views, Kant, said in effect that the extension of judgment from experiences in the observable sensible world to the world of the suprasensible, or spiritual, is invalid because the rules which govern the latter would not necessarily, or even likely, correspond with those of the sensible world. Therefore, it must always remain unknowable, even unthinkable, in any real, rational way by the sense-bound beings of this world. Specifically, just because there is an observable relationship between cause and effect in this world until one gets to the outer boundaries of knowledge does not justify the extrapolation of the causal principle across that unknowable boundary.

If now we examine the statement "Everything that comes into existence requires a pre-existing causal agency," it is obvious that in this form the statement is a proposition universal in application. It would apply to an angel, to man or to God if God "comes into existence" rather than comprising, in His essence, eternal existence and being. In Part III, one of the two leading cosmogenic theories— that of the continuous creation— postulates that the observed continuous expansion of our universe can be explained by the "spontaneous generation" of one atom of hydrogen per cubic foot of space "every few billion years." That still amounts to a tremendous amount of hydrogen or energy if converted, by the Einstein equation, even for the universe within the range of our current radio telescopes. It would comprise several equivalent solar systems per year, in fact. But that is itself beside the point. Across the unknowable boundary an atom of hydrogen "comes into existence." There is no conversion of energy involved here. An instant before there was no atom or anything else. Suddenly, an atom is there where nothing had been. According to our universal proposition, there must necessarily be a causal agency. Neither Ockham nor Kant, of course, were faced with such a potential particular; only the total existent universe. But, quite obviously, if an atom of hydrogen can self-generate, so could everything else as in Holbach's solution. The difference is purely quantitative.

The question will not go away here or at any other point where the physical sciences come to their boundaries, as they have in physics in the areas of both microphysics and macrophysics where causalities are explainable only in terms of statistics, or in the biologic sciences, where the ultimate explanation lies hidden in the behavior of organisms. The "causal" limits available to physical science have been reached in these areas, and as the present boundaries are passed the scientists will face another set. The causal inference remains at the boundary, wherever that boundary exists, staring at all of us, not only the scientists. It is a matter far more pervasive than just the world of the empirical sciences. It stands at the heart of the entire logical complex. What it tells us, intuitively, if you will, is that some universals do indeed extend beyond the boundaries of sense data. It is intellectually repugnant that a state of non-being—total absence of resources, will or essence—can give being to itself, can bring itself into existence spontaneously. It is also mathematically repugnant for the symbol of non-value, zero, to take on a value. Non-A equals A. This is a contradiction necessarily false.

In 1800 the West, Europe and the Americas were still largely agricultural, and the rural people, traditionally conservative, remained undisturbed by the intellectual disputations taking place in the great urban centers. They were solidly theistic in orientation. But with the one-way push of people out of rural areas into industrial cities, a relatively slow process in 1800 but becoming a headlong rush by 1900, that picture changed drastically.

Chapter 5

THE POSITIVISTS AND MATERIALISTS

The nineteenth century was one of great change. It was a time of shifting power and revolution in Europe and, by extension, in the colonial empires throughout the world. It is proper that it should begin with the reign of Napoleon (1769-1821), who came to power in his coup d'etat of 1799. After his brilliant military campaigns, particularly his triumphs in Austria and Italy, his successes stood in deep contrast to the general bumbling and discord of the First Republic. Although the First Republic survived in name until 1804, it was finished.

Most of the French people were more than somewhat tired of Madame Guillotine by that time though the Republic in its last years had moderated to some extent. The militant attack on all organized religion had reached its climax early in 1793 with appropriate services at Notre Dame and authorization by the National Convention to turn churches into temples of the atheistic "religion of reason." By the end of the French Revolution, as at the beginning, after incredible slaughter, cultural disruption, and destruction throughout Europe, the poor were just as poor and just as unequal.

Although the Napoleonic period was short, about 15 years in all, it was dramatic. Napoleon crowned himself Emperor Napoleon I in Paris at Notre Dame Cathedral on December 1, 1804, placing the crown on his own head. While he established a strong and efficient central government and accomplished much in the way of public improvement, he was also hopelessly and fatally ambitious and vain. He possessed an almost superstitious awe of himself as a man chosen by destiny. His reign was one of continuous warfare until his last defeat at Waterloo and abdication into exile in June 1815. But his defeat and death did not end the Napoleonic era. In his short reign, he succeeded in placing members of his family into "royal" positions everywhere.

In France, national patriotism was the theme and continued to be so after Napoleon. It was taught even in primary schools, along with, and co-equal to, Christian morality. Schools were nationalized in a program to insure continuation of the secularization policies of the First Republic. Napoleon's reign spread the predominant French political and intellectual attitude throughout all of Europe. National sovereignty, only a concept in England in the thirteenth century, was well-established there in the seventeenth. The principle quite successfully extended during the eighteenth century in Europe was now, largely as a result of Napoleon's activities, essentially dominant in the early nineteenth century.

Though the monarchial form of government continued and lingered for another 100 years on the continent, it was largely defeated intellectually. Only in Russia did the two-century-old idea of the divine right of kings continue to exhibit real strength. Nationalism was the coming mode. The nation was the sovereign, not the king. Although there would be tyrants, they would tyrannize in the name of the nation, not their own. In Germany, Spain, Italy, Poland, Ireland, Finland, Estonia, Latvia, Norway, Sweden, Greece, Yugoslavia, Croatia and Serbia, and in all the colonies in the Americas, nationalism took on a dominant role. It was even felt in the Ottoman Empire. First in the Balkans, then later in Turkey itself.

Probably because both Russia and England had been victorious against Napoleon, the intellectual impact of the Napoleonic era was less in these places. In addition, the mass of the people in England were already progressive and those of Russia probably too backward to be impressed by the egalitarian ideal. But even in Russia, at its western edge, nationalism was an important theme. It was halfheartedly fostered by Czar Alexander, who saw himself as enlightened, having been tutored by French philosophers. He was to some extent in sympathy with the national aspirations of the Poles, Latvians and others on the European frontier of his vast empire.

Following Napoleon, Count Clemens Metternich (1773-1859), claimed center stage. He had had a hand in the defeat of Napoleon whom he hated passionately. By his shrewd diplomacy, he had succeeded in playing Russia and France against each other to weaken them both and to strengthen Austria, where he was Chief Minister under Emperor Francis I. At the Congress of Vienna in 1814, Metternich's plan was to provide a counterweight to the rising revolutionary spirit. The results of the Congress were to once again pull together a coalition of dynastic forces. It led to the Treaty of Paris in November, 1815 and the Quadruple Alliance. That alliance involved the so-called Concert of Great Powers: Austria, Russia, Prussia and Great Britain. Its aim, not openly expressed, was to prevent a revival of the French imperialism dominant for two centuries. But by its disregard of the not-to-be-denied principles of nationalism, it was doomed to failure, although it lasted to mid-century. Discussing the close of the age of Metternich, historian Hayes gives a panoramic view of the times. He says (796-797),

Yet 1848 is an arbitrary date for the ending of any era. Certainly, the reactionary principles of the "era of Metternich" continued to be cherished and practiced in central and northern Europe considerably after 1848, considerably after the disappearance of the era's namesake from the scene. They reemerged victorious from the revolutionary storms of 1848-1849 in central Europe and remained the guiding stars of the public policy of Austria and Prussia until the 1860's, and of Russia long thereafter.

On the other hand, quite as certainly the central tenet of the "era of Metternich" was repudiated in a large part of southern Europe considerably before 1848. It was liberalism and nationalism, not conservatism and reaction, which registered enduring triumphs in the July (1830) Revolution in France, in the establishment of an independent Belgium (1831), an independent Greece (1832), and an autonomous Serbia (1829), in the loss to Spain and Portugal of their American colonies (1810-1830), in the gain of constitutional government by states of Southern Germany, and in the defection of France from the police-system of the "Concert of Europe." And by 1848 it was apparent that the tide of revolution was rising and that, despite recurrent setbacks, it would eventually engulf all Europe—and probably the whole world.

What was most significant in the situation was the rapidly changing character of England. For England, aristocratic and properly Tory in the first years of Metternich's sway, was irrevocably liberal in the 1830's. A revolution had occurred in England, and a revolution much more fundamental in character and far-reaching in effect than the French Revolution or the revolutions in British politics and European thought in the seventeenth and eighteenth centuries. It was the Industrial Revolution.

The Puritan Revolution, the "Glorious" Revolution, the American Revolution, the Intellectual Revolution, the French Revolution, the revolutionary changes of the era of Napoleon, and the revolutionary upheavals of the era of Metternich, including the Greek Revolution and the Latin American Revolutions—all these had been wrought in a European society which was still predominantly agricultural. It was a society in which the masses were farmers and peasants and the classes enjoyed prestige in some direct proportion to the wealth which they derived from landed estates. It was a very old and traditional society, one which still did its travelling by foot or horse and got its news from stage-coaches, and one which was relatively static.

The rise of modern capitalism, it is true, had been introducing a dynamic element into European society since at least the sixteenth century. Agriculture was gradually becoming more and more capitalistic, and its profits were being invested more and more in commercial enterprise. More and more, therefore a commercial bourgeois class was coming to the fore. And it should be borne in mind that it was the rising bourgeoisie which tended to upset the social equilibrium of Europe and which actually provided the platforms and the most zealous leaders for all the revolutions. Being more numerous in Britain and France than in Germany or northern Europe, the middle class was more immediately successful with its revolutionary endeavors in the former countries than in the latter.

Nevertheless, in every country of the European Continent, as late as the "era of Metternich," the persons dependent on commerce and industry were greatly outnumbered by those dependent on agriculture; the bourgeoisie was but an island in a sea of peasants and landlords. So long as this situation lasted, there would be at least an even chance that the conservative principles of a Metternich could be maintained.

In England, however, during the years when Napoleon's peasant soldiers were fighting with flintlock muskets and when Metternich was riding to international congresses in a coach pulled by four horses, an amazing revolution occurred in the industrial arts and society. Machinery was invented. Factories were built. Production of goods multiplied. Capitalism grew by leaps and bounds. Cities drew hundreds of thousands of men and women from the country-side. The era of real bourgeois supremacy dawned.

Little can be added to Hayes' analysis, the industrial revolution was at hand, and in its long-term effect, made the more glamorous exploits of Napoleon and Metternich as but terminal reflex spasms of a dying social organism. But even as the bourgeois supremacy dawned, a new contender appeared.

The Manifesto of Karl Marx, the formal gauntlet being flung down for the laboring class before the bourgeoisie, opened with the dramatic words, "A specter is haunting Europe—the specter of communism. All the powers of the old Europe have entered into a holy alliance to exorcise this specter. Pope and Tzar, Metternich and Guizot, French radicals and German police spies."

However, before discussing Marx and his tremendous impact on world political, sociological, economic and philosophic thought, we should take a look at the transitional philosophies which led from Kant on the continent and from Hume in England into the dialectic materialism of Engels and Marx. For like every other philosophy, Marxism did not appear *ex nihilo*. If we recall Kant's insistence on the gap which existed between the world of matter and the world of the aesthetic and the spiritual, the truth in the latter two areas was inaccessible to logic. The non-sensory world was a concept of idea alone not reasoned to by the logic from the material world. And, as to the material world, reason in turn was dependent upon the sensory perception received by *a priori* intuitions into the mind. Although the matter of the world was real and objective, existing in some way as "thing in itself" outside the human subject, our perception could not reach it directly and our grasp was necessarily subjective. But Kant's philosophy was highly complex, in some areas frankly ambiguous, and those who followed him took divergent views. Yet, each claimed to be his true disciple—like Elisha bearing the mantle of Elijah.

The period of German Idealism which dominated the early decades of the nineteenth century on the continent had a baroque character which seemed to match the Wagnerian mood of the same period in music and art. We will concentrate on Georg Hegel as the most important of the period in the ongoing theme of the concept of man, but mention also must be made of his principal contemporaries who also influenced that picture.

Johann Fichte (1762-1814) was rector of the newly founded

University of Berlin and Dean of its Philosophical Faculty. For
Fichte, philosophy was a science first and foremost and hence
could be explicated in a mathematical model. Experience of
whatever kind demands a subject or one expressing experiences,
and an object or that which is experienced. Otherwise, the term
itself has no meaning. But how does this relate to Kant, who
mediates the two through an intuitive faculty? In his characteristic way of setting up two decisive alternatives, Fichte says
this mediation is totally fictitious, and he proceeds to establish
his dichotomy. Either the "thing in itself" exists and is perceived as it is by the subject, or it is only a creation of the
subject's mind and has no other meaning. But that latter route,
unless one postulates a universal mind, leads to the conclusion
that only the subject exists. There is nothing else, and that ultimate solipsistic view is manifestly ridiculous. There are other
beings besides oneself. The first view, Kant's, that the perception is a direct effect of the "thing in itself," eventually leads,
on the other hand, eventually to a dogmatic materialism and
determinism. Only the material is real.

Fichte says the decision which must be made is up to each
of us and depends upon the personal character of the individual
subject. But of the two approaches the pure idealistic, "no thing
in itself" at all, contains the higher human value. The philosopher who is mature in moral consciousness will choose that
route, and thus Fichte takes the route of pure idealism. This
leads him to discussion of the "I" or "ego," the subjective self,
and the "it" of everything else. And Fichte emphasizes that the
subject ego and the non-ego are in opposition until one hits
on the ultimate of the "I" and the "it," the idealized subject
and reflected object in the eternal unlimited pure Ego—God,
in whom all the apparent dichotomies are resolved. Thus, there
is not pantheism, but panentheism. There is the individual ego
subject, but, in a holdover from Kant, his direct relationship
to the pure Ego is inaccessible to reason.

Man's life depends on himself; he is free in spite of the difficulties in rationale, and his world view depends on him—how he
handles himself in his freedom. The living and operative moral
order is itself God. "We need no other God and we can concern no other. . .Only reason exists; the infinite in itself, the
finite in it and through it. Only in our minds does He create
a world at least that *from which* and *by which* we unfold it;
the voice of duty and harmonious feeling, intuition, and the
laws of thought." (Emphasis Fichte). Later in his life, he turned
to a somewhat more Christian personal view of God: "Only

one Being exists purely through itself, God...And neither within Him nor outside Him can a new Being arise." In the political field, Fichte accepted the concept of the "general will" of Rousseau, and the state which resulted was truly sovereign. He thus strongly supported the rising national German state.

Friedrich Wilhelm Joseph von Schelling was born in 1775 at Leanberg in Wurttenburg. His father was a Lutheran minister who himself had a broad background in theology, philosophy and the humanities and early developed in his son earnest study habits and a love of learning. When he was only 23, Friedrich was appointed professor in the University of Jena. At that time, he was a disciple of Fichte and had earlier, while at the University of Tubingen, became acquainted with Hegel and Holderin, both of them older than he by several years. His earliest writing, however, showed an individuality of approach to philosophy, and he later broke decisively with both Fichte and Hegel. Hegel, in fact, became to him almost a symbol of opposition in this thought. There are hints that Schelling suspected Hegel of plagiarizing his ideas. Of all the German Idealists, his philosophy seems the least extravagant and fanciful. It was one showing a pattern of development out of Idealism. It can be said he lived through the age of Idealism and matured out of it. Since he outlived all of his colleagues—he died in 1854—to some extent, Schelling had the last word.

Schelling was not satisfied with the duality which had been developing from the time of Descartes, nor the "thing of nature" merging in the absolute intelligence of Spinoza, emphasizing a pantheism founded in nature, nor the strict gap in the dichotomies of Kant, nor the subject worshipping ego or non-ego of Fichte, nor yet was he satisfied with the triadic thought of Hegel. As we shall see, however, there are significant similarities to Hegel's syntheses.

Schelling strove for a unity in syntheses rather than duality in the Kantian mode and in his later years was obsessed with the question, "Why is there being rather than non-being?" For our purposes, the later position in his developing philosophy is perhaps the most important, though possibly it also has been most neglected by the historians of this period of philosophy. It seems to me to be the richest part of his work, that to which all else had been tending. The philosophy of religion became the center of his thought, and he showed a continuity, or continuum, between the pure myth of the most primitive mind and pure revelation in the ultimate phase of the continuing manifestation of the absolute. Religion, at any point, is a mixture of the two and is symbolic of man's ascent to God. And both are necessary. Man is not purely matter, nor purely spirit, but a synthesis of both.

In his analysis of the Christian religious trend, Schelling sees it as a passage from that of Authority "The Petrine period," symbolized by the Father to the second; the Pauline, and its idea of freedom of man in making his decision—the Son's filial yet independent relationship to the Father. He sees, approaching, the third or final phase of ascent to a pure intellectual relationship or the synthesizing of the two earlier phases plus the outpouring of Divine Love symbolized in the Holy Spirit. This would be the Johannine period, the true Christian community in love—religion in its purest form. This was not an entirely new idea. The monk Joachim of Flora had suggested the same three-stage sequence related to the Trinity in 1190—before Thomas Aquinas was born.

For Schelling, the philosophy that leads to the existence of a personal God is *Positive* philosophy and applies to existence as it is lived. The philosophy that leads to its negation, purely abstract mental construction, is *Negative* philosophy. Schelling says, "The good must be brought out of darkness into actuality that, through it, man may live everlastingly with God; and evil must be separated from the good that it may be cast into non-being."

In some ways, Schelling seems to anticipate the thought of Teilhard de Chardin in his upward spiraling of a coming to perfection of the human essence in approach to God. Yet Schelling's God certainly is not a developing God but the eternal absolute. During his life Schelling passed from an initial idealistic pantheism similar to Fichte's in solving the problem of the one and the many, where Ego and non-ego are fused in the Absolute syntheses, to a final view of a personal theism, more Augustinian than Kantian, in a philosophy which still had many of the flights of fancy characteristic of his original idealism. Among his various audiences in later lectures at Berlin were Soren Kierkgaard and Freidrich Engels, who took mutually antithetical positions in the future and whose thought we will consider. But Schelling, like Fichte, did not have a profound influence on the future trend in philosophy.

Georg Wilhelm Hegel, a philosophical antecedent of Marx in a strange way, was born at Stuttgart, Germany, August 27, 1770, of a family of substantial middle class civil servants. His father was a revenue official. He went to school at Tubingen after primary grades at Stuttgart. His parents wanted him to go into the ministry, and that apparently was his first intention. After he received his Ph.D in 1798 with major work in philosophy and the humanities, he continued in theology, but became disgusted with the curriculum and his teachers. It appears he did not impress his teachers, either.

After he left the university, he became a private tutor in Berne, Switzerland, and devoted most of his effort to the political philosophies of his time, those of the French Revolution and early Napoleonic era. He also studied the philosophic works of Kant, to whom he was attracted and whose work he sought to advance. He was impressed with the genius of the Greeks, particularly, the tragic drama. Their theme of conflict between man's ambition and his fate is carried into Hegel's philosophy. Despite his early disillusionment at the university, he was quite theologically oriented in his views—much more so than Kant had been. In 1799 his father died and left him a small inheritance which was sufficient for him to continue his career as a private student. In 1800 he went to Jena in Prussia. There, for a short time, he worked with Schelling who, although his junior by some five years, was already actively publishing. Though Schelling was more inclined at this time to romanticism, they had common interests.

Hegel taught at the university in fields of logic, metaphysics and, it is believed, mathematics. At least, he was competent in mathematics. He was successively professor of philosophy at Heidelburg in 1816 and Berlin in 1818. A perfectionist, dedicated to working out the last detail to its very end, he was forever in completing anything for publication. However, after lengthy procrastination his first important work, *Phenomenology of Mind,* appeared in 1807 and *Science of Logic* in 1812. These were later followed, after some delay, by his *Aesthetics, Philosophy of Religion, Philosophy of History* and *History of Philosophy.* In 1830 he was named rector of the university. However, before accepting that responsibility, he died of cholera at Kupfergraben on November 14, 1831.

The Triad is Hegel's trademark. Like Schelling, the question of being versus non-being was a constant companion in his thought, and Hegel saw all existence as a movement from non-being toward being. Here was the primary dialectic: being the thesis and non-being the antithesis. The becoming of being to *actual existence* is the synthesis that completes the triad. This becoming to being was a groping, upward striving of the becoming absolute in being to achieve self-consciousness. This urge to self-consciousness by the absolute was reflected through the human spirit. As the human spirit evolved its universalizing self-consciousness, the becoming absolute likewise achieved a synthesis of all the unit self-consciousness into its own being and became conscious of itself. The absolute thus knows itself and approaches the point of absolute knowledge to the extent, and only to the extent, that the comprehensive human spirit or mind rises toward infinite itself. It is a strangely anthropocentric viewpoint in which one can hear the strains of the Wagnerian tetrology *Der Ring des Nibelungen* in the wings. If God was important to man's existence, man was essential to God's becoming God, a subconscious, gigantic, blind deity, with all its power, striving to attain its own fullness of being and identity and its only rational tool the bumbling, inefficient creature, man.

This is an obvious over-simplification of Hegel's complex thought. Hegel was no idiot or hopeless romantic. But in the constant pursuit of his triadic dialectic solutions he gets himself into such positions. He applied the concept universally in art, politics, religion and culture generally, always the conflict resolving itself in a synthesis which is yet higher than either of the conflicting concepts. His is a total teleologic viewpoint; everything, particularly all conflict—has its pre-established purpose in achieving ever higher and higher levels of perfection. The concept of dialectic obviously agrees with many day to day observations of life as it is lived with its social, economic, cultural and political interactions. It is at the extreme extensions that credibility becomes tenuous.

In the political field Hegel, like Fichte, was attracted to the "general will" concept of Rousseau, and he saw the state as it emerged and evolved through the dialectic of ideological conflict at any given point in time as the supreme manifestation of the world spirit which is uniquely the state at these various times. The dialectic involved the individual and general wills as reflected at each successive social grouping from the family to the state, dialectics that are simultaneous and multi-faceted. Hegel says, for instance, of this dialectic at the political-cultural level, "This people is the dominant people in world history for this epoch—and it is only once that it can make its hour strike." He constructed a world history pursuing this theme.

In the moral sphere Hegel says: "Conscience expressed the absolute right of subjective self-consciousness to know itself and through itself what is right and duty, and to recognize nothing as good other than what it knows to be good, at the same time asserting that what it knows and wills as good is in truth right and good."

In spite of what has been said, if one looks at practice rather than pure concept, Hegel's philosophy was related to the Christian religion, though not as thoroughly so as in his own view. He saw the philosopher's role as one of clarifying the God and universe of revelation and making it comprehensible and rational. He started with the Aristotelian concept of a Supreme Being as pure intelligence. He welded that to the idea of man's mind as also, in knowledge of itself, an intrinsic intelligence and hence compatible with a Supreme Being. He felt that truth is an idealized object as the intelligence perceives it and consists in the absence of error in perception. Error in turn is known by experience and eliminated from perception by the process of intelligence. It is in the victory of truth over error that the intelligence is vindicated.

After Hegel's death, his disciples split into two wings. The right wing represented best by Karl Goschel (1784-1861) tried to relate Hegel's philosophy to a Christian theology, and Goschel himself published a number of works emphasizing the relationship of the triad to the Trinity, as Hegel himself had done in attempts to demonstrate the compatibility of his thoughts with those of a personal God and personal immortality. Thus, Hegel became a force in the Protestant religious field. The left wing started with the emphasis on the pantheism of Hegel and denied personal immortality. Later, as we will see, it led into the atheism of Engels and Marx because they seized upon the political-social dialectic concept and made it their own.

Hegel has also been considered as the first existentialist with his emphasis on the becoming of being. His dialectical juxtaposition of being-in-itself, being-for-itself and for-others has been echoed by existentialists since the time of Kierkegaard, whose own philosophy, as we will see, was developed in opposition to Hegel but also used many of Hegel's insights. It could easily be said that Hegel foreshadowed both Nietzsche and Kierkegaard. For all three, life was constituted as "being in process," which is almost a definition of existentialism.

In some ways Hegel offered something to everyone. For decades after his death, his philosophic teaching virtually coincided with German thought and greatly influenced French philosophy as well. In England and in Scotland, Hegelian thought took hold in the late nineteenth century when it was already waning on the continent. In very recent times, Hegel's work has strongly influenced Heidegger, Sartre and other existentialist philosophers.

Hegel's concept of man was clearly (as he thought) that man

is a transcendental being and his dignity lies chiefly in his intellectual acceptance of the idea of his role as the spirit knowing itself as spirit. In his religious life, man made his closest approach to absolute knowledge and value.

Karl Marx, the principal author of the Manifesto and the chief philosopher of socialism, was born in 1818 at Trier, Germany, the son of a prosperous middle class lawyer, a distinguished advocate who was honored by membership in the top legal fraternity of the time, but who also joined illegal clubs toasting a republican Germany. Heinrich Marx was originally Jewish, but converted to a liberal Christianity. He trained his son, Karl, in the liberal philosophies of Voltaire and Diderot. He wished Karl to be a lawyer, as he was, but at the universities at Bonn and Berlin, Marx found philosophy more to his liking. It was the time of the young Hegelian movement, and Karl became a part of it. The subjects were those of the time. Everything was included, from pure communism and atheism to the iron clad German State, "God walking on earth." Karl liked the flavor and decided to make philosophy his career.

After receiving his doctorate in philosophy, Marx changed suddenly to journalism, which he saw as the vehicle for his ideas. He was soured on the academic life by the firing of one of his favorite professors, Bruno Bauer, for being too liberal in his views on constitutionalism and irreligion or anti-religion. Marx's journalistic career was a disaster. His position was guaranteed to ruin any publication that pursued it. He acted as editor of the *Rheinische Zeitung* at Cologne until 1843 when it closed.

Marx's meeting with Engel (1820-1895), who preceded him in socialist activities, established, beginning that day in 1844, an association and friendship that remained until Marx's death and even after. Engels continued to work on Marx's unfinished manuscripts and published them after Marx's death. Engels supported Marx throughout these years, financially and every other way, yet they were utterly dissimilar. Freidrich Engels was epicurian, quick and witty, like Voltaire. Marx was slow and studious, determined and exact, but in his way a man of great depth. His personal life was one of pure pathos. He was so dedicated to his ideas and ideals that he let no personal matters ever take precedence over his work, *Das Kapital* and his political, economic and social theories.

He was a loving husband and father, apparently the only really sensitive emotions he ever displayed, but even there neither the welfare of his wife, Jenny, whom he had known since childhood, nor of his children deterred him from the road he had chosen. He was so absolutely convinced that capitalism would bury itself in its own greed that it obsessed him. The squalid London sweat shop area, where he had moved in 1849, and in which he lived most of his active years, certainly gave the picture of the class of bourgeoisie industrialists and commercialists as totally ruthless and the working class as utterly exploited, suffering 80-hour work weeks and the lowest pay the market and survival would bear. It seemed inevitable to Marx that class warfare would erupt and result in the takeover of the means, forces and agencies of production by the working class.

Scenes of the French Revolution were not too long past, and they were still fresh in peoples' memories as well as in Marx's thinking. Marx had been expelled from Paris in 1845 and then from Brussels after the revolutionary outbursts in 1848 following issue of *The Manifesto*. He spent a brief time in Germany, during which he edited another newspaper until it closed. Then he moved to England, where he stayed the rest of his life.

Marx was almost entirely dependent upon Engels during his period in London. He lived in poverty until almost the end of his life, when he received a small bequest from a friend which eased his last days. He sold a few articles, including some to the New York Tribune. However, his income from his writing was minimal. His was not a popular subject. Marx died in March 1883 and left as his monument nothing more substantial than a single book in four volumes—*DAS KAPITAL*. All but the first volume published in 1867, were in manuscript form and barely legible. The last volume was not published until 1910. The second volume was published by Engels in 1885 and the third in 1894. Of his last days, Heilbroner says (Heilbroner, 1962, page 126):

> In 1881 Jenny died; she had buried two of her five children including her only son; she was old and tired. Marx was too ill to go to the funeral; when Engels looked at him he said, "The Moor is dead, too." Not quite; he lingered for two more years; disapproved of the husbands whom his two married daughters had chosen; grew weary of the bickering of the working-class movement and delivered himself of a statement that has never ceased to bedevil the faithful ("I am not a Marxist," he said one day); and then on a March afternoon, quietly slipped away.

What had he produced, this strange, brooding, quarrelsome man? His philosophy was that of dialectic materialism, his vision, a classless society with all the forces and agencies of production working for the good of man, "To each according of his means, from each according to his abilities." Strangely enough, his world, Utopian surely in concept, would not be produced out of the universe of ideas, of abstractions, of philosophy, of soul, as with Plato or Thomas More, but out of the brute inanimate stuff of the earth—for that is all there is. He saw ideas as necessary, but subordinate to their environment. The effect would come about because of the inevitable application of the changing forces of society and the physical environment. No metaphysics here! No higher good, no moral qualities; sheer matter in action. But yet not economic determinism—only deducible interplay and exhaustion of class conflict to its final concluding position, the last state of social entropy, the heat sink, though Marx would not have thought of it that way. To Marx, the dialectic would be continuously to higher levels, a sort of Darwinism of class survival.

Of course, if that were all, Karl Marx would only be another name in a turbulent period. But Marx's logic, ponderously complex as it was, was also convincing, step by step. Later critics have pointed out errors in his assumptions, but nonetheless, within 100 years of his death, many things he forecast from his thesis came to pass, such as the ubiquitous growth of monster industries. Many nations are dedicated to at least the general concept of Marxism, though his "ideal" end position is as unattainable as ever.

Both Engels and Marx were thoroughly familiar with the dialectic philosophy of Friedrich Hegel. In 1842 while he was working as an editor of the *Rheinische Zeitung,* Marx attempted a criticism of Hegel's idea of the state, which we have seen was dialectical in the sense of a development in a horizontal sequence from the concept of synthesizing individual wills through the family and tribal levels to the general will of the national state proposed by Rousseau. The state was the contemporary expression of the world spirit, uniting the individuals in concert. This, says Marx, alienated man's fundamental nature. The dialectic is vertical between the individual and the superimposed organization at every level, not between individual will versus individual will being finally synthesized in society. What is demanded in the ultimate is still a dialectic solution. But, it is a synthesis found in the complete withering away of the superimposed organization and substitution of the true communistic society where each individual achieves his true self-fulfillment. The collectivist aspect of the Lenin and Mao versions of Marxism would be abhorrent. Further, the idea of private property and religion were antithetical to man as the thetical concept, because restrictive to the individual will. Nevertheless, Marx congratulated Hegel for having exposed the dialectical nature of political reality. However, what was required was not philosophy, but action; and this is in a sense another dialectic which will be resolved through social revolution and whereby a new higher historical plateau will be achieved in its broadest sense. History becomes a progression of dialectic victories or defeats for the individual from primitive communism to fully developed communism. The bourgeoisie society was one step above the feudal in the progression, but it must likewise go in the continuing dialectic of developing humanity. When the bourgeoisie society is at its apex in industrialization, the working class will emerge and seize control of the agencies of production as a true dialectic evolution into the communistic society.

Marx's philosophy represents somewhat the bargain-basement assembly of the most material-oriented views of Kant, Hume and Hegel as well as the ideas of French social theorist Pierre Proudhon (1809-1895). Proudhon and Marx were personally acquainted, and their ideas on private property and the non-necessity of government were compatible. This is not all there was to his philosophy, it is true, but those trends in thought were intimately woven into his own and Engel's dialectic emphasis to form the philosophy which bears Marx's name to this day, despite the obvious heresies.

Marx seemed to shortchange people in their spiritual dimension and erred chiefly in making his assumptions of their nature. They are not always, nor even usually, predictable cogs, and they are neither entirely Hobbesian nor Rousseau's idealization of nature, not always greedy, not always unconcerned in the good of others, not always even in large numbers statistically predictable as totally egocentric. Perhaps in his life he had reason to feel as he did. Marx undoubtedly would be overwhelmed at the position of labor in the modern capitalist world and the standard of living in the West he lived in. Much of it is a result of public acknowledgement of the evils which Marx encountered and portrayed, and most of the improvement is from intellectual direction rather than brute social class dialectic interaction.

Marx's concept of man was that of a gifted animal in an atheistic, materialistic world—a strange ideal to evoke such complete dedication. For a rational man, how could such self-sacrificing to such a pointless humanity be rational? Perhaps his last words "I am not a Marxist" explain it.

Auguste Comte was the father of sociology and putatively of the positivist school of philosophy. He was born at Montpellier, France, January 19, 1798, of a family of modest means. His father was a tax official. In 1814, he entered the Ecole Polytechnique at Paris and remained until it was closed temporarily in 1816. During the interim in his studies he remained in Paris as a teacher of mathematics. It was there, in 1818, at the age of twenty, that he met Henri de Saint-Simon. Out of this relationship which lasted until they finally disagreed in 1826, came many of the concepts which Comte was to embody in the yet unnamed science of man in relation to society.

Comte lectured briefly on his own ideas in Paris, but suffered a nervous breakdown and was forced to abandon his career for a time. For ten years, 1832-1842, he was a private tutor and an examiner at the Ecole Polytechnique, but after a series of quarrels with officials, he left his post, and together with it his livelihood. He was supported on the beneficence of admirers for the rest of his life, principally by John Stuart Mill and Maximilien Litre. His marriage to Caroline Massin in 1825 was unhappy and ended in 1842. The remaining time until his death September 5, 1857, was one of determined effort to establish his ideas in the positivist concept of man in which he saw the ultimate idea of human betterment.

Comte's personal relations, even with his benefactors, Saint-Simon and Mill were poor. He was known openly as a moody, ungrateful, self-centered person of considerable conceit. He visualized the advancement of society through sociology as a priesthood of the intellectuals which, using positivistic scientific concepts, would lead the way to peace, contentment, and prosperity. The French Revolution's deification of reason was to him a sufficient repudiation of Christianity or of any supernatural religious motivation. With Comte, if there was to be a religion, it would be the secular religion of reason.

In spite of his unimpressive background in philosophy, Comte was one of the most powerful figures in the development of scientism or of the positivistic orientation in the nineteenth century, extending into contemporary times. This was true, even though his own formal background in science was sparse. Comte's Supreme Being was the reification and personification of humanity of all ages in terms of the Great Being a deity having no existence in reality.

Comte considered sociology as the highest science, since it dealt with man himself. In decreasing order of importance he ranked the sciences: sociology, biology, chemistry, physics, astronomy and mathematics. This was almost the reverse of the way Descartes would have built the series with his strong concentration on mathematics and physics.

His lasting contribution to sociology rests in his naming of the science and in his earnest efforts to standardize the field. Even though most of his work has long since been superseded, it was a start. Of his basic ideas, the most important was his postulation that civilization passed through three stages, even as men do in progressing from childhood to maturity. The schema was an amplification of the similar hypothesis put forward by Anne Robert Turgot (1727-1781) almost a century earlier. Comte designated them the theological, the metaphysical and the scientific (positive). Each one was a step upward as men advanced and matured in knowledge. But as with individual men, some aspects of the earlier stages remained, even in the most advanced state, which accounted for the persistence of religious ideas even into such a highly civilized scientific environment as was France in the nineteenth century. The idea of the three stages is probably now most utilized in a historical context to show development into later concepts.

Discussing how it would be when the positive state is fully established, Comte says: "Finally, in the Positive state, the human mind, recognizing the impossibility of obtaining absolute truth, gives up the search after the origin and destination of the universe and a knowledge of the final causes of phenomena. It only endeavors now to discover, by a well-combined use of reasoning and observation, the actual laws of phenomena—that is to say, their invariable relations of succession and likeness. The explanation of facts, thus reduced to its real terms, consists henceforth only in the connection established between different particular phenomena and some general facts, the number of which the progress of science tends more and more to diminish." Science, far from diminishing the "connections" or the "particular phenomena" and "general facts" as Comte foresaw, has caused them to develop in profusion.

Comte had an important influence in social work and in reform movements, chiefly in England, as a result of his relationship with Mill. His idea of an intellectual elite has also been seized upon by various far-right groups from time to time to justify their ideals. To some extent, Comte foreshadowed Nietzsche's idea of the superiority of the "morality of the masters." Comte probably influenced the Italian sociology of Pareto and Mosca in their thinking along this same line. Comte's concept of man was that of a materialist, with some overtones of a metaphysical humanity. Man was a gifted animal and his dignity lay in recognizing the greatness of the species to which he owed his nature and for whose advancement he should live, work and die.

Emil Durkheim was born in Epinal in the Lorraine province of France in April, 1858, less than a year after the death of Auguste Comte. He was from a family of long Jewish tradition, and Emil was expected to continue the family role in the rabbinate following his father, who was one of the most eminent rabbis in Europe of his time. At the Ecole, however, first from Emile Boutroux, a French philosopher, he got his initial interest in sociology via the works of Kant and Comte. It was there that Durkheim first conceived of the idea that society could be thought of as an entity in itself distinct from the individuals which comprised it. He concluded, therefore, that the psychology and biology of individuals did not answer questions in sociology. During a brief period of teaching in the secondary schools in France he was able to include a year of advanced work in sociology in Germany. It was in the midst of this that he became interested in the evolutionary concepts in the sociology of Spencer, Espinas, and Schaeffle.

In 1887 he went to the University of Bordeaux where he was the first instructor in sociology. At that time, the discipline was still thought of as a premature sub-scientific discipline. Five years later, he received his doctorate at the Sorbonne. His thesis was on the subject of division of labor in society. His educational background was particularly rich in the humanities and in psychology and biology, but lacked great depth in the other physical sciences and mathematics.

Durkheim saw society and hence sociology in everything involving man: religion, science, literature, economics, art, family life. He termed this view sociologism. He was recognized in his lifetime as the chief figure in sociology of his period, even among those who did not share his views. Hence along with Auguste Comte, he is recognized almost universally as one of the founders of the discipline. His span of interest in sociology, as indicated, was almost universal and on one point he was particularly insistent. Sociology was a science. Hence, it must be approached in accord, and with full attention to scientific methodology, specific rather than general research, and objective rather than subjective orientation. He viewed his classic work on suicide as proof of the validity of society, as an entity and of the applicability of true, empirical research, though some critics claimed his empiricism was more apparent than real in this case.

His work had a tremendous impact on the direction sociology and anthropology took in the twentieth century, particularly as to the concept of man and the place of values in analysis of social phenomena. Durkheim claimed to be a positivist and, given his definition of society as an entity in itself, he was. But his ideas of a collectivity of psychic and biologic phenomena conveying moral obligation and the derivation from that of an implicit collective mind which made society possible is stretching positivism to a point beyond its definition by Comte.

Durkheim conceived of society as a subject of investigation independent of the individual idiosyncracies of its members, and, in itself, amenable to discoverable scientific laws as a predictable whole. In his early years, he saw moral obligations arising almost exclusively as a result of duty to humanity as perceived in this common view. He later, perhaps influenced by his Kantian background, modified this exclusivity by adding the idea of some innate tendency for virtue, of an interior gratification which made morality something to be sought for—its goal, happiness itself. In a sense, Durkheim went back to Plato and Aristotle who saw happiness as the end good to be sought by man. Though it is difficult to conceive of a collective happiness, it was nevertheless, in this free commitment to moral obligations thus arrived at, conjoined with a sense of duty that collective man was fulfilled.

For Durkheim, religion served its purpose in society by assisting man to integrate the realization of that society, by universalizing the disparate phenomena around them, and thus achieving the community of viewpoint necessary for society to exist. Religion was a means to secular ends, a cohesive agent to offset "anomie." A term proposed by Durkheim to express normlessness, which in later times was to be applied to almost every form of human disenchantment with humanity. Thus, unlike Comte, Durkheim did not see religion as hostile to science, but as something necessary in some form to promote or even make possible social life. Religion provided an answer to the Hobbesian question. Nevertheless, pursuit of science was the only way in which man the collective could achieve his eminence, here again, not so much as the individual, but as society.

Durkheim had a deep sense of the need for moral order and the universality of moral law and of the need for ethics based on that law. He promised to establish a sociology of morals but was never able to come to grips with the dichotomy of the moral obligation as purely man's duty to society, as a member of society, and of man's virtually innate felt-need of individual morality in pursuit of true happiness. But Durkheim himself had no particular religious leanings. Man was still only an atom in an organism not much different than Karl Marx would have him, but animate not mechanical. At his death in 1917, Durkheim's entire life had been devoted to the cause of sociology and anthropology. He left behind as a legacy a devout group of disciples who spread the Durkheimian principles throughout the sociological world.

It is perhaps unfortunate that sociology would have its beginnings in a period of history dominated by positivistic ideas. Both Comte and Durkheim were positivists, Durkheim somewhat less so. It is perhaps also almost inevitable that it should be so. Until this period of history, there had been no particular need for a science of society or of anthropology either for that matter. People in the West had been content with society as a matter-of-fact way by which people got along. There had been no wide-spread pluralism in belief generally as to man's beginning or his destiny as a child of God. Hobbes, Rousseau and Locke were the first to raise the question as to how society was possible and that because God was beginning to be visualized in an impersonal deistic way in intellectual circles. The positivistic term of sociology has lingered on beyond the demise of its philosophic source and no new philosophy of sociology has replaced it. Had its roots and the roots of anthropology been deeper in philosophic time, the present crisis in sociology would not be so severe.

Charles R. Darwin was born in Shrewsbury, Shropshire, England, February 12, 1809, of a distinguished intellectual family. His grandfather was Erasmas Darwin (1731-1802), pioneer English scientist, physician and poet. Educated at Edinborough University, Charles Darwin studied to be a physician, then later decided to become a clergyman and went to Christ College, Cambridge where he received his degree in 1831.

In December, 1831, he embarked on HMS Beagle as a naturalist on its voyage of exploration into the South Seas, which lasted until October, 1836. It was in the course of his investigations and surveys in geology and zoology, primarily of the Galapagos Archipelago, that he formulated his theory on the transmutation of species. In 1837 he published his tradition-shattering treatise *On Origin of Species by Means of Natural Selection of the Preservation of Favored Races in the Struggle for Life,* usually cited as "On Origin of Species."

If the effect on man's thought in general was shattering, it was even more so for Darwin who had been thoroughly indoctrinated in the Durham-Paley School of natural theology whose base for the existence of God—the teleologic argument—the design and order of nature, was badly shaken by his theory. In 1856 he wrote, "What a book a devil's chaplain might write on the clumsy, wasteful, blundering law and cruel work of nature." And in 1870 he said, "My theology is a simple muddle. I cannot look at the universe as the result of blind chance yet I can see no beneficent design or indeed of a design of any kind in the details." Darwin gradually shifted his philosophical position to one of agnosticism. Morality was the result of evolutionary forces.

The impact of Darwin's work and thought, piled on top of the spiritually debilitating Age of Enlightenment, brought about the sudden decline of the idealistic philosophies based on the Kantian concepts, which were themselves fragile in the extreme although the thought of Hegel in one form or other continued to dominate continental philosophy. The prevalent misconception of the Newtonian Basis of the universe added to the disaster. It was this combination which brought the "discrediting" of a theistic viewpoint and hence of the transcendental nature of man and its replacement by the purely biologic concept of man which persisted into this century. It still persists in the behavioral sciences generally, though the basis, in the pure empiricism of Locke and Hume, has long since evaporated. Darwin died on April 19, 1882, a man who regretted his own disillusionment, but whose intellectual honesty would not permit him to modify his views even for himself. He did not recognize the radical changes in the concept of the universe which were dimly coming into focus at the time of his death.

Before moving ahead into the last of the nineteenth and the early twentieth centuries, combined in this section, it is advisable to catch up on the changes which occurred since the times of Metternich and the Communist Manifesto. As was clear, the stew was bound to get thicker. The central powers had committed themselves to the reactionary policy of Metternich. Frederick William IV came to power still within the Metternich era in 1840. He was an odd combination of romanticist, mystic and unconvinced liberal, but crushed the revolution of March 1848 which saw Marx abandoning Germany for England. At that time he was offered the imperial crown by the weak

Frankfurt parliament, but rejected it on the peculiar grounds that as a divine-right monarch, he could not accept it from an elected parliamentary assembly.

After various schemes to achieve a union of all Germany were nullified in 1850 by the treaty of Olmutz, he became mentally unbalanced. His brother, William I, took over as regent in 1858. Four years later, William appointed Otto von Bismark as chancellor and from that point, Prussia became completely militaristic. Bismark dissolved parliament for opposing his armament budget in 1862 and on pretext attacked Denmark in 1864. This was quickly followed by the Austria-Prussian War of 1866 which forced Austria to recognize exclusive sovereignty of Prussia to contested territories and to accept Prussian leadership in the North Germany Confederation. On a blatant pretext, he provoked the Franco-Prussian War of 1870-71, and had William I crowned Emperor of Germany at Versailles on January 18, 1871.

Bismark then formed alliances with Austria in 1879 and Italy in 1882. He was, however, unable to bring either the church or the socialist movement to heel, despite earnest efforts to do so. Bismark was dismissed by William II, the Kaiser of World War I, whose own over-bearing attitude clashed with Bismark's. Nevertheless, the stage was now set with development of two rival forces: the Triple Alliance of Germany, Austria and Italy in 1883 and the Triple Entente of France, England and Russia, which evolved into its final form in 1907. This situation needed only the suitable incident to set off the continental war which eventually escalated to world scale. One effect was the movement of the Unites States into final position as a great world power.

In this frame, one must view Max Weber who was born in 1864 at Erfurt, Germany of a well-to-do family. His father was a prominent figure supporting the National Liberal party which was sponsored chiefly by business interests. The Weber house was the scene of many political discussions. It was a stimulating intellectual environment, so that Max early developed a keen interest in sociology and in government and political affairs. His brother, Alfred, also became an important sociologist.

Max's early schooling was at the Gymnasium, a school for pre-university maturation of prospective outstanding students. Under the German system, Weber was able to attend at several different locations with no difficulty and, thus, to accommodate his chief interests. First, in 1882, he studied law at Heidelburg; this was interrupted by one year of military duty at Strasbourg. Weber then shifted to the Universities of Berlin and

Gottingen. His entire educational program was intermingled with periods of military service, readily understandable given the history of his time.

Weber completed his law studies in 1886 at Berlin and continued there, taking his Ph.D. in 1889. His chief scholastic interests were law and economics, and he published several works in these fields. In the years between 1891 and 1896 he worked as a consultant to government agencies and professional organizations. His first sociologic study as such was one of rural labor in East Prussia in 1892. In that study he outlined the effect of industrialization and commercialization on cultural values and demonstrated that these effects were both favorable and unfavorable. Weber also developed the relationship of ethical and sociologic motivation in economic conduct, a theme he referred back to many times. In his early work Weber indicated his interest in specific contemporaneous sociologic problems in contradistinction to the earlier grand planning of Comte or the generalized science in approach of Durkheim. He appears to have been influenced in this regard by the philosophy of sometimes Neo-Kantian philosopher of life Wilhelm Dilthey (1833-1911), whose interest in social values and social ends was similar to Weber's. Dilthey's ideas of *Erlebniss* and *Verstehen* were united in providing the individual the comprehensive understanding of his own life in the experienced interaction with his social environment, a concept which Weber himself was to use. Later Weber's ideas seem to correspond more closely with the right-wing Hegelian's and the emerging existentialism.

In 1894, Weber became a full professor of economics at Frieburg University. In 1896 he returned to Heidelburg as professor of economic history. Apparently Weber drove himself too hard, for he had a complete collapse in 1897 and did not return to the world of scholarship until 1904, though he traveled and studied intermittently. In 1904, his period of truly productive work in sociology began with the writing of two important works: *Protestant Ethic,* relating capitalism to a particular religious asceticism, and the *Spirit of Capitalism* in which he undertook to contest Marx. Not until 1918 did he resume academic life, first at the University of Vienna, and then at the University of Munich. But the time between had been tremendously active, primarily as a private scholar, though with some administrative service at one time in a hospital in Germany during World War I. Most of his writings were unpublished at the time of his death of influenza in 1920, and have been pulled together, edited and issued—largely piecemeal—over the years.

Weber undertook much of his work to counteract Karl Marx. Even his Protestant Ethic was an effort to demonstrate the need of motivational factors to which, as has been noted, Marx gave little or no place in any positive sense. Marx's motivation was the dialectic stemming from the left-wing interpretation of Hegel. Weber did a large part of his work on bureaucracy to show that the socialists had the same problems as capitalists if they were going to achieve a technologically advanced society. It was an effort going back to Weber's earliest theme that traditional and cultural values were inevitably sacrificed for efficiency and the resulting technologic values. It was not a one-way benefit, and a balance was necessary. In another very similar way it went back to opposing Kantian idealism against Marxist materialism, and ideas as prime movers versus the mechanical response to environment.

Currently, Weber's work in bureaucracy in which he drew up a set of idealized operating characteristics and his work on differentiation of types of leadership and power relationships are most fruitful in sociological studies. His ideas concerning the need to recognize a subjective vector even in objective research, his expression of the idea of *Verstehen,* roughly, a comprehensive understanding including subjective elements, is also of wide interest and becoming increasingly so. Weber shows that there are many ways that the subjective viewpoint entered into the research and had to be considered in all propriety if realistically acceptable conclusions were to be reached from studies in sociology. It was a counterpunctual view to those of the Comtean positivism which was in Weber's day coming into dominance in Germany as a general philosophy and not limited to science.

For purposes of this study, Weber's concept of man is of paramount interest since it is an exception in an era of strict scientism. While much of Weber's work, and important work, was related to the sociology of religion, it was not in itself particularly revealing of Weber's own views. However, looking at his entire field of interest and his basic themes, he appears to have leaned to Dilthey's naturalism. He was an idealist (not in the Kantian philosophic sense), strongly opposed to materialism. Thus, Weber necessarily accorded man a higher status than that of a gifted animal. His concept of morality was primarily culture-related, not unlike that of contemporary Emile Durkheim. But in the Germany of his time, with the Hegelian right wing and theologically-oriented philosophy perhaps dominant in the culture, this took a religious orientation. He discussed various aspects of the dignity of man, mostly in conjunction with establishing a basis for ascribing status in various groups. His concept of motivation for the underprivileged usually assumed the form of other-worldly ambition, the transcendental, and for the positively privileged, worldly esteem. From this picture man's dignity was his worth in his own eyes. He saw himself as valuable for whatever reason, but of intrinsic value nonetheless. Weber was, like most sociologists, remarkably noncommittal in any specific way on the subject of his views of man as man. I believe he was a modified Hegelian in his view of man's relationship in the world. Man likely has a non-biologic vector in his nature which is largely unknowable through reason and should not be used as a basis of any scientific investigation, although it must be considered as a conditioning subjective agency in any investigation.

Soren Kierkegaard was born May 5, 1813 in Copenhagen. His father was originally a farmer in West Jutland but moved to Copenhagen and made a fortune in wool merchandising. His father was a man who considered himself accursed by God as a result of an early blasphemy and was given to periods of intense depression. This bothered Soren, who was a religious young man. It seemed to turn his mind into deeply introspective and many times depressing themes. Kierkegaard was a student of theology at the University of Copenhagen between 1830 and 1840, where his views conflicted with those of the established church of Denmark, then dominated by the Hegelian philosophy. It will be recalled that Kierkegaard was one of those attending Schelling's lectures. And he joined Schelling's attitude in opposition to Hegel's thoughts, though from a different viewpoint. Kierkegaard admired Hegel's dialectical approach. It seemed to reflect his own tension between the one and the crowd.

Apparently to avoid being ostracized Kierkegaard published under numerous pseudonyms—some quite bizarre—though his identity was well known. Kierkegaard's philosophic roots lay somewhere between the romanticism of Rousseau and the Hegelian dialectic, but he tended to emphasize interiority more than the romanticists, generally, and from this blending he developed his own view—the distinctive Kierkegaardian and the first aspects of existentialism. He constantly questioned rather than answered and eventually held that all truth is subjective, depending solely on the individual's viewpoint. Hence when man must make a decision in Kierkegaard's view, religious or worldly, he must decide totally for himself, within himself. With Kant, he believed there is no outside rational basis such as Hegel had held (somewhat tenuously it is true) for coming to a knowledge of a Supreme Being or of His moral law. Kierkegaard contrasted the various aspects of human motivation—the biological with the sociological, the pride in possession with man's assertive independence of things and finally all of these with that of utter and complete dedication to God as the Ultimate Thou toward which all else becomes irrelevant. But the individual, the "I" which responds must be authentic, not a facade, not directed to human respect, but as he is—an individual standing over against God in dialogue. Kierkegaard lived only forty-two years and died November 11, 1855, so that there is not a great deal which could be classed as "mature Kierkegaard." He had little influence in his own day. His chief impact was a century away. He had a great influence on the existentialist philosophers, including Heidegger and Sartre, and on theology generally, but particularly in the twentieth century on the theology of process. Kierkegaard's existentialism was not atheistic. He took what may be called a subliminal approach to the idea of a Supreme Being. While one has no direct way of comprehending God, Kierkegaard felt deeply that each individual, if he gives his attention to the spiritual way of life, will come to some positive personal relationship with the infinite. He did not develop any ethical or metaphysical system, nor a dogmatic affirmation of religion. Thus the requirements for a "school of philosophy," of a comprehensive philosophical theory, process and methodology is not present in his existentialism. As a true prototype existentialist, he emphasizes the authentic individual versus the crowd, the collective, and the partial over the general.

To Kierkegaard, man is far more than only a gifted animal. He is a transcendental being in some evanescent sense which defies rational analysis, but which is individually true when apprehended. Kierkegaard's insistence on the reality of eternal truths, revealed through complex personal reflection, and their opposition in temporal life is a constant theme in his works.

Friedrich Nietzsche was born October 15, 1844 in Rocken, Saxony, the son of a Lutheran minister and grandson of two. His father died in 1849 and he was raised by his mother, who was a very pious woman, his grandmother and two maiden aunts. There was almost no male influence in his boyhood years. He attended university, first very briefly in 1864 and 1865 at Bonn, then moved to Leipzig. He taught Greek literature and philosophy and appears to have abandoned Christianity in his early twenties while still at Leipzig. He was preeminently a philosophical psychologist. At the age of 25 he was made professor of philosophy at the prestigious University of Basel. During the Franco-Prussian War he interrupted this work for a stint with the ambulance corps but was forced to leave because of illness. He returned to the university but was forced to abandon this post within ten years as a result of increasing mental disturbance, becoming hopelessly insane in 1889. He was a close friend and to some extent protege of Richard Wagner for several years, and some of his first works were devoted to extolling the Wagnerian influence on German culture; but the friendship cooled and was broken completely in 1878.

In a relatively short period of fruitful activity, Nietzsche established himself in history as a man of tremendous influence during his age, and more importantly, in the following century. Along with Soren Kierkegaard he has been identified as a precursor of existentialism. He has had a profound influence on the development of both political and philosophical thought and literature. His best known work, *Thus Spake Zarathustra,* produced between 1883 and 1891, during the period of increasing mental illness, was a powerful poetic and symbolic work condemning the estabished Christian morality of the late nineteenth century. He criticized particularly the increasing decadence of western civilization which he saw as slavishly following a code of ethics to which it was less and less authentically dedicated. It was to him a sham and facade behind which the powerful hid to mulct the weak. While he scorned the Christian-oriented establishment, he did not yet appear to object to the enslavement of the lower classes. He was convinced of the superiority of the minority—an elite—forerunners of a master race of supermen which the "Will to Power" would eventually create and which would restore, in its own way, a morality completely secular in form. This concept was seized on by Hitler in his rise to power, but there is no evidence that Neitzsche foresaw such a monstrous adaptation of his philosophy. The Nazis, on the other hand, merely used Nietzsche's popularity as an instrument of convenience.

The conviction of Nietzsche that man has the last word in his moral actions was pronounced in the symbolic person of Zarathustra in the statement that, "By chance it is the oldest nobility in the world. I conferred it upon all things when I proclaimed that above them no eternal will was exercised." The *Will to Power,* which enunciated the philosophy symbolically presented in *Thus Spake Zarathustra,* was a compilation of notes put together by Nietzsche's sister and was not published until 1908. Whether it is a solid representation of Nietzsche's actual thought is a moot question, but as noted in this writer's preface it predicted a tidal sweep toward nihilism in which men would be engulfed. In the preface to that work, Nietzsche also had indicated that the Christian ideals and values were doomed because they were the device of an inferior majority to control the superior minority and had been discredited. In an analysis of Nietzsche's logic toward that conclusion, it becomes apparent that it is not the values and ideals which were at fault. It is, instead, the loss of the justification and motivation to sustain the ideals and values, when their theologic basis had been demolished which made them obsolete and without sanction. This, Nietzsche was convinced, was the case.

In his work *The Gay Science*, Nietzsche gives his own philosophy of life:

> . . . I welcome all signs that a more manly, a warlike age is about to begin, an age which, above all, will give honor to valor once more. For this age shall prepare the way for one yet higher, and it shall gather the strength which this higher age will need one day—this age which is to carry heroism into the pursuit of knowledge and wage wars for the sake of thoughts and their consequences. . . For believe me, the secret of the greatest fruitfulness and the greatest enjoyment of existence is: to live dangerously! Build your cities under Vesuvius! Send your ships into unchartered seas! Live at war with your peers and yourselves! Be robbers and conquerors, as long as you cannot be rulers and owners you lovers of knowledge. Soon the age will be past when you could be satisfied to live like shy deer, hidden in the woods. At long last the pursuit of knowledge will reach out for its due: It will want to rule and own, and you with it! . . . For one thing is needful: that a human being attain his satisfaction with himself—whether it be by this or by that poetry and art: only then is a human being at all tolerable to behold. Whoever is dissatisfied with himself is always ready to revenge himself therefor; we others will be his victims, if only by always having to stand his ugly sight. For the sight of the ugly makes men bad and gloomy.

Nietzsche sees beneath the civilized surface vital forces which are "wild, primitive and completely merciless." His man was obviously Hobbesian, more power-driven and self-centered even than Hobbes would have liked to portray him.

Nietzsche lived when the positivistic philosophy was at its dogmatic apex, though not at its point of greatest influence, which would come later. But it counted among its membership some of the greatest scientific minds of the age. It was not so much an academic philosophy as a pervasive attitude of the professional class. The God of theistic philosophies certainly seemed to be outgunned and doomed to extinction, and Nietzsche rejoices in the funeral preparations. He appears to be in a double revolt—first against the idea of the uniformity of the masses, the collectivized mass society then taking shape under a technological aegis, and second, against the pious lip service being given that which he considered to be moribund Christian cultural values and ethics. Since no values could come out of empirical materialism, he saw nihilism as the logical outcome of this conjunction of social driving forces.

Whether Nietzsche was an atheist is debatable—he seemed to protest too much. But he was convinced the God of theism was dead, though there might have been a Supreme Being in the deistic image. His law of the Eternal Return seems to have been an attempt to avoid a deity. If so, it was an idea borrowed from the Pythagoreans of whom Eudemus had said, "According to the Pythagoreans a day will come when you will be all gathered again sitting in the very same places to listen, and I shall be telling you the same story once more." It was the Pythagorean solution to the problem of the "one and the many" which Nietzsche also conceived. There was no "one," only an eternal repetition of the same sequence of the "many." Man's dignity appears to consist solely in his being authentic in pursuit of his own innate drives—an attitude quite close to Holbach's a hundred years before.

Nietzsche joyfully welcomes "this most gruesome of all guests," the advent of nihilism, because it signalled the concurrent end of the decadent, western, Christianity-based civilization and the law of the masses and made way for the eventual rise of the age of the supermen, those lofty creatures who would stand above all the trivial demands of a morality foisted on the human race by the slave mentality of mediocrity. Not that the mediocre were not necessary to support the masters—but their fear-driven, herding instincts would not affect the elite!

Nietzsche saw himself as the prophet of a real and imminent *Gotterdammerung:* "There will be wars such as there have never been on earth before. Only from my time on will there be on earth politics on the grand scale." And out of the catastrophic, ideological struggles foreshadowed by the great power groupings of the late nineteenth century, the Triple Alliance and the preliminary negotiations for Triple Entente, plus the coinciding intellectual struggle between the decadent Christian and rising atheistic concepts, Nietzsche visualized the execution of his judgment. His erstwhile friend Wagner himself could not have done as well in the clash of sound and fury. And for almost a century his prophecy has been becoming reality—his scenarios letter perfect. Yet, one can visualize Nietzsche sick, lonely, knowing his mind was being ravaged and imagining himself as one of the supermen, "the Roman with Christ's soul," fully realizing, in his torment, that there was really no solution in the remedies he was prescribing in his philosophy.

At the close of the period in the early twentieth century, the world was greatly changed from a hundred years earlier. The Industrial Revolution had initiated an irreversible population migration from rural to urban areas. The constitutional national state with sovereignty in the people, at least in theory, controlled the political scene.

The philosophic thought in the West had become highly diversified, almost splintered, and unfortunately, in this necessarily foreshortened work, the true extent can only be dimly shown as it exists in the hazy background of the central action. There was a rather sharp cleavage between the philosophic thought on the continent of Europe and that in England and in the United States, which tended to follow the British pattern.

A brief word should be said about the British trend, though the chief seminal lines in philosophy were developing on the continent. At the end of the century, empiricism in the tradition of Berkeley, Locke, Hume and a new champion, J. S. Mill (1806-1873) dominated British thought, though there were the loyal oppositions representing the faculties of the major universities. These followed the path of the "Cambridge Platonists" and idealists, the latter chiefly a Neo-Kantian form and not the typical Kantian and Hegelian offshoots which were evident in Europe. The Marxists were also gathering strength. But in the main, the Utilitarians represented by Mill, a movement in the empiricist model, held center stage. Hume was considered to have established that all virtue and all other human mental activity, being in its end only a reflection of the sensed apprehension of the material environment, was justified only as it was useful. And while the actual origin of the movement dated back before Hume, his thought brought it into prominence.

Utilitarianism was completely materialistic, its creed as enunciated by Mill: "Happiness is the universal good. Not the agents, own greatest happiness, but the greatest amount of happiness altogether." Certainly, as to the individual, that is an ancient thought. Occasionally, though grudgingly, Mill bowed to man's intrinsic intuition that there are other criteria than sheer mass happiness. Mills admitted "It is better to be a human being dissatisfied than a pig satisfied; better to be Socrates dissatisfied than a fool satisfied." Nor does Mill say that raw empiricism is sufficient to advance knowledge; logic, both inductive and deductive, are essential.

As we saw earlier, Mill was an admirer and patron of Auguste Comte and incorporated much of the latter's positivism into his own thinking; but he was not Utopian in his thinking, as was Comte, and he was not, like Comte, an atheist. He said, "I think it must be allowed that, in the present state of our knowledge, the adaptation in Nature affords a large balance of probability in favor of creation by intelligence." But that intelligence was limited; in fact, "Every indication of design in the cosmos is so much evidence against the omnipotence of the designer." Mill was fundamentally "hung up on" the ancient problem of conflict between the ideas of omnipotence of God and of evil in the world. Mill's view of the deity probably represents a weighted consensus of the British philosophers, but there was no widely held common position on the point at the end of the nineteenth century.

In continental Europe, during the early nineteenth century, the idealists certainly dominated thought. But, by the end of the century, there was virtually no common position that could be said to be dominant other than the statement "broadly Hegelian." And again, in spite of the variety, the end consensus as to the existence of God would be well summed up in Mill's statement. The approach was more romantic than that in England, but the result was about the same.

The scholastic philosophies which had suffered such a devastating blow with the suppression of the Jesuits had begun to revive toward the end of the century, being given strong impetus by the encyclical letter, *Aeterni Patris,* by Pope Leo XIII in 1879 and the so-called Leonine Restoration which followed. The previous half century had seen a much diluted Thomism embracing many of the rationalist ideas, introduced from Descartes onward, including some attempts at a Hegelian theology. Leo called, not for a reestablishment of Thomism, but a restoration of a Christian philosophy based on the wisdom of St.

Thomas viewed in the light of scientific advancement.

In general intellectual life, humanism was the central driving force, but as in philosophy, also generally, the theme was now strongly atheistic, materialistic and positivistic; theism had contracted in all areas under the impact of Darwinism. Except for the rear guard action of a slowly reemerging scholasticism in religious centers, a rational direct approach to theism had been abandoned to successively weaker idealistic positions such as Hegel's or the many-faceted, reflective insights of Kierkegaard, both skirting the approach to God through reason. Among the leading intellectuals, particularly in the field of the social sciences, God had been reduced to an artificial construct, if considered at all. Nietzsche's view of the dead God was not far from a statement of the intellectual position. Man was only a gifted animal; any dignity lay in his ability to expand his giftedness. But the mass of the people had not yet received the message and persisted in living dedicated moral lives guided by strong religious faith.

While it is hard to see any pattern, other than an empirical materialism, developing out of the melange of viewpoints existing in 1900, looking back from the vantage point almost a century later we can see how the threads would form in the future. While, in England, the positivist-empiricist-utilitarian philosophy did indeed continue to dominate the philosophic thought in the first half of the twentieth century, there was a turning more toward the analytic and mathematical view under Bertrand Russell's influence. In Europe other winds were blowing. The idealist image persisted, and the three radical offshoots from Hegel's thought—indeed almost in opposition to Hegel's thought—came to the fore in the Marxist atheistic, dialectical materialism, the Kierkegaardian theistic, existentialism and the Nietzschean atheistic existentialism. There were also two paths leading out of scholasticism: the infant phenomenology of Franz Brentano (1838-1907) and the mainline Neo-Thomism resurfacing especially at the University of Paris and under the Jesuits at Louvain University in Belgium. The confrontation for men's minds now begins to form into two major groupings, a theistic wing including subdivisions into theist realist and existentialists and an atheistic wing divided into materialist and existentialist subgroups.

But obviously, this grouping also tends to be oversimplified, for there are other drives at work within and around these major movements. A major source of differentiation centered on man's idea of the need for social cooperation which stands over against his individualizing instincts. In this vein there were, among the atheists, the Marxist ideological solution, the dictatorship of the proletariat, a theoretical classless society that was communistic in economy and self-regulatory in government, and there was, in contrast, the existentialist viewpoint—the individual best achieves his destiny by living life to the full in intimate, but free, interaction with his associates in a conflict against the absurdity of life.

Among the theists, there is the idea of the individual living freely in community, attaining fulfillment through participation in the divine love through a loving response to the fellowman's needs. This ideal takes two paths: one, that of the existentialists which places emphasis on the individual, *qua* individual—the intimate I—Thou dialogue of the individual achieving his authentic self in a lived intimate interaction with his associates. Two, the theist realists, on the other hand, emphasized the responsible individual achieving social progress by cooperation within the context of a stable social community. So that, in both the theist and atheist wings, there is a duality of thrust which in reality is probably a continuum from total individuality to total collectivity. On the one hand, the theists within the tension of the insistent dialectic and, on the other hand, the atheists transforming the insistent dialectic to a tension between free individual and individual subject to the totalitarian state. Regardless, the dialectic tension remains.

As we noted, from the time of Grosseteste, in the early thirteenth century, there was a trend toward empiricism in the philosophies being developed in England. This culminated in the epistemologically dominated empiricism of Hume and utilitarianism of Mills. The impact of the British empiricism was intruded as a development into the continental system in spurts rather than continuously, as Hume influenced Kant, for instance. But the question asked by the epistemologists, of whatever basic school, turned increasingly from that of exploring the mechanism by which men acquire knowledge to that of a questioning if, and to what extent, man can acquire knowledge. The first mode was typified by Descartes' physiological-psychical interchange, which never for the moment questioned that man did, in fact, acquire real knowledge in both physical and metaphysical concepts. Descartes' entire system of "universal doubt" was devoted to arriving at substantive truth from a sure base. The second aspect, perhaps, is illustrated best by Bertrand Russell's semi-serious remarks, "Science is what you more or less know and philosophy is what you do not know." Knowledge is very tenuous and tentative at best even in science, and, "Philosophy arises from an unusually obstinate attempt to arrive at real knowledge," and, yet again, "Order, unity, and continuity are human inventions." Both the latter statements imply futile, almost perverse effort even though real knowledge was impossible. Viewed from the existentialist side, Albert Camus' statement, "The only thing certain is uncertainty"—gives the same picture, a helpless throwing up of hands. Though, as we will see, Russell did not by any means hold that man could not "know" anything, and as to Camus' view, one frankly cannot be "certain."

The main trend has not been a total denial of man's ability to know, but rather a severe limitation on that capacity as a response to the sense data and the scientific method of analysis of that data. The main battle between ontologic and epistemologic emphasis on man's nature remains to be fought on the field of rationalism versus irrationalism, and existentialism can go either way. The outcome of the Nietzsche scenario depends upon victory of irrationality, that of Toynbee on the supremacy of rationalism, in its broadest and original positive sense of man's ability to acquire and use knowledge, freed from artificial fetters of rigid empiricism or of a narrow linguistics.

Chapter 6

PHILOSOPHIES OF THE
LATE TWENTIETH CENTURY

In reviewing the history of the concept of man as seen by man, the writer has discussed certain individuals who in light of history have been important in forming the concept of man. Now, however, he is dealing chiefly with those who are forming it in the late twentieth century, and hence who may or may not be considered important a century or so from now. Some who are still unknown will become the leaders in thought. The writer is also looking in some areas at individuals who are still forming their own views, and if it is hazardous to discern a man's thought in the light of history, it is even more difficult without that illumination.

Nevertheless, as in the past, the writer will let men's works speak for them to the extent that it is possible, bearing in mind that opinions do change with time and analysis is always subjective to some degree. Hopefully, in considering those still active, biographies will be shortened and in some cases eliminated. Thus the amount of substantive work offered will be proportionately increased with broader coverage in the same reading time.

The term "the late twentieth century" is perhaps misleading in the chapter heading since the preceding chapter included only the very early part of this century, and thus the transition into twentieth century thought. The last chapter was intended to give a picture of prevalent thought during that total period which has come to signify the end of the "Modern Age" which in fact intruded into the twentieth century. This chapter is intended to portray the picture of the beginnings of a new epoch. It concerns that period in which American viewpoints, particularly in sociology, came to the forefront, reflecting the rising, even dominant position of the United States in world affairs at mid-century following the emergence from the great depression and World War II. In other ways it is even more current and looks at the prevailing thought today, foreshadowing the closing decades of the century.

One of the things that is characteristic of the relationship of intellectual thought to behavior patterns in any culture is

the time-lag between the former and the latter. This has historically been in the order of fifty to seventy-five years. In spite
of the acceleration in change generally in this century, the lag
still exists. Much of the materialism in behavior patterns today
reflects the philosophy of fifty or more years ago.

The merging patterns of thought, as almost everything else
in human affairs during the past fifty years, have been changing
at an accelerated pace. And whereas one could earlier speak
of transitions in terms of centuries, now it is appropriate to
speak in terms of decades. Although the generational span remains much the same, the overall intellectual span does not.
In spite of the latter fact, the teacher-student relationship remains basically genetically generational. Many educators reflect
the intellectual pattern which they developed as students one
or more decades past. In that regard, and of considerable interest, are the views of the modern Spanish philosopher, Ortega
y Gasset, that the real generational span, the intellectual rather
than genetic, is 15 years. His view is that at every period there
are three age levels active in a culture: the rising generation,
the young adult, age 15 to 30; the challenging generation, age
30 to 45 and the establishment, age 45 to 60. The terminology
is my own, not Ortega y Gasset's. The shift in general thought
follows those patterns; it is dialectic in interactions as each group
seeks to establish its identity. Those younger or older, those
less than 15 or more than 60, are for the most part out of
the current competitive scene. The popular slogan among the
young in the 1960's, "Don't trust anybody over thirty," is reflective of this idea. That group of young adults rejected the values
of both the establishment and the immediate challengers. That
same group now constitutes the challengers.

While the developments following out of World Wars I and
II were historically of top importance in the first half century
and made tremendous geographic, political, sociologic and economic change, the quiet emergence of Einsteinian physics, sup-
planting the two-century Newtonian mechanical theme of the
universe, had a greater impact on intellectual development and
ultimately on cultural and technological change as well. For
the great advances in industrial technology after World War II
were fed by the sense that technology, which had created the
nuclear bomb, could accomplish anything else which it might
set its mind to, even an ascent to the moon. Nevertheless, there
were subtle implications which evolved from the Einsteinian
physics which were not assessed until quite recently by the
intellectual leadership.

Whereas the Copernican and Newtonian ideas of the universe had a relatively quick reflection in philosophy—probably faster than in technology, with the greatest impact in metaphysics— the Einsteinian universe had not had similarly dramatic repercussions, although it is of greater significance. The technological interpretation of the new physics has affected the sociological attitudes primarily because of the general reaction of society to man's capability to utilize it destructively as well as constructively. Not to belabor the point here, because it is covered in some depth in Part III, it is interesting to observe as the various individual philosophic and sociologic thinkers are studied, how few of them, other than the ontologists, even mention the modern physics. Two or three generations previously, the "scientific revolution" provided the central thrust of philosophy, the conversion of a supernatural metaphysics to one of natural science. The "Copernican Revolution" of Kant is an example. Comtian positivism is another.

Yet the Einsteinian physics and its sequelae have demolished the basis from which those earlier philosophies sprang. Concepts of time, space, matter, energy and their interrelationships have all been drastically changed. While in the eighteenth and nineteenth century all philosophers prided themselves in being in the forefront of all of natural science, the modern philosophers for the most part, those whose main work has been in the last half century, seem to stay away from it. In fact, some commentaries on this situation have attributed the rapid growth of existentialism to a negative reaction in the face of the implications of the new physics and the resulting technology.

Another characteristic of the active philosophers today seems to be a tendency to dedicate themselves to a particular limited field of thought, a methodology contrary to that of virtually all previous times. They seem to sense the need to specialize, to focus on some part, since it seems hopeless, individually, to advance the entire front. A Kant or a Hegel would never conceive of such an approach.

Since there tends to be specialization within schools or systems, the approach in this chapter will be to take a look at the overall concepts and discuss individual thought within the overall system. The philosophical categories I have chosen follow generally those of I.M. Bochenski, in his book *Contemporary European Philosophy* (Bochenski, 1956).

While in the previous chapters we have been emphasizing the development of thought concerning man's nature and his relationship with God and the world through the eyes and the ideas of individual men, this chapter, though it uses somewhat the same methodology, is devoted to a study of the content of the thought of a category of philosophy. What is the binding central theme that, in spite of individual differences, provides a recognizable unity in intellectual thrust and commonality in viewpoint of man in the universe. Earlier, we had observed a tendency toward a split into Ontological (philosophy of being) and Epistemological (philosophy of knowledge) lines. Then in the last century two more branches were becoming discernible, Existentialism (philosophy of existence) characterized by Kierkegaard and Nietzsche and Phenomenology (philosophy of essence) introduced by Franz Brentano. These divisions continue but the epistemological branch can be conveniently subdivided into two separate wings the idealists (philosophers of the idea) and the materialists philosophers of matter). Both are chiefly centered on the relationship of man and the outside world keyed to his acquisition of knowledge. Kant and Hegel versus Hume and Marx it could be said. The influential relationship within the thought framework represented by those four names has been previously noted: Kant by Hume; Hegel by Kant; Marx by Hegel and Hume—the common root lies in Hume and continues in the British empiricists. A sixth group identified as the philosophers of Life, a biologically oriented group, could be said to have descended immediately from the evolutionary thought of Spencer and Darwin. But, in fact, this school of thought extends back through Spinoza, to Giordano Bruno and Nicholas of Cusa, in the Renaissance Period.

Before embarking on the review the writer believes it fitting to give an outstanding specialist's view on some of the things we may encounter. Walter Kaufmann, Professor of Philosophy at Princeton University, in his introduction to his critical work, *Existentialism* (Kaufmann, 1956), has this to say on the status of current philosophy:

> It is one of the saddest features of our age that we are faced with an entirely unnecessary dichotomy: On the one hand, there are those whose devotion to intellectual cleanliness and rigor is exemplary but who refuse to deal with anything but small and often downright trivial questions; on the other hand, are men like Toynbee and some of the existentialists who deal with the big and interesting questions but in such a manner that the positivists point to them as living proofs that any effort of this kind is doomed to

failure. Aware of their opponent's errors, both sides go to ever greater extremes; the split widens; and the intelligent layman who is left in the middle will soon lose sight of both. . .That the existentialists and the analysts will get together is not likely. But if the feat of Socrates is really to be repeated and philosophy is to have a future outside the academies, there will have to be philosophers who think in the tension between analysis and existentialism.

In the last chapter it was becoming obvious that the cleavage between British and European continental thought had developed on exactly this issue—rigor versus imaginative speculation. There are hopeful signs that the situation is improving along the lines Kaufmann suggested thirty years ago.

The atomic age began when the theories of Einstein had been scientifically demonstrated by the work of Otto Kahn and Lisa Meitner with the fission of uranium at the Kaiser Wilhelm Institute and by the work of Lawrence at the University of California at Berkeley in the middle and late 1930's. This was followed quickly by verification of the enormous potential supply of energy for productive or destructive use. All that was needed was the technology to carry this scientific fact into being. This in turn was accomplished with the detonation of the first atomic device near Alamogordo, New Mexico, July 16, 1945. If there was needed a fitting burst of sound, like a Wagnerian finale ending the "Modern Age," certainly the event that day provided it. There have been a few curtain calls since, but the opera was over. The theme of the new age, however, was not clear.

The present indifference to physical science did not exist among the philosophers who were active at the time Einstein's theories of relativity were first announced. All schools of philosophy seized upon the radically and only sketchily understood ideas and attempted to demonstrate how the theories corroborated their viewpoints, but this initial enthusiasm had largely died down by World War II when the larger and somewhat more grim, implications became better known.

What were Einstein's own philosophic views? They tended to the positivistic, yet he early opposed the rigor of the strictly positivist's school and later that of the "Vienna Circle" form of logical positivism and the ideas of Ernst Mach, a fellow physicist and philosopher, who espoused the physical theories of Niels Bohr, theories which intervened briefly between concepts of Newton and Einstein in certain aspects of physics. Einstein must be classed as a modified logical-positivist. If there were such a peculiar thing, he could be called an intuitionist-positivist, as he placed an intuitional intellectualism and the abstract capacity of the free intellect ahead of the empirical methodology. Yet, he properly held to the positivistic need of experimental verification of theories. In a series of lectures at Oxford in the summer of 1933 he expressed his viewpoint as recorded by biographer Phillip Frank, (Frank, 1963, page 282):

> To Einstein, the physical theory is a product of human inventiveness, the correctness of which can be judged only on the basis of its logical simplicity and the agreement of its observable consequences with experience. This is exactly the description of a theory and the criterion of its validity which has been advocated by the Logical Positivists. To them, the belief in the "existence of a correct theory" means the "hope to make a certain invention." The expression "the correct form of a theory" has no more meaning than "the correct form of an airplane" which is obviously a meaningless expression.
>
> But here Einstein deviates definitely from the conception of Logical Positivism. In his Oxford lecture he replied to the question whether there is a "correct way" as follows:
>
> "To this I answer with complete assurance that in my opinion there is the correct path and, moreover, that it is in our power to find it. Our experience up to date justifies us in feeling sure that in nature is actualized the idea of mathematical simplicity.
>
> "It is my conviction that pure mathematical construction enables us to discover the concepts and the laws connecting them, which give us the key to the understanding of the phenomena of nature. Experience can, of course, guide us in our choice of serviceable mathematical concepts; it cannot possibly be the source from which they are derived.
>
> "In a certain sense, therefore, I hold it to be true that pure thought is competent to comprehend the real as the ancients dreamed."

His definition of the "correct path" does not coincide with the "correct theory" of the logical positivists. That he was not an atheistic materialist has previously been pointed out, but his personal views undoubtedly are not consistent with any religious orthodoxy. Man is more to him than just a gifted animal; just what more is not clear. But man's dignity lies in his intellectual capacity to conceive and appreciate the wondrous innate simplicity and order which is apparent in everything in the universe and which to him demonstrates in its design an intelligence of high order, again quoting Frank:

> The cosmic religious experience is the strongest and the noblest, deriving from behind scientific research. No one who does not appreciate the terrific exertions, the devotion, without which pioneer creation in scientific thought cannot come into being can judge the strength of the feeling out of which alone such work, turned away as it is from immediate practical life, can grow.
>
> What deep faith in the rationality of the structure of the world, what a longing to understand even a small glimpse of the reason revealed in the world, there must have been in Kepler and Newton!

In this chapter the philosophical aspects of the concept of man are considered under the following broad headings, representing a general continuum from most materialistic to least materialistic. But as will be noted, individuals within these broad headings have great differences in their views of the concept of man and in his relationship to the totality of the "other" regardless of its perceived form.

1. Philosophy of Matter
2. Philosophy of the Idea
3. Philosophy of Life
4. Philosophy of Essence
5. Philosophy of Existence
6. Philosophy of Being

This breakdown also permits a consideration of individuals in terms of their specialization. But it should be borne in mind that at the present time there are certain characteristics or usages of the schools which cut across these categories. For instance, the methodology of the materialist in analysis has been used by the other groups, and the theistic question cuts across all of them in various degrees.

Section 1—Philosophy of Matter

The leading thinker of the twentieth century under the heading of philosophy of matter is Bertrand Russell, the third Earl Russell, who was born in 1872 of a family which first appeared in prominence in England at the time of Henry VIII, John Russell, the first Earl of Bedford, arranged the marriage in 1554 of Mary I of England to Philip II of Spain. Russell thus represents a family of long aristocratic tradition. His parents both died when he was young and he was reared by his grandfather Lord John Russell. He was educated at Cambridge, being a fellow at Trinity College in 1895, and a lecturer there from 1910 to 1916. His original education was in mathematics. Then, largely through his own scholarship, he gradually changed to a tone of pure philosophy. Russell undoubtedly is the best known of all the British philosophers of this century. His long life and bizarre behavior assured that and he was a prolific writer on a wide range of subjects.

Russell was a noted pacifist since before World War I, during which he was imprisoned for his efforts. In his long life, he produced a tremendous volume of work in addition to his popular writing, largely fostering a scientistic view of philosophy and reflecting his predelictions for logic and mathematics in his thought. While other materialistic philosophers have waivered down through their aging process, Russell was steadfast until his death in his materialism although fully aware of how tenuous matter is in the new physics. Yet his philosophy was remarkably changeable in its methodological approach to the constant theme of materialism. In his collection *Contemporary British Philosophy*, C.D. Broad remarked "As we all know, Mr. Russell produces a different system of philosophy every few years." And some of his ideas are downright odd; yet still acute. In many ways his philosophic thought, when disassociated from his analytic work, seems like a colossal bit of leg-pulling but it must be taken seriously.

His joint work with A.N. Whitehead, *Principia Mathematica,* 1910-1913, a leading work in symbolic logic, but now largely of historical rather than mathematical interest, is perhaps his best known. For him natural science offers the only solutions to man's problems. He says, echoing the positivist's theme, "The particular sciences are the *only* source of knowledge about the world and we *cannot know* about anything else" (emphasis supplied). In spite of being a philosopher, he did not see any answers coming out of philosophy, only questions, since philosophy is "prescientific" as a discipline. He was a positivist in the true tradition of Comte and a utilitarian in Mill's footsteps, although much more a detailist in both regards than either. His attitude toward religion and metaphysics was the same as theirs, a skeptical negative. Russell held that man is an insignificant part of nature, yet the most important.

From his early philosophic years, Russell began to doubt that there is an immediate knowledge of the self, and essentially adopted Hume's attitude, that the human soul is simply an association of ideas. In *The Analysis of Mind*, Russell expressly sets forth this concept, but on his own terms. While mental and physical worlds coincide, mental and physical laws differ. Mental events are established by "mnemonic determinism" in turn derived from the determinism of the nervous system. Subjectivity is also a characteristic of mind and is materially explained as a concentration of sense data in the brain. The fact that mental concepts exist in consciousness is not enough to identify them as intrinsically mental because they are not a constant presence in consciousness, nor can they be equated to concepts such as habit, memory or thought because these are mere elaborations on mnemonic determinism. He early considered British empiricism primitive and at first turned to Hegel's thought, but about 1900 he was attracted to the analytic aspects of empiricism. At about the same time, he apparently gave up any hope of arriving at a knowledge of God through reason.

Russell admits the present conditions of science and his own doctrine prevent him from accepting Humean materalistic teaching in its entirety. Nevertheless, he maintains firmly that mental phenomena are a reaction to physiological phenomena, and so denies the existence of any transcendental soul. Yet mental events are more real than matter because the latter is not immediately given but is established only by deduction and construction. Natural science, the only real source of knowledge, gives no support whatever for the belief in God or immortality. The doctrine of immortality is nonsense. Because, to be immortal, the soul would have to occupy the whole of space. Shades of the medieval angelologists who allegedly used to debate that, since pure spirit occupied no space, how many could occupy the point of a pin! Religion, at least organized religion, is evil because it is based on and fosters fear. It is the enemy of all that is good and decent in the modern world and is for Russell, after Comte, a sign of man's immaturity. Yet man, while he is only an insignificant bit of matter in the universe, is highest in the order of values and the good life is Russell's answer. On that point, his view is much like that of Montaigne, though it also resembles the existentialists—man should live an authentic life forgetting moral laws which are only artificial. There is no immortality so why foist off behavior based on that idea. Be a man but be kind and loving. Abandon the metaphysical and accept the utilitarian and be happy. Life is short enough so make it pleasant. Russell agrees with Hume's conclusion that while the self or mind is only a logical construction, that is to say a convenient fiction, we cannot live in accord with that concept. We must think ourselves as selves in our day to day lives and in our language. If it is more poetic than real in our expression, nevertheless, it is justified because it agrees with the way life appears to us. A strange philosophy.

Russell's final position was still as a hard-core, empirical materialist and, if not an atheist, then most certainly a strict and dedicated agnostic. He belongs to the English neo-realistic movement, and his thought is typical of that group. It could almost be said that he was the group in thought process of the middle twentieth century. The school is waning in strength and essentially died with Russell.

A second level under the philosophy of matter is the neo-positivist or logical positivist. This was the outgrowth of the positivistic philosophy in Germany and Austria perhaps dominant among the scientists at the turn of the century and represented in the early decades of this century by the "Vienna Circle," which switched from a rigid positivism, almost completely dogmatic, to logical positivism with the change from Newtonian physics to that of Niels Bohr. Physicist philosopher Ernst Mach (1838-1916) was one of the leading geniuses of that group. As would be expected, the philosophy was, and it no longer is a dominant philosophy, strongly analytic and devoutly scientistic, but not atheistic nor even agnostic. It merely denies that metaphysical or theological language is philosophically meaningful. As noted previously, Einstein's views, less any dogmatic attitude, would probably come closest to the attitude of this group.

The Vienna Circle was formed by Morritz Schlick (1882-1936), professor of philosophy at the University of Vienna in 1924. It included a number of outstanding scientists in addition to Mach. Phillip Frank, biographer of Einstein, quoted above, was a member. It broke up with Schlick's death in 1936.

An outstanding representative of this group was Ludvig Wittgenstein. He was a lecturer in philosophy at Cambridge from

1929 and, at the time of his death in 1951, head of the department. Wittgenstein, while acquainted with the Vienna Circle membership and representing its thought, was not himself a member, preferring to work by himself. But he had a profound influence on the movement, particularly directing it toward the linguistic analysis mode which increasingly characterized its later life. But Wittgenstein, if he was important in the birth and direction of the Logical Positivist movement, almost served as its undertaker as well. For in a posthumously published work (1953), *Philosophical Investigations,* he effectively gutted the movement in its dogmatic pretensions that the language of science, or better, the scientific view of language was the model toward which all philosophic usage in language should, or even, must adhere. Whereas he had been the pillar of the rigorous view, he now admitted that there are many correct usages equally valid. He said, "The meaning of a word is its use in the language"—not a very dramatic statement except for those who had been utterly dedicated to a strict usage interpretation and to elimination of metaphysics on that score as chief target. To them, it was a disastrous apostasy and the apostate was out of reach for extirpation. It was not Wittgenstein, however, who finally laid the main program to rest. It was the failure of the empirical verification principle to provide the sieve which would permit the physical science propositions to pass, while retaining those of the metaphysical.

Anticipating early demise of metaphysics in 1955, Gilbert Ryle, a leading British member of the logical positivist movement, said, "The theological fire has died down, but it has not quite gone out and the kettle of theological philosophy, though far from even simmering, is not quite stone cold. . ." Yet, some 30 years later logical positivism, in its dogmatic form, is in fact stone cold and metaphysics is still with us. Currently the analytic philosophers, almost exclusively devoted to linguistics, are the surviving element and are doing much useful work in a truly positive sense in language applications. There is even a modest interest in metaphysics being shown. Yet, the analyticists characteristically, in spite of their formidable language structure, oversimplify the relationships of a complex world. For example, Wittgenstein had written in his *Philosophical Investigations,* "Philosophy simply puts everything before us, and neither explains nor deduces anything—since everything lies open to view there is nothing to explain."

Wittgenstein was not a materialist in any strict sense of the word except as the sense factor and logic therefrom served as the limit to knowledge. Writing in 1918 in his work *Tractatus Logico-Philosophicus* (Wittgenstein, 1915) he had said:

> The sense of the world must lie outside the world. In the world everything is as it is and happens as it does happen. *In* it there is no value—and if there were, it would be of no value. If there is a value which is of value, it must lie outside all happenings and being-so (brute fact). For all happening and being-so is accidental. What makes it non-accidental cannot lie in the world, for otherwise this would again be accidental. He must lie outside the world. . . Not *how* the world is, is the mystical, but *that* it is. The contemplation of the world *sub specie aeterni* is its contemplation as a limited whole. The feeling of the world as a limited whole is the mystical whole. . .We feel that even if *all possible* scientific questions be answered, the problems of life have not been touched at all. Of course there is then no question left, and just this is the answer. My propositions are elucidatory in this way: he who understands me finally recognizes them as senseless, when he has climbed out through them, on them, over them. (He must so to speak throw away the ladder, after he has climbed up on it.) He must surmount these propositions; then he sees the world rightly. Whereof one cannot speak, thereof one must be silent. (Emphasis Wittgenstein).

Wittgenstein believed that no accurate questions could be asked or answers provided outside the realm of the natural sciences and refused to speak of them philosophically. Yet, he believed there was a reality beyond the material order which explained the material order and gave it meaning. That meaning was forever beyond our reach.

The third level under this philosophy is dialectic materialism—that of Marx and Engels filtered through Lenin. It is the philosophy which is also an ideology—that of international communism. It is the only philosophy officially tolerated in countries which are controlled by communist governments. As a philosophy distinct from its economic, social and political aspects it has little standing in other countries except for those which are ideologically completely oriented to a Leninist or Maoist communism. Paul Sartre, the existentialist, discussed in a later section, was influenced by this school through his sympathies with the communist ideology. He, of course, does not belong with this philosophic group.

This school, in its doctrinal approach, sees mind or consciousness in the tradition of Hume as only a product of the brain as it is stimulated by exterior excitation. "Pavlov's dog" is the well-known model, long since superseded in the behavioral sciences. These philosophers are by dogma dedicated to a materialistic atheism, and their view of man is that expressed by Marx himself, as representative only of matter in motion along with all other forms of existence in a continuous Hegelian dialectical conflict through which change and progress emerge. They deny the existence of problems which have a source other than in matter or economics stemming from that matter, a dogma which today makes their position almost untenable, for manifestly other problems exist, they are not nonsense, they will not go away. With Engel's dialectic contribution, it is a stagnant philosophy, but obviously, in its ideological extension, an important one.

The outstanding exponent of this philosophy in the United States is the late Herbert Marcuse, former professor of philosophy at the University of California at San Diego who was educated at the Universities of Berlin and Frieburg. In his book *Negations* (Marcuse, 1968), Marcuse republishes a number of essays explicating his position and that of Marxism in Germany in the years just prior to World War II and adds some more recent ones.

> At a low level of productive forces, bourgeois society did not yet have the means to administer soul and mind without discrediting this administration through terroristic violence. Today total administration is necessary, and the means are at hand; mass gratification, market research, industrial psychology, computer mathematics, and the so-called science of human relations. These take care of the nonterroristic, democratic, spontaneous-automatic harmonization of individual and socially necessary needs and wants, of autonomy and heteronomy. They assure the free election of individuals and policies necessary for this system to continue to exist and grow. *The democratic abolition of thought,* which the "common man" undergoes automatically and which he himself carries out (in labor and in the use and enjoyment of the apparatus of production and consumption), *is brought*

about in the higher learning" by those positivistic
and positive trends of philosophy, sociology, and psychology that make the established system into an in-
superable framework for conceptual thought.
(Emphasis supplied).

Thus things are really worse today rather than better because
of the higher level of thought control—only in the capitalist
world of course. The need for the Marxist take over is all the
more urgent, yet made more difficult by technological advance.
Marcuse continues:

Productivity and prosperity in league with a technology in the service of monopolistic politics seems
to immunize advancing industrial society in its established structure. . .
Is this concept of immunity still dialectical? In view
of the capacity and productivity of organized capitalism, should not the "first phase" of socialism be more
and qualitatively other than it was projected to be
in Marxian theory? Is not this the context in which
belongs socialism's affinity for and successes in pre-
industrial and weakly industrialized societies? The
Marxian concepts of capitalism and of socialism were
decisively determined by the function of human labor,
physical labor in social reproduction. Marx's image
of the realm of necessity does not correspond to today's highly developed industrial nations. And in view
of the frantic expansion of totalitarian mass
democracy, the Marxian image of the realm of freedom beyond the realm of necessity must appear
"romantic." For it stipulates an individual subject of
labor, an autonomy of creative activity and leisure,
and a dimension of unspoiled nature that have long
since been liquidated in the progress of domination
and industrialization. . .
Has not late industrial society already surpassed,
in a bad form, the idea of socialism—as in bad planning, bad expansion of the productive forces, bad
organization of the working class, and bad development of needs and of gratification? Of course, all the
wealth, the technology and the productivity of this
society cannot match the ideas of real freedom and
of real justice which are at the center of socialist

theory. Nevertheless, these ideas appear in forms worked out substantially as the potentiality and negation of a capitalism that was not yet fully developed. Developed industrial society has already won for itself much of the ground on which the new freedom was to have flourished. This society has appropriated dimensions of consciousness and nature that formerly were relatively unspoiled. It has formed historical alternatives in its own image and flattened out contradiction, which it can thus tolerate. Through this totalitarian-democratic conquest of man and of nature, the subjective and objective space for the realm of freedom has also been conquered.

The world is not the same as the one viewed by Marx but the need to free man from the historical social structure of superior and subordinate remains undiminished. In a recent essay on Max Weber in his collection "Industrialization and Capitalism" first published in 1964, Marcuse leaves no doubt that the dialectic is still the same. He says:

> In the continuum of history, in which all economic action takes place, all economic reason is always the reason of domination, which historically and socially determines economic action. Capitalism, no matter how mathematized and "scientific," remains the mathematized, technological domination of men; and socialism, no matter how scientific and technological is the...demolition of domination.

The philosophy remains solely an ideologic tool unchanged basically since 1848. All problems are economic at root, their solution only to be achieved by eventual dialectic victory of the economic-materialistic views of Marx himself. It is a philosophy of polemic not of reason.

As a total system, the philosophies of matter are viewed as reactionary, as outdated, as holding no promise for new insights or philosophical progress. Their vivifying sources have dried up, exhausted with the definition of matter even while fundamental matter, the atom, has become materialistically elusive. The chief contribution of the group is as a counterpose to the totally "dematerialistic" groups at the other end of the continuum who see matter as having no reality. But the philosophers of matter offer no real solutions to the major problems facing man at this point. The problems cannot even be addressed within their context.

Section 2—The Philosophy of the Idea

The modern thinkers grouped under the philosophy of the idea are those whose "modern" roots lie in the work of Kant, but, in most aspects, reflect Hegelian overtones. Their thoughts are those, therefore, predominant among adherents to older Protestant religious views yet who, to some extent, desired to remain close to the main theme of an idealist school of being in the right wing Hegelian tradition. The movement has in its most general form been designated as "Neo-Kantian," its proponents are almost universally objective idealists, and it includes the "Neo-idealists." For the most part, they regard the entirety of reality as inherent in the objective spirit, whose manifestations include both the human soul and nature and may, in fact, be coexistent and identical with both. They are distinguished from the Kantian philosophy in not believing that "thing-in-itself," the noumena, is an existent, but rather a limiting concept, a concept purely of the mind. They are Fichtean of Hegelian in that sense. Reality itself is a construct of the mind. The phenomenal material world is real under that ideational definition. And, as with Kant, only the material world as mental construct can be correctly said to be within man's cognitive grasp.

Although this school is currently in a state of virtual eclipse from its powerful position in the nineteenth century, and even more so in the United States than in Europe, it still is influential through its impact, particularly in the early twentieth century, in the zone where philosophy is conjoined with theology. In its broadest sense, it spans the gap between the materialist and the positivist on the one side and the existentially oriented groups on the other. It is to this extent a philosophy of the middle ground, but one not having well-defined theistic connotations. There is no outstanding thinker in this group to compare with Russell among the materialists for example, so that three individual viewpoints will be given without particular biographical reference.

Benedetto Croce (1866-1953) was at one time minister of education in Italy, including a short term after the liberation at the end of World War II. He was influenced not only by Kant and Hegel, but also by the positivists and Marxian philosophers. His position, therefore, is toward the pragmatic side. At one time, one could have said the "left" but the former "radical" philosophies are now seen as ultraconservative in philosophy. In Croce's thinking there are but two ways of possessing knowledge. The first is the conceptual, which can be defined as cognitive or purely rational; the second is the intuitive (not the Kantian intuition of the senses), which has its origin in the aesthetic, emotive aspects of human nature. Croce denied any intellectual capacity to this latter faculty. In addition, Croce held that the intellect can have no grasp of the thing's essence. Somewhat like the thing-in-itself for Kant, it apprehends only the impactive response which an object evokes in the subject in one of the two ways indicated. But there is nonetheless objective knowledge seen in the first way as the universal and in the second way as the personal sensuous linkage between the universal cognitive reality and its mode of recognition by the individual. The function of the intellect is to combine and analyze the various singular recognitions thus apprehended.

For Croce there was nothing permanent in this world or in man's existence in it. There was merely a continuous stream of events in a somewhat Humean sense. Each instant was discrete from the one preceding and the one following. Nevertheless, they were related by a complex, almost circuitous, causal relationship, which was itself manifested in four modes—aesthetic, logical, economic and moral. Philosophy in viewing reality must look at each event in these four modes.

The function of the moral mode of apprehension is to point the spirit to the universal, not to gainsay the place of the other modes, but to elevate the manner of acceptance. Croce expressly denied that emotion is the criterion of moral activity, although it can act to motivate moral activity. Moral man, therefore, as he is ordered toward a universal and spiritual end, does not thereby cease to be motivated by the useful or to tend toward happiness which in fact must coincide with this very activity. Yet moral and economic activity though directed to a common spiritual end are not completely within the realm of the spirit.

While Croce denied that religion, as such, is a specific form in which the spirit adhered, he believed that religious morality is far superior to any morality which can be based on secular moral codes, and that in its highest expression it contained nearly all of the true morality of the spirit. Yet, with Kant, the true moral viewpoint is true only to the individual. It is subjective. Man himself is individually his own moral law as Kant himself had said in his introduction to the *Metaphysics of Morals*.

Leon Brunschvicg was born in 1869 and was professor of

philosophy at the Ecole Normale in Paris until he was dismissed by the Germans in the occupation in 1941. His thoughts were influenced not only by Kant and Hegel, but he also drew heavily upon Plato, Spinoza, Descartes, Pascal and Schelling. His philosophy is an idealistic synthesis of all of these. He placed special stress on the creative role of philosophic thought in the expression of cultural history as well as in the natural sciences. His influence was strongest during the period immediately prior to World War II. He continued to publish afterwards, but was an old man even when the Nazis removed him. He is an idealist in two ways: first, in his extension of the ideas of Kant and Hegel to their conclusions and synthesizing them and, second, by subjecting this synthesis to added idealistic extrapolation from their antecedent philosophies beginning with Plato but especially related to Spinoza.

Brunschvicg saw a pervasive duality even greater than that expressed by Kant in his dichotomies. For instance, there are two constituents of mind, first an internality—rational, judgmental, where a subject is related to a predicate—and second an externality—that which the mind considers but which lies beyond the rational cognitive ability and is intellectually impenetrable. This latter mode seems to agree somewhat with the noumena of Kant. However, Brunschvicg formed a mediating third category, a mixed form of the contingent which permitted integration of the total concept again almost like Kant who assigned this role to judgment which Brunschvicg appeared to limit to the first constituent.

Brunschvicg's thinking is not much removed from Croce, except that he accords religious questions a much higher place, to the extent that the philosophy of religion is his dominant interest. But he seems to take a view of God and religion not unlike that of Spinoza, in that his God also seems to be unloving; a groping spirit seeking fulfillment of its intellect and man's end is to be absorbed in that intellect. There is fundamentally nothing apart from the spirit in its creative surging mode unfolding itself in creation as it comes to consciousness.

One other group, the Baden German School, is personified by its principal founder Wilhelm Windelband (1848-1915), noted especially as a historian. It closes the span in this overall school, though as was indicated there is no broad spread in the Neo-Kantian thought. The Baden group is less dominated than the other Philosophers of the Idea by the Kantian relationship to the natural sciences, which limits knowledge to sensed apprehension of phenomenon, and also by the Kantian strict duality of "knowledge" which flows from that concept. Its theme is that of the unity of culture in providing man the essential integrative element in support of human existence.

The proponents recognize an irrational element in reality and hold that the essence of objective being is not found exclusively, nor even preponderantly in logical laws, but also in the validity of a value system fundamental to culture. The two standards are of a different genre. The logical is unchanging and has absolute validity, the normative or value-oriented is relative but nonetheless valid within its sphere of reference. Among the normatively defined concepts are those having a transcendental value and having no place in a reality of logic, but having a subjectively oriented reality nonetheless. The highest class of these are the religious values. The chief difference between Croce's view and Windelband's is the addition of the cultural value concept to an objective morality which in a way seems to introduce a social as well as a subjective distortion. When viewed in the overall idealistic frame by the idealist, objective and idealistic tend to coincide so that this is seen to add an additional dimension rather than distortion.

The continuing theme of idealism in the contemporary world remains Kantian, but as previously indicated, it is individually modified to bring into focus the uniqueness and pervasiveness of spirit and the idea of real being and objective and logical law. But at the same time, as was clear in the Baden School, there is the developing concept of certain normative or value-oriented "realities" which are relative in their application in time and space, and there is also a creative aspect to knowledge. Knowledge is more than a passive reception of images from the senses. The total group thus stands between the materialists, on the one hand who hold that there is nothing else or at least nothing else knowable than matter since we are limited to our sense perceptions, and the complete irrationalists and subjectivists on the other.

But the idealist's concepts remain constricted. Suffering from the need to reconcile a dualism in approach to reality, they tend to obscure not only the concrete world as it exists to the senses, but also the world of the "spirit," their chief realm of activity. Because of its extension, the spirit thus conceived becomes one of little depth. The idealist's world is one of pure constructs. Again, as with the pure materialists, they lack any real ability to come to grips with the problems of human existence as they are in fact experienced.

Section 3—Philosophy of Life

In the previous two basic aspects of philosophy in reference to man's concept of man—the materialistic and idealistic viewpoints, man did not emerge as a human being in any real way. In the first case, he was viewed as an object of laboratory investigation, the subject of empirical research and inductive logic based thereon or a creation of economic significance. Human nature was passed through a coarse sieve. Any aesthetic, not to mention spiritual qualities, would pass through and only the gross material chunks were considered. In the second, man was oddly split and examined as two separate entities as though screened through two sieves in sequence, the first coarse, the second fine and only the coarse elements retained by the first and the fine passed by the second were examined and then in separate processes, thus leaving the center fractions unexamined.

The philosophers of life make an honest attempt to take an integral view of man. They want to avoid both materialism and idealism and view man as he lives. In doing so, they have, however, looked at only the center fraction, leaving the coarsest and finest unexamined. The characteristic of this group is "actuality." Bochenski describes their attitude in the following quotation (pages 100, 101):

> Another feature which distinguishes them from the idealists and empiricists is the fact that they are striving to break away from the general framework of "modern" (1600-1900) philosophy, and especially of Kantianism. They wish, above all, to avoid both mechanism and idealism. However much they differ from each other in details, they are at one on the following issues:
>
> (1) They are absolute actualists. For them there is only movement, becoming, life. So far as they recognize matter or being at all, it is only as the by-product of movement; in this respect each of them echoes Bergson's verdict "there is more in becoming than in being."
> (2) Their conception of reality is an organic one, in which biology enjoys a status comparable to that of physics among the representatives of scientific materialism. History also plays an important role with

some of them, especially for Dilthey's school. At any rate, none of them think of the world as a machine, but as pulsating life.

(3) They expound their own philosophy of knowledge in the light of this biological attitude; without exception they are irrationalists and resolute empiricists. Concepts, a priori laws, logical deduction are an abomination to them; they consequently will not accept rational method as the touchstone of philosophy but replace it by the test of intuition, practice, and a vital understanding of history.

(4) For all this they are but rarely subjectivists and they assume the existence of an objective reality which transcends the subject; therefore they will have nothing to do with transcendental or absolute idealism.

(5) Finally the majority of these philosophers betray a marked inclination toward pluralism and personalism. If this inclination does not entirely harmonize with their basic teaching concerning the evolution of life, it may perhaps be explained as a reaction from materialistic or idealistic monism; in any case this has been one of the movement's most powerful tendencies.

The leading representative of this group is Henri Bergson who was born in Paris of Irish-Jewish parentage October 18, 1859. He was educated at the Ecole Normale Superieure in Paris and was a long-time professor of philosophy at the College of France. In 1927, he won the Nobel Prize in literature for his philosophic writing, which underscores the quality of his presentation. He was quite naturally influenced by the work of his teacher, Emile Boutroux (1845-1921) who it will be recalled was also one who influenced Durkheim in his development of sociology. He also was influenced by Herbert Spencer (1820-1903), the social evolutionist. Bergson has stated that his own philosophy was an inverted outgrowth of his work to provide a better basis for Spencer's system which he eventually came to oppose completely. Yet, there always remained a certain kinship between Spencer and Bergson. Bergson was a painstaking researcher and totally devoted to the idea that only after one had established a solid basis in fact could he start the superstructure of a philosophic system.

Concerning his concept of man, Bergson visualized two

spheres of reality which man can apprehend. The first is that of the practical intellect—the sphere of spacial and rigid matter; the second, that of intuition which he did not, as the Kantians did, totally eliminate as an intellectual activity. His definition of intuition is likewise different from that of Kant, for Bergson it is the sphere of life and enduring awareness. And while this was an intellectual activity, nevertheless the intellect is always directed toward practical ends, hence, the intuitive "concepts" cannot be reduced to logical proof nor properly incorporated in them. Bergson places great emphasis on the importance of the intuitive aspects as the proper, if not the major, area of philosophic inquiry, and it is largely from this emphasis that the philosophic system is designated the life philosophy.

Intuition, for Bergson, corresponds to the instinctive faculty in the non-human animal life and, as the evolutionary extension of instinct shows us, the genuine reality of life. Human life, in turn, is a constant intuitive, striving for freedom which is the human goal. To some extent, mankind represents this soaring impulse toward freedom, the expression of the *elan vital*—the life force—seeking freedom from matter, from its animality, freedom of the spirit from its earthbound limitations, perhaps even to survival beyond death.

Bergson sees in morality an expression of the striving for mankind's emancipation from the animal-material surround. He sees two types of morality somewhat Durkheimian, one from duty, the pressure exercised by society; the other an inner vocation, which might correspond with Durkheim's "search for happiness." This second type of morality seemed to Bergson to be the motivation of heroes and saints. He makes the same distinction in religion. The first is a static "myth making" religion. The second, dynamic, the religion of mysticism coming from the original, striving, life impulse to freedom. It is in this life impulse, this mystic extension of life into the ecstatic drive for freedom in union with something infinitely lovable and desirable that Bergson sees the grounds for asserting God's existence and the immortality of the soul, which he believes, along with Kant, cannot be demonstrated on logical grounds.

In the same group, but more pragmatic and materialistic, and illustrating the breadth of this school, is John Dewey.

John Dewey was born in 1859 in Burlington, Vermont, and after attending the University of Vermont, taught at various rural schools for about two years. In 1884, he received his Ph.D at Johns Hopkins University and taught philosophy at the university in 1888-1889. He moved to the University of Michigan for five years, then went in 1896 to the University of Chicago, in the Laboratory School, which he directed until 1904. He then went to Columbia University as professor of philosophy and remained there until his retirement from active teaching in 1930. Initially, he was an idealist in the Hegelian right-wing mold—but, finding no adequate answers to the challenge of Darwin there, he gradually shifted in the years between 1884 and 1909 to his own philosophy of life, yet he commented that there remained a "Hegelian bacillus in my blood."

During his long life, he had many assignments as a consultant, and as a guest lecturer, or as an honored visitor, to foreign governments. His main interest was that of educational reform. He has been called the father of the progressive educational school system widely adapted in the United States and elsewhere in the 1920's and 1930's. His central theme was that "science is the organ of general social progress." All schools should be embryonic communities and give the sensed feel of humanity in history, art and science. In many ways, he echoed the ideas of Rousseau—that the education of the child should be one of natural adaptation. Dewey himself, though, disavowed many of the innovations in education made in his name.

While Dewey's philosophy has been called pragmatic, he himself saw it as experimental or instrumental. The model of all inquiry should be scientific investigation. He denied the existence of ethical absolutes and believed that morals were basically adaptations to fit social needs at the time, and hence, were continuously varying. He believed there is no reason to bring in a set of universal moral norms which would imply "That one method obtained in natural science and another, radically different, in moral questions." The only effect would be creation of a disunity in the intellectual life of our time and denial of the promise which scientific empirical methods hold even in the field of ethics. Dewey was insistent upon that point. In his essay, *Intelligence and Morals,* originally presented at Columbia University in March 1908 he said:

> From this point of view, there is no separate body of moral rules, no separate system of motive powers; no separate subject-matter of moral knowledge, and hence no such thing as an isolated ethical science. If the business of morals is not to speculate upon man's final end and upon an ultimate standard of right, it is to utilize physiology, anthropology, and

psychology to discover all that can be discovered of man, his organic powers and propensities. If its business is not to search for the one separate moral motive, it is to converge all the instrumentalities of the social arts, of law, education, economics and political science upon the construction of intelligent methods of improving the common lot. . . All men require moral sanctions in their conduct: the consent of their kind. Not getting it otherwise, they go insane to feign it. No man ever lived with the exclusive approval of his own conscience. Hence the vacuum left in practical matters by the remote irrelevancy of transcendental morals has to be filled in somehow. It is filled in. It is filled in with class-codes, class-standards, class-approvals—with codes which recommend the practices and habits already current in a given circle, set, calling, profession, trade, industry, club, or gang.

Class-codes of morals are sanctions, under the caption of ideals, of uncriticized customs; they are recommendations, under the head of duties, of what the members of the class are already most given to doing. If they are to obtain more equable and comprehensive principles of action, exacting a more impartial exercise of natural power and resource in the interests of a common good, members of a class must no longer rest content in responsibility to a class whose traditions constitute its conscience, but be made responsible to a society whose conscience is its free and effectively organized intelligence.

In such a conscience alone will the Socratic injunction to man to know himself be fulfilled.

Of course, such a conception means something for philosophy as well as for psychology; possibly it involves, for philosophy, the larger measure of transformation. It involves surrender of any claim on the part of philosophy to be the sole source of some truths and the exclusive guardian of some values.

Dewey left a tremendous task to science in translating scientific evidence into a total conscience for society. But he plainly felt it would be equal to the task, given a little time.

In an essay, *Consciousness and Experience,* presented at the University of California in May 1899, he had said:

It means that philosophy be a method; not an assurance company, nor a knight errant. It means an alignment with science. Philosophy may not be sacrificed to the partial and superficial clamor of that which sometimes officiously and pretentiously exhibits itself as Science. But there is a sense in which philosophy must go to school to the sciences, must have no data save such as it receives at their hands; and be hospitable to no method of inquiry or reflection not akin to those in daily use among the sciences. As long as it claims for itself special territory of fact, or peculiar modes of access to truth, so long must it occupy a dubious position. Yet this claim it has to make until psychology comes to its own.

Clearly when psychology finally would come of age, philosophers could cease worrying about the human mind and its moral problems. Morality would flow automatically from the well-organized, scientific, conscience of society. This narrowness of view reflected the provincial scientism of much of the early twentieth century thought. In Dewey's case his words have a polemical sound to them akin to the later Marxist-Leninist pronouncements. Still this is a characteristic which must flow from an abandonment of organized deductive logical thought as a road to truth.

As already suggested, Dewey's most important works were in the area of education, and that is the field in which his impact on the concept of man took greatest effect. The thoughts expressed in the foregoing quotations extended through all of his works. It is hard to over-estimate his influence on the American school system or on modern thought in the United States through that system. He conceived liberal democracy as the one which free men should seek, more as an association than as a government and concluded that his methodology would give the greatest opportunity for experimentation and growth. He clearly saw the progress of humanity as a function of natural science, but science somehow directed toward an evolving condition of higher personal satisfaction and biological happiness. There is little to suggest that Dewey had any concept of man other than as a gifted animal or that he saw the dignity of man in any other light than living decently and freely in concord with his fellow man—an end which would result through the instrumentality of an experimentally-determined, scientifically-directed way of life. His ideas, while still persisting in the social sciences and education, have largely been bypassed in the emerging philosophies of the later twentieth century.

While the life philosophers as a group have clearly seen that life is not completely dominated by the material nor yet by the spirit as a separately constituted entity, they are oriented to the biologic view of man. Bergson sees a possible, even likely, transcendental life, but in the case of Dewey, man is confined solely to an earthly existence. They both reduce reason to a relatively minor function in the analysis of man's being. One ascribes higher value to knowledge by intuition, though not a completely intellectual intuition; the other, exclusively to empirical induction. For both, deductive logic has an inferior position. By their limitation of man's sphere of knowledge either in the cognitive or intuitive sense to the biological they are effectively sealed off from any consideration of man in his spiritual, existential relationships or of any problems arising in that context. For Dewey, the problems are mythical, for Bergson mystical.

Section 4—Philosophy of Essence

The philosophy of essence is represented by the phenomenologists, a group of thinkers largely independent of the older schools, yet still having roots in the older scholasticism and the Kantian system. It thus takes both an ontological and epistemological view of man and his environment in arriving at an understanding of essence. Phenomenology is in many ways better described as a methodology of philosophy, rather than a philosophic system although the latter certainly has been attempted. This method is a systematic way of looking at phenomena, at anything which is presented to an individual for analysis, as it is immediately presented. Hence, it is opposed to strict materialistic empiricism, and at the same time to Kantian idealism. In its origins, it runs counter to the dominant schools of thought in the late nineteenth century and thus does not place itself in an epistemological box. Yet it does not extend to a consideration of being, *qua* being, but on the "whatness" of individual phenomenal objects in the broadest sense. In a sense it is a seminal philosophy, many of its disciples having moved to existentialism or philosophy of being.

As a free-standing approach, it is properly classified as philosophy of essence since it seeks to discover the at-root nature of objects of intellectual concern (intellectual here interpreted in its very broadest context to include the intuitive). The analysis is as a discovery, the object completely divorced from preconceptions—as though it were being viewed for the very first time. The methodology brushes aside empiricism, idealism, and conceptualism, correctly pointing out that all three are hedged around by dogma which prevent a clear look at the totality of the object. They hold that there is a possible knowledge of objectivity of essence as well as an objectivity of knowledge and that in the assessing of the true nature of something, every aspect must be completely defined as it is given or presented.

From our standpoint, the definition of "human spirit" as provided by the phenomenologists is of chief importance, and it is in many ways the most important in phenomenology in its totality which also relates heavily to human behavior. This aspect is best exemplified by reviewing the specific points held by its leading representatives, Edmond Husserl and Max Scheler.

Edmond Husserl, the father of phenomenology as a school of philosophy, was born at Prossnitz, Moravia, on April 8, 1859, of middle class Jewish parentage. He attended several German universities concentrating in mathematics and then went to the University of Vienna in 1884, where he became a student of Franz Brentano (1838-1917). Brentano had been a Dominican priest in early life, but left both the order and the Church, and as we noted earlier was a precursor of phenomenology as a school of philosophy. Thus, to some extent the ideas of Aristotelian and Thomistic scholasticism were brought into the new school and influenced Husserl. Husserl was attracted also to Kant's ideas as translated through the Neo-Kantian system. He also studied under psychologist Carl Stumpf (1848-1936). He taught philosophy as a private instructor in Halle beginning in 1887, then became a professor at the University of Halle. Husserl was professor of philosophy at Gottingen in 1901 and Freiburg in 1916, where he remained until retirement in 1928. His works in their systematic organization are in the Aristotelian/Thomistic tradition, although the language of phenomenology is greatly different.

Husserl's first works were in mathematics, and it was not until 1901 that his first work in philosophy, *Logische Untersuchungen,* or Investigation of Logic, was published. In the first edition of this work, Husserl defined phenomenology as "descriptive analysis of subjective processes." It was thus closely related to psychology. Husserl, at this time under Kantian influence, saw no relationship to metaphysical problems though he came to include such problems later. After that first work he produced voluminously, progressing gradually from purely mathematical works through a rational objectivity and eventually to idealism, so that he in effect brackets the entire field—but in an evolving schema.

Husserl tried to free philosophy or, for that matter any systematic thought process, from assumptions or preconceived notions of being. What one knows is limited to "that prime consciousness which presents the given immediately." What is it that one apprehends when an object presents itself to him? What is given to his comprehension? That "given" is called phenomenal as it is apprehended by the individual. This by no means says that reality is subjective. It has an objective existence which is what gives verity to perception. In a paradoxical way it could almost be said that through a process of psychological reduction, an attitude of what Husserl called *Epoche* is achieved. By a mental removal of the intending ego from his own subjectivity, the phenomenologist is able to view that subjectivity objectively.

The method, therefore, is one of defining any object, not necessarily material, as the object of any activity of man, emotional, aesthetic, intuitive or cognitive, so that it constitutes that which presents itself to man, what is known, or lived, or desired, or conversely is doubted, hated or repelled. It applies in modified forms to abstraction, a geometric figure, a circle or square, to the purely imaginative, a pink elephant or to any material object of the senses. Its chief importance, and it is highly important, lies in the adaptation of its methodology to the emerging philosophies of this century and to the scientific field particularly psychology. It attributed to a material object no greater significance than to any other object. Hence, it is strongly opposed to the various predominantly materialistic systems of thought, such as those of Hume, Marx, Dewey or Russell, which attribute special position to knowledge gained by purely sensory empirical methodology. It is not empirical, nor is it deductive—it is "elucidative." When something is presented to man, he suspends judgment as to its "eidos," its essence, roughly until it is stripped to reveal its true nature. The opinions of others are not accepted at this point, or at all, except in a subsequent comparative situation after the analysis is complete. The method returns approximately to where men stood before Descartes' attempts to understand the physics of perception led to the duality separating man from the actual perceived world in which he lives and the later concentration on the philosophy of knowledge. Man once more is a being in the world and of the world which surrounds him. It almost returned to Descartes' own intuitive answer "man sees with his soul."

Husserl holds that there are two modes of science active in any investigation. The first is factual, resting on scientific experience, and the second essential (eidetic) aiming at the intuition of essence. As he developed his system, he progressed toward an idealistic attitude, and his system followed a somewhat similar evolution. This process was in terms of "add on" steps in analysis leading Husserl intentionally, and finally, to a transcendental reduction. At this time, Husserl reasserted his Idealistic background and terms this philosophic viewpoint, Transcendental-phenomenological Idealism. The end point is a total system which, is related to the Neo-Kantian idealism—except that the Kantian formal *a priori* logical laws do not have a counterpart in phenomenology.

Husserl pointed out the developing crisis in thought which was becoming apparent in his later years. Regarding this situation, James Collins says (Collins, 1969, page 372):

> In his final period, Husserl was not confident about working out all the lines of intentional genesis and thereby displaying the evidence for his philosophy in a coercive way. But he did maintain that a study of the crisis between Western sciences and humanism leads to three unavoidable conclusions. First, the cultural crisis is being generated by the philosophical dilemma between objectivism or naturalism and transcendentalism. Next, the remedy for this situation is not to be found in some higher synthesis but in recognizing that the proper intent of modern philosophy is to achieve that integral rationalism or transcendental doctrine of the intending ego and its world which is fundamental in Husserl's own thought. And finally, it is one and the same thing to accept this integral rationalism, to maintain the self-founding will to rationality or practico-transcendental faith in reason, and to realize an authentic humanism.

There appears to be at least a familial resemblance in the relation of subject to object in empirical research between Husserl's phenomenological perception and Max Weber's sociological concept of "Verstehen." At the time of Husserl's death at Freiburg, April 27, 1938, the majority of his followers did not accept his idealism and this aspect of his philosophy, uniquely his, essentially died with him.

Max Scheler was born in Munich in 1874. He was originally

a pupil of Rudolph Euken (1846-1926), and taught at the Universities of Jean, Munich and Cologne. He drew from Euken much of the spiritualistic idealistic metaphysics which he showed in development of his metaphysical concepts in the phenomenologist group to which he became attached early in his academic career. Euken contributed much to the chief difference between Husserl and Scheler which lay in their concept of man's knowledge. Where Husserl saw two kinds of knowledge, Scheler saw a third kind, the metaphysical, that which is at and beyond the borders of cognitive science but yet touching the intuitive. It is like a cluster of three mutually overlapping circles, but having greater commonality between the metaphysical and the intellectual. The new concept was applied to man; it was called meta-anthropology. While Husserl continues to dominate the phenomenologist group to the extent there is such an independent school, Max Scheler probably currently has a greater following largely in extension into other philosophic systems and is of greater current importance. On this point, Collins says (page 106):

> In Europe and America, the philosophy of Max Scheler (1874-1928) is undergoing a remarkable and paradoxical renascence. He has been hailed by diametrically opposed groups as a saving guide in the midst of intellectual chaos. His emphasis upon philosophical anthropology as the basic, unifying discipline has met with renewed approval in the wake of the second World War and its shattering effect upon European humanism. Many searching individuals have turned also for religious support to his speculation about God as a component in the travail of mankind. Scheler's "partnership pantheism," in which God realizes Himself by means of human efforts, has exercised the same attraction as the evolutionary notion of a finite developing deity. Man is no longer alone and worthless, if he can be shown to be a co-worker with divinity in the furtherance of cosmic ends.

Scheler's life, short as it was (he died when he was 54) may be broken into three periods. The first is dominated by Euken and even more by St. Augustine, whom Scheler saw as the great doctor of the concept of love between God and man. The second (1913-1922), one in which he produced his mature works as a convinced Christian. The third, a brief period until his death in which he veered to pantheism with the concept that the love God had for him was, in a sense, God's love for His own emanation. He died before completing any really substantive work on this theory. Because of the differences in the three separate periods, it is hard to identify Scheler's views on the basis of any one of them or to say of any single work, "This was Scheler's view."

We are indebted to Scheler for a clear formulation and explanation, or elucidation, of the millenia-old philosophic question, "Why is there something rather than nothing?" Aristotle had termed an understanding of that *question* the beginning of wisdom. When Scheler turned the question around and produced the awkward answering proposition "not nothing is" or "there is not nothing" to convey the idea of the universe that observably is, he was drawing profound, if gauche, attention to a *fait accompli*.

But let us let Scheler speak for himself. On this matter Scheler had written:

> But the *first* and most direct self-evident insight is that already postulated in establishing the sense of the expression "doubt about something" (about the being of something, the truth of a proposition, etc.): put in the form of a judgment, it states that *there is something* (in general) or to put it more acutely, that *there is not nothing*—the word "nothing" here denoting not simply the non-being-anything or non-existence of a thing, but that *absolute nothing* whose negation of being does *not*—"as yet" discriminate in the negated being between thusness (So-sein), or essence, and existence (Dasein). The situation that *there is not nothing* is at one and the same time the object of the first and most direct self-evident insight and the object of the most intense, the ultimate philosophical wonder, though I grant that this emotional response cannot come to fruition until it has been preceded, among the emotional acts conducive to the philosophical attitude, by the adoption of that humility which abolishes the taken-for-granted, self-evident character of being as a fundamental fact and even undermines it as an *obvious* fact. *This* insight, then, is evident to me with invincible clarity, no matter where I turn my attention, whatever I look

upon and however it be more closely determined according to secondary categories of being—whether it be quality or existence, noumenal or phenomenal, a real or objective non-real entity, an object or subject, an ideal or a resistant object, valuate or value-neuter "existential" being, whether it be substantial, attributive, accidental or relational; possible, necessary or actual; timeless, purely durational, past, present or future; true (as e.g. a proposition), valid or prelogical; purely mental and fictive like the wholly imaginary "mountain of gold" or a merely imagined feeling or extra-mental or both mental and extra-mental. Choose where you will, with *every* example within one or more interlinked and overlapping "kinds" of being, as with every one of these categories themselves, the clarity of this primary insight is such that it outshines *everything* which can in any conceivable way be brought into comparison with it. But whoever has not, so to speak, looked into the abyss of absolute nothing will indeed completely overlook the eminent positivity inherent in the insight that there is something and not rather nothing; he will begin with one or other of the perhaps no less self-evident insights which are, nevertheless, posterior and subordinate in self-evidence to this insight, as for example the insight in *cogito ergo sum,* or such intuitions as that there is truth, that there is judgment, that there are feelings, or that we have a "picture" or the world.

The something that exists *de facto* renders the contrary situation impossible—a phenomenological and ontological contradiction. Since the condition existence, or being-in-existence observably stands before us as a phenomenological object, necessarily the condition "nothing" has no status in phenomenology, not even as imaginary, it is literally inconceivable. Scheler put the statement in the negative form partly to emphasize how impossible it would be to make the companion reverse statements "not anything is" or "there is not anything." It is somewhat like Descartes' "cogito" to which it is closely related. Its simplicity repels its refutation—"I think, therefore I am" or "not nothing is" make the contrary positions ridiculous even to contemplate. No amount of intellectual reduction will provide an idea of the contrary essences of a state of non-being or thought without an existent-intending ego. With Descartes, the reason for the present tense is obvious—he was temporal. In the latter case, however, Scheler subtly suggests, through usage of the negative form and the present tense, that the case "not nothing," so apparent around us might be temporal also in its individual forms just as Descartes was, just as Scheler was. Thus, it might not always have been or always continue to be. The case "not nothing is," might not necessarily be the case. It invites, even demands, that the intrinsic necessity of the situation be next considered.

For the situation "nothing" to be the case, there must be complete absence of thing or being since by definition, which reduces to a necessary tautology—if not nothing is—thing is, and—nothing is not. It remains to be shown that thing or being necessarily is the case. That is, for us to be able to say that it is inconceivable that the condition, not nothing is, is not the unalterable situation or, to simplify the terminology, that being in existence as essence or essences in being is necessary intrinisically and hence eternally. "Intrinsic necessity" here is defined as a characteristic possessed by a state, condition or being such that its imputed absence involves a contradiction in terms such that the state, condition or being is denied. For example, it is intrinsically necessary that all points on a circle be equally distant from the center. If the points are not equidistant, the figure is necessarily not a circle. If the points are all equidistant, the figure is necessarily a circle. If, and only if, all points are equidistant from the center, the figure is a circle. We want to be able to say if, and only if, there is being in existence eternally, is there a possible current condition of not nothing or being in existence, as the case observable.

The relationship between "the nothing" and "being-in-existence" is not that of a dialectic-produced, competitive tension between opposing polar positions both having actuality. The case "nothing" is a mere theoretical monopole having actuality only if the case "being in existence" is denied. Being and non-being are mutually exclusive absolutes.

As would be expected, there is a parallel in pure mathematics. A continuum of magnitude exists from greatest to least, but it does not include the concept zero. The continuum exists between the infinitesimal and the infinite, neither of which are numerically achievable. The infinitesimal is less than any pre-assigned value, however small, and infinity is greater than any pre-assigned value, however large. But at every position between, value or magnitude exists. The qualitative difference from zero at any magnitude is absolute. A function is said to "vanish" if it assumes the position zero. The difference between being and non-being is qualitatively complete. There is no definition of one in terms of the other, only a negation of one or the other. The extent to which being exists in terms of specific differentiating essences is quantitatively relative, but its distinction from non-being is absolute.

By very definition then, a condition nothing or non-being has no magnitude, resource, or capacity, however small. A statement to the contrary is necessarily false since that statement would be intrinsically contradictory in terms. The observable current state "there is not nothing," therefore cannot owe its present actuality to any growth from, or development out of, a previous state "there is nothing," or "there is not anything." Since there are only two possible absolute positions with no middle ground—"there is not nothing"—or—"there is not anything," then the state "there is not nothing" must owe its present observable condition to a continuation of the same state previously existing.

The condition "there is not nothing" then must be an intrinsic and necessary one since no sequence, however long, could produce a state of "there is not nothing" from one of "there is not anything." The concepts are totally incompatible; there is no possible blending or grading of one into the other. We therefore can indeed say, "If, and only if, there is being in existence eternally is there a current condition of "not nothing is?" Further, the constituitive "stuff" of being in existence in whatever manifestation, has no external resource to draw upon to increase or contrariwise "heat sink" in which to dissipate, for either resource or heat sink implies a form of being and the exchange would be merely a transformation in form. Therefore, all the *resource* of being must have been eternally existing. Being is absolute!

Have we forgotten the concept of spontaneous generation or Holbach's spontaneous matter in motion? Bertrand Russell had said that it was certainly an odd concept but he was not about to say that oddness was equivalent to impossibility. What is involved is a problem of the intellectual coherence of a "free-standing-predicate" a generation without a progenitor—a motion without the mover (something). The proposition is excessively odd, and even rigorously illogical. There is absolutely no way of filling in the blank of the missing subject—that from which, or by which, or out of which, the designated activity proceeds—by which the case "not something" becomes the case "not nothing."

The case or state or condition "nothing," thus, in view of the observable being in existence, including the observer's own, is inconceivable, a negation of what is observable. In attempts to conjure up an idea of such a situation—nothing—we must necessarily relate it to the situation, something, by subtraction. The question, or perhaps, the answer, as to why is there something rather than nothing becomes a statement of the necessity of being-in-existence. It is so necessarily. The non-existence of being-in-existence—the case of not anything is inconceivable in view of the extent case, being is. The situation "nothing" necessarily has no actuality presently or eternally.

Scheler concludes from the fact that, "there is not nothing, a second self-evident insight":

> And so the insight that there is an absolute entity, or an entity through which every non-absolute entity has, and holds, its attributive being, forms the *second self-evident insight*. For if (as we clearly recognize with each example of an entity, no matter what) there is something (in general) rather than nothing, then in our "examples," to be reviewed at will, that part of them which is relative not-being (both not-being-anything and non-existence) can indeed be attributed to the possible contingencies and relativities which their being possesses from other entities including even the knowing subject), but this is never possible in respect of their positive being itself. It is no inference merely, but a direct intuition, which tells us that this being demands a source in an entity pure and simple which is *devoid* of any more restrictive determination. (Emphasis Scheler.)

Thus flowing from the concept of absoluteness of being, Scheler sees the necessity of an absolute being. This is an intuitive determination in the strong phenomenological sense of the word. Scheler sees the relative being (relative to total being in existence) in the universe about us as grounded in the absolute. The absolute being is the undergirding fact of all being, actual and potential. In his "intellect," all external, and hence relative, being and existence, actual and potential, have eternal reality in accord with his eternally efficacious "will." Scheler in fact defines philosophy as "the intuitive understanding of individual essences in their relationship to the absolute being and its essence."

In his final pantheistic phase, Scheler saw in the unfolding of existence the fulfillment of the Godhead, and this primarily through man as an agency. Hence, his viewpoint acquired its label "the partnership Pantheism." There were viewpoints in the Kantian derivation quite similar, Hegel for instance, but Scheler saw it somehow as one of developing essence and somehow a function of time in a "becoming" mode of being. The "stuff" of essential being in existence was eternally there, but the texture and realized essence were of a developing pattern.

It is interesting to compare and combine essentialist Scheler's concept with that of St. Anselm, a devoted philosopher of being, in his ontological "proof" of the existence of God which we briefly looked at earlier. As we saw, Anselm's was a concept used by Descartes and others—as a coercive proof—but denied in that usage by Aquinas and Kant. That concept hinges on two definitions: (1) God is that being—that something—than which nothing greater can be conceived of and, (2) God is that being, that something, inconceivable as not existing. It also, at least implicitly, hinges on the fact that there is not nothing carried to its conclusion as to the necessity of being in existence. As we have seen, Anselm pursued that point in his *Monologium,* before his *Proslogium,* but did not proceed to its conclusion as to the necessity of being in existence, apparently considering it self-evident, as in fact so does Scheler.

The terms "being," "essence," and "existence" are all intimately involved in the mysterious concatenation of circumstances which results in the situation "there is not nothing." The sequence normally followed is, that there is no existence of essence without being in which to subsist, but the actuality of being requires its existence and an essence which distinguishes it from other forms of being and makes "it" what "it" is— therefore, yielding the relationship—of being in existence, having some specific essence, or essences. Being has actuality only in the existence of specific essence or essences.

All natural existents we have experienced, or can conceive of, are also conceivable as not existing. Thus, any real existent material entity, an atom or a galaxy, can be conceived of as "not there," as having vanished from the scene. We can in fact go down the entire catalog of such existents and conceive of them as non-existent—we can conceive of a time or situation when they did not exist or when they will no longer exist. But should we subtract all of the known existents, we must still admit that we can conceive of their existence. Since they would, in fact, have existed, they are clearly "existable." Their incidental absence does not constitute a partial nothingness—only the lack of existence of a particular essence or form of something "existable." What is inconceivable, in fact, is that either their specific existence or non-existence is inconceivable. The *duality* possible in state, condition or circumstance of either existence or non-existence in the *particular* material form is therefore intrinsically necessary since the contrary constitutes a conceptual contradiction. But, while the duality is necessary, it is not self-necessitating. There is no intrinsic capacity of intentionality in the individual forms, including man, to modify their absolute state from non-existence to existence. They cannot self-create. Somewhere within that being in existence, globally conceived and previously shown to be necessarily existing, therefore inconceivable as not existing, must be a determining, intentional essence upon which all the real and potential but non-absolute (since their existence or non-existence are both conceivable) existents depend and have depended for their conceivability and reality. "Somewhere," there must be that absolute being inconceivable as not existing whose own existence is explicit in its essence. Its very nature demands its existence and is its existence.

But if being in existence has an intentional and determining essence which characterizes it at some level, it must have a corresponding characteristic being at that level in which to subsist in the sense of "I think, therefore I am," and therefore, in that sense, to be personal. The non-existence of the being inconceivable as not existing would render the previously established necessary condition "not nothing is" unnecessary—a contradiction in terms. The statement, "The being inconceivable as not existing does not exist" is false, necessarily. And here the statement is not, as with the ontological argument of St. Anselm, one standing by itself, since the being's *actual* existence has been established as necessary and not left implicit. Further, since controlling the existence or non-existence of all being in existence, the being inconceivable as not existing must be greater than any being or existence whose state of existence it determines. It must be greater than all such being of which we can conceive. Therefore, the necessary being must be greater than any being of which we can conceive within our possible knowledge. Anselm's further definition becomes a mere corollary. Since a real being is greater than the equivalent being in concept only, to avoid contradiction, we must conceive of the being inconceivable as not existing as a real being. If it is necessary, it is real. That Being, than which nothing greater can be conceived, exists in reality as the necessary being. That being is called God.

It has been argued that, yes, we can agree that individually no observable entity has within its essence the characteristic of intentionality relative to its own self-creation or self-annihilation, but it may be that, in the total complex, they collectively have that characteristic. Cannot an intentionality or a willing be other than personal—the analogy of nuclear detonation indicates a possibility? The reason why an aggregate of certain critical mass of Uranium 235 can self-detonate, whereas a smaller mass cannot, is not an example, though it has been used. The mass action entering into the chain reaction is a composite effect of identical characteristics possessed by all Uranium 235 atomic essences to fission individually with a certain probability. Accumulation of the critical mass only permits the action to be accelerated by conditioning the environment. The mass required is determined by the individual probabilities. But intentionality does not exist in the same way. The problem of spontaneous fission has previously been mentioned and will be looked at again critically in Part III.

But what constitutes the characteristic of intentionality? What is it that distinguishes intentionality? We saw that Descartes' "cogito" draws attention not only to existence of the thinking person but also the reflective consciousness of that existence which could as an intending ego direct itself to and consider itself as an object of its own thought—however biased that view might be. There was thus a degree of autonomy not possessed by any other known physical creature. Man can thus conceive of various courses of action, reflect on the consequences, decide between the courses of action then evaluate the actual results of his action and, further, even reflect on what might otherwise have been. Intentionality requires a combined act of intellect and will in the decision process. It is the antonym of randomness.

The ideal "General Will of Rosseau" was the consensus of individual wills and did not give to a state as a freestanding legal entity any intentional power not possessed by the individuals. It could not direct attention or consider or decide except as individuals within the corporate body decided. The characteristic existed at the *personal* level *before* it could exist at the corporate. If the characteristic, intentionality, exists in an essence it is prima facie evidence that that essence is personal and possessed of self-consciousness; intentionality is a personal not a distributive characteristic.

The combination of Scheler and Anselm gives few handholds for logical attack and is logically coercive rather than only intuitive even in the strong phenomenological sense of Scheler's derivation. Scheler of Anselm would have spurned this detailed analysis, both relying heavily on the leap of intuitional insight which at least in the case of Scheler he considered superior to rational analysis. Being more earthbound, we have to follow the more tedious procedure and reduce the extent of the leap while arriving at the same conclusions.

The critical difference between an approach through "essence" and an approach through "being" is also apparent. Both Husserl and Scheler, while they discussed the "intending ego" as subject, were more concerned with the "characteristics" or "essential qualities" of objects of the intention than they were in the being in which the intending essence resided. It was thus a natural tendency for Scheler to apply the characteristic of intentionality to a generalized universal being, comprehending all being, than to identify a discrete personal being possessed of these essential characteristics. He went back to the solution of the one and the many proposed by Heraclitus "unity in diversity." On the other hand, Anselm was far more concerned with establishing the nature of the being in whom the characteristics resided as an existent being. In his route, the tendency to move toward Pantheism and a role of intentionality as process disappears.

For the purposes of this approach to God's existence it does not matter whether our personal individuality is the case or not. If we are real conscious selves in this natural, i.e., created order, we had a causal base in the natural order. If we are real, it is real. Further that causal base, if proximate had a causal base in the causal order to the limit of causality in the natural order. It is *intuitively* evident that nothing in the natural order is eternal. There *is* a natural limit on time. At some real remove in time, there was a real first natural entity, a first event, a first activity—a first real situational set. But the fact that "nothing is" is the present case and the fact that in the natural order alone the case "not nothing is" comes to a limit in time faces us with a past condition in which either "nothing is" is the case or there is a case "not nothing is" beyond the natural order from which the natural order came into being. But coercively the case "nothing is" can never be an antecedent to a real condition "not nothing is" where non-being defines being where non-A becomes A when non-A equals A. There must be a time-unlimited being in some supernatural order in which the natural order *finds* its causal base.

If we take the contrary position that we are mere pseudo-selves, projections of an external-self, we come to the same

conclusions. That external projecting self as being either itself
unlimited in time or again dependent upon being which is time-
unlimited. We are faced inexorably with the conclusion that
there is time-unlimited being which is to say external being external to the natural order in time.

The impact which the thought of Max Scheler has had on
current thinking has already been mentioned. It should be added
that probably the most important contribution of phenomenology to philosophy in this period is that it has served as a bridge
between the nineteenth century thought and that of the late
twentieth century. It has been the seedbed of concepts in both
the new philosophy of existence and the ancient philosophy
of being, the two truly challenging systems of philosophic
thought now apparently moving into position of dominance
and we will encounter additional phenomenologists in those
contexts. In the main, the phenomenologists failed to achieve
their objective (as did the life philosophers who had the same
goal) to somehow "actualize" being, man in particular. The
"eidos" of man is characterized by the phenomenal processes
of living, thinking and acting. The ideational or spiritual and
material vectors in man are not integrated. God remains an essence involved in phenomenal process. The "whatness" of man
and God does not provide the answers to who is man and who
is God. Thus, in the long run, the phenomenologists failed also
to establish a credible metaphysics. With them, man still remained a Kantian split personality though the individual can
never see himself that way, for to him he remains one person—a
unique being.

Section 5—Philosophy of Existence

Undoubtedly existentialism, that philosophic doctrine which
gives the human experiencing of life the highest place in defining reality is the most widely known of the modern philosophies
in spite of the fact that it is in many ways the "least knowable."
Its chief representatives frequently have been individuals who
were themselves dramatists in one sense or another and used
the media of stage and popular literature, including both prose
and poetry, to attain public exposure for their concepts. Albert
Camus, probably the most dramatically gifted of the highly gifted
group, has said, "Feelings and images multiply philosophy by
ten" and this expressed both their approach and appeal. It is
hence the popular image of existentialism which comes to most
people's minds. Thus, also, existentialism has been described
as a current of thought or movement at least as frequently as

it has been described as a philosophic system. However, these chief representatives are philosophers in the deepest sense of the word in methodology as well as conceptuality. But for some, the better known, their presentation is much more in the order of an art form—a mode of conveying a sense of meaning by overall impression than it is a methodology of coercive logic. It is very close to being an inverted logic, in fact.

The existentialists see themselves as addressing the fundamental problems of human existence from the viewpoint of the individual as he confronts the problem. Existentialists' cornerstone is man in his experiencing of his existence. Everything else, all other reality, including God Himself for those of the theistic wing, is viewed in the light of interplay in terms of man's existence. Man's highest attribute is freedom to be himself.

Existentialism is a new approach, though its subject matter is ancient. Its deepest systemic roots go no farther back than Kierkegaard, and it has borrowed heavily from the recent methodology of the phenomenologists. The key to the existentialists' thought is experience, which is closely related to the idea of the phenomenal. Their hyphenated, synthetic language is strange to older philosophic usage. An example is the recent popular cliche "togetherness," and its antonym "one-selfness." The first is an expression which connotes that intimate relationship wherein one man's experienced existence and problems are inextricably intertwined with those of his associates. All are bound together in a tight, multi-faceted interaction in conflict or in community with God or against God. It is this aspect in fact which makes dramatization such an excellent vehicle for existentialistic ideas. "One-selfness" thus, obviously has a highly unfavorable connotation.

Each representative has a different grasp of the way he sees reality, but all agree that there is no division between subjective and objective reality. What reality is for the individual, it is, as the individual experiences it and copes with it. Knowledge is not divided into intuitive and intellectual knowledge. Again, how "it," anything, is perceived and experienced in a single package by the individual comprises his unique knowledge. His life is, life for him, what he makes of it. It is the authentic life for him that is all that matters. Authenticity is the key to life fulfilled. As would be expected, the range of viewpoints is enormous. As a consequence it is necessary to examine a fairly large number of the existentialists to get a real idea of the scope and detail which this "series of systems" involves. For instance, Sartre and Merleau-Ponty were closely associated at one time, but one can scarcely imagine two more divergent approaches to philosophic questions. Further, at this juncture in history and in the theme of this work, existentialism seems to hold the key to the direction of future thought and must be examined in both extent and depth.

As was stated before, there is a deep cleavage within the school. In fact it has two wings, the theist wing and the atheist wing. The writer thinks this analysis can be viewed best by "experiencing" its representatives Sartre and Camus, atheists; Jasper, Marcel and Buber representing Protestant, Catholic and Jewish viewpoints respectively; theists, Heidegger, generally classed as an atheist but seen rather at the middle ground, who, in fact, even disclaims being an existentialist, and finally Merleau-Ponty, psychologist-phenomenologist who while searching remained uncommitted, but seemed to be tending toward theism at the time of his premature death. Before discussing the individual representatives, it is necessary to mention something about the general attitude of the group toward religion. For this purpose a statement by Collins is appropriate:

> Where do the existentialists leave us in their treatment of the theme of religion? Precisely where they want to; as individuals responsible for our own interpretation of that aspect of human existence. The existentialists do not impose a decision upon us about the nature of religion, and they do not even confront us with a uniform final answer of their own. Their achievement lies in another direction, and it is two-fold. The first result is to make the questions dealing with man's religious relationship important ones, not only for a specialized philosophy of religion but for the whole tissue of philosophical inquiry today. In the second place, they present us with a wide spectrum of possible positions which can be taken on religion from a starting point in philosophy. Their positions are by no means exhaustive alternatives, but they do sharpen many of the issues involved in any discussion on religion and thus invite us to make our own reflections about it.
>
> Another common premise shared by the existentialists is that, in our human world of widely diverse religions, the Judeo-Christian tradition conserves the most values and achieves the highest unification. Consequently, religious transcendence is usually interpreted

by them to mean a reference of the human person to the transcendent personal God. The intentional meaning of religious faith is only fulfilled through a reference to a personal being which is other than the human self. Hence the I-and-Thou pattern is accepted as characterizing the human existent's relationship with the Transcendent Reality. The practical commitment characteristic of the theistic religious response provides another piece of testimony, since it intends to be a response to the holiness and the demanding initiative of a personal God, not merely of an ideal standard.

Where the existentialists part company is over their evaluation of this description of the religious situation. Sartre will call for a reconsideration of every statement in the description, in order to show that the whole religious structure leads to frustration rather than fulfillment. Heidegger will put a large set of parentheses around the entire matter by declaring it outside the bounds set for philosophical inquiry. Marcel will use the description as a basis for uncovering some enduring traits of participating being and its real ordination to God.

The common characteristic of the Existentialist philosophers of all persuasions is the dialectic in-built under their concept of man as a being in the world. The dialectic is that between man as an ontological being—being-in-itself—that which he in sheer reality is and the epistemological being—being-for-itself—man's knowledge of himself and his relationships in his self-consciousness and his consciousness of the outside world. They ask the question, "Can we know ourselves in our relations to self and others?" and follow this with another compound question, "How do we conceive of ourselves—how do we arrive at authentic self-knowledge and hence self-realization?" In most instances, they arrive at a situation in duality. While we are conscious of the fact that we are the same individual extant today that we were yesterday or when we were children—and in spite of Hume's hypothesis, we are also aware that we are far from being the same person in viewpoints, capabilities, interests, aspirations, behavior patterns and emotions—that "person" changes as it were momentarily. We became the person we are today and we will become the person we will be tomorrow and next year. Further, we become what we are principally through our lived experience in existence. How is the being we are this instant distinguished from that being which we in sheer actuality are? A colt matures and becomes a horse in a far different way than a child matures and becomes a beggar, merchant, or a chief. In the former process there is no dialectic. It is that human "momentariousness" of the being-for-itself as it has progressively modified being-in-itself which distinguishes man from all other beings. To personalize for a minute, myself is my actuality—the myself I am for me causes the difficulty. I see myself for differently than I in actuality am or as others see me—Socrates admonition to "know thyself" may be a total impossibility. And it may be that true self is only an instantaneous differential from the past moving to the future.

Each of the existentialists sees the problem and its solution differently. In general, the atheists see man as a futile exercise in absurdity, almost as a freak of nature—an unfortunate chance occurrence that we, the victims, must nonetheless make the best of. Each moment must be lived for its own sake. The theists view man as life in an encounter, in temporality—of a searching and growing through temporal relationship for the final encounter with the ultimate "other"—the infinite, timeless, relationship with God. It almost seems once the existentialists have locked into a position, one way or the other, that they are obsessed by it.

With a few exceptions, the existentialist dialogues are conducted at right angles in terms of the rational world—it is there but the rational vector has little bearing on their theme. One notable exception, the late Merleau-Ponty, through his detailed phenomenological work on the structure of behavior had finally arrived at a synthesis of being-in-itself and for-itself as a singular rather than dualistic concept, as we shall see. Whether he could have remained an existentialist in philosophical posture afterwards, we of course, will never know.

Jean Paul Sartre was born in Paris, June 21, 1905. He was raised from infancy by his grandfather, Charles Schweitzer, who took the boy upon his father's death. His grandfather was an uncle of Albert Schweitzer, the famous doctor, philosopher and missionary. Sartre did not emulate Schweitzer in the least, however, for Schweitzer saw the conditions of the world in terms antithetical to Sartre. In 1923, Albert Schweitzer had written that the tragedy of the West lay in the decline of spiritual values which in turn led to the "state of uncivilization" in which we find ourselves. Sartre is a graduate of the Ecole Normale Superieure in Paris and there developed an early dislike for the mathematically-oriented philosophy of Descartes. In fact, it seems to have had a reverse impact on him. It was too mechanical. In 1933 and 1934, he spent a year at the Institute of France in Berlin in between his work as a teacher, chiefly in the outskirts of Paris. During this period he became acquainted with the works of Heidegger and Husserl, both were oriented to phenomenology and both greatly influenced the philosophy Sartre was to develop in later years.

His first published works were in fiction, chiefly short stories. In the period of World War II, he introduced the phenomenology of Husserl and existentialism of Heidegger to France. He has said of himself that he was in his early years obsessed with metaphysics which grew from fantasies in his own lonely childhood, and that in middle life he was delivered from it by his adoption of Marxism with its idea of salvation through action.

Sartre is a master of many forms of literature, something in which he resembles Voltaire, though their style is greatly different. He has written, in addition to short stories, two novels, *La Naussee,* his first and perhaps greatest, and *La Chemins de la Liberta.* In drama, *The Flies, No Exit,* and *The Condemned of Alma,* in 1960, are his best known general works. The essays *Existentialism and Humanism,* published in English in 1964, and a longer monologue, *Critique de la Raison Dialectique* are probably his best known works in philosophy as such. He was a co-founder of the review *Les Temps Modernes.*

In all his works, he utilizes the dramatic theme to carry forward his basic philosophical ideas. The theme has changed over the years from his earlier works emphasizing mere fantasy, with salvation seen in art, to his later Marxist action theme, "The man who would do good must soil his hands." Sartre's view is the opposite of a determinist. And he sees existentialism as its necessary counterpoise. He sees the fact of human freedom as evidence of this characteristic. He sees freedom as a heavy burden to mankind, since it brings as concomitants responsibility, guilt and internalized remorse and punishment. He also sees in it the foundation of his idea of the dignity of man, since it is this freedom which makes man like a god.

In his later life, Sartre became involved in politics. He helped found the Republican-Democrat Rally, a left facing organization, and then shifted to support of communism when the Rally failed. He supported Cuba against the U.S. and also chaired Russell's Viet Nam War Crimes Tribunal in Stockholm and openly advocated Russian intervention for North Viet Nam even at the risk of global war. He was already nearly blind when Russia invaded Afghanistan. It is said he opposed that adventure, but as a true Marxist found excuses.

It is obvious from the outset that each existentialist philosopher is going to look at man, *qua* man, differently because of the composite objective-subjective, variegated image each will develop. It has been said that each existentialist philosopher's work tells us much more about him as an individual than it does about the world and its denizens. But the range of viewpoints is made more tractable by concentration on their views of man as being-in-the-world as it is modified by the emphasis each puts on the dialectic concept being-in-itself and being-for-itself which puts an ontological bias on the two existential aspects.

For Sartre, a consciousness is a nothingness of being, "which manifests ifself in its own nihilation of being." It exists, "as at a distance from itself" and this "empty distance which that being carries in itself is nothingness." His is almost a Humean concept—there is no real individual self represented by a consciousness of self, only a series of events through which the individual lives. Thus, instantaneous being-for-itself becomes almost the totality of man as being-in-the-world the ultimate form and role of man in life.

From this attitude we expect and find Sartre emphasizing man as a totally independent being who should seek to find fulfillment in living each discrete instant which must stand on its own feet as an event of existence to be savored or despised depending upon the mood.

Speaking of the dialectic itself Sartre says, "This perpetually disappearing contingency of the in-itself which pervades the for-itself and attaches it to being-in-itself without ever letting it be captured is what we shall call the *facticity* of the-for-itself."

Sartre's influence among the young intellectuals, particularly the students of the 1960's, was great, since the theme he espoused was the pursuit of freedom of the human spirit, regardless of cost or morality, a theme which characterized that period. Sartre's philosophy seems to reveal a reaction to the sheer materialism which dominated the mainstream of modern thought. Yet, he is attracted to the most materialistic theme of them all—Marxism—and Sartre's logical antecedent is Hume. In his *Critique of Dialectic Reason,* he has said "Nothing happens to man and objects except in their material being and by the materiality of being." To this writer, the only thing that saves his works from the hackneyed Marxist polemic is his sense of drama and his dedication to the phenomenological method. He nevertheless refuses to look critically at Marxism in that light.

Sartre tried to unite Marxism with Existentialism into a single philosophy but failed completely. Marxism was not compatible for a variety of obvious reasons.

Sartre sees man to be a pensive animal whose gifts may be more apparent than real. In *L'etre et la Neant,* Sartre argues that there is no moral law—"Man is a useless passion." In *St. Genet,* he describes men an "impossible nullities." This view is compatible with Hobbesian and Nietzschean ideas. No one respects the freedom of others. All relations between human beings are conflicts. In his later work, *Existentialism and Humanism,* Sartre changes this to say that morality consists in the obligation and pursuit of our own freedom and in respecting and even assisting in securing the rights of others. Each man is responsible to all for the values he affirms in his way of life. Life has no other meaning. On this point Sartre in that work had written:

> If, on the other hand, existence precedes essence, and if we grant that we exist and fashion our image at one and the same time, the image is valid for everyone and for our whole age. Thus, our responsibility is much greater than we might have supposed, because it involves all mankind. If I am a working man and choose to join a Christian trade union rather than be a Communist, and if by being a member I want to show that the best thing for man is resignation, that the kingdom of man is not of this world, I am not only involving my own case—I want to be resigned for everyone. As a result, my action has involved all humanity. . .
>
> When we speak of forlornness, a term Heidegger was fond of, we mean only that God does not exist and that we have to face all the consequences of this. The existentialist is strongly opposed to a certain kind of secular ethics which would like to abolish God with the least possible expense. About 1880, some French teachers tried to set up a secular ethics which went something like this: God is a useless and costly hypothesis: we are discarding it: but, meanwhile, in order for there to be an ethics, a society, a civilization, it is essential that certain values be taken seriously and that they be considered as having an *a*

priori existence. It must be obligatory, *a priori,* to
be honest, not to lie, not to beat your wife, to have
children, etc., etc. So we're going to try a little device which will make it possible to show that values
exist all the same, inscribed in a heaven of ideas,
though otherwise God does not exist. In other
words—and this, I believe, is the tendency of everything called reformism in France—nothing will be
changed if God does not exist. We shall find ourselves with the same norms of honesty, progress, and
humanism, and we shall have made of God an outdated hypothesis which will peacefully die off by
itself. . .

The existentialist, on the contrary, thinks it very
distressing this God does not exist, because all possibility of finding values in a heaven of ideas disappears along with Him; there can no longer be an *a
priori* Good, since there is no infinite and perfect
consciousness to think it. Nowhere is it written that
the Good exists, that we must be honest, that we
must not lie; because the fact is we are on a plane
where there are only men. Dostoevsky said "If God
didn't exist everything would be possible." This is
the very starting point of existentialism. Indeed,
everything is permissible if God does not exist and
as a result man is forlorn, because neither within him
nor without does he find anything to cling to. He
can't start making excuses for himself.

Sartre died April 15, 1980.

Albert Camus was born at Modovi, near Constantine, Algiers,
November 7, 1913. He scarcely knew his father who was killed
in World War I. He attended the University of Algiers but did
not pursue post-graduate studies at that time because of illness.
His early and continuing primary interest lay in technical aspects
of the stage. His first work, *L'Envers et L'Endroit* was a collection of sensitive essays centering on man's evanescence and fragility. He went to France in 1939 and joined the resistance
movement there in 1942, which in a way symbolizes his philosophy of life. He had a passionate regard for the plight of man
in the constraints of the surrounding world throughout his life.
In his works, essays, novels and plays the theme is of the absurdity of life—the irrational nature of the world. *La Peste, The
Plague,* published in 1948 was typical in its dramatic appeal

in that central theme. Camus prepared adaptations for the theater of works which carried out this same idea. For Dostoevsky, *The Possessed* in 1959, and for William Faulkner's *Requiem for a Nun* in 1956. His concept of life in this world was of man in revolt against all restraints, yet in a spirit of close-knit comradery in which humanity can best cope with the absurdities of life. It was a concept of an atheistic humanism in an environment of pathos. Camus was killed in an auto accident in 1960 at the age of 46.

Camus was a philosopher who always maintained that he was not a philosopher but only an artist. Yet he was interested in philosophy, was a student of philosophy—and he wrote almost exclusively in a philosophic vein. He further strove to establish his philosophical ideas particularly through his literary works. While he was very much an independent thinker, Nietzsche was the dominant influence on his thought; and through Camus, Nietzsche, in renewal, has had a substantial impact on current thought in promoting a philosophical speculation placing rationality and irrationality in dialectic juxtaposition. For a good many years Camus was a close associate of Sartre although the two became estranged in later years by Sartre's preoccupation with Marxism and Camus' disinclination to involve himself in activist politics after a history of unselfish dedication to the French resistance. Camus was a quiet, unassuming individual but thoroughly courageous in upholding his viewpoint either philosophically or politically.

For Camus, both man as being-in-itself and for-itself were real and extant, though Camus' avowed thesis that only uncertainty is certain would indicate doubt as to the nature of either. But in the ever present theme among the existentialists expressing that dialectic relationship of conflict between man and his world, Camus' was that of man the revolutionist over against all the established values and constraints and it is being-for-itself striving to become being-in-itself as being-in-the-world. Life is a positive, active, groping of the consciousness to establish supremacy over the world "out there." Man is a rebel by nature even more than he becomes one. This attitude distinguishes the two outstanding atheistic existentialists one from the other. For Sartre, since being-in-itself has no permanent actuality the dialectic is conflict thrust upon man as being for-itself. The world "out there" impinges on man at every instant and man, being for-itself seizes it, throttles it as it were to squeeze his own gratification from it. He does not revolt, eventually he even becomes cooperative. Yet in their works, Camus comes through as being the less individualistic—for his revolt is always a work of a common action by a group—it is the revolt that gives the solidarity, which makes man men in confrontation against the environment not as individuals against each other or as individuals against the environment. But for both, life is a sickness—the absurd for Camus, *La Nausee* for Sartre.

In *L'Homme Revolte,* Camus says, "The solidarity of men is founded on the movement of revolt which in turn, finds its justification only in this complicity. We shall, then, have the right to say that all revolt which denies or destroys this solidarity loses at the same moment the name of revolt and actually coincides with a murderous consentment." The value of revolt is that it promotes solidarity—without solidarity it becomes a negative value.

In looking at the atheistic wing of existentialism, Camus is more explicit in his atheism, yet less overtly hostile in attitude than Sartre, hence he is more useful for purposes of this study of that aspect of existentialism. Just as we were indebted to Scheler for his "elucidation" of the concept "there is not nothing" we are indebted to Camus for his enunciation of the concept which is the theme of the atheistic wing of existentialism, regardless of how expressed, "the unreasonableness of life." Although Camus' work, *The Myth of Sisyphus* is his best known philosophical work expressing the concept of the absurd in allegory, his essay, *An Absurd Reasoning* is a statement in clear direct prose of the same concept.

Of the current prominent atheistic philosophers, Camus is the only one to state formally his reasons for his belief and the reasons are profoundly revealing as to his total philosophy as well. It is thus doubly rewarding to consider it in an analytical way. The other modern atheistic philosophers from Hume to Russell to Sartre rely on negative evidence to support their positions and as we saw in the strange case of Hume he was not an atheist except in his philosophy. The use of the negative approach is well exampled in the story of La Place in explicating to Napoleon his theory of the origin of the universe. When La Place had completed his presentation, Napoleon asked him where God fitted into the explanation; whereupon La Place is reported to have replied, "Sire, I have no need for that hypothesis." He started with Holbach's hypothesis instead—spontaneous matter in motion. The fundamental question of origin—of the fact that there is not nothing—is ignored.

After devoting a major portion of the essay, *An Absurd Reasoning,* to a discussion of philosophers and the philosophical literature of preceding history from Parmenides to Kierkegaard and Husserl and without engaging in any rational criticism of these works, but only general polemics, Camus begins to develop his own thesis. He says:

> It is futile to be amazed by the apparent paradox that leads thought to its own negation by the opposite paths of humilated reason and triumphant reason. From the abstract God of Husserl to the dazzling God of Kierkegaard the distance is not so great. Reason and the irrational lead to the same preaching. In truth, the way matters but little; the will to arrive suffices. The abstract philosopher and the religious philosopher start out from the same disorder and support each other in the same anxiety. . .Just as reason was able to soothe the melancholy of Plotinus it provides modern anguish the means of calming itself in the familiar setting of the eternal. The absurd mind has less luck. For it the world is neither so rational nor so irrational. It is unreasonable and only that. With Husserl, the reason eventually has no limits at all. The absurd, on the contrary, establishes its limits since it is powerless to calm its anguish. Kierkegaard independently asserts that a single limit is enough to negate that anguish. But the absurd does not go so far. For it that limit is directed solely at the reason's ambitions. The theme is irrational, as it is conceived by the existentialists, is reason becoming confused and escaping by negating itself. The absurd is lucid reasoning noting its limits.

Camus never describes what is considered lucid nor what are the limits, although he implies that only the absurd understands; then he continues:

> My reasoning wants to be faithful to the evidence that aroused it. That evidence is the absurd. . .Hence what he [the absurd man] demands of himself is to live solely with what he knows to accommodate himself to what is, and to bring in nothing that is not certain. He is told that nothing is. But this at least is a certainty. And it is with this that he is concerned: he wants to find out if it is possible to live *without appeal*. (Emphasis Camus.)

Gratuitously, Camus accepts as evidential fact only that nothing is certain but uncertainty. He will not make the step Descartes or Scheler did. But the conclusions of Descartes or Scheler are better supported than Camus'. That the thinker exists as a conscious subject, which Descartes considered certain or the fact that there is an existent world of things, beings as objects of thought as Scheler concluded as certain, appear in any rational approach to be of greater "certitude" than the "certitude" of uncertainty and a far better basis for a plan of thought. If Camus really believed what he preached, he should have stopped immediately. But Camus takes the same stance toward a philosophy of life as a complete skeptic or agnostic: nothing is knowable with any certitude, and then he comes to the crux of his problem:

> Knowing whether or not a man is free involves knowing whether he can have a master. The absurdity peculiar to this problem comes from the fact that the very notion that makes the problem of freedom possible also takes away its meaning. For in the presence of God there is less a problem of freedom than a problem of evil. You know the alternatives: either we are not free and God the all-powerful is responsible for evil, or we are free and responsible but God is not all-powerful. All the scholastic subtleties have neither added anything to nor subtracted anything from the acuteness of this paradox...Now if the absurd cancels all my chances of eternal freedom, it restores and magnifies, on the other hand, my freedom of action. That privation of hope and future means an increase in man's availability.

Virtually all of Camus' various theses are based on that formula. As we did with Scheler and his basic thesis "There is not nothing," we must take a critical look at Camus' fundamental concept and test its validity.

To begin with, the position that there is "nothing certain except uncertainty" is a cliche and lacks probity as evidential fact in the real world of men. It is truly an unjustified universalism; it hangs on the definition of certitude as the asymptote of truth—that which is unachievable in the created order, though it may be approached as closely as the infinitesimal. It is not the definition of certitude as decision coercing truth or facticity—the basis of all human existence. On the other hand, the conclusions of Descartes and Scheler do yield decision coercing truth, and they are antonymic of Camus' starting point. If either Descartes' or Scheler's position is tenable, Camus' is not.

Now in expanding his basic position from this foundation, Camus concludes that if the only fact is uncertainty, we may as well take that approach to life which best pleases us and proceed on that course. Camus does not deny the existence of God directly—His existence is uncertain, as is everything else, and moreover God is an inconvenient hypothesis. To restate and summarize his problem of God, Camus says in effect: If there is an omnipotent God and He, in spite of His omnipotence, permits physical evil such as the suffering of an innocent child, He is a cruel God and a cruel God is intrinsically evil. Not only is He contrary to the theistic concept of God, but if He exists He should in no event be obeyed; He should be defied, we should rebel against such tyranny. But if, on the other hand, He is not omnipotent and hence helpless to prevent evil, He is an impotent God and likewise should not be allowed to interfere with our personal freedom. But compounding this, one is conscious of the freedom one has to choose—for example, to affirm or deny God. But if He were the omnipotent God one could not be free. Camus says, "I cannot understand what kind of freedom would be given me by a higher being. I have lost the sense of hierarchy. The only conception of freedom I can have is that of the prisoner or the individual in the midst of the State. The only one I know is freedom of thought and action."

Camus has mingled two ancient problems which should be considered separately to avoid circuitry. The first proposition affirms the intrinsic incompatibility of the concept of an omnipotent, merciful God and the existence of physical evil. The second affirms the intrinsic incompatibility of the concept of an omnipotent God and human free will or freedom of choice. In a logical argument, the apparent alternatives of a cruel God, a negative attribute, or a God of limited powers are metaphysically unsound. The two problems are independent and need not, in fact ought not, be considered together.

Camus' first proposition fails, if under any conceivable conditions the infinite mercy of the omnipotent God is not incompatible with the existence of physical evil in the world, because then the apparent conceptual conflict is not intrinsic and therefore does not support the proposition. The "scholastic subtleties" referred to by Camus would go like this: Finite man is in no position to judge the purpose or motivation of the infinite

God, who is able to weigh all factors in every case. We cannot evaluate the balance between the 'malice' of particular, temporal, secular suffering and the possible value of eternal, spiritual as well as temporal benefits which result to mankind universally. God's omnipotence is preserved if the means used were the *optimum* to secure the ends God had intended, though it might entail human suffering—so does the painful warning of an abscessed tooth. Pain often serves a useful purpose, in fact it is fundamentally necessary to organize life at all levels.

Camus' second proposition fails if, under any conceivable conditions, the omnipotence of God is not incompatible with man's freedom of choice. His argument may be restated: If God is omnipotent, He is by that fact responsible for my acts, but I am conscious of my responsibility and freedom to act and I do so act. Therefore, there is no omnipotent God. The first premise puts the case, if two independent beings are involved in an act, one of which beings is omnipotent and hence *capable* of imposing its will completely on the other, the first will *always* so act and control and hence be responsible for the acts of the second. The second's freedom of action is impossible. The argument equates capability and execution. In fact, under that interpretation every conceivable possible act would have to be fully executed since within God's capability. But, capability and execution are not identical, only related through the decision of the will to exercise the capacity. Further, if capacity and execution are identical, that would deny God's own free will to elect to execute or not to execute to His full capability in every case. In that event, neither God nor man would have freedom of action. Let us take a well-known example of both theses of activity of the omnipotent and merciful God of theism.

If a Man dearly beloved of God as His only Son should freely choose to die a most miserable death by execution, maliciously contrived, thereby providing all mankind the highest model of love as well as tremendous spiritual benefits, should or would God *necessarily* interfere with that Man's free will and the free will of His executioners and murderers and prevent the suffering of the Beloved, though He surely had the capability of doing so. Was God thereby cruel, or evil, or thwarted in His own omnipotent power or was man's free will expropriated? On the contrary, even though it was considered only a pious fable, it is a conceivable situation because it has been conceived. It has been the most admired paradox of all human history, the paradox of the absurd made infinite.

Camus' thesis therefore cannot be sustained; the hypothesis of an omnipotent and merciful God is not falsified by either the fact of physical or moral evil in the world or of man's free will. Camus' argument is primarily emotional, not logical in formulation; but the answer can be given on either emotional or logical grounds. Camus takes an anthropomorphic view of God. He uses the term omnipotent, but in context he does not connote the absolute, the infinitude of infinity and the concomitant incommensurability of the finite in juxtaposition with that infinity. His rejection is on the same basis as that of J. S. Mill and Bertrand Russell before him. They reject God because they cannot have Him on their own terms.

Camus must also rely on negative argumentation: one cannot be certain God exists; therefore one elects to act as though God does not exist. One cannot be certain that life has any meaning but the absurd; therefore one elects to act as though the absurd is the only way. He says:

It was previously a question of finding out whether or not life had to have a meaning to be lived. It now becomes clear, on the contrary that it will be lived all the better if it has no meaning. Living an experience, a particular fate, is accepting it fully. Now, no one will live this fate, knowing it to be absurd unless he does everything to keep before him that absurd brought to life by consciousness. . . .One of the only coherent philosophic positions is thus revolt. It is a constant confrontation between man and his own obscurity. It is an insistence upon an impossible transparency. It challenges the world anew every second. Just as danger provided man the unique opportunity of seizing awareness, so metaphysical revolt extends awareness to the whole of experience.

Camus like Nietzsche before him revels in the concept of revolt against any constraint. He accepts as his paradigms in revolt, Cain and Prometheus. In *The Myth of Sisyphus* in which Camus outlines how Sisyphus, having been unjustly condemned by the gods to rolling a huge stone up a mountain perpetually, only to have it roll back down, has nonetheless defied the gods and by such defiance the futility becomes worthwhile. In that work Camus concludes, "I leave Sisyphus at the foot of the mountain! One always finds one's burden again. But Sisyphus teaches the higher fidelity that negates the gods and raises rocks. . . ." ". . .This universe henceforth without a master seems to him neither sterile nor futile. . . ." "One must imagine Sisyphus happy." Camus was Sisyphus.

Camus' "atheistic" humanism would in view of his argument of uncertainty have to be classed as agnostic rather than as classically atheistic; but he was agnostic with a trenchant and defiant, not a passive, acceptance and—that requires a revolt against God if He exists. His idea of the dignity of man clearly lay in being master of himself, recognizing no higher level of authority but yet maintaining a passionate humanistic solidarity with his comrades in revolt in defying the absurd to the last breath.

Martin Heidegger was born at Messkirch in the Black Forest or Baden, Germany September 26, 1889. He attended the University of Freiburg. In 1915, he became a private instructor in philosophy at Freiburg, and in 1923 became a professor of philosophy at Marburg. While at Freiburg, he was influenced by his association with Husserl, thirty years his senior, and also by the works of Kierkegaard. Like many others in phenomenology and existentialism, Heidegger was raised a Catholic and was schooled in the scholastic tradition. Heidegger turned away from belief in an infinite, just, and merciful God as a result of his experience in World War I—much like Camus—he could not equate the existence of physical evil with that God.

Using Husserl's phenomenological concepts, the ideas of Nietzsche to which he turned after World War I, together with his own thoughts, he developed a system of philosophy which has been called atheistic existentialism. The first indication of this vein of thought is contained in his first and major work, *Being and Time* (*Sein and Zeit*), which was published in 1927. This work, while incomplete (there was to be a second and even a third volume), expresses his main ideas and is considered his greatest work. It was left incomplete largely because he, in fact, could not complete it within the frame of his philosophy. It has nevertheless exercised a profound influence on the main thrust of existentialism.

Heidegger succeeded Husserl as head of philosophy at Freiburg in 1929 and was later appointed rector of the university when the Nazi Party came into power in 1933. He resigned in 1935. After World War II, he was prevented from returning to his former position because of alleged Nazi sympathies. This is certainly a moot point; however, Heidegger used to open his classes with a stout "Heil Hitler" during that early period. He retired from the academic world into a life of private study. However, he was not particularly creative. Most of his publications during this period were nothing more than restructures and reissues of work which he had done earlier while with the university. Heidegger died May 26, 1976 at the age of 86. He returned to his Catholic Faith in his last illness.

Heidegger viewed man as an oppressed and anxious animal. He rejected the conventional religious answers, including those given by idealism, such as those of Kant and Hegel, which were still prevalent in Germany. He believed that by questioning, man can learn of the nature of existence, and by accepting that particular aspect which adapts best to his needs, can assert his own being, and achieve his destiny. He was obsessed by the problem of death and how man should face it. Virtually all of the existentialists, perhaps following Heidegger, are preoccupied by the end of man. In *Being and Time*, Heidegger stated his position:

We may now summarize our characterization of authentic Being-toward-death as we have projected it existentially: *anticipation reveals to Dasein its lostness in the they-self, and brings it face to face with the possibility of being itself, primarily unsupported by concernful solicitude, but of being itself, rather, in an impassioned* FREEDOM TOWARD DEATH—*a freedom which has been released from the illusions of the "they" and which is factical, certain of itself, and anxious.* (Emphasis Heidegger's.)

Heidegger was a Greek scholar and seems overly preoccupied with establishing what the Greek words, particularly those of Parmenides and Heraclitus, actually meant to Greeks in their time. The result is a constant reference to original Greek terminology, which makes his main effort and thought difficult to follow in the original German. English translations are scarcely better, being subjected to one more level of difficult interpretation, because Heidegger's German is also highly specialized. Heidegger concluded from his Greek studies that the Greek translations available have greatly modified the original intent, inferring thereby that the philosophies supported by the translations have a false base. The point is at best argumentative. But when Heidegger leaves his linguistic detail and existential jargon his thought and language flow with great power.

Heidegger's work has been an important source for those, such as Sartre, who continued in existentialism, which in Heidegger's main active period was indeed more a current of thought than a school of philosophy. Heidegger is classed as an atheistic existentialist, though he denied being an existentialist, and though, likewise there is no evidence that he was ever an atheist. A more factual observation is simply, that for him, God was not a proper subject of philosophy.

Heidegger's attitude is more like that of the stoics, particularly Epictetus or Seneca, who held that all reality is material though not materialistic; that good is within oneself, and that a unified dynamic force pervades everything. Therefore, whoever sought to "live consistently with nature, and put aside passion, impatience, unjust thoughts and indulgence, and perform his duty, would then gain true freedom in the brotherhood of man." This attitude also relates very closely to that of the ancient Eleatic School of Parmenides or of Xenophanes, who believed, as Heidegger did, that being is the ultimate reality, since perception and change are illusory or a caricature. Heidegger's own assessment of his position is that of a pre-Platonic or pre-Socratic individual. Certainly, his insistence on excluding any idea of God from philosophy fits the earlier group best. His questioning approach is Socratic. His existential variation is purely the Heidegger adaptation of numerous philosophies. It blends aspects of Husserl, Kierkegaard and Nietzsche with Heidegger's own concepts and with the older schools.

In relation to the question of man's status as being-in-the world, Heidegger's man is displayed in *Being and Time.* He takes it for granted that man is being-in-the world at the superorganic level—at a level of complexity above that of perception and the sensible. Living adequately is the placing of oneself so as to grow as part of the world "out there" by constant questioning and adjustment. In this way, the individual achieves not only contemporaneous realization of being-for-itself but also ultimate being-in-itself at the conjunction of the right action at the right moment.

Authenticity is that life which is thus lived experientially meeting the momentary exigencies courageously. Heidegger says,

> Only as questioning, historical being does man come to himself; only as such is he a self. Man's selfhood means this, he must transform the being that discloses itself to him into history and bring himself to stand in it. Selfhood does not mean that he is primarily an "ego" and an individual. This he is no more than he is a we, a community. (Heidegger, 1959, page 121).

The question then does not appear as a true dialectic to

Heidegger. Man is in an organic unity with the world "out there" in which he plays or fails to play a historic role. When Heidegger said (Heidegger, 1961, page 7), "Philosophy is essentially untimely because it is one of those few things that can never find an immediate echo in the present. When such an echo seems to occur, when a philosophy becomes fashionable, either it is no philosophy or it has been misinterpreted and misused for ephemeral and extraneous purposes," he was emphasizing two things. First, the undoubted fashionableness of existentialism in his later years, and his disavowal of it. His disavowal may in fact have been prompted by its fashionableness and liberal use of showmanship. The second point is the reaffirmation, and an important one, of the role which philosophy has traditionally taken and ought to take in guidance rather than mere reflection of thought in the world at large. It echoes Nietzsche's attitude. On one occasion, Heidegger had said of Sartre that "he was more a propagandist for philosophy than a philosopher."

On balance at this point in philosophic thought, Heidegger's works place him, even if reluctantly, in the ranks of the existentialists—if there were conservative existentialists he would be one. Heidegger's God was the dead God of Nietzsche, *"Gott ist tot,"* but yet he hedges on saying that there is not another God, a living God. The last two paragraphs in his work *An Introduction to Metaphysics* relate to this point and are typically more stoic than existentialist:

> To know how to question means to know how to wait, even a whole lifetime. But an age which regards as real only what goes fast and can be clutched with both hands looks on questioning as "remote from reality" and as something that does not pay, whose benefits cannot be numbered. But the essential is not number; the essential is the right time, i.e., the right moment, and the right perseverance.
>
> "For," as Holderlin said, "the mindful God abhors untimely growth." ("Aus dem Motivkreis der Titanen," Samtliche Werke, r, 218.). (Heidegger 1959, page 172).

His concept of man, then, is essentially that of the stoic, less their pantheistic view of the universe. Perhaps, man is only an animal. Perhaps, something else. In any event, he is a naturalistic animal and there is no need in philosophy to bring in any relationship to a spiritual god who may or may not exist. Man's dignity lies in gaining true freedom and authentic self through self-knowledge in relation to reality as the individual perceives it eventually, through constant and unhurried questioning. Heidegger did not die as an atheist.

Gabriel Marcel was born on December 7, 1889, in Paris of a prominent family. His father was French Minister to Stockholm for several years beginning in 1898. His mother, a Jewess, died when he was four years old, so to some extent he had a lonely boyhood. He was educated at the Sorbonne, and took his doctorate there in 1910. His dissertation, pointing the way his career would tend, was on the subject of the "Metaphysical Ideas of Coleridge, as related to the philosophy of Schelling." While in Switzerland for his health in 1912, he began his journal, *Metaphysique,* which occupied him until 1921. During World War II, he worked with the Red Cross and became interested in paranormal cognition, which is also a clue to his interest in the psychological and metaphysical.

He taught only briefly in 1940 and 1941. His chief occupation has been as a playwright and dramatist. He wrote some 20 plays between 1914 and 1960, the first *Le Soleil Invisible.* His best known work is probably *Homo Viator,* in which he develops a metaphysics of hope deliberately to counteract Sartre's pessimism.

Along with his fellow existentialists, Marcel is deeply artistic and earnestly philosophical. His work is a brilliant blend of the two different, yet closely related, aspects of life. He rejects the outlook that life is a thing to be endured—an unceasing struggle against the stifling pressures of the world on that sole unfortunate island of consciousness in a sea of hostile incomprehending and incomprehensible matter. In the same way that art attempts to express the unexpressible, philosophy must somehow bring out the full richness of the sensed—only spirit of community—that enduring love which pervades the ultimate mystery of conscious life. Marcel's plays are designed to convey an impression in spiritual maturity through the intimate human relationship. Collins (1969) well describes this aspect of Marcel's work in contrast to Sartre, who develops the same technique to the opposite end.

> Marcel's plays pursue the common theme that man finds his vocation in learning to participate in being. This participation is not achieved by dissolving the individual in some vague cosmic embrace, but by gaining awareness of one's personal significance and joining in the community of persons. In dramatic terms,

this means a sharp antithesis between the theater of Sartre and that of Marcel. The former sets his stage in the packing-box of Hell, with the individual character bedeviled by his past deeds and tortured by the staring presence of other men. For the protagonists in Sartre's plays, there is no possibility of communion with each other or of liberating movement toward the Father of light.

Such a possibility is always there in Marcel's dramatic world, not as a sop but as an open path which human freedom is enabled to take. Instead of the room with no exit, the typical setting is found in the home, where there are plenty of doors and windows symbolizing our capacity for becoming accessible to others and for living with each other.

This is not to say that Marcel takes an easy, sentimental view of our human predicament. In an interview, he has stated that his concern in the theater is the presentation "of the soul in exile, of the soul which suffers from the lack of communion with herself and with others."

Marcel had religious leanings from the beginning, but his philosophy had not changed to a theistic realism or a metaphysical extension of existentialism. Moreover, Marcel did not consider himself a "Christian existentialist," but preferred to be regarded as Neo-Socratic, because of his preference to a questioning approach in his work. For Marcel, the personality matters most. Fears and desires belong to the realm of "having." They are things which are "possessed" by the individual yet which somehow possesses the individual in almost the same way as health or sickness.

Since he holds about the same approach to reality, though of opposite polarity, in its existence as do Camus and Sartre, it is best to look at the area where he sees matters differently, and that is basically in the ideas of God and man's relationship to him. On this point, Collins (1969) says:

> One of Marcel's earliest contentions was that we are confronted with an initial option of regarding reality either as closed off from every reference to the transcendent God or as being open to that reference. But . . . he is not aware of two difficulties in this theory of the initial option. For one thing, it fits the

opposition between his own theism and Sartre's atheism, but it does not explain very incisively Heidegger's position of not ruling out the reality of God or even our ability to become related in some fashion with him, and yet of refusing to bring the issue within philosophical range. Another drawback is that it does not deal effectively with minds which claim to be still uncommitted philosophically on the question of God and religion. Such minds cannot be told that the question has already been settled within the terms of their philosophy, but on the contrary they must be given same philosophically specifiable grounds for settling it in some definite way.

With his fellow existentialists, Marcel is almost obsessed with the idea of the intimate interaction of the relationship between people in any group, whether in opposition or cooperation, toward the sensed grasping at reality of existence. This is reinforced in Marcel's work by the concept that through the living, free collaboration of individuals, all are thereby assisted to attain being, the total impact being greater than the sum of the individual activity. It is in this intimate interaction that humanity achieves its closest approach to real being. Marcel gives a theologic example from the Trinity, the perfect communication in community achieving unity. If we now examine being-in-the-world in this context we arrive at Marcel's position by what he termed the "orchestration of themes" through which we arrive at the ". . . hidden identity of the way which leads to holiness and the road which leads the metaphysician to the affirmation of being. . . the philosopher must realize that. . . here is one and the same road." Being-for-itself, the conscious, striving inwardness to fulfillment, is itself of itself incapable of attaining its completeness except as it is forced through interaction with all its close associates in the context of conflict and reconciliation to plumb its inmost depths. Thereby it discovers what it is that commands its highest attention, toward attainment of which it will sacrifice all else—will literally stake its life. Being-in-the-world is the development of that vision which the being-for-itself has identified. To the extent the vision is fulfilled, being is fulfilled.
Marcel's view of man as being-in-the-world is radically different from Sartre's and Camus'. It is closely akin to the opposition of Jungian and Freudian psychology. For Marcel, man is a being with a destiny. The being-in-itself, the self-conscious ego, is not opposed to the being-for-itself. Both are initially

immature and remain basically unchanged except, as through the lived experience in the interaction with our fellowmen we either grow and achieve fulfillment, being-in-itself working as being-for-itself in a spiritual realization of our communality with all men, or we shrink into a contemptuous, cynical, self-centered shell of a man, being-for-itself either destroyed or forced into the being-in-itself an egotistical, intelligent beast—no more. As we see from Collin's analysis this does not face the problem of Heidegger. Yet Heidegger and Marcel are not that different, other than the former's skepticism. Both are questioning and questing philosophers—Marcel, emphasizing the contemplative aspect; Heidegger, the broadly empirical theme of trial and error. Marcel sees the great problem in our modern age in the distortion which impersonal mass society and its materialistic goals have forced in man's ideals—those for which he is willing to commit himself. No longer involved in a community of intimately-felt common interests which gives and deepens a sense of values, man has become a diseased organism with shallow roots. To Marcel, we no longer are able to discover ourselves, and, being unable to do so, remove ourselves from reality. Ours is a "world under condemnation."

Karl Jaspers was born on February 23, 1883, in Oldenberg, Germany, the son of a bank director and former sheriff. It was not a religious family, and Karl had no formal upbringing in any religious confession. His family, however, was close-knit and loving with a strong sense of what could be called a deep moral awareness. His original education at the university was for the practice of law, but he quickly changed to medicine. He was disappointed in this venture, and in the incidental courses in philosophy he took in the course of these studies. But he was strongly attracted by philosophy, nevertheless, even after beginning the practice of medicine. He eventually hoped to return to an academic career in psychology or psychiatry. In 1913, he qualified as lecturer in psychology, but the experiences of World War I changed his orientation completely toward philosophy. It was not until he was 39 years of age that he made the break to devote his life to philosophy.

Jaspers brings to existentialism, then, a totally different background from those whom we have looked at up to this time. This reveals the other face of existentialism—that face which is not dramatized and popularized—the non-flamboyant scientifically-supportive rather than scientifically-suppressive view. Merleau-Ponty, who follows, is also of this orientation—perhaps even more so than Jaspers.

Of these who influenced his thought most, Jaspers indicates in his autobiographical work, *On My Philosophy,* that Kant was originally *the* philosopher for him and remained so though Spinoza, Plotinus, Bruno, Nicholas of Cusa and Schelling were early influences. Eventually Kierkegaard and then quite late Nietzsche became prominent in his thought. Concerning personal influences, Jaspers says, "Among my deceased contemporaries I owe what I am able to think—those closest to me excepted—above all to the one and only Max Weber. He alone, through his being, showed me what human greatness can be." Jaspers does not mention Hegel as an influence, but rather as a milestone—"the culmination of two and a half millenia of thought and a break point to what happened after the collapse of idealism."

Looking at modern civilization, Jaspers says, "We are so exposed that we constantly find ourselves facing nothingness. . . .The alternative 'nothing or everything' stands before our age as the questioning of man's spiritual destiny." That also, of course, expresses the theme of this book and, in many ways, the dialectical orientation existentialism has taken between its two wings from the beginning. Nietzsche versus Kierkegaard, or Nietzsche and Marx versus Kierkegaard—a dialectic which sprang from the cleavage in Hegel, a cleavage which rather than dialectic appears as irreconcilable polarity *"Gott ist tot"* or *"Gott ist."*

Jaspers, though influenced by Nietzsche and Kierkegaard, does not subscribe to their irrational—willfully irrational—methodology. He felt reason must be exercised to prevent such brutal, unreal, exclusive alternatives which contain no proper communicative value. They are blind alleys to those who follow.

Jaspers emphasized six main points throughout his work: (1) The knowledge of science is tremendously important within its proper scope but it is limited. (2) Truth extends beyond science and it is in that metaphysical or transcendental extension that the philosopher chiefly finds "a new, more urgent, more exciting task." Indeed, the philospher's primary task lies precisely in the development and communication of the broad outlines in which the truth may be found. (3) The communication of truth fails chiefly in the breach between scientific knowledge and that which lies beyond it. (4) Man, alone, is the reality through which anything and everything else becomes real to man. He is the only means of communication. What man is, and can become, is the foundation question which the communication must convey. (5) Man as being-in-the-world becomes himself only through his relationships—only through interaction and communication with "the other" considered both as human and as impersonal objects. (6) Man, in the twentieth century, lives in a world where the lines of communication have become weirdly entangled yet foreshortened. We no longer subsist with our fellow-communicators in a nexus of shared values, goals, commitments and spiritual aspirations but as a mechanically-coupled—staccato—binary—monosyllabic—impersonal bedlam of discordant messages. In explication of these points, Jaspers is tremendously complex. I find his thought, along with Kant's, the most difficult to describe briefly.

The existentialist concept, being-in-itself, for Jaspers, is almost synonymous with his own unique expression, *"Existenz."*

> As an existent, I am present in the world as body, character, past, and present action. These are all aspects of myself, as through them I am aware of myself, but they are not individually me, they must be integrated and interpreted by a decision process which transcends them. Only then, do I become a fully self-conscious unique human being having transcendental value in myself, knowing myself fully—my total being-in-itself. The ultimate level of Existenz, for the individual, is established only as it is lived. It is a process: "Decision makes Existenz real, forms life and changes it in inner action which, through clarification, keeps us soaring upwards."

Intimately related to the concept, *Existenz,* is that of the "Encompassing." This is the source of all truth. It is that ". . .truth that makes itself felt at the boundary of science." It cannot be obtained by philosophizing, though it may be clarified. If we try to understand, ". . .we fall back again at the boundary where the leap to transcending thinking must be made." Then Jaspers adds, "Perhaps a few words may *suggest* even if not *explain* what is meant."

"Everything that becomes an *object* to me approaches me as it were from the dark background of Being. Every object is a determinate being (as *this* confronting me in a subject-object division) but never all Beings. No being known as an object is *the* Being." (Emphasis Jaspers'). It is more than the sum of all objects. This idea seems closely related to Schelers' Absolute Being in which all being is grounded. The Encompassing is Being: "We inquire after the Being which, with the manifestation

of all encountered appearance in object and horizons, yet re-
cedes Itself. This being we call the Encompassing. The Encompassing, then, is that which always makes Its presence known,
which does not appear Itself, but from which everything comes
to us. . . ." ". . .Only if all horizons met in one closed whole,
so that they formed a finite multiplicity could we attain, by
moving through all the horizons, the one closed Being—Being,
however, is not closed for us and the horizons are not finite.
On all sides we are impelled toward the infinite." Jaspers'
thought, then, is reminiscent of Spinoza. But, for Jaspers, the
Being is also personal, loving—the God of theism. He says:

> No proof of God succeeds in philosophy if it at-
> tempts to provide compelling knowledge; but it is
> possible for "proofs" of God to succeed as ways of
> transcending thought. . . .The question "What is Tran-
> scendence?" is not answered, therefore by a knowl-
> edge of transcendence—the answer comes indirectly
> by a clarification of the incompleteness of the world,
> the imperfectibility of man, the impossibility of a per-
> manently valid world order, the universal failure—
> bearing in mind at the same time that there is not
> nothing, but that in nature, history and human exis-
> tence, the magnificent is as real as the terrible.

This description would seem to say "Transcendence" is a montage of intuitive insights conveying an overall impression of the
unexpressible, even unthinkable, beyond the scientific boundary. The overall idea is somewhat Kantian, but the "Encompassing" is not an idealistic concept.

Jaspers was satisfied with a non-coercive proof of the existence
of God, while Scheler was not. This reflects a major difference
between the true existentialists, who shun hard logic, and the
phenomenologists and philosophers of being. As in many other
things, the existentialists prefer an "arty" approach to reality.

The existential concept, being-for-itself, can be discovered in
Jaspers' thought then as being-in-itself, Existenz, as it emerges
from the continuous communication with the world "out there"
and with God, the Encompassing, in a subject-object dialogue.
Jaspers says, speaking in context of the foregoing:

> How I understand this language, however, is based
> on what I really am myself. What I am myself is based
> on my original relations to Transcendence: In defiance

and in surrender, in falling away and the passion of the night. When I philosophize I clarify and remember and prepare how, through these relations I can experience Eternity in Time. The experience itself cannot be forced and cannot be proved: It is the fulfilled historicity of my Existenz.

Being-for-itself, then, can be Sartrean or Marcellian or the revolutionary of Camus. The decision is a process, and the process depends upon the individual. Being-for-itself is the instantaneous role being-in-itself experiences and plays throughout its life. The role may be authentic or false. The distance between the in-itself and for-itself may be small or great. Both its interim and ultimate nature depend on each of us as we experience our lives and decide based on those experiences.

Martin Buber was born in Vienna in 1878 and raised by his grandfather Solomon Buber, a well-educated, traditional Jewish scholar. During this period, Buber developed strong ties to Hasidism, perhaps the predominant influence on his subsequent writing. He attended the Universities of Vienna and Berlin with major work in philosophy, history and art. He was greatly influenced and attracted by the works of Nietzsche and Kierkegaard, though disagreeing violently with both on major aspects of their thought. The turn of the century saw him join the Zionist movement. Soon, however, he disassociated himself from the pure activist wing and remained essentially spiritual and cultural in his approach to the development of Zionism. In 1923, he was associated with Catholic theologian Joseph Wittig and Protestant psychiatric physician Victor von Weizsacher in publication of the religiously oriented journal, *Die Kreatur.* His first major work, *Daniel,* published in 1913, established him as an existentialist. His preeminent and best known work, *I and Thou,* was published in 1923. He published numerous other works covering philosophical and religious themes.

After many vicissitudes during the early Nazi period in Germany, in which he courageously took charge of the Frankfort Jewish community and where he was a university professor, he left for Palestine, in 1938, to take the chair in social philosophy at the Hebrew University. In 1951, he retired from that post and lectured extensively in the United States, where he made a profound impact on the then, just emerging, existentialist movement. At the time of his death in 1956 he was Professor Emeritus of Social Philosophy at the Hebrew University in Jerusalem. Unlike many of the contemporary prominent existentialists, he was not deeply involved in dramatic work forms, relying instead on a clear and forceful, but yet almost poetic, prose to convey the deeper emotive expressions of his thought.

In his work, *I and Thou,* he sets forth the main elements which guided his thought, and most of this analysis of his position is based on that work. Buber sets up two primary "words," I—Thou and I—It. The first "word" is an expression of a personal relationship between individuals. Among primitive peoples the Thou could be animals or even inanimate objects having deep personal significance, as in animistic religions. The second word, the I—It, denotes a pragmatic subject-object relationship, even though the "It" be a fellow human. Buber very nearly equates the fulfilled human life with that of summation of authentic, human, I—Thou meetings, including in that concept the multitudinous meetings between the I and the eternal Thou, God. He says:

> The present, and by that is meant not the point which indicates, from time to time in our thought, merely the conclusion of "finished time"; the mere appearance of a termination which is fixed and held, but the real, filled present, exists only in so far as actual presentness, meeting and relation exist. The present arises only in virtue of the fact that the Thou becomes present.
>
> The I of the primary word I—It, that is, the I faced by no Thou but surrounded by a multitude of "contents" has no present, only the past. Put in another way, in so far as man rests satisfied with the things (including persons) that he experiences and uses, he lives in the past, and his moment has no present content. He has nothing but objects. But objects subsist in time that has been.
>
> The present is not fugitive and transient, but continually present and enduring. The object is not duration but cessation, suspension, a breaking off and cutting clear and hardening, absence of relation and of present being. True beings are lived in the present, the life of objects is in the past.

Buber sees the human "its" continuously being changed to "thous" as relationships develop and "thous" devolve into "its" as relationships deteriorate. The "I" also changes in the two relationships, but not as drastically. The more close relationships one has the richer the "I" becomes in human value.

Turning to his concept of man's relationship with God, Buber says:

> The extended lines of relations meet in the eternal *Thou*. Every particular *Thou* is a glimpse through to the eternal *Thou;* by means of every particular *Thou*, the primary word addresses the eternal *Thou*. Through this mediation of the *Thou* of all beings, fulfillment and non-fulfillment of relations comes to them; the inborn *Thou* is realized in each relation and consummated in none. It is consummated only in the direct relation with the *Thou* that by its nature cannot become *It*.
>
> Men have addressed their eternal *Thou* with many names. In singing of him who was thus named, they always had the *Thou* in mind. The first myths were hymns of praise. Then the names took refuge in the language of It; men were more and more strongly moved to think of and address their eternal *Thou* as an It. But all God's names are hallowed, for in them He is not merely spoken about but also spoken to. . . .
>
> . . . For me he speaks the word of God and really has *Thou* in mind (whatever illusion by which he is held) addresses the true *Thou* of life, which cannot be limited by another *Thou* and to which he stands in a relation that gathers up and includes all others.
>
> But when he, too, who abhors the name, and believes himself to be godless, gives his whole being to addressing the *Thou* of his life as a *Thou* that cannot be limited to another, he addresses God. (Italics Buber's).

In the preceding two paragraphs Buber develops a concept quite similar to that of theologian Paul Tillich, whose work we will review briefly in Part V, also considered an existentialist, in his concept of God as "Ultimate Concern." Whatever is that concept which a man places above all others and before all others—even though it be such a thing as wealth or power—that is God for him, however the individual would wish to disguise it. In a great many ways Buber's concept is richer than Tillich's, for to Buber that reverse side is completely secondary and unworthy. On that point Buber says:

> To look away from the world, or to stare at it does not help a man to reach God; but he who sees the world in Him stands in His presence. "Here world, there God" is the language of *It;* "God in the world" is another language of *It* but to eliminate or leave behind all, to include the whole world in the *Thou,* to give the world its due and its truth, to include nothing beside, God but everything in Him—this is full and complete relation.
>
> Men do not find God if they stay in the world. They do not find Him if they leave the world. He who goes out with his whole being to meet his Thou, and carries to it all being that is in the world, finds Him who cannot be sought.

Buber also seems quite close to Soren Kierkegaard in his concept of God but here, again, Buber appears to have a richer concept. Where Kierkegaard emphasized the idea of the "Single One" of a personal exclusiveness between the I and God, Buber emphasizes the community participation—the intertwining of all the thous of one's life in relationship to the eternal Thou.

Buber's approach to God is like his fellow theistic existentialists, one of a sensed feeling, a hunger fulfilled, rather than an intuitive grasp as with the phenomenologists or the rational, logical approach of the theistic realists or the other philosophers of being to be considered in the next section.

Buber's feeling has much in common with Augustine in his deep sense of the eternal Thou as the "Beloved One," a sense also closely related to the themes of the psalms and wisdom literature generally of the Old Testament. His idea of the dignity of man lies in man's relationship first to the eternal Thou and then to all of his associates in a relationship of extended personal depth and not a shallow utilitarian acquaintance.

Buber did not directly reflect Heidegger's existential influence of the transcendent importance of the question of being. This theme for Buber is generally more "ontological" in tone rather than "essential" or "existential" in the three-cornered relationship. His emphasis is upon individual beings as they are related to other individual beings in the network of existential relationships. Yet, he is as concerned with the idea of authenticity of the individual in achieving fulfillment in his lived existence as his more dramatic colleagues. We can interpolate a meaning for the duality—the in-itself, for-itself or being-in-the-world from his I-Thou, I-It primary word context. Being-for-itself the developing consciousness of self is a blank at the beginning of life as with the others, but with Buber it develops with experience along one of two ways, either that characterized by the impersonal I-It, of which Buber says, "But the mankind of mere It that is imagined, postulated and propagated by such a man has nothing in common with a living mankind where Thou may truly be spoken." The world of the "It" is a world in the past tense a world of role-playing pretense without authenticity; to repeat a bit, ". . . In so far as man rests satisfied with the things he experiences and uses, he lives in the past and his moment has no present content. He has nothing but objects. But objects exist in time that has been." Along the other path, being-for-itself in terms of the objective world "out there" but participates in the present by maximizing the human relationships in the I-Thou context. "The primary word I-Thou can be spoken only with the whole being. . . . I become through my relations to the Thou; as I become I, I say Thou. All real living is meeting." Only as the being-for-itself is oriented to others in the I-Thou context, does the primal being-in-itself become fulfilled in the merging of the dual aspects of being-in-the-world. For Buber, the structure of authentic being arises to its supreme height as the Eternal Thou is brought into this picture meeting in present timeliness. As Will Hersberg states in the introduction in his collection *The Writing of Martin Buber* (Hersberg, 1956), for Buber, "God is the center of the circle of existence, the apex of the triangle of life."

Maurice Merleau-Ponty was born at Roche-sur Mar in 1902 and died in May of 1961 at the age of 53; he was at the height of his ability at the time of his death. He for eight years had been the successor of Bergson and Gilson in the chair of philosophy at the College de France, a position of great prestige. Prior to that he had been professor of philosophy at the University of Lyon and later at the Sorbonne. His academic qualifications therefore are exceptional. In the introductory paragraph to this section the writer had noted that Merleau-Ponty did not belong to either set—the theist or atheist wing—but was still searching. What to him was to be his major work was still largely in the planning state and is still largely unavailable, although preliminary work has been done in compiling and editing his efforts toward that work. Some has been issued piecemeal and is only partially available in English translation. The first of his two most celebrated works, *The Structure of Behavior* was originally published in 1942 and has been available generally in English translation since 1963, published posthumously, though the proposed translation had been reviewed by him and approved. The second,

The Phenomenology of Perception, was published in France in 1945 and has been available in English since 1962. These were, then, both fairly early works written while he was in his mid-thirties and both dealt heavily with the problem which has plagued the philosophic world since Descartes: Man, as he is to himself, and as he is related to the world in which he is situated, in existential terminology the conflict Being-in-itself and Being-for-itself. The thing which stands between for Merleau-Ponty and for Descartes is our means of acquisition or perception of knowledge. A problem of epistemology, then, lies between the ontology of the conscious self and that ontology as related to self and as modified to the "all else." While Merleau-Ponty's interests as shown in his work have spanned everything from politics to art, he has always been preoccupied with this central theme. From the notes pulled together for what was to be his major work, *Le Visible et L'invisible,* indicate it was again to be on the same subject but at the next level up from the purely perceptual. It was to be a work in which the Being, man, was to be looked at as the "Incarnate Consciousness," as an ontological unity in fact, as well as in concept. In the two published works cited earlier, which are the chief source documents used in this narrow analysis of his position, Merleau-Ponty comes through more as a phenomenologist than as an existentialist, although the idea of the experiential in life is not ever very far below the surface. But, if the root thought in theoretical approach is existential, his methodology is phenomenology at its very best. In fact, these works constitute a clear example of the potential of the phenomenological approach when followed detailedly. Their study is thus doubly fruitful.

Politically and sociologically, Merleau-Ponty was originally influenced by Marx's early works but became disenchanted with Marxism as it was developed in the communist world. He saw France caught between the United States and Russia in the battle of opposing power-hungry ideologies and strove for a middle world position. Early he had been closely associated with Sartre and Simone de Beauvoir, both dedicated to the communist principles, and was co-founder with them of the influential review *Les Temps Modernes* but with his, Merleau-Ponty's, outspoken criticism of communist activities he alienated both.

Like many of his colleagues, Merleau-Ponty was a disciple of Husserl—not the final Husserl of the "Transcendental Reduction"—but of the earlier "Phenomenological Reduction," which leaves behind all presuppositions in investigation of phenomena and considers only the world as it is experienced by the observer.

Merleau-Ponty goes one step further in the cited major works and places the object whose behavior is to be investigated in context of its associated behavioral surroundings—the background field against which the object is displayed. My own analogy would be that of a solitary electric charge in an electric force field: the behavior of the charge would not relate solely to its own state of charge, but would be profoundly affected by the polarity and intensity of the force field in which it is surrounded.

Merleau-Ponty's other chief philosophical influence appears to have been Hegel in his dialectical approach—but Merleau-Ponty uses the expression in such a varied set of contexts that the Hegelian idea is almost lost. The range varies from the pure thesis-antithesis-synthesis-through intense interaction and denouement, to one which is little more than the compromise in dialogue on a disputed matter. In the *Structure of Behavior,* Merleau-Ponty takes almost a "Humean" interest in the empirical side of the problem of perception as he follows animal and normal and abnormal human behavioral laboratory studies to thoroughly discredit their extended application in some cases, or to point out where the findings should more properly lead if applied in their proper context. His viewpoint of man, as it is revealed in these studies, is greatly different from Sartre and was one point of friction between them. Merleau-Ponty shows little of the influence of either of his two outstanding immediate predecessors at the College de France, Henri Bergson, the philosopher of life, or Ettiene Gilson, a philosopher of being in the Thomist tradition.

In the introduction to *Structure of Behavior,* Merleau-Ponty says, "Our goal is to understand the relation of consciousness and nature: organic, psychological or even social. By nature, we understand here a multiplicity of events external to each other and bound together by relations of causality." The bulk of the work is then devoted to a meticulous demonstration of the inadequacies of present theories to explain behavior at any level of the organism from the invertebrate forms to man himself. The inadequacy results largely because of study of the organism as a mechanical device, as an assemblage of parts each of which can be analyzed in an isolated way. He begins with the earliest theories—those of the early reflex concepts of Pavlov, Koehler and Watson, and advanced to the more sophisticated ideas of Gestalt Theory. In all, he notes the limitations of the idea of causality taken directly from physics, which excludes completely any hint of purposefulness on the part of the organism. He says:

It is known that in Watson, following, the classical
antimony, the negation of consciousness as "internal
reality" is made to the benefit of physiology; behavior
is reduced to the sum of reflexes and conditioned
reflexes between which no intrinsic connection is admitted but precisely this atomistic interpretation fails
even at the level of the theory of the reflex (Chapter I)
and all the more in psychology—even the objective
psychology—of higher levels of behavior (Chapter II)
as Gestalt theory has clearly shown. By going through
behaviorism, however, one gains, at least in being able
to introduce consciousness not as psychological reality or as cause, but as structure. It will remain for
us to investigate (Chapter III) the model of existence
of these structures.

Interesting as it is, we cannot of course, here, accompany
Merleau-Ponty in that work, only summarize what it reveals
as to his viewpoint on man and those things in which man
achieves his highest fulfillment. He arrives at three basic distin-
guishable levels of behavior: the physical, the vital, and the
human orders which do not grade one into the other. Merleau-
Ponty believes that these levels of behavior:

. . .do not represent three powers of being, but three
dialectics. Physical nature in man is not subordinated
to a vital principle, the organism does not conspire
to actualize the idea, and the mental is not the motor
principle in the body but what we call life is already
consciousness of life and what we call mental is still
an object vis-a-vis consciousness. Nevertheless, while
establishing the ideality of the physical form, that of
the organism, and that of the "mental" and *precisely
because we did it,* we could not simply superimpose
these three structural orders. . . . Man can never be
an animal; his life is always more or less integrated
than that of an animal. But if the alleged instincts
of man do not exist apart from the mental dialectic,
correlatively, this dialect is not conceivable outside
of the concrete situations in which it is embodied.
One does not act with mind alone. Either mind is
nothing, or it constitutes a real, not an ideal, transformation of man. Because it is not a sort of being
but a new form of unity, it cannot stand by itself.

Man is a unique being, an integrated symbol-making and symbol-using unit characterized by the ability to think and to be conscious of that thought and to carry out multiform activity, including all perception, purposively using all physical, vital and mental functions without any necessary reflection on this use in the subject-object sense relating to its internal operations.

The concept of man as a being uniquely distinguished from all other beings by communicating chiefly through use of "symbolizing" was later (1949) repeated by anthropologist Leslie White, who declared "The symbol is the universe of man" in his work *The Science of Culture*. This was a position which, even that late, was considered to run counter to the predominant concept of "Comparative mentality," which rated man's thinking power as qualitatively the same as the lower animals though quantitatively superior. The latter view remains a prevalent concept in the anthropological and sociological field.

In amplification of this point, Merleau-Ponty says:

He (the subject) lives in a universe of experience, in a milieu which is neutral with regard to the substantial distinction between the organism, thought and extension; he lives in a direct commerce with beings and things and his own body. The ego as center from which his intentions radiate, the body which carries them and the beings and things to which they are addressed are "not confused," but they are only three sectors of a unique field. Things are things, that is, transcendent with respect to all that I know of them and accessible to other perceiving subjects, but intended precisely as things; as such they are the indispensible moment of the lived dialectic which embraces them.

For Merleau-Ponty, then, his phenomenological study of behavior brings him to this conclusion in existential theory that Being-for-itself becomes a conscious witness to the activities of the Being-in-itself. Man as being-in-the-world is exactly that, with no artificial subdivisions into "in-itself" and "for-itself." He says, "We want to make consciousness equal with the whole of experience, to gather into consciousness for-itself (*pour soi*) all the life of consciousness in-itself (*en soi*)." His studies also bring him to the other conclusions only hinted at in *The Structure of Behavior* and *The Phenomenology of Perception* but revealed in his notes for his proposed work the *Visible and the Invisible.* Here he suggests there was to be a radical change in his approach—not to the unity of the being, man, but in man's intrinsic nature. Merleau-Ponty was concerned that the idea of perception generally was too shallow, that there was in each of us a center of subconsciousness—a place within the inmost ego where the "me" not reachable even by our deepest introspection yet radiates the idea self to the consciousness. This is the "me" that is really "me" stripped of all the conditioning we have been exposed to and crowded into our conscious selves. Man was "incarnate consciousness" but what was the ultimate depth of that which was enfleshed. Perhaps, Merleau-Ponty seems to say, I didn't really solve the problem at all but merely pushed the interface one level deeper. He turns once more to the meaning of experience, but not toward the lowest levels of awareness of passivity, unconsciousness, sleep. He seeks to descend into the "cellar" of self. He believes there is an area in which the present is really recognized only by reason of the "immense latent content of past, or future and of elsewhere that it conceals." This is an idea strongly Jungian in psychologic approach.

Merleau-Ponty hints in the conclusion of *The Structure of Behavior* that what he is seeking requires a sharper focus; in a passage which may be deliberately ambiguous he says,

> It is a problem to know what happens, for example, when consciousness disassociates itself from time, from this uninterrupted gushing at the center of itself, in order to apprehend it as an intellectual and manipulable signification. Does it lay bare only what was implicit? Or, on the contrary, does it not enter as into a lucid dream in which indeed it encounters no opaqueness, not because it has clarified the existence of things and its own existence, but because it lives at the surface of itself and on the envelope of things? Is the reflexive passage to intellectual consciousness an adequation of our knowing to our being or only a way for consciousness to create a separated existence, a quietism? These questions express no empiricist demand, no complaissance for "experiences" which would not have to account for themselves.
>
> If. . .our knowledge depends upon what we are; moral theory begins with a psychological and sociological critique of oneself; man is not assured ahead of time of possessing a source of morality; consciousness

of self is not given a man by right; it is acquired only by the elucidation of his concrete being and is verified only by the active integration of isolated dialectics—body and soul—between which it is initially broken up and finally, death is not deprived of meaning, since the contingency of the lived is a perpetual menace for the eternal signification in which it is believed to be completely expressed. It will be necessary to assure oneself that the experience of eternity is not the unconsciousness of death, and that it is not on this side but beyond; similarly, moreover, it will be necessary to distinguish the love of life from the attachment to biologic existence. The sacrifice of life will be philosophically speaking impossible; it will be a question only of "staking one's life," which is a deeper way of living.

In this writer's opinion this statement is a somewhat wistful look by Merleau-Ponty at what might derive from the philosophic critical tradition if subjected to the phenomenologist's detailed searching and evaluation. He did not believe like Descartes that there were "isolated dialectics—body and soul" but an integrated conscious being. Almost ten years later at his death he had still not found the answer. His words almost echo those of Martin Buber, "life on the narrow ridge" between abysses taken by the one who "stakes his life on his thinking."

Despite a religious family background, Merleau-Ponty virtually never broached the subject of God. He himself appears to have been an agnostic, but a searching agnostic in a philosophical sense. It seems, like Heidegger, he did not consider God a proper subject of philosophy but apparently found it impossible to arrive at solutions to life "from below" without some consideration of source. He even admits in *The Phenomenology of Perception* that, "it is of the nature of man to think of God." He appears to adhere strictly, even though Husserl, the founder, did not, to the concept of phenomenology that there is no validity in a concept unless it can be achieved through "experiencing" it. To him the concept, God seemed still "unexperienceable" and, for him, the search had to continue.

Existentialism has certainly played a major part in the dramatic turn which intellectual thought has taken away from the hard line positivist or dialectical materialistic philosophies prevalent at the beginning of the twentieth century, although Sartre calls himself a materialist monist. Yet, in some ways, it has gone perhaps too far in its reaction. The reaction has two modes which are yet differentiated into the theist and atheist phases. First, there is a general rejection of the past as significant to the present existent moment and to its implications of a future shaped by the present, but absolutely beyond the control of the present. Among the atheists, it is an almost stereotype oriental stoicism in its dedication to fatalism, the unavoidability of failure, suffering, and death. Its tone is somber and without elan. Life seems pointless and valueless. Among the theists, there is hope, but as a subdued yearning—not as a buoyant, dynamic, surging force. The second mode is the turning away from the basic thought system pervading Western culture from the time of the Greeks. Even Heidegger, who quotes the Greek origins so incessantly, pays little attention to the Platonic-Aristotelian main thrust and prefers that of the pre-Socratic Eleatic school, and even seemingly of the later Stoics. He leaps over 2,000 years. Marcel is Platonic in many of his philosophic conceptions yet, even here, he seems preoccupied with a pathos which is totally non-Platonic though he says he is Neo-Socratic in his questioning methodology. The existentialists, with the exception of Jaspers and Merleau-Ponty, have largely eliminated the sense of any objectivity in essence and the value of scientific investigation which searches for knowledge in that objectivity and which evolved from the Platonic-Aristotelian tradition.

Existentialistic solutions to the problems of man are for the most part non-solutions. They are largely in the nature of internalized reconciliations of man to his fate. Although the theist branch sees man of preeminent value in his transcendence, it does not do so in the joyous, exulting vision of Augustine, even though Augustine himself was to some extent an existentialist. In their relations between God and man, the theist existentialists still see a struggling anxious groping in the mists of self-realization, remaining somber to the end.

One of the subtle effects of the existential emphasis on the preeminent reality of the present moment vis-a-vis time past and future is the devaluation of the concept of a moral obligation. If at some point in time past, one had made a commitment in good faith as evaluated under the then existent circumstances to a certain course of action, a marriage for instance, why should he remain pinned down to that commitment, under the changed condition of the present instant. Is not the spirit of faithfulness to the ideal of love better served by the courageous free choice made at each instant to serve that instant's demands in support of the generalized ideal of love than in a slavish sacrifice reluctantly given to some past commitment now overtaken by crisis. One owes the obligation to one's self to be the authentic person he has become. One must live one's life momentarily, experientially to the full. Let the dead past, the dead love be buried and forgotten.

From an atheistic existential viewpoint the case is flawless. But from the theistic existential viewpoint, it is the eternal Thou of Buber to which moral obligations have primary reference. Faithfulness in a relationship of duty, trust or love with the individual "thous" of one's life are not mitigated by the deterioration of the relationship to the I—It level. The responsibilities of real obligations remain because all the I's and Thous and Its, if persons, are all "Thous" to God's "I." Moral commitments made "in good faith" between "Thous" have Him as eternal witness, regardless of the individual's transitory viewpoint. Faithfulness in a relationship becomes a faithfulness before God, and it is not a faithfulness only in a momentary situation.

As Merleau-Ponty seems to have apprehended, the present is not instantaneous for human beings. For us, like it or not, life is a historical experience. The past blends into the future through an interface which is the transitional present. The evenings of distant past and the dawns of the distant future are as surely real as the current instant. Man lives a lifetime with past satisfactions or regrets and future hopes and fears which always condition the present.

Section 6—Philosophy of Being

The philosophers of being, the last in the series, are placed after the existentialists since, in their overall orientation, they are further removed from the pure materialists in thought and because of the great prominence which metaphysics, in the sense of that which is beyond the physical, takes in their work. But on the other hand a characteristic of the group is that these philosophers do, in fact, consider the entire band of "reality" from the most material to the purely spiritual. If the cornerstone of the existentialists is human existence, and reality through that existence, the cornerstone of the philosophers of being is that of the "knowability" of all being, and hence of reality viewed through being. If existentialism is shallow-rooted, the philosophy of being is deep-rooted. And as the existentialists divided into two wings these do also. The one wing goes back to Platonic thought, its primary representative in this century being Alfred North Whitehead; the other, to Aristotle—chiefly those of the Neo-Thomist scholastic tradition whose outstanding representative for the present era is Jacques Maritain. Whereas the scope and detail of the work of individual existentialists was highly differentiated, this group is characterized by its solidarity on its main approaches, though there are, of course, significant differences in methodology and foci of interest. The solidarity reflects the many centuries of background in this overall tradition.

This area of thought will be studied chiefly through the ideas of Whitehead and Maritain. Today, the philosophers of being constitute one of the largest groups of philosophers in the academic sense. They are, here, late in the twentieth century, rising in importance in western Europe, outside of England, sharing the stage with the existentialists. They are becoming increasingly important in the United States with the decline of idealism, and naturalism. Undoubtedly, the analytical school, with whom this group is in strongest contrast, remains the dominant viewpoint in the United States and England as successors to the positivists and materialists.

As a general group, the philosophers of being are theistic in orientation, although one prominent philosopher of being, who is almost exclusively an ontologist, and not a metaphysician, Nicolai Hartmann (1882 - 1950), is an atheist. An Aristotelian, he is almost the only important member of the group who concludes his philosophy on the atheistic note, and also the only one who ascribes to philosophy the primary task of stating problems. Almost universally, the others are dedicated to the proposition that the primary task of philosophy is seeking answers or solutions to problems once they are stated. Oddly, Hartmann's main contribution is in the field of ethics and he was, and still is, important in Germany and England in that area. He proceeds from the doctrine of Max Scheler in terms of values which, like his, have their foundation ultimately in freedom of being. For Hartmann, man determines for himself the real world, his place in it, and the standard to which he himself, as a human being, should aspire and remain faithful. Obviously he does not arrive at the same conclusion as Scheler.

In many ways, the philosophers of being are the universalists. They draw from all of the other philosophic thinkers past and current and, by comparative analysis, take those elements of each which appear to be compatible with their own main line of thought. Also in many ways, they attempt to formulate a "perennial" philosophy, one which can be continuously reappraised and adjusted to fit new problems as they appear and to comprehend and utilize other viewpoints as they are developed. Because of their emphasis on metaphysics, they always refer problems to first principles, seeking to trace each to its roots. With Hartmann, once the problems have been stated in those terms, the philosopher's task is done. He is resolute in regarding the final definition of spiritual existence at the level of conscious being and rejects the Platonic idea of the higher, the more sublime, the infinite goodness.

It is, perhaps, worthwhile to sketch out the very close relationship which must exist among the philosophers of essence, existence and being. As was noted in discussing Scheler, the three descriptive factors must be conjoined in any real entity. They constitute the "Gordian knot" of reality which cannot be separated without total destruction. Real being is specific essence in actual existence. None of the three or no two of the three elements can "survive" in isolation. Yet, they are not merely different aspects of the same thing, and can thus be considered in speculative isolation in a limited way.

We have just seen how the existentialists sought to examine being, human being, as a development of existence. Lived existence in duration determines the momentary human being which, in fact, is. The *essence* of the being somehow changes with time. If the essence changes with time so logically must the being since essence defines the being.

The philosophers of being start about where Merleau-Ponty finished. They deny that being-in-itself and for-itself in dialectic provide the legitimate point of departure. They start with "being is" and then seek to determine its specific nature or essence and then move to its mode of existence or occurrence. The existentialist's dialectic disappears when one attributes to man's specific nature, or essence, the characteristic of growth and maturity in a historic existence; and, as Merleau-Ponty concluded, in *The Structure of Behavior,* that is what man is. Man is not just an animal with an add-on peculiarity of intellectual self-consciousness. As with man so with all other beings, philosophers of being seek to discover the total reality which that being has. Unlike the philosophers of essence, they are not content to view being, including man, as an object of analysis in isolation but as the being stands in relationship to all being through a reduction to first principles. They are generally dedicated to the validity of universal concepts, to the extent that what one says about human beings, or human nature, applies legitimately—to the entire species, as a category, not merely to a series of individuals that happen to have certain characteristics.

The concept "man" means more than just a collection. And the beings under study are in a relationship with their environment—a true relationship which both affects, and is affected by, the beings' existence. Whitehead has said that universals or generalities provide the bridge between "specific notions, applying to a restricted group of facts, for the divination of the general notions which apply to all facts."

Alfred North Whitehead was born in Ramshead, England, February 15, 1861. He specialized in mathematics at Cambridge, being a fellow at Trinity College. He later taught mathematics and physics, and was Dean of Science at the Imperial College, University of London. In 1924 when he was 63, he moved to Harvard as Professor of Philosophy, where he taught until his retirement in 1937. He is considered, and deservedly, by a wide margin, the outstanding philosopher of Anglo-Saxon origin in this century, completely overshadowing both of his principal contemporaries, John Dewey and Bertrand Russell, the latter with whom he collaborated in *Principia Mathematica.*

The first work incorporating Whitehead's philosophy, *Science and the Modern World,* was published in 1926, and established him as a metaphysician. His major work, *Process and Reality,* in which he presents his complete system of thought, was published in 1929. He was a man of tremendous versatility and depth of thought. He covered everything from symbolic logic in mathematics through mechanics in physics and biology to his premier field, the philosophy of religion. In the latter, he is in complete contrast with his early associate, Russell.

Whitehead's background is so diversified and rich that he could be reasonably placed as a representative in any one of several fields—except that he does insist on going to first principles. Science is not the last word. He says, for instance, that the principle of relativity is the key to developing understanding of metaphysics, yet this principle, in turn, can be adequately explained only by resort to metaphysical principles.

Like Russell, Whitehead has been considered one of the English Neorealists because he employs their analytical method, and because he shares their high valuation of science and realism. Whitehead has worked up the results of the natural sciences into a more complete synthesis than any other contemporary philosopher. Consistent with his emphasis on mathematics and logical analysis, he is a Platonist in the strictest sense. Despite Whitehead's assertion, however, that all of Western philosophy consists of footnotes to Plato, his Platonism is different. Plato would never have said that ideas possess no actuality but are pure possibilities. Aristotelianism is found in his works where his intellectualism is united with his broad empiricism. In some respects, he reflects Liebnitz and Spinoza and his aesthetics follows the Aristotelian tradition generally. Whitehead is as devoted to natural dynamism and evolutionism as firmly as Bergson and Dewey, but his naturalism is only an adjunct to his ontological viewpoint. Despite his variety, Whitehead's thought is not shallow. It is as deep as it is extensive. The dominant feature of his system is its extraordinary unity. In discussing his views on the philosophy of Whitehead, Bochenski says (page 227):

His fundamental notions of creativity and prehension are entirely original, and he stretches them to their logical conclusion through applying them at every turn. Thus, he seems to have been thoroughly modern in the sense that he was one of the leading and most modern of philosophers in an age wholly given over to twentieth-century physics, mathematics, biology, and philosophy; yet, at the same time, he maintained his metaphysical speculation on the timeless level at which Plato dealt with these problems.

[For Whitehead] Thought is abstract and we cannot think without abstractions. But abstractions are as dangerous as they are useful. They are often developed from inadequate foundation, as in modern natural science, for example, and can lead to intellectual intolerance, since one may overlook all those concrete elements which do not fit into an abstract scheme. Once abstractions are set up, one tends to take them as dogmas and to regard them as realities. The fallacy of misplaced concreteness can condemn a civilization to sterility. Now, the primordial task of philosophy is the critique of abstractions. The basic ideas assumed by scholars to be free of contradictions must be tested and comparisons made between the abstract schemata of the different sciences and between those of religion and the sciences. Philosophy also develops its own system relying upon more concrete intuitions than are used by the sciences. Philosophy appeals even to the testimony of poetry and religion. Therefore, it is not one among the sciences, but goes beyond all of them. It is indispensable, for without it man would develop synoptic theories without the sober guidance of understanding and reason.

Thus philosophy may also be defined as striving for the complete rationalization of human experience.

Methods of philosophy, then, must be comprehensive in scope and rational. The surrender of reason to brute fact which has characterized the "modern age" must be ended—and quickly— because its effects are now resulting in impoverishment of the human race—its fruits have turned bitter. Whitehead's confidence lies in his conviction that the intelligibility of the universe around us, as revealed by research in depth, demonstrates the capacity of the human reason to, in fact, arrive at true first principles from which the intelligibility takes its source. It is increasingly apparent that it is only this pervasive intelligibility which makes science possible.

The insight displayed so amazingly by Plato and the Greek classicists is but a reflection of what the human mind can achieve given the far greater resources in scientific knowledge and methodology now at its disposal. Speculation in the metaphysical order is not only justified, it is becoming an urgent demand. While metaphysics can only be descriptive and not definitive, the reciprocal contrasts exercised by empiricism and metaphysics are the key to true balance in human progress. Whitehead had written that metaphysics seeks:

> . . .those generalities which characterize the complete reality of fact, and apart from which any fact must sink into an abstraction. But science makes the abstraction, and is content to understand the complete fact in respect to only some of its essential aspects. Science and philosophy mutually criticize each other, and provide imaginative material for each other. A philosophic system should present an elucidation of concrete fact from which the sciences abstract. Also, the scientists should find their principles in the concrete facts which a philosophic system presents.

In his work, *Science and the Modern World,* Whitehead expresses his views concerning the microphysics of that time (1926) and gives a prognosis not much different than is developing in the late twentieth century as we will see in Part III. But of course, Whitehead was the head of the science department of the University of London just before moving to Harvard. He felt deeply the change in philosophic thought implicit in the change from the Newtonian to the Einsteinian models—from continuity to discontinuity. He says:

> One of the most hopeful lines of explanation (in quantum physics) is to assume that an electron does not continuously traverse its path in space. The alternative notion as to its mode of existence is that it appears at a series of discrete positions in space which it occupies for successive durations of time. It is as though an automobile, moving at the average rate of thirty miles an hour along a road, did not traverse the road continuously; but appeared successively at the successive milestones, remaining for two minutes at each milestone. . . .
>
> But now a problem is handed over to the philosophers. This discontinuous existence in space, thus assigned to electrons, is very unlike the continuous existence of material entities which we habitually assume as obvious. The electron seems to be borrowing the character which some people have assigned to the Mahatmas of Tibet. . . .
>
> A new problem is now placed before philosophers and physicists, if we entertain the hypothesis that the ultimate elements of matter are, in their essence, vibratory. By this I mean that apart from being a periodic system, such an element would have no existence. With this hypothesis we have to ask, what are the ingredients which form the vibratory organism. We have already got rid of the matter with its appearance of undifferentiated endurance. . . . The field is now open for the introduction of some new doctrine of organism which may take the place of the materialism with which, since the seventeenth century, science has saddled philosophy.

Here the term "organism" does not imply "a living being," but a developing pattern which each of the discrete events tends to bring to fruition.

Does intelligibility of a product imply intelligence in its production? It will be recalled the Paley theology was based on the "design" of the universe and theoretically "lost" its validity with the findings of Darwin—all was explainable through chance. In fact, the statement has been made that, contrary to there being design, we perceive purpose in such things which is to say intelligibility in such phenomena as the bee's activity because that is the way we think. Our brains are organized to project purpose into all of our sense data acquisition.

If our brains are thus constrained, why are we not thoroughly consistent? For example, why do we distinguish between random and systematic errors in data acquisition and analysis? We know random errors will tend to converge to the true values given a sufficiently large sampling. We know systematic errors will not—there is an intelligible bias in one direction.

It is a fact that we seek to find intelligibility in any data collection. Because we are intelligent, we do seek intelligibility. We subject everything to analysis. We know that once we have identified the consistent relationships between variables, we can, from that point on, provide solutions—not through trial and error—but by direct calculation from one side only. The relationships we identify are real—not imaginary.

The point in the chain of events at which purposive intelligence is directly applied may not be visible. The bee is a case in point, the configuration of its wax honey cell is the optimum. But no one believes the bee at some point sat down and calculated this relationship, and then went to work. The biologic mechanism that directs the bee's specific activity defies analysis. Similarly, in the lifeless world, the crystalline structure of specific minerals is intelligible and can be projected on the basis of the molecular structure. To find the basic reason why there is the observed intelligibility, the research has to be moved back into the atomic and sub-atomic levels. At that point, we are effectively stopped by the state of the science of high energy physics. We are still intelligently seeking for the intelligible relationships and we feel sure that we will ultimately find them.

One can speculate, with some confidence, that, ultimately, we will find some characteristics of pure energy such that, when transformed into pure matter, it takes on the specific forms it does—and in the proportions that it does—so that the chain can be projected forward—link by link to the specific mineral and its specific crystalline structure. It will be an intelligible chain.

Inevitably we will try to find the source of the pure energy from which the material universe derives. We will have to seek something which has being as an actual entity. For energy is a capacity to act and capacity to act resides only in being—an entity—a something with real existence. If the capacity to act is real, then the being in which the capacity inheres is real and the intelligible chain, in fact, will begin with that being.

It seems obtuse to hold that that being, source of all that is intelligible, is not itself intelligent and that somewhere between the source, being, and the bee or the crystal, the pure energy or pure matter acquires, of itself, this characteristic of intelligibility.

Because of Whitehead's deep interest in religion as a field of philosophy, standing in sharp contrast to his criticism of "scientism" in his approach to ontology, he is placed at the forefront in this grouping of philosophers of being, or of what is being regarded in this century as the "new metaphysics." He has a deep-seated faith in reason, as, of course, did Einstein. Although he is, by no means, a rationalist in the limited sense most commonly used since the time of Descartes. His "rationality" is based on the conviction that the ultimate nature of all things is in harmony in a concatenation which is approachable through reason. And, as has been found in the more sophisticated mathematical approaches in physical science, the identification of the basic principles is achievable only through an insight into the nature of things. This insight, as it has been exercised in this century in the basic sciences, shows an immanent set of logical laws in both the aesthetic and scientific orders. Pure deductive or inductive processes, particularly the latter in strict empiricism, are incomplete and inadequate tools. Whitehead stands in clear opposition to the materialist school. Yet Whitehead says, "Our datum is the actual world, including ourselves; and this actual world spreads itself for observation in the guise of the topic of our immediate experience. The elucidation of immediate experience is the sole justification of any thought."

In his earliest work in philosophy, shortly after his move to Harvard, Whitehead viewed God in the Aristotelian image, that of a rather disinterested, detached being. Later he conceived of what might be called a "duality" in God as man can conceive of Him. First, God possesses a "primordial nature" more like Aristotle's than Plato's—infinite, changeless, timeless; second, a "consequent nature" in which God acts in His creative power. In this second sense, Whitehead sees Him in a becoming mode, constantly growing and enriching Himself through His creative activities. It is in this mode that He can be seen as involving Himself in the affairs of His creation. It is a viewpoint reminiscent of Scheler and Schelling and prophetic of Teilhard de Chardin where God becomes, in a sense, the champion of the good in the battle against the degrading entropy of evil. He is battling continuously against evil with the unfailing loyal support of those who suffer and fight against the problems of the world. In presenting this concept Whitehead says:

> There is another side to the nature of God which cannot be omitted. Throughout this exposition of the philosophy of organism we have been considering the primary action of God on the world. From this point of view, He is the principle of concretion—the principle whereby there is initiated a definite outcome from a situation otherwise riddled with ambiguity. Thus, so far, the primordial side of the nature of God has alone been relevant.
>
> But God, as well as being primordial, is also consequent. He is the beginning and the end. He is not the beginning in the sense of conceptual operation, in unison of becoming with every other creative act. Thus, by reason of the relativity of all things, there is a reaction of the world on God. The completion of God's nature into a fullness of physical feeling is derived from the objectification of the world in God. He shares with every new creation its actual world. The concrescent creature is objectified in God as a novel element in God's objectification of that actual world.

This writer views the duality in the nature of God as proposed by Whitehead as an attempt to solve the problem of the one and the many. The "many" relate to the consequent nature of God only—the "one" to His primordial nature only. But he has treated a larger problem by splitting that which is the Unchangeable One. Whitehead provides the philosophical base for the "process theologians" so prominent in the later twentieth century and who stand in sharp contrast to the Neo-Thomist theologians for whom God is the Unchangeable One. We will look at this problem later.

The mystery of God's intrinsic nature must remain hidden to us, but the various religious insights reveal in the personality of God deep concern and almost anguish in sympathy for our earthly plight. Whitehead sees the dignity of man in his position as a transcendental creature of God, who by his free will can contribute toward the eventual victory of good. For Whitehead, the true spirit of Humanism can be attained only in consonance with our growth in appreciation of man's relationship to himself, his fellowman and the world in relationship to the overall harmony of God.

Jacques Maritain was born in Paris, November 18, 1882, and was brought up in an atmosphere of liberal Protestantism. He went to the Sorbonne and was exposed to the ideas of the rational materialistic philosophers—that natural science could provide all the answers. At the Sorbonne, he met Raissa Oumansoff, a Russian Jewess and fellow student. They agreed on their disagreement—on the philosophies being taught, and apparently on other things, for they were married in November 1904. Over the years the two collaborated in several philosophical works.

Maritain took his degree at the Sorbonne in philosophy in 1905 and that same year was converted to Catholicism. He spent two additional years at Heidelburg studying biology and then returned to Paris and the study of Thomistic philosophy. From 1914 to 1939 he was professor of modern philosophy at the Institute Catholique. From 1932 on, he gave yearly courses at the Institute of Medieval Studies in Toronto and was professor at Princeton from 1941-1942, and Columbia from 1941-1944, under sponsorship of the French government. After World War II, from 1945-1948, he was French ambassador to the Vatican; and following this, he was professor of philosophy at Princeton from 1948-1955.

Maritain bases his philosophy in Thomas Aquinas, but he has incorporated much from other philosophies of both classical and modern times and from data supplied by anthropology, political science, sociology and psychology. His principal theme is that there are different ways of looking at reality, much as this writer has indicated, science, philosophy, poetry, mysticism, each with its proper sphere. For Maritain the individual is supreme in relation to the society or state in his personal dignity. There is a need for a personal moral philosophy in relation to tradition and revelation for guidance of the individual in the existential state of man, and for the pluralistic cooperation of man in the pursuit of the common good in political life. As Collins sees him (Collins, 1962):

> Jacques Maritain's arresting quality springs from his sensitivity to what is specifically new in our world, as combined with his fidelity to St. Thomas and some commentators. This crossgraining of old and new underlies his approach to natural philosophy and modern science. He sees no need to sacrifice the essential points in either standpoint, provided that we recognize them to be distinct types of knowledge. He refuses to reduce the modern scientific analysis to an

already anticipated subdivision of the Aristotelian philosophy of nature, just as he finds no good grounds for eliminating that philosophy itself in the line of ontological explanation. To observe Maritain's mind working on the testimony of the French poets or on the data of social scientists is to learn how a philosopher proceeds at the very frontier of research. There, the modern esthetic and social discoveries of the human spirit retain their freshness, without being put off from all relationship with the Thomistic metaphysics of knowledge and theory of society.

Maritain is no proponent of abstruseness in philosophic language. He writes with the ease of a master who has no need to demonstrate his erudition by constant use of philosophic technicalese. He makes a point of the need for clarity if thought is to be communicated. In the preface to his book, *Man and the State* (Maritain, 1954), he says:

> Finally, there is an issue—quite extraneous to this book which I should like to raise, for it relates to a point with which I have been long concerned. To the extent to which philosophy is wisdom, philosophical language should not be confined to an academic museum of abstract formulae or logistic symbols, or to a literary heaven of distinguished and highbrow angels intent upon not speaking like the people. Philosophical language should use images—which are the wellspring of ideas—and current, common, everyday idioms—which are the vehicles of people's creativity and insure the contact of thought with concrete life.

In his work, *Human Knowledge and Metaphysics* (Maritain, 1952), Maritain addresses the current problem of man and the approach to God through reason. He says:

> If civilization is to survive, the coming age must be an age of spiritual as well as social integration.
> Today the human mind is torn and divided between Positivism and Irrationalism. Pragmatism succeeded in obliging philosophers to take certain basic aspects of reality into consideration, and in developing what might be called the sociology of knowledge; as a

philosophy—however, pragmatism has been a failure. The same can be said of Idealism's attempt at a supreme synthesis, an attempt which at times had unquestionable grandeur, but which wound up in a dream of dialectical reason, because it was centered solely upon the human mind.

What is essentially needed is a renewal of metaphysics. The conceptions of modern science—the unification of matter and energy, physical indeterminism, the notion of space-time, the new reality vouchsafed both to quality and duration, the concept of a cosmos of stars and electrons in which the stars are the heavenly laboratories of elements, and which is subjected everywhere to genesis and transmutation, a universe finite but whose limits cannot be attained because of the curvature of space, a world which dynamically evolves in a definite direction, namely, both toward the highest forms of individuation and concentration and toward a simultaneous degradation of the quality of its total energy—all this is, no doubt, external description and scientific imagery rather than ontological insight, and cannot directly serve the purpose of any philosophical or metaphysical extrapolations; yet all this constitutes, at the same time, a basic representation of the world incomparably more favorable to the edification of a philosophy of nature and more often to the deepening labor of metaphysical reason than the old Newtonian physics. The opportunity is now given for that reconciliation between science and wisdom for which the human mind thirsts. What is needed first and foremost is a rediscovery of Being, and by the same token a rediscovery of love.

This means, axiomatically, a rediscovery of God. The existential philosophies which are today in fashion are but a sign of a certain deep want and desire to find again the sense of Being. This want is now unfulfilled, for these philosophies are still enslaved by Irrationalism and seek for the revelation of existence, for ontological ecstasy, in the breaking of reason, in the experience of Despair and Nothingness. True existentialism is the work of reason. The act by virtue of which I exist and things exist, transcends concepts and ideas; it is a mystery for the intellect.

But the intellect lives on this mystery. It does so in its most natural activity, which is as ordinary, daily and vulgar as eating or drinking: for the act of existing is indeed the very object of every judgement. It is perceived by that intellectual intuition, immersed in sense-experience, which is the common treasure (all the more precious as it is natural and imbues the depths of our thought) of all our assertions, of all this mysterious activity by means of which we declare either *ita est* or *fiat*! in the face of the world or at the moment of making a decision. Now, when the intellect passes the threshold of philosophy, it does so by becoming aware of this intellectual intuition, freeing its genuine power, and making it the peculiar weapon of a knowledge whose subject matter is Being itself. I do not here refer to Platonic essences. I refer to the act of existing insofar as it grounds and centers the intelligible structure of reality, as it expands into activity in every being, and as, in its supreme, un-created plenitude, it activates and attracts to itself the entire dynamism of nature. At their ontological peak, in the transcendence of the Pure Act and the Abso-lute, Being and Reason are one and the same reality. In the created realm Reason confronts Being and labors to conquer it, both to transfer Being into its own immaterial life and immaterially to be or be-come Being. In perceiving Being, Reason knows God—the self-subsisting Act of being—in an enigmatic but inescapable manner.

Amplifying the difficulties which Maritain sees confronting the existential philosophers is the momentariousness of mean-ing in life. Each instant of existence is its own measure. It builds upon the past and it looks to the future but it is only this dis-crete fleeting instant which has reality. It is Humean in its se-quencing of life frame by frame only one of which is fully illuminated. The self is reduced to receiver of impressions and a spontaneous reactor to the impressions. Their dialectic of being-in-itself and being-for-itself is integrated into an authentic being only with difficulty. For the philosopher of being, exis-tence is an experiencing through a duration of life. Man lives in a real history—his own—his plans are an extension into fu-ture history. He is self from beginning to end. His life is real. The experiences are real. His fellow beings are real. His history is real. He, as a being, is real. Maritain goes on to contrast the two philosophies of existence and Being. He says:

> So the prime intuition of Being is the intuition of the solidity and inexorability of existence; and, secondly, of the death and nothingness to which my existence is liable. And thirdly, in the same flash of intuition, which is but my becoming aware of the intelligible value of Being, I realize that the solid and inexorable existence perceived in anything whatsoever implies—I don't know yet in what way, perhaps in things themselves, perhaps separately from them— some absolute, irrefragable existence, completely free from nothingness and death. These three intellective leaps—to actual existence as asserting itself independently from me; from this sheer objective existence to my own threatened existence; and from my existence spoiled with nothingness to absolute existence—are achieved within that same and unique intuition, which philosophers would explain as the intuitive perception of the essentially analogical content of the first concept, the concept of Being.
>
> The tragedy of the philosophers who call themselves existentialists, whether they be Christian existentialists like Gabriel Marcel, or atheistic existentialists like the French disciples of Husserl and Heidegger, lies in their having the feeling or apperception of the primacy of being, or existence, while at the same time denying, under the pretext that it is abstract, that the notion of being has any value: so that they see in it only an empty word. If I, on the other hand, am a Thomist, it is in the last analysis because I have understood that the intellect sees, and that it is cut out to conquer being. In its most perfect function, which is not to manufacture ideas, but to judge, the intellect seizes upon existence exercized by things. And, at the same time, it forms the first of its concepts—the concept of being, which metaphysics will bring out, in its own light, at the highest degree of abstractive visualization.
>
> I believe that the central intuition on which the Existentialism of Kierkegaard lived was, in the last analysis, the very same which is at the core of Thomism: the intuition of the absolutely unique value and

primacy of existence, *existentia ut exercita;* but then
this intuition arose in the midst of an anguished faith,
stripped of its intelligible or super-intelligible organism, a faith which desperately awaited miracle and
refused the mystical possession after which it thirsted,
and was born of a radically irrationalist thought
which, rejecting and sacrificing essences, fell back
upon the night of subjectivity. And I believe that the
central intuition on which contemporary Existentialism lives, or dies, is the negative aspect of that Kierkegaardian intuition, henceforth emptied of the faith
which once animated it—I mean the intuition of the
absolute Nothingness of the creature, henceforth without a Creator, and the radical absurdity of existence
uprooted from God.

Then in discussing where the roots of philosophy ought to
lie, Maritain says:

> The universe of intelligible objects, to which, first
> and foremost, we owe our loyalty is not that uni-
> verse of verbal conclusions which serve all too often
> as material blinders which keep a man from gazing
> into the eyes of other men. It is the universe of real-
> ity itself, made intelligible in act and objectivized be-
> fore the mind, and that universe is transparent, not
> opaque. From the perceived object, and through the
> perceived object, it leads to that other reality which
> is the thought that also seeks to grasp it, albeit per-
> haps clumsily, and which must in its turn be made
> intelligible in act and objectivized before the mind,
> and respected in its depths.
>
> If the notion of objectivity is thus taken in its real
> meaning, as including existing reality and even that
> of the subjects which seek to grasp it, it must be
> said that the more a philosophy possesses objective
> value and derives its life from the object, the more
> it has the sense of intellectual justice. And the more
> a philosophy discards the object in order to seek it-
> self in the folds of subjectivity—a subjectivity en-
> trenched within the individuality of the ego, instead
> of being spiritualized and universalized by its com-
> munication with objective being—the more it loses
> the sense of intellectual justice.

Although the ideas of St. Thomas were looked at in a general way at the beginning of this review of the concept of man, it seems a good idea to take a look at them in modern times. Thomism is above all an intellectual system. It holds we acquire knowledge of truth by intellectual insights obtained through rational analysis as applied to the observation of the nature of being. It is largely a deductive process, inductive processes being necessary, but secondary. For while it is a necessary process to draw correct inferences from the data presented, it is also necessary to take the induced conclusions and see to what further principles they will lead. In this way only can one arrive at the first principles.

One induces, even predicts, with high confidence, that because we have observed the sun rising every morning in the past that it will probably do so the following morning. The fact that the earth is itself turning and causing this phenomenon, can only be deduced by taking this observed fact and relating it to yet other observations in the universe as Copernicus, and before him the Pythagorians had done. Thus, the intellectual or speculative manipulative role is of the essence in all true advance in knowledge. But for this to be valid, one must also hold that it is possible for man to perceive reality. The relationship of God to the world in Thomism is arrived at by such processes. They are different than Whitehead's.

The intent of the philosophy of being generally in all of its various aspects is to go to the root of all problems facing man. With Hartmann, the correct formulation of the problem is the primary product. With Whitehead and Maritain and their supporters, the proposal of principles of solution is as much an essential step, as is stating the problem. In Part III as an extension of the discussion on various current scientific hypotheses we will look at alternatives in first principles including those of the metaphysicians.

In the writer's view, the difficulty, if it is a difficulty, with the philosophers of being is their very dedication to "sobriety" which makes their works of very limited appeal. In an age looking for "shock," their methodology is scarcely adaptable to making the best seller lists. It does not seem impossible, however, to make the treatment more palatable to aesthetic appetites through lively analytical work in poetry and art—which, in fact, Maritain has done but in a secondary way. This requirement is essentially artistic or dramatic and the blend of strict reason and art is a rare one. Thomas Aquinas did produce some excellent poetry of course but as an adjunct to his theologic rather than philosophic role. Perhaps there is still room for the ancient appeal of Augustine and Bonaventure who never bothered to make strict breaks between the two fields which, at least in metaphysics, are closely related. It also might help the current malaise of the process in theology.

In summarizing the position of the philosophers of being with the others looked at previously, Bochenski says:

> Of course each of the philosophical systems discussed has its own weaknesses. But in evaluating these systems, one has always to bear in mind how much their achievements surpassed the capacity of late nineteenth-century philosophy, for they have produced an ontology and an organic conception of reality. Whitehead and the Thomists adopt an intermediate position by propounding both an ontology and a metaphysics. Yet Thomistic ontology is not inferior to Hartmann's and it affords the basis for a more comprehensive and coherent conception of reality than is to be found in Hartmann.
>
> Much more striking, however, than the differences between the tendencies within the philosophy of being, is the fundamental agreement which these differing conceptions exhibit. This is all the more remarkable in that these tendencies spring from such varied sources—Einstein's physics, the Marburg school, scholasticism. Running through most of their statements about the nature of knowledge and the hierarchical structure of the world, or about the spirit and its freedom, there is broad agreement among the philosophers of being, and their systems are examples of all that is best in the achievements of contemporary philosophical study.

Before leaving the philosophers it is worthwhile to take a look at what attempts are being made to achieve a true "perennial" philosophy. On this score Collins (1962) says (page 266, 267):

> Philosophical progress does not consist in replacing one limited utterance by another, but in the deliberate program of orchestrating all the individual efforts in the interests of the whole. Among the major configurations of philosophic insight, Haberlin lists the philosophies of Parmenides and Heraclitus, Plato

and Aristotle, Augustine and Aquinas (in their non-dogmatic aspect), Descartes and Leibnitz, Kant and Hegel, Fechner, Wundt and Fischer (in their nonempiricist aspects), Schopenhauer and the contemporary existentialists.

This impressive roll call makes perennial philosophy practically equivalent to all forms of Western philosophy. Nevertheless, there are some persistent efforts being made today to widen its scope even more, so as to include the Eastern philosophies as well. In the concluding chapter of his survey of Eastern and Western philosophy, the eminent Indian thinker and statesman, Sarvepalli Radhakrishnan, makes an eloquent plea for a perennial philosophy conceived on a worldwide scale. For, a comparative study of human intellectual history shows that philosophy recognizes no national, cultural, or religious frontiers. Although the different systems of thought are conditioned by temporal circumstances, there is a universal and abiding core of method and doctrine.

Radhakrishnan experiences no difficulty, for instance, in establishing a detailed rapprochement between the Upanishads of India and European existentialism. Both movements are concerned with the nature of man, treated not merely as a natural object of scientific investigation but also as a conscious center of freedom. They exhibit a common, perennial awareness of man's plight, at the moment when he becomes aware of eternal horizons beyond nature, and yet is in anguished dread about his ability to make the flight of transcendence. "Lead me from the unreal to the real: lead me from darkness to light. Lead me from death to immortality." This cry for divine help is sounded in the Upanishads, but it is reechoed in all the epochs of history. Radhakrishnan quotes Plotinus, Augustine, and the Koran as witnesses to the central human intuition that man can find fulfillment of his aspirations only in a union with God. Every doctrinal effort is an elaboration upon this theme, a one-sided attempt to express it within a special historical situation. The worldwide perennial philosophy appears in many garments, yet through them all it displays but one inner spirit: the nisus of man's transcendence toward God.

It cannot have escaped the notice of the reader that all of the "current" philosophers he has reviewed in any detail are either dead or very old men. Where are the young ones? Where are the women: What are their views? Aside from the fact that philosophy is not a field promising high financial rewards so that there are no doubt fewer outstanding individuals who enter it while still young, but also among those now in the field there seems to be a pause of uncertainty. The writer quoted Walter Kaufmann in the introduction to Part II in which he pointed out the dilemma of modern philosophy—trapped between the analytical and the existential. One gets the picture of a group of young, or middle-aged, lions circling the carcass for a likely place to begin the feast. But there is a sensing that the choice existential and phenomenological areas have been fairly well cleaned out by the experts, the old lions. The materialist area is almost completely exhausted and the pure analytical area as Kaufmann has said is trivial. What the writer would like to see as an interested spectator is not a compromise between the analytical and existential viewpoints, which he cannot visualize, but a true synthesis of methodologies in a contrapuntal mode using the analytical and the dramatic existential in the exploration of the rich and rewarding ontological and metaphysical area providing both dark and light meat.

Chapter 7

SOCIOLOGICAL VIEWPOINTS

This book was initially conceived as a vehicle to promote a broader scanning of mankind in its total humanity by sociologists for sociological purposes. The writer feels that there is no way society can exist over any long period of time without a general conviction in society of the transcendental nature of man. There is no other rational answer to the Hobbesian question. The social contracts of Locke, Rousseau, Hobbes and others are pure myths and not myths in their purposive role of illustrating reality. Hobbes identified the problem correctly: He held that "All passions may be reduced to the Desire of Power" and unless man stands in awe of something beyond him, some force or being more powerful than himself which can use reward or punishment as sanctions to behavior, rational man would follow his own self-interest in seeking power to his own destruction.

That something and its enforcement capability has to be real and credible to the individual. The number of absolute philanthropists in society is small, so the abstract concept of the advancement of humanity is of no great value. As our current age has revealed, governments made up of men may do as much to foster disobedience as obedience and disobedience with public approbation in many cases. That leaves little else to control man's aggressiveness. Man's instincts, such as they are, have from the beginning been predatory with the exception of his relations to a very close circle. The instincts provide no fall back position. If man is nothing else than a gifted animal, this is exactly how he should and inevitably will respond. Unfortunately he does not have the built-in self-control imposed by instinct which the animals have. The conscience or consciousness of guilt, which in most people is the mediate guide to moral behavior, is largely conditioned by the attitudes internalized since infancy. Few people feel guilty after having successfully avoided established speed limits and, given no higher morality, a law against murder or rape has the same qualitative sanction. Alvin Gouldner summarizes well the situation in sociology on this point. He says (Gouldner, 1970, pages 140-141):

The internal structure of sociology may be usefully characterized in terms of what it does not do and in terms of what it excludes. In addition to sociology's systematic neglect of economic factors, there is another generally evident intellectual omission from the internal structure of academic sociological practice: this is the absence of a sociology of morals or values. Despite the fact that Academic Sociology, beginning with Sociological Positivism, had hailed the significance of shared moral values, despite the fact that Emile Durkheim had called for and promised to create such a sociology of morals, and despite the fact that a concern with moral values was central to Max Weber's sociology of religion as well as to Talcott Parsons' "voluntaristic" theory, there still remains no concentration of scholarship that might be called a "sociology of moral values."

This omission is paradoxical because the concerns of Academic Sociology, seen as a patterned arrangement of scholarly energies and attention, have traditionally emphasized the importance of moral values both for the solidarity of societies and for the well-being of individuals. Structurally, then, Academic Sociology is characterized both by the importance it attributes to values and by its failure to develop—in its characteristic manner which transforms almost everything into a specialization—a distinctive sociology of moral values. This omission is, I believe, due largely to the fact that a full-scale analysis of moral values would tend to undermine their autonomy.

Moral values, in fact, cannot be autonomous. They must be based on values of the spirit, in some sense. Sometimes, sociologists are also philosophers, but generally they are not, at least in their professional approach to social problems. Thus, they rarely explicate their broad personal views on the nature of man. Man is viewed by sociology as a member of society, rather than as an individual and hence, his activities in the societal arena and only his secondary motivations are seen as the proper objects of sociological investigation.

The writer earlier noted that sociologists must do better in conveying their understanding of man if they are to maintain public credibility and relevance. But by and large, one cannot take their readings and from those deduce their personal ideas regarding the nature of man, or the source of human dignity if indeed there is such a thing. Most sociologists construct a model of man and then play back observed behavior against that model to determine conformance or lack of conformance. The analysis responds to behavior in various situations so that one can evaluate man only *as though* he were actuated like the model. When the model is apt for those situations for which the model was developed, man's behavior can be predicted with fair reliability at least statistically. As limited purpose tools, the models are useful.

Where such models are discernible, the comments in the following personal sketches will discuss them very briefly. These sketches do not necessarily represent the sociologists' personal view of the nature of man although certainly they may reflect that view in some cases. Greater attention will be given to the extrapolation of the model to the solution of the Hobbesian question. What is the cohesive which the model will give to society in its broadest sense so that it provides for the preservation of society?

Talcott Parsons was beyond doubt the best known and most widely read and followed sociologist of the mid-twentieth century. He still represents the dominant American viewpoint, although his system is coming increasingly under critical attack. Alvin Gouldner's work, *The Coming Crisis in Western Sociology,* cited earlier, is chiefly a criticism of the Parsonsian sociology. Parsons was born in Colorado Springs, Colorado, December 13, 1902, and received his doctorate at the University of Heidelburg in the fields of sociology and economics. He has been professor of sociology at Harvard from 1944 until his death in 1979. He has been widely honored and has done much professional work outside of his university activities.

He is the father of the "school of sociology" known as the Structural-Functionalists and in his best known work, the *Structure of Social Action,* Parsons developed a functional model of society which holds that it is self-sustaining. Through the interplay of structure and function, those activities, or those modes of life, which are functional will continue; those which are dis-functional will disappear. The mechanism is somewhat like the drive of biologic evolution. Parsons in his later works, since about 1960, having previously attacked the nineteenth century social evolutionist theories of Herbert Spencer (1820-1903), has adapted some of those views to accommodate change in his social mechanism.

Parsons' main thought hinges on the interplay of forces tending to return stability to an established structure threatened by any disturbing elements. For purposes of this study, looking at the Hobbesian question, if one were to examine an existing stable society, and one in which there was a culturally induced morality under attack by disruptive forces, how will it respond? If the attack springs from sources in human nature induced by such motivation as avarice, sex drive, aggressive instincts and opportunism, then there is the natural, almost homeostatic, stability-seeking functional reaction of increased social emphasis on the culturally-induced morality to counterbalance the disruptive forces. Theoretically, feedback into the system from effects of any increased crime or criminality induce greater emphasis on the insemination of morality to restore stability. The process is similar to that of temperature control. If the weather gets colder, the thermostat "tells" the furnace to burn longer to maintain the desired temperature.

Obviously, if this stabilizing mechanism is overpowered, the device of culture-induced morality is not of itself adequate. So increased law enforcement comes into the picture as a primary or supplementary device to maintain stability. This is in accordance with Nietzsche's observation, "Some say virtue is necessary but, in truth, they only believe that police are necessary." Inevitably under Parson's schema, societies will develop the necessary structural adjustments and functional responses to maintain society in a stable form. Parson's reply to the Hobbesian question would be that society will find a way to maintain stability largely within its present structural-functional framework which has survived many crises by increasing emphasis on the effective homeostatic function. The writer leaves this question to the judgment of the reader to decide how effectively this has worked in practice in the current age.

Alvin Gouldner was born in New York, July 29, 1920. He received his A.B. degree at City College of New York, and his M.A. and Ph.D degrees at Columbia University. He is the Max Weber Resident Professor of Social Theory at Washington University, St. Louis, Missouri. He too has been widely honored in his profession and has lectured as a visiting scholar at many universities and at many seminars.

Gouldner is not a formulator of general systems or theories in the sense of Parsons. In many ways, such general schema appear to be one of his main critical targets. As was seen in the introduction to this book, he is critical of current sociology and announces an imminent crisis, primarily because sociology has taken a too detached view of society. Society, and man in it, have been examined in the manner of laboratory specimens in a control group when society is better conceived of as an arena of action, one in which the sociologist is himself a participant. In many ways, Gouldner's position as the Max Weber professor is appropriate because his ideas on the close relationship between objective and subjective viewing of social phenomena are closely allied to Weber's. As will be recalled, Weber used the concept of *Verstehen,* a total combined understanding of the subjective and objective nature in observation of social phenomena. But Gouldner, even more than Weber, adds the subjective "background assumptions," which the viewer brings to bear on the investigation, whether he is conscious of them or not. Therefore, in coming up with an explanation of social behavior from individually observed and interpreted empirical evidence, quite likely the resulting explanation (or ultimately theorizing therefrom) will be conditioned by subjective factors not within the control limits of the experiment or observation.

Thus, if a group of theorists views a series of social phenomena and they as individuals independently explain them, each would tailor his observations to fit certain preconceptions of "what ought to have been" and he will explain these preconceptions rather than the actual phenomena. Each will explain the observed sequence of events according to his own system of theorizing, or if they are absolutely impossible to explain, will write them off as anomalous events and of little significance.

If Gouldner is in fact, as he seems to be, basically Weberian in his outlook, he is a middle of the road sociologist in his own viewpoints of man's motivation. Looking at the Hobbesian question directly as to what is the cohesive force which holds society together, he would probably conclude that the vast bulk of people comprising society represents a combination of open utilitarianism and honest personal morality in various mixes—a continuum between extremes. The ordinary individual would be constantly seeking a balance point in being a fair and decent person, but at the same time in getting his proper or greater share of the rewards. There are few absolute scoundrels and few absolute saints. Thus, there is inherent conflict and also inherent stability. The opposing interplay results in a gradual shifting in the "morality" of the social composite as the center of gravity moves in accordance with weights given by the individuals in society at various times and places to the selfish or unselfish motivation. The collective sense is made by the individuals in society. Gouldner's view of the current level of morality is not encouraging (pages 389, 390).

In this new period, traditional moralities and religions continue to lose their hold on men's faith. Once sacred symbols, such as the flag, are mingled defiantly with the sensual and become, as in some recent art forms, a draping for the "great American nude." "Pop Art" declares an end to the distinction between fine art and advertising, in much the same manner that dramaturgy obliterates the distinciton between "real life" and the theater. The "Mafia" become businessmen; the police are sometimes difficult to distinguish from the rioters except by their uniforms; heterosexuality and homosexuality come to be viewed by some as akin to the difference between righthandedness and lefthandedness; the television program becomes the definition of reality. The antihero becomes the hero. Once established hierarchies of value and worth are shaken, and the sacred and profane are now mingled in grotesque juxtapositions. The new middle class seeks to cope with the attenuation of its conventional standards of utility and morality by retreating from both and by seeking to fix its perspective in aesthetic standards, in the appearance of things.

The main point in Gouldner's ideas for a "Reflexive Sociology" which he also terms a moral sociology is that under this concept the sociologist takes the individual as the base point. Society is made by man and for men, and not the reverse. In his epilogue he discusses and summarizes the role of reflexive society in *The Coming Crisis in Western Sociology.* He says:

A Reflexive Sociology, though, insists upon the reality of these different levels and of the tensions among them. It sees that history, culture, and society never exhaust biography, that everywhere men live with the "loose ends" of an existence that they are constantly striving to pull together.

In some measure this effort at integration was once the task of religion. Western religions sought, among other things, to bridge the different levels of existence by affirming their common origin in and governance by a Supreme Being. As the traditional religions broke down in the eighteenth and nineteenth centuries, science came increasingly albeit surreptitiously to serve as an integrating philosophy of life. Instead of seeing man, society, and species as part of a God-created whole, science sought to integrate existence by tacitly premising the unity and the hegemony of the human species. Instead of placing God at the ideological center of gravity, it placed man and society. From this standpoint the rest of the universe was an empire that stood waiting to be claimed, conquered, and exploited for man's advantage. Presumably, it was there to be known, and it was to be known in order that it might be used. Science, in fine, sought to unify human experience by sanctioning and empowering the imperialism of the human species, and by dangling before men the promise of undreamed riches born of its new power. It may be that, underlying the world of science fiction, or, for that matter, the recent scientific efforts to scan the universe for signals of intelligence elsewhere, mankind has begun to have a value sense of the grim deficiencies of human ethnocentrism: the suspicion that homosapiens is not alone in the universe is a suspicion that the universe may not be ours. It is part of the absurdity of our time that the world of science fiction may sometimes be based upon a more humane ethic—if not a sounder perfection of "reality"—than the world of social science. (Page 510).

This is about as close as Gouldner ever gets to saying perhaps there is something else which can influence mankind. Aside from the subtle "dig" at the absurd transparency of our scientific self-deception, he would have done better going to the writers of non-fictional physics rather than science fiction.

Those in the hard sciences are among the least complacent in our self-centeredness. Nevertheless, as in the Parsonsian structural-functional approach, Gouldner finds there has to be a balance of moral motivation from some source or society would, in fact, collapse.

While Parsons uses an "as if" morality to stabilize, Gouldner seems to offer some "at root" human goodness which will come to the forefront. He feels that morality is not so much learned at "intuited." Gouldner insists that morality requires personal, historical, and cultural responsibility in freedom. Therein lies the problem. What is the source of responsibility within the purely biological approach?

In my view, both Parsons' and Gouldner's models for stability in society in any autonomous stance end in fiction, the former a construct, suspended from a theocentric history no longer applicable, the latter a hopeful imponderable—an awakening of man to his real responsibilities. There seems no reason to believe man, the gifted animal, as a gifted animal, is either inherently good or bad. In fact, goodness or badness are meaningless terms in that context. Pure biologic man is just intelligent and selfish. Unless man has a motivation to use his intelligence unselfishly, society is in poor hands with such animals. Neither Parsons' model nor Gouldner's apparent viewpoint provide that motivation. Although, in all honesty, Gouldner does not claim to, he merely emphasizes there is a problem.

Dennis Wrong was born in Toronto, Ontario, Canada, November 22, 1923, and received his Ph.D. degree in sociology at Columbia University in 1956. He had been a professor of sociology at New York University since 1963. Wrong, like Gouldner, is disaffected with the prevailing structural-functional theory of sociology and, generally, for the same reasons as Gouldner. He feels that it portrays a dehumanized society which it then manipulates in its models in an artificial world.

Wrong goes further than Gouldner in his criticism—or, perhaps, he is only somewhat more precise in his points of difference. But he does go beyond Gouldner in attacking some of the overemphasis on the extreme models, which truly take a look at man at a very short focal length—an example of Henri Poincare's satirical view of the elephant through a microscope. As in Poincare's case, revealing the elephant as a multicellular organism—the conclusions are true, but such a view does not tell us very much about the elephant. It is a less informative approach in fact than that of the groping Jainian blindmen. At least they were getting some appreciation of scale.

Wrong's criticism is perhaps best indicated in his article, "The Oversocialized Conception of Man," (Wrong, 1961) in which he states, "The view that man is invariably pushed by internalized norms or pulled by the lure of self validation by others ignores— to speak archaically for the moment—both the highest and the lowest, both the beast and the angel in his nature." In this article, Wrong addresses the Hobbesian question directly, saying that, in some ways, Parsons' entire system is an attempt to explain it, first on Positivist lines and then later, on Freudian lines. Because Wrong addresses the Hobbesian question in some detail as it is seen in current sociology, this writer feels that it is worth quoting at some length to clarify the total picture and not just Wrong's view. In looking at current views, Wrong says,

The first secular social theorist in the history of Western thought, and one of the first clearly to discern and define the problem of order in human society long before Darwinism made awareness of it a commonplace, Hobbes was a dialectical thinker who refused to separate answers from questions, solutions to society's enduring problems from the conditions creating the problems.

What is the answer of contemporary sociological theory to the Hobbesian question? There are two main answers, each of which has come to be understood in a way that denies the reality and meaningfulness of the question. Together they constitute a model of human nature, sometimes clearly stated, more often implicit in accepted concepts, that pervades modern sociology. The first answer is summed up in the notion of the "internalization of social norms." The second, more commonly employed or assumed in empirical research, is the view that man is essentially motivated by the desire to achieve a positive image of self by winning acceptance or status in the eyes of others.

The following statement represents, briefly and broadly, what is probably the most influential contemporary sociological conception—and dismissal—of the Hobbesian problem: "To a modern sociologist imbued with the conception that action follows institutionalized patterns, opposition of individual and common interests has only a very limited relevance or is thoroughly unsound." From this writer's perspective, the problem is an unreal one: human conduct is totally shared by common norms or "institutionalized patterns." Sheer ignorance must have led people who were unfortunate enough not to be modern sociologists to ask, "How is order possible?" A thoughtful bee or ant would never inquire, "How is the social order of the hive or ant-hill possible?" for the opposite of that order is unimaginable when the instinctive endowment of the insects ensures its stability and built-in harmony between "individual and common interests." Human society, we are assured, is not essentially different, although conformity and stability are there maintained by non-instinctive processes. Modern sociologists believe that they have understood these processes and that they have not merely answered but disposed of the Hobbesian question, showing that, far from expressing a valid intimation of the tensions and possibilities of social life, it can only be asked out of ignorance.

The degree to which conformity is frequently the result of coercion rather than conviction is minimized. Either someone has internalized the norms, or he is "unsocialized," a feral or socially-isolated child, or a psychopath. Yet Freud recognized that many people, conceivably a majority fail to acquire superegos. "Such people," he wrote, "habitually permit themselves to do any bad deed that procures them something they want, if only they are sure that no authority will discover it or make them suffer for it; their anxiety relates only to the possibility of detection. Present-day society had to take into account the prevalence of this state of mind." The last sentence suggests that Freud was aware of the decline of "inner-direction," of the Protestant conscience, about which we have heard so much lately. So let us turn to the other elements of human nature that sociologists appeal to in order to explain, or rather explain away, the Hobbesian problem.

Parsons' model of the "complementarity of expectations," the view that in social interaction men mutually seek approval from one another by conforming to shared norms, is a formalized version of what has tended to become a distinctive sociological perspective on human motivation. Ralph Linton states it in explicit psychological terms: "The need for eliciting favorable responses from others is an almost constant component of (personality). Indeed, it is not too much to say that there is very little organized human behavior which is not directed toward its satisfaction in at least some degree."

Of course, such an image of man is, like all the others mentioned, valuable for limited purposes so long as it is not taken for the whole truth. What are some of its deficiencies? To begin with, it neglects the other half of the model of human nature presupposed by current theory: moral man, guided by his built-in super-ego and beckoning ego-ideal. In recent years sociologists have been less interested than they once were in culture and national character as backgrounds to conduct, partly because stress on the concept of "role" as the crucial link between the individual and the social structure has directed their attention to the immediate situation in which social interaction takes place. Man is increasingly seen as a "role-playing" creature, responding eagerly or anxiously to the expectations of other role-players in the multiple group settings in which he finds himself. Such an approach, while valuable in helping us grasp the complexity of a highly differentiated social structure such as our own, is far too often generalized to serve as a kind of ad hoc social psychology, easily adaptable to particular sociological purposes.

But there is a difference between the Freudian view on the one hand and both sociological and neo-Freudian conceptions of man on the other. To Freud man is a social animal without being entirely a socialized animal. His very social nature is the source of conflicts and antagonisms that create resistance to socialization by the norms of the societies which have existed in the course of human history. . . . All cultures, as Freud contended, do violence to man's socialized bodily drives, but this in no sense means that men could possibly exist without culture or independently of society. From such a standpoint, man may properly be called as Norman Brown has called him, the "neurotic" or the "discontented" animal and repression may be seen as the main characteristic of human nature as we have known it in history.

Wrong does not himself formulate an answer to the Hobbesian question in the article, but merely says sociologists must do better. But even closer to the matter at issue he seems to have missed the central point that Hobbes is making. The social contract is only Hobbes' answer, and that, likely, with tongue in cheek. Because, as Wrong noted in his article, Hobbes was probably too sophisticated to take the "social contract" as an actual agreement in any real sense. It is another "as if" construct. Hobbes' point, as stated earlier in this work, is that man has to "stand in awe" of something more powerful than himself—something he believes will hold him individually responsible for himself. Hobbes' realistic answer for his time, and he was not addressing a society of convinced gifted animals by any means, was a strong central government. Yet, here Hobbes recognized a higher norm—but not a higher government. In case of conflict between spiritual and temporal "orders" man can do nothing but accept the former and "take his lumps" from the latter. The illustration of Thomas More's tragic choice was not too long past.

Wrong believes we will not find the answer to the Hobbesian question any place in current sociologic thought because it refuses to look at man as he is, a very complex being, with a very complex pattern of motivation, of which the "rational" in the sense of susceptibility to scientific analysis may be of far less significance than previously supposed. Yet Wrong's statement of the psychological or psychoanalytical aspects using the Freudian or even Neo-Freudian "animal" models only, completely bypasses the equally as important Jungian viewpoint, which makes the problem more difficult by several orders of magnitude. For Jung, from the sociological perspective, opened a whole Pandora's Box of trouble. If man's behavior as a gifted animal, a big smart Rhesus monkey, is difficult to predict, how much more so transcendental man? For that in fact is Jung's contribution.

Freud traced the phenomenon of the psyche backwards in time, bringing in all the primordial instincts both in the individual and the race to infancy or remote primitive times, so that man's problems individually and, hence, as reflected in society, are conditioned by these largely unconsciously held drives, inhibitions and complexes. Jung reverses the direction of the psychic thrust and says in effect that while his former associate's concepts are valid as far as they go, they are completely inadequate to explain man's total behavior or even the larger part of it.

The orientation of the psyche toward the future is of even greater importance. Its aspirations and drives toward fulfillment, toward in-built but undefined goals, have been implanted in man's spirit, just as instincts have been placed in the animal. Jung thus sees an infinity extending into the inmost recesses of the psyche as well as extending into the vast infinity of God's being. If Jung is correct, this is the total and integrated social being which sociology has to address in answering the Hobbesian question. And it provides an answer, but not in terms of biologic man.

Three additional sociologists: David Riesman, Erving Goffman and George Homans, will be discussed, not so much because of their different approach to an overall sociologic position, but because they illustrate three facets of the sociologic

position, but because they illustrate three facets of the sociologic viewpoint of man which are quite widely accepted by
the general public. These concepts are useful but are far from
being explicitory of the entire man. They are typically constructs
of behavior which apply under ordinary day-to-day modern living. They are revealing of general attitudes, attitudes which as
Wrong says are over-emphasized by sociology in defining human
behavior.

The first of these, that of the "other-directedness" of man
in the twentieth century, is that of David Riesman. Riesman
was born in Philadelphia, September 22, 1909. He was educated in law, receiving his J.D. degree in 1934 and was for a
short time law clerk to Supreme Court Justice Brandeis in 1935
and 1936. He has been since 1958 Henry Ford II Professor of
Sociology at Harvard University. Riesman looked at man historically and found that in earlier (or even present day) "folk"
societies man looked to tradition and the past for guidance,
his was "tradition-directedness." He was the man typified in
the mores and folkways of William G. Sumner.

Later, particularly in the nineteenth and early twentieth centuries, Riesman believes man began to look within himself for
guidance. His was designated an "inner-directedness," typified
by the tycoon and industrial baron of pre-World War II. His
ideals were wealth, knowledge and the self-conceived moral
life. He was the self-reliant individual.

Then Riesman saw emerging from mid-twentieth century the
"other-directed" man of our time described in his book *The
Lonely Crowd,* published in 1950, in collaboration with Den-
ney and Glazer. Man makes his way through life by sensing what
his contemporaries expect of him, and directing his own behavior in accordance with that sense to obtain their approval.
The "peer group" approval becomes the criterion for action.
The "other directed" man is not any less success-energized than
his predecessors were, but he relies on this sensed approval to
discern what success really is. It reflects somewhat the switch
from the production to the consumer philosophy. Prestige and
success are measured by approval of the peer group. Morality
consists in going along with what the crowd approves of. It
will be recalled that John Dewey, writing in 1908 had said that
with the decline and prospective early demise of the religiously
based morality there would be one quickly supplied by "class
codes." He saw developing even then a temporary "fix" in the
form of "class standards, class approvals" by "a given circle,
set, calling, profession, trade, industry, club or gang." Ultimately

science would create "a society whose conscience is its free and effectively organized intelligence." The ultimate day seems a long time "abornin'."

Testing Riesman's outlook by the Hobbesian question and looking at the entire progression, the shift has been from culture-oriented to self-oriented to peer-group-oriented and in the last-named with no norms except what the immediate local crowd approves. Riesman saw, today—in man, with his psychological thrust in anxiety—the ultimate moral evil was being disapproved by one's associates. If one is a member of a terrorist gang, he must aspire to excel as a terrorist. Conversely, of course, if the aspirations of the group are constantly ascending toward some state of perfection for some external reason, the result is toward perfection, but not for that reason, but only because it is the way the crowd approves. The preservation of society under such a concept would depend on the level of motivation which can somehow be perceived by the crowd as the crowd's. Given a biologic man—the trousered ape—society is not in good hands in such a group of crowds. What are the prospects of Dewey's prognosis? It appears, given Dewey's rationale but Freud's man, highly improbable; with Jung's man of course, Dewey's rationale is contradicted.

The second special concept to be reviewed is that of Erving Goffman, who was born June 11, 1922, in Mansville, Alberta, Canada. He has been the Benjamin Franklin Professor of Anthropology and Sociology at the University of Pennsylvania since 1968. The Goffman model has been called the dramaturgical schema. It is one in which modern man goes through life playing at various roles. He is an "image projector." He moves into a given situation, looks at the other members of the cast, and decides what image projected by him in that group will give him top billing. He then directs his behavior to best convey that picture of himself. It is a totally selfish portrayal, even though he plays to perfection the generous, loving, moral or whatever other type of part will assure him not only the most applause (as perhaps Riesman's man would seek), but the biggest share of the rewards however he measure them. It is reminiscent of Machiavelli's advice to Lorenzo. Once our hero achieves his goal, he changes costumes and makeup to fit the character in the next scene. It is of the same genre, but a more self-seeking model than Riesman's. Desire of approval of one's associates is a true and universally recognized human characteristic, and Reisman's model reflects that trait, perhaps to excess. But Goffman's model exaggerates a perversion of intellectual honesty.

It has always existed in man, but has never been admired. Few would care for a Machiavellian world though they may live in one. At its extreme, Goffman's is the model of the con-artist. God help society in that milieu. The boy scout would help the old lady into the middle of the intersection and then abandon her if she gave him a quarter too soon.

The comments of Gouldner on a different aspect of the dramaturgical model are worth repeating here:

> Dramaturgical models are most convincing when adapted to only partial social sectors or limited periods of time. When life is looked upon as a drama, the focus must be given over to necessarily restricted situations and personnel. The story can be told only under the spotlight and while the curtain is raised; each drama is an entity independent of the others. In effect, then, the dramaturgical model invites us to live situationally; it invites us to carve a slice out of time, history, and society, rather than to attempt to organize and make manageable the larger whole. In this respect it is vastly different both from the more traditional religious standpoints of Western society and, for that matter, from the more classical evolutionary social philosophies and the theories of total society that emerged in Western Europe during the first half of the nineteenth century. Rather than offering a world view, the new model offers us "a piece of the action."
>
> And yet it does this in a world that is becoming increasingly interdependent. This would seem to imply that the drama to which it invites us is a game to be played within the interstices of social life and within the framework of the dominant institutions. A dramaturgical model is an accommodation congenial only to those who are willing to accept the basic allocations of existent master institutions, for it is an invitation to a "side game." It is for those who have already made out in the big game, or for those who have given up playing it. It has appeal to those members of the middle class who generally mask their alienation out of a concern to maintain a respectable appearance, and to those "dropouts" in the Psychedelic culture who feel no need to conceal their alienation; both groups are alike in that they are not

moved to protest against and actively oppose the system that has alienated them.

Goffman's dramaturgy is a revealing symptom of the latest phase in the long-term tension between the middle class's orientation to morality and its concern with utility. In its earliest development, the middle class had denied the existence of such a tension, or, if it perceived one, often vigorously came to the defense of morality. (Gouldner, 1970, page 385, 386).

The third model is that of George Homans, who was born in Boston, Massachusetts on August 11, 1910. He has been a professor of sociology at Harvard since 1953. His model is significantly different from the others. For Homans, society is not just an artificial construct, a totally "as if" world. The other constructs saw society in that light. Homans would attempt to view society in a world of "real people." He takes the rather general anthropological viewpoint of the world as one of exchange. He sees society existing because every man needs something from others, and the most reliable means of obtaining it is by offering something in exchange. It can be affection or potatoes, both are commodities in the market. The mechanism is much more apparent in the primitive societies, where the inlanders exchange yams for the shoreline inhabitants' fish and where marriage and every other facet of life is a matter of barter and interchange. Its basic truth cannot be denied.

To Homans, society exists because people found cooperation in exchange more useful than war. He believes that society persists into modern times as a kind of conditioned reflex. Man is used to performing some act and receiving some reward in exchange. Man is like the behavioral psychologist's pigeon which is trained to peck at a target because corn drops into the cage when it does so. It is a form of exchange, a peck for a grain of corn. He will continue to peck at the target for a time even after it has failed to reward him, though becoming a bit frustrated after repeated failure.

Considering now the end game in this model, man's behavior is geared and conditioned to obtain rewards in exchange. His rewards, in turn, are measured in terms of the values he attributes to life, in terms of his specific goals. If his goals lie in pure self-gratification, he degenerates into Goffman's dramaturgical schema. He puts on a good act and expects a commensurate reward. Both act and expected reward are largely subjective. Modern man is, therefore, different from primitive man whose objectives and basis of exchange are clear and present and recognized by the entire community. Unless there are community or social objectives which stand out as the universal goals which all men seek or recognize as of commanding value and worth a corresponding sacrifice in exchange, the system breaks down. Then "war" may be considered more useful than exchange. Power again becomes the criterion of correctness and, lacking other motivation, desire of self-gratification—always present— will be imposed as the norm of behavior by a process of moral entropy or statistical sorting. So even here, the Hobbesian question is not given a positive answer with biologic man. Here also a value system with a moral base is necessary.

Before leaving the sociologic viewpoint one strong voice of dissent with the biologic model should be cited. Pitirim Sorokin, the internationally-renowned sociologist and historian and the first head of the sociology department at Harvard University, and long-time professor of sociology there, has been a voice crying in the wilderness since the mid-twenties. In 1959 he teamed with fellow Harvardian and sociologist Walter A. Lunden in the book *Power and Morality* in which what they hoped was an emerging view in the behavioral sciences was discussed. Sorokin and Lunden wrote:

> In contrast to the superannuated, though still intoned, cliches of mechanistic, materialistic, and deterministic biology, psychology, and sociology, the rising, significant theories in these disciplines clearly show that the phenomena of life, organism, personality, mind, and sociocultural processes are irreducible to, and cannot be understood as, purely materialistic, mechanistic, and sensory realities. According to these theories they have, besides their empirical aspect, the far more important mindfully rational and even supersensory and superrational aspects.
>
> This replacement becomes clear if we take a few basic problems in physical, biological, and social sciences. We can begin with the problem of the true and total reality. As mentioned before Sensate science of preceding centuries explicitly and implicitly tended to reduce this reality either to matter or to the sensory reality as it is perceived by our sense organs. Such a science either denied or had an agnostic attitude toward any non-sensory reality. At the present

time this conception of reality is already largely abandoned by all sciences as too narrow and inadequate. It is already superseded by an incomparably wider and more adequate conception of the total reality. Today this total reality is thought of as the infinite X of numberless qualities and quantities: spiritual and material, temporal and timeless, everchanging and unchangeable, personal and superpersonal, spatial and spaceless, one and many. In this sense it is conceived as the veritable *coincidentia oppositorum, mysterium tremendum et fascinosum.* Of its innumerable modes of being, three basic forms appear to be important: (a) empirical-sensory, (b) rational-mindful, and (c) superrational-supersensory. The new conception does not deny the sensory form of reality, but it makes it only one of its three main aspects. This new conception of the true reality, being incomparably richer and more adequate than the old one, is at the same time much nearer to the true and total reality of practically all great religions, especially of their mystical currents.

The same can be said of the old Sensate and the new—Integral—theory of human personality and of human mind. The Sensate theories viewed man mainly as an animal organism of the homo sapiens species. They tended to interpret his nature and behavior predominantly in mechanistic, materialistic, reflexological and other "physicalistic" terms. Some of these Sensate theories have even denied the reality of the human mind. Some others saw in it only two forms of mental energy: unconscious (or subconscious, or preconscious) and conscious. The recent decadent form of Sensate theories, exemplified by S. Freud's yarns, largely reduced mind or human psyche to the pan-sexual unconscious libido or id, with epiphenomenal ego and super-ego representing a modification of the same unconscious under the pressure of the family and society's censorship. This sort of Sensate theory of personality represents but a decadent and atrocious variety of the previous, more sound Sensate conceptions of man. In the Freudian and similar recent conjectures the distortion and degradation of human nature reached its lowest level.

If man were only an organism, motivated and

guided only by the libidinal or other forms of the unconscious, he would have had as little chance to become the highest creative agent in the total universe as other biological species endowed only with the reflexological-instinctive unconscious and with the rudiments of the conscious mind. Exactly, the endowment of homo sapiens with a developed rational mind and with the superconscious genius is responsible for a truly astounding and ever-growing creativity of man. As we see, this new—Integral—theory of human personality again appears to be quite congenial to the religious idea of man as a son of God, created in the image of the Supreme Creator. This triadic theory of personality is a more precise formulation of the triadic conceptions of man prevalent in great religions. These conceptions viewed man as a triadic creature having three forms of being: (a) the unconscious (reflexo-instinctive mechanism of body), (b) the conscious (rational mind), and (c) the supraconscious creator ("Nous," "Pneuma," "Spirit," "Soul," "Divine Self"). In the rational and the superconscious properties of man lies the answer to the ancient question: "What is man, that thou shouldst magnify him?"

From this outline of the new theories in this field one can see again that these theories are in complete agreement with the religious verity that God is Love and with the moral precepts of the great religions.

It has been shown elsewhere that drastic revision of many other basic theories of psychosocial sciences have taken place for the last few decades; in the problems of methods of social research, of causality, of sociocultural structure and dynamics, of the total character of explanation and interpretation of politics and economics, ethics and law, fine arts and other cultural values. It is enough to say that in all these problems the discussed struggle between the decadent varieties of Sensate and the newly merging Integral theories relentlessly goes on.

This struggle proceeds also in other compartments of today's culture and social life. In the field of philosophy this double process has manifested itself in increasing sterility and decline of recent materialistic, mechanistic, positivistic, and other Sensate philosophies; and in emergence and growth of the Phenomenological, the Existential, the Intuitive, the Integral, the neo-Mystical, the neo-Thomist, the neo-Vedantist, the new Integral theories of the total reality, cognition, human personality, and so on.

Among other things, this brief analysis shows that the new rising sociocultural order promises to give a spontaneous unification of religion, philosophy, science, ethics, and fine arts into one integrated system of supreme values of Truth, Goodness, and Beauty. Such a unification signifies the end of conflicts of science, religion, fine arts and ethics with each other.

This struggle between the forces of the previously creative, now largely outworn Sensate order, and the emerging creative forces of a new—Integral—order is proceeding relentlessly in all fields of social and cultural life, and in the inner life of every one of us. The final outcome of this epochal struggle will greatly depend upon whether mankind can avoid a new world war. If this Apocalyptic catastrophe can be avoided, then the emerging creative forces will usher humanity into a new and magnificent era of its history. (Sorokin, 1959, pages 122-134).

A quarter of a century later the budding changes so rosily projected had not bloomed and Sorokin in 1966 in a major work, *The Shape of Society to Come*, said,

Today's sociology has excavated so many facts that it often does not know what to do with them. Likewise, in its analysis of various—important and unimportant—techniques of research, it has become as finicky as the angelology of the medieval Scholastics. In its revolt against the "grand systems of sociology," it has increasingly neglected a study of the fundamental problems of sociology and has progressively wasted its creative energy in research on comparatively trivial, cognitively unimportant problems.

Furthur research along these lines will yield not bigger and better scientific harvests but progressively diminishing returns, not new break-throughs but an increasing stagnation and routinization of sociology.

Whether we like it or not, today's sociology has

come to a crossroad: one road leads it to the new peak of great syntheses and more adequate systems of sociology, the other leads it to a hackneyed, rubber-stamped, greatly mechanized set of dogmas devoid of creative elan and cognitive growth. (Sorokin, 1966, page 649).

Now, in 1987, we hear "the superannuated cliches of mechanistic, materialistic, and deterministic biology, psychology, and sociology" still "being intoned." The prestigious voice of Sorokin is resoundingly ignored in the current works of social theory being only occasionally referred to in footnotes. Wrong, Gouldner and others are not in consonance with the claquous routine but appears not as ready to come out in opposition as Sorokin was fifty years ago.

Chapter 8

AN ANALYSIS OF THE CONCEPTS OF MAN

When one has finished such a hurried tour through the historic development of the concept of man probably the first reaction is that there are no answers having permanent value and validity. Everything is relative to the particular environment in which the various individuals lived and which guided their reflections. That, as Heraclitus had held, all is flux and change—permanence is an illusion. This is probably followed by a conclusion that philosophy is indeed a vain endeavor claiming to give answers to life's meaning, yet, in fact, offering none upon which one can depend. The sociologists seem likewise to be in considerable disarray in approaching the problems besetting man. But, on deeper reflection, there is a discernible pattern or rhythm to the thought, and, if each sequence seems to open more doors to inquiry than it closes, why should we complain? Life is inestimably richer because of the great variety in viewpoints presented and, if questions are not answered with finality—and few are—yet each major question which is raised is subjected to so many varied approaches in seeking an answer that virtually all alternatives available during a period are exposed and offered to following generations for further analysis. There is a movement from "crudity" toward refinement of the points at issue. If there is no reduction in the number of the issues, at least there is a far better definition of what it is that is at issue and what distinguishes each from the others.

We have looked at six broad approaches to man in the universe and from these we can arrive at what these major philosophic systems used as a basic principle of operation. These principles can now be restated in the following more or less systemic language:

1. The universe and man as matter in motion.
2. The universe and man as idea.
3. The universe and man as organic process.
4. The universe and man as experienced phenomenal process and being.
5. The universe and man as experiential relationship in

developing being.

6. The universe and man's being in actuality of essence in existence.

Each of the sytems has its basic problems which are addressed differently by the individual philosophers in attempting to make their theory cohesive and explanatory of man's position over against the world "out there."

At this point, the writer believes we can say that we have fairly well opened all the closet doors in the historic structure housing man's concept of man in the western tradition. Are there any conclusions to be drawn impinging on the Nietzsche versus Toynbee dialectic scenarios? First of all, as a minimum, the writer believes that there is clear evidence of a slackening of the headlong plunge of intellectual thought toward the materialistic order. The philosophic rhythm-makers have explored that system thoroughly and are now moving to new ground. Since the horrendous episode of World War II the promise of unending vistas of rising expectations in human happiness through science and technology has been gradually replaced with a cynicism and skepticism which, since the French Revolution, has been reserved for the metaphysical order.

The attitude is far different than that which we saw was Condorcet's and Comte's at the apex of the enlightenment. It is far different than that of Karl Marx foretelling how it would be when the fully classless society had emerged which would free men to experience leisure in joyous exploitation of the rich material environment. The scene today is far different from the world under the illusion that efficient technology can be accomplished by a bunch of happy and classless farmers or workmen each with no "boss" but his own noble Marxist dedication. Each year the tension differential between the Marxian dialectic and capitalistic poles becomes less and hence the driving potential also becomes less. Both are cynically materialistic practically speaking. Nietzsche's nihilistic scenario would come to pass automatically if no new movement captures man's imagination in the meantime and a new movement requires new motivation.

The review of philosophy permits the conclusion that the most profound intellects in every age, up to, and including, the present, support the spiritual values as the most worthy motivators though recognizing that at many times they are used as motivation in unworthy causes. We have observed that course of thought, essentially from the time of William of Ockham and the renaissance nominalists, attacking the creditability of man's capacity to acquire knowledge beyond the level of the particular and the material. This attack had in effect two facets— the first, that of Ockham himself, was anti-humanistic. Man was making undue pretensions of ability to acquire knowledge— God had revealed Himself in the prophetic works which the metaphysical efforts tended to reduce in importance. Man should acknowledge that he is a creature of very limited ability—he should not insist that God, who is omnipotent, is constrained by any principle of universals or fixed laws of logic beyond the particular which He presents to us directly through the senses.

The second facet was humanistic. The ontologic viewpoint inevitably resulted in ascribing powers to a being above man which seemingly threatened to reduce man's independence. This mode was a later development and moved from the Cartesian duality—really a double duality—of splitting man into two strictly separate spheres for knowledge acquisition. These were, the internal rational processes purely intellectual and ontological in application confined to the soul of which the "Cogito" was typical and the bodily externally-actuated sense perceptive mode characteristic of John Dewey. In this epistomological mode, the liberated man under the aegis of the scientifically directed intellect would live full and orderly fruitful lives without the noisome burden of religious superstition. A searching, questing period in philosophy is now emerging. It is a dissatisfied world looking for new answers—and that is always the attitude necessary for a change. The current attitude among the intellectuals of virtually all stripe is one of recognition of man at a crossroads and of reflection on the probable future course. That is the attitude which Nietzsche's scenario cannot tolerate. He postulated that it would not happen. But at the same time we seem to be a long way from following Toynbee's scenario. For the atheistic existentialist to whom spiritual values are meaningless there still is the absurdity pervading consciousness, the absurdity of the useless passion which is man. That attitude, if widespread would be more disastrous than a continuation of the myth of an invincible scientific materialism. It was only in the deifying of science—the making it as a god able to provide all things and in the resulting closing off of true spiritual values to all men that the error arose.

The Toynbee scenario, as we saw, is completely dependent on establishing a spiritual basis for man's next phase of civilization. The quasi-spiritual thrust which has sparked the tremendous Marxian march in the current century is a close-ended movement.

It requires physical lands to conquer—the villian, Capitalism, must be expunged from the world maps. The villain and the Marxist motivation can be destroyed in two ways—by actual conquest and destruction of capitalism or by a convergence of the, two worlds in practice, if not in theory. With either eventuality, and the second seems more likely at this time, the "spiritual" force is dissipated and the movement grinds to a halt. The bureaucratic structure as Max Weber had pointed out is a concomitant of technology and, Marcuse notwithstanding, is no respecter of ideologies, and we either technologize or starve.

Reference to man's use of symbols as a characteristic which separates him from the lower animals was made at the middle of this century by both philosopher Merleau-Ponty and anthropologist Leslie White. They observed that we do all of our communication and almost all of our intellection by manipulating symbols. It is our chief mode of learning and communicating learning. The phonetic alphabet is a symbolic system for expressing sounds which in turn are symbolic of meaning. We live in a world of analogy which is just another aspect of symbolism. In the early days of electrical engineering, problems were solved by hydraulic analogy. Then as expertise developed and sophistication in electrical theory and engineering increased, hydraulic problems were solved by electrical analogy. The entire cybernetic science is developed as an analogy to electric circuitry and it is applied by reverse interpretation both to the study of the human nervous system as well as to its main use in computerization. Analogy is the basis for most laboratory research on animal behavior for later application to man. It is one of man's most powerful tools and used constantly in going from the symbol to the thing symbolized in exploring relationships of all types. Why should analogy be despised in application to the world of metaphysics?

The use of analogy in working with the causal principle is obvious—all of our information comes from observation. Any time we wish to generalize from that data in the slightest degree we must use analogy. If we never observe "free-standing" effects, we universalize, by analogy, that effects always demand causes. We compare, we see this case is similar to that case in the following respects and dissimilar in the following respects. In reviewing Kant's epistemology, from which the view against the causal principle was projected—Kant's concept of "thing-in-itself"—that which provided his representation in perception—that which he needed as a base from which to move his idealism, was shown to be an extension of the causal principle into the forbidden area of intelligibilia. Nonetheless, the effect of Kant's criticism on subsequent philosophy was restriction of the causal principle, only to process in its epistemological context, responding to the question, "How?" and not to the ontological avenue, or, the purposive context responding to the question, "Why?"

Aristotle, in his *Metaphysics* had said, "No man would start to do anything, if he did not expect to reach some end. Nor would there be any intelligence in the universe, because an intelligent man certainly always does things for a purpose and that is their terminus, for the end is a terminus." All motivation implies purpose. Thus, in the causal relationship, there are two chains of questioning, one vertical in time via process, the other horizontal via purpose which is time independent. The same purpose exists throughout the process or the process is changed.

Let us look analytically at the causal relationship which will be the subject of our first logic gates at the conclusion of this chapter. First, we will look at the vertical series of causality via process. Each of us recognizes that we are a product of a very long process. We talk of our ancestors—particularly if they are famous. A father and mother never say we have just made a son or daughter, knowing full well, that while they are essential mechanisms in the process, the raw material was none of their deliberate doings. If, now, the process is extended back in generational pairs a few million years, the raw material is still "provided by others." Yet, around ten billion or so years ago—far short of infinity—there were absolutely no biological "others," only miscellaneous inorganic chemical molecules and atoms bouncing merrily around in the chaos which was to become earth. Were the raw materials still "provided by others?" If not, at what point was the essential raw material supplied and, if so, then, how? If the raw material was still further back we can speculatively drift back another 20 billion years or so—infinity is no closer—and ask the same question. Time and space as we know it becomes meaningless. Now, how about the nameless original "others" who furnished the raw materials? If from that remote age we turn around and look speculatively to the future, does the process appear random that resulted in us as individuals? Why not just the continuing chaos or nothing? Once the *process* started, it was continuing and progressive in complexity. Now, to speak of a random process is a misuse of both terms. A series of events is either systematic and intelligible, in which case it is process, or it is unsystematic and nonintelligible, in which case it is a random series.

Now let us look at the horizontal chain briefly on the assumption that the vertical chain reveals a process. Why do we as individuals exist? For what purpose do we exist? If there is a purpose there is an intending ego, a personality which formed a concept requiring a solution for which our existence is either the final end or a mediate end, a partial means to a further end. But if we are an end in either sense, we should examine our capabilities. The purpose of our existence, as we are constituted, is revealed by our capabilities and we should look at our highest capability. It is the intellectual faculty which is the distinguishing characteristic in man. Then our purpose must lie in utilization of the intellectual faculty as directed to its highest capability. The highest capability only need be identified because a process, since intelligible, does not overextend. A mechanical system is designed to perform its required function. Its auxiliary systems support that function. But its highest function is that for which it was intentionally provided, its ultimate use or purpose. While a major computer center contains air conditioning equipment as a basic requirement, the highest function of the center is not to provide air conditioning. The air conditioning is only supportive to the computer. For man the intellectual capabilities point to an advance to the summit of intellectual life. As to the summit of intellectual life, there are not too many alternatives. Starting at the bottom, for easier elimination, there is the solution that intellectual direction is provided to promote self-gratification. This is a final end, but hardly one fitting to a process started for that end so many eons ago. It is a possibility, but low probability. At the second level, our intellectual powers are to achieve species progress in the biologic order—a mediate end to a later life situation. These are not really appropriate uses for intellectual capabilities. The apes could certainly do much better. As a species, we do more tearing down than building up. Intellectual development remains a possibility of low probability on a biological utilization basis. The next higher solution is that the intellectual efforts are directed toward improvement of the human condition or to maximize survivability in society. This idea has been used frequently by the philosophers we studied. It was certainly Dewey's solution. It certainly must be considered. The top of the series would be that of the theists. The ultimate purpose is intellectual effort toward the honor and glory of God, the others are incidental. Is the writer making an unjustified value judgment in stating this as the top of the series? Perhaps, but if this one is not valid, the others are largely a matter of indifference and mouselike offspring to such elephantine laborings. In truth, the candle may just as well be brief. But the basis of validity, whatever it may be, requires greater study of the causal principle in depth. Let us start with the nature of the intending personalities we know, ourselves.

Personality has been defined as the expression or manifestation of self-consciousness of a being having the capacity to reflect on itself as a specific identity in relationship to all else. It would have been an impossible concept in Hume's epistemology. In the natural order, it exists only in man.

Max Scheler had written in his work, *On the Eternal in Man*, that, in sharp contrast to Hume's idea of the pinpointedness of our life occurrence:

> Every single one of these life-moments, corresponding with just one indivisible point of objective Time, contains within itself its three extensions: the experienced past, the present being experienced and the future, whose ingredients are constituted by awareness, immediate memory and immediate expectation. It is by virtue of this wonderful fact that— perhaps not the material reality—but the *sense* and *worth* of the whole of our life still come, at every moment of our life, within the scope of our freedom of action. We are not the disposers merely of our future; there is also no part of our past life which— while its component natural reality is of course less freely alterable than the future—might not still be genuinely altered in its *meaning* and *worth*, through entering our life's total significance as a constituent of the self-revision which is always possible. . . .
>
> Since, however, the total efficacy of an event is, in the texture of life, bound up with its *full* significance and *final* value, every event of our past remains *indeterminate* in significance and *incomplete* in value until it has yielded *all* its potential effects. Only when seen in the whole context of life, only when we are dead (which, however, implies "never," if we assume an after-life), does such an event take on the completed significance and "unalterability" which render it a fact such as past events in nature are from their inception. Before our life comes to an end the whole of the past, at least with respect to its significance, never ceases to present us with

the problem of *what we are going to make of it.*
For no sooner does a section of objective time enter
into that extension-category of our experience which
we know as our past, than it is deprived of that fatality and completion which past events in nature possess. As *past* this time content becomes "ours"—is
subordinated to the power of the *personal Self.* Therefore, the extent and nature of the effects that every
part of our past may exercise upon the sense of our
life lie still within our power at *every* moment of
our life. This proposition is valid for every "fact"
in "historical reality," whether in the history of the
individual, the race or the world. *"Historical reality" is incomplete and, so to speak, redeemable.* I
grant that everything about the death of Ceasar which
appertains to the events of nature is as complete and
invariable as the eclipse of the sun which Thales
prophesied. But whatever belonged on that occasion
to "historical reality," whatever is woven of it as
meaning and effect into the fabric of man's history,
is an incomplete thing, and will not be complete until
the end of world-history. (Emphasis Scheler's).
(Scheler, 1972).

Human personality, in short, is the reflection of the individual
human essence as the individual has formed it. It is "experienced" by the individual himself and also by other "personalities," although the projected personality can be a far cry from
the true personality. But even then the "felt need" of disguise
is a reflection of the real personality. The "authentic self" sought
by existentialists is the personality which is "real." If one takes
a phenomenological examination of the concept "personality,"
cutting it away in isolation, and mentally cataloging its prime
characteristics, the following would be a basic list:
   It is moldable—Personality is that which reflects the life experiences. It makes the self-conscious self recognize that while
one is the same "ego" that one was as a child, one is not the
same in physical capacity, mental traits, outlook on life, or in
external relationships. The personality has changed, has been
molded by life events.
   It has a physical vector—Personality is affected by brain modification, by narcotics, injury, disease, surgery or aging. In its normal state, it compares and evaluates its own physical status in its
various life relations such as physical capacity, health, and vitality.

It has a mental vector—Personality is that which thinks and wills: "cogito ergo sum." It is the seat of introspection. One constantly compares that which he considers himself actually to be, with what he would be, should be, or will strive to be. The trend in life's pattern stems from this constant internal scanning.

It has a spiritual vector—As an extension of the preceding capacity, the personality is the seat of normative expression and the conscience. It extends the analysis of life possibilities to value judgments in aesthetics, moral subjects, and to assessments of what is the awesome and the holy, however conceived.

It is integrative—The personality functions to take these vectors and interrelate them introspectively and to bring out what the self-conscious self visualizes as its life meaning in the broadest sense. The overall behavior pattern of the individual at any time reflects this integration.

It is purposive—Through the life process, the self-conscious self uses the integrated viewpoint at any given time to plan ahead (consciously or unconsciously) for the oncoming life increments. The picturesque language of Whitehead comes to mind. "What we perceive as present is the vivid fringe of memory tinged with anticipation. . . .The past and the future meet and mingle in the ill-defined present." This present future-planning in light of the past is the case only for man. It is this capacity which distinguishes human life and makes it fully free and relevant. The individual, regardless of his life condition, is not a prisoner of his past or of his present. His future remains his to form. He has the ability to direct himself, at least by intent, into other channels in which he can seek fulfillment. He can be, in fact, he must be purposive, if he is to be human. It is this function of personality which gives significance to life. Without it human beings would be less than human, with it, human beings are unique in the world.

From this, we see that personality is not in a dialectic with the naive self, although there may be other dialectics involved. The personality at any stage is the naive self, as it has developed itself, in accordance with its basic nature as man. It is man's nature to mature intellectually and grow and it is in his exercise of the intent and purposive function in relationship to all else which makes him a responsible human being.

There is another side of the coin of intentionality and purpose. While we are conscious of our ability to direct our intent to particular ends and adapt means to meet those ends—to take purposeful action—it is also true that a purposeful act signifies intent and demands a rational, intelligent, source of that intent. This can be stated in two propositions: only if there is intent is there a purposeful act and only if there is a rational personal source is there an intent. The first statement is really a tautology since the concept of intent is carried within the meaning of purposeful act. The second one, at one time, would have been classed as self-evident but Kant raised a question. He said in effect, "While it seems there is purpose behind phenomena we cannot bring the purpose under definite concepts." A bird builds a nest. It is purposeful, or seems so. Can the bird form an intent so as to make the act truly purposeful?

Among the ancient Greeks, the "purpose"—the answer to "why?"—was the primary causal significant. The motivational, the instinctive, are the most fascinating aspects of animate creatures, whether insects, birds, or mammals. It is the most inexplicable. And of these, the secondary and tertiary levels, those levels beyond the immediate biological, alimentary, sexual or survival reactive instincts are of greatest interest. The levels of migration, food storage, and nest building are but a few examples. They show a problem solving facet to the creature's behavior—providing for a future contingency under varied given conditions in individual cases. How is this programmed? It is not learned. The first attempt at nest building is as successful as the succeeding—for the artificially incubated as for those in nature. Is this "skill" carried in the DNA chains as inert chemical elements comprised of very common chemical elements that have no faculties or intentionality whatsoever—either individually, or, as far as can be ascertained, collectively? As Montaigne had argued—doubtless to inculcate a proper spirit of humility—the animals do many things better than men and with much less fuss and bother. That is, in fact, the problem. We recognize how difficult it is, as humans, to solve even simple problems intellectually. Yet, the lower animals do it without intellection. How? Answers are provided without intellection. How? Pavlov, or the gestalt theorists, could not really handle the primary level instincts as Merleau-Ponty so brilliantly demonstrated. Both the biologist and the physicist come to a barrier at the atomic and subatomic levels. And all of these specialists recognize that fact.

In *The Structure of Behavior,* Merleau-Ponty had written,

> But, as we have seen, physical laws do not furnish
> an explanation of the structures, they represent an
> explanation within the structures. They express the

least integrated structures, those in which the simple
relations of function to variable can be established.
They are already becoming inadequate in the
"acausal" domain of modern physics. In the functioning of the organism, the structuration is constituted according to new dimensions—the typical
activity of the species or the individual—and the preferred forms of action and perception can be treated
even less as the summative effect of partial interactions. Thus the properties of the phenomenal field
are not expressible in a language which would owe
nothing to them. The structure of the "thing perceived" now offers a new support to this conclusion.

The answers are not forthcoming from an isolated view of
animal behavior but only of the behavior in context with the
totality of the living experience. In this same work Merleau-
Ponty had noted in criticism of the early work in the reflex
and gestalt theories that there was an inexplicable purposefulness, "a problem solving purposefulness" in the instinctive animal organisms below man which these theories could in no
way address.

A problem must be formulated and its parameters assessed
before a solution can be begun and as Aristotle had said in
Chapter 1 of his work on *Parts of Animals*,

The causes concerned in the generation of the
works of nature are, as we see, more than one. There
is the final cause and there is the moving cause. Now
we must decide which of these two causes come first,
which second. Plainly, however, that cause is the first
which we call the final one. For this is the reason,
and the reason forms the starting point, alike in works
of art and works of nature. For consider how a physician or how a builder sets about his work. He starts
by forming for himself a definite picture, in the one
case mental, in the other actual, of his end—the physician of health, the builder of a house. This he keeps
in mind as the reason and explanation of each subsequent step that he takes, and of his acting in this
or that way as the case may be.

Now all of the secondary and tertiary level animal instinctive
response to problems are completely purposeful. Take the case

of the nest-building bird; it must select an appropriate site, select the right materials from those available, organize them so as to provide for both insulation and drainage as well as for the structural requirements. It must put forth great effort unselfishly; no direct physical reward is apparent to build a nest of a particular design in advance of and during egg development timed to coincide with the need. It must do it the first time correctly, with no memory and no models to proceed from.

All of these activities reflect a recognition that a situation presents a problem to a being which then proceeds to address the matter of its solution. It is an activity directed to a future purposeful outcome. The effort is intentional and intent demands a personal formulation. Having solved problems of one nature or another ourselves, we can recognize others in process of solving problems and by analogy project the capacity of problem solving to others whom we see performing that process. We also can project that the same principles involved in problem solving for us are involved wherever problems are solved. We can speculate on whether a personal intent is present for the beaver, the spider, the bird, the bee or the ant—which all carry out purposeful activity, not immediately biologic in reward or in external execution, selecting sites, materials and setting schedules each time under different circumstances involving different problems. And there is no "learning curve." The work is done as correctly and efficiently the first time as the last.

We saw earlier that the objection is raised that only because we apply our human viewpoint to the creature's activity does it seem purposeful—from the creature's viewpoint it is not. Regardless of the viewpoint the activity preeminently fits the definition of purposefulness. This writer is not for an instant suggesting that there is specific intent in the organism. But if the writer is working in an office and a teleprinter starts up and transmits a message, likewise he does not for an instant think the machine intended to carry out a purposeful act and present him a piece of information. If he could think of a machine's viewpoint it would "see" a series of signals and carry out the responses required by those signals through its mechanism specifically designed for that purpose. But he is also totally certain that there was somewhere an intending ego which did formulate the signal and provide a special purpose mechanism to respond. The writer would agree that the creatures are likely responding to a signal passed by their genetic code over thousands of generations. He would be inclined to be in awe at this display of expertise in microminiturization technique. But that is bypassing the point, which is a question of purpose and the need for an intending ego regardless of how the activity is remoted. The point is that the concept "purposefulness" is a valid universal subdivision of causality and is not limited to human activity. Where there is purpose there is intent. If the immediate agency does not, by its nature, show the capacity of forming intent as the teleprinter, the answer is not that there was no intent but that the intent was elsewhere. It does exist. It is real. One should no more logically say that the intent was missing from the activity of the nest-building bird than the teleprinter, even though the former methodology was far more sophisticated than the latter.

In the naive way of children, always inquisitive, asking their insistent "why?" is revealed how important that question ought to be, for it cuts through the sophistry of modernism and goes to the root. It scarcely appears in philosophy after Descartes. Only the "How?" aspect of causality was considered important—a complete reversal of the importance given by Aristotle—and he the prototype empiricist! "Why do the flowers smell sweet, Daddy?" "Because it attracts the bees." "Why does the flower want to attract the bees?" Aristotle came to the proper conclusion: there was an intending ego that set it all in motion; and his was a multi-purpose solution not only symbiotic to flowers and bees, but the fragrance and beauty also delighted the sons of men and the honey provided sweets to his larder. How dull-witted and unenlightened the ancients were to suggest such things. Intent and purpose indeed! Just a lovely statistical coincidence, and those stupid bees—until Liebnitz we could not prove that the configuration of their wax cell was the optimum possible.

We are instead back to the answer given by the desperate parent to the precocious offspring: "They just do, that's why!" Yet we, as curious human beings, cannot stop there. That insistent itch, that incessant tickle of the consciousness demands a final, satisfying, conclusion. We likewise know with a frustrating clarity in opaqueness, that the line of questioning in the realm of science is fruitless. It may eventually extend to the subatomic level which was mathematician, physicist, philosopher Whitehead's enigmatic suggestion that matter is merely vibrational phenomena of the primal energy form—a first cousin of light. But that, even if fact, while it might be bad news to the materialists, is of little value to theists. Light is as impersonal and unintentional, or purposeless, in its essence of itself as a pavement block.

If one intends to perform any act there is an object which he, the intelligent subject addresses with an intent to know, to love, to destroy, or to create. In the latter case, the object of intent exists in the mind of the subject before the act—a builder of a house has at least a concept in mind when he starts—an example we have already used from Aristotle. It is, in the case of pure creation, incomprehensible that a non-existent subject can, in advance of its existence, form the intent to bring itself into existence as an object. Or, one step further, it is incomprehensible that in any purposeful act, the building of a bird's nest for instance, that the "purpose" can be carried out without the specific intent, first being formed, to carry out the act for that purpose. At some level, a purposeful intent is formed and the act proceeds from that point of intent. The instinctive act of the bird—its very invariability in form and of success of such a complex undertaking, the first time—points to its non-intellection and its source as an automatic instinctive reaction. The bird carries out a purposeful act which it is specifically designed to do. It does not extend its problem solving ability to other problems. It is a special purpose organism. A robin builds a robin's nest because it is a robin and not a swallow or an oriole. The bird does not form a specific intent. It is impelled, by its instincts, to behave as it does to include the instinctive solving of particular problems which the environment presents. As we noted in Kant's view, the act was deprived of intent and hence regardless of appearance could not be purposeful since the concept purposeful includes the idea of advance intent. Kant could not bring the purpose under "definite concepts" and so he slid away from the problem. He refused to concede an intent formed at a level beyond the bird which would be the cause of the bird's activity. Is this a viable answer? What is the alternative? If it is not a purposeful act, it is a random act, an *aimless* act and yet an invariable, sought for end is achieved.

A bird's nest provides a solution to a specific problem. There is no randomness associated with the bird's behavior. It goes about its task with consummate skill adopting means to ends. The definition of "purposeful" in *Webster's New World Dictionary* (1970) is: "1. Resolutely aiming at a specific goal; 2. directed toward a specific end; not meaningless." The bird's activity certainly meets both definitions. The answer lies in the response to a second question.—Can an instinctive act be purposeful?—There is no doubt that the answer is yes. Virtually all instinctive acts are purposeful. There are cases, where the purpose may be no longer valid. Some migrations, of the East Coast lobster, for instance, are specific examples. This answer goes back to "intent." In the definitions above, the intent is implicit in the two words "resolutely" and "directed"—both signify intent. Lacking ego—as in our teleprinter analogy—there is neither in-built resoluteness nor deliberate direction while the bird gives every evidence of having both characteristics "in-built." Following Merleau-Ponty, the bird is internally instructed, by its biological structure, responding instinctively to some internal or external environmental signification. In contrast, the teleprinter is externally motivated by its mechanical structure, responding mechanically to some external environmental signification. The machine is an extension of man's intellectually-motivated activity. The question next arises: Since there was the carrying out of an intent, both by the bird (instinctively) and the machine (mechanically by extension), can an instinct carry in itself its own intentionality or is it not, like the mechanical response of the teleprinter, merely an extension of the intellectually-motivated activity located, by preprogramming, external to the bird itself? The instincts, qua instincts, reveal no self-generational capacity to form an intent to act or to plan the execution of the act nor does the definition include the idea.

Again referring to the dictionary, the appropriate definition of instinct is "an inborn tendency to behave in a way characteristic of a species. A natural, unacquired, mode of response to stimuli." Like the machine, there is no capacity in the bird to form intent as a part of its biologic life. The bird is faced with an imperative "must" just as the machine is. The preprogrammed "must" controls the instinctive act. Therefore the intent, and since the activity is purposeful there is intent, must lie remote from the bird. The hard-line evolutionists contend that the present apparent purposefulness of the bird's actions are only the result of a long line of random chance happenings which began eons ago and is the result of a survival bias which tended to produce organisms which could solve progressively more difficult problems culminating in man. This is a position difficult to maintain beyond the purely mechanical level. In a classic example moths of a certain color tend to survive in an environment which makes them inconspicuous. That can be an illustration of a "random" activity which is survival biased toward a specific color. It improves the odds of survival of moths of that color in competition with others in the particular environment. At the second level removed, a feeding preference enhances survival. This can also be seen as a selection by chance or accident. At the third level removed, animals sense danger and can "voluntarily" change appearance on alarm as chameleons and certain fish do. The solution, by random act, becomes a quantum order more difficult, the beginning of truly purposeful instinct; but, since it is strictly an interior automatic biological process, "perhaps" it can evolve by random chance, as a result of mutation of the genes, and change in genetic codes which are survival biased. At the fourth level removed, the organism acts to camouflage or otherwise protect itself using unmodified external materials. This feat becomes very difficult, and there are not many examples except those chiefly in the insect and fish species at the lower end of the animal series. The hermit crab is an example. This development is hard to see as the result of a pure chance response regardless of gene modification by random mutation. Can a learning of a specific skill in use of external materials be randomly developed and transmitted? Can a gene modification include a learned skill? And we are not addressing an "infinite" duration or "infinite" quantities.

The fifth level removed, is that of "purposive" acts such as were described for the bird in modifying and adapting materials to meet a new requirement. A wide variety of materials are selected and blended to form a nest of soft, close, texture that has comfort and insulating value near the point of occupancy and open texture at the outside surface for structural strength, anchorage and drainage. In other words, a sound structure is developed making good use of design and construction methods for a purpose. The very commonality of this type of development not only makes it one which we accept as a matter of course but also makes it totally inexplicable through random action. The variety of specific solutions is almost endless— each case presents the organism with a different problem, but the end solution is likewise invariant except in minor detail for the particular species. Yet, this trait is not common in the more advanced, the higher animal species, such as apes or baboons. Among mammals, the beaver and other rodents seem most adept.

It seems almost to have an inverse relationship to the species' complexity and intelligence. The more complex and intelligent the species, the less natural skill is provided in instinctive purposefulness. Only where the instinct is needed is it provided. If one tries to turn that argument around—that it was evolved only where survival necessitated it—the word "necessitated" is by no means a random concept. Why should any survival be necessary—necessary for what; by whom determined? The species would just disappear, or better, not appear at all. More logically, only because a species was to develop and to survive were the appropriate instincts provided. Without instinct at some level there would be no species at all. Viewed in this way, the species did not develop the instinctive trait by reason of random natural selection. These advanced instincts did not preexist but always emerged. The trait was provided when and where needed so that the species could survive. The eggs of warm-blooded oviparous animals had to be incubated, and the instinctive skills were provided at that stage of development. This would be a teleological viewpoint of evolution. If instinct is anything, it is purposeful. But the "intent" essential for purposefulness is not contained in the organism's instinctive response at any level, including the human.

In an incredibly anthropocentric passage of his work *The Influence of Darwin,* John Dewey concluded that there was no intelligence in the world until man came along. He says,

> Not then, when Nature produces health or efficiency or complexity does Nature exhibit regard for value, but only when it produces a living organism that has settled preferences and endeavors. The mere happenings of complexity, health, adjustment, is all that Nature effects, as rightly called accident as purpose. But when Nature produces an intelligence—ah, then, indeed Nature has achieved something. . . . Because in consciousness an end is preferred, is selected for maintenance, and because intelligence pictures not a world just as it is in toto, but images forth the conditions and obstacles of the continued maintenance of the selected good.

What is the nature of this "Nature" which John Dewey euphonizes in the production of man, the first intelligence in the universe. It will be recalled Kant substituted the word "Nature" for "providence" not because he didn't believe in Divine Providence but because it seemed more appropriate in a technical work. Dewey had no such concept. The fact is, that here is a "universal" which is not, in any sense, justified except in a figure of speech. There is no such inert "global" entity possible, even in concept. What is meant is a *process* not an *essence.* It is in the nature of a process that Dewey finds all these things. It comprises a tremendously complex entropic energy process

running from the gross gravitational to the microbiological, as
we will see in more detail in Part III. But for the purpose of
the philosophic viewpoint, it is an energy system which is capable of being broken into many subsystems for easier analysis.
John Dewey takes the biologic subsystem and describes it as
characterized by production of "mere happening of complexity, health, adjustment"—and the "mere happening" can be as
correctly defined as "accident" or as "purpose." Now, process,
as we have just seen, is never accidental. Something can result
from an accident—a broken leg for instance, but the broken leg
is healed by a process, a detailed process, not correctly called
accidental by the widest stretch of the imagination. An organism comes to life, matures and carries out its biological existence by process—the process may well be interrupted by
accident. The question still is, "Is process—all process—
intelligible, patterned, or is there some other word John Dewey
should have called attention to between that which is intelligible and that which is accidental? Process is intelligible and predictable. Unless there is some extraneous problem, a doctor can
specify the nature of the healing of a broken bone and predict
the course of recovery. Are accidents intelligible? One knows that
if he accidentally falls from a roof he is likely to suffer injury
and could predict that outcome even half way down. But what
he would be predicting is the outcome of the process of falling,
not the accident which was the occasion of the fall. One could
deliberately jump from the building to escape greater danger and
make the same judgment. Accidents, by definition, are not predictable except in a statistical way. Every so many vehicle miles
will produce a fatality. But the fatality will result from a process
which once begun will run its course unless interrupted.

The next question is, "If a thing is intelligible—as process
is—can it be the result of 'mere happening'? bearing in mind
that 'Nature' is a fictional essence?" There is no fairy godmother
called Nature waving a wand. Search as much as one might
he can never find a process which is a "mere happening." Even
the elimination of the less fortunate moths mentioned earlier
was no "mere happening." They were eliminated because of
a process of selection. If one should elect to outfit an army
in red coats and send them into battle in a green forest, one
could rather expect to have high casualty rates. It is not the
process which is a "mere happening." Mere happenings themselves are hard to find. It takes a good deal of effort to work
up a table of random numbers—systemization is hard to evade
in the universe. And there is the crux of the problem.

If one were to say there is a "survival bias" in the evolutionary process, what lies in back of that term? The survival bias
depends upon two non-random traits, the "urge" to survive
and the "urge" to reproduce. In the first life forms, both the
potency and actuality had to coincide. In both traits, the "urge"
had to precede the act and the capacity to respond to the "urge"
had to precede the act. Both "urge" and capacity had to be
present potentially and for both survival and reproduction. Why
is there a survival instinct for self-preservation, for reproduction, for feeding, for dominance? There is some REASON that
survival has a preferred status. The classic case of the moths
does not begin to answer the question. Those individuals in
a species favorably situated with respect to the survival bias
will be perpetuated to reproduce and extend that strain. Why
should that process result in greater complexity if it does? The
amoeba is a highly durable organism and, assuming the original
"happened" organisms were somewhat like the amoeba and
inexplicably had the instincts and capacity necessary to survival and reproduction, can we expect that a series of random
happenings, being a finite number, even with a bias to survival,
in the limited sense of that term, would do anything but to
further and further specialize the strain of the original amoeba-
like organism. It does not tend to generalization. Let us take
a look at those moths again. They were caught in a period of
industrialization which saw the trees begrimed. The light-colored moths were done for. Only the darker moths survived.
Now suppose that there is a rigid clean air policy and the trees
regain their light color; that does in the dark-colored moths,
leaving only a marginal group of narrow neutral shade which
would survive. Many sequences like that and the moths' position would be precarious indeed. But if the insect is provided
a new instinct which tells it to match itself in color with whatever surrounding it finds itself in, it is the new instinct starting
a new trend which saves the day. What is the alternative to
a new instinct? Can it be logically said that the instincts to color-
select preexisted in the insects where it later developed and
that only those who had it survived and reinforced the trait
in the species? That must mean that every possible instinct which
was to emerge was to some extent contained in the most primitive amoeba-like forms to some degree if nothing new is ever
added. That is preprogramming with a vengeance! How large
would "n" have to be to bring about the complexity of current
biology? The survival and development bias is far more likely
keyed to primal survival instincts from the beginning, and the

timely incorporation of new instincts as the need arose in a planned process of development, than to the accidents of environment alone.

Is systemization not antithetical to randomness? There is always a reason or cause for systemization though it may be difficult to find. That fact is the great motivator of physical science and philosophy. Both seek answers in viewing the world as intelligible. If something in an activity is intelligible there is a principle which governs the activity and which when discovered leads to the causality both in terms of how and why. The physical scientist is interested almost exclusively in the first question; the philosophers ought to be most interested in the second. Why is the world intelligible, which is to say, not random—not a "mere happening?" If the world is purposeful in process, and it is in all of its major aspects, wherein does the purpose lie and wherein does the intent reside which that purpose implies?

All the biologic activity can be broken down into the two categories of voluntary and involuntary acts. These are, in turn, subdivided into several classes as follows:

Voluntary Acts
Appetitive, physically pleasurable (or in avoidance of pain)
*Appetitive, intellectually pleasurable
*Dutiful

Involuntary Acts
Compulsive
*Duress, intellectual
Duress, physical
Physical, organic, functional
Physical, reactive
Accidental
*Human beings only

The first group provide no difficulty as to intentionality. The class we must key on in the second group is that of compulsive behavior. It is observable in both human and lower animal life. In the latter case, compulsion is the motivation that seems to drive the creature to purposeful external activity. It is an activity which uses means to ends and in which both the means selected, and the ends sought, are, to some extent, beyond the actor's apparent control of intent.

In psychology, the definition of "compulsion" is an irresistible, repeated, irrational, impulse to perform some act. It is closely allied to hypnotic action in which the intent is exterior to the actor. Its characteristic sensation in the actor of the human order is one of "must" or "ought"—closer to a sense of duty than to the appetitive motivation. The case of the compulsive alcoholic would constitute a condition closer to a physical addictive response from a physical malfunction than a true compulsion, though the sense of "craving" is perhaps borderline.

Does a compulsive act signify that there is no intent although the act itself is purposeful to all outward appearance? In the human being compulsion appears to be of two types. One type of compulsive act may be a result of a mental disorder. There is the *imagined* need to act and the intent is formed to meet the need. The activity is intentional though the motivation to form the intent arises from the disorder. In the second type of compulsive act, the actor executes the act under a temporary external motivation. Post-hypnotic suggestion is a good example. The actor performs some purposeful act—some impulsive furniture rearranging for example—and he knows that he intends to move the furniture, sensing that he is doing what he should do. The motivation to the intent was provided by the hypnotist in the form of a subconscious suggestion.

The activity under direct hypnosis is probably similar, although there the intent, even if actual on the part of the actor, is unconscious, but it is conscious on the part of the hypnotist. Since bodily actions are extremely complex, it is likely there would be a subconscious intent to carry out the activity on the part of the actor in response to the hypnotist's conscious intent transmitted with the suggestion. The act is in no case deprived of a "personal" intent.

Control of animal instinctive behavior beyond the physically appetitive appears to be supplied in the form of in-built compulsion to behave in a prescribed way typical of the species. The biological condition or the environment provides the signification to which the structured organism responds. The intent is in-built and unconscious in the organism. The bird would never inquire into its motivation in building a nest or "intend" to build it in a certain way. It would, however, "sense" what was correct in its behavior under the compulsion.

Can a process, an instinctive process, provide its own intent to be purposeful? Can the atom call itself into existence, "boot strapping" at its quintessence? The answer appears to be No.

If, however, the intent is provided as an organic response to the stimulus which initiates the act, then a process can be said to provide its own intent to be purposeful. The compulsive sense of "must" and sense of "correctness" in execution is on the operative level. That is, the intent is on the level of the prime motivator, the designer of the organism, still purposive, still personal. There is no reason that a "sense" of compulsion or of "satisfaction" with progress cannot be preprogrammed into the organism's basic structure. But it must be programmed. It is not contained in the stimulus or in the instinctive act as process. It is a function of the structured being. It is in the specific nature of the organism. Nor does incorporation by chance seem any more likely than in our most sophisticated computer which is still crude in comparison with the organism. Computers are utterly valueless unless they are carefully, purposefully, personally programmed to respond to the data stimuli.

The involuntary purposive acts described in the Table as physical, organic, functional, and physical, reactive the eye blink for instance are virtually identical in man and the lower animals. Here the programming is complete. The organism exercises almost no control over these activities. Is there a specific intent? Obviously there is none on the part of the creature. Yet, manifestly, the activities are not chance happenings for the most complex or for the most primitive organism. There is no reason to believe that these activities were, in any essential way, different for the first organisms.

Is our hypotheses of the universality of the causal principle about to founder, not on the highest level and instinctive behavior but on the lowest? If analogy can be carried up a chain, can it not likewise be carried down the chain? Here is a situation where the preprogramming is almost identical in nature across the range of organisms, though differentiated in degree, by complexity of species. Like the teleprinter, the organism is designed and fabricated to carry out its intended function and the auxiliary subsystems are likewise all designed to support the organism's primary function. Indeed, there is every evidence of intent leading to a purposeful activity.

Now, John Dewey's solution demands that the entire structure arises as a result of the last mode of involuntary acts which is, conceivably, but with difficulty, accidental. That is the only alternative to an intellectual intentional ordering of the series. In my opinion, after analysis, the credibility of the solution is minimal. Though the origin of the problem was largely Ockham's doing, his razor would find a difficult and luxuriant beard, in its end state. The hypothesis is impossibly complex and difficult to support.

There are two facts which are evident beyond any rational doubt. There is being and there is consciousness—an awareness—that there is being. We have seen, with Scheler, the derivative fact that there is being absolutely and absolute being. The "abyss of nothing" is fiction. It is deprived of meaning by the absoluteness of being. Its conception as a "possibility" resides only in a negation of that which, in fact, is and has being.

The intellectual awareness at some level that there is being derives from the consciousness of our own being, undeniable—except through denial of the experienced self. Our awareness of the absolute self consciousness is brought into our full consciousness by a process of induction. First, there is consciousness. Merleau-Ponty saw, in man, "incarnate consciousness" without, at the same time, reflecting that there must be a consciousness that is not incarnate. For him, consciousness in man was integral with the organism man—a phenomenon which was in no way isolable from matter as it constituted man.

Consciousness and being are correlative. When we looked at the concept of being with Scheler we concluded with him that the observed experience of existing time-limited being led to the affirmation of absolute being. In an analogous way, the experience of our own consciousness of our own being leads to the affirmation of an absolute consciousness of being. We participate in that consciousness just as we participate in absolute being in a relationship of dependency. Our being is not absolute, nor is our consciousness absolute. Our own human consciousness is polarized by its incarnation. It must view itself and all else through and in context of its embedment in space-time. It must recognize its own contingency—that the specific circumstance of its *being here* is incredibly unlikely, yet, that the facticity of *some* consciousness *being here* is unavoidable.

The individual could be or not be but the individual consciousness of men once established is not satisfied with its carnal environment. It is oriented toward freedom in asserting itself against its limitations, in directing its activities, in acquisition of knowledge. Overcoming constraint is its perpetual occupation or preoccupation. The challenge of every consciousness is to expand and grow toward—to approach the absolute consciousness of absolute being. It is not the Absolute, the One, which evolves—a concept fraught with contradiction—but the finite, the Many under impulse of the Absolute seek to image forth the Absolute as closely as possible. The Absolute wills that all creation, animals and inanimate the Many, reflect Him to the maximum extent their individual natures permit.

Whitehead's "consequent nature of God" in which God is seen to enter into and be affected by the processes of the world yields to the absolute consciousness "from the beginning." God's awareness of and concern for our predicament in specific space-time reflects from eternity the situation as it evolves in history, in time. The state of our consciousness as it is at this instant is totally apprehended by God. He is not a mere "partner in travail" sharing our anxieties—which indeed He is not—He is the master of history infinitely loving and compassionate, totally in command who in His infinite wisdom has provided for all contingencies in advance. If we pray for assistance in trouble and are answered—as we will be—it is because from all eternity God is aware of our problems and of our response, whatever it is, and has provided for its solution in the light of our response from all eternity. The point is that our response is ours, known and considered by Him. But since we do not know all of the parameters of the problem in any trial, we are free to respond as we will either in rebellion or in resignation to God's will. We may be sure moreover that the outcome will reflect our action as it in fact took place. Though God is master of history, we are uniquely masters of our lives within that history. God is not process nor affected by process, yet is the ultimate cause and controller of all process.

The god of deism was closely related to the process of nature, but nonetheless was construed as a conscious personal being even if he were disinterested in the petty things of men. During and shortly after the "enlightenment" the early positivists extracted what was left of personality and sought to deify process. "Science" was the ritual of deified process. In recent times the confusion of process and being has deepened. After Hegel, especially, and the process of dialectic, the tendency was to make a process out of deity and everything else. Hegel's and even Scheler's "groping" deity seeking to come to consciousness in man reflects this effect. Both viewpoints are errors stemming from a failure to distinguish between the two concepts, process and being. Any actor in any activity carries out a process or is the object of a process. The deity initiates process but is not a part of it—the "One" does not become the "many" nor do the "many" constitute the "One." Parmenides and Heraclitus are not telescoped. There is rather the "One" who is of Plato—from whom the many proceed, a result of process as manifestations of His creativity in an endless proliferation and profusion. The teleprinter is not part of its designer, fabricator or operator; it merely manifests those designing fabrication and operating capabilities, though the machine executes purposeful intent and carries out a process.

Existentialism with its stress on becoming is a process philosophy and of course so are naturalism and materialism. With them, in a large sense, all is process. Now, there is no question but that the intelligibility of process and its implicit purposefulness are intriguing to the human intelligence. What must not be forgotten is that specific intent which lies behind any planned process and further that personality which inevitably lies behind that intent wherever process, purposefulness and intelligibility are exhibited.

The philosophers of being habitually seek to go behind the process and to identify first principles—to locate the intending personality—the being which is responsible and then from observation of its process to form some opinion of the being's nature through relationship to the process. This brings in the matter of "relationship" in process and, with that idea, we will summarize to some extent what has gone before. It will be recalled that Ockham had denied the relevance of "relationship" as well as the universality of the relationship. Thus, one had fathers and sons. No need to talk about the relationship "paternity" which is just another name for the process of bisexual generation in the male line. Ockham says in effect, "we observe the relationship in specific instances but should not conclude as to its universality." Ockham felt, in the cited case, that the relationship, to the extent it was relevant, was implicit in the terms father and son and hence the relationship "paternity" was an unnecessary term. He was thus, consciously or not, also denying the relevance of process and the universality which that has as the expression of true relationships.

Process always involves relationship between things. A simple chemical reaction is a process which expresses a relationship. For example, there is a relationship between oxygen and hydrogen. Their union brings about an energy release in the overall entropic system such that the process is not reversible without bringing in energy from an external source. All these characteristics define the nature of the process. All are intelligible if the relationship between the "actors" is known. Thus chemists were able to predict the characteristics of the missing elements in the early Mendeleyev series before they were isolated and identified, because they recognized the relationship which existed throughout the chemical series.

The more complex the relationship, the more complex is the process. In analyzing the structure of the causality principle exhibited in process we note that there is first a conscious intelligent being, a personality which forms an intent to undertake an activity, a process, and all for a specific end. The intelligent being relates itself by intent and purpose in the process by means of which it will carry out the activity to produce the desired end. There are of course many processes which cannot be analyzed as to specific intent. The process of erosion, of oxidation, of orogeny, of virtually all of the mechanical processes of the universe are of this nature. Yet, our inability of analysis only points to our own limitations. These processes are purposeful but are at a level beyond our detailed comprehension. Viewed from the position of an observer who can see only the things-in-process, which is the human position vis-a-vis the universe, we have to look both ways, back toward the Initiator and forward toward the end which the Initiator had in His intent. If we look only at the pieces of process, as empirically revealed, we form a picture of that very narrow and fragmented band and all is unrelated matter in motion. A particular bird's nest is only a complex structure instinctively constructed by a particular bird. The only way that the band of intellectual perspective can be widened, would be to extend our "vision" by rational process, interrelating the fragments of process which we observe, and which appear unrelated when taken in isolation. This can be done only through analogy with our own purposeful activity, and by extending the observed causal relationship in specific fields to causal process in the universal field. The validity of the extension was what Ockham, Kant and the modern empiricists following Kant denied absolutely. But absolute barriers occur only at absolute boundaries, and there are none here apparent.

As we saw, there are two absolutes contained in the overall idea of being and non-being. These are the absolute of nothingness and the absolute of infinity in being. If there is a condition of nothing in existence, there is absolutely no existence, actual or potential, and if there is a condition of existence there is an infinity of existence without limit. Now, the proper antithesis of nothingness is inifinity and, as we saw earlier in looking at Scheler, there is no continuum between these terms. The concept of magnitude bears the same relationship to infinity as time does to eternity—neither finite magnitude of being nor time are segments of infinite being or eternity respectively. But both the former exist because of the existence of and in relationship to the latter two. At its interface, this relationship represents the "twilight zone" of our ability to exert our powers and reason. We literally cannot form a well-illuminated analogy to the intrinsic infinite or to the intrinsic eternal "condition," which is really "uncondition." However, this is far beyond Kant's limit which is artificial and within time and finiteness. We can go to the interface and define the interface itself, and this is sufficient. The causal relationship is not limited to the specific case but can be extended to any situation in which we observe process. If an atom comes into existence, it is an effect—a result of a process. . .and the "horizontal" causal chain is as applicable there as for the teleprinter or the nest.

Now the primary purpose of this discourse was to manipulate the various causal relationships in context, to demonstrate how closely they interlock, and to illustrate how far-reaching the implications are. It is perhaps appropriate now to try to formulate a definition of the causal principle that covers these relationships. The concept of causality is similar to the concept of time. Everybody knows what it is, until they are asked to define it. The simplest definition is as follows: "A cause is that without which nothing happens." But that is scarcely a sufficient definition for analytical purposes. The writer's definition, with that objective in mind, is: "Causality is the relationship which exists between two sets of situational parameters (a mix of entities, processes, and events), such that, the first, called the antecedent, has the capacity to produce or alter the second, called the subsequent, and that the second derives both its purpose and methodology of development from the first. The antecedent set completely defines the subsequent."

It is time to attempt some logical conclusions from the study. The first logic gate presents the proposition: The causal principle is not limited to the specific observed case, but can be extended to any activity in which process is explicit in the nature of the activity. Process is here defined as "a patterned change or series of changes between two sets of situational parameters identified as antecedent and subsequent." It had been noted earlier that "accidental" or "uncaused" events are very hard to find—even the "broken leg" which was used earlier or the elimination of the unfavorably situated moths are reducible to process at some point. The coin toss would come close to a purely random activity. The results at least are practically unpatterned. Whether heads or tails results from a particular coin toss would be considered sufficiently unpatterned as to affirm that in the real world the outcome is in no sense related to the toss. The execution of the toss itself of course would be a process and under this proposition subject to the causal principle. What are the alternatives to the proposition?—only its denial. This causal principle is accepted by the human mind first of all because we observe effects in relationship to their causes. The alternative—true spontaneous happenings—literally cannot be conceived. Analyticist Ludwig Wittgenstein, no particular friend of the metaphysicians, said: "We do not believe, *a priori*, in a law of conservation. But, we know, *a priori*, the possibility of a logical form. All propositions, such as the law of causation, the law of continuity in nature, the law of least expenditure in nature, etc., etc., all themselves are *a priori* intuitions of possible forms of the propositions of science. What can be described can happen too, and what is excluded by the law of causality cannot be described." (Wittgenstein, 1951). Rigorously, however, the causal principle cannot be extended universally if process in at least one possible instance can be shown to be acausal. That is the reason that the writer stated earlier that a rigorous proof is one of induction and hence impossible. For our logic gates, the propositions will be stated in terms of confidence level in correctness of the position. For instance, in this case, based on all available evidence, it can be stated at a high level of confidence that the causal principle is not limited to the specific observed cases but can be extended to any activity in which process is explicit or implicit in the nature of the activity. The reader should interpolate such probabilistic language in all the subsequent logic gates. From a *practical* standpoint there is certitude.

The second logic gate is really only an extension of the basic definition of "process." As defined, the concept of process implies that there is an intelligible relationship in the "patternedness" in the changes between the two situational sets. What are the alternatives?—denial that there is always an intelligible relationship implicit in "pattern." The process of elimination of the moths was patterned and was intelligible. The elimination of the moths was determined by the color of the moth related to its randomly selected background—as the color of the general background darkened from air pollution, the percentage of light-colored moths destroyed by preying birds increased disproportionately in the subsequent condition compared to their number in the population in the antecedent condition. There was process, the process is intelligible. Since we are dealing only with implication in definition between terms, the denial can be rejected on the basis that it results in a contradiction. The term "patternedness" does contain the notion of being susceptible to explanation, of "non-randomness," and hence of intelligibility.

The third logic gate states the proposition that the principle of causality as applied universally is capable of intellectual analysis regardless of the nature of the process. This proposition flows from the combination of logic gates one and two. The writer's frank intent here is to open the door to "analogic" analysis and of denying Kant's limitation of the range of the intellect to the sensory. If process is intelligible, it is, by that fact, capable of intellectual analysis.

The fourth logic gate presents the proposition which is a specific application of the causal principle as defined in approaching logic gate one. It is stated in the form, "Nothing comes into existence without an external cause." This does not say that anything does come into existence, only that if it does, there is a cause outside of itself.

A "coming into existence" is an intelligible concept in theoretical terms. One can clearly conceive of a thing "not being there" and then of its "being there." If such an action occurs, it is clearly patterned between before and after conditions. There is process. Comparing it with the coin toss, the after condition is always differentiated from the before condition in the same direction and with the same result—existence in some form—the result is not random. There is therefore a causal relationship in the process "coming into existence." Now since "coming into existence" is process, assume the isolated antecedent condition, nothing, and the subsequent condition, something. These situational sets are separated by an act which must be performed. A process must be carried out. But the assumed antecedent set "nothing" has by definition no capacity to act. Therefore the process is not possible as assumed. The act must be performed by an external agency not in the assumed antecedent situational set, nothing. The *actual* antecedent situational set must contain an actor, a causal entity preexisting the posited act of coming into existence.

The fifth logic gate approaches the question of purpose and intent in the universe on the basis of the previous conclusions and involves an appeal to reason on the "mass of evidence" basis. If there is, and, as there is, a predominance of intelligibility in the continuous changes in situational sets in the observable physical universe, there must be an intelligent source (cause) of intelligibility which is the primal antecedent set to which all the subsequent observable sets bear the relationship of effect directly or at some finite remove. Intelligibility as a characteristic of process is the effect of intelligible activity between situational sets. Reversing the order of this statement the proposition is made:

There is an external antecedent intelligent situational set which either modified a preexisting unintelligible antecedent situational set to provide an intelligible subsequent situational set, or caused the intelligible subsequent set to come into existence. The first explanation would be Aristotelian—the second Platonic. We will now examine this proposition in some detail.

Up to this point we have been concentrating on the methodology in causation—its epistomological mode; now let us look at its ontological mode. The ontological mode or view of causality, as the name suggests, emphasizes the impact on man as a being, as a being in a relationship. Any relationship involving human beings in its highest form is a personal interaction—a dialogue between I and Thou in the intimate "Buberian" understanding—although the "I, It" relationship is also present. The causal relationship thus conceived is one in which the intelligible process between any two situational sets reflects the comprehension by an intelligent being present in both the antecedent set and the subsequent set or in the subsequent set alone that the process in which it finds itself is the outcome of an intelligence *intending* the process. An intelligible act in this context can be defined as one in which an intelligent being is "dissatisfied" with a given situational set—which might be that of no entity, event or process external to itself—and intentionally sets in motion a process of change toward a different situational set. This process would continue uninterruptedly through a sequence of situational sets until an intelligent being, either the same or another, forms the intent to change the course from that originally started.

"Time" may be conceived as comprising the sequence of situational sets from "the beginning." In this view, a single situational set would be a complete instantaneous picture of the simultaneous conditions of the total universe. "Evolution" as popularly conceived would be the historical account of this process of "sequelity." The concept implies that if one could freeze a situational set in time and make a detailed analysis it would reveal the shape of the subsequent set which would emerge inevitably following the entities, events and processes then active in the situational set under observation. An accident, in reality, is termed so only because we cannot analyze in detail sufficiently fine to predict the outcome from the immediately antecedent conditions. The outcome of a coin toss, though random as to the human observer in time, is determined by the detailed totality of the existent situation during which the toss process takes place.

John Dewey was right to the extent that (so far as we know) until man arrived on the scene there was no being *internal* to the world which could change the pattern of "sequelity" by deliberate premeditated action, and no other action could change it—that action requires an independent intelligence. Dewey was wrong when he said that until man, there were "mere happenings." He denied the intelligibility and hence intelligent origin of the vast series of situational sets prior to man. The strict "determinists," on the other hand, would hold that even man is so controlled by his submergence in the detailed situational set in which he momentarily finds himself, that independence of action is impossible. The individual does not know it, but his decisions are totally dependent upon the pressures which control his motivation—he is no better off than the lower animals with their instinctive drive for motivation—or even the apple in the tree which falls to the ground and rots. Now they might be right if man, in fact, could freeze the antecedent set and make the required detailed, unemotional analysis before acting. The fact is, he cannot have absolute knowledge—and it is precisely in this inability, that man can—and does—exercise an independent judgment in his actions and that there is variability in his decisions. Each individual's decisions are peculiarly his own. Judgments connote opinions, not absolute knowledge, in the human order.

Now the fact—if it is a fact—that an external independent intelligence *does know* the detail including the shortcomings which beset the other intelligence internal to the process and *does know* the answer, which will result from that independent being's action inside the global process, in no way affects the latter's independence in judgment. It does, however, permit the former from "the beginning," to take into account that independent activity, project the outcome and preprogram the course which will still result in the net outcome it desires. Man's efforts, while ineffective in changing the end position, remain independent and reflective of his individual will under his personal intentionality in direction. The unforeseen consequences of intentional acts apply only to beings unable to foresee all aspects of their deliberate acts. In these unforeseen consequences the process leading to the consequences is not intentional, but the causative agency remains.

Without independent beings internal to the process there would have been cause and effect in the universe, as there certainly was in the world before man appeared, but there would have been no being internal to the process which recognized the process between situational sets. Thus the causal "relation-ship" could have been said to have had no "meaning" in the world until man appeared and could recognize it. When man did appear and did recognize process for what it was, even in an inchoate way, he also recognized his own ability to modify it because he realized that it was intelligible, not random, not accidental. He also recognized that there was something "out there" that also possessed the same intelligent capacity to "cause" things to eventuate in accordance with advance plan-ning that man himself possessed, only to an incomprehensibly great degree. The work, *Insight,* by Bernard Lonergan (Loner-gan, 1958) is an excellent, detailed development of the logic in support of a metaphysics of the created universe and the essential characteristics of the necessary being responsible for its creation.

Several questions arise at this point. Does intelligibility in ac-tivity *necessarily* imply intelligence in formulation of the ac-tivity? What are the alternatives? There are two somewhat related alternative explanations which are frequently given. The first states that intelligible acts are random happenings that "hap-pen" to form an intelligible pattern. The second goes one step beyond and would explain the "intelligibility" as appearance. These activities appear intelligible to us in our human view-point. Actually, we formulate the laws based on the way we think which gives them, then, the appearance of intelligibility.

In looking at the first alternative, let us take a simple example from human activity. The popularity of the various word games like cryptograms lies in the characteristic of the human being to seek answers to events in nature which show a pattern of intelligibility. In this case the puzzle solver has been assured by the intelligent producer of the puzzles that there is an an-swer if the former can respond to the clues which are given by the latter. When the participant finds the pattern by which the cryptogram was constructed, he can find the "message" that cryptogram conveyed and all similarly constructed crypto-grams as well. He would have "broken the code." Now if the same curious human being is given a bowl of alphabet soup, he does not try to "solve" the soup and find the deeper mean-ings conveyed. If he did, he would be classed as slightly balmy. No number of bowls of soup would produce an intelligibility such that clues would lead to an intelligible message or lead to a conclusion of an intelligent formulator as the cryptogram would. There is no pattern discernible because none was intended.

Man's universal quest for answers to the "puzzle" of the physical universe is studied with consummate dedication because the patterned relationships are intelligible and point out that an intelligent pursuit will provide intelligible answers to an intelligent observer. The reverse implication is clear that the intelligible puzzles solvable by intelligent action were provided only by an intelligent formulation. One of the problems of sociology as a science is that the basic units forming the puzzle are themselves intelligent and can change their pattern individually or in groups, making a solution of the puzzle several orders more difficult.

The second alternative is more complex. It has two points of attack. The first is ontological. The nature of man is such as to seek causal relations because we "see" causal relationships where none exist. We formulate models of what we observe and label them as physical laws. Then we say these laws make the universe intelligible. In this form, there is denial that there is intelligibility and the answer lies in the same approach in answer to the first alternative. The laws are possible because there is a relationship that can be identified—the relationship is not a result of the laws. Any attempt to arrive at laws in the alphabet soup beyond the statistical—on the average each handful will contain a certain number of each letter—is fruitless because there is no relationship to be found which can be used in a predictive way for application to that bowl of soup or any subsequent bowls of soup.

The second facet is epistemological—Can we know from our perception that there is intelligibility even if we discern it? This is the Kantian skepticism and goes to the ability of human beings to know beyond the particular and to the validity of analogy in extending observations from the "puzzle" for instance to the universe—and to that which lies behind the universe. This question, in turn, leads to the basis of intelligent analysis of all perception. We form conclusions from our perceptions so that we can act rationally in the situational set in which we find ourselves. We must and do act on the basis that our perceptions are a real, not imaginary, reflection of what is really the case and that the case is intelligible. If virtually everything human beings have observed over the ages appears intelligible, the only basis of action is that the relationships we discern are intelligible as real knowledge on which decision can and must be based unless we are to sit in perpetual idleness. Attempts to meet radical skepticism by rigorous rationality is a tilting with windmills—the question "Can we know anything?"

is not rational. It is an expression of querulous pessimism concerning man's condition—and the answers cannot be given exhaustive detailed rational formulation. One's own existence can be held unknowable argumentively. But unfortunately for our age, the skeptical view which is so common, is an invitation to the agnostic non-solution—one cannot know either way—Lippman's view in this writer's preface—therefore one should act as though the question does not exist. One should submerge the question in happy thoughts. It cannot be important anyhow. It is the viewpoint that appeals to a lazy intellect and leads to Nietzsche's outcome—for nihilism is the child of skepticism.

The fifth logic gate then, which is crucial, can be passed with high confidence in its correctness. It can now be stated thus: The observed intelligibility of processes in the universe is clear evidence of an intelligent, purposeful being, external to the universe in essence, who established these processes in a causal relationship by his direct intent.

Thus, the observable existence of being and process both point to the existence of a Supreme Being, the intelligent intending ego source of being and process.

In Part III the implications of this logic gate will be explored as they relate to the observations of physical science late in the twentieth century in relationships of intelligence, energy and informational systems. The Supreme Being as pure act will also be viewed as pure energy, pure intelligence in possession of all possible information. From this sequence it will be adduced that "prior" to the active physical existence of space, time and matter they had potential existence as conscious possibilities. The actuality of space, time and matter from eternal possibilities required eternal intent of self-sufficient eternal being and the actuality eventuated from the intent.

Before moving away from the review of the concept of man through the centuries, the writer would attempt to show graphically what has taken place in this concept.

See CURVE—Figure 1

Figure 1 is a pictorial representation showing two relationships in a time scale over the past 800 years. The first depicts the effort toward technological advance measured by gross energy production. The second depicts the cultural advance measured only relatively to a somewhat arbitrarily selected balance position about the year 1850 which coincides with general onset of the Industrial Revolution. It also coincides with the

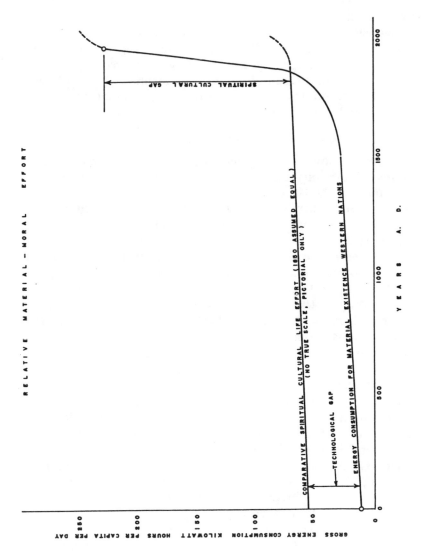

RELATIVE MATERIAL — MORAL EFFORT

GROSS ENERGY CONSUMPTION KILOWATT HOURS PER CAPITA PER DAY

SPIRITUAL CULTURAL GAP

COMPARATIVE SPIRITUAL CULTURAL LIFE EFFORT (1850 ASSUMED EQUAL)
(NO TRUE SCALE, PICTORIAL ONLY)

TECHNOLOGICAL GAP

ENERGY CONSUMPTION FOR MATERIAL EXISTENCE WESTERN NATIONS

YEARS A. D.

500   1000   1500   2000

0   50   100   150   200   250

FIGURE 1

general application of social theories which came out of the Age of the Enlightenment. Prior to that date, certainly man was under-technologized and most higher education was directed to the nontechnical fields; these comprised the humanities, including philosophy and religion, medicine and law. Relatively little effort was given to the sciences, and those chiefly astronomy and the associated mathematics. Obviously, thereafter, what had been a slow climb for both remained a slow climb for the cultural advance. The slow climb changed, however, to a continually accelerating high speed ascent for technology. Virtually all of the human effort freed by technology was plowed back into technology. There was no corresponding new input for cultural development.

See CURVE—Figure 2

Figure 2 shows at the extreme left the major source philosophies of antiquity and at the extreme right the philosophic groupings in the last half of the twentieth century just discussed. While a strict parallelism is not possible, the pattern at both right and left is from the materialistic end of the spectrum at the bottom to the spiritual end at the top.

In between, the writer has placed the names of those reviewed on a horizontal time-scale and in the approximate vertical position which the writer feels the individual would fit in his corresponding attitude toward man. The location of the philosophers of idea near the bottom of the scale next to the materialist, is perhaps arbitrary, but it has to do with the Kantian limitation of knowledge to the sensory perception even though much of Kant's philosophy had "moral" connotations. But in that form his thinking was not so much "philosophy" as "faith." Hegel, Fichte and Schelling largely disassociated themselves from that attitude, yet Hegel was the basic source of Marx's dialectic materialism. If the positions of philosophers of idea and of life were reversed the general picture would not be much changed. As was noted in the text earlier, the modern philosophic "systems" tend to have considerable range in the spiritual and materialist spectrum. An additional comment should be made concerning the graph and that is that a continuous scholastic philosophy generally of a "low profile" continued in the Platonic-Aristotelian-Augustinian-Thomas tradition across the centuries.

Two asterisked points have been plotted. The one at the left reflects the convergent position on the monastic scholasticism at the time immediately preceding Thomas Aquinas. The one

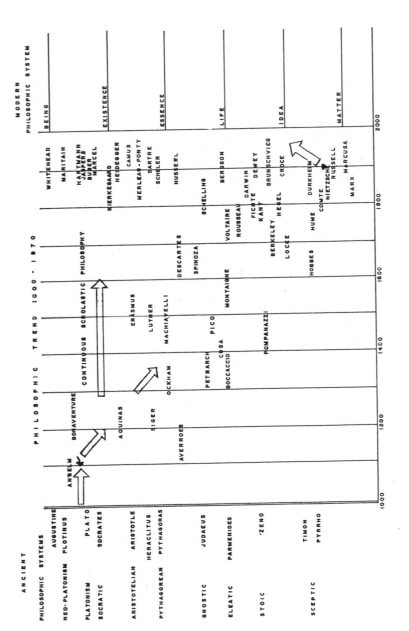

FIGURE 2

at the right reflects the convergence on materialism at about the beginning of the twentieth century. From these points, two trend paths are shown, both indicating a period of divergence for the period ahead and the direction the divergence takes. The upper opens into the Renaissance; the lower into the emerging new age. It is clear by now from the review of the emerging thought some half century after the lower asterisk that indeed the philosophic trend has begun to spread the spectrum once more. A move, still inchoate but active, has begun toward the transcendental and more balanced viewpoint.

If God was dead for Nietzsche at the latter's death in 1900, He is now being revitalized in what may be called the New Renaissance. For, if the new trends in philosophy are allowed to survive their birthing crisis, they give promise of a fullness of human existence never before conceived or physically realizable. No one should deny the enrichening potential which the modern age scientific and technologic advances have provided. What is needed now is a companion spiritual enrichment. This means we must avoid starving the emerging infant pattern of thought by separating it from nourishment in the long western tradition of man's belief in a beneficent God and man's own transcendental nature. This tradition alone can supply the spiritual values needed to fashion the emerging world into one of deeply satisfying fulfillment.

See CURVE—Figure 3

Figure 3 is a plot of the technological advance as measured by the gross per capita energy consumption in the West, the same as shown in Figure 1. Added to this plot is the trend in philosophic thought—a purely subjective estimate based by the writer on the results of our tour down through the centuries. This comparison displays the situation in the modern world: almost complete concentration on the material way of life, contrasted with the indifference if not outright denial of spiritual values in the early decades of this century. Continuation of this situation for an extended period would be bound to end in disaster. But in the last few decades the rebound which we have noted occurred, if not toward the spiritual, at least away from the materialistic aspects.

In the writer's opinion it has been fairly well demonstrated that the Hobbesian question can be answered in a free society positively by no other philosophy than one based on moral values developed from considerations of man as a being responsible to his Creator for his actions. The philosophy of any period

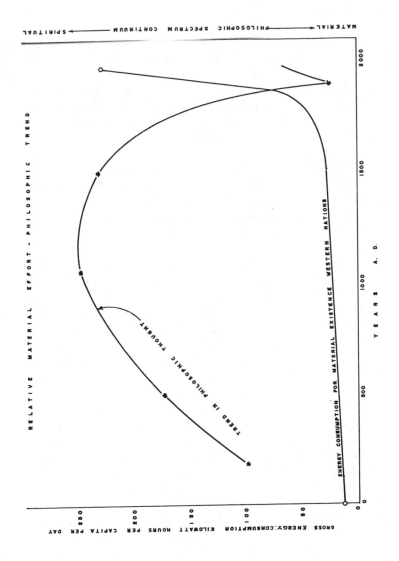

FIGURE 3

is the intellectual embodiment of the efforts to provide man of that period with the mental conditioning to permit accommodation to the facts of life as then perceived. Viewed in this light, the Augustinian-Platonic philosophy gave man the necessary fortitude to strive and endure in a period of great physical disorder during and following the collapse of the Roman Empire. Aristotelian-Thomism modified the older philosophy to adjust to the then incipient intellectual quickening of the city universities and the political turmoil surrounding the breakup of feudalism.

Similarly, the Renaissance philosophic divergence was an attempt to come to grips with the new commercial development, the accelerating growth of natural science, the phenomena of the national academies and to digest the heavy infusion of ancient classics.

Sometimes a philosophy reflected a strong reaction to an existing concept which yet reinforced that concept. Marxism was such a case; it was a reaction to the abuses of a materialistic exploitation of the laboring class by the bourgeoisie. Yet it strengthened the very materialism which was at the root of the exploitation.

The pattern of philosophic change up until the time of the introduction of the Copernican concept of the universe was one of a fairly smooth transition, for the change in world view was gradual. The concept of the universe was essentially what it had been for all previous history. The Copernican-Galilean concepts were, however, thoroughly disruptive in their cosmological effect. All of the sciences were affected and burst into action. The philosophers were suddenly, for philosophers, forced to review all of their previous concepts. There was no new neat package to hand to people in explaining the individual's place in the new world which was so ebulliently emerging.

The religious upheaval and the shallow toyings of kings, princes and prelates in science and philosophy pointed up the fact that the philosophic answers were not at hand. The questions far outdistanced the philosophers. In many ways, the entire period since that changed world view has been one of trial and error in philosophy and the social sciences in attempts to come up with satisfying answers. Gradually, a convergence started in what appeared to be the logical solution. That is, a split package solution in fact, Kantian in approach, dichotomatic.

What was spiritual was reduced to feelings. The moral imperative, intellectually unknowable. What was matter was empiricized, knowable by the senses, a matter of purely scientific resolution, yet still idealized. We were in a way captives of our sense limitation. With the impressive advances in science and technology at the turn of the century and afterwards, idealism, a poor, weak, fanciful, concept in the first place, fell by the wayside. Positivistic, naturalistic, pragmatic and Marxian materialism became the dominant and almost the only widely active advancing philosophies in the early twentieth century.

But now a new and radical physical universe, a new cosmology, thrust itself forward in the acceptance of Einsteinian physics. Compounding this were the sociologic, political and economic repercussions of materialism. All things seemed to point to materialism's dismal shortcomings in its efforts to provide lasting answers. Now, once more, the philosophies began to diverge and on a trend toward the re-emergence of a transcendental concept of man.

Part II has shown that the duration of the atheistic materialistic viewpoint has been short. It has lasted less than two hundred years. Its birth, in its militant form, took place in the French Revolution. Prior to that time, the only open sponsor of the "atheistic wing" was Holbach in his *Systems of Nature,* published in 1770. Further, the biographies show that the leaders of the enlightenment thought were not true scientists, nor were they true philosophers. They were clever, articulate dabblers in both, and they were, above all, politically active. None were men of challenging intellectual depth. What happened is this, the philosophers and theologians of real scholarship, with few exceptions (Kant being the notable one), were so busy beating each other about on their religious differences that they let the mainline intellectual initiative swing to non-professionals—those who were far less qualified.

Meanwhile, the man in the street, and on the farm, went his own way. Then, when the Industrial Revolution came, working men moving into the cities in large numbers lacked a strong philosophical background to support them. In the absence of a spiritual thrust, the surging materialistic advancement—so apparent—so full of vitality—took over and remains with us, although the philosophic tides have changed. It is the task of reintroducing the transcendental philosophic viewpoint at a meaningful level in society that poses the greatest challenge to men of the new age.

PART III

GOD AND MAN IN THE UNIVERSE

Chapter 9

GOD AND MAN, AN ANALYSIS OF ALTERNATIVES

As a consequence of our historical study of man's view of man through the philosophical and sociological systems, we have been able to conclude, with a high-derived-probability, from essentially intellectual considerations, that God exists. The principle arguments were from the de facto existence of being—for -us to being-in and of-itself following St. Anselm's, Descartes', and Scheler's development of the concept. The other principle argument was from the concept of causality in its ontological, rather than empirical, formulation. The universe was viewed as intelligible—the consequence of intelligible processes. These processes, not being "free standing," are initiated and maintained by an intelligent being called God.

In Part III we will look at the physical universe as it is being revealed by modern scientific investigation. The approach here is not from a rigorous scientific exposition, which will change with tomorrow or next year's experiment, but more from the trends which are being disclosed with deeper and deeper development of the actual structure of the universe about us. It is more a survey from an engineering viewpoint. What do the scientific results taken at face value permit us to say about their applicability in their relationship to man's physical and spiritual needs?

The themes of Being and causality are here examined again in the context of the world—part of a physical system—as viewed in the closing decades of the twentieth century. Again, no claim of "proof" of the existence of God is made. There is only a claim of a high-derived-probability, particularly in the apparent convergence of all of the accumulating evidence in the various subsystems on the existence of a nonphysical "system," from which the physical systems depend. The resultant high probability is considered coercive of the existence of God.

Central to any concept of man as a transcendental being, is the idea of an ongoing existence which is independent of the material universe. If there is no such existence, there is no

320

possibility of a transcendental vector in man's nature. The term is meaningless. Establishment of a credible basis for such an existence is of necessity the first task which a proponent of man's immortality must undertake. A second, but closely related, concept which also must be established is that of the possibility of an interface between a material and an immaterial existence. The development of both of these crucial elements lies in the answer to that evasive cosmological question of the nature and origin of the material universe. Fortunately for us, the responses to that question are converging in this century, after two centuries of divergence. This convergence is not being brought to a focus by wishful thinking. It is being brought about by the analysis of data from many disciplines and mathematical solutions to the complex, simultaneous equations of time, space, matter (mass) and energy.

Section 1—A View From Cosmology

There are only three fundamental ways to explain the universe:

a. It always existed.
b. It is self-created, or self-generated and sustaining.
c. It is created by an agency not itself created and therefore itself unchangeable. For convenience, this mode is designated "externally created."

The idea of a material universe of an infinite duration in the past is no longer held by responsible scientists. This is evident to the extent that one cosmologist and the basic originator of one of the two leading concepts—Reginald Kapp—in his book, *Toward a Unified Cosmology* (Kapp, 1960), felt it was necessary to apologize to his colleagues for raising this issue as one of his possibilities, saying, (page 57), "Many will say in refuting it I am only flogging a dead horse." He says, on pages 47 and 48, "For the foregoing reasons, the notion that the contents of the material universe have existed for all time, seems today to have but a few sponsors among serious scientists. It fails badly by any acceptable scientific criteria and certainly by that of minimum assumption."

The basic reason for its rejection can be put in express mathematical terms, or rather, more correctly, it can be rejected, since it cannot be expressed as a mathematically, viable solution. The notion of any continuous occurrence of events—the ticks of a clock, the scintillations of atomic decay, the pulses of the cephides, can be expressed mathematically as a numerical sequence as 1, 2, 3, 4 . . . 1,000—2,000—3,000—10,000 . . .

10^5—10^{10}—10^{100}—10^n. The number, regardless of how great, if real, always bears a fixed sequential relationship to a first event. On the other hand it is a mathematical contradiction to speak of a "nowness" from an infinite past in any changing existence as the physical universe observably is.

As a very simple example, if we make an attempt to write the fraction 1/3 as a decimal we can go on mindlessly adding "3's" to the sequence 0.333333. Yet, the end point is never precisely reached. The mathematical sequence expressing the value starts at the decimal point and from that point has a real value, although only approximate. The sequence itself has no finite end. The residual error becomes an infinitesimal. If we flip our decimal over and now try to approach the value from the other end—from the infinitesimal end, we find that—not only can we never arrive at our decimal point, but we also can never arrive at any specific "3" in the sequence. We cannot even begin the assembly. It has no reality, because it has no beginning point. The same is true of the idea of a physical universe infinitely existing from the past.

The concept of infinite material existence, from the past, also fails badly in terms of the observed winding down or entropy in the universe. This is the principle which states that in any process of heat transfer—although the total quantity of heat remains the same—the quality or availability continuously degrades. From the infinite past, our universe would have wound down, unless it were infinitely energetic, which again, observably, it is not.

These conclusions leave the two other possibilities. Either the universe was self-created or externally created. As will be seen, this includes a concept bridging the two, which is basically Kapp's position. The current popular theories, the single creative act, popularly known as the "Big Bang," and continuous creation, while they are almost at opposite ends of the spectrum, are both amenable to analysis from the viewpoint of the two remaining basic possibilities. Neither, for reasons stated, are amenable to the first—and discarded concept—of an infinite past existence of the material universe.

The modern seeking of answers in cosmology in the light of Einsteinian physics can be said to have begun with Einstein himself in what has been called a static universe model. In 1916, he published his first ideas in which he considered the universe as a sort of superfluid of stellar and galactic molecules, having a fixed average density. It was a time-independent, fixed structure of fixed dimensions. It seems strange coming from Einstein.

However, in 1916 the concept of an expanding universe had not yet been brought into being by the deep space observations of Edwin Hubble (1889 - 1953) and others. Under his general theory of relativity, the curvature of this space would be directly related to the density of the "fluid." An empty space would have an infinite radius and be Euclidean in geometry. Densely packed space would have a relatively short radius and severe curvature. It was found that this model was disastrously unstable. It would quickly collapse under gravitational forces. To avoid this observably incorrect conclusion, Einstein assumed an opposed "repulsive force" which would exactly counterbalance the gravitational attractive force. His universe was now in a precarious state of unstable equilibrium. The slightest disturbance of balance would either send it flying apart, or, as before, collapsing. Einstein repudiated the concept even before the later observations of the expanding universe destroyed it as a complete hypothesis.

In 1917, William de Sitter (1872 - 1934), a Dutch astronomer, attempted to work out a stable variation of the Einstein model by proposing that the Euclidean, infinite-radius, zero-density aspect of Einstein's model was, in fact, the limit to which the present universe was expanding. It was a remarkable insight considering that there was not the slightest indication, empirically, at that time, of the expansion now taken for granted. De Sitter built his model on that limit and it is not far from the present concept. The actual average density has now been evaluated at about the equivalent of one atom of hydrogen per cubic meter. We cannot achieve such a close approximation of a true vacuum either in our laboratories or in our space probes. Our own galaxy is of high density by comparison. His space had the peculiar, yet not so peculiar, characteristic that time was a function of distance from the observer. Rather than space being "curved," time would be "curved." De Sitter's model, though later shown mathematically unstable—and no solution to Einstein's dilemma—remains as the "limiting" condition of the current expanding space models. Einstein's original remains the "limiting" condition of a collapsed universe.

The third significant model was that of Abbe Georges Henri Lemaitre, a Belgian astrophysicist and mathematician, who was, like his intellectual forebearer Copernicus, also a priest. Born in 1894, he was named president of the Pontifical Academy of Sciences in 1960. This model, first published in 1927, is also the currently accepted and most probable solution. It is the forerunner of the "Big Bang" theory and will be described as now viewed.

The "Big Bang" concept states, in effect, that all matter and energy now in the universe have existed for the same length of time, from $t = 0$, which the proponents designate as creation.

Their position is reached because all estimates of the age of the universe from the most distant galaxy to our own, regardless of how measured, whether by radioactive decay, ratio of helium to hydrogen in the stars, or by kinetic energy between the stars, seem to give a point of origin of about thirteen billion years ago, within a probable error of about three billion years. The point is, in the theory, the age of the universe is a fixed date throughout the universe. This, coupled with observations of the rate of expansion of the universe, postulates a central concentration of all the mass and energy in a "primeval atom." At time, "t," this atom detonated and the kinetic energy thus released accounts fairly well for the phenomenon which can be observed. Now, those who still grasp at the infinite existence theory, say, "Fine—the current expansion is only one phase of a series of expansions and contractions, divergence and convergence, if you will." They, of course, are still hoist, so to speak, by the impossibility of getting their petard to a current sequence. The "Big Bang" theory could still live with the postulate of a self-generated "primeval atom" if that could be supported on its own merits.

The Lemaitre model has, of course, been given many variations by other cosmologists over the years. In the main, however, the original concept remains substantially intact. It well matches observations and other requirements of other disciplines. For example, the model provides physicists and chemists the high densities they require for a nuclear reaction to form the chain of heavier elements from hydrogen, and the hypothesis provides astronomers with a necessarily slow phase in which the galaxies and individual stars could form. The constant creation universe has great difficulties in these regards. A description of the mechanism in some detail is given in the following excerpt from the book, *Survey of the Universe,* by Menzel, Whipple and de Vaucouleurs (Menzel, 1970, p. 781-783):

Lemaitre's Primeval Atom and the "Big Bang" Theory.

We explained how the evolution of the homogeneous model universes of general relativity can be represented by a graph of the radius of curvature $R(t)$ vs. time. Lemaitre favored a model in which $R(t)$ is mathematically zero (or physically very small) at a time t_0, the instant of "creation." He postulated that, no matter how this "creation" may have occurred (something he did not discuss), the universe started in this model as a hyperdense sphere of matter or "primeval atom," which physicists later described as a giant neutron ball.

We know that matter, at nuclear densities, is highly unstable beyond atomic number $\cong 100$ or a mass of $\cong 250$ nucleons. The original neutron in this picture had a mass equal to that of the whole universe, some 10^{78} to 10^{79} neutrons packed into a volume not much larger than that of the present solar system, an extremely unstable configuration. The superatom must have almost instantly exploded with a violence that defies description. The neutrons rapidly decayed into protons and electrons, forming deuterons by neutron capture, then helium nuclei, and so on, until an immense number of nuclear reactions built up the various atomic species of increasing atomic number.

The nuclear reactions in the primeval fireball have been investigated by many physicists. At the extremely high temperatures (billions of degrees during the first few minutes) and intense radiation and particle fluxes of the fireball a much greater variety of nuclear transmutations is possible than even in a hydrogen bomb. The complication of the chemistry of this initial cosmic brew, dubbed "ylem" by G. Gamow, defies a complete analysis. But a plausible scheme can be outlined through which nearly all the higher elements up to iron can be formed in the first thirty minutes or so, and in about the correct observed cosmic abundances. Because of this rapid explosion, proceeding initially at the velocity of light, the temperature of the fireball had to drop rapidly from perhaps $10^{12}\,^\circ K$ [Kelvin] within the first microsecond, to $10^9\,^\circ K$ after five minutes, to $40 \times 10^6\,^\circ K$ after one day, then more slowly to $6{,}000\,^\circ K$ after 300,000 years. According to Gamow, most atom-building reactions stopped after about thirty minutes. The heavier elements must have been produced much later in the secondary nuclear reactions that are still taking place in stellar interiors.

In the early phases of this explosion tremendous pressure forces were present, and the idealized cosmological models with zero pressure do not apply. The universe was a big ball of nuclear fire and radiation. Thus, in the era of the hydrogen bomb, the "primeval atom" hypothesis of Lemaitre has become popularly known as the "Big Bang" theory. After several hundred million years, matter had dispersed and cooled enough and radiation had been diluted to a point where the laws of ordinary macroscopic physics could take over, and more conventional cosmogonical mechanisms came into play. Most of these mechanisms require long periods of time to be effective. If it takes millions of years for interstellar matter to condense into stars, the formation of galaxies and clusters of galaxies may have taken hundreds of millions of years or more.

In order to provide a long period of quasi-stable conditions during which small density and temperature fluctuations could initiate condensations on galactic and supergalactic scales, Lemaitre argued that the initial expansion was slowed down and finally almost brought to a standstill by the force of gravitational attraction, which was very strong in the initial dense phases of the universe. Thus, the universe may have spent perhaps a billion years going through the quasi-stable Einstein phase. While the universe as a whole was almost in equilibrium, local fluctuations occurred—regions that were slightly hotter or cooler, denser or more rarefied, than the average. Eddies of the cosmic fluid could react to the usual physical laws of gas and radiation and, according to Lemaitre, start the formation of clusters of galaxies. Observation suggests that galaxies form in groups, clusters, or superclusters and not as isolated individuals in intergalactic space. Lemaitre visualized the great clusters of galaxies having mean densities of the order of 10^{-27} g/cm^3 as remnants of the Einstein phase of the universe. Thus. . .the radius of curvature of the universe while it passed slowly through the quasi-stable phase was $R \cong 300$ megaparsecs. (As we saw. . .with the present density of 10^{-30} g/cm^3 or so the radius of curvature of an Einstein universe is much larger.)

Eventually, as matter collected into vast clouds, that later condensed further into galaxies, the cosmic repulsion overcame gravitation, at least in the vast low-density intercluster spaces. The universe as a whole resumed its expansion, at first very slowly, then at an increasing rate following the R(t) curve for the Lemaitre model.

The "Big Bang" concept fairly recently received what its proponents and most others also, consider conclusive support as a result of experiments conducted at the Bell Laboratories in New Jersey which show a steady and consistent microwave radiation from all areas of the universe radiating a base temperature of a few (2.5-3) degrees above zero Kelvin. This condition had been predicted by the "Big Bangers" far in advance of its verification. It was, and is, seen as a consequence of the gradual expansion and cooling of the "fireball" resulting from the initial "detonation" of the primeval "atom." The time of the detonation would be placed by this thermal effect at about 13 billion years ago which coincides well with other estimates.

The idea of a sequence of expansion and contractions of such events on a cycle approaching 75 to 100 billion years is being pursued. Currently, however, evidence points to a one-time occurrence. The density and quantity of material in the observed universe is insufficient for gravitational forces to counteract the observed energy of expansion. There are also serious questions on the complete reversibility of the energy flow required in reconstituting the basic neutron atom. In no event, as we have seen, does it yield an existence having no beginning.

In 1940, Reginald Kapp, a long-time Professor and Professor Emeritus of Electrical Engineering at University College, London, postulated a solution to the expanding universe in terms of what he later called the Theory of Symmetrical Impermanence in which matter was continuously being created and annihilated in space. Because of the connotation of a self-created universe implicit in his presentation, this theory will be discussed in more detail a bit later. It was the prototype of the continuous creation or "Steady State" universe.

The principal theorists of the "Steady State" hypothesis comprise a group of British cosmologists (Bondi, Gold, and Hoyle) who put forth their version in 1948. The current state of this theory is well summarized also in *Survey of the Universe,* (Menzel, 1970, p. 760-761).

The Steady-State Universe of Bondi, Gold, and Hoyle.

All attempts to build models of the universe are based on explicit or implicit assumptions or principles: homogeneity, isotrophy, conservation of energy, and so on. Overriding is the so-called cosmological principle: "The universe looks very much the same from any location and in all directions." There is no privileged position in space. This principle, however, overlooks time; models based on it have different properties at different times. For example, the Lemaitre-Eddington models evolve from a dense past to a tenuous future. Cosmic evolution is a one-way street, and the present state is unique. A school of British theoreticians began in 1948 to question the validity of this hidden assumption of previous relativistic models.

"If the universe is homogeneous and isotropic in space, why not also in time? And so they completed the cosmological principle by the added requirement". . ."and at all times." On the largest scale, everything is very much the same anywhere, anytime. There is nothing unique in here and now. The universe was, and will always be, as we now see it. This assertion, which they dubbed the "perfect cosmological principle," is in a sense a logical extension of the Copernican view of the universe: neither our place nor our time is in any way remarkable.

This apparently innocent addition to the cosmological principle leads to some drastic conclusions; in particular, it leads to the rejection of another fundamental assumption, the principle of conservation of mass and energy. Observation shows that the universe is expanding. If the total mass and radiation are constant, its density must decrease with time as the volume of space increases. But then the future is not equivalent to the past. In other words, instead of assuming that mass (energy) is a constant, we may assume now that the density p is a constant. To maintain a constant density in an ever-expanding universe, matter must be created in space at a rate precisely compensating the rarefaction caused by the expansion.

The postulated spontaneous creation of matter out of nothing is the most disturbing feature of this theory of Bondi, Gold, and Hoyle. But it is a logical deduction from the hypothesis that the universe is simultaneously expanding and in a steady state. That this creation of matter violates the principle of conservation of mass and energy is not in itself a serious objection. Just as any other principle of physics, the conservation principle is justified by experience and with a precision that is quite limited. No one has verified it to, say one part in 10^{12}. The creation rate required by the steady-state theory is much less than that. The universal expansion rate causes a given volume of space to increase each second by a fraction given by the H constant and, according to Hoyle, the creation of just one atom of hydrogen per cubic foot every few billion years would be enough to keep it constant. No conceivable experiment could ever detect the stray brand new nucleus. Thus, we cannot discard the steady-state theory just because of this infinitesimal departure from the law of conservation.

The theory has some attractive features. Hoyle has shown that the metric of the steady-state universe is similar to that of the De Sitter universe, but, of course, it is not empty and it is infinite in space and time. [In a universe "infinite in space" 1 atom per ft^3 every few billion years would still be at an infinite rate!] The steady-state model also leads to some definite predictions that may be compared with observations. In particular, distant galaxies should not be younger than nearby ones, as in the Lemaitre-Eddington models, and some very old galaxies should be present, much older than allowed by the Lemaitre model. Recent observations of cosmic evolution and counts of radio sources tend to disagree with the predictions of the steady state model. If it is finally disproved, it will at least have played a useful role in forcing scientists to question and investigate more deeply the basic principles of physics and cosmology.

Commenting on the idea of creation from nothing fundamental to the concept, although the rate "one atom of hydrogen per cubic foot every few billion years" is lightly passed over, we are still speaking of creation at a tremendous rate even in a limited universe—several complete solar systems per year. The inference is left that we are well within the limits of error in our observations in the Law of Conservation of Energy and matter, and hence the small relative amount is of no real consequence. The writers did not distinguish that it is a systematic aberration in principle always applying and not casual or random. Matter can either "happen" (or be externally created) into existence or it cannot. If the principle stands, then logically all matter in the universe came into existence in that way. In the continuous creation theory that would be the basic assumption. It is an area impinging directly on metaphysics. Sooner or later, the question must be addressed. Man, the questioning animal, will not be denied.

Both systems, the "Big Bang" and "Steady-State" and, of course, any conceivable other system require a creation of matter. The crucial question of how it is brought about, whether by "self-generation" or "externally created," is a question that remains unsolved at the scientific level. We will later address it in the logic of metaphysics.

Kapp's theory of "symmetrical impermanence" though, makes the rate of creation by Bondi and others pale into insignificance. Since his matter is being annihilated continuously as well as created, he must also make up for that being lost to the system. He states (Kapp, 1960, p. 57) that this expanding universe could be maintained with creation at the rate of 500 atoms of hydrogen per cubic kilometer of space per year which is several times greater than Hoyle and others of his group apply. They are not as definite as Kapp. Kapp supports this hypothesis with a postulation of the continuous decay of mass and energy. This results in giving all matter a predicted half-life of around 300 to 400 million years. (Kapp, 243). (This is unlikely, as viewed today, since apparently too low by many orders of magnitude.) His view therefore, is that matter is being "originated" and "annihilated" continuously throughout the universe at a prodigious rate. The steady-state would, in effect, require an equivalent universe replacement about every billion years. It must be clear that what he is referring to is not a change in state between energy and matter, but an absolute origin from and annihilation to nothing. There was absolutely nothing before the particle appeared and will be absolutely nothing left after it disappears. If space is expanding continuously (currently), it is because there is an excess of origins. If origins and annihilations were exactly equal, there would be a steady-state. If there were less origins than annihilations, the universe would contract. In the Kapp hypothesis, there is a critical point which has to be examined—the origin and annihilation of matter. He postulates these individual events as "uncaused events" meaning that in the most literal way possible—that they are not only totally random events that just occur any time, any place, but also totally causeless. However, if we examine closely his example of a causeless event, atomic disintegration, what he is really saying is not "causelessness" but "unpredictability." For he says (page 65), "In the latter (atomic decay) it is found that *there is no reason* why a given atom should disintegrate *at a given moment* rather than any other atom," emphasis supplied.

This is far different than saying there is no cause interior or exterior, and even if you say there is no *discernible cause,* you still have not closed the loop; nor even approached a closure. You could only say it follows no known physical law. Physicist Pierre Auger says on precisely this same point, (Auger, 1963, pages 350, 351):

It was, however, during the year 1900, on December 14th to be exact, that the storm finally broke. On that day, physics entered the predicted new era, and it did so by suddenly breaking with the classical principles. The continuous theories of thermodynamics, too tenuous to keep up with the results of experiments, fell away.

Since the atomic nuclei contain but a limited number of particles, the explanation of a long period of life in certain unstable (radioactive) elements on the basis of the mechanics of the relative motions of these various particles became very difficult. Who could believe that it might be ten thousand million years before the decisive configuration necessary for the breaking apart of an ensemble composed of a few dozen particles in rapid motion would occur? The collapse of all conceptions as to the universe of continuous laws—and the corresponding Newtonian determinism—became evident. Since it was necessary to connect these phenomena to some notion of causality, physicists found themselves reduced, as it were, to adding to the two kinds of causality invoked by the ancient philosophers—that is, efficient causes and final causes—a probable causality; a system placed in conditions such that it is capable of undergoing various spontaneous transformations is affected or governed by coefficients representing the probabilities of these transformations in time units. No sufficiently precise description of the makeup of the system can be given that will permit a certain prediction as to whether it will undergo such and such a change. One can say that its interior structure eludes fine analysis, and that thus it has no real existence; what it presents as reality are its coefficients of probability.

Let us examine Auger's statement a bit critically, particularly that part of the concluding statement which says, "One can say that its interior *structure eludes fine analysis* and that *thus it has no real existence*." This statement clearly shows the limitations placed on knowledge by the scientific analysis and also the limit the more narrow thinkers try to place on any other form of analysis or knowledge. *Reality* is defined as what can be analyzed scientifically when yet, manifestly, reality extends beyond that limit. Auger's admission when rephrased slightly says as much. "It has an interior structure *which cannot be analyzed, therefore it is not real.*" Phenomena which result from that unanalyzable structure are, therefore, without cause or can be called "acausal." This conclusion stems from a view of causality which the positivists early espoused which, in Wiggensteins's language, though it is not Wiggenstein's concept, is, "The case where it is observed that event B always occurs when, and only when, event A occurs defines the relationship between event A and event B as causal." Note that, however, if event C occurs and no such event A can be *observed* the case is defined as "acausal." For purposes of empirical science, the definition may be adequate, although, for the scientist, as a curious human being, it is unduly pragmatic and not very "elucidative" of the observed phenomenon C. It is little better than the exasperating ultimate reply of the exasperated father to the ubiquitous "why?" of the precocious offspring. It is the reason Aristotle could not stop with his physics and had to look into the first principle of causality in what has been since called metaphysics.

Causality, then, has more than just its scientific form. As we saw earlier, in Part II, it has also an ontological aspect—the relationship which exists, first between the two possible "states" of individual being, existence and nonexistence, and a second between two states of a being's existential situation in an environment, or the relationship of agency. The case when: event B occurs when, and only when, agent A acts in respect to event B, is defined as causal on the part of agent A in producing the effect, event B. Until the "Epistemological Revolution," the agency aspect of the causal relationship predominated, although the other causal relationships were recognized. The actual agency advanced through a series of secondary, or intermediate, causes to a final cause which, from Aristotle, was considered the prime-mover of all things. But, beginning with Descartes, the question of the nature of our perception of the outside world came to dominate the philosophical scene and this led, by stages, to the empirically determinable causality principle of science. With the denial of a speculative metaphysics by Kant, the scientific definition of causality was moved in unmodified form to the philosophical field.

The current confusion in the matter of the nature of being also stems from the Kantian dichotomy of being between phenomena and noumena. There may even have been confusion in Kant's mind. Although, even a hurried reading of Kant reveals he considered the noumena the "real" and the phenomena the "unreal." Oddly, the "real" could not be "known." Only the "unreal" sensed, and artificially categorized, world could be "known." In the various manipulations of Kantian thought between pragmatic and positivistic schools of philosophy in England and on the continent, respectively, being became identified with materialism, or materialistic things, which could be physically sensed and measured. No other form of being was "real" since not measurable by physical means. That this was an unjustified conclusion from Kant's premise, an extension of hypothesis far beyond applicability is clear. Manifestly, if one can measure light phenomena only in the visible spectrum, one is not justified in stating, that because this is true, ultraviolet and infrared light do not exist. They are unreal. Yet, during this same period of materialization, of being "Ether," which could not be sensed (and which most certainly does not have any real existence even in modified form), was being solemnly accepted as the medium by which light phenomena were propagated even though some of its characteristics— extreme rigidity—would have been indescribably difficult to reconcile with other required characteristics—complete penetrability. Angels on pinheads would have been easier to conceive.

In the present period, half-seriously referred to as the age of "Dematerialization of Matter," there has been no corresponding reinstatement of immaterial being as a possible being form— better all being should be denied. Unexplicable phenomena are not real. While it may be said that it is "unscientific" to propose a solution to a problem which involves agencies beyond the material order, the statement reflects a narrow scope and definition for science having a history of less than 200 years. Newton certainly did not view it that way. It is true that no such solution should be treated under the subject heading "physics." But it also should not be denied under the heading "physics" either.

Physics has not, except in very recent times, been considered to define the limits of science. The fact is, that "Being is" and that fact cannot be explained by the phenomena of physics. Once that proposition is established, the arguments that investigations into that area of being beyond the scope of physics are unscientific is of little significance. The labeling of an event as uncaused (if the structure of the event defies analysis by physical means) and the labeling of any postulated cause as "unreal" (because it also cannot be analyzed) is totally unscientific. Explicability and reality are not synonymous. The rules of the universe should not be hammered into convenient shapes to fit preconceived notions. Further, where the universe situation refuses to fit the assumed rules or physical models, the universe's situation should not be declared "unreal." But that is the tendency when a physical model has been conceived to explain reality. When the inevitable disagreement with reality is found, the model is accepted rather than reality. We are back to Plato's cave.

Returning, then, to Auger, the more adequate statement would have been: "One can say that its interior structure eludes fine analysis and the cause is indeterminable at this time." This would prevent the naive or the devious from seizing the example to "prove" the non-existence of a universal efficient causal principle in the material order. It is clear that science cannot answer the "Why" or "How" or "What." Does that mean that there are no final causes? Does that mean that the causal chain and the line of inquiry must stop at the boundary, quickly reached, in empirical methodology? Scientific or sense-acquired empirical knowledge is only a relatively narrow band in the total spectrum of possible knowledge. Limiting philosophic thought to that band reduces man to a mechanism only quantitatively differentiated from the computer and, in many ways, unfavorably differentiated.

The zone beyond the boundary of the physical sciences—the subatomic world—is not made less "real" by reason of the "immateriality" of matter which microphysics leads us into, nor is it merely idealized as with Berkeley or Kant. It is only that we have been, in our age, conditioned to think of matter and reality as that to which the senses can respond. That was not Aristotle's view, nor was it St. Thomas Aquinas' thought. Matter, or substance, with them, was whatever the essence of the being was—and that essence, in the case of a pure spirit, was obviously not impenetrable, visible, tangible, space-occupying, solidified essence. The fact that the electron is ephemeral in its overt manifestations does not imply that it has no existence. Light from an alternating current source is just as real as light from a direct current source. There is the same power requirement for the lumen output although its value varies between positive and negative limits. Light from an alternating current source has a cyclic quality in its quantitative duration and is just as subject to the laws of causality as light from a direct current source.

The very fact that the different radioactive isotopes have different rates of decay, points to the conclusion that the difference in rates is a function of a difference in structure regardless of how infrequent the necessary configuration occurs in any isotope. Thus there is a cause, and even if the "uncaused" decay is accepted, it does not imply "uncaused" creation. It is only a change to a different form—that of energy. Further still, the proof of annihilation does not demonstrate a state of self-creation. Suicide and self-conception are of a different genre.

The reason for discussing the point here is that the only way that the necessity of an external creation can be avoided, whether one by "Big Bang" or continuous creative mode, the difference is purely temporal and quantitative not qualitative, is by a hypothesis that a physical entity, matter, energy, or any other form can "call" itself into existence spontaneously where no other form previously existed. It will be recalled that Holbach, the original atheistic philosopher of the enlightenment period used the notion of the universe as "spontaneous matter in motion" without, of course, giving any explanation of its nature. Our fourth logic gate addressed this point.

It could easily be pointed out, for purposes of this work, that the "Big Bang" is only a special case of Kapp's, given his basic assumption. All of the particles or whatever could "happen" to originate in a given instant, at a given location, given sufficient time. Theoretically, from a rigorous probability standpoint, all would and all could self-destruct at a given instant, given sufficient time. The distinction that they all originated over a period of billions of years instead of instantaneously is beside the point.

Let us consider a hypothesis. If we take the amount of energy represented, that is, just the differential of origin over annihilation, represented by Kapp and the other constant-creation protagonists, as a constant supply to the expanding universe as currently conceived and remembering that the energy/mass ratio is almost 35 billion to one, the "gratis" input in energy becomes a tremendous input regardless of its form. Significantly, in our finest laboratories, we are unable to produce the slightest bit of matter by conversion of energy. Yet, this theory would have matter form spontaneously—from nothing—with no available energy and at a tremendous rate. When Kapp states that the "concept of the perpetual motion device is refuted as false by principle alone" (page 31), he is completely right. Nevertheless, Kapp, himself, creates a gigantic one. Whether it is one atom or 10^{100} atoms is of no consequence—the principle is identical. By what possible means can we construe a "Material" non-thing creating or "energizing" itself where nothing exists to call it or will it into existence.

In the modern physics, space is defined as the environment of matter in its most general meaning. In other words, where there is no matter, there is no space. When the atom is created, so also is its corresponding space. Both space and its correlative time began in this universe with the first atom and, since sequential and durational, there was a first atom. The writer hastens to point out that Kapp does not exclude a Creator nor, really, do any of the others. It is, in Kapp's view, a special case of his hypothesis of symmetrical impermanence approached by his principle of minimum assumption, which states: "When you form a hypothesis, you first try that one which requires fewest assumptions." Indeed, a sound principle—"Ockham's razor." Kapp did not wish to assume a Creator, which he considered the other possibilities did, and locked his heels on the same point against assuming a cause in the statistical realm of decay configuration occurrence, infrequent as it is. But if Kapp can postulate his uncaused events, occurring continuously, why not postulate the "Big Bang"—a one time, uncaused event—different only in scale.

Looking a bit closer at the alternatives, if we were to choose the viewpoint of the self-created universe, what rational concessions must we be prepared to make? First, there is a mathematical interpretation of the expression "zero" as having potential value which is contrary to any concepts in the theory of mathematical logic. This would be an interpretation that would be nowhere else applicable. Because zero is that precise condition having no magnitude which separates negative from positive. It is the only condition under which a function "vanishes"—has no value. In terms of existence, it is the absolute absence of any existence. Not even a theoretical point, it has, of itself, no actual or potential location. Second, in the physical order we must assign to that concept absolute non-existence that has no possible resources, an internal volitional capability to become existent, and the activating ability to call itself into existence. To restate, we must assign to this concept a capacity for pure will pure act without source and, for the first such event, under conditions of no pre-existing location, no space, no energy, no matter, and no time. These are concessions which are certainly unacceptable to reason. They are incompatible with both mathematics and the logic of physics. Descartes' "Cogito," "I think, therefore I am" expresses the idea that volition or any intellectual act (and one would add any act) necessarily carried with it the assumed pre-existence of the essential actor that thinks or acts, as we have seen earlier in Part II.

It may be argued that the postulation of a Creator only changes the terminology. How did the Creator come into existence? Is the problem not just as rationally unapproachable from that viewpoint? The difference in the argument lies in the distinction between the nature of the Creator and the observed nature and behavior of physical matter in the universe. This latter is observed as changeable, time-oriented, particulate and limited, all qualities which prevent the designation "eternal" or "infinite" being applied to matter in its modern sense in any of its forms.

The Creator, by definition, and to be mathematically coherent, must have an existence such that these characteristics do not apply. That is, it must be immaterial, infinite, simple, changeless and eternal. That this is the same view of the Creator held by most of the great philosophers since Plato is no accident. What rational concessions must we be prepared to make to accept this viewpoint? None, although, the *possibility* of an immaterial existence must be granted. First, the concept of creation proceeds not from "zero existence" but from an on-going existence of power absolutely beyond limit. Is this mathematically or logically repugnant? There is no contrary observable evidence as there is with matter. Nothing in the theory of mathematical logic is opposed. The extent of the Creator, as defined, is beyond any preassignable limit. The created material universe would thus flow from a Being possessed of all resources, pure will, pure act. There is no logical or mathematical incompatibility.

There remains the difficulty of the relationship between a time-oriented physical universe and an eternally-existing Creator. Are these concepts incompatible? We have some suggestions of the answer in the model of the universe provided by Einsteinian physics. Theoretically, as the higher extremes of velocity are approached, time as a measure of rate of physical change would be modified. There would be a condition approaching timelessness. The concept of time-collapse or slow-down of physical process as the velocity of light is approached is a familiar one and one which has now had some empirical verification in modified atomic decay rates at extreme velocities. By inference, our particular time-orientation is a function of the level and limits of velocity and energy in this universe. Within our own universe, time may have significant differences. For example? Observations recently performed indicate Quasar OQ 172 near the "edge" of space, almost 10 billion light-years away, is moving at 91 percent of the speed of light. At such velocities, the time-collapse effect would likely change the "dimension" of time. "Our world" and a world in that area would have significantly different time viewpoints if we could somehow see each other, bearing in mind that we "see" it by radio astronomy as it was 10 billion years ago, before our solar system was even formed. There is, therefore, no absolute time in any real sense. Time might be conceived of as a random line which passes through a sphere which is eternity. It has its beginning and end in eternity but serves in no way to define eternity.

The Creator is free to choose any limits in time or energy levels. His own existence being eternal and infinite, energy level and time provide no constraints. The answer in logic therefore is that there is no incompatibility. Our universe occurred in whatever mode and in whatever relationship to eternity that the Creator eternally willed. In our case, it is time-oriented at a particular energy level, and that energy level is only one level in a vast range of possibilities that are all uniquely present to Him. Time, space, and matter began, as we apprehend it, when He willed.

We now stand at a decision point in the cosmological approach to the origin of the material universe. The three choices remain as before:

1. It always existed (eternally existed).
2. It was self-created.
3. It was externally created.

Only the third choice does not involve unacceptable mathematical and logical concessions. It alone is compatible with reason. There are not at this time, nor foreseeably, any viable alternatives. The probabilities therefore are clearly adequate to form the basis for our decision to select the created origin of the universe. The gate can be passed with the highest confidence that the selection is correct.

The question naturally arises. Why, if the conclusion that there must be a Creator seems so apparent in logic, do we find philosophers and scientists—people of vast erudition in mathematics as well as in the individual sciences—not unanimously concluding that the Creator is an essential point of departure in philosophy or cosmology? It is the writer's view that the reason is similar to his own in not speaking of proofs of the existence of God, or of anything else for that matter. He has deliberately elected to speak in terms of probabilities. We cannot know, in a rigorous sense, that there are not alternatives beyond our current levels of cognition, but we can subjectively assess the probabilities of such alternatives. In this case, the writer's view is that they are infinitesimal; others might assess it differently. The writer believes the great majority of thinkers in current cosmology do conclude that the universe demands a Creator for its explanation. A number of statements have already been provided in that regard. The range extends from the view expressed by Einstein, who probably held to a deistic god, perhaps not much interested in man, to Lemaitre, a priest, who undoubtedly held the view of a god as a being in the same absolutely infinite, yet personal way, as does this writer. Each individual makes his own subjective appraisal of the probabilities at the various levels.

The problem goes to the scope of the universe as it is being revealed. That scope is so great that Sir James Jeans (1887-1946), one of the great physicists, astronomers, and cosmologists of the early twentieth century was led to ask rhetorically, almost overawed as he looked at the stars: "Are they all perchance only a dream, while we are but brain cells in the mind of the dreamer?" (Jeans, 1961, p. 422). Jeans was no pantheist. Yet, he almost could not believe what he experienced in his views into space. Nevertheless, the last thing he would have given up was the Creator. He would give up his own identity first. The difficulty is that while we speak of God being infinite, we still want to place constraints on that term. We want Him somehow to be of human dimensions—not to be so overwhelmingly powerful and omniscient. Our minds continually refuse to even place Him in the same scale as the universe, far from infinite, which yet may contain some 10^{20} or even more stars like our own sun—numbers literally like the sands on the seashores. If we do conceive of Him in those terms, we cannot then envision Him being as concerned for one of our grains of sand, or of an atom within the grain, or an electron within the atom as He is with the whole galactic wonder. Moreover, we have difficulty comprehending the idea or the fact that scale means nothing in infinity. This is what being infinite really means. And the alternative to the infinite God is truly far less acceptable. If we do not accept Him, we must accept "nothing" and then have that "nothing" make itself into a thing of the same "dimensions" as the universe with all its intricacies and potential in life, its laws, and in its evolution through time. It is an utterly preposterous idea. The reluctance to accept the idea of a Creator seems principally emotional. If we accept Him, we must draw the inevitable comparison of our personal worth in contrast to Him and all creation. We cannot conceive that one rational, freely-willed human being worshipping Him is greater in His sight than all of the rest of the inert matter in which that tiny being is placed. Another reason is simply that we are all products of the predominant thought of the period in which we live. This period still reflects the dying materialism.

In this regard, of all the modern philosophers we reviewed in Part II, the most inexplicable to me is Bertrand Russell, who was a leader of thought in the early part of the century. Russell held that natural science is the unique support of knowledge and gives no support whatever for the belief in God or immortality. Now Russell lived well into the period of modern physics and cosmology; he was an eminent mathematician in the area of symbolic logic. It is inconceivable that he was unfamiliar with the other works of Alfred North Whitehead, with whom he collaborated in *Principia Mathematica*. Yet the views expressed above are not only incorrect in the light of the evidence, regardless of how you wish to assign probabilities, they are utterly contrary to Whitehead's clear position—unless he held Whitehead a fool. Russell's apparent concept of soul with relationship to space is irrational. Soul and space by any definition and regardless of realities do not have any common "dimensions." The only answer seems to be an ingrained bias, almost hatred, on Russell's part, of the concept of a Supreme Being to whom man might be subject. In Russell's view, this constituted an unacceptable limitation on man's freedom. This emotional block destroyed Russell's reasoning faculty when the question of God was involved. His pacifistic extremism seems similarly emotionally driven. It is the "passionate disbelief" referred to by Albert Camus.

Some people of great intellectual ability—chiefly skeptics and agnostics—say flatly there is no way of arriving at an answer. They refuse to look at and examine evidence of any sort on the subject. They do not agree that probabilities can form a basis of decision. Yet, virtually all the decisions on which we act, whether we like it or not, are based on our unconsciously-assigned probabilities of correctness of judgment of the selected line of action. Absolute certitude is a rare thing, as our tour through philosophy should have demonstrated. Russell, of course, was not alone among the non-Marxists who influenced Western thought toward the materialistic bias. John Dewey, a strictly "biologic" philosopher, tremendously influenced American thought of the first half of the twentieth century toward materialistic views—particularly in education.

In the introduction, the writer referred to the "biologic" psychology being taught particularly during the middle decades of this century in contradiction to the attitudes of the prominent physical scientists of the same period. It was a time when the liberal arts schools from journalism to psychology were profoundly under the influence of Sigmund Freud (1856-1939). It was probably natural. The world was emerging from a prim Victorianism, and sex was being generally rediscovered in the aftermath of World War I. The repeal of prohibition in the United States stimulated the cocktail party fashion and Freud was seen as somewhat risque, even *avante garde,* and therefore, eminently appropriate to popularization. In a series of lectures he gave in 1932 and collected in his *New Introductory Lectures on Psycho-Analysis* (Freud, 1933, p. 219, et seq), Freud expresses, among many other things, his views on approaches to knowledge and truth, views which were being absorbed by the students and general public.

Of the three forces which can dispute the position of science, religion alone is a really serious enemy. Art is almost always harmless and beneficent, it does not seek to be anything else but an illusion. Save in the case of a few people who are, one might say, obsessed by art, it never dares to make any attacks on the realm of reality. Philosophy is not opposed to science, it behaves itself as if it were a science, and to a certain extent it makes use of the same methods; but it parts company with science, in that it clings to the illusion that it can produce a complete and coherent picture of the universe, though in fact that picture must needs fall to pieces with every new advance in our knowledge. Its methodological error lies in the fact that it over-estimates the epistemological value of our logical operations, and, to a certain extent, admits the validity of other sources of knowledge, such as intuition. And often enough one feels that the poet Heine is not unjustified when he says of the philosopher: "With his nightcap and his nightshirt tatters, he botches up the loop-holes in the structure of the world."

The struggle, therefore, is not yet at an end. The followers of the religious Weltanschauung [roughly a comprehensive philosophy of life] act in accordance with the old maxim: the best defense is attack. "What," they ask, "is this science that presumes to depreciate our religion which has brought salvation and comfort to millions of men for many thousands of years? What has science for its part so far accomplished? What more can be expected of it? On its own admission, it is incapable of comforting or ennobling us. We will leave that on one side, therefore, though it is by no means easy to give up such benefits. But what of its teaching? Can it tell us how the world began, and what fate is in store for it? Can it even paint for us a coherent picture of the universe, and show us where the unexplained phenomena of life fit in and how spiritual forces are able to operate on inert matter? If it could do that we should not refuse it our respect. But it has done nothing of the sort, not one single problem of this kind has it solved. It gives us fragments of alleged knowledge, which it cannot harmonize with one another, it collects observations of uniformities from the totality of events, and dignifies them with the names of laws and subjects them to its hazardous interpretations. And with what a small degree of certitude does it establish its conclusions! All that it teaches is only provisionally true; what is prized today as the highest wisdom is overthrown tomorrow and experimentally replaced by something else. The latest error is then given the name of truth. And to this truth we are asked to sacrifice our highest good!"

Ladies and Gentlemen—insofar as you yourselves are supporters of the scientific Weltanschauung I do not think you will be very profoundly shaken by this critic's attack.

Freud was expressing a dominant viewpoint in the behavioral sciences of that time. He obviously expected his audience to applaud. At this point, some forty years later, the real scientists in the world would admit they cannot answer these cosmologic and metaphysical questions from scientific evidence with any degree of certitude and that the situation he describes for religion is close to where we stand in the physical sciences today. They would say humbly, far from Freud's hauteur, that they do not have all the answers there are. They would never say or imply that there are no other viewpoints of merit which must be considered. These scientists would say that deductive logic is of great value—particularly those scientists in modern physics. It has been the basis of their most outstanding achievement. For indeed, while objective truth is one, the subjective viewpoints which man must evaluate to approach it are many.

Freud probably remains the most quoted authority in the area of broad social-psychological behavior by writers for the general public. His name has a residual magic to it which reflects his high academic eminence in the second quartile of the twentieth century particularly. That academic eminence has affected much of the thinking today through that generation of students now passing from the scene, but still important.

Returning, however, to cosmology, Kapp, in his epilogue (pages 294, 295) so as not to give any aid, assistance, and comfort to the materialistics, says:

> Here I have only discussed structures in the rough untouched world of lifeless things. I have attributed these to the action of matter on matter, but, in doing so, I have also shown that they can be accounted for without attributing to matter anything in the nature of a capacity for creating order, for selection, guidance, control, coordination. Therewith, I have implied that it is erroneous to idealize matter as is done in the various materialistic schools. The true inference from what has been said here is that the kind of order observable wherever things are touched by life must be attributed to the action of non-material influences.

Section 2—God and the Universe as a Dynamic System

At this point, to get an appreciation for just how critical is the kind of order we see in the universe as a dynamic system, we should look in a rather extensive way at the article in *The Scientific American* by Freeman Dyson, referred to in the introduction. For it truly points out the fundamental orderliness makes human existence possible and points to the need of an intelligent Creator in its explanation.

As we look out into space we see no sign that life has intervened to control events anywhere except precariously on our own planet. Everywhere else, the universe appears to be mindlessly burning up its reserves of energy, inexorably drifting toward the state of final quiescence described imaginatively by Olaf Stapledon: "Presently nothing was left in the whole cosmos but darkness and the dark whiffs of dust that once were galaxies." It is conceivable, however, that life may have a larger role to play than we have yet imagined. Life may succeed against all the odds in molding the universe to its own purposes. And the design of the inanimate universe may not be as detached from the potentialities of life and intelligence as scientists of the 20th century have tended to suppose.

When one views the universe in broad outline in this way, a set of paradoxical questions at once arises. Since thermodynamics favors the degradation of gravitational energy to other forms, how does it happen that the gravitational energy of the universe is still predominant after 10 billion years of cosmic evolution? Since large masses are unstable against gravitational collapse, why did they not all collapse long ago and convert their gravitational energy into heat and light in a quick display of cosmic fireworks? Since the universe is on a one-way slide toward a state of final death in which energy is maximally degraded, how does it manage, like King Charles to take such an unconscionably long time a-dying? These questions are not easy to answer. The further one goes in answering them, the more remarkable and paradoxical becomes the apparent stability of the cosmos. It turns out that the universe, as we know it, survives not by any inherent stability but by a succession of seemingly accidental "hangups." By a hangup I mean an obstacle, usually arising from some quantitative feature of the design of the universe, that arrests the normal processes of degradation of energy. Psychological hangups are generally supposed to be bad for us, but cosmological hangups are absolutely necessary for our existence.

The first and most basic hangup built into the architecture of the universe is the size hangup. A naive person looking at the cosmos has the impression that the whole thing is extravagantly, even irrelevantly, large. This extravagant size is our primary protection against a variety of catastrophes. If a volume of space is filled with matter with an average density, d, the matter cannot collapse gravitationally in a time shorter than the "freefall time" t, which is the time it would take to fall together in the absence of any other hangups. The formula relating d with t is $Gdt^2 = 1$, where G is the constant in Newton's law of gravitation. The effect of this formula is that when we have an extravagantly small density d, and therefore an extravagantly big volume of space, the free fall time, t, can become so long that gravitational collapse is postponed to a remote future.

Another form of degradation of gravitational energy, one less drastic than gravitational collapse, would be the disruption of the solar system by close encounters or collisions with other stars. Such a degradation of the orbital motions of the earth and planets would be just as fatal to our existence as a complete collapse. We have escaped this catastrophe only because the distances between stars in our galaxy are also extravagantly large. Again, a calculation shows that our galaxy is barely large enough to make the damaging encounters unlikely. So, even with our galaxy, the size hangup is necessary to our preservation, although it is not by itself sufficient.

The second on the list of hangups is the spin hangup. An extended object cannot collapse gravitationally if it is spinning rapidly. Instead of collapsing, the outer parts of the object settle into stationary orbits revolving around the inner parts. Our galaxy as a whole is preserved by this hangup, and the earth is preserved by it from collapsing into the sun. Without the spin hangup no planetary system could have been formed at the time the sun condensed out of interstellar gas.

The third hangup is the thermonuclear hangup. This hangup arises from the fact that hydrogen "burns" to form helium when it is heated and compressed. The thermonuclear burning (actually fusion reactions between hydrogen nuclei) releases energy, which opposes any further compression. As a result any object such as a star that contains a large proportion of hydrogen is unable to collapse gravitationally beyond a certain point until the hydrogen is all burned up. For example, the sun has been stuck on the thermonuclear hangup for 4.5 billion years and will take another five billion years to burn up its hydrogen before its gravitational contraction can be resumed.

The discovery that the universe was originally composed of rather pure hydrogen implies that the thermonuclear hangup is a universal phenomenon. Every mass large enough to be capable of gravitational collapse must inescapably pass through a prolonged hydrogen-burning phase. The only objects exempt from this rule are masses of planetary size or smaller, in which gravitational contraction is halted by the mechanical incompressibility of the material before the ignition point of thermonuclear reactions is reached. The preponderance of hydrogen in the universe ensures that our night sky is filled with well-behaved stars like our own sun, placidly pouring out their energy for the benefit of any attendant life forms and giving to the celestial sphere its historical attribute of serene immobility. It is only by virtue of the thermonuclear hangup that the heavens have appeared to be immobile. We now know that in corners of the universe other than our own violent events are the rule rather than the exception. The prevalence of catastrophic outbursts of energy was revealed to us through the rapid progress of radio astronomy over the past 30 years. These outbursts are still poorly understood, but it seems likely that they occur in regions of the universe where the thermonuclear hangup has been brought to an end by the exhaustion of hydrogen.

It may seem paradoxical that the thermonuclear hangup has such benign and pacifying effects on extraterrestrial affairs in view of the fact that, so far at least, our terrestrial thermonuclear devices are neither peaceful nor particularly benign. Why does the sun burn its hydrogen gently for billions of years instead of blowing up like a bomb? To answer this question it is necessary to invoke yet another hangup.

The crucial difference between the sun and a bomb is that the sun contains ordinary hydrogen with only a trace of the heavy hydrogen isotopes deuterium and tritium, whereas the bomb is made mainly of heavy hydrogen. Heavy hydrogen can burn explosively by strong nuclear interactions, but ordinary hydrogen can react with itself only by the weak-interaction process. In this process two hydrogen nuclei (protons) fuse to form a deutron (a proton and a neutron) plus a positron and a neutrino. The proton-proton reaction proceeds about 10 times more slowly than a strong nuclear reaction at the same density and temperature. It is this weak-interaction hangup that makes ordinary hydrogen useless to us as a terrestrial source of energy. [In a thermonuclear reaction]. The hangup is essential to our existence, however, in at least three ways. First, without this hangup we would not have a sufficiently long-lived and stable sun. Second, without it the ocean would be an excellent thermonuclear high explosive and would constitute a perennial temptation to builders of "doomsday machines." Third, and most important, without the weak-interaction hangup it is unlikely that any appreciable quantity of hydrogen would have survived the initial hot, dense phase of the evolution of the universe. Essentially all the matter in the universe would have been burned to helium before the first galaxies started to condense, and no normally long-lived stars would have had a chance to be born.

If one looks in greater detail at the theoretical reasons for the existence of the weak-interaction hangup, our salvation seems even more providential. The hangup depends decisively on the non-existence of an isotope of helium with a mass number of 2, the nucleus of which would consist of two protons and no neutrons. If helium 2 existed, the proton-proton reaction would yield a helium-2 nucleus plus a proton, and the helium-2 nucleus would in turn spontaneously decay into a deutron, a positron and a neutrino. The first reaction being strong, the hydrogen would burn fast to produce helium 2. The subsequent weak decay of the helium 2 would not limit the rate of burning. It happens that there does exist a well-observed state of the helium-2 nucleus, but the state is unbound by about half a million volts. The nuclear force between two protons is attractive and of the order of 20 million volts, but it just barely fails to produce a bound state. If the force were a few percent stronger, there would be no weak-interaction hangup.

I have discussed four hangups: size, spin, thermonuclear and weak-interaction. The catalogue is by no means complete. There is an important class of transport or opacity hangups, which arise because the transport of energy by conduction or radiation from the hot interior of the earth or the sun to the cooler surface takes billions of years to complete. It is the transport hangup that keeps the earth fluid and geology active, giving us such phenomena as continental drift, earthquakes, volcanoes and mountain uplift. All these processes derive their energy from the original gravitational condensation of the earth four billion years ago, supplemented by a modest energy input from subsequent radioactivity.

While Dyson does not point out why this is a fortuitous development, it surely is. If it were not for these agents of orogeny constantly building up the elevated areas, the earth would be nothing but a vast sea. The energy resources represented by coal, oil and other fossil fuels would never have been formed, the present vast array of life forms impossible.

Last on my list is a special surface tension hangup that has enabled the fissionable nuclei of uranium and thorium to survive in the earth's crust until we are ready to use them. These nuclei are unstable against spontaneous fission. They contain so much positive charge and so much electrostatic energy that they are ready to fly apart at the slightest provocation. Before they can fly apart, however, their surface must be stretched into a nonspherical shape, and this stretching is opposed by an extremely powerful force of surface tension. A nucleus is kept spherical in exactly the same way a droplet of rain is kept spherical by the surface tension of water, except that the nucleus has a tension about 10 times as strong as that of a raindrop. In spite of this surface tension a nucleus of uranium 238 does occasionally fission spontaneously, and the rate of the fissioning can be measured. Nonetheless, the hangup is so effective that less than one in a million of the earth's uranium nuclei has disappeared in this way during the whole of geological history. [Remembering Pierre Auger's statement that the fact of delayed radio-active decay was an example of the acausal notion of fission. Dyson explains why it takes so long a time and has such a low probability.]

No hangup can last forever. There are times and places in the universe at which the flow of energy breaks through all hangups. Then rapid and violent transformations occur, of whose nature we are still ignorant. Historically it was physicists and not astronomers who recorded the first evidence that the universe is not everywhere as quiescent as traditional astronomy had pictured it.

The cosmic rays must certainly originate in catastrophic processes. Various attempts to explain them as by-products of familiar astronomical objects have proved quantitatively inadequate. In the past 30 years half a dozen strange new types of object have been discovered, each of which is violent and enigmatic enough to be a plausible parent of cosmic rays. These include the super-novas (exploding stars), the radio galaxies (giant clouds of enormously energetic electrons emerging from galaxies), the Seyfert galaxies (galaxies with intensely bright and turbulent nuclei), the x-ray sources, the quasars and the pulsars. All these objects are inconspicuous only because they are extremely distant from us. Once again, only the size hangup—the vastness of the interstellar spaces—has diluted the cosmic rays enough to save us from being fried or at least sterilized by them. If sheer distance had not effectively isolated the quiet regions of the universe from the noisy ones, no type of biological evolution would have been possible.

The main sources of energy available to us on the earth are chemical fuels, uranium and sunlight. In addition, we hope one day to learn how to burn, in a controlled fashion, the deuterium in the oceans. All these energy stores exist here by virtue of hangups that have temporarily halted the universal process of energy degradation. Sunlight is sustained by the thermonuclear, the weak-interaction and the opacity hangups. Uranium is preserved by the surface-tension hangup. Coal and oil have been buried in the ground and saved from oxidation by various biological and chemical hangups, the details of which are still under debate. Deuterium has been preserved in low abundance, after almost all of it was burned to form helium in the earliest stages of the history of the universe, because no thermonuclear reaction ever runs quite to completion.

Humanity is fortunate in having such a variety of energy resources at its disposal. In the very long run we shall need energy that is absolutely pollution-free; we shall have sunlight. In the fairly long run we shall need energy that is inexhaustible and moderately clean; we shall have deuterium. In the short run we shall need energy that is readily usable and abundant; we shall have uranium. Right now we need energy that is cheap and convenient; we have coal and oil. Nature has been kinder to us than we had any right to expect.

As we look out into the universe and identify the many accidents of physics and astronomy that have worked together to our benefit, it almost seems as if the universe must in some sense have known that we were coming.

At this point the writer will repeat the words of despairing Charles Darwin, "My theology is a simple muddle, I cannot look at the universe as the result of blind chance. Yet, I can see no beneficent design or indeed a design of any kind in the details." He lived a century too soon.

Dyson's article describes a gigantic energy system of tremendous sophistication, yet far from infinite. Its size is appropriate to its function. It had a beginning in time and is proceeding inexorably to its conclusion in time. It obviously has not eternally existed. Its vast energy levels, its utter sophistication, its purposefulness, literally scream out against any idea of a random, causeless, purposeless self-generated occurrence out of the void. Yet it exists. How did it come to be? The only explanation consistent with observation, as well as the only viable alternative in the possible modes of origin and continuance through time as a dynamic system, is that it was designed and brought into existence by an intelligent Being not Himself created. Is it possible to formulate a model of such a Being?

Section 3—A MATHEMATICAL MODEL OF THE CREATOR

It has been said that, of all men's knowledge, only mathematics is qualitatively the same as the divine (Galileo). It is utterly abstract and immaterial in its essence. Because of this nature, mathematics is completely universal in its application. We must always be wary of a concept in any system which cannot be conceived of or modeled in some sort of a mathematical way. One of the great beauties of the Einsteinian physics is its mathematical purity and at-root simplicity. For it remains, in many ways, a mathematical construct of the universe which is reflected into ever widening areas of physical application. As we attempt to develop a mathematical model of the Creator, it must be remarked beforehand that it is indeed only a model, a construct, and as such, it is a more or less useful tool to conceive of the reality it represents. In actuality the power and existence of the Creator are one with His essence and being—Infinite. We must turn to the basic concepts of the differential and integral calculus in an elementary way to begin the construct.

The concept of the infinite—of infinity—at least dimly perceived—was familiar to the philosophers from classical Greek times. Mathematicians, at least from the time of Descartes, had perceived the existence of such a concept. But, like the concept "zero," it was one which had no real universal understanding and took many years of mathematical groping before it was grasped. We still have difficulty with the idea of "absolute nothing" which, as we have seen, is different than "vacant space." Space itself is something defined as the environment of matter. In a strictly limited universe, located within celestial spheres, both infinity and zero seemed unnecessary. A hand with zero fingers was no hand. But the calculus needed two concepts at opposite ends of a continuum. These two concepts defined the infinitesimal and the infinite. Now the infinitesimal did indeed approach a limit "zero" as the number of successive divisions increased indefinitely (became infinite). The other direction, the infinite itself, remained, not a limit but beyond any preassigned limit. The infinite was unachievable, indeterminable forever. This truth is expressed by the definitive equation, $\lim_{x \to \infty} cx = \infty$. The equation states that the limit of the value of the product of a variable and a constant, as the value of the variable, becomes infinite—is infinite. The value of the constant, no matter how large, has no bearing on the result. The same is true concerning the infinitesimal at the opposite end of the mathematical spectrum, where x approaches zero.

If we were to define x as a variable expressing existence in any of its forms and all of its forms, as a continuous function of the power of the Creator, p, we would, in accordance with the differential calculus, say that at any point for an increment of power $\triangle p$ there would be a corresponding increase in existence $\triangle x$ and we would express this increase in the ratio $\frac{\triangle x}{\triangle p}$. Now we further establish the limit and say that $\frac{dx}{dp} = \lim_{\triangle p \to 0} \frac{\triangle x}{\triangle p}$. This equation states that as the magnitude of the increase, in the independent variable p, approaches "zero" or becomes infinitesimal, the value of the ratio between the increments of the variables approaches and becomes a fixed quantity at specific points as the function changes in value. Graphically in Cartesian coordinates, the value of $\frac{dx}{dp}$ is the instantaneous slope of the function plot at any point. We can now say that both dx and dp are infinitesimal increments in existence x and power p regardless of the numerical value represented by $\frac{dx}{dp}$ since the product of any constant c times dx or dp would remain an infinitesimal value. Going on to the integral calculus, we can further state that the power of the Creator p can be explained by the following formula:

$$P = \lim_{n \to \infty} \int_0^n c \, dx = c \, [x]_0^n = cn = \infty$$

where p is measured by the summation of all of the infinitesimal increments of existence between "zero" and an upper "boundary," $n = \infty$, and where c is the constant or summation of constants which defines the elements of existence. Thus, the power of the Creator is infinite and He Himself is infinite. As in the integration, the constant, defining all the elements of existence, is absorbed in His infinity. Infinite existence and essence coalesce in the Creator's infinite being. As His existence, measured by His power, is infinite; so, by implication, is His essence. Thus, in the model, the Creator is infinite in being, essence, existence and power. It should be remarked, in passing, that there is no way a mathematical model can be conceived for a self-created universe. It would require the development of an expansion from the term "zero" with no operating function. By definition, it has "zero" power and "zero" existence, hence "zero" creativity.

At this point, in expanding from our model, we must perforce leave the realm of physics for metaphysics. However, rules of mathematics and logic still apply. The Creative Agency has been described as the uncaused Being, Essence and Existence. It was observed that It must therefore be infinite, at least, as to Its existence. Creation was an event brought about by the

Creator. The Creator has an eternal existence without sequential change. The first agreement to reach is this: there is nothing gained by postulating another physical creative agency or event because that merely pushes the sequence back one more step. Whatever the ultimate Agency is must Itself be uncaused and also inherently uncaused in Its very essence. It must therefore not be something in the space, time, mass concept which has no such quality, but independent of it. It must have reality. It is not just an "as if" construct. It is at least as real as the physical universe—since originating it—and It must be changeless in any terms we can apply to that concept from time and space considerations. It was not changed in Its essence in any way by the creation of the material universe. If It had been, It would in turn be as subject to the mathematically bankrupt idea of an infinite, regressive sequence of events which would apply here with equal force. The Creator constitutes only "one event." It has only one "event"—Its existence—and that necessarily changeless and eternal.

Since changeless and eternal, the Creator must be immaterial in any sense we can apply from the physical universe. This is, of course, the source of the "hang-up" which stemmed from the strict concentration on empiricism in the physical and social sciences, and, by reflection, in philosophy after the Age of Enlightenment. It was a point raised by Freud. By definition, an immaterial substance could not be measured by physical material instrumentation. This is not the same as saying that it cannot exist, although that is the conclusion of the rigorous materialist.

There are many things which have real existence but do not yield to such measurements. For example, anything in the realm of human symbology, which was real enough to convey information from which civilization and everything within it has been built, is physically unmeasurable. Even prototype materialist, Karl Marx, in his *Manifesto*, had reality and produced effects not subject to physical measurements. But all these are only the signatures reflecting the materially even less measurable personalities behind the symbols. Yet, they are a far more significant measure of the total individual personality than his height, weight, girth and color. Even our "ultimate" material "particles" are directly unmeasurable and likely will remain unmeasurable except by their effects. Yet, they are matter in its most fundamental state.

The Creator, therefore, is an immaterial Personality measurable in the physical sense only by His effects. He must also be completely unaffected intrinsically by any sequential acts or form of existence which He had set in motion, as in the time and space manner of the physical universe. This Being is infinite in the most absolute context possible—to the extent that there are no possible powers excluded. If there were, He could not be infinite. He would be lacking something. He could be changed by the addition. There could not be a change in His power and creating—only a fulfilled willing to have a creation come into being as He had personally conceived it eternally. As there was no beginning to the exercise of power, there will be no end to its exercise. The beginning and end are merged as one, continuous, yet ever present exercise.

The mode in which we see our existence is as a time-oriented existence. It is real in that mode—but as the enactment of a drama in a preprogrammed scenario—a video tape—which the Creator sees eternally in the present. His manner of knowledge is qualitatively different than ours, as is His manner of existence. Ours is necessarily sequential. His is not sequential. The first, and last, events in our knowledge are, at once, present in the Creator's knowledge, plus all possible variations which might have been played stemming from all alternatives.

Further, the concept of "economy" has no meaning in the Creator's actions, although we may so speak. With any species of existence, the smallest, the most simple, the most easily conceived in human terms, is, to the Creator, as important, as valuable, as worthy, as the most complex or the most elaborate. To the Creator, an atom or a galaxy are of the same "weight" and in neither case insignificant and one as easily created as the other. One instant or ten billion years are the same. However, in one aspect, both are apprehended by Him as they are by us. Our objective and our subjective universe is also real to Him since our awareness is also in His knowledge.

It could be said that that is stretching the model a long way. Since, however, by the definition of His power and existence as infinite, the Creator is absolutely comprehensive—having no possible positive boundaries or dimension, it is possible to go further. It is noteworthy that the model does not extend in the negative direction, in the region of nonexistence or of a negative power, which would imply a contradiction. The Creator is thus totally consistent in all of His concepts. From this point, it is possible to say that the Creator is purposeful. While the lack of need for "economy" might suggest wild extravagence, the requirement that the creative acts be consistent means they are balanced and ordered to achieve the end willed. In other words, the willing is guided by an infinite, purposeful, constructive intelligence—a quality also one with the Creator's essence.

From the nature of the Creator thus seen in the model, through the metaphysical perspective, the physical universe, since it is a possible form of existence, would always have been creatable—though not necessarily in this form. There could be many, and if transcendental beings are possible (i.e., conceivable without intrinsic contradiction) they would likely be created, though not necessarily in human form. There could be many such forms. For, implicit in the concept of infinite creative power in the Creator, is comprehensive exercise of that power to the extent it is consistent with His will.

The model, moreover, provides an answer to what might be called the anthropocentric "hang-up." Probably, the single thing which contributed most to the estrangement of the intellectuals of the eighteenth and nineteenth centuries, and their academic progeny, from the idea of a Creator was the vastness of the universe as it was being revealed by the science of astronomy with its newfound tools and concepts. If there was a God, He was manifestly too great a being to concern Himself in any personal way with man.

The traditional view of God was in the image of man, a very great being, and the universe, centered on the earth or, at most, the sun, was conformable with that view. He was still manlike in many ways even though He might have been called infinite and eternal. Suddenly, the vastness was seen as so great as to overwhelm any such manlike being, as to be utterly beyond any control of any conceivable being in the older terms. The scientifically immature concept of the infinitely pre-existing universe and a paradoxically shrinking and disinterested God, brought with it an erosion of the idea for a need of the existence of any God to explain it. If man, with his great intelligence, could not visualize Him in terms of the scale of the universe, He must not be. The biblical creation became a tinker toy for children or the unsophisticated.

The new physics at last has brought the physical universe, vast as it is, back into terms far from infinite. Now, a concept of the Creator, for what He really must be—truly infinite—is dimly reflected on the stage of the universe. Existence—all existence—including His own—is great so as to be limitless. However, His being is even greater, for His power comprehends and controls all of it.

The model also comprehends the infinitesimal, the very

minute, so that man is not confronted with a being solely involved in throwing great forces around with wild abandon. The physicists are still unable to say just how small the final basic element of matter really is. Every step seems to bring with it further subdivisions. The ultimate component or corpuscle may be but energy in some other form, yet the elemental forms in that microcosmic existence show the same careful attention to design and order as the galaxies which, in essence, are made up of such almost infinitesimal particles. So, if the comfortable anthropomorphic God has been dethroned, an even more considerate and truly infinite and more God-like God has replaced Him. He is being, independent of the physical universe which He created, but one who, in all His creative function, has shown concern for its development and preservation. He is as infinitely concerned with the least as with the greatest. Each one of us could individually be as big as a galaxy or as small as an atom without the slightest difference to God. Or our lives might be as a milli-second or as a billion years, yet all would be the same. The Almighty and Eternal God can be completely present in the slightest photon, if such things be, and in all of them in all the universe, yet not be comprehended in the slightest manner by all possible universes.

In the preface, the writer quoted a few sentences from the Freeman Dyson article and Dyson, in turn, had quoted a few lines from William Blake's *The Marriage of Heaven and Hell*, written in 1793. In that poem Blake said:

Energy is the only life and is
from the body; and Reason is the
bound or outward circumference of
Energy. Energy is Eternal Delight.

Dyson's opening paragraph in this article then said:

One need not be a poet or a mystic to find Blake's definition of energy more satisfying than the definition given in textbooks on physics. Even within the framework of physical science, energy has a transcendent quality. . . . We do not know how the scientists of the next century will define energy or in what strange jargon they will discuss it. But no matter what language the physicists use, they will not come into contradiction with Blake. Energy will remain in some sense the lord and giver of life, a reality transcending our mathematical descriptions. Its nature lies at the heart of the mystery of our existence as animate beings in an inanimate universe.

It is on that theme that I would like to approach the second central concept—that of the possibility of an interface other than creation itself between the material universe and the immaterial surround—for if man is, in fact, a transcendental being with "one foot in this world and the other in the next," he, himself, must constitute such an interface, the only one we know. And so it is to the way man displays his energies just as it is with the Creator that we must look for evidence in support of such a hypothesis. The writer plans to approach the problem from three viewpoints. First in the light of matter as it is now conceived in modern physics. Second from the standpoint of man's position in the chain of energy utilization, the entropy chain if you will. And third, that from anthropology—a functional approach. As was stated, there is of course a close relationship between the support for the existence of an infinite, eternal Creator in any argument for transcendental man, and here metaphysical logic is of even greater importance.

Modern science has eschewed attempts, and properly so, within the defined context of modern scientific methodology to explain first principles in the nature and being of reality. That is the subject of metaphysics, and the very soul of all existence and self-knowledge. There is need however to make a very strong point that physical science of itself does not provide the final answers to questions in the metaphysical realm, which many of its detail-blinded exponents claimed. Now modern science, by its self-imposed limitation of knowledge to that which is observable within the state of the art, in fact limited itself to the existing instrumentation. It can support this by logical and mathematical conceptualization which the data justify, but this must always define "reality" in terms of the available data and logic. It will hence be constantly changing reality with improved instrumentation and logic, hopefully convergent on true reality, the unchangeable, the absolute.

Section 4—A View From the World of Microphysics

Obviously the nature of the universe, as man conceives it from physical science today, is vastly different from the views of the late eighteenth and early nineteenth centuries. That period in which the philosophers and social scientists lived who remain the seed bed of much which shares a man's concept of man at this time some 200 years later was a period, primitive in science. It was far different even than it was at the end of the nineteenth century, when Newtonian mechanical models no longer explained the observed behavior of phenomena associated with extremes of distance or velocity, but before the Einsteinian revolution. And yet, it cannot be denied that their concepts of man, and his relationship with society, and in the universe, were profoundly influenced by the Newtonian view of cosmology and the nature of matter. This is true though Newton himself was far from being a materialist; in fact his system could only be made to work if metaphysical considerations were incorporated (Frank, 1963, p. 35). But that latter point was missed, or dismissed, by Saint-Simon and Auguste Comte and their immediate followers who were not sufficiently deep in Newtonian science to comprehend it.

But, if someone, speaking as a serious scientist, were to have told Isaac Newton in spite of his genius, that matter and energy—and space and time—are but manifestation of closely related phenomena, perhaps even largely interchangeable, in a unitary force field—that his newly discovered concept of gravitation was only one aspect of the interaction in a comprehensive energy matrix relating matter and energy in a space and time continuum—a time continuum in which time is only a space coordinate which, however, has no relationship in its dimension to Euclidian geometry, Newton would have had that speaker committed—or, at least, banished from the circle of mathematicians and physical scientists. For instrumentation and data therefrom were not available to support such views. But that is the direction in which the physical sciences have been heading for fifty years, are heading, and in fact are at the very threshold of establishing. Very recently, the number of different force field configurations which the theory must explain was reduced from four to three with demonstration that the weak atomic nuclear force was an aspect of electromagnetic phenomena and not an independent energy configuration.

Not to be repetitious, but to summarize, before looking at the microphysical world, matter is almost literally nothing but space. We have not arrived at that point at which energy and its resultant forces define the universe and where the manifestations we observe are only energy being exercised in various ways, but we are trending that way. Space itself appears to be nothing but the environment in which these energy phenomena exist. Where they exist, space exists; where they do not, there is literally nothing. And space expands or contracts, if it should, with the expansion and contraction of the energy environment. That a change in philosophical orientation is necessary is seen in the following quotation from the essay, *Philosophy of Physical Science in the Twentieth Century,* H. Margenau and J. E. Smith (Margenau, 1963, pages 382 et seq.):

Three things have happened in this century, which, more than any other, succeeded in exerting profound effects on the philosophy of science, and we shall deal with them in sequence. One is the progressive revelation that matter, the good old stuff of ancient Greece or the impenetrable atom of the nineteenth century, is much less solid, uniform, and simple than was originally supposed. At the risk of seeming paradoxical, we shall term the series of events and interpretations documenting this assertion the dematerialization of matter. Next on our list of significant discoveries is a group of facts indicating a failure of the continuity of motion in the atomic world, the failure of a deep-seated postulate whose disavowal threw philosophy of science into peculiar gyrations that have not completely subsided even today. And thirdly, we must recall certain developments that draw into question a principle ordinarily called causality, a principle whose rejection is sometimes said to entail freedom. Finally, as a sort of unconventional excursion it will be shown how, in this seemingly uncoordinated melee of scientific facts, there may be found the elements that account for the tenacity of so "unscientific" a philosophy as the existentialism of our day.

If any label serves to characterize the scientific philosophy of the Western world at the beginning of the present century, it is probably materialism, the doctrine that regards all the facts of the universe as explainable in terms of matter and motion, and in particular explains all psychical processes as material changes in the nervous system. Its basis lay in the belief that science has shown matter to be ultimate, not reducible to anything else and yet exceedingly versatile as a carrier of phenomena. Coupled with these qualities was its visual familiarity, and ease of comprehension and a pictorial obviousness which beguiled the scientists into thinking that matter was as simple and devoid of problems as it was versatile.

The whole development culminated in the ingenuous conception of Rutherford, who demonstrated beyond doubt that the atom has essentially the structure that is now common knowledge. Its core, or nucleus, is positively charged and heavy; around it move, in planetary fashion, enough negative electrons to make the entire atom electrically neutral. And, as to its size, the following description may be revealing. If our bodies were enlarged until they extended from the earth to the North Star, a hydrogen atom within them would have a nucleus the size of a tennis ball, its electrons would be 300-foot spheres and revolve about the tennis ball in orbits some ten miles in diameter. The hard and solid atom had become mostly empty space.

It should be noted that the ratio of "open space" to "solid mass" in the atomic structure may not be the same under all conditions. Einsteinian physics, in fact, predicted that under extremes of gravitational forces the open spaces, at least between atoms, would be compressed to approximate a "solid" mass. In modern astronomy, the pulsars (pulsating stellar radio sources) are conceived of as stars which have undergone gravitational collapse and, as a consequence, have squeezed out open space to the extent that the matter equivalent to our earth would be squeezed into a sphere having a diameter about equal to the length of a football field. The so-called "Black Holes" in space are believed to be collapsed stars so dense that not even light or any electromagnetic radiation can escape the gravitational field. Hence, they are invisible. Obviously matter and atomic particles in those environments could be a great deal different than under terrestrial ambience as being described in this essay.

This picture is still too simple. The nucleus is not a uniform sphere but has its own structure and is subject to change. The electrons are not simple objects but possess a spinning motion and other more baffling and poorly understood properties. Science is no longer sure that a nucleus has size: they may indeed be points, mathematical singularities, haunting space. The riddle has not been solved, but one conclusion stands out above all uncertainties: the concept of the atom, too, has undergone changes which are hardly misrepresented by the term dematerialization.

In principle, of course, this development does not argue against the philosophic doctrine of materialism, least of all in its dialectical form, for matter can be the last instance of explanatory appeal even if its structure is highly complicated. Nevertheless, the philosophic mind wonders whether anything so far from simple, so mysterious and impermanent can provide the ultimate resolution of all problems, and indeed whether there is such an ultimate resolution at all. It is for this methodological reason that materialism has largely lost its point.

Consider the appearance of a firefly in a dark summer night. To the eye, the motion of this insect is not continuous; what it presents is a succession of bright spots or streaks at different places in our field of view. The judgment that this phenomenon represents the uninterrupted passage of an object from one point of space to another is based, strictly speaking, on an interpolation between the bursts of luminosity that are actually perceived. Yet common sense, and indeed scientific description, regard themselves fully justified in performing that ideal supplementation of immediate perception that the interpretation of these sporadic darts as continuous motion demands. The chief reasons for this attitude are the following.

First, the hypothesis of continuous motion is testable through other experience. It is possible to watch the firefly in the daytime, when its progression from point to point becomes visible. This settles the issue in large part, although it may not convince the inveterate skeptic who feels that, when unilluminated the firefly behaves like the angels to whom St. Thomas attributed the ability of emerging at separate points without having to traverse the intervening distances. To answer the skeptic, we must demonstrate the simplicity and convenience of the continuity hypothesis. Thus we add to the fact of testability a second item of evidence of a more rational sort, namely, the simplicity of the geometric curve on which the luminous dots are situated. If the interpolated path were very irregular, showing unlikely curvatures and strange convolutions, doubts as to continuity might arise; the smoothness of the plotted trajectory goes a long way toward removing them.

In the last analysis, the validity of every scientific theory rests on two kinds of evidence: (1) empirical verifiability of some of its consequences, and (2) rational coherence, or economy of thought, or simplicity conveyed by the ideas composing the theory. It is because the hypothesis of continuity in reference to the motion of the firefly satisfies both of these criteria that common sense accepts it.

Atomic entities, like electrons, present phenomena that, on the purely empirical side, are not unlike the sporadic emergence of a firefly at night. To be sure, the electron in an atom cannot be seen. Nevertheless if the results of experiments and observations using the refined techniques of modern physics can be trusted, an electron in what is called a Bohr orbit reveals its position as a random set of points located throughout a region of space in the neighborhood of the so-called classical orbit. More precisely, if a series of position measurements were made while the electron is in the unvarying state known as the ground state of the hydrogen atom, the results would form a probability aggregate of known spatial distribution; the individual positions thus established will dot this region in a curious manner, offering no immediate suggestion as to continuity of motion.

Thus, it is seen that the atomic realm confronts the physicist with a novel kind of problem in interpretation, with a challenge to explain or rationalize, perhaps, in ways to which he is not accustomed. And nature is not generous in providing hints for the solution of this methodological puzzle; the difficulties of direct verification we have already noted are so great that theories cannot readily be exposed to tests. The sphinx is noncommittal. The physicist has an embarrassing amount of freedom in making his interpretations.

Largely because of the impossibility of making road maps for scientific research, because of the growing realization that the constructions of science are not merely inductive generalizations of numerous facts, recent philosophy seems to be moving away from the extreme forms of positivism (e.g., of the Vienna Circle type) that inspired the earlier decades of this century.

It is now accepted that atomic motions are not necessarily continuous—that the microcosm need not satisfy those propensities for visual intuition of all happenings with which experience in the molar realm has endowed man. Things intrinsically too small to be seen may be quite unlike the visual, factual, and intuitable models that seem so clear to us; the denizens of the microcosm may be subject only to more subtle and more abstract human considerations, perhaps considerations of purely mathematical or logical sort. Scientists have begun to speak of mathematical and logical models!

In the human sciences, there occurs a class of observables that, although useful, do not exhibit the unvarying attachment to systems that characterize the possessed observables of classical physics. Anger, happiness, composure are psychological qualities of man, often used in the same way for the purpose of describing his mental state as the physicist uses position, velocity, and mass of an electron, for example. But there is this important difference: anger, happiness, and composure may be present or not; man is sometimes angry, happy, or composed, but there are states in which the attribution of these qualities is meaningless. Anger, happiness, composure are sometimes present and sometimes not. They might be called "latent" observables, which come into being and then disappear, and no one would be disposed to claim continuity of anger, happiness, and so forth.

Could it be, that the observation of atomic particles are of this latent variety? Could it be that an electron in certain states simply has no position but manifests this quality upon measurement, the observable being elicited as it were by the act of human interference? Anger, happiness, composure can be called into being by human intervention, indeed by acts of inquiry. This interpretation of atomic observables, which amounts to a radical denial of continuity as that phrase is usually understood, is by no means generally accepted, but it presents itself for discussion and study in the face of the facts.

There is another way of stating the salient features of the recent discoveries in quantum mechanics. We have seen that the electron in the hydrogen atom, when its position is measured, gives widely divergent and apparently inconsistent answers to the experimental query of its whereabouts. We noted that its "path," when interpreted continuously, is erratic and complicated. There is no simplicity and no great significance in the result of a single measurement. Nor are there laws that connect the individual observations. But the average of a multitude of observations does obey a simple principle embodied in the equations of quantum mechanics. Individual observations are lawless and chaotic, yet there resides within the totality a measure of regularity on which analysis and mathematics can seize. This is where probabilities enter the scene. Single, unique events in the atomic domain are unpredictable, but the probabilities are determined by mathematical laws.

It is not idle, however, to ask the question whether the new law of quantum mechanics (Schrodinger's equation) selects, or is compatible with, states in terms of other variables, and whether these variables permit a causal description in the more formal sense of our principles. That is, in fact, the case. Only, it happens to be the misfortune of these new variables, and of the states they define, to be somewhat strange and elusive when judged from Newton's familiar standpoint. As we have seen, they turn out to be probabilities.

Here, then, is the situation with respect to causality today. Those who insist on retaining the old "classical" definition of states, which ties state variables to single observations, in particular to an assignment of x and p, are forced to relinquish the causal principle. If, however, one is willing to modify the meaning of state, is willing to accept a statistical definition of state that sees significance (perhaps exclusively) in probabilities, then there is no need to reject causality. For, as a formal relation between states at different times, it continues to hold.

Regardless of this choice it is true that individual

events are no longer subject to rigid determination by natural laws. Prediction of a single future event on the basis of a single present or past event is often impossible. This means, of course, that something philosophically noteworthy slips through the net of scientific determination. If the lawful states, which satisfy differential equations, but are related to events through probabilities only, are called essences, while the unique contingencies of our experience are regarded as existences, then the existentialist is right in claiming that essences have lost control of the world of existences.

In addition to its main emphasis on the current disarray of the philosophy of physical science and the decline of materialism and positivism on that account, the article points up the fragility of matter as now conceived. The "dematerialization of matter" as the authors termed it may well lead to the ultimate postulation that matter is nothing else but configured energy and all the physical properties of matter we observe and measure only the result of the particular form and structure which the energy has been given in this time and space continuum. The measurements have no universal validity or application. There is no discernible final continuity in either structure of motion.

The relative "immateriality" of the physical universe offers no problems to man as a transcendental being. At the same time, of course, it offers no direct support to the concept, but the intangibility of ultimate matter renders the materialistic philosophies impotent and, to that extent, it increases the viability of the less materialistic. It literally forces the physical scientist to move to the metaphyscial for advance in logical projection. When states of existence are only definable in terms of probabilities, as they are in microphysics, not only has "something philosophically noteworthy slipped through the net of scientific determination," but it appears science must now attempt to assess probabilities in terms of "intentionality" in first principles and therefore turn to logical models. "Probable causality" reflects alternatives of varying degree of likelihood, for probability is not itself a cause. It is only a predictive methodology resorted to when the actual causation is too complex to be analyzed or is subject to pure chance. Human behavior studies are an example of the first. People act in individually unpredictable ways, but in large numbers react fairly consistently so that reliable probabilistic forecasts in society can be made. The causes or motivation of the specific action in individual cases are usually quite varied. It seems likely that the "behavior" of the atomic particles is more of this type. As was pointed out in the article by Pierre Auger (1963)—previously quoted—in relation to atomic disintegration the small number of particles involved, "a few dozen," cannot of itself support a randomly selected solution in terms of thousands of millions of years.

Whatever the causality, that phenomenon serves a highly useful purpose, referring now to the Dyson article on energy in the universe, the criticality of the "weak interaction hang-up" and of the availability and control of nuclear energy in all its forms which rely on this activity. Thus, contrary to the conclusion in the final paragraph of the article by Margenau and Smith, just quoted, essences have not lost control of existences. The determination of the state of existence is forced to a much higher level and beyond the material. Existences in their most fundamental material mode are now more clearly shown to be carefully controlled and serve the purposes of the Highest Essence. While the secondary cause of the phenomenon (and there could be one or many) may remain a mystery, the ultimate or final cause lies in the intentionality of the Creator. This development, in fact, provides strong support for the created universe. The only alternatives appear to be (1) the assignment of "intentionality" or a "willing" capability to the particle to elect to change its state or even to bring itself into existence in some inconceivable way a la Kapp, or (2) to assign the "intentionality" to an external entity—God. The first choice seems completely irrational, a probability approaching zero. The second is consistent with other evidence of the Creator's purposeful activity. There is a choice: The capacity of intentionality can be ascribed to an inert or even non-existent particle, or it can be ascribed to an eternally existing, infinite, intelligent Being. There are no other options.

Stephen Hawking, the British theoretical physicist has developed the mathematics of the "Black Holes" in space to a point comparable with that of the theory of relativity in the 1920's. If Hawking's calculations stand the test of verification possible through the technological advance anticipated during the 1980's, the science of macro-physics and micro-physics will undergo a change, the equivalent of that following verification of the expanding universe in the 1930's.

It is of little value now to speculate on the nature and extent of the changes involved since the uncertainties are too great. It is sufficient to note that the "Black Holes" tend to substantiate the "Big Bang" theory of creation and to suggest that the "Black Holes" may provide the methodology of reverting matter to the timeless, spaceless energy form from which the universe was brought into existence.

Having seen how immaterial matter has become, how discontinuous in structure and motion, how totally unpredictable is the behavior of the atomic units in terms of small numbers, one should now reflect on the biologic phenomena resulting in species differentiation. The current theory, and it is increasingly substantiated by indirect evidence, is that the joining in the mating process of two molecular chains called DNA (deoxyribonucleic acid) is the determinant. The structure of the two chains each a few millimicrons in length comprising nothing which physical science can detect but such elemental atomic particles. These particles however carry all the genetic codes. The mating of these chains determines whether the resulting offspring will be a mouse or a man, and additionally will include all of the individuating characteristics blended from the parents.

The DNA molecule is complex, comprising some 10^6 atoms of carbon, nitrogen, oxygen, hydrogen and phosphorus. Although there are a great many combinations possible, the viable chemical configuration limit is far below the strict mathematical potential. The mating of the molecules results in passing along genetic characteristics many orders of magnitude greater in number. The number of discrete genetic characteristics is impossible to estimate considering all the life forms, and individuals within those life forms over the last three to four billion years that the process has been under way. The potential number of forms and individuals is of course far more horrendous. Probabilities provide no help. In the first place, the total number of particles included in the DNA chain is too small a sample to provide answers to even the simplest question in terms of ordinary atomic behavior in situations described by Auger or by Smith and Margenau. The effect of the mating of the DNA complex molecules, if anything, should be chaotically unpredictable. Yet, unless externally damaged or mutated by some other rare and unknown cause, the DNA chains carry out the assignment with almost total predictability. If the atom is so unpredictable in its individual behavior how can a combination of a relatively small number of such elements be so purposive and predictable? Neither biologists nor physicists care to answer the question. Or, if we look at the matter from another viewpoint, why should the few million inert particles predictably collect themselves and take on the same configurations so as to repeat that of the parents except as modified to reflect the merger? They follow an established pattern and established rules exactly, although produced in many different ways in many different organisms. Why should the process be to continuously more complex forms of life and yet continue those lower forms which remain useful? In the usual response, the mechanism is substituted for the cause resulting in circularity of logic. Mosquito DNA always produces mosquitoes, never elephants, nor ever elephant-like mosquitoes, because the mosquitoes produce mosquito DNA and elephants produce elephant DNA—but small changes can occur by mutation.

There is obviously something else involved in DNA aside from the purely chemical linkage. Using micro-surgical techniques, biologists have been able to combine DNA from dissimilar species. The resulting life form bears characteristics of both parent species. In some circles this has been advanced as evidence that the phenomenon of life itself is purely chemical. What is demonstrated, is the versatility of the DNA programming and the persistence of the life impulse to seek ways of fulfillment in spite of the genetic tinkerings.

There was a point in time some 3.5 billion years ago or so when there was no life—no DNA. Now there are innumerable forms of life—no two individuals in any species exactly alike, likely no two strands of DNA exactly alike—but totally consistent within species. Can all this concurrent consistency yet constant change and upward development be attributed to the erratic, logic-defying atom plus chance probability?

This writer finds it amusing that the same scientist who finds a goal-seeking teleological development of the universe impossible, has no difficulty with the goal-seeking teleological development of a human being from the mating of two DNA chains comprising a few million atoms of common elements.

Looking back at the initial life impulse in the remote Pre-Cambrian times, some biologic philosophers have visualized the spontaneous development of life in the rich chemical broth provided by warm primeval seas where lifeless polymers were already randomly coagulating. Then, in the course of violent thunderstorms, or other highly-energized natural phenomena, some polymers were impelled into the biotic age. The life process was then biogenic as to existing life forms. Still, it must be understood that only process is being discussed. If this process were granted as the plausible origin, why did the process have that effect? Is there something in the nature of lightning, or other observable phenomena, or in inert chemicals, or their combination, which can account for life which at its base level involves a system of energy use and conversion into a self-perpetuating mechanism? Is there something in the nature of chemicals, once energized, to develop that everywhere-observed instinctive drive for self-preservation and reproduction? This condition implies an "intent," self-contained, or exteriorly induced, to survive and to proliferate. This process has observably involved constantly more complex forms emerging eventually as an intellectual being able to think about the process and try to imitate it. If we relate the initiating condition in the process to the product, now observable, there is a colossal disproportion between the process and the result.

Every new life in the natural order requires a process to bring it into being. Yet, few parents say to their child, "I produced your life." Certainly they were instrumental in the child's here and now existence. That human personality would not exist without them, but they did not create its life. Nor does the hen sitting on her clutch of eggs or the industrial incubator give life to the chicks. Yet, this process would come to a halt, in these instances, without them. Life, in the material order, is more than a chemical process. It is a chemical process infused with—some very special energy utilization mode—a quantum jump above the chemical. The cause of life is not the process. It is not the application of calories to a collection of chemicals. Lurking somewhere, there is an intelligence and a will which directs the execution of the plan—provides the process—and supplies the energy.

It is common, in popular journals, to make the statement that, "They have uncovered the mystery of life" and then to proceed to describe in tremendous detail the *processes* through which a living being carries out its functions whether that being is a single cell or a polycellular being such as man. DNA and RNA are not life of themselves, though they are living tissue. They are complex arrays of common chemicals. Life, on the other hand, is a characteristic of certain "being forms" to execute intrinsic and specific internally-directed objectives peculiar to their specific "being forms" as an organizing and energizing principle. Life is not a form of energy itself nor a process but a *capacity* to create, modify, and utilize energy through process in pursuit of internally directed objectives.

Process was previously broadly defined as a patterned activity or sequence of activities in the course of which change was produced between two situational sets. Process is intelligible but not necessarily intentional at the level of identification. The process of life differentiation, development and evolution is frequently ascribed totally to random selection under a survival bias. The concept "survival bias" is, in turn, based on the observed situations that those traits or characteristics tending to promote survival will tend to be increased in succeeding generations. The case of the moths discussed earlier is illustrative of a new condition imposed on a species previously well adapted to camouflage in its habitat over many generations. The selective picking off of the light-colored moths in the darkened trees was a result of a process which is subject to ready analysis. The intentionality involved is highly complex and not identifiable though we could say quite properly that darkening of the trees was an unforeseen consequence of many intentional processes at the human level. Meanwhile, the predation was selective until a balance was achieved. If there were no urge to reproduce, on the part of the moths, obviously, the whole process would quickly come to a halt. If there was no urge to survive—to nourish, on the part of the birds, they would ignore the moths.

It is a fair statement that every "ecological niche" will be filled by the species or subspecies best suited to survive in that environment. The term "best suited to survive" can, and does, cover a vast range of traits. However, two things are certain. The reproduction rate must equal or exceed the mortality rate and, in a situation of scarcity, which is the usual case, the species or subspecies best able to utilize the nutrients available will survive and those less capable will die out. The question goes to the nature of life itself. The "elan vital" of Bergson is, in fact, that bundle of urges present in every life form, requiring it to strive to surmount the difficulties and hazards of its environment. Thus we see that the chain of process leading always to higher, more complex, life forms is not even philosophically random but fiercely, actively, biased by a force which is not explainable by the material constituents at all. The survival bias is merely an expression of the "will to function" in accord with its form of being. A tree, for example, clearly exhibits this characteristic in its existence. From the germinating seed, until maturity and production of seed, all activities are directed to that final end in spite of the most adverse circumstances and setbacks. The tree succeeds or dies in the attempt, sacrificing all to that end, though its own form is stunted and warped in the process.

A mineral crystal, though highly organized and invariant in its form, does not have the characteristic of internal "compulsion" to attain the end which described the "elan vital." Nor does the complex polymer, which tends to provide a chemical linkage pattern for other similar formulations in a chemical broth. The crystalline and the amorphous chemical forms are far closer to each other than to those primordial organisms exhibiting life. The purely chemical activities are differentiated from the biologic or biochemical processes by the additional characteristics—the integral capacity and necessity to direct energy utilization to the desired ends which the latter form possessed. It is an either/or situation, not a continuum. If the specific being possesses that capacity, it is a life form. If it does not, it is not a life form. The virus presents a problem, because it presents the picture of life form in one environment and of inanimate matter in another—but clearly in those phases in which it acts as a life form it is a life form.

If life, then is best defined as a capacity to utilize energy in an internally self-directed way, we are forced to conclude that there is something in which that capacity must inhere. But, if it is not inherent in the specific chemical forms; that is, the chemical forms separately, or in combinations, which comprise the material base, there must be a substrate in the living being and peculiar to its essence, in which that capacity does inhere. Thomas Aquinas called it the animating principle, or soul, and posited souls for the vegetal, animal and human beings. In each case, the lower capacities were subsumed in, and subordinate to, the higher principles. Because of this, man's soul possessed the inherent capacity of the vegetal and animal forms as well as the intellectual.

Husserl, in his final stage, called the understanding of the "Lebenswelt," the life world, the most universal problem of philosophy. Agnostic, Merleau-Ponty called man "incarnate consciousness" without further definition of what that consciousness consisted in. What we have done is provide a series of tautologies for the sake of convenience. The specific life principle is the principle of that specific life. In these definitions, we have not even speculated on what that principle must be. What can we say about it? First, we can say that this principle has the obvious characteristics of providing specific and detailed direction of activity. Second, it has the characteristic of controlling complex processes in detailed ways for carrying out directions in growth, damage control, and repair. Third, as to the world about us at least, this principle is persistent, ubiquitous and yet, extremely fragile in individual beings. Death, which here seems to equate with a withdrawal of the animating principle from the material form, takes place universally. Sometimes death takes place after maturity of the organism and many times before, when that noncorrectable malfunction occurs in the purely physical structure of the being.

In the urge toward perfection—the "elan vital"—perhaps an inchoate form of love, we see a compulsion toward completion of perfection in being. We see a common pattern emerging. There is a demand, an "obligation," placed on every form of being to fulfill its destiny. Only rational beings are free to refuse. We see inexorably emerging, perhaps reminiscent of Spinoza's thought which emphasized the natural, that pervasive consciousness in the universe which, through the agencies of the specific material beings, carries out an overall plan of development in space and time. The animating principle of life is the most sophisticated of these agencies and it is a reflection of the active intervention of that supreme infinite consciousness—"The spirit which moves where it wills." The animating principle—the soul—is the inherent vehicle for the vital capacity which is provided for that particular life form through which the will of the consciousness, primary and universal is exercised. In man, the soul has been provided the gift of intelligent self-direction. Man is, in effect, a willing or unwilling participant in the development of that total conscious plan. He is given the capacity to use energy at the intellectual and spiritual levels and it seems likely he is the only being in the physical universe which has that capacity. The likelihood of man's immortality is intimately related, and dependent upon, the existence of that capacity.

But what of that capacity of life? It is, perhaps, easier to define life after the analysis of the condition, death. Our materialistic definition of death as the result of a noncorrectable malfunction of the process mechanism given earlier is essentially correct. But, it is properly applied only to a mechanism of material form whether mechanical or biologic. It represents a "machine"—an energy converter, which has lost its essential capacity. A man dies—no question—and all that is biological and material in that individual loses its capacity to function. But this definition of death can only apply to a termination of process which flows from, or is intrinsic to, material capacity. When a tree dies, it is no longer able to convert the ambient energy forms to its appropriate functioning as a tree. If life in man is intrinsically material in its capacity, as is a tree, then man is equally as dead.

Death is an inappropriate term, however, when applied to a non-material, or spiritual, capability above the biologic order. Love is, literally, deathless; although it can be withdrawn. That there is such love or charity can scarcely be questioned. Most human aspirations are of this same immaterial order. An ideal strongly held—one for which one will die—does not spring from material capability. An in-built capacity to die for a principle would be totally incompatible with a materialistic life capability. It would constitute a system-destroying malfunction. Suicide, as pointed out by Merleau-Ponty, for principle or otherwise, is an exclusively human activity.

Having looked briefly at the characteristics of being and of life we can conclude that a capacity—a capability—for life, for instance, can only occur in a being. Being is the necessary vehicle, or frame, in which all capacity is grounded. If there is a capacity or a capability, there is a being in which that capacity or capability resides. We can say further that there is the intrinsic capability, at least in potency, in any form of being, to execute those activities which that form of being exhibits and to become that final form to which its activities are directed. If a form of being exhibits life, that being is intrinsically capable of life. An acorn is intrinsically capable, at least it has the potential capability of becoming an oak tree. If it does not have that capacity, it is not an acorn. Further, the activities between potency and fulfillment are all directed to that fulfillment. An acorn germinates—puts down roots—thrusts up leaves—and all of this is done toward that final end of becoming an oak tree. In the human being is exhibited the capacity for divine worship; supernatural love, hope of immortality, abstract intellection and moral judgment all aimed at becoming a being giving personal service to God. The being, man, is intrinsically capable, at least in potency, of performing those supra-material activities and becoming that ultimate being in the service of God.

If we go back to Avicenna's "Flying Man" or Descartes's sublimated human intelligence, the intrinsic capacity of thought is intellectually demonstrable as disassociated from sense perception, though dependent on the material body for human existence and on proper functioning of an organic material brain for rational acts. It will be recalled, Descartes' original dichotomy, in epistemology—relating mind to soul—and sense perception of the eternal world to body—stemmed from his attempts to place these characteristics in aspects of the human being, to which they could pertain in capacity. He could see no purely intellectual capacity intrinsic in a material brain nor could he see sense perception in a completely spiritual soul. *The crucial point in demonstrating his existence was that he could think.* He was self-conscious of his existence. This self-conscious thought was independent of the existence of the external world—dependent solely on his own existence as a thinking human being possessing a thinking soul. The idea therefore, that the personal human soul is the seat of the capacity, in the human being, for activities having nonsensory, nonmaterial objectives is well grounded in philosophic literature.

It seems to go almost without saying that a functioning, living, being can, itself, be of no lower level of intrinsic nature than that of the activities which it exhibits. The acorn has the intrinsic potential for life as an oak tree. The bird is a flying nest-building creature. The capacity and activity of the species are in consonance with their nature. The potency eventuates in capacity and activity. Man has the intrinsic potency for supra-material activities—he performs such activities, therefore he has the capacity and must have the intrinsic potency of supra-material life. It is but a short step to the conclusion— since in all forms of being experienced, where the potency is exhibited, capacity precedes activity—the activity eventuates—so with man, if the potency for supra-material life, that life style will also eventuate. It does eventuate in this life in attenuated form.

In the discussions in Part II, on the "purposefulness" of animals, an intuitive approach was made to an "intending ego" which "preprogrammed" the organisms instinctively to respond to stimuli so that they did, in fact, respond and act compulsively in a problem-solving way even though there was no individually formed intent to "solve" problems. At this state, in considering the associated problem of "energy in the universe," there is a question of how the energy series is extended into the biologic field. We are aware that, entropically speaking, it is the least efficient form in conversion of energy as we now know it. There is a severe degradation of energy as it passes into the biologic sequence which is also, chronologically, the latest sequence to appear in the universe. But what are we really saying? Though often described as a measure of disorganization it appears that the entropy series really measures the complexity of the process. It is the sheer number of transactions rather than sheer inefficiency of individual internal interchanges in biochemical activity which produces the rapid reduction of general reaction energy and increased entropy. The material living beings "degrade" energy at a high rate because they are highly complex and demanding in contra-distinction to the mechanical processes.

The phenomena of life, then, is exhibited at several levels of sophistication—the vegetal—insensitive and compulsive, the animal—sensitive and compulsive and, in addition to the others, man—experiential and intellectual. Occasionally, there is exhibited in man, examples of higher level of life activity. An activity that could be called an induced intellection—that rare insight typical of clairvoyance, for instance, and other phenomena included in the catchall expression "extra sensory perception" which would include religious experience of an ecstatic nature. Forms of energy, in themselves, not oriented to matter but totally capable of impinging on matter, also, therefore, likely exist at "frequencies" beyond the physical. These forms would be exhibited when, controlled by beings capable of utilizing them, they do impinge, by phenomena not explainable by the purely physical laws and then primarily in the vital, intellectual, and spiritual field. They are likely non-entropic.

The entire range of life phenomena, in spite of the volumes of work written on the subject, remain unexplainable at the physical level. As we have seen, life is not just a form of energy. It is a capacity to use energy of various forms in particular ways. The life principle, the soul, is the agency within the physical form by which, and through which, the various biologic species utilize energy—physical and supra-physical in the case of man—to carry out their life purpose. Chaotic though the world of life may seem in overall view, the behavior, in detail, is purposeful and exhibits an intelligent source behind the activity providing the energy and the specific life forms to utilize it. Finally, in the consciousness of man—his capabilities, drives, and aspirations—beyond the biologic order—there is the clear indication of an ultimate end of those capabilities, beyond the biologic order.

The greatest certitude is not "I think therefore I am," but "There is thought (consciousness of being), therefore being is." It is not inconceivable, since it has been conceived, that I, as an individual, think or am conscious of my own being and yet, do not have real individual existence. But it is inconceivable, in view of my consciousness of self and other selves, that there is not consciousness at some level of the existence of being which my consciousness reflects. It is almost inconceivable, Dewey not withstanding, that there could be a state of being without a consciousness or awareness of that state of being at a level which comprehends the totality of all being. Schrodinger, the father of the quantum theory of wave-mechanics, held almost passionately that he was that conscious "I" acting at that point in time and space which he occupied. All other conscious beings were similarly that "I" in their particular situation. It is a multi-form pantheism quite difficult to maintain in view of the innumerable intellectual conflicts always erupting in the world of consciousness which we know. The complete "I" is a very strange intending ego in action, yet Schrodinger's view reflects the sense of the ubiquity of consciousness.

It is certainly true that there is consciousness only because there is being. Intuitively, the reverse is likewise true that there is being only because there is a consciousness by which being is. At the supreme level of being and consciousness—God—being and consciousness are identical in His eternal essence. The mystery of God and the promise of man's spiritual immortality are clearly related to the mystery of self-consciousness in man and in that being in which resides the totality of consciousness of being.

Section 5—God and Man in a View of an Extended Entropy System

In terms of the concept of the universe as it is now unfolding in science, in the science of matter itself throughout the universe, in the nature of the Creator as developed by the mathematical model and metaphysical logic and in the face of many unanswered questions, perhaps the first question which should be examined is the possibility of existence of life forms beyond our observable physical forms here on earth. The response, "It is the only one we know," is not sufficient. As an example, if we could imagine a creature limited to two dimensions, it would be constrained by the line of the periphery of its plane. It would have absolutely no concept of a being which existed in three dimensions from what it could see or experience. It could never look up to see anything else above, although a footprint might cause it to wonder. But that would not limit reality to its two dimensions—though it might say so. It is the height of intellectual arrogance to say "This is all there can be" and at this point in time it is on the verge of stupidity to add "because it is all I can sense." So, at least, the possibility of some other forms of living existence must be left open.

What can we now develop as the essential difference between an existence in this universe and in one which is completely free of matter as we know it. We have already seen from the foregoing discussion of the material world that the former concept of "continuity" of solid form, real though it is to man, is interpreted rather more as the effect of interplay of "forces in structures" than of mass.

Before Einstein's world-shaking formula $E = Mc^2$ was made public, that formula, in essentially the same form, was used in 1904 by Hasenohrl, an Austrian scientist, to explain the observed pressure which light exerts on a surface, which, in our own day, solar "wind" experiments in space have well demonstrated and made general public knowledge. He postulated that if it were possible to confine light radiation in a massless vessel of some sort, under the pressure developed by the impacting light "corpuscles" the massless vessel would behave exactly "as if" it did, in fact, have mass. And the apparent mass would be proportional to the enclosed light energy. As the vessel would radiate the enclosed energy, the "mass" would diminish proportionately. Hasenohrl was attempting to relate, in some way, the kinetic energy of the light to its apparent "mass." In some sense, it has the characteristic of momentum. If Einstein's law is restated, in the terms $E = Mv^2$, in which the general symbolic terms for velocity, "v", is used for the velocity of light, we have a very close resemblance to the normal equation of kinetic energy. Energy is directly proportional to the product of the mass times the square of the velocity, or, specifically, Mv^2. In the case of light, the velocity in this universe is constant (approximately); hence the substitution, "c", as a constant is appropriate. Einstein's law further universalized the concept to all matter and energy. It begins to appear, by reason of the pervasiveness of that constant, in terms of all energy and all matter, to be a short step to say metaphysically that our particular universe is the one which the Creator keyed to that particular phenomenon which may be only one aspect of a truly primal energy. There could be countless others keyed to other conditioning realities. Perhaps the photon, the light "corpuscle" which has no electric charge, no mass, but as we have seen possesses "momentum," is the fundamental particle in our universe.

Imam Gazali, Muslim philosopher and mystic of the late eleventh and early twelfth centuries, wrote in his *Misket al Anwar* (Gazali, 1924): "God has seventy thousand veils of light and darkness, were He to withdraw their curtain then would the splendours of His aspect surely consume everyone who apprehended Him with his sight....That ultimate light is the final Fountainhead, who is light Himself," and "But that which has no existence for others nor for itself is assuredly the very extreme of darkness. In contrast with it is Being, which is therefore light. Thus, God most high is the only reality, as He is the only Light." This magnificent comment was foreshadowed by Augustine in the fifth century, and prophetic of Grosseteste in the twelfth and Whitehead in the twentieth.

Could light, that strange phenomenon which acts as pure energy in some modes, corresponding to the wave theory, and as matter in other modes as in the quantum theory, somehow be the ultimate "stuff" of the universe? The behavior of the photon is remarkably like that of the elusive electron. The point being made here is that we can very well conceive that our physical universe, as it reveals itself, is no more "material" than a ray of light. The discussion of the immaterial nature of the infinitely intelligent Creator and the developing ultimate "immateriality" of matter obviously establishes that there is nothing in these concepts to suggest intelligent life, as such, is, in any way, dependent upon material form, as, for instance, operating through a "solid-state" brain. Quite the contrary in logic, the solid-state form would likely be the great exception since vastly limiting the mobility and intelligence acquisition of the being. Intelligence is, therefore, not in logic dependent on matter, as such, for its existence. It appears to be far more allied to energy and there is no restriction that energy must be confined to a material form. A logical extension of both the "Big Bang" and "Constant Creation" theories is that matter is produced by transformation of an immaterial energy via creation.

Almost the only essential unforged link in logic to a free intellectual interchange between a material and an immaterial universe is one on the material side and that is the capacity of a material being to have an immaterial vector. What must be the nature of an intellectual being which could exist in both environments since that is really what the problem leads to? Obviously one independent of matter and its dimensional limitations—that is to say, one dimensionally indeterminate would qualify. For it seems clear that a being not subject to the Einstein constant or any fixed velocity limitation would be completely unaffected by it. Time, space, mass, would only exist to the extent it "wished" them to exist in the sense that it "wished" or elected to recognize them. This could be true, just as a three-dimensional creature could step over a line or not, while the two-dimensional creature referred to earlier would be stopped by the line.

Thus, a being, or faculty of a being, which could approach the Aristotelian concept of pure intellect, pure act, could operate in either mode and would satisfy the requirement. It would just not be, itself, subject to inertial or dimensional laws. The only thing left that we must accommodate to the concept of potential transcendentalism of man is the answer to the question: Does man have, as part of his essence, a quality or faculty which is pure intellect and capable of pure act, or is his humanity totally sense-limited and material?

The atheistic materialistic philosopher would say the latter, citing Pavlov's dog. What is the contrary evidence? Eventually, and perhaps not too remotely, a physical demonstration may be possible. It is known that one of the astronauts attempted some direct thought transmission experiments from the moon with unstated results. If it becomes possible to evoke this real phenomenon on command, and time the responses accurately, it would, in fact, then be possible, using the long distances in space, to overcome instrumentation difficulties and to determine if thought does travel at "infinite" velocity, or instantly. Such evidence would be almost conclusive as to the immateriality of the intellectual powers. But the existing inferential evidence is significant and convincing. Man's ability to develop and hold such abstract thoughts as human nature, human existence, God, beauty and all of his symbology in communication are disassociated from any particular material reality. Further, his capacity to be motivated to act by such thoughts and symbols and to motivate others to act by communicating such thoughts is not dependent on matter. Everything which makes a man a distinctive personality is of this genre. There is an ability to reflect on, to react to, and to affect other individuals by such purely intellectual activity, which has no materially-based quality other than action through the agency of the brain, an organic computer, faulty and slow, but with tremendous programming potential—this is the crux—it must be programmed. It is in the programming essence that man's transcendence must lie.

Studies in neurophysiology have resulted in defining the manner in which the brain functions both in purely instinctive ways and also personally when "the will" which is the self-identifying element of man takes over the functions and directs an act. Professor J.C. Eccles of Oxford University described the methodology of acts when "the mind was in liaison with the brain." In his work, *The Neurophysiological Basis of Mind,* he first establishes the facticity of mental phenomenon (self-consciousness). We recognize the difference between hallucinations and our knowledge of our real self. Our exercise of free will is our act.

When man directs his operations the activity in the cerebral cortex is of a different mode than otherwise. The electroencephalograph when in "liaison with mind" is that of a rapid irregular and low voltage mode, but of greatly elevated activity— covering a relatively large area of the cerebral cortex indicating the simultaneous stimulation of a very large number of neurons. The subsequent activity of the brain is characterized by "waves of fields of influence. . .with temporal sequences of milliseconds." The integration "within a few milliseconds, of influences picked up at hundreds of thousands of nodes would be unique." From this, Professor Eccles concludes that "thus the neurophysiological hypothesis is that the will modifies the spatio-temporal activity of the neuronal network by exerting spatio-temporal fields of influence that become effective through the unique detector function of the active cerebral cortex." By some device, the will, acting internally, impresses upon the cerebral cortex a patterned "demand for action." This pattern is detected by the neurons in the cerebral cortex and then relayed to the brain generally for execution. This hypothesis would identify the human programming activity with the mind acting on the cerebral cortex by impressing a "field of influence" which must itself be some form of energy since it derives from a capacity to act. The "mind" is identified with "soul" acting through the brain without inferring a Cartesian dichotomy.

This programming ability is the one characteristic which distinguishes man from everything else in the material surround. It is not an incidental difference; it is an essential difference. The only other being which we have been able to identify as having that same characteristic is God, the Creator. Though He is of infinite rather than of limited capacity, the nature of the programming activity, purely intellectual in its concept, is the same. God, the Creator is pure spirit but He achieves His observable material end by extension of His power through material means—for example through the instincts of the animal world, for the animals have no rational independence in the application of their instincts. They are programmed. Therefore, it is compatible that man, the intellectual and also material being, should be designed to accomplish his intellectually-conceived programmed ends through material means—a part of his very being.

Brand Blanshard, Sterling Professor Emeritus of Yale University, in an article "A Verdict on Ephiphenomenalism" in the volume, *Current Philosophic Issues,* published in 1966, discussed the nature of man's intellectual processes. He said,

If we grant that the thought process is at times purposive and under rational control, we are committed to a theory of mind and body that is far removed from epiphenomenalism. We need not deny the epiphenomenalist thesis that mind has its roots in the body, if that means that certain states of the brain provide the necessary condition of certain states of mind. We must, however, deny that they are the sufficient condition. For the urges, pushes and strivings that are essential to mind are activities with ends. These ends have patterns of their own. These patterns affect the course of their conscious realization. The patterns are not physical, nor can they be the replicas or reflections of any merely physical whole. Thinking in art and morals and even mathematics is neither the reflection in consciousness of a mechanical order in the brain nor the tracing with the mind's endeavour to realize in thought an ideal order which could satisfy an inner demand. The nearer thought comes to its goal, the more it finds itself under constraint by that goal, and dominated in its creative effort by aesthetic or moral or logical relevance. These relations of relevance are not physical or psychological relations. They are normative relations that can enter into the mental current because that current is truly, not just seemingly, teleological. Their operation marks the presence of a different type of law, which supervenes upon physical and psychological laws when purpose takes control. (Blanshard, 1966, pp. 118-119).

In the same general vein, but emphasizing the criticality of the higher mental processes to all human activities, sociologist Pitirim Sorokin said,

The integral cognition is particularly necessary in the cognition of man and of psychosocial and cultural phenomena, because the superorganic human world is made up not only of physical and biological forms of being, but also the "immaterial"—unconscious, conscious-rational, and superconscious-superrational forms and energies of the total reality; and because man is not only physical object and biological organism, but a rational thinker and doer, and, particularly, a "super-sensory and superrational" creator, he is an eminent participant in creative processes of the cosmos. (Sorokin, 1966, p. 257).

But we still have to satisfy ourselves that the programming essence, the soul, if you will, even given this immaterial capability does not nevertheless destruct simultaneously with the body. This represents the difference between possession of the capability and its exercise. Since it is not itself directly material nor dependent on matter for its field of action but only for its function in a material universe, it need not perish with the material if there is a purpose for it beyond this life. We have noted before that the intellectual operation through matter, the subordination of an intellectual faculty to a material environment, would in logic be the exception. Hence an operation of the human intellectual capacity apart from its bodily supportive mechanism would appear to be consistent with that idea. Here again, recourse must be made to the realm of metaphysics and to the attributes which we have said must flow from the Creator's essence. We have said He must be infinitely purposeful and consistent. If He has designed a creature and given it certain powers, He must, to be consistent, will that it exercise those powers, and that those powers, in turn, should work toward the implicit ends for which the creature was designed, as identified by those powers. What about man's powers and their implicit ends? One of these obviously has been the ability to conceive of the Creator, a deity system, and to worship Him. This is almost a universal human characteristic and power.

But more generally, there is absolutely no need for a rational being in a material universe if that materiality is the end product, and an infinitely consistent Creator must adapt means to ends. In fact, things generally in the biologic realm, get along much better without man. Man has consistently assumed, by his activity, that the world was his to exploit for his benefit. He has, in fact, severely overplayed the part by assuming he was its owner. And—if the hierarchy of existence through levels—inorganic, organic vegetal, organic animate, organic animate rational—as it has appeared in the history of the earth, is the result of the Creator's purposefulness, is it not a proper conclusion that the end of this chain, this building to support an immaterial consciousness, was not also the end for which man was created—to achieve a transcendent existence by some process like the butterfly from the earthbound caterpillar? If man has the power and capability to live a transcendent existence, must it not also be an implicit end? Is it not a more fitting answer that the end of all the material activity, for all the billions of years, at least in this solar system, and perhaps in countless others was to exercise the Creator's powers in producing a being or beings with physical material origins which might still transcend through his power to the higher spiritual life; a creature He designed from such low beginnings to share in His programming powers and thus glorify Him in His creative mode by a freely-willed spiritual response? What other purpose can we discern for the Creator—pure spirit, pure intelligence, pure act? And there would be a purpose.

As before, what is the alternative which we must examine? The alternative is that the soul does not survive, in any form, after death. There is no reincarnation, no reabsorption to the "eternal intellect" of Aristotle—nothing. Now, how does this look from the standpoint of an infinitely purposeful, consistent Creator? The rational programming powers are merely to serve a biologic end, and a higher quality, and it is higher, thereby designed to serve a lower end, and unnecessarily as has been noted. The apes do quite well without man and his programming and so did the mosquitoes and cockroaches for a long period before man—though surely they would miss him.

Now, we might well repeat Einstein's observation recorded on the wall in the Institute of Advanced Study at Princeton: "God is sophisticated, but He is not malicious." (Frank, 1963, p. 284). For in giving man this in-built craving for happiness unachievable in this life, and dangling this bright hope before his intellect, urging him to strive and sacrifice donkey-like for an impossible goal would be malicious, as well as unpurposeful and inconsistent, to a high degree. The alternative, thus, does not appear a very probable one, given the Creator and the evidence previously provided.

The concept of entropy is one derived from the field of thermo-dynamics and, in its broadest application, is related to the observed phenomenon that, in the universe, neglecting any creative agency, the *availability* of energy steadily decreases while the quantity of kinetic and potential energy remains the same in consonance with the law of conservation of energy. It states, in essence, that the differential in temperature between the heat source and sink would continue to diminish so that, eventually, and it is asymptotic only, heat transfer (the basic mode) would cease. It is, as far as can be observed, an irreversible trend.

Looking at the universe, as we did with Dyson, in terms of

a thermodynamic system it is apparent that vast quantities of energy are constantly being transformed. But, of all these, only gravitational exchange and the related energy of orbital and rotational motion took place at 0 entropy. This is to say that no degradation of energy took place in the process since heat transfer was not involved. Some others, notably nuclear, were very efficient, which taken together explain the great potential duration of the universe. As the life processes, chemical in nature became involved, the entropy was greatly increased culminating in the biologic interaction, from initial photosynthesis to the final bacteriological decomposition.

All of the universe is powered by this hierarchial energy structure. The system calls for an explanation and, in a sense, goes back to Kapp's concept of the uncaused events. It will be recalled that the source of this energy was itself zero energy—"nothing." And, that the universe, in its origin, gradually emerging, and its continuation, was supplied by "nothing." Energy units in the form of hydrogen atoms were creating themselves "from nothing" continuously and at an enormous rate, and always on the same unchangeable design. The alternative to this unattractive logic, and it is scarcely logic, must lie in the metaphysical, in the infinite, immaterial Creator previously developed and defined as pure intellect, and, at this point, it would appear appropriate to add, pure source of energy in all its forms. For it appears necessary, as Dyson suggested, that the spiritual existence have a close kinship to energy in a form from which the "mechanical" energy of the universe could flow.

If we admit the existence of the physical universe—as we have seen some philosophers do not—and then try to deny any other form of being, we are placed in a dilemma which makes Camus' problem of evil child's play by comparison. We must select one of two options: (1) accept the idea of a limited physical universe in isolation, or (2) accept the idea of an infinite physical universe; i.e., one with infinite and temporal extension. Hartmann could be an ontologist as an atheist only because he said, and rigidly followed, his dictum that it was not the responsibility of the philosopher to provide answers, only to formulate the question. He would not attempt the solution of this dilemma.

The physical universe presents to us the picture of a real energy system—a system as Dyson also pointed out having an origin in time and gradually approaching burn out. A characteristic of systems in the physical order is that they interface with other systems. A true "closed" physical system: i.e., one which is totally self-contained, is only an inexact theoretical concept. There is an overall entropic decay rate in physical systems. They are not steady-state. If, however, they are to maintain operations of a constant output level, there is a need for an energy source equal to the output plus internal entropic decay and further for a "heat sink" to dispose of this residual energy at the lowest level of the system operation. An energy differential or gradient must be maintained or operations cease. It is the flow of energy from high to low "potential" which produces "work"; e.g., an expansion in space. If the physical universe is currently operating as a "closed" system, and it appears to be, it will gradually lose efficiency and approach a quiescent base level. This is in accord with the "Big Bang" idea. But at some point in time (or at time zero) it must have received an enormous energy charge from some source external to what was to become the physical universe we know. The universe is still apparently working on that "charge." This is obviously not a universe in isolation.

Of course, under the constant creation theory, we are not dealing with a closed system at all but one constantly receiving energy from some external source and by constant expansion maintaining the constant energy differential—some "transducer" is providing energy, from an external system, to maintain the expansion. Either way, there appears to be no conceivable universe in isolation.

The second horn of the dilemma, that of a physical universe of infinite extent, is a contradiction in terms. In the constant creation mode, it was said that the universe is so vast in extent that it can be considered infinite. However, the universe cannot have *physical reality* without extension in space and it cannot be infinite if it has extension in space. If it is expanding, there is still a "frontier" into which it is expanding.

The usual fallback position following Kant is that we cannot know the "unknowable"—the nature of the interface. Even if that be granted, we *can* "know" that there must be, or has been, an interface and that at the "other side" it is not "physical." Further, it must be as real as the physical universe, since it supports the physical universe. That there is a real, non-physical, "system" in being is the only way out in logic.

It must be non-physical. That is, it must be without extension in space—else it is only an appendage to the present physical universe—a part of the same system and subject to the same limitations. For the interface, the "boundary" through which the energy passes in Kant's world would be a phenomena/noumena impasse. But here, there is a physical predicate demanding a non-physical subject—a physical effect from a non-physical cause. If there are no other answers and this provides the answer with no contradiction or difficulty except that the nature of the noumena cannot be known, then this must be accepted at least *ex hypothesi* until some other "not now known" possible answer is forthcoming. Further, this interfacing non-physical "system" must be a-causal—something impossible to say about any physical system. This poses no particular problem. Strictly speaking, causality implies a temporal relationship—a before and after situation which would have no real meaning in eternity in which *dependency* better expresses the relationship of a subordinate system to a superior system.

At the interface, at t = o, marking the beginning of time either as a point, a line, or a zone, a physical universe came into existence or began coming into existence. On the physical side it is viewed as a time and space-caused event, or series of events; on the non-physical side as a fulfillment of a specific free commitment in eternity to energize and maintain a subordinate physical system in time. As to the intrinsic nature of the supporting system we can know very little. There is no need to know much—enough that it is non-physical and competent to create and support the physical universe, which it is since the latter exists and is maintained. The non-physical system provides an answer to those free-standing predicates, those causeless effects which stand staring at us at the temporal boundary of the physical universe, however conceived. There is something unfinished in concept or rather unbegun in reality about those freely appearing hydrogen atoms that happen into and out of existence willy nilly like the smile of the Cheshire cat.

Where does man stand in the entropy series? As to the world about us, we are in the biochemical series having a relatively high entropy. But there is another aspect of entropy in common usage. With the development of complex information systems, information was conceived as energy. As we have seen information is accepted by the brain from sense input by energetic stimulation of neurons. This process is analogous to the way in which data is fed into computers. In the language of communicating and data processing entropy is a measure of disorganization (chaos) and information is "negative entropy." A rule following the entropy analogy is that information cannot increase in any operation. Now, the essential difference between man and computer in terms of informational entropy is that man defies the rule. He increases information as a result of his data processing. The entire world shows forth this fact. If we combine the two sets of ideas entropy in mechanics and entropy in communication and information and, acknowledging that both are forms of energy but quite different forms, man is continuously converting mechanical biochemical energy at high entropy into information at decreasing entropy—negative entropy in fact. His *creational* mental activity is primarily nonmaterial. He becomes a transducer of energy from mechanical to intellectual which is to say spiritual forms. He is in this view a net producer of energy.

Intelligence, whether that of God or man, can be viewed as a personal information and energy management and control system. With God it is intrinsic, one with His complete essence. With man it is also intrinsic, but as a characteristic of his human nature. The entire human organism, material and spiritual vectors is dedicated to acquisition, development, exploitation, management and control of information for deployment of energy to further previously selected personal ends. This is intelligence in man controlling human activity. The material vector is subordinate to, and under control of, the spiritual vector but is essential in a material environment. It is the primary information acquisition system at the data input level.

Man, as a being, having certain powers which are not physical in their ends of application, acts through material means supplied by the physical energy source. But man is, in some manner, supplied by "energy" independently in his "control circuitry," to draw a crude parallel with sophisticated automated heavy equipment where the "quality" of energy required is quite different in the production and control modes. The terms, inspiration, insight, grace, aesthetic intuition, have been variously applied to the immaterial energy which is dimly perceived, yet acknowledged almost universally, as having a real, rather than an imaginary, existence. And, while the terms are applied usually to mean the more exotic aspects of true creative thought or action, yet all men, even the most worldly, must acknowledge that it exists in virtually all their acts. Every significant decision follows a process in which the "higher" functions of the intellect are involved and which utilize this energy. It lies at the roots of the nature of human rational life itself.

Induced by the immanent symmetry observed throughout creation, I would make the following proposals. As a parallel to the basic entropy system which leads to the postulation of a spiritual, infinite source of mechanical energy, there is a corresponding "entropy system" or better, perhaps, a negative entropy system which leads from the same infinite source. There is also the absolute or infinite form of rational existence to provide spiritual energy to a sequence of rational life forms. In man, the end of the chain in this material order, the capability to utilize this energy at the purely spiritual level, implies his capability to exist at the transcendental spiritual level, independently of his mortal, matter-constrained life.

The naive mind historically, and almost universally, viewed the universe as the work of God. It was accepted as fact as naturally as the facts of birth and death. Only when the true informational situation was obscured by all the "noise" of materialism was the idea of God found difficult. The information entropic situation deteriorated with the disorganization of modern society.

It has struck the writer that in the outpourings of science fiction the human characters in their relationships with the various rational beings—malevolent or benevolent they encounter of all configurations and composition show a greater kinship to those beings than they do to their closest terrestrial cohabitants such as their pet dog or the great apes. And most major modern industrial nations spend a substantial amount, continuously scanning the universe for signals from some other rational beings in the deep regions of space, fully aware that, if such a signal in rational symbolism should be received, our relationship with that being or those beings would be closer than any relationship to any animal here on earth because that being would also possess access to the spiritual energy source, that inspiration necessary to intelligence. The conclusion seems inescapable that the spiritual and mechanical orders of energy are qualitatively different but from the same infinite source. Man not only considers himself, but is, more than just a biological extension of terrestrial animal life and the mechanical energy system. The alternative, that an extension of the biologic material structure can produce a non-biologic immaterial emanation, leaves too wide a gap to be spanned by logical inference. Man does not consider he has, nor does he have, a close fundamental kinship to the beasts in his rational life. To limit man's existence to the purely biological is, in fact, a highly illogical and improbable proposition.

To close this entropic viewpoint a quotation from *Einstein, His Life and Times* by Phillip Frank, concerning the Newtonian system which largely spurred the Age of Enlightenment and its materialism seems appropriate. It shows Newton's concept of God in relation to energy and that the whole chaos of

Materialism resulted largely because the "dabblers in science" of the time, failed to understand Newton's concepts in their very basic principles.

For a long time, no one had realized precisely what was the actual link between Newton's theological reflections and his scientific work. It was often asserted that they had no logical connection and that his reflections were significant only from a purely emotional standpoint or as a concession to the theological spirit of his time. But this is certainly not so. Although, there might have been some doubt about this point earlier. Yet, since the discovery of the diary of David Gregory, a friend and student of Newton's, we know definitely that Newton introduced the theological hypothesis in order to give his theory of empty and absolute space a logically unobjectionable form. Gregory's diary for 1705 contains an entry concerning a conversation with Newton on this topic. It says: "What the space that is empty of body is filled with, the plain truth is that he (Newton) believes God to be omnipresent in the literal sense: and that as we are sensible of objects when their images are brought home within the brain, so God must be sensible of everything, being intimately present with everything: for he (Newton) supposes that as God is present in space where there is no body, He is present in space when a body is also present.

E. A. Burtt in *The Metaphysical Foundations of Modern Physical Science,* published in 1925, interprets correctly:

"Certainly, at least, God must know whether any given motion is absolute or relative. The divine consciousness furnishes the ultimate center or reference for absolute motion. Moreover, the animism in Newton's conception of force plays a part in the premise of the position. God is the ultimate originator of motion. Thus, in the last analysis, all relative or absolute motion is the resultant of an expenditure of the divine energy. Whenever the divine intelligence is cognizant of such an expenditure, the motion so added to the system of the world must be absolute."

Section 6—A View from a Functional Anthropology

Looking now at the anthropological aspect, there are two possibilities, and only two, which must be appraised and the evidence weighed. One will be that man is only a gifted animal—the "trousered ape"—a biological entity and nothing more. The alternative will be that he is both a biologic being and a being which has the extra dimension which is spiritual or immaterial and hence capable of survival in some manner independent of the physical universe. The manner of the spiritual existence is not at issue at this point. Anthropologists do not address this question any more than physicists do the origin of matter as a part of the discipline, but some of the data develop concepts which tend to point, with greater probability, toward one possibility than to the other. Regardless of which of the two alternatives we take, there are common grounds which can be stated as agreed points for departure. Those should be stated, and settled, so as not to be brought in later and held up as arguments for one side or the other.

Over the thousands of years of known human existence, man's survival has depended upon his ability to adapt himself or his environment to meet his needs. This adaptation has been primarily non-biologic, though there are exceptions, such as modified pigmentation and minor adjustments of bodily configuration under climatic and nutritional influences. But, in general it can be stated that it was through man's ability to reflect on observed physical phenomena, and the consequences of his alternative responses, which permitted man to dominate his surroundings. To this extent man has been oriented to empiricism from the beginning. Those practices which were functional over the long term survived. Those practices which were not functional were discarded or reduced to symbolic vestiges.

One of the ubiquitous responses to man's observations has been a belief in some deity system, a transcendental relationship between man and some being or group of beings in which there was a personal involvement—in which his personal behavior was reflected by reward or punishment—requiring at times propitiation and sacrifice and having a profound impact on his social relationships. The idea of morality did not evolve from a sense of love of neighbor as the "noble savage" of Rousseau, because man naturally would tend to be more Hobbesian as he left the competitive jungle, or Eden, for that matter. The idea of morality rose, instead, from the functional requirement, readily observable, that if he were to survive in a hostile world, he needed cooperation, and in turn was expected to cooperate.

Anti-social acts were thus observed to be self-defeating and non-functional. They were labeled immoral, and because they were immoral, they became an object of moral sanction of some form, or other—in most cases, by an avenging or rewarding God.

To this point, there would be general agreement by proponents of either the pure biologic or transcendental viewpoint. The separation comes when we look at man, the rational being as compared to the rest of the physical-life forms which either instinctively cooperate or perish. The ants, bees, wolves, baboons, all cooperate. In a broad sense, any enduring ecosystem is a cooperative enterprise. But, in these there is clearly no concept of morality, only biologic drive.

One would be led to question the functionality of a rational intelligence which the strict evolutionists must hold was gradually purchased only at the price of gradual and very significant loss of strict biologic capability. The increased brain capacity demanded several disadvantageous biologic changes, emphasizing somewhat more in the female. The larger cranium of the offspring required a larger pelvic structure in the female and resulted in loss of agility, and the longer gestation and extended period of helpless infancy of the offspring were a great drain on the total adult resources. Further, the configuration of the skull to accommodate the increase in brain size was detrimental to the physical strength of neck and jaw. The fully upright stance was scarcely functional, as all of our sacroiliac problems tell us.

Under early primitive conditions, the sacrifice of agility, physical strength, and natural weapons for a modicum of increased intelligence and their result, modern man, would at best be marginal. Viewed objectively from the purely biologic position—including that of the gross ecology—human intelligence is a disaster, an utterly nonfunctional monstrosity in an otherwise rather satisfactory, functional, physical universe. The only creature able to reflect on his multitudinous problems, to anticipate the future pain and agony of life, and the certainty of his decreasing capacity with age and ignominious end—it is a hideous denouement to the biological series of changes which brought him about. Is this horrible anomaly, man, the logical result of any truly adaptive biologic process, the result of functional selection and regrouping of characteristics at each step then and there adaptive to survival? For we dare not base it on predictive conditions ten years, one hundred years, or ten thousand years in the future. Among primates, the baboon appears to have a far better solution, most of the advantages and few disadvantages.

It is important now to look at that point in time when the

trend to rational man began. In accordance with strict evolutionary principles—and—it is clear, if we could visualize a universe that somehow kicked itself into existence, there is no other possible route but random selection between alternatives in the statistical sense. Any tendency toward rational behavior would be adaptively, but randomly, selected in preference to continued instinctive behavior by a survivability coefficient. By reason of randomly selective biologic processes, a line which could have run parallel to that followed by the instinctive great apes, headed down the path eventually leading to man. When the separation began is argumentative, but it had to break someplace. Thereafter, the option was made virtually at every step, at every selection point—which is really to say at every generation until man was evolved, the probable number being between 50,000 and 100,000 sequential events. The lack of paleontologic evidence to the contrary suggests a small population throughout this period for all the logical ancestors of man, so there was no great number of concurrent events.

Let us examine the hypothesis mathematically. In order for the process to have progressed in accordance with the laws of adaptive selection, the increment of survivability $\triangle$ s for increased tendency to rational capacity $\triangle$ R must have exceeded the negative increment or decrement in loss of biologic capacity $\triangle$ B . This selection would have been made only when $\frac{\triangle s}{\triangle t}$, the increment of survivability at that increment in time was positive. That is when $\frac{\triangle s}{\triangle t} \geq 0$, or when $\frac{\triangle s}{\triangle t} + \left(\frac{-\triangle B}{\triangle t}\right) \geq 0 \leq \frac{\triangle s}{\triangle t}$. Yet, reasoning capacity in any true human sense must have been a very late stage after much preliminary development. Even 50,000 or 100,000 generation decision points do not allot much leeway for setback in this train. By a great preponderance, the original split and succeeding splits must have been positive, $\frac{\triangle R}{\triangle t} + \left(\frac{-\triangle B}{\triangle t}\right) \geq 0$.

Oddly, from a purely statistical point, there appear not to have been any offshoots except that resulting in man—in which the trend was positive—for all men are genetically of the same species, fully capable of continued reproducibility—no races in which mating produces sterile hybrids. Vision developed independently among virtually all animate forms of life. Such an exotic faculty as flight developed among insects, reptiles, and mammals, yet rational intelligence developed only in man.

One other point: since the appearance of Cro-Magnon man: during the Magdalenian period, some 15,000 to 20,000 years ago, there have been no significant changes in man. In fact, perhaps, a retrogression. He was tall (approximately 5 feet 11 inches and had a significantly larger cranial capacity than to-day's modern man—1650 cc vs. about 1350 cc). He had a high forehead, strong, well-developed chin and nose, and was highly artistic. Cro-Magnon man, of course, was a modern man. But it is estimated that some 95 percent of all the human species have existed since his time and yet, suddenly, the trend stopped for the last thousand or so generations. The enhanced chances for mutation which the larger population would have en-couraged, have produced nothing in the way of a higher bio-logic type of rational being.

Now, all of this is not related to argue against evolution. Be-cause such an argument is of no significance to this study, only against evolution by random chance, with a survivability bias but not in accordance with some intelligently planned sequence (without teleological development if you will). The human brain is only one of many physical developments in the history of life which appear highly improbable unless an intelligence was directing the sequence. Vision is another. Countless generations would have proceeded toward the development of the struc-ture of the eye before any vision was possible.

As it develops with regard to rational man, it is not enough to state the usual reply: given sufficient opportunity, anything can happen. The opportunities are limited. We are talking about one chain. All others, if there were any, were dead-end streets, long past. And we find no trace of them in the last forty thou-sand years at least.

The biologic evolutionary principle of itself, standing alone, is contradictory to the otherwise universal principle that things tend to move down the potential gradient, from high tempera-ture to low temperature, high elevation to low elevation, high voltage to low voltage, high intensity radiation to low intensity, and from superior to subordinate. Why should the trend in the observable thrust of life be from lower forms to higher forms of existence unless there were an external source of energy to cause the counter flow? Just as one needs heaters, pumps, gener-ators, microwave boosters or training facilities to reverse the trend in the other forms of energy mentioned—and life is an energy-dependent form—it seems logically clear that an exter-nal "booster" is required.

The paleontologic record is plain, there has been a trend to higher life forms. But is the record plain enough to indicate that there was no planning, programming or energizing to bring it about as the strict evolutionists hold? I think not. Quite the contrary, why should the single-cell animal organisms, by a long series of quantum jumps by species and genera, eventuate in man—a rational, intellectual, being where there is no evidence of material precedent? Biologic survivability. By no means! Survivability is certainly on the side of the durable amoeba. Complexity, for complexity's sake? No. Where else is it exhibited? Complexity fosters breakdown. Simplicity is a more consistent theme in the universe unless there is a contrary functional purpose. But what function could there be in a non-purposeful biologic world with only a biologic randomly selected end? And if there is a non-biologic end, it must be to fit a non-biologic program and purpose.

We have seen that the survival bias itself is critically dependent upon the existence of two non-random traits—the "urge" to survive and the "urge" to reproduce. In the first life forms, the potency, capacity, and "urge" had to be present. The urge had to precede the act and the capacity to act had to exist in potency to respond to the urge. The complex organic molecules in the primordial seas, postulated by the evolutionists, had to have these non-random traits *ab initio* before the life process could begin. The urge and capacity to seek and use nutrient and the urge and capacity to reproduce.

Concerning the probity of non-purposive evolution, Brand Blanshard, in the previously cited work, said:

> He (Aristotle) would have rejected, and would surely have been right in rejecting, the conception of evolution as a process which, looked back upon from the attitude it has reached, reveals itself as a chapter of accidents. The story of the emergence of mind as a set of blind lurches by matter, all but a few of which were terminal, and of the surviving lurches being allowed to lunge and stagger on till they produced an organism that somehow floundered aimlessly through *Hamlet* and *Principia Mathematica,* seems, to me, a fairy tale. And how can it be denied that if there is nothing in human activity inexplicable in the end by physics, this is the story we are being told?
>
> If we find ourselves swept away by that tale, I suggest that it is because we are suffering a sort of hypnosis, not by science—I should want to reject that emphatically—but by a philosophy of science that is dogmatic and unempirical. It is dogmatic because it accepts too uncritically the assumption that science,

in the end, means physics. It is unempirical in the sense that it closes its eyes to a range of facts that can be ascertained about mind by directly examining its higher processes. The facts about invention, discovery, creation, dialectical thinking, are as truly facts that require explanation as any others and to me at least they seem to be facts in which the operation of purpose and necessity is too importunate to be explained away. If it cannot be explained away, then science, instead of ignoring them should look at them straight and steadily, and revise its methods to deal with them. The revision would have to be considerable. For science would have to start dealing with man not only as a cybernetic marvel, but also as a thinking reed. (Blanshard, 1966, pp. 119, 120).

Turning now to the cultural sequence in the "pre-civilized" world, we can perceive that the change between human and instinctive existence appears suddenly linked in a four-way manner. Talcott Parsons, whom we met before, dean of U.S. sociologists, lists religion as one of the four evolutionary universals, with the need of such a device recognized as functional. In an article "Evolutionary Universals in Society" in *The American Sociological Review*, Vol. 29, 3 June 1964, he says:

From his distinctive organic endowment and from his capacity for and ultimate dependence on generalized learning, man derives his unique ability to create and transmit culture. To quote the biologist Alfred Emerson within a major sphere of man's adaptation, the "gene" has been replaced by the "symbol." Hence, it is not only the genetic constitution of the species that determines the "needs" confronting the environment, but this constitution, plus the cultural tradition. A set of "normative expectations" pertaining to man's relation to his environment delineates the ways in which adaptation should be developed and extended. Within the relevant range, cultural innovations, especially definitions of what man's life ought to be, thus replace Darwinian variations in genetic constitution.

Cultural "patterns" or orientations, however, do not implement themselves. Properly conceived in their most fundamental aspect as "religious," they must be articulated with the environment in ways that make

effective adaptation possible. I am inclined to treat
the entire orientational aspect of culture itself, in the
simplest, least evolved forms, as directly synonymous
with religion. But since a cultural system—never any
more an individual matter than a genetic pattern—is
shared among a plurality of individuals, mechanisms
of communication must exist to mediate this sharing. The fundamental evolutionary universal here is
language: no concrete human group lacks it. Neither
communication nor the learning processes that make
it possible, however, is conceivable without deter-
minately organized relations among those who teach
and learn and communicate.

The evolutionary origin of social organization seems
to be kinship. In an evolutionary sense, it is an extension of the mammalian system of bisexual
reproduction. The imperative of socialization is of
course a central corollary of culture, as is the need
to establish a viable social system to "carry" the culture. From one viewpoint, the core of the kinship
system is the incest taboo, or, more generally, the rules
of exogamy and endogamy structuring relations of
descent, affinity, and residence. Finally, since the cultural level of action implies the use of brain, hands,
and other organs in actively coping with the physical environment, we may say that culture implies the
existence of technology, which is, in its most undifferentiated form, a synthesis of empirical knowledge and practical techniques.

These four features of even the simplest action system "religion," communication with language, social
organization through kinship, and technology—may
be regarded as an integrated set of evolutionary
universals at even the earliest human level. No known
human society has existed without all four in
relatively definite relations to each other. In fact, their
presence constitutes the very minimum that may be
said to mark a society as truly human.

Systematic relations exist not only among these four
elements themselves, but between them and the more
general framework of biological evolution. Technology clearly is the primary focus of the organization
of the adaptive relations of the human system to its
physical environment. Kinship is the social extension

of the individual organism's basic articulation to the species through bisexual reproduction. But, through plasticity and the importance of learning, cultural and symbolic communications are integral to the human level of individual personality organization. Social relations among personalities, to be distinctively human, must be mediated by linguistic communication. Finally, the main cultural patterns that regulate the social, psychological, and organic levels of the total system of action are embodied (the more primitive the system, the more exclusively so) in the religious tradition, the focus of the use of symbolization to control the variety of conditions to which a human system is exposed.

How did this unique linkage evolve? Human society began, as Parsons implies, when the four universals appeared and then were not separated, but appeared as an integral basis of activity. And man does not exist separate from society. If it was evolutionary in process, the probabilities point, as in Dyson's cosmic "hang-ups," to a result of purposeful activity by some external agency. For a linkage was necessary. All four must proceed concurrently and did so, and do so in primitive groups today. And the metaphysical, cosmological, moral orientation involved in Parsons' "religion" was based not on a theoretical construct, but what the given tribal group saw as a reality. What their community view was, may have been only a "first approximation," but it was an attempt to interpret existence holistically in all its aspects. The compartmentalization process was far in the future. Alfonzo Ortiz, an anthropologist, and himself a Tewa, demonstrates this among the Tewas. The members of the tribe met socially, discussed, worked, hunted and worshipped all in a unified, closely coherent activity. Respecting the Tewas of the Pueblo Indians in New Mexico, Ortiz says,

> For Geertz [another anthropologist] as for me, culture refers to a system of historically derived meanings and conventional understandings embodied in symbols; meanings and understandings which derive from the social order, yet which also serve to reinforce and perpetuate that social order. More specifically I focus here on the more intellectual aspects of Tewa culture—on the ideas, rules, and principles, as these are reflected in mythology, world view, and

ritual, by means of which the Tewa organize their
thought and conduct. I believe further that the symbolic statements, representations, and acts reflected
in Tewa mythology, world view, and ritual are more
than epiphenomenal to social relations. Rather, as I
shall attempt to demonstrate, they serve not only to
reflect these social relations but to give them direction and continuity as well.

While I concern myself primarily with thought
rather than action, with the rules governing conduct
rather than the conduct itself, there is such a goodness of fit between the two among the Tewa that
such an approach does not serve to mislead.

Clifford Geertz defines world view as "a people's
picture of the way things, in sheer actuality are, their
concept of nature, of self, of society. It contains their
most comprehensive ideas of order." I have attempted
to determine, then, how a reasonable Tewa every man
would answer for himself questions such as the following. Who am I? Where did I come from? How
did I get here? With whom do I move through life?
What are the boundaries of the world within which
I move? What kind of order exists within it? How
did suffering, evil, and death come to be in this
world? What is likely to happen to me when I die?
The general point of view from which I have approached the hypothetical Tewa every man is the
"view of man as a symbolizing, conceptualizing,
meaning-seeking animal which...cannot live in a
world it cannot understand." (Ortiz, 1969).

And the idea of just how non-functional the solely biologic
viewpoint is can be gained if we now consider the strict evolutionists biologic development of man in the rational mode, conjoined with the physical.

If we take as our model of conjunction the point of "initial
rational development," the situation in an advanced "tribal"community among the present day non-human primates, the baboons, we see a "social" group with strongly developed instincts
of group survival, even to the "sacrifice" of the individual for
the group as under attack conditions. As the rational mode takes
over from the instinctive, what rational mechanism would replace the purely biologic physical drive for group survival, even
recognizing the fact that there would be a gradual exchange

if the process were purely biologic? If the rationality were basically biologic, could it be enlightened self-interest? There is no body of culturally-derived habits and mores of millenia of the theistic background to guide the poor semi-beasts as exists in modern civilization. Though manifestly unprovable, the likelihood is the transition would have been Hobbesian and fatal. How much more functional was the instinctive in a biologic world! Man is indeed intellectually over-qualified in his physical environment!

Auguste Comte in his concept of the three stages of civilization postulated that observations show the first levels of society are theologic, the second metaphysical, the third scientific, or rational. He presumed an initial theistic orientation in the primitive civilization, but if that orientation came from the biologic source, how was it derived? Can a biologic source conceive a non-biologic existence? How did the original "myth" come about? Certainly baboons and apes do not have them. Comte was not a functionalist in the Parsonsian sense or he would have had to say that the development, as he envisioned it, was "functional to survival at each state. The theistic orientation was necessary for primitive survival regardless of its source but if he pondered further, how can he have avoided the conclusion that a theistic-basic orientation was as necessary for survival of the species in advanced civilization as in primitive, or, more so, given the suicidal pressures and murderous capability of society even in his day.

The theistic orientation was functional, even necessary, to survival initially and it remains so today. If, as seems logically unavoidable, the development of man as a rational being was the purposeful result of a purposeful Creator, again the inescapable conclusion must be drawn that the rational function was to serve the rational end of producing a transcendent creature capable of an ultimate spiritual, material-independent existence in union with that Creator.

As sociologist Wrong says in the article previously cited,

> But I do not see how at the level of theory, sociologists can fail to make assumptions about human nature. If our assumptions are left implicit, we will inevitably presuppose a view of man that is tailor-made to our special needs: when our sociological theories over stress the stability and integration of society, we will end up imagining that man is the disembodied, conscience driven, status-seeking

phantom of current theory. We must do better if we really wish to win credit outside our ranks for special understanding of man, that plausible creature whose wagging tongue so often hides the despair and darkness in his heart. (Wrong, 1966).

We are at another logic gate, this time to make those assumptions about human nature that Wrong suggests and this time we have but two alternatives: These are:

1. Biologic man, the gifted animal, the "trousered ape," intrinsically irresponsible, the evolutionary descendant from nothing, doomed to nothingness.

2. Transcendental man, the intelligent, free-willed being responsible for his acts, selective of his future, destined for immortality, the well-loved creature of an infinitely powerful, intelligent and loving God.

It could be charged that expressing the choice in this way is a cheap emotional appeal. The writer has placed the options in the stark contrast in which they actually stand, and which the evidence delineates both ways. The statement and the evidence show just how futile and nihilistic the biologic concept must be to a rational being. On the one hand, the statement on biologic man presents a view stripped of the perfume and funeral parlor pink gauze. On the other hand, the statement on transcendental man shows how rich and suggestive of happiness and rewarding of our efforts in this life is that concept.

The point being made is that a sociologist, if he is going to do as Dennis Wrong suggests, must stop at this logic gate and decide before traveling on. Only one of these selections has objective reality, the other is a fiction. The writer believes the probabilities are strongly supportive, again approaching certitude, of the second option of transcendental man. So why should we spend so much time basing theory on the improbable first option. It offers no solution whatever to the Hobbesian question to a society convinced of that viewpoint. Sociology from that perspective looks like a science doomed to predecease its doomed clientage. Freud in his *Introductory Lecture on Psycho-Analysis* given in Vienna in the winter session of 1915-16 said,

> We believe that civilization has been created under the pressure of the exigencies of life at the cost of satisfaction of the instincts; and we believe that civilization is to a large extent being constantly created anew,

since each individual who makes a fresh entry into human society repeats this sacrifice of instinctual satisfaction for the benefit of the whole community. Among the instinctual forces which are put to this use the sexual impulses play an important part; in this process they are sublimated—that is to say, they are diverted from their sexual aims and directed to others that are socially higher and no longer sexual. But this arrangement is unstable; the sexual instincts are imperfectly tamed, and, in the case of every individual who is supposed to join in the work of civilization, there is a risk that his sexual instincts may refuse to be put to that use. Society believes that no greater threat to its civilization could arise than if the sexual instincts were to be liberated and returned to their original aims. (Freud, 1963, pp. 22, 23).

A person is led to ask, looking around at Western society today, how much longer the convinced "trousered apes" are going to be willing to make such sacrifices in such a patently foolish cause—and, of course, Freud was not suggesting that they should or would—but, what a tragedy it is if, as is highly probable, that projected exclusively biologic viewpoint is objectively incorrect. What a loss of human talent, of fruitful human capacity, of happiness, is entailed in the error. And, on the other hand, to complete the picture, what is lost if the second viewpoint is taken and then, even remotely, is incorrect? No one will ever know. Is there anything which would not be better because of its exercise as the ages past so clearly show? Even the "as if" construct of the second alternative is preferable to the reality of the first in terms of preservation of society. And to speak of intellectual "honesty" is a ridiculous argument in such circumstances. Honesty is a meaningless concept to a piece of protoplasm. As Sartre would say, "To whom is honesty owed?"

Voltaire aptly said, "If God did not exist, we would have to invent Him." Ironically, the few, but highly visible modern "God is dead" theologians, widely publicized by a red blazoned cover of *Time* magazine a few years back, take the second part of Voltaire's statement literally, and say this is exactly what happened though just as we have seen, certainly this was not Voltaire's view, anticleric though he was and, just as certainly, all signs point the other way.

Even Bio-psychologist Sigmund Freud could not stand his own materialistic conclusions. As he said somewhat wistfully,

We may insist as often as we like that man's intellect is powerless in comparison with his instinctual life, and we may be right in this. Nevertheless, there is something peculiar about his weakness. The voice of the intellect is a soft one, but it does not rest till it has gained a hearing. Finally, after a countless succession of rebuffs, it succeeds. This is one of the few points on which one may be optimistic about the future of mankind. But it is, in itself, a point of no small importance. And, from it, one can derive yet other hopes. The primacy of the intellect lies, it is true, in a distant, distant future, but probably not in an infinitely distant one.

The chances are man is *now* as inherently intelligent as he ever will be. The time for the primacy of the intellect which is to say the nonbiologic man must be now or it likely never will be.

Given the thesis of evolutionary development to continuously higher forms what appears to be the future of life forms on earth. As was noted earlier, there appears to be no progressive physical changes in man himself over the past thousand or so generations. The increase in stature of certain groups of human beings during the past fifty years has been a result of enhanced nutrition. It remains to be seen whether that has been a thing favorable to survival or not. Miniaturization might be more appropriate. Again, one can discern a stagnation, a sense of "topping out," as though the actual apex, or better, a plateau—the goal of physical evolutionary development on earth has been attained. The balance between availability of resources and their rate of utilization, by all life forms, particularly man, shows a certain oscillation characteristic of physical systems at peak output. The remaining resources, particularly of energy, are enormous, but their exploitation requires continuously increasing levels of effort. We predicted earlier a topping out of the rate of use per capita. This, in spite of the fact that, the populous developing world is greatly below Western standards. Man needs to continue the technological advances at ever-increasing rates to supply the increasing demands.

As to the intellectual and spiritual potential, in view of low priority given to the moral and spiritual values currently, one is tempted to say that the peak in spiritual values has been passed and we are on the declining limb of the curve leading to nihilism as Nietzsche projected. However, looking at the role man plays in our primary thesis as the purposive end in the material order of a purposeful Creator, that at the peak of maturity the crop will turn bitter and fail seems defeating of that purpose. It seems more reasonable to assume there will be at least one last brilliant burst of the intellectual and spiritual *elan vital* to coincide with the physical peaking out before the drama closes.

Section 7—A Summary of the Viewpoints

At the biologic interface of life and matter on the unit-genetic level, at the physical boundary between matter and energy in the subatomic range, the problems of "causeless" events remain to be explained by science. Events occur—inert particles come into existence and combine to form a universe of vast energy, complexity and extent. Inert chemical chains take form at the submicroscopic atomic level and accept a modulation from some source to carry the genetic codes of life. Events occur—atoms fission or fuse and a fraction is conveyed to energy which provides heat to make life possible. All these happenings are observed but there is no available explanation of why, although, in some cases, processes are described. The ubiquitous existence of these events, all so closely interrelated, to make biologic life possible implies purpose, intentionality, and instrumentality at some level not approached by random probabilities. The events demand an explanation, and it is apparent the explanation lies beyond the material world we know. It is clear that whether the universe is scanned through the telescope or the microscope, at its boundaries we do indeed reach the "psychic abyss" where the material and immaterial existences must interface. The situation corresponds in symmetry to the Jungian idea of the inward extending infinity of the human psyche as well as the outward extending infinity in the vast recesses of God's being. In Part III, we have sought the answers to the unexplained events by metaphysical extension in logic and in evaluation of alternatives in physical and metaphysical terms. The conclusions are brought together in this summary section.

First, it appears appropriate to sum up where we stand in terms of the relative probability of the three possible modes of origin of the physical universe in terms of the current cosmology, mathematical concepts and four aspects of scientific development which were reviewed. This is best done by formulating a matrix of relative compatibility. This is shown in Table 2.

The only explanation, in fact, which is compatible with all of these aspects, and I know of no others which are generally applicable, is that the universe was created, and that the Creator was intelligent and purposeful. In the last column under "Anthropology" the possibility of the other explanations is contingent on the physical world, having somehow come into existence, and then only in terms of a signally improbable occurrence. It would require a specific set of initiating circumstances and a sequence of on-following accidental, but survival-biased events occurring against incredible odds. It is therefore not truly compatible in any logical sense since dependent on incompatible conditions.

Similarly, the probability of the transcendental nature of man is displayed evidentially in Table 3. While not as clearly demonstrable as the created universe, yet since man's transcendental nature flows from the nature of the Creator and man's relationship to the Creator, the probability remains convincingly high, far higher than the alternative. We will develop further evidence of man's transcendental nature in Part IV and at the same time demonstrate the personal, intimate, loving relationship which God has with His rational, transcendental creature, man.

The sixth logic gate which flows almost coercively from analysis of Table 2 states that, the universe was created by an intelligent and purposeful Being who preexisted and is external to the universe in essence. This is an extension and reinforcement of the logic gate five in Part II.

The seventh logic gate states that the Creator is unchangeable in essence and eternal in existence possessing all possible knowledge and power. This conclusion stems from the mathematical and metaphysical analysis establishing the characteristics of an uncaused Being which had produced the observable universe.

The eighth logic gate proposes the following: There is no logical barrier or incompatibility to preclude the intellectual interchange between material and immaterial forms of life. This conclusion is based on the general analysis of the necessary conditions for existence of both forms.

The ninth logic gate is based on Table 3 and states that man has both the potency and capacity in his intellectual aspects to survive death of his body in its material form.

PART IV

THE PHYSICAL ANOMALY— SIGN OF GOD'S CONCERN

Chapter 10

A DIFFERENT WORLD

The purpose of this chapter is to extend the ideas of man's role as a transcendental being as it can be rationally developed from available physical evidence. Its purpose is really two-fold: first, to establish that there is a basis for morality other than culturally-internalized norms or teachings projected by the various religious groups based on faith. Yet, the purpose is also to reinforce the validity of a morality based on faith. Secondly, the purpose is to establish that the relationship between God, the Creator, and His transcendental creature, man, is personal. It is the author's intention to demonstrate with high probability that God is a being who shows a personal interest in the affairs of man and strong predilection for some patterns of behavior as opposed to others. The anomalies will demonstrate that God's interest is revealed always as one of compassion, concern, and love, never cynicism or brutal exploitation through terror. In short, they show Him as the God of Augustine's writings.

The investigations which I performed in preparing this study meet the criteria for empirical research. They are repeatable in detail by anyone else who would care to do so. The writer attempted to take the phenomenologic attitude of accepting what he saw as it was presented and of evaluating the data as he would evidence in any other investigation, without preconceptions from opinions of others. What does the evidence show stripped of its surrounding emotional environment? How credible is it? What are the alternative explanations? How plausible are they? Where does the weight of evidence lie? The methodology, hence, is broadly investigative of alternatives rather than rigorously scientific. It is, nonetheless, valid. In this part of the work, the existence of God is presumed accepted. These cases, while they may reinforce that previously established high probability of His existence, are not presented for that purpose. For, if one denied the existence of God, he would also deny that

405

there would be exceptions to the physical laws, regardless of the contrary evidence.

Oddly, for an age when sensationalism is so much a part of life, where science fiction has a large and avid following and various esoteric cults are popular, serious research into this important and very real class of phenomena is considered eccentric and unorthodox. Yet, there the anomalies are. They stand enigmatic but visible, tangible, and testable. They demand an explanation as fully as any other phenomena. That they are not physically explainable does not cause the question to go away. As we have seen, the physical sciences do not comprehend all of the universe of knowledge, which is to say all of science in its authentic meaning. Although the physical hypothesis and examination should be the first approach to a physical phenomenon, it is not the only approach available.

These happenings are rarely reported and, when they are, they are covered in sentimental pseudo-pious, condescending articles with the clear implication that if one really believes them he needs a guardian. It is the blasé view taken of the traditional, supernatural religions prevalent in the current age. It reflects the attitude commented on by one of Isaac Singer's characters in his collection of stories, *A Crown of Feathers* ". . . if the heavens would part and the angel Gabriel were to fly down with his six fiery wings and take a walk on Broadway they would not write about it for more than a day or two." Yet, if there were a report of a little green man in a shiny space suit on Broadway, half the city would be ready to commit suicide.

Returning to the previous chapters briefly, we have stated that the nature of the Creator was one of infinite intelligence, purpose, and power. Such a Creator does not make mistakes, so that if there are physical anomalies, they are not the result of correcting for a slip-up in design or execution. The universe unfolds and moves as He eternally willed it to. For even man's free-willed behavior, its actual and possible outcomes known eternally, would have been compensated for one way or another, depending upon how man selected from his alternatives.

The only reason there would be an intervention would be for a definite purpose that God wills to have His existence and His desires, His compassion and concern known and recognized, and thus to encourage man to search for His way of life. Yet God does not so overwhelm man with His presence that the free will of man is precluded from making its own choice. He does not will that He be served by a race of slaves but of free men and women. Interventions would be rare therefore, since His Creation, as He wills and maintains it, carries out His primary purposes. For that reason, this investigation is rather like the search for the cosmic ray. One photograph out of thousands under carefully staged conditions might show the trace by its effect on surrounding matter.

In this search and study these would be exceptions to the physical laws—purposeful anomalies unexplained by physical science, but indicative that God does desire human beings to turn to Him for assistance and guidance. In short, that He desires men to love Him, and, therefore, that He gives their lives transcendental value. The last conclusion is derived from the point that the writer could find no anomalies which are aimed to strike terror. Quite the contrary, they are all beneficent. The individuals they honor are kind, loving, and self-effacing.

The cases which the writer has selected and, in general, personally investigated at the site, are those to which no hysteria or psychological interpretation can be made, except by a person of obdurate and emotional bias. The term "selected" should also be clarified at this point. Just as the experimenters in high-energy particles select photographs which best show the phenomenon they wish to explain, so here, too, neither time nor space permits every likely case to be presented. Only three "cures" out of thousands reported each year are included, one because of the high professional qualifications and competence of one of the witnesses, a Nobel prize winner in the field concerned; another because she remains, in 1974, a living "impossibility"; the third, arbitrarily selected, the last case recorded at Lourdes, at the time of the investigation to show a typical anomaly of the cure category which has been officially affirmed rather than exposed by prestige of one witness.

In spite of the fact that the cases selected are predominately of one religious group—a condition which was determined by availability of evidence—no implication is intended that they are limited to that group. Further, although sometimes the term is used in quotations, no reference is made by the writer to these phenomena as "miracles," which is, in its most correct application, a canonical term. For purposes of the study, the cases are classed as "preternatural" rather than "supernatural," although in most of them the distinction is a fine one.

This is, by far, the most difficult section of the work to write and still maintain an attitude of true objectivity. By their very nature the phenomena are imbedded in emotion and hence quotations of witnesses and others have to be "detuned" to arrive at a factual evaluation, but yet somehow leave a personal sense to avoid stripping them of their essential human character.

The attitude which ought to guide all scientific research is one of truth-seeking. The scientist should seek the true solution regardless of where that path leads him. The anomalies demand an explanation, just as validly, in terms of true scientific pursuit of knowledge, as did Bequerel's accidentally fogged photographic film which led to the discovery of radioactivity in minerals. These physical phenomena, regardless of their peculiar circumstances could lead to important findings, to affirmation or denial of some currently held theories of the nature of man. The pursuit is scientific in its broadest sense.

The writer would hope others will engage in similar studies and that the custodians of the information will also recognize the importance of such studies in an age where faith alone has been widely rejected as an acceptable basis of rational action in moral situations. The writer is also convinced that the more investigations there are, and the wider the search, the more compelling the evidence will be. He believes this field of investigation is on the same level of importance as those which Dr. L.S.B. Leakey and his successors are engaged in at Olduvai Gorge in trying to trace our biological antecedents.

The tools of science and mathematics, and the test methods now available, are the best means to legitimize preternatural physical phenomena. Test procedures do need to be beyond suspicion. The critics are many, aggressive and vocal, and that is for the best.

The three propositions which the writer attempts to establish are:

1. The anomalies of this type are not randomly dispersed, but on the contrary, are patterned. They occur only when related to events, or ways of life, having spiritual significance. The term "spiritual," in this context, being defined in a limited way as of, or relating to, the human soul in its relation to a Supreme Being.

2. The nature of the anomalous event in every case is one to
    (a) reflect honor to an individual who lived a dedicated
        spiritual life, or
    (b) inspire devotion to a facet of spiritual life.

3. The anomalies are in all cases of a nature to suggest beneficent, personal concern of the Creator.

The first proposition is one of induction, generalizing from the specific to the universal, and therefore is subject to the valid criticism that the writer has not examined all cases. That is a situation common to empirically-based conclusions, yet it is the method most valued by modern science. The usual and valid answer is to let the critics offer exceptions and let these be examined.

The writer deliberately avoided selecting numerous examples from the many thousands of supporting medical events because he could not eliminate the problem of the "state of the medical arts." In that connection, the reason for the rejection of many "cures" in the past and the writer's reason for generally excluding them was to forestall the very slick response that physical science cannot answer the question today, but it will tomorrow with our advancing knowledge. Out of curiosity, the writer checked to see if any of the "cures" which had been canonically defined in the past fifty years at the major sites had been overturned by the notable advances in medicine in the interim. None had, nor were any in doubt. As a side comment—if this attitude is sincere—every possible investigation should be undertaken to determine what is the physical explanation of the cases. What valuable information for applied medicine!

I have selected 27 cases to report on in this section in the belief that they are the most important of those which I investigated. They are all physical, none psychological. Some are fairly well known, others are not. The writer has established four categories of phenomena. The first, the "cures" already mentioned. Second, a group of three, representing inanimate objects which have been given preternatural connotation by some related event. The third, three cases of human tissue or blood which have survived for centuries in ambient condition and which have additional preternatural phenomenal characteristics. And the last, of a related nature, but more numerous, fifteen cases of human corpses which have remained incorrupt for long periods under varied ambient conditions, which are hence fundamentally anomalous and have common backgrounds suggesting correlation to the preternatural for the anomaly. There are undoubtedly many others of the latter category, but it is a process of search, location by location.

In support of the three stated propositions, the four categories of anomalies are studied together to identify common correlative features.

Section 1—Category I Phenomena—Cures

Gemma Di Giorgi was born blind in Ribera, Sicily, having a congenital deformity in which her eyes had no pupils. The doctors told her parents what was obvious, there was absolutely nothing that could be done for her. Her parents accepted this. Her grandmother did not. When the little girl was about seven in 1947, the grandmother undertook the trip to San Giovanni Rotondo and the Capuchin Monastery near Foggia, Italy, where Padre Pio, the humble and, to his embarrassment, well-known stigmatist lived. The following excerpt from the book, *Padre Pio the Stigmatist* by Carty (1963, p. 160), describes the case:

> They were both lost in the crowd of the faithful attending his Mass, when at the end, while the silence was still intense, everyone heard a voice calling: "Gemma, come here!" The grandmother pushed her way up to the altar with the child and knelt down before the holy man whom they had come so far to see. He smiled at Gemma and told her that she must make her first Communion. He heard her confession and then stroked her eyes with his hand. She received Holy Communion by herself and when afterwards her grandmother asked her if she had begged for any favor from Padre Pio the little girl answered, "No, Little Grandmother, I forgot!" Padre Pio saw them later and said: "May the Madonna bless you Gemma. Be a good girl!" At this moment the child gave a frantic cry, she could see.... The cure was permanent and complete, although her eyes still have no pupils. She has been examined by many doctors who have testified to the case and are able to offer no scientific explanation.

There was still, in 1973 at the time of the writer's investigation, no explanation. She sees as well as anyone, but she has no way of seeing in the ordinary physical sense.

The story of Padre Pio himself, who died in 1968 at the age of 81, having had the stigmata for fifty years, is almost a one-man defense of the thesis of the transcendental nature of man—if even ten percent of the phenomena attributed to him in the several books concerning his life are true. He was a gentle man of utter self-effacement and a mystic who led a life of extreme asceticism, having consented to photographs only under obedience to his superiors. The cause for his beatification is underway because of the manifest sanctity of his life. He made very clear that no works are performed by him, but only his beloved Master working through and in him. Of all the phenomena in which he was involved, only this one was selected because the cure, purely physical in its effect, is continuously visible and verifiable. There is no hysterical or natural psychological explanation, and numerous doctors have so testified. The probability that it is a natural phenomenon is very low.

The second case is that of Marie Bailly, a native of Lyons, France, 22 years of age, who was, in the collective view of the examining doctors, suffering terminal tubercular peritonitis when, with a group of sick, she went to Lourdes in France in November, 1903. The thing which makes this an acceptable case for the study is that one of the examining physicians was Dr. Alexis Carrel, at the time on the staff of the medical school at the University of Lyons, and accompanied a group of patients from Lyons. He had been raised a Catholic, but had given up religion and become a skeptic, influenced by the stoic and Kantain philosophies (Cassagnard, 1971, p. 76). In the following excerpt from the book, *Voyage to Lourdes,* (Carrel, 1950), Carrel, using the name Lerrac and Marie Ferrand for Marie Bailly, writes,

Lerrac leaned over her bed and studied Marie Ferrand. She was laying on her back, inert. Her head, with its white, emaciated face, was flung back on the pillow. Her wasted arms lay flat at her sides. Her breathing was rapid and shallow.

"How are you feeling?" Lerrac asked her, gently.

She turned her dim, dark-circled eyes toward him and her gray lips moved in an inaudible reply.

Taking her hand, Lerrac put his fingertips on her wrist. Her pulse was excessively rapid, a hundred and fifty beats a minute, and irregular. Her heart was giving out. "Get me the hypodermic syringe," he told the nurse. "We'll give her an injection of caffeine."

Pulling back the covers, the nurse removed the cradle that held up the bed clothes and the rubber ice bag which hung over the patient's abdomen.

Marie Ferrand's emaciated body lay exposed again. The abdomen was distended, as before. The swelling was almost uniform, but somewhat more pronounced on the left side. Gently, he let his hands slide over the smooth surface of the belly, lightly palpating it. The solid masses were still there; at the center, under the umbilicus, he could still feel the fluid.

Again Lerrac thought to himself that a small two-inch incision below the umbilicus would have been more useful than sending her to Lourdes. . . .

He turned to A.B., who was standing a little way off, visibly moved by the sight of this sickness and suffering.

"It's just what I told you," said Lerrac, "advanced tubercular peritonitis. The fluid is almost gone. You can feel the solid masses at the sides. I told you that both her parents died of tuberculosis. At seventeen, she was already spitting blood. At eighteen, she had a tubercular pleurisy; more than half a gallon of fluid was drawn from the left lung. Then she had pulmonary lesions. And now, for the last eight months, she has had this unmistakable tubercular peritonitis. She is almost completely wasted away. Her heart is racing madly. Look how thin she is. Look at the color of her face and hands. She may last a few days more, but she is doomed. Death is very near."

He walked past the lines of little carts and through the crowd toward the Grotto. Pausing for a moment at the edge of the stream, he observed the crowd. A young intern from Bordeaux, Mr. M., whom Lerrac had met the day before greeted him.

"Have you had any cures?" Lerrac asked him.

"No," replied M. "A few of the hysteria cases have recovered, but there has been nothing unexpected, nothing that one can't see any day in a hospital."

"Come and look at my patient," said Lerrac. "Her case is not unusual, but I think she is dying. She is at the Grotto."

"I saw her a few minutes ago," said M. "What a pity they let her come to Lourdes. She should have been operated on. Bringing her to the Grotto does not seem to have helped her. . . ."

In front of the iron grille and almost touching it, a stretcher was already lying. . . . He and M. made their way toward the Grotto where they could have a close view of the sick and the pilgrims. They stopped near Marie Ferrand's stretcher and leaned against the low wall. She was motionless, her breathing still rapid and shallow; she seemed to be at the point of death. More pilgrims were approaching the Grotto. . . .

Lerrac glanced again at Marie Ferrand. Suddenly

he stared. It seemed to him that there had been a change, that the harsh shadows on her face had disappeared, that her skin was somehow less ashen.

Surely, he thought, this was a hallucination. But the hallucination itself was interesting psychologically, and might be worth recording. Hastily he jotted down the time in his notebook. It was twenty minutes before three o'clock.

But if the change in Marie Ferrand was a hallucination, it was the first one Lerrac had ever had. He turned to M. "Look at our patient again," he said. "Does it seem to you that she has rallied a little?"

"She looks much the same to me," answered M. "All I can see is that she is no worse."

Leaning over the stretcher, Lerrac took her pulse again and listened to her breathing.

"The respiration is less rapid?" he told M., after a moment.

"That may mean that she is about to die," said M. . . .

A Miracle

Lerrac made no reply. To him it was obvious that there was a sudden improvement in her general condition. Something was taking place. He stiffened to resist a tremor of emotion, and concentrated all his power of observation on Marie Ferrand. He did not lift his eyes from her face. A priest was preaching to the assembled throngs of pilgrims and patients; hymns and prayers burst out sporadically (the Blessed Sacrament was reserved in the Grotto), and in this atmosphere of fervor, under Lerrac's cool, objective gaze, the face of Marie Ferrand slowly continued to change. Her eyes, so dim before, were now wide with ecstasy as she turned them toward the Grotto. The change was undeniable. The nurse leaned over and held her. . . .

Suddenly, Lerrac felt himself turning pale. The blanket which covered Marie Ferrand's distended abdomen was gradually flattening out.

"Look at her abdomen!" he exclaimed to M.

"Why yes," he said, "it seems to have gone down. It's probably the folds in the blanket that give that impression."

The bell of the basilica had just struck three. A few minutes later, there was no longer any sign of distension in Marie Ferrand's abdomen.

Lerrac felt as though he were going mad.

Standing beside Marie Ferrand, he watched the intake of her breath and the pulsing at her throat with fascination. The heartbeat, though still very rapid, had become regular.

This time, for sure, something was taking place. "How do you feel?" he asked her.

"I feel very well," she answered in a low voice. "I am still weak, but I feel I am cured."

There was no longer any doubt; Marie Ferrand's condition was improving so much that she was scarcely recognizable. . . .

Lerrac stood there in silence, his mind a blank. This event, exactly the opposite of what he had expected, must surely be nothing but a dream. . . .

Abruptly, Lerrac moved off. Making his way through the crowd of pilgrims whose loud prayers he hardly heard, he left the Grotto. It was now about four o'clock.

A dying girl was recovering.

It was the resurrection of the dead; it was a miracle!

He had not yet examined her; he could not yet know the real condition of her lesions. But he had seen with his own eyes a functional improvement which was in itself a miracle. How simple, how private, it had been! The crowd at the Grotto was not even aware that it had happened. . . .

At half-past-seven, he started for the hospital, tense and on fire with curiosity.

One question alone filled his mind. Had the incurable Marie Ferrand been cured?

Opening the door of the ward of the Immaculate Conception (hospital) he hastened across the room to her bedside. With mute astonishment, he stood and gazed. The change was overpowering. Marie Ferrand, in a white jacket, was sitting up in bed. Though her face was still gray and emaciated, it was alight with life; her eyes shone, a faint color tinted her cheeks. Such an indescribable serenity emanated from her person that it seemed to illuminate the whole sad ward with joy. "Doctor?" she said, "I am completely cured. I feel very weak, but I think I could even walk."

Lerrac put his hand on her wrist. The pulse beat was calm and regular. Her respiration had also become completely normal. Confusion flooded Lerrac's mind. Was this merely an apparent cure, the result of a patient's stimulus of autosuggestion? Or was it a new fact, an astounding, unacceptable event—a miracle? For a brief moment, before subjecting Marie Ferrand to the supreme test of examining her abdomen, Lerrac hesitated. Then, torn between hope and fear, he threw back the blanket. The skin was smooth and white. Above the narrow hips was the small, flat, slightly concave abdomen of a young, undernourished girl. Lightly he put his hands on the wall of the abdomen, looking for traces of the distension and hard masses he had found before. They had vanished like a bad dream.

The sweat broke out on Lerrac's forehead. He felt as though someone had struck him on the head. His heart began to pump furiously. He held himself in with iron determination.

He had not heard Doctors J. and M. entering the ward. Suddenly he noticed them, standing beside him. "She seems to be cured," he said, then "I cannot find anything wrong. Please examine her yourselves."

While his two colleagues carefully palpated Marie Ferrand's abdomen, Lerrac stood aside and watched them with shining eyes. There could be no doubt whatever that the girl was cured. It was a miracle, the kind of miracle which took the public by storm and sent them in hordes to Lourdes. And the public was justified in its enthusiasm. Whatever the source of these cures, the results were not only breathtaking but positive and good. Again it swept over Lerrac how fortunate he was, that among all the patients at Lourdes that day it was the one he had known and studied carefully whom he saw cured!

. . .When a scientist tried to apply his intellectual techniques and convictions to metaphysics, he was lost. He could no longer use his reasoning, since reason did not go beyond the establishing of facts and their relations to each other. In the search for causes, there was nothing absolute, there were no sign posts along the way, there was no proof of right or wrong. All things in this mysterious realm were therefore possible. Intellectual systems no longer seemed to count. In the face of life and death, the mere theories were void. It was not science that nourished the inner life of man, it was the faith of his soul. He had to reach a conclusion. He was certain of his diagnosis. It was incontestable that a miracle had taken place. But was it by the hand of God? Some day he would know. Meanwhile, it was safe to say it was a cure; that much he could guarantee. Yet deep within himself, he felt that was not all. . . .

He climbed the steps of the church in the glitter of lights while the organ boomed and a thousand voices chanted. He sat down on a chair at the back near an old peasant. For a long time he sat there motionless, his hands over his face, listening to the hymns. Then he found himself praying: ". . . I believe in Thee. Thou didst answer my prayers by a blazing miracle. I am still blind to it. I still doubt. But the greatest desire of my life is to believe, to believe passionately, implicitly, and never more to analyze and doubt. . . . Beneath the deep, harsh warnings of my intellectual pride a smothered dream persists. Alas, it is still only a dream but the most enchanting of them all. It is the dream of believing in Thee and loving Thee with the shining spirit of men of God."

Subsequent examinations over the years revealed that her cure was indeed instantaneous and permanent. Marie Bailly entered the Order of Sisters of Charity of St. Vincent De Paul the following August as a postulant and then later as a novice at the mother house of the sisters at Paris on Rue de Bac. She lived for 35 years as a Sister of Charity at various locations in France and Italy taking care of the poor, the sick, and the infirm. She died in February 1937 at the age of 57 of causes unrelated to her earlier illness.

In the short term, the event cost Carrel dearly. His colleagues at the University of Lyons at first laughed at his naivete, then grew angry when he refused to deny what he had experienced, and he was shortly after forced to leave his position. He left France and came to the United States, where he joined the Rockefeller Institute for Medical Research. There he had a long and brilliant career in the course of which, in 1913, he won the

Nobel Prize for his studies in biology, the first by an American (Cassagnard, 1971, p. 150). Eventually in his late years he teamed with Charles Lindberg in development of a mechanical heart. He won the Nordhoff-Jung Cancer Prize in 1931, the United States Distinguished Service Medal, and the Newman Foundation Award in 1937. He died in November of 1944, having lived a life dedicated to science, during which he published several books on themes basically spiritual, but showing the relationship of the infinite with the world of science. The incident described changed his life entirely. It was included in the excellent book, *Turning Point* (Dunaway, 1958), as one of the fifty or more examples of where a single event is identified as the crisis in life. It was also well covered in the book, *The World's Greatest Secret,* by John M. Haffert (Haffert, 1967).

The very number of cases in the cure category is of great significance, in itself, in establishing the nature of these anomalies. Yet, neither of the previously described events have been canonically defined as miraculous. This is not surprising. For instance in the 25-year period, 1945-1970, of the 964 anomalous phenomena which occurred at Lourdes and were considered significant enough for official recognition, only 22 have been declared miraculous and as much as 33 years has elapsed between the event and its declaration. Many things, other than the event itself, have a bearing on the definition.

The third case in this category is the case of Elisa Aloi, who was born at Patti near Messina, Italy, November 26, 1931. It was the last of the canonically established cures reported in the official updating published in 1972 (Olivieri, 1972). No attempt was made to secure an outstanding case. Miss Aloi's mother died of tuberculosis and her father died of heart complications deriving from tuberculosis. There were two other children in the family, both of whom are in good health (1970).

In 1950, Elisa was admitted first to the solarium of Palermo and the hospital of Patti, and finally the Hospital Regina Margherita at Messina where she was found to have tuberculosis of the twelfth vertebra and also in her right knee. She previously (in 1948) had had a painful swelling of the right knee in which an infection was found and an abscess formed, but the lesion closed after about six months. She was given usual therapy but in 1951 a new focus of tuberculosis was found in her right thigh.

She recovered sufficiently to leave the hospital, but was again stricken in 1953 and was in a very serious condition with anemia and general debilitation, with many suppurating ulcers in the muscular tissue. Many new foci of tuberculosis were found. X-rays showed invasion of the disease in the right sacroiliac; from that point the patient was forced to wear a brace to make movement possible. In February 1955, she was operated upon and found to have tubercular infection of the right thighbone. She was in and out of the hospital, gradually becoming more and more incapacitated. In March, 1957 she entered the hospital of the House of the Sun (Casa del Sole), and remained almost a year, being treated with penicillin and streptomycin while she alternated between improvement and worsening of her condition.

That year, she made a pilgrimage to Lourdes and seemed to improve somewhat, but after a fall, she was as bad or worse than ever. In May 1958, Professor Di Cesare of the Hospital of San Angelo in Messina reported her condition, as of May 1958, and in addition to his usual historical record, stated that she had many lesions of the right thigh, of the right knee and foot. The lesions were "of tubercular osteomyelitis which first appeared in 1948." She had never received any improvement either by surgery or medication. The osteomyelitis extended to the second rib at the sternum and the twelfth vertebra. She was completely paralyzed. She could not move nor bend feet or knees. During her stay in the hospital there was no improvement. She had general tuberculosis with not only bone invasion, but also muscular erosion and running abscesses, opacity in her right lung and other physical deterioration. Her general condition to say the least was bad.

Dr. Zappia who accompanied the pilgrimage (Treno Bianco) to Lourdes and remained with her, described her condition in basically the same terms as Dr. Di Cesare, reporting that on the train her abscesses were running and malodorus. Her fever was 39.5 degrees C. (103.1 degrees F.), at arrival in Lourdes. During the first two days, June 5th and 6th, by application of bandages soaked in water, and subcutaneous injection of the Lourdes water, at the request of the patient, the abscesses were healed. The third day there was no more suppuration and by the time she left Lourdes on June 11th, the abscesses were all healing and the open sores closed. The patient refused medication. She felt well and was able to move her feet and toes. She wanted to remove the brace, but Dr. Zappia refused, preferring that the doctors at the hospital make the decision. Before the train arrived at Messina, the bandages were dry and scabs had formed on all open sores.

The doctors back at Messina on June 13, 1958, reported "Miss

Aloi returned from Lourdes completely cured and in good health *(cosi bene in salute)*. We are not able to believe that this is the same person who left in such desperate condition. Elisa Aloi is completely cured."

The case was reviewed in June 1959 and June 1960. There was no relapse. Elisa is married and has two children and now (in 1972) lives a completely normal life with her husband, Signor M. Varacallia, a carbiniere, near Abruzzi, Italy.

The report of the second examination stated in effect that all of the conditions revealed in the report of the previous year remain unchanged. The affected parts are covered with scars, more or less deep, but perfectly dry and without pain. The joint movement and articulation of the joints are all normal. Numerous radiographs showed the perfect cure of the diseased bone.

On June 4, 1960, the fourteen doctors present at the official medical office at Lourdes reported they have agreed unanimously the illness described existed with certainty at the time of the pilgrimage, that there was at that time no improvement nor any tendency toward improvement. It was a true cure and is herewith transmitted to the International Medical Commission. The official report of the International Medical Committee signed by Professor Salmon of the faculty of medicine of the University of Marseilles on April 23, 1961, contains the unanimous conclusions of the Board as follows:

1. Miss Elisa Aloi was truly sick at her arrival at Lourdes on June 5, 1958, of multiple tubercular lesions of the bones and joints (di tuberculosi multipla osteorarticulari fistoloso).

2. The illness and condition of the patient was suddenly modified in its evolution when there has been no sign of any tendency for betterment.

3. Miss Aloi on that day, June 5, 1958, was cured without any special medication.

4. In the view of the Medical Board, the cure is real and without explanation.

The canonical determination of the miraculous nature of the cure was made on May 25, 1965. Disregarding the official ecclesiastical finding and evaluating the evidence, the view that the event had no physical or psychological explanation seems clear. Damaged and decayed bone and tissue were suddenly replaced by clean, healthy bone and tissue with no intervening time for normal curative processes to take effect and with no special medication. Probabilities of the preternatural explanation must be considered very great. The subject is alive, well and living a completely normal life after ten years of the gravest illness.

Section 2—Category II
Phenomena Related to Inanimate Objects

The first of these, the image of the Virgin of Guadalupe which is continuously displayed at the Basilica of Our Lady of Guadalupe in Mexico City is the product of an event which took place on December 12, 1531, at the site, at that time called Tepeyacac, less than forty years after Columbus' first voyage of discovery and fifteen years before the death of Cortez, conqueror of the Aztecs. There is no question of the authenticity of the present image being that of the original because of its uninterrupted exposure since construction of the first chapel on December 26, 1531, only two weeks after the event. It has been the object of continuous popular veneration since that time. The image was displayed unprotected for 116 years until 1647 when two sections of glass were sent from Spain to protect it. These were replaced in 1766 by a single sheet of glass, also from Spain, provided by the Duke of Albuquerque, the Spanish viceroy.

The phenomenon has been the subject of continuous correspondence and record from the first. This history is of crucial interest from any point of view which is directed at the physical manifestation, rather than strictly religious phenomenology. The image is presented on a rough cloth woven from the fiber of the maguey plant. It is a tilma, or mantle, worn by the natives of Mexico at the time of the event, and is composed of two pieces of cloth, loosely stitched together and roughly bisecting the image, which is 66 inches long and 41 inches wide. It is totally unsuitable for a painting or for a photosensitive print. The maguey plant fiber is quite subject to bacterial decay and the life of a piece of exposed cloth of this size under these conditions has been variously estimated at between 25 and 70 years. The image is 456 years old. The religious story, based on contemporary accounts, is fairly well known, but certain facts are important for purpose of this study and bear repeating.

A historical figure—not a legend—a native—Juan Diego, a man of middle age was a weaver of petates, a type of mat. He was not an impoverished peon as some legends would have him. He was a grown man at the time of the Spanish conquest. He accepted Christianity, apparently with genuine fervor since he was on his way to get a priest to assist his uncle who he thought was dying from a wound (or an illness, *cocolistla*, by some versions) when a young women appeared to him the fourth time. In going for the priest he was not keeping an appointment he had previously made with her and was deliberately avoiding her, but she intercepted him. She had told him on three occasions previously to have the bishop (Bishop Juan Zumarraga, a historical figure and writer on the subject of the image), build a chapel or sanctuary to her at the site. His first and second meetings with the bishop on the subject were not outstanding successes, but the second time the bishop was sufficiently impressed so that he told Juan Diego to have the woman give him a sign. On the third meeting with the young woman she promised Juan Diego she would give him a sign, and now she confronted him.

She listened to his excuse for avoiding her and told him not to fear, that his uncle would recover. She told him that she would now give him the sign; that he was to go to the top of the rocky hill where they had first met. There he would find Castillian roses blooming. He was to cut the flowers and bring them to her. It was an impossibility at that location any time, but in the middle of December, doubly so. But he nonetheless went, found the flowers and put many into his tilma which he bound up and took to the young woman. She rearranged the roses in the tilma and tied up the mantle in a knot at the back of his neck, and told him to bring them to the bishop. This he did. After a bit of delay—but not too long, because the people were curious—as he undid the knot before the bishop and others and let the flowers cascade to the floor, simultaneously the image, as it is today, appeared on the tilma. An unlikely story?

The image and story were responsible, far more than brutal oppression, in the historical conversion of some eight million natives of Mexico to Christianity in a period of less than ten years. Of these circumstances, Friar Toribio de Benevente, called "Motolinia," the Poor One, by the Indians wrote (Behrens, 1964, p. 51):

> . . . In five days at the Monastery of Quecholac another priest and I baptized 14,500 Indians, anointing them with oil and chrism. There were two days on which as many as 750 couples presented themselves to be married and in the Monastery of Tlaxcala and in another Monastery more than 1,000 couples were married in one day.

In the village of Tehuacan in the year 1540 on Easter Sunday, I witnessed an extraordinary event. From 40 different provinces and villages, some as far distant as 50 or 60 leagues, the Indians came with their chiefs to be present at the festivities of Holy Week in the Church of the Immaculate Conception. They had not been called nor compelled to come. They represented twelve nations and spoke twelve different dialects or languages. After having taken part in the regular ceremonies, all offered flowers and prayers to the Blessed Virgin.

What can be said about the image itself which is the subject here? There were casual studies over the first three centuries by painters and others of scientific bent trying to establish what was the method used in its production. Agreement was reached early that no artist of any then existing or pre-existing known school could have produced this image which, in spite of the rough texture of the material, presents a smooth surface. There are no brush strokes and the detail of the work is exquisite and of minute refinement and delicate hue.

In 1964 a detailed examination of the picture was made by technical experts of Kodak de Mexico. Their conclusions were that the image is in the nature of a photographic reproduction of exotic process and impossible today. Of course, photography in any form was unknown in 1531. The image is presented as though it were a thin film, which accounts for its smoothness. The color does not penetrate the fiber. A study of an enlarged (25x) section of the eyes of the image was made in 1962, showing a portrait of three persons reflected in the eyes. The reflection is clear in the right, but blurred in the left because of a knot in the thread. Subsequent optical studies show the images were as though the Virgin were looking at the scene at the time. One of the images is remarkably similar to a from-life portrait of Juan Diego. This aspect of the phenomenon has been studied by specialists in optics and photography and seems to support the photographic origin of the image (Whalig. 1973). In the spring of 1980 a complete scientific investigation of the image was initiated using the most sophisticated photographic techniques. Initial reports support that the image is not a painting.

No physical explanations have been found for the total anomaly. The site has been the scene of tens of thousands of physical anomalies of the cure category since 1531.

As an interesting sidelight, on November 24, 1921, a dynamite bomb had been placed on the altar, hidden in a bouquet of flowers and was detonated in an attempt to destroy the image. The explosion tore marble blocks from the altar, broke the windows near the altar, and bent a heavy crucifix below the image into an ogee, but did not even crack the ancient glass protection of the image.

In appraising the credibility of the event, as described above, from the current physical tests, the timing is crucial. The episode was explosive in its suddenness; there was no long period of legend-building. The importance was instantly recognized and made a matter of record in correspondence between Cortez and Bishop Zumarraga. The first chapel was completed within two weeks. The flowers which Juan Diego had brought to the bishop, and they were real flowers, had scarcely faded. The whole history was written within a few days when memories were fresh and events verifiable. The word was spread among millions of the natives, not so much by the Spaniards as by the people themselves.

What are the probabilities of a natural physical explanation of the total event and the image, which is here for study to substantiate the story? Even if one wished to stretch his imagination into the realm of science fiction or an adventure, and a pointless one, by extraterrestrial natural, intelligent creatures, he runs into difficulties no good science fiction writer would touch.

The name "Guadalupe" results from a misinterpretation by the Spanish of the words spoken by the Virgin to Juan Bernardino, uncle of Diego, to whom she appeared and cured while Juan Diego was absent at the bishop's residence. The Aztec words, "tecoatlaxopeuh," she used mean to the Indians "to crush the stone serpent," whereas the Spanish thought the similar sounding words referred to Guadalupe, a town in Spain, and so named the Virgin. The Indians took it as the end of Quetzalcoatl, the serpent god and of human sacrifices to him.

The second item in this category is that of the Shroud of Turin. It is probably better known, at least worldwide, than the Image of the Virgin, and there are a number of fairly recent books on the subject. The writer has relied most heavily on that of Peter Rinaldi (Rinaldi, 1972).

Unlike the Image of the Virgin of Guadalupe, its historical background is unclear, although its known history is over a longer period. It can be traced with good reliability to June 20, 1353, when it was exposed by Geoffrey de Charney, Lord of Savousie and Lirey in the Collegiate Church of Lirey. He referred to it as the "true burial sheet of Christ." Its whereabouts before that are somewhat clouded, although there are traditions of the existence of the Shroud extending back to apostolic times and historical reference as early as the year 120 when St. Braulio of Seville wrote of it in terms of a relic of common knowledge. In 670, Arculph, a French bishop, testified that it had been shown to him in Jerusalem and he had been allowed to kiss it.

There is a record of the existence of a "shroud of Christ" in Constantinople in 1201. It is logical that the relic would have been taken by the Byzantine Christians to Constantinople from Jerusalem prior to the first invasion by the forces of Islam. This appears to support the subsequent record of a shroud at the Church of St. Stephen at Besancon, France, between 1203 and 1349. That shroud was reliably believed to be the one which had been brought to France from Constantinople in 1203 by the Crusader, Otho de la Roche, and delivered to Besancon. The Besancon shroud had been presumed lost in a fire which destroyed the church.

It seems probable, and in fact is now generally accepted, that the shroud which Geoffrey exposed was the one which had been presumed lost in the fire, since only three years lapsed between the events. It even might be suggested that the fire was a convenient bit of arson to cover up an important case of larceny.

There are gaps, but in consideration of the state of communications and the violence of the intervening years, this is understandable. There is now (1980) little doubt that the shroud dates from the time of Christ and that it originated in Palestine. Preliminary reports on studies still under way have satisfied all but the most biased of its authenticity.

Looking at the shroud as a physical anomaly, there are two basic, and several collateral, aspects which should be taken together. This phase of it can really be said to begin when some photographs were made of the shroud in 1898. The photographic negatives revealed an extent of detail not indicated in the original cloth. These early photographs, in turn, have now been supplemented by others of more recent age which have been examined by physicians and surgeons. Virtually to a man the examiners have identified the figure beyond question as the image, front and rear, left by the body of a man who had been incredibly abused. All of the wounds attributed to the biblical accounts of the Crucifixion of Jesus are present. The details presented in the doctors' reports are astounding! The number of scourge blows, approximately 120—the type of scourge—and the shape of the crown of thorns—the blows on the face, and the detailed description of the path of the lance which, as Rinaldi says, "From the position of the wound, Dr. Pierre Barbet of Paris could easily determine the trail of the lance. It penetrated between the fifth and sixth ribs, bore through the right lung and pierced the right auricle of the heart." Sufficient to say, it is a picture of an agonizing death that no crucifix ever approaches. There are no longer any serious questions but that it is the imprint of the body of a man who was maltreated and executed in precisely the way in which the accounts say Christ was executed. Details on the cloth were not revealed until modern photography permitted them to be. Debate now centers on how the images were formed on the cloth, what chemical processes were involved and other similar details.

Photo enhancement studies conducted at the U.S. Air Force Academy in 1977 (reported in an Academy news release October 2, 1977) have produced interesting information concerning the nature of the image of the shroud. Recently, it had been surmised that it was a "vapographic" process, that is, that vapors rising from the body and herbs and spice used in burial had reacted with the cloth. The studies by Dr. Eric Jumper and others at the Air Force Academy indicated that the unique three-dimensional nature of the image revealed by their studies would suggest rather that the image was projected by a form of radiation from the body in all directions. They suggest this might have occurred at the instant of the revivification of the body at the resurrection—like the radiation image of a man recorded on a wall at Hiroshima after the nuclear detonation ending the Second World War in the Pacific. This idea is strengthened since their studies also revealed, for the first time, two circular coin-like objects over the eyes of the image. The coins would not have given off any such vapors, yet their configuration including thickness is clearly delineated by the three-dimensional studies. On the other hand, coins could well have concentrated a radiation-like emanation. Other studies had previously revealed that the stains are surface phenomena and do not penetrate the fibers—a fact which also supports a "radiation" or "photographic" rather than chemical process. As a matter of considerable interest, the latest studies centering on photographs made in 1978 using all modern techniques and exhaustive physico-chemical examinations made by an international study team of high competence have revealed that one of the "coin-like objects" is a coin having Greek inscriptives dating it to the time of Pontius Pilate.

The second aspect now being studied intensively is the preservation of the shroud, if, as is likely, its age will be verified at some 1,950 years. The preservation, in fact, was one of the early points of attack by the opponents of its authenticity. The proponents, of course, took vigorous action to prove that natural linen can survive that long—and it can, if it is properly protected and cleaned.

For our purposes, we are not talking about just any piece of linen, but this specific and unique piece of linen which, if the authenticity is admitted, some 1,950 years ago was wrapped around a particular human body—a highly controversial body. The piece of cloth changed hands many times, was handled and protected in different ways at many times, went through wars and fires, sea voyages and all the vicissitudes of the rise and death of empires, and now is here in our secure possession for us to photograph. It was even plunged into boiling water on Good Friday in 1503 when the Duke of Canbery sought to remove the stain and washed the linen, fortunately unsuccessfully. What were the odds back in 33 A.D. that the cloth would survive?

And now let us draw a comparison with the preceding case of the Virgin of Guadalupe, for the symmetry is compelling point and counterpoint. The two pieces of cloth, one of short natural life, the other long life. One a life of single location, and generally, with but one violent exception, without any external peril. The other a violent existence in many perils, but both survive to the present. The images, one instantaneously revealed and spectacular, its "process" unexplainable, until the present, as photographic. This explanation only adds to the significance of the mystery. The second, basically mute for many centuries, the cloth more venerated than the image. Suddenly in the present, its true nature is revealed by photography, its basic processes unexplained—and yet—also appearing to be exotic. Now which of these has a more probable purely natural explanation?

In both cases, a purely "natural" explanation is of low probability, that of the Virgin of Guadalupe being less probable. For someone who has considered, side by side, the even more puzzling case of the image of the Virgin of Guadalupe, this one of the shroud is by no means mind-boggling. If an image can be formed on a tilma of rough fiber of the maguey plant by a "photographic process" almost 400 years before photography was invented, with no visible photographic subject, and by an unknown process even today, then an image formed by a body, in close proximity or contact with, the relatively smooth linen fabric is not difficult to conceive. As in the case of the Virgin of Guadalupe, regardless of the process, chemical or otherwise, which results in the image, the view that the detailed bodily condition reflected represents ordinary operational physical agencies is far more difficult to accept than its alternative.

The third and last item in this category is truly an eyebrow raiser. It is the weeping Madonna of Syracuse, an event of the last forty years. It owes its validity, in fact, to its modernity and to modern scientific analysis. There have been other weeping madonnas, probably equally as authentic from the standpoint of testimony of witnesses. Most lack hard physical evidence to back up the testimony and are thus evaluated by the skeptics as instances of hysterical hallucination. An example is the Mater Dolorosa in the Chapel of Campocavalla, Italy, a small village near Ancona, in which the eyes reportedly moved and wept in 1892 and 1893. The writer visited the site in the fall of 1973. The image is more appealing in appearance than the one at Syracuse, but since the only evidence is all human testimony, it is of little significance outside its village. For some reason, testimony of witnesses has little value outside the courtroom—if even there. But when the rather ordinary little wall plaque, many from the same mold had been produced by a firm at Bagno di Lucca, near Livorno, Italy, began weeping on August 29, 1953 at 8:30 A.M., in the room of a very sick young woman in a poor section of Syracuse, it created a sensation. For the madonna wept profusely, even while the police, hoping to stave off a traffic disaster for the city, confiscated and took it to the police station for examination. There was little to examine, a little painted plaster of paris figure attached to a simple glass mounting board. But it continued to weep. It soaked the vest of the policeman carrying it; it wept at the desk of the sergeant; it wept for more than three days.

Fortunately, the phenomenon was photographed by movie cameras as well as by still cameras and from close up. Pictures in slow motion revealed the tears, welling up at the corners of the eyes of the madonna and coursing down her face. It was viewed by thousands—the police had their traffic jam.

The officials of the pharmaceutical licensing laboratory at Syracuse collected samples of the effluent (about thirty drops with a pipette as they came from the eyes) and examined them and made the analysis a matter of official record. They were, chemically, human tears, containing the same traces of protein as real tears and totally absent in plaster of paris. Microscopic examination showed no pores which could produce the tears; there was no cavity in the plaque to hold them. Yet there they were, and there the evidence is.

Since the event, a major basilica has been constructed at Syracuse in which the madonna is exposed continuously and venerated. It has never wept again, but there have been hundreds of physical anomalies of the cure category recorded at the site, some 300 referred to the commission the first year. A major hospital has been built in connection with the shrine. Every possible physical theory has been explored from all pertinent scientific disciplines, biology, physics and chemistry, mineralogy, hydroscopy, climatology, and apparently there is none.

Why this madonna? Why this time? Why Syracuse? Why that house? Why tears at all? Answers to these questions are beyond this study, except to say that the results in terms of numbers of human beings being affected in a religious sense have been astounding. If that was the purpose, it was eminently successful. In view of the physical evidence alone, with none of the collateral phenomena, the probabilities of a physical explanation of this anomaly are minute. It may be protested that statues do not cry—of course, they do not. Neither do pictures paint themselves nor pupilless eyes see, nor atoms form from nothing without an intervention by a Being with the power and the purpose to cause them to do so.

Section 3—Category III
Phenomena—Anomalous Existence of Incorrupt Human Tissue or Blood Having Associated Preternatural Events

The first of these is the "Miraculous Eucharist of Lanciano," an event which dates from the eighth century A.D. There are written records of it, including stone inscriptions beginning about 1258 when the relic was at the "new" Church of St. Francis of Lanciano. At that time, apparently this anomaly was considered a relic of great antiquity. The event is of importance now as a physical anomaly for two reasons. First, the survival of a small isolated piece of tissue and congealed blood, in ambient condition for some 700 years and probably as much as 1,200 years is, in itself, remarkable. But, secondly, and of more importance, is that in 1970 and 1971, the tissue and the blood were subject to a series of intensive and very carefully executed and observed scientific tests using the most modern techniques to verify the authenticity of the relic. These tests, described subsequently, were under the sponsorship of the University of Siena in cooperation with the clinic of pathological anatomy at the hospital of Arezzo.

According to the legend (not to imply myth), the event occurred in an ancient church long since destroyed, dedicated to San Legaziano at Lanciano. Legaziano (Longinus) was the Roman soldier who, by tradition, pierced the side of Christ. The church was, at that time, part of a monastery of the Basilian monks of the Byzantine Eastern Rite. Records show that this circumstance would place the event not earlier than the first half of the sixth century, when Belisarius of the Byzantines, in 537, acting under Emperor Justinian, had driven the Goths out of the territory. The latest date would have been sometime in the eighth century, after, but soon after, Lanciano had been established as the Episcopal See under the Latin rite. The later dating is more probable. The legend attributes the anomaly to doubts of the Basilian monk as to the efficacy of the Consecration. He was saying Mass in Latin, using the unleavened circular host rather than in Greek and using the square leavened bread of the Greek rite at that time.

According to the legend, the monk immediately after having completed the consecrating act was assailed by doubt, whereupon the Host turned into a piece of bleeding flesh and the wine into blood before his eyes. He was horrified, and started to "bolt the scene," but then conscience-stricken, revealed to the Basilian community what had happened. The circular piece of flesh, and the blood congealed in five irregularly shaped masses, were immediately considered items for exalted veneration and have been preserved and venerated until this time.

The relic has remained in the Lanciano area, though in different churches, and in different chapels or locations within the church and under several religious orders. Since 1258, the relic has been in custody of the Franciscans except for an interval of about 142 years following the suppression of the Franciscans by Napoleon Bonaparte in 1809 until 1953 when the custody of the church and relic were returned by the diocesan clergy to the Franciscans. The people of Lanciano have from earliest knowledge been dedicated to the veneration of the relic. It has been in the present reliquary since 1713.

I was fortunate in having Fr. Luigi Laurello, O.F.M., who was one of the witnesses to the tests, show me the relic at close view and with intense illumination, both front and rear, of the ostensorium glass. As seen today, the Host is roughly circular in elevation view, of about ten centimeters maximum diameter. It is more of an annulus than a disc since there is a large irregular area missing in the center portion. Illuminated from the front, the relic is a yellowish maroon color, with fibrous texture, thin in section, but considerably thickened at the edge. Illuminated from the rear it is translucent, and is of various shades between yellow and red, darker in color at the edges. In section, it is very thin, not more than two millimeters at its thickest. The congealed blood in five small separated masses, has the appearance of a brownish maroon wax. The total weight of the blood, according to the recent tests, was 16.5 grams, a little more than one-half ounce. It is contained in a glass flask at the base of the ostensorium which contains the Host.

The series of tests were begun on November 18, 1970, when the relics were examined synoptically and the specimens of tissue and blood were taken and witnessed, and concluded March 4, 1971, with the final report of the commission. The tests span the full range of microscopic and microphotographic examination, biologic examination, including hematology, immunology, chromotographics and microchemical, and electrophoretic examination of protein. Great care was taken in identification of the specimens and separation of studies of the blood and tissue so as to discourage collaboration. The results were in three phases: first identification as animal tissue and type of tissue and blood; second, determination of human origin; and third, determination of compatibility between tissue and blood. The results are summarized below:

1. The tissue is of human miocardic muscle origin with isolated bits of interstitial adipose tissue. The section was taken parallel to the heart fibers rather than a crosscut through the organ.

2. The blood is of human origin, type AB, and further the blood contains the same fraction of proteins as fresh normal human blood not of that of a cadaver or of exposed blood, which separates quickly.

3. The blood and flesh are compatible, which is to say it could come from the same donor, but is not necessarily from the same donor.

4. The chemical analysis of the blood and tissue were normal; there was no sign of any preservative agency.

5. Of collateral importance, there was no evidence of starch on the specimen of tissue or in the ostensorium.

A white stain on the tissue had been identified visually by the last examiner in 1886 as fragments of bread. It was found instead to be a fungus residue. The last point clarifies the condition of the Host which, as was noted, has a large vacant area. It has been conjectured for many years that the vacant area represented bread which had not been changed and had subsequently deteriorated and been lost. The whitish stain had been interpreted as being the zone of contact between the tissue and the bread. The new interpretation is that as the circular tissue dried, it ruptured near the center, perhaps because in the original reliquary it was constrained at the edge, and withdrew toward the periphery which contributed to the observed thickened edge. The evidence appears conclusive that there never was any starchy substance in contact with the tissue.

We are now left with the task of trying to explain the anomaly.

The first physical explanation is, of course, that the tissue at some time in the past or several times in the past had been cut from a human heart immediately after death and placed in the reliquary to perpetrate and perpetuate the fraud. The examining doctors expressed the view that to take a section as large in diameter and thin as this one, painstakingly parallel to the fiber, would require skilled technicians, and instruments including optical aids of the very best dissectionists. We would also have to suppose that the individual or individuals in ages past had the foresight to assume that at some future time equipment to make a determination would become available and provide for that eventuality at tremendous expenditure of energy and time, not to mention risk. Otherwise, why not take a section of pork or lamb and any blood they could find. There was certainly no way until this century that the examination and tests could be conducted.

The second explanation is, of course, falsified laboratory work. The number of people and professional reputation of the people involved do not in any way support this view. The third explanation is that the event took place essentially as described. Additional support for the authenticity of the anomaly is that the tissue and blood have not decayed, but remain in excellent condition without any preservation and in ambient conditions. But even today to obtain five specimens of solidified human blood containing normal fresh blood characteristics would be straining the state of the medical arts.

All of the explanations strain the credibility levels, but if there were a readily understandable explanation, it would not be an anomaly. When considered with the other anomalies we have looked at, this one is no more inexplicable than the instantaneous replacement of diseased bone and tissue with healthy bone and tissue as in the case of Elisa Aloi.

There are numerous other instances of the same or similar phenomena more recent and without detailed scientific corroboration. Among them an additional case at Lanciano occurred in 1273, two cases near Siena, one in 1330, now conserved in the sanctuary of St. Rita in Cascia, and the other in 1730 at the Basilica of St. Francis in Siena; at Santarem near Fatima in Portugal, also in the thirteenth century; at Ferrara in 1171, Alatri in 1228, and Florence in 1230, all in Italy. The most famous of all was at Bolsena in 1263, which was the subject of a painting by Raphael now at the Vatican Library and the motive for establishing the Feast of Corpus Christi in 1264. Oddly enough, the anomalies other than the last named are not well known, even within the Church. The writer would hope the results of Lanciano would spur scientific analysis of the others, not expressing doubt, but—on the contrary—confidence.

As in the other previously considered anomalies, at Lanciano, there is the matter of assessing the probability of a preternatural explanation when viewed in the light of all the circumstances. Certainly that view is far more likely than the physical alternatives, both leaving questions of physical anomaly in the survival of the blood and tissue and both hinging on fraud with little or no potential reward and tremendous difficulty and personal risk. It should be noted that the alternatives are not truly separable because if the substances are not blood and human tissue, then there were two fraudulent representations, the original perpetrators and "conclusive" scientific tests separated by centuries. If it is human tissue, but particularly if it is human blood, which eliminated the second fraud, there still is no physical explanation. Solidified blood under natural conditions is not merely a change from liquid to solid state as in freezing water, but of entirely different molecular composition as a result of highly complex biochemical change involving enzymatic action. It is not a reversible process. The adding of distilled water and agitation as was done in the tests are largely mechanical in effect.

The blood protein profile for the specimen was determined by the Kohn technique and electrophoretic electrodialysis and gave the following protein profile:

Albumine (61.93%; Globuline Alpha-1 (2.38%);

Globuline Alpha-2 (7.14%);

Globuline Beta (7.14%), and Globuline Gamma (21.425),

The ratio of albumine to total protein is within normal range. (Sammaciccia, 1973, pp 59, 60, translation by the writer).

This corresponds with the profile of normal fresh blood. The writer verified the fresh blood profile by inquiry in the United States. Although the percentage of Globuline Alpha-1 is a trifle below normal lower limits (2.38 vs 2.50) as calculated using normal gram-percent ratios of total protein used more commonly in the United States, this variation would not be considered unusual.

If there was fraud by the original perpetrator alone, he was truly a genius, having to synthesize in his solidified "blood masses" a pattern of protein which, when examined centuries later, would correspond with fresh blood and preserve it without preservatives; quite a trick, even today.

The second case of this group is that of the annual liquefaction of the Blood of St. Januarius (San Gennaro) in the cathedral dedicated to him in Naples, Italy. This is a well-known phenomenon, often referred to in the same joking way as Saint Patrick and the snakes. It is not a joke to the bulk of the Neapolitans, who on the rare instances when it has not occurred became very upset, since historically it has been accompanied by disaster. The last time it failed to occur was in 1944, at the height of World War II, when Naples was heavily damaged both by the Germans retreating to Naples from Salerno in the fall of 1943 and the Americans later driving them out. In 1973 when the phenomenon occurred on schedule on the Saint's Feast, September 19, the city heaved a collective sigh since a threatened epidemic of cholera would have been both a medical and economic disaster had it developed. The people took the liquefaction as a sign that a disaster would not occur. That, of course, has little bearing on our case. The case is an oddity and appears to make little sense in any hardheaded way, except it is a very real cohesive force among the people of the Saint's ancient city. This case and the following one were selected because of:

1. The tremendous impact on the concept of the transcendental nature of man, if tests under way, projected, and contemplated, are carried out and verify the phenomenon, and

2. The illustration it provides for the recognition and appreciation which the Creator has for the affection of man, and even for the whimsical man, for whimsy is a basic human characteristic and totally human. Even Scrooge eventually became whimsical when he became human.

Saint Januarius was beheaded and buried about the year 305, at a place called Marciano between the present cities of Naples and Pozzuoli, during the persecutions of Diocletian. Written records from the period show that in 431 his remains were transferred to Naples by Bishop St. John I, of Naples, in response to the request of what appears to have been a long established cult in the Naples area venerating the Saint. The cemetery where he was buried in 431 is called the Catacomb of Saint Januarius from that event.

In this age, we have difficulty in comprehending the jealousy and competition which existed in the early centuries for the relics of the saints; it seems somewhat macabre. But St. Januarius was not to be excluded from its effect. In 831, Sicone, Duke of Benevento, opened the catacomb and had the relics transported to the Church of Saint Mary of Jerusalem in Benevento. Then in 839 the relics were ordered transferred to Reichenau, on Lake Constance, by the Emperor Lothario. Apparently, in the midst of wars and plagues they were transferred again to Montevergine and almost forgotten. There is now considerable argument whether all of the relics ever were in Reichenau.

In 1480, the relics were rediscovered under the main altar of the Basilica at Montevergine and after difficult negotiations were returned to Naples in 1497. Of crucial interest in our case is the fact that all the records of these translations of the relics are silent as to the relics of the head and the blood. There is no information concerning these specific relics, but in 1306 there is a record of a French artist being brought to Naples to make a silver reliquary for the head of Saint Januarius. There were celebrations in Naples, including one which became the subject of a Papal Bull by John XXII, in 1331, indicating some relics or at least the head was already in Naples. But also, in none of these documents is there any mention of the blood, or hence of the anomaly of the liquefaction. It is not a scientific inference, but one suspects the Neapolitans held out on the original transfer in 831 and were quiet about it afterwards.

The first mention of the liquefaction was on August 17, 1389, at which time a chronicle item in an ecclesiastical diary or log recorded incidentally the liquefaction of the blood of St. Januarius of Naples when brought together with his other relics, presumably his head, since the other relics were still in Montevergine at the time.

On December 31, 1390, the official archives of the new Cathedral of Naples, which had been completed earlier in the fourteenth century, records that the relics of the head and blood were both there. They are still in the same reliquaries as when first reported, which appear to date from the thirteenth or fourteenth century. Some embellishments have been added over the years and make visual identification of the age difficult. The blood is contained in two glass ampules, one of which appears to be about three inches long and about 1.5 inches in maximum diameter. The second ampule is about of equal height, but much smaller, perhaps one quarter of the volume. Together, the contents could not be more than three or four fluid ounces. It appears these ampules must be the original containers of the blood and antidate the glass windowed ostensorium in which they are displayed, which is about three inches in diameter and about two inches deep (visual estimates).

The liquefaction occurs on September 19, the Feast of the Saint, so celebrated as a matter of record since the fifth century in Naples, and also by the cult of St. Januarius among the Cathagenians in Africa from the sixth century. It also occurs on the Saint's Feast Day in May, which honors the first bringing of the relics to Naples, and on December 16, the anniversary of the terrible eruption of Vesuvius in 1631, when the Saint's help was implored to save the city. It has also occurred rarely on occasions of public disaster or special events in honor of the Saint. The last such occasion officially recorded (1972) was on February 28, 1964, when Alfonso Cardinal Castaldo was debating the results of the visual examination of the bones completed the previous day.

The liquefaction has failed to occur only four times—in May and September 1527, in May 1835, and May 1944. These dates correlate much better with military, political, economic and religious upheavals in Italy generally than with disastrous eruptions of Vesuvius, as some writers have indicated. (Since this section was written the blood failed to liquefy in May 1976. This failure coincided with the disastrous earthquake in Udine, Italy and with a period of political turmoil and the first election of a communist mayor in Rome.)

The liquefaction of February 28, 1964 apparently convinced the Cardinal and he gave the previous work his official approval and signaled the continuing of the scientific examination. The first phase of work, anatomic identification of the bones as all of the same individual, was completed in July 1964, and indicated they were not a complete skeleton. Some bones were missing, but those that there were appeared to be of the same individual.

The second phase was a radiographic examination to determine the approximate age of the bones. Again this established the probability of the early fourth century. Since carbon dating involves destruction of the material tested, the examiners were reluctant at this time to proceed with those tests. The results of the radiographic study have suggested that other supposed relics, including some remaining in the abbey in Reichenau on Lake Constance be also tested to resolve that debate and perhaps supply answers to questions about the missing bones.

Phases of work proposed involving the blood have been held in abeyance. The blood was tested earlier, using spectroscopic methods which confirmed that the spectrum absorption profile corresponded with that of oxyhemoglobin. It seems likely in the not too distant future that tests similar to those at Lanciano will be conducted to identify positively the nature of the ampule content. At least such tests are being discussed (1974). The reluctance to proceed is more emotional than rational, but it is nevertheless real and understandable. These ampules were not designed to be sampled. It will probably be necessary to penetrate the ancient glass with a drill or similar means to withdraw a bit of the matter for test. The total volume involved at Lanciano of original material and in any required samples are quite similar, but these samples will be more difficult to obtain.

The phenomenon has great significance relative to demonstration of the transcendental nature of man. If the blood is shown to be of human origin, it is absolutely unexplainable in physical terms. As has been pointed out in the first case, the process of coagulation of blood is nonreversible outside of a living body, and largely so otherwise, even when using special anticoagulants and large quantities of fresh blood to dissolve and absorb the clots. To have the actual process repeated and recorded several times a year for almost 600 years is utterly fantastic. Further, blood outside the body in a container soon separates gravitationally with the serum rising to the top. There is no evidence of this in this case. Not to mention the specificity of dates of occurrence and the conjunction with other relics involved in the whole process. The preservation of blood for that period alone, even in the solid state, would be an anomaly.

Currently the condition is one of high probability that it is human blood, particularly when viewed in the light of the tests at Lanciano and results of the previous spectroscopic examination. There are at this time no alternative explanations to offer. Hence, also, there is high probability of its being a physical anomaly of preternatural origin and explanation.

Where were the relics of the blood before 1389 and hence why was there no record of the liquefaction before that date?

Probably there never will be an answer to those questions. It is quite likely (if tests verify the relics) that the ampules of blood were held completely separate from the bones from the time of the martyrdom of the saint; that they were collected in secret by one of the intimate followers of the bishop and concealed only to be discovered many years later. In view of all the other anomalous aspects of the case, that would be of very minor concern.

The third case in this category is that of the liquefaction of the blood of St. Pantaleon in Ravello, Italy, near the coast about halfway between Salerno and Naples. St. Pantaleon, a physician of Nicomedia, was, by tradition, physician to the Emperor Maximilian, in what is present day Izmir, Turkey. He was put to death in 305, the same year as St. Januarius, under Diocletian who had established his Eastern Empire capital at Nicomedia. Before death, Pantaleon was tortured on the rack and burned with flaming torches. He is the principal patron of the medical profession after St. Luke. Our history can only begin with a description of the special relationship which existed between the citizens of Ravello and Amalfi, its coastal outlet, and the Byzantines and Arabs of the late Middle Ages. Amalfi had won its independence from Byzantium and Naples in 810 and controlled the southern approaches to Italy and the Tyrrenian Sea. From the tenth to the thirteenth centuries, in spite of almost perpetual wars, a sturdy maritime commerce had built up between the Republic of Amalfi and the communities in Asia Minor and other Adriatic and Eastern Mediterranean states. Ravello became a populous city of about 30,000 (it is now about 2,500). As we saw earlier the forces of Islam steadily moved westward and reduced the Byzantine Empire, forcing retreat of much of its main cultural and economic activity into European areas of the Eastern Empire and adjacent western Christendom. Sometime during this period, certainly prior to 1453 when Constantinople fell to Islam, the relic of the blood of St. Pantaleon which had been previously (about 535 A.D.) transferred from Nicomedia to Constantinople under the Christian Emperor Justinian, was carried to Ravello. A church on the main square dedicated to St. Pantaleon dates from 1288, and since 1112 there has been an altar dedicated to him in the Church of St. Augustine.

Official notice of the phenomenon of liquefaction of the blood began in 1577, which is not to say it had not occurred before that, and the anomaly has occurred every year since. The solid substance liquefies on the feast day of the saint, July 27, and remains liquid until the Feast of the Holy Cross on September 14. In the description of the phenomenon, the color of the blood is said to change to deep clear crimson. The relic is contained in what appears to be a glass urn decorated in gold and silver, although it is described as a "chiseled ampulla of gold and silver of the thirteenth century" (Einaudi, 1956). At the time the writer first viewed the relic in the fall of 1973, it was in its solid state. The quantity of the blood which appears as a maroon waxy mass is much greater than at Lanciano or Naples. There appears to be about a half liter or more of the material. The ampule has a bad crack which dates from 1577 (the same year liquefaction was first recorded and which may account for its being recorded) and appears to be far from airtight yet the liquid has not tended to evaporate. The ampule is contained in an altar in the Church of the Assumption and St. Pantaleon. In the summer of 1975 the writer again visited Ravello during the period September 12 to 15. The blood was in the liquid state on September 13, being dark red and somewhat translucent and showing the meniscus upturn at the sides of the vessel. By the afternoon of September 14 the blood had congealed into a solid waxy mass.

There seems to be no extant body of knowledge on the phenomenon and nothing in the way of scientific examination. It is included in this study because of its close relationship in type to that of Lanciano and Saint Januarius. There, of course, has been no pressure in the little community for such tests, probably on the contrary. But in view of the large quantity of material, its unexplainable precise liquefaction regardless of its nature, the long period it remains in the liquid state, more than six weeks—and the probability that it is an identical phenomenon to that of Naples certainly makes it a likely candidate for scientific test and verification.

If it is verified as human blood, it would be of importance equal to that of the blood of St. Januarius as a preternatural event, particularly since the relatively long period it remains in the liquid state under ambient conditions would be absolutely impossible with blood under purely physical control.

Section 4—Category IV
Phenomena—Incorrupt Human Bodies

In this fourth category, the nature of the study changes from that of discussing well-defined singular cases, even though related in general categories, to one of a search for and explanation of a type of physical anomaly which has been observed but rarely. It is well known that a human body, like that of any organism comprised of soft tissue, under usual ambient conditions deteriorates rapidly after death, decomposes and is reduced by bacteriological and other action to its bony skeletal remains, which themselves slowly deteriorate and crumble. In the last section we saw some exceptions to this physical order which were related however to other anomalous circumstances of preternatural significance.

In this category of cases, however, we have a human body which in most cases has been interred in a casket below ground and after a period of years has been exhumed, examined and found to be incorrupt—one, in China, after almost 2200 years. The writer took the purely scientific view that there are no accidental anomalies. The general physical laws stand unviolable unless some special condition, physical or otherwise, causes a change. Among physical causes, freezing would be one, intense radiation would be another, embalming or mummifying preservations would be another, and desiccation under continuously very arid conditions, or as in some observed cases direct embedment in asphalt, volcanic ash or dense calcareous clays and in peat bogs seem to have produced these results to some degree. But if having covered all of these plausible answers and still finding certain cases which have commonality of circumstances, but defy natural explanation, it is surely permissible to look to other sources.

The cases are not publicized. There is little literature the writer could find in English, French, Italian or Spanish on the general subject. His search for cases eventually took the form of checking out likely candidates—people who had a local reputation for a life of devotion to transcendental matters. All other avenues seemed to be of no avail. This it can be argued puts a very strong bias on the overall study because there might be just as many cases among thieves and murderers, and scoundrels, in general, as well as among the bon vivants, or just ordinary people. If that were the case, there would be no anomaly at all for the percentage of cases among the humble, dedicated, and intensely spiritual is high. The writer's sample is not yet large enough to do a reliable statistical correlative study and the type of definition is still too vague. The writer searched for other cases having no specific religious connotations and found three which he investigated and will report on. The writer covered some fifteen instances of the anomaly which represents several months of research in libraries and on the ground.

The first case, the one which prompted the writer to undertake this line of investigation, in fact, is fairly recent. Placido Riccardi was born in Trevi near Spoleto June 24, 1844, and died March 15, 1915. In January, 1959, the writer was in Rome on a business-related vacation and happened during a standard guided tour to go through the Basilica of St. Paul outside the Walls. There was, before the main altar, a glass casket in which a monk's body had been placed, apparently ready for a funeral service, though it seemed strange to have him in a glass casket. The writer was shocked to hear that the individual had been dead, at the time, almost 44 years. Everyone else in the group was equally astounded—even unbelieving—that this was not the body of a middle-aged person who had just died. In fact, he looked scarcely dead. Nevertheless, the tour went on and the writer did not even know the man's name. But occasionally, the event would come to mind and disturb him, though he was not at the time much concerned with such matters. Over the next ten years, he was in Rome several times, and at every opportunity would go back to see if the body was there again. It never was. In the fall of 1973, however, when he had decided to make a project out of gathering physical evidence of man's transcendental nature for this study, that case was uppermost in his mind.

After some persistent inquiries, in October 1973, I learned that the monk was Placido Riccardi and that his body had been returned to his own abbey at Sabina in Farfa about 50 kilometers from Rome toward Rieti. The writer went to Sabina and there, in the chapel, was he, looking just the same, and meanwhile the writer had aged some 14 years! The writer was even more surprised to find that Riccardi had been over 70 years of age when he died, he looked to be between 50 and 60 years of age. There were no efforts to maintain his condition, no cosmetics, the glass casket was lightly jointed and there was a 100-watt bulb to illuminate the space. No one paid any attention to him. He was a part of the Benedictine community at Farfa where he had been rector. He had never really left. His life from his late teens had been one of absolute unobtrusiveness, of humility, of meditation and prayer, and most of all of great devotion to the service of God, expressed largely in little things rather than great. In his last years he had been subjected to intestinal illness which incapacitated him to the extent that he was unable to leave his cell and, in fact, needed almost constant assistance. He could take little food. He hung between life and death his last two years. His greatest worry was the difficulty he imposed on others.

His case is really somewhat typical. The writer never would have found Blessed Placido Riccardi (beatified in 1954) had it not been for a chance observation some fourteen years before. Even the book on his life prepared by Ildefonso Cardinal Schuster in 1954 (Schuster 1954) shortly after his beatification makes no mention of the fact. It is not considered miraculous, but it is certainly anomalous!

The second case is Saint Marie Bernadette Soubirous, who as a result largely of the movie "The Song of Bernadette," is the best known of all the "incorrupts" though not in that context. Few people, in fact, have heard that her body is in the chapel of Nevers at the convent of Saint Gillard rather than at Lourdes, or that it is incorrupt. St. Bernadette was born at Lourdes January 7, 1844, the same year as Blessed Placido. She was 14 at the beginning of the apparitions for which she is famous. She joined the Sisters of Charity at Nevers in 1866 and died of tuberculosis at the age of 35, April 16, 1879, after a short life of poverty, suffering and intense devotion and dedication to the service of God in the most menial occupations.

She was buried on the confines of the convent on April 30, 1879. On September 22, 1909, as part of a formal action for her beatification, her body was exhumed and found incorrupt. After examination and certification, it was reinterred the same day in a new coffin. On April 3, 1919, it was again exhumed for another examination, this time in the presence of the Bishop of Nevers, the commissioner of police and other municipal officials. The condition was the same. The body was again reinterred. On April 18, 1925, the body was brought into its present resting place in the glass enclosed casket under the altar in the chapel. St. Bernadette's face had darkened in time and a light cosmetic mask of wax made from an impression of her face after the last examination in 1925 was applied. Similar cosmetic action was taken for her hands, which had also darkened. The result is breathtaking, considering how sick Bernadette had been for the last years of her life, and after 100 years her condition is truly remarkable.

The third case is St. Catherine Laboure. Catherine Laboure was born May 2, 1806, at Fain Les Moutiers, Cote d'Or in the Bourgogne district of France. She was the ninth of eleven children and had been an exceptionally spiritually-minded child. When her mother died in 1821, it is reported she had already dedicated herself to the religious life in service of the Blessed Virgin. After much opposition from her father, in April 1830, she entered the convent of the Sisters of Charity of St. Vincent de Paul on Rue Du Bac in Paris (the same convent that Marie Bailly, Dr. Carrel's patient entered some 75 years later.).

The same year, 1830, the series of private apparitions of the Blessed Virgin during which the disastrous war of 1870 and siege of Paris were predicted and which culminated in the Miraculous Medal devotion (important among Catholics) took place. The cult was authorized in Paris in 1838 and other dioceses in France in 1839-40. Because of her great desire to avoid the public notoriety, not even other members of her community, including the Superior, knew of Catherine Laboure's part in the devotion until May 1876, eight months before her death on December 31, 1876. Meanwhile, she had devoted her life to the poor and sick at the Hospice d'Enghien near Paris. St. Catherine was beatified in 1933 following which her body was exhumed on March 21, 1933 and found to be incorrupt. It was examined by two doctors and other officials. *"Telle on l'avait couchee le 3 Janvier 1877, telle on la retrova le 21 Mars 1933. Le chairs etaient intactes, les members souples, les prunelles bleues."* "Thus as she went to rest on January 3, 1877, so she returned on March 21, 1933. Her flesh fresh and firm, her limbs pliant, her eyes blue."

It was that same year placed in the unpretentious glass casket where it still remains at the side altar in the Chapel of Apparitions, Rue du Bac, Paris. St. Catherine was 70 years of age at her death. She looks much younger than that. To the best of the writer's knowledge, and from observation from about five feet away in good illumination, there appears to be no cosmetic work involved as there was in the case of St. Bernadette.

The fourth case is that of Jacinta Marto, the youngest of three children who were the central subjects of the apparitions at Fatima, and whose case for beatification is currently in process. Jacinta was born on March 11, 1910 in the village of Cova da Iria, about 25 miles from the present railroad station of Fatima, Portugal, which is in turn about 70 miles northeast of Lisbon. Jacinta died during the influenza epidemic in February 1920, being still less than 10 years of age. The apparitions took place in 1917 when she was but seven. The short period between, her life would have to be classed as one of heroic virtue if that can be properly said of one so young, but she had a full appreciation of the significance of the events of which she was a major part. Her life in that period was one of dedicated prayer, humility and suffering.

As part of the inquiry into the beatification process, the body of Jacinto was exhumed in 1935, was examined and found to be incorrupt. Her body was reinterred so that in 1973, there was no way of viewing it. The written testimony is however available. Presumably, if and when the beatification process is completed the body will once again be exhumed as has been the pattern in these cases. If the pattern of incorruption also holds (the writer has heard of no exception), her body will again be found incorrupt.

The fifth case, and most recent in terms of death, is venerable Father Balbino del Carmelo, a Carmelite monk born on March 7, 1865 and named Ildefonso-Tomas Sanchez y Mayorga in El Fresno, Avila Province, Spain. He died on May 12, 1934, at the age of 69 and was buried at the Carmelite Monastery in Avila, where he had spent most of his life. After a boyhood of earnest dedication in school and in religion, at the age of 16, he entered the Carmelite Order at the Novitiate de Larrea at Viscaya. His life is almost a duplicate of Placido Riccardi, except even more humble, of lower rank and of great simplicity. The small book on his life (San Jose, 1961) speaks of him, *"He aqui santo que, sin haber heco cosas grandes no extraordinarias, encontro su perfection en las pequenos y ordinarias de cada dia."* "Here is a saint, without having done anything great or extraordinary, found perfection in the small and ordinary things of each day." In connection with the beatification process, his body was exhumed and found incorrupt and was brought to the chapel of the Carmelites and is in a small room adjacent to the tomb of the great 16th century mystic St. Teresa of Avila, who is also incorrupt and whose case is discussed later. The lighting of the tomb of Venerable Balbino is not the best, but he appears to be in good condition considering his age at death; but he looks his age.

The sixth example is Blessed Marie-Assunta Pallotta. This was another case the writer was unable to check personally since she was interred in China at the site of her death, but the records are clear. This account is adapted from the series *The Saints Go Marching* by the late Archbishop Robert J. Dwyer. Maria was born near Ascoli, Italy, on August 20, 1878, the eldest of five children. Her parents were the poorest of the poor, so that when she was only a child she was sent out to work as a hired hand as a hod carrier for masons and carrying stones for the building of roads and courtyards. She also at a later period was hired as a helper to a tailor. She had almost no education but from her earliest childhood had a deep devotion to the spiritual life and because her sanctity was well known locally, she was admitted as a lay sister for a newly founded order, the Franciscan Missionary Sisters of Mary.

She was trained in the scullery as a cook. While in the novitiate near Rome, she captivated all who knew her with her bright smile, cheerfulness and warmth. In addition to all her normal arduous duties she worked at any other menial tasks she could find in the infirmary or on the farm.

She asked for a mission assignment among the lepers and was sent in February 1904 to the mission of T'ai Yuan in Shangsi province, the scene some five years previously of the savage Boxer Rebellion. She was assigned as the convent cook. The spring following her arrival, a typhus epidemic broke out and she cared for the sick, at last becoming infected herself. She died on April 7, 1905. At the time of her death, the room was filled with the pervasive and compelling odor of flowers—roses and violets, so that her funeral was one attended by crowds of natives who filed by the bier in awe and wonder. Her burial took on the proportions of a triumphal procession. In 1913 when action for her beatification was being initiated, her body was exhumed and found incorrupt, the perfume of flowers still apparent. She was formally declared blessed on November 7, 1954 by Pope Pius XII.

The seventh case is that of Pope Pius X, born Giuseppe Melchiorre Sarto at Reisi in Venice, Italy, on June 2, 1835. Again, he was the child of poor parents, but was known even as a young boy for his religious devotion, particularly for his attention to the old and crippled among the poor, of which he was, of course, one. He had no aspirations for religious rank, but was a man of great intelligence and energy so that it was thrust upon him and he was named pope in 1903. During his reign he fought the secularization of the Church in France and the rise of the materialistic-positivistic trends in Church affairs, which are lumped together under the heading of "Modernism."

He was best known for his love for the common people. He did not court the political greats in Europe on the eve of World War I. His life has been termed a dedication to the "folly of the Cross" and his simplicity of life and humility shone through all of the pomp of the papacy. His final will was keyed to those words, "I was born poor, I have lived in poverty and I wish to die poor." He died on August 20, 1914. During the beatification process his body was found to be incorrupt. He was canonized on May 29, 1954.

Nothing can be determined about the condition of his body, which lies in a glass enclosed tomb at St. Peter's basilica, since his face is covered by the burial death mask.

The last of what may be called the modern examples of incorrupt bodies is truly strange and one which because of the "Yom Kipper War" and subsequent disturbances, the writer has not seen. Yet, as will be pointed out, it is quite similar in one aspect to the oldest of all. The account here is adapted from the work of John Haffert (1967). It is the body of St. Charbel Makhlouf, a priest of the Oriental rite who died in 1898 at the Maronite monastery just north of Beirut in Lebanon. Christened Joseph Makhlouf, St. Charbel was born on May 8, 1828 in a Lebanese mountain village of Biqua-Kafra and against family wishes entered the monastery of Our Lady of Mayfoulk north of Biblus. He was ordained in 1859. The last twenty years of his life were spent in a hermitage not far from the main monastery, where he lived a life of strict asceticism. The final eight days of his life after collapse at the altar appeared to be re-enactment of the sufferings of Christ.

Aside from that, his l'fe was not on a dramatic note. He was not known outside of his monastery, but was known there for his great devotion to the Eucharist, spending long hours in preparation daily for his Mass and long hours afterwards in thanksgiving. After his death he was buried in the monastery cemetery. For years a light had been observed emanating from the tomb, and in 1950 the monastery received permission to exhume the body. The body was found to be absolutely incorrupt, but to have exuded a liquid reddish in color like a mixture of water and blood. The body has since been moved to an above-ground tomb in the ancient monastery. The tomb, which is closed to view, is opened each year, and the body, still incorrupt, is found to be semi-floating in the liquid which collects to a depth of about three inches. There seems to be no explanation for the liquid at all in the above-ground tomb. The liquid appears to be highly corrosive to metals, causing deterioration of the caskets even when a zinc lining was provided, and corroded the metal documentation box in which doctors had placed their certification. The paper which the doctors used, however, was unaffected.

The writer has found no evidence that the liquid has been chemically analyzed. Father Makhlouf was beatified on May 12, 1965, and canonized in October 1977. Many physical anomalies, primarily of the cure category, have been reported at the tomb, several thousand since 1950. The pattern of St. Charbel's life is consistent with the others which have been discussed previously. Reports have come out of Lebanon that since his canonization the phenomenon of the fluid has ceased and corruption of the body has occurred.

Because of certain similarities with the case of Blessed Makh-louf, the oldest case is chosen to begin the review of those instances of bodies which have remained incorrupt for centuries. The case is that of a woman identified as Lady Tai. Her tomb on the eastern suburbs of Chong Sa in Hunan Province, has been dated by Chinese archeologists from 190 B.C., the early part of the Han dynasty (206 B.C.-A.D. 24). Buried with the body are several items of burial goods marked with the inscription, roughly translated "Household assistant of the Marques of Tai" and "family of the Marquis of Tai." The investigators believe Lady Tai was the wife of the first of four nobles with that title, conferred in 193 B.C., and who held that title for about eight years. The grave was found as a part of a general archaeological investigation by the Chinese People's Republic in 1972. This report is taken from an article by Richard C. Rudolph in the magazine, *Archaeology*, of the American Institute of Archaeology, Volume 26, April 1973, pages 106-115. Rudolph is Professor of Oriental Languages at the University of California at Los Angeles. The article is accompanied by excellent photographs of Lady Tai and the burial goods. Her body looks typical of the condition of these older cases, incorrupt but shrunken and desiccated to some extent. Quoting from the article,

The innermost coffin contained the body of a woman interred on her back with her head pointing north. She has now been identified as a certain Lady Tai. Her body was clothed and wrapped in some 20 layers of silk and was in an excellent state of preservation at the time of the discovery, a fact which stirred great interest in scientific circles. This is by far the earliest find of its type ever made in China. The original excavation report says that the body was partly immersed in a reddish fluid which apparently helped to preserve it, but strangely enough, no analysis of this fluid has yet been published. An autopsy showed that the subcutaneous loose connective tissues were still elastic and the fibers still distinct; the color of the femoral artery, moreover, was similar to that of a recently deceased person. Calcified areas in the bronchi and lungs indicate that the lady probably died from tuberculosis, and she was estimated to be about 50 years old at the time of her death. The body has now been preserved by modern scientific methods....The most important and interesting of the textile items is a large, T-shaped piece of silk fabric directly beneath the lid of the innermost coffin and situated on top of the layers of other textiles protecting the body. This piece, which is 205 centimeters long, 92 centimeters at the top, and 47.7 centimeters wide at the bottom, appears to have been designed to be vertically suspended. It is completely covered with a very well executed painting in bright and contrasting colors, and can be divided into three general sections according to the subject matter: the heavenly world, the world of man, and the under-world. Some of the myths and legends represented are well known, including among others symbols of the sun and the moon, and eight suns in a tree that recall the myth of the archer Yi, who shot nine of the original ten suns down from the sky. Other motifs are more obscure, and possibly reflect local beliefs and traditions. Painted fabrics earlier than this piece have been found, but they are small and fragmentary, and the Lady Tai silk is now considered one of China's art treasures.

Subsequent to Rudolph's report, an article appeared in the *National Geographic Magazine*, Vol. 145, No. 5, May 1974 which states (page 663), "Chemists analyzed a reddish fluid that partly covered the body and some of the grave goods. It contained a mercurial compound and organic acids that could have retarded deterioration. Since the tomb has been airtight, so that few decay-causing bacteria could live, many experts speculate that the lack of oxygen also aided the preservation." This would indicate a substantial difference then, than in the case of Blessed Makhlouf. The later article also indicated death of Lady Tai as from a heart attack rather than tuberculosis and suggested she might have been of higher rank than Lady Hsin Chui.

This is the only case the author could find which exhibits the same general physical condition as others discussed under incorrupt bodies, the case of the liquid being almost identical with that of St. Charbel, and the only other case in which that phenomenon has been reported. Two things are different which might explain the preservation on purely physical grounds.

A cross section through the tomb shows the coffin was surrounded by a bed of charcoal about 30 centimeters in thickness. Outside that is a packing of "white" clay about a meter thick. Calcareeus clays, and the description of "white" would indicate that they have characteristics fostering decay resistance as mentioned earlier and which appear to have application in another case discussed later. This condition has been observed however, only when the bodies were in intimate contact with it, which is not the case here.

The description of the symbology on the drape or banner described in the article would imply that she also had been a very devout person in her religion (logically, Taoism at that time) and from that viewpoint alone, would be a candidate for the class of anomaly under study. In this connection in the center of the banner is what appears to be a symbol of Lady Tai. The caption of the photo enlargement of this section says, "Here appears an elegantly dressed elderly woman, leaning on a long walking stick, attended by two servants and three other women. The central figure probably, represents Lady Tai, the occupant of the tomb." The other two identified as servants appear to be men, kneeling at the foot of the woman in an attitude of profound respect. The three women standing in the background appear to be Lady Tai's attendants. It is as though she were revered by the men as a person of great wisdom.

The writer investigated available literature on the religious situation in Hunan Province during the period. The following quotation from the book *Everyday Life in Early Imperial China,* (Loewe, 1968, p. 114) appears to offer some possible enlightenment.

> The cult of immortality, which was of paramount importance in the growth of religious practices in Han China, derived from early origins. A desire to prolong life is seen in some of the first records of thought and emotion that date from the eighth century B.C. or even earlier. It was probably inspired not only as a matter of personal interest for the individual but also as a means of ensuring the continuity or survival of the man's family or community, and it is possible to discern two distinct ways in which the concept was being advanced in the fourth and third centuries B.C. . . .
>
> In the first place, there was a longing for physical immortality, for the continuation of life in the world of flesh without suffering the failures, corruption and destruction of the body; such an idea of immortality

was essentially this-worldly. But, at the same time, there was developing a belief that it was possible to attain the bliss of an endless life in the totally different circumstances of another world; and the characteristics of those who attained a non-worldly immortality of this type were those of the ascetic or the hermit.

Both these objectives could be reached by the intervention of intermediary experts. These were the magicians who could lay their hands on the medicaments and drugs that would preserve the body; alternately they could devise means of introduction to those who had already achieved a state of non-worldly immortality and who could possibly lead others to the enjoyment of the same life of enchantment. On several occasions in the late third and the second centuries B.C. emperors sent expeditions to search for the non-worldly immortals, whose abode was thought to lie beyond the confines of the known world: and in this way we hear of parties who explored the Eastern Isles of the Ocean, to find immortal beings, and of the thought that the Queen Mother of the West who would confer these blessings would be found in the deep recesses of Central Asia.

Also of possible application is an excerpt from the book *The Religions of Man* by Houston Smith, discussing certain aspects of Taoism (Smith, 1958, page 199).

There are books whose first reading casts a spell never quite undone, the reason being that they speak to the deepest "me" in the reader. For all who quicken to the thought that anywhere, anytime, Tao can swell within us, the Tao Te Ching is such a book. Mostly it has been so for the Chinese, but a contemporary American poet equally can find it "the straightest, most logical explanation as yet advanced for the continuance of life, the most logical use yet advised for enjoying it." Though obviously never practiced to perfection, its lessons of simplicity and openness have been for millions of Chinese a joyful guide.

There is a being, wonderful, perfect;
It existed before heaven and earth.
How quiet it is!
How spiritual it is!
It stands alone and it does not change.
It moves around and around, but does not on this
account suffer.
All life comes from it.
It wraps everything with love as in a garment, and
yet it claims no honor, it does not demand to be Lord.
I do not know its name, and so I call it Tao, the
way, and I rejoice in its power.

The poem is from the twenty-fifth chapter of the *Tao Te Ching* translation by Reichelt.

The next oldest case is some 1,400 years later, St. Clare, the founder of the Order of Poor Clares, who was born in Assisi in 1193 and at a very young age dedicated herself to a life of poverty and prayer. At the age of 19, she and several other young women joined together and sought assistance of St. Francis of Assisi in establishing the order. His "constitution" for the Poor Clares was patterned after the very strict rules of St. Benedict as they were originally. They slept on the ground, walked barefoot, and made poverty the basis of their lives. St. Clare died on August 11, 1253 and was canonized only two years later.

She was renowned for her life of holiness all over Christendom. It does not appear that her body was ever interred, rather the records indicate it has been continuously in a transparent tomb, as it is today, in the great triple church in Assisi in a baroque glass-encased tomb. Her body appears shrunken, and the skin very dark, almost mummified. Since the thirteenth and fourteenth century descriptions indicate her great beauty, there appears to have been a gradual deterioration, but not decay over the centuries. It is almost like sublimation in the chemical sense of direct vaporization of the solid substance. It might be asked if it was God's will they be preserved incorrupt why would they deteriorate? A suitable answer would appear to be that devoted to God as they were, they were yet not perfect and hence the ultimate fate of return to dust must still overtake them.

St. Zita of Lucca, Italy, is undoubtedly one of the most humanly lovable characters we will run across in these pages. She is the patron saint of domestics. St. Zita was born in Monsagretti, near Lucca, Italy in 1218 of a poor but religious family. One of her maternal uncles was St. Graziano, who has had a small town near Lucca named after him. At the age of 12 she was placed in the service of the Casa Fatinelli, a prominent family in Lucca, where she worked until her death on April 27, 1278. Her life—much of it documented, much more by legend—was one of constant prayer and humble personal help to the poor, even if it took a bit of scheming to accomplish it. In one legend buns changed to roses so that she would not be caught by her master giving away bread from his kitchen. She really was not—she had an inexhaustible store of grain like the widow of Sarepta.

She was evidently loved by all because at her death practically the whole town came to a halt. All labor was stopped for three days. The Basilica of St. Frediano and the whole main square and adjacent squares were filled with people paying homage to the poor house servant to whom many marvels were attributed during life. This history of the city's mourning is a matter of record at the cathedral where she was entombed at an altar within the church, a thing itself highly unusual for other than a person of high rank. St. Zita does not appear to have been entombed in the usual sense. The people would not let them bury her.

Sometime in the middle of the fifteenth century, the increase in devotion to St. Zita was such that a new chapel was built for her where the old sacristy had been, and it is in this chapel that her body has been for the last 500 years. Her body appears to be in somewhat better condition than St. Clare's, but to have shrunk and her skin is a dark brown, but not truly mummified in appearance. She looks old, but she may have looked old when she died.

St. Rita of Cascia was born in 1381 at Roccaporena in the Italian Apennines of a humble peasant family. From her earliest childhood, she had wished to devote herself to God but her parents refused and she was married to a son of a prominent family, a dissolute and brutal man. For 18 years, during which she bore two sons, she put up with drunken beatings and every other abuse. Then at last, her husband somehow was induced by her patient endurance of his rages to change but, shortly afterwards, he was surprised by a group of his former intimates and murdered. Her two sons vowed vengeance but again through their mother's solicitations, they were deterred. Both were shortly after stricken with the plague and died.

Rita was given special dispensation and entered the convent of the Augustinian nuns at Cascia in 1413 where she lived a life of great austerity and suffering, being marked by the stigmata of the crown of thorns. She was pitiless to herself in her work, and suffering while always attending to others with great compassion. She died on May 22, 1457. The mark of her stigmata which during her life had been an open sore closed immediately following her death, leaving no scar. (A similar phenomenon occurred at the death of stigmatist Padre Pio in 1968.) St. Rita's body was subsequently found to be incorrupt and placed in an elevated crypt behind the altar of the church, where it remains in excellent condition. It reflects a not unusual appearance for a person of 75.

St. Catherine of Siena was born in 1347, the twenty-third of twenty-four children and from an early age resolved to devote her life to prayer and good work. At the age of 18 in 1365 she joined the religious group of women known as the Third Order of St. Dominic and in the great plague of 1374 was distinguished for her help to the sick and dying. She died on April 29, 1380 and is entombed in the Church of Santa Maria Sopra Minerva in Rome. It is a matter of official record that her body remains incorrupt and was observed over the centuries, although it is in a solid sacrophagus and cannot be generally viewed. It would be expected from other cases of the same age that her body now is in about the same condition as St. Zita and St. Clare.

St. Antoninus was born in Florence, Italy in 1389, and died on May 2, 1459. At 16 he entered the Dominican order in the convent at Fiesole. He was a brilliant student, but even more noted for his dedication to a life of reflection and prayer. He nevertheless was not allowed to have a life of quiet contemplation and was prior of several convents before being ordered to the office as the first Archbishop of Florence in 1446. In that office, in his role as pastor and in practice of austere virtue, he was distinguished for his personal activity in the care of the sick, particularly in the pestilence of 1448. His reputation for holiness was widespread. His incorrupt body has been under a side altar at the Church of St. Marco at Florence almost since his death. Aside from a darkening of the skin, he may have been dark anyway, his body appears to be in good condition today, considering he was 70 at the time of his death.

St. Teresa of Avila was born on March 28, 1515 and is known as the model of Christian mystics. She and St. Catherine of Siena are the only women who have been named doctors of the church. She is foundress of the Discalced Carmelites, an order dedicated to prayer and contemplation. Teresa was 12 when her mother died and her father placed her with a convent of Augustinian nuns. There she decided to enter the religious life and entered the Carmelite Convent of the Incarnation near Avila in November of 1534. Working with the other great Spanish mystic of the time, St. John of the Cross, she returned the Carmelite order to the original austerity from which it had departed with time. She died on October 4, 1582. Her body is entombed in the Carmelite monastery in Avila, about 75 feet from the room in which she was born. After her death, her body remained incorrupt and appears never to have been interred. It is however, enclosed in a solid tomb so that it is not possible for the general public to view it. Though it may sound strange, her heart was removed shortly after her death and is in a glass reliquary at the convent, where it is venerated. It looks perfectly fresh and certainly incorrupt.

Mary Magdalene (Catherine) Di Pazzi was born of a noble Florentine family in 1566. From the age of seven she had a great compassion for the poor and on going to school, habitually gave her lunch to prisoners in a jail she passed. When she was 14, her father was made governor of Cortona, and she was placed in the care of the monastery of St. John in Florence and entered the Carmelites in 1582, taking the name of Mary Magdalene. She lived a life characterized by contemplative mysticism and had the gift of prophecy. The last years of her life were of intense suffering. She died on May 25, 1607. After her death and until this day, her incorrupt body has exuded a sweet perfume. Her body is at the chapel of the cloistered convent of the Carmelites on the outskirts of Florence but administered from the Church of St. Mary of the Angels in Florence. Getting permission to view the body requires prior approval in the church in Florence and is not easily obtained.

The collateral phenomenon of the fragrance of the mystics was noted earlier in the case of Blessed Maria-Assunta Pallotta. It is frequently referred to in early religious writings as the "odor of sanctity." Padre Pio, also mentioned earlier, was characterized by this phenomenon during his lifetime and also at his death. If this pattern holds, one would expect that his body also will be found incorrupt if, and when, it is exhumed.

St. Josaphat was born in Poland of noble parents in 1580. After a youth of singular innocence, at the age of 20 he entered the Basilian Order (the same Byzantine order that was involved in the Lanciana anomaly). He was later Archbishop of Polotsk in Poland. He worked constantly for the reunion of the Schismatic Ruthenian Church with that of Rome and was martyred by his enemies in 1623 for those efforts. He was noted for his life of contemplation and prayer in spite of indefatigable efforts in his official duties. His body rests in St. Peter's Basilica in a glass-faced tomb. His face appears to have darkened and the tissue also seems to have shrunk in the same manner of the older incorrupt bodies.

St. Jean Baptiste Marie Vianney, the Curé of Ars, was born and raised at Dardilly near Lyons, France in May, 1786 and so lived during the turmoil of the French Revolution and the Napoleonic Empire—the age of greatest anti-clericism in France. He was a poor student and though he early sought to become a priest he was not ordained until his thirtieth year. He was pastor of Ars for forty-two years—during which time he transformed the village into a model of sanctity. His life was marked by austere penances and by many preternatural events so that this poor humble man became known throughout Europe—more than 100,000 visiting Ars in a single year to see him. He died on August 4, 1859 and was canonized on May 31, 1925. During the beatification process his body was found incorrupt and now rests in a glass casket at a side altar in the church to which he gave his life. The condition of his body cannot be determined since a death mask covers his face and he is fully vested.

It may be asked now, what is the relationship, what is the correlation, even granting there is one, between the fact of their incorrupt condition and man's transcendental nature? The relationship which seems to develop (with the ambiguous exception of Lady Tai) is that although the bodies represent people of both sexes, high and low status, young and old, some buried in the ground, some not, the one common factor was dedication to the service of God and to humanity for the sake of serving God. They were characterized by a humble life, even though some were of exalted position. They deliberately lived their lives in close union with God—lives of intense devotion to His service.

The chief hallmark which stamped their behavior is the abnegation of self and detachment from any thought of worldly advancement, even though that might have come to them by their circumstances. They are almost the antithesis, in fact, of the picture we get of modern man from the models of Riesman, Goffman, or Homans. In these people, the theme of the transcendental aspect of man has been developed to its highest level.

Characteristically, also, this way of life developed within them at an early age so that it might be said truthfully their entire lives had been free of worldly materialistic influence. This is not to say they were unaware of the world or of worldly needs. It is told of St. Teresa of Avila, the model of mystics, for instance, that on one occasion she was displaying obvious relish with a dinner of wild game and was chided for her enthusiasm. She eyed her accuser and said, "Penance is penance and partridge is partridge." If there is one thing these people were not, it is hypocritical. They were not acting out a role for peer group approval. If they seem pious and other-worldly to us, it is because they were.

Now, the point behind all of this is not, that the anomaly was produced by the peculiar life they lived—it was not, by some chemical or biological influence of religiosity, although that would have to be considered. It is far more probable that it was worked in their inanimate remains as a sign of the pleasure and approval with which God viewed their lives. It is a pointer to His beneficence. In terms of logic, the necessary condition was an intensely spiritual way of life. The sufficient condition, the intervention by the preternatural agency. Not everyone who lived such a life was "rewarded" in this way, but everyone who was so rewarded had lived this way. Thus, it could be said the Creator, by these acts, has indicated His preference for a life of gentleness, of kindness, of humility and above all, of confident prayerful recourse to Him. That is also what all of the major religions of the world teach. It is the transcendental attitude which, of all earthly creatures, only man is able to accept or reject.

I stated earlier that I had investigated other cases which I found in an attempt to determine if there were any anomalies of a similar type which would tend to discredit a preternatural explanation of the anomalies or of their symbolic approval of a particular lifestyle.

The case of Lady Tai was the one clear exception which the writer was unable to eliminate because of peculiar natural conditions associated with the burial, although the later report would indicate natural causes were a factor. In her case, the question is moot. There is evidence either way and both ways.

In addition there is a fairly well-known case (locally) of the so-called "mummies of Bordeaux." The mummies are a group of about 25 bodies now exhibited as a sort of display in a room at the base of the campanile of the Church of St. Michael in Bordeaux, France. The bodies were discovered in foundation excavations several centuries ago in what had been the cemetery for a church at that location before the twelfth century.

Nothing is known about the individuals, who range in age from children of a few years to old men and women. The brochure which is distributed at the site says the bodies were all found in a calcareous seam which cut through the cemetery and attributed the preservation to that fact.

The bodies are in various stages of advanced disintegration but are not decayed nor truly mummified in the sense of Egypt or of the next case discussed, and they have been outside the earth for a very long time. There is no odor other than a mustiness which is usual in old underground areas. This case would be difficult to assess, and there is too little known to even attempt it; again the answer might be either way, though natural causes seem to be suggested. The "Bog People" of Denmark is another case of apparent natural preservation by the peculiar ground in which the bodies of "victims" apparently sacrificed during pagan rites survived for many centuries.

The other case which was investigated personally by the writer is at Paracas, Peru, about 160 miles by highway south of Lima. There in the new *Museo de Sitio de Paracas* is a display of archaeologic finds dating from 500 to 1000 B.C. They are related to mummified remains found in caverns in the desert area during the middle 1930's. With the mummies were found rich burial goods which were taken to the museum and are the chief part of the display. The bodies were especially processed before burial by "secret mummification techniques" and the climate also would have fostered mummification. The situation seems quite similar to that of early Egyptian ceremonial burials. The anomaly seems explainable completely by physical circumstances. The writer has found no anomalies of preservation beyond these mentioned. Undoubtedly, there are some.

Section 5—Summary

What can we say about the combined impact of all four classes of anomalies we have looked at, bearing in mind that they represent but a small portion of the similar unexplained events which have happened throughout history and continue to occur today. First of all, it should be said that they are as available to any investigator as they were to the writer, and the research can be repeated by anyone so disposed.

Let us examine the three propositions which the writer set out to defend at the start of the section.

1. The anomalous events of this type are not random happenings, but occur only when related to events or way of life having spiritual significance.

As each event was reviewed the spiritual significance was pointed out and, in the first three categories, the relative probability of preternatural versus purely physical causation was discussed. Some seemed clear. Others are in need of additional investigation but are at least probable on prima facia evidence. Verification tests are possible, some are under way. In the last category the group effect was used to establish the spiritual basis. In most cases, the probability was high and in the totality overwhelmingly so. Just as in photographic evidence of the cosmic ray, here also the mass effect of the summation of evidence exceeds the weight of individual events taken separately.

None of the events could be called random occurrences in any sense of the word. As described, they are unique, having fixed relationships between purpose, causation, and phenomenon. They are patterned events. All are indications of a purposeful intent to provide man with physical evidence of the Creator's presence in the physical world and His control over the physical laws of nature, but most of all of His kind and beneficent concern for man.

2. The nature of the anomalous event is to:

    a. reflect honor to a dedicated spiritual individual, or

    b. to inspire devotion to a facet of spiritual life.

Clearly, the events in all cases are personal though they may affect directly only inanimate objects. The events are never degrading, but on the contrary, are inspiring. They reflect honor to the individual or individuals affected and demonstrate the Creator's approval of the individuals concerned and/or the circumstances in which they occur.

3. The anomalies are, in all cases, of a nature to suggest beneficent, personal concern of the causative agency.

The writer could find no examples of a threatening nature. The message conveyed by all of the phenomena was one of deep concern of a kind and loving father who would guide, but not physically constrain, humanity toward a life of peace and fruitful tranquility.

What does this do in the way of demonstrating the high probability that man, in fact, does have a transcendental nature, one which will endure after his physical death? What does it imply as to the future life being dependent in some way on actions in this life? In Part III, we developed the idea that the Creator is purposeful. Therefore, His acts affecting human beings and having preternatural causes, that is, beyond the natural laws, must also be purposeful. They must be for the specific purpose of demonstrating a preternatural effect. If man is to but live and

die as all other purely physical creatures, any preternatural intervention to demonstrate his concern is purposeless. The physical
laws will take care of man one way or another, even if it be eventual species extinction. His existence has no possible preternatural significance. In fact, what happens to man in terms of good
or bad and any idea of a moral law is absurd, as it is with the
other animals. For the Creator to give indications which would
support an inefficacious moral law would be utterly purposeless
and cruel in addition. From the Creator's very nature, then, the
preternatural events themselves are evidential of God's preference for a life based on His morality and of a future existence
wherein man will be rewarded for a life so lived. The fact that
the events do occur in a patterned way, associated only with
a certain way of life indicates His approval for that way above
others and, in a sense, marks it with His seal.

We are now in a position to look at the logic gates suggested
by the analysis of these anomalous events.

The tenth logic gate states the proposition: The existence of the
anomalous events demonstrates both capacity and actuality of intervention in the action of physical laws by extra-physical forces.

The eleventh logic gate states the proposition: The nature of
the anomalous events—as responses to devotion to God—are
evidential of God's direct intervention in the physical laws on
behalf of individuals.

The twelfth logic gate states the proposition: The existence
and nature of the anomalous events is evidential of God's personal benevolent regard of His creature, man, not only in general,
but also as individual persons and of a life devoted to Him.

The thirteenth logic gate states the proposition: The concern
of God in man's behavior evidenced by the anomalous events
implies the existence of preferred codes of morality on the part
of God in relation to man.

The fourteenth logic gate states the proposition: The anomalous events and the implication of God's concern for man's
behavior are evidential of man's nature as a transcendental being
destined to survive death in response to the love of God.

The fifteenth logic gate combining those of Parts II, III and
IV states the proposition: God the infinite, the immutable, the
omnipotent is also God the merciful, the loving, and the personal. This logic gate puts us back almost where we started
800 years ago, in fact clear to Socrates. Those ideas have been
tried in the intervening years—yet, how philosophically sound
in logic they still are!

PART V

GOD—THE HOLY—THE REVEALED

Chapter 11

REVELATION AS AUTHENTIC HISTORY

Having passed the logic gate which would affirm at a high confidence level that God, the infinite, the immutable, the omnipotent, is also God the merciful, the loving, and the personal, we come in Part V to the final series of logic gates of our comprehensive thesis. They consist in defining God in His relationship to man—God, as He communicates with man, in defining morality as a rational behavioral system of free man, legitimized, in concept, by the existence of God and grounded in the mutual love of God and man. We wish to affirm with high confidence that God, having the other attributes we have accepted, loves and cares for man, His transcendental creature, and hence would most certainly also wish to communicate with man—to make Himself known so that He also might be loved in return. We will show how that concept, with its moral accompaniment, carries in it the motivation for a strong social movement.

All of primitive man's surroundings were full of mystery. It was the various forms and displays of nature that man first deified. He saw God in everything and everywhere—in the sun, the clouds, the storms, the calm seas, the flowering of the fields, the shadows of the forest, the grandeur of the mountains, the beckoning stars, the fruitfulness of his own body. Everything was to him a form of communication of the pervasive numinousness. In that sense, there was and is, as we have seen, a form of silent communication which tells us something about the nature of nature's God. As in Psalm 19, "The heavens declare the glory of God and the firmament shows his handiwork," so that as in Psalm 14, "Only the fool says in his heart, there is no God." Further, man always and everywhere sought ways of communication in return—some way of giving homage. But is it reasonable that, through the long course of ages, as the plan of creation moved into its maturity and towards its fulfillment, the intelligent God we have studied would wish only to communicate with His intelligent creature in silent symbology,

459

leaving totally to man the task of unravelling what the God he worshipped desires of man? If He "wished" men to strive and seek, would He not have also "wished" man to know something about His nature—things totally unknowable to man unless God, Himself, were to intervene and tell him? If God desired man's love, He must provide man the knowledge from which love could spring. Only in the vague speculative way could that knowledge be made accessible to man without some form of revelation, as we also have seen.

All of the world's great religions, which probably embrace 75 percent of living man, have traditions and writings which are held to be either directly or indirectly inspired by God. It is those transmissions converted to writing and then reinterpretated, to men, generally, which contain the philosophies and which give spirit and coherence to those religions and to their supporting cultures. The *Bhagavad-Gita, Bhagavatapurana* and the *Upanishads* of the Hindus; the collected wisdom of Buddha in that offshoot of Hinduism and the many faceted writings of his disciples throughout the Orient are major examples. The writings of the First Teacher, Kung the Master, Kung Fu tza—Confucius—contemporary of Buddha were works primarily providing a way of life in society dedicated to counteracting the decadence which had infiltrated China in the sixth century B.C. Confucius has said, "Heaven sends down its good and evil symbols and the wise act in accord." His concept of Jen, conduct of life in fullness of love of your fellowman—respect for yourself engendered from your respect for your brother were supported by the compassionate concepts of Chuntzu-courtliness in behavior and Li-truth. These promoted the balance in behavior without pride, but self-respect without excess in anything—neither indifference nor fanaticism. The beauty of *Tao Te Ching* of Taoism, was noted in the brief selection quoted in Part IV. Last and of preeminent importance in Western history are of course the *Koran, Haddith* and *Sunna* of Islam; the New Testament of the Christian Bible and that upon which both, the two preceding rest—the Old Testament of Judaism.

It was not only among the organized systems of religion as now conceived that revelation existed in some form. The oracles of Delphi and the Sibylline oracles of ancient Rome were also held as special vehicles of divine revelation. In the latter case some prophecies of seemingly amazing significance occurred and were recorded. Unfortunately these have been so intermingled with spurious "oracles" that it is impossible, at least at this time, to accept any as genuine. Of interest in this same "pagan" sense is the belief of Socrates as recorded in Plato's biographical work on Socrates' trial, *Apologia,* that he was divinely inspired in his activity. It is worthwhile to recall how much Socrates was influenced in his ideas by this sense of God in relation with the world. Plato has Socrates making the following statements during his trial.

> If you say to me, Socrates, this time we will not mind Anytus, and you shall be let off, but upon one condition, that you are not to inquire and speculate in this way any more, and that if you are caught doing so again you shall die; if this was the condition on which you let me go, I should reply: Men of Athens, I honor and love you; but I shall obey God rather than you, and while I have life and strength I shall never cease from the practice and teaching of philosophy, exhorting anyone whom I meet and saying to him after my manner: "You, my friend—a citizen of the great and mighty and wise city of Athens—are you not ashamed of heaping up the greatest amount of money and honor and reputation, and caring so little about wisdom and truth and the greatest improvement of the soul, which you never regard or heed at all?"
>
> Someone may wonder why I go about in private giving advice and busying myself with the concerns of others, but do not venture to come forward in public and advise the state. I will tell you why. You have heard me speak at sundry times and in diverse places of an oracle or sign which comes to me, and is the divinity which Meletus ridicules in the indictment. This sign, which is a kind of voice, first began to come to me when I was a child; it always forbids but never commands me to do anything which I am going to do. This is what deters me from being a politician. And rightly, as I think. For I am certain, O men of Athens, that if I had engaged in politics, I should have perished long ago, and done no good either to you or to myself.
>
> But if death is the journey to another place, and there, as men say, all the dead abide, what good, O my friends and judges, can be greater than this? If indeed when the pilgrim arrives in the world below, he is delivered from the professors of justice to give

judgment there, Minos and Rhadamanthus and Aeacus and Triptolemus, and other sons of God who were righteous in their own life, that pilgrimage will be worth making. What would not a man give if he might converse with Orpheus and Musaeus and Hesiod and Homer? Nay, if this be true, let me die again and again. I myself, too, shall have a wonderful interest in their meeting and conversing with Palamedes, and Ajax the son of Telamon, and any other ancient hero who has suffered death through an unjust judgment; and there will be no small pleasure, as I think, in comparing my own sufferings with theirs. Above all, I shall then be able to continue my search into true and false knowledge; as in this world, so also in the next; and I shall find out who is wise? and who pretends to be wise, and is not. What would not a man give, o judges, to be able to examine the leader of the great Trojan expedition; or Odysseus or Sisyphus; or numberless others, men and women too! What infinite delight would there be in conversing with them and asking them questions! In another world they do not put a man to death for asking questions: assuredly not. For besides being happier than we are, they will be immortal, if what is said is true.

Someone will say: Yes, Socrates, but cannot you hold your tongue, and then you may go into a foreign city, and no one will interfere with you? Now I have great difficulty in making you understand my answer to this. For if I tell you that to do as you say would be a disobedience to the God, and therefore that I cannot hold my tongue, you will not believe that I am serious; and if I say again that daily to discourse about virtue, and of those other things about which you hear me examining myself and others, is the greatest good of many, and that the *unexamined life is not worth living,* you are still less likely to believe me.

The hour of departure has arrived, and we our ways—I to die, and you to live. Which is better, God only knows.

Some look upon the diversity of religious belief and ritual as indication of the lack of validity of any of them. However, upon reflection, one would have to as fairly—or unfairly—conclude that the diversities of cultures would also indicate the validity of none. That would be an absurd conclusion. God, though one, might be considered as symbolized by the diamond; His many facets enhance the brilliance and attractiveness to those who would seek Him.

In spite of the diversity of presentation and belief, which does not much if any exceed the diversity of the cultures, regions and ages from which they sprang, the basic teachings on conduct of man's life and his relationship to God are closely parallel. If mankind truly lived up to the teachings of any, the world would be a place of peace and bliss indeed. And the vision of God which comes through all is the same, with only variation in emphasis. For instance, despite the frequent charge that Hinduism is polytheistic because of the multiform of "idols" which are seen in the temples, they are but human interpretations of different aspects of the one Brahman. One of the most common Hindu invocations is:

> O Lord, forgive three sins that are due my human
> frailty;
> Thou art everywhere, but I worship you here;
> Thou art without form, but I worship you in these
> forms;
> Thou needest no praise, yet I offer you these prayers
> and salutations.

In this Part V, the first logic gate to be passed is an affirmation that God has communicated to mankind, through revelation of one form or other, knowledge about Himself and of how man should respond to Him and how man should respond in relationship to his fellowmen because they are all, alike, God's well-loved creatures—indeed, His sons and daughters.

In the sublime picture of God, as He must be, from the standpoint of metaphysical speculation as well as from the sheer magnificence and magnitude of the universe as it is being revealed to us by modern science, one can intuitively grasp that, if God sees fit to manifest Himself to us, that manifestation at its climax in time must be equally sublime. It must, to paraphrase St. Anselm, be that greatest and most inspiring revelation in love and holiness beyond which no greater or inspiring can be conceived. Further, intuitively we sense that God's revealing act requires a corresponding act of man. God sets revelation in man's view, but man must look.

Only one example will be looked at in detail in this study—that work which has had, either directly or indirectly, the most profound impact of any work in the world upon mankind—it is the Old Testament of the Bible, itself as noted, the foundation and basis of the New Testament and the Koran. This work is selected not only because it is best known, having been the most widely studied and being most widespread in geographic dissemination, but also because it has also been the one whose validity has been most heavily challenged by the positivistically inspired exegesis of the past century.

Positivism as a philosophy was reviewed briefly in Part II. It was noted that it was a philosophy of empiricism and materialism and basically opposed to anything which gave implications of the supernatural. Its main philosophic target was metaphysics. Positivists held that there were no topics of knowledge beyond the sensory, and metaphysics disputed that view. As we have seen, positivism and its child, logical positivism, have largely strangled themselves in their own rigor within the past three decades. Their influence, however, on recent religious thought, finding continuing expression in the analytical philosophies which survive in the United States and England, is extensive and deep. Its mode of attack carried on in Bible scholarship of the Old Testament was from two directions. First, it promoted a skeptical outlook on the authenticity of the work as a historical document and second, it popularized a scientistic "rationalizing" or "demythologizing" of any attribute of the supernatural in the events which were described. The Bible was to be viewed in no way differently than the imaginative works of Homer or Virgil. On this point in 1957, Ian M. Crombie, a prominent analytical philosopher, had written in his work, *The Possibility of Theological Statements:*

> Granted then, that we might discover that our understanding of life was deepened by conceiving of it in Christian terms: in that case, the Bible could be regarded as the work of serious fiction. The Christian interpretation would vie with the Dostoevskian or Kafkaesque interpretation. It might indeed surpass them all. But success, even supreme success, in interpretating life could only confirm it as an interpretation of life. It would still be open to me, the critic may say, to admit its validity as an interpretation, but nevertheless to regard all reference contained in it to things beyond experience as

simply the device by which the illumination is thrown.

Speaking in refutation of this attitude of the Bible as "serious fiction," K. A. Kitchen, lecturer in the School of Archaeology and Oriental Studies, University of Liverpool, says in his book, *Ancient Orient and Old Testament,* (Kitchen, 1966),

Following on the period of "Deist" speculation in the eighteenth century, Old Testament studies during the nineteenth century carried the mark of reaction against older beliefs about the Bible and its constituent writings, a mark still perceptible today. In contrast to earlier epochs in which the main concern of biblical study was the exposition of the sacred text and the formulation of doctrine, Old Testament studies of the nineteenth century were more concerned with literary and historical criticism, especially in connection with philosophical treatment of early Hebrew religion. Certain dominant tendencies became apparent. Beside the desire to break with the weight of inherited later tradition (often of dubious value), there was an eagerness to experiment with literary and history-of-religion theories like those then current in Homeric and other studies, and also a wish to view the history of Old Testament religion and literature in terms of the evolutionary philosophies of the age.

One result of all this was the emergence of a marked skepticism not only towards traditions about the Bible, but also towards the historical veracity of the Old Testament books and towards the integrity of their present literary form. The existing structure of Old Testament religion and literature could not, as it stood, be fitted into the prevailing philosophical schemes, so it was drastically remodelled until it did. The resultant physiognomy presented by Old Testament studies needs only the briefest summary here; the role of theory is preponderant. Thus, the Pentateuch and other books were split up into various supposed source-documents of different authorship of varying epochs (traditionally designated J (ahwist), E (lohist), P (riestly code), D (dueteronomist), etc., and considered to have been assembled into the present books at a relatively late date. Various literary, linguistic and theological criteria were produced in order to justify these divisions and late datings. The prophetical books were also fragmented across the centuries, and the poetry and wisdom-literature assigned to a very late period. Concepts that were held to be theologically "advanced" (universalism, personification, etc.) were also considered to be late developments. With innumerable variations in detail, and some modifications in view of the recent developments, Old Testament studies have remained fundamentally the same up to the present day. To this picture Gunkel and others added *Gattungsforschung* or *Formgeschichte* (form-criticism), and the Scandinavians have laid stress on the supposed role of oral tradition, while Alt and Noth have combined part of these methods with literary criticism and their own theories about aetiological traditions allegedly linked with specific localities.

Contradictions are said to abound in the Old Testament, and its history is still treated with skepticism, especially the earlier periods (e.g., Patriarchs, Exodus and Conquest). It is not merely that (for the historic Christian faith) these results leave a wide gulf between the vision of a dependable and authoritative Word of God, and the spectacle of a tattered miscellany of half-mythical and historically unreliable literary fragments. Rather, on the fundamental level of "What actually happened in history?" there is above all a very considerable tension between the development of Israelite history, religion and literature as portrayed by the Old Testament and the general reconstructions so far offered by conventional Old Testament studies. An example is afforded by W. Zimmerli who brings out the vast change proposed by Wellhausen in making the "law of Moses" (especially "P") later than the prophets instead of preceding them. Nowhere else in the whole of Ancient Near Eastern history has the literary, religious and historical development of a nation been subjected to such drastic and wholesale reconstructions, at such variance with the existing documentary evidence. The fact that Old Testament scholars are habituated to these widely known reconstructions, even mentally conditioned by them, does not alter the basic gravity of this situation which should not be taken for granted.

The net effect of the work of the butchers of the Pentateuch was a tremendous cleavage in viewpoint of the Old Testament between its traditional role as the basis for dependable faith in God and—as visualized in the new teaching—that, after all, it was no more than a "tattered miscellany of half-mythical and historically unreliable literary fragments." If the latter described situation corresponded with reality, those faiths which had accepted the Bible as truth found their basis in sad condition indeed. While there likely is indeed some blending of historical traditions—the Pentateuch was not composed overnight—and perhaps even more blending than Kitchen would propose to admit, the wholesale mishmash which the "scholars" would make of it is clearly unjustified—particularly their shift to a mid-first millenium date of composition. Kitchen goes on to comment on the caliber of the "studies":

> One more point must now be briefly considered. Through the impact of the Ancient Orient upon the Old Testament and upon Old Testament studies a new tension is being set up, while an older one is being reduced. For the comparative material from the Ancient Near East is tending to agree with the extant structure of Old Testament documents as actually transmitted to us, rather than with the reconstructions of nineteenth century Old Testament scholarship—or with its twentieth century prolongation and developments to the present day.
>
> Some examples may illustrate this point. The valid and close parallels to the social customs of the Patriarchs come from documents of the nineteenth to fifteenth centuries B.C. (agreeing with an early-second-millennium origin for this material in Genesis), and not from Assyro-Babylonian data of the tenth to sixth centuries B.C. (possible period of the supposed "J", "E" sources). Likewise for Genesis 23, the closest parallel comes from the Hittite Laws which passed into oblivion with the fall of the Hittite Empire about 1200 B.C. The covenant-forms which appear in Exodus, Deuteronomy and Joshua follow the model of those current in the thirteenth century B.C.—the

period of Moses and Joshua—and not those of the first millennium B.C. The background to Syro-Palestinian kingship in 1 Samuel 8 is provided by documents from Alalakh and Ugarit of not later than the thirteenth century B.C.; this suggests that late enough date for the content of this passage, and would be much more realistic of abstracts, like wisdom in Proverbs 8 and 9, finds its real origin not in Greek influences of the fourth century B.C. but in the wide use of precisely such personified concepts throughout the Ancient Near East in the third and second millennia B.C., up to 1,500 years before even Solomon was born. Words once thought to be a mark of post-Exilic date now turn up in Ugaritic texts of the thirteenth century B.C., or in even earlier sources.

The proper implications of these and many similar facts are that large parts of the Pentateuch really did originate in the second millennium B.C., that Samuel really could (and probably did) issue the warnings recorded in 1 Samuel 8, and that the connection between Soloman's reign and the first few chapters of Proverbs (cf. Pr. 1:1-7) is something more than just the idle fancy of some late scribe, and so on. At least, this is the rational approach that would obtain if this were any part of Ancient Near Eastern literature, history and culture other than the Old Testament.

There is thus a tension between the basic theories and procedures of much Old Testament scholarship and the frequent and increasing agreement of Ancient Oriental data with the existing Old Testament-written traditions. As yet, this tension has barely begun to emerge, but it will inevitably do so increasingly. After all, even the most respected theories are only a means to an end, not an end in themselves. In the light of the vast new knowledge that is becoming available, old problems are amenable to new treatment; they must be dealt with afresh, from the foundations up, taking no current theory for granted or as the equivalent of fact, as is too commonly done, for instance, with the methods and general results of conventional literary criticism.

The first effort then of this study will be to establish the credibility of the Old Testament as reliable history rather than fiction regardless of its religious significance. The writer will rely on recent and current archaeologic investigations and studies.

Many of the nineteenth century archaeologic investigations were religiously inspired and made in the hope of shedding some light on biblical history. However, the more recent studies have been based on the gathering of basic scientific data concerning the peoples of the Ancient Near East for its historical value alone. Thus, they are not warped, or romanticized, or pragmatically colored, to support pet theologic and philosophic theories. In this true scientific stance, paradoxically, the recent studies have incidentally provided strong evidence for the historicity of the Old Testament Bible. It is an accurate reflection of the time it claims to represent and not of some far later and largely imaginary construction of wishful-thinking Theocrats, as the positivistic studies had held.

The oldest existing biblical manuscript dates from the third century B.C. It is a fragment of *Exodus* found among the Dead Sea Scrolls. It is only a copy of an earlier text, but it shows that current texts are in complete consonance with those of 2,000 and more years ago. The absence of earlier manuscripts stems chiefly from the perishability of the organic materials used, either papyrus or parchment vellum. The Hebrews, being traditionally nomadic in culture, did not use baked clay or stone—not only because of the burdensome weight, but also because engravings seemed idolatrous to the Hebrews.

To the Semitic peoples, generally, the word—written or spoken—has, and still has, in many places, a significance of spirituality and finality which moderns, so besieged by words, can only faintly grasp. To the Semites, the word was, somehow, an emanation of "self"—once given-forever beyond recall. The lack of really ancient documents had permitted the growth of speculation and fanciful theorizing about the origin of the current texts. There is no physical evidence, in the form of original documentation, to permit falsification of any theory—or authentication either, for that matter.

However, while there is a scarcity of biblical documents there is a fair number, almost a plentitude, of manuscripts both in stone and baked clay from the Assyrian, Summerian, Hittite and Egyptian peoples in the area. The works generally have been found historically accurate, and these peoples were the cohabitants of the Hebrews in Palestine and the Near East throughout biblical times. These manuscripts are securely dated, some to 1800 and 1900 B.C. One of the Hittite writings, specifically an eclipse of the sun during the tenth year of Mursisis II which has been identified with an actual eclipse which occurred on March 12, 1335 B.C. (Guerney, 1966). Further, whereas earlier critics were prone to doubt the accuracy of copyists and resort to wholesale emendation of texts, later archaeologic studies have revealed great attention to prevent copy errors. Kitchen says on this point:

> Until recent decades, Old Testament scholars were much too partial to emendation of the consonantal text of the Hebrew Bible (the notes in the *Biblia Hebraica*, edited by Kittel, exhibit this fault to a degree, as is widely recognized), but nowadays they show a much greater and commendable caution in this regard. The evidence of the Dead Sea Scrolls and the rich harvest of linguistic gains from Ugartic or North Canaanite have repeatedly demonstrated the essential soundness of the consonantal Hebrew text at many points where obscurity had hitherto tempted to emendation. In the Ancient Near East, moreover, there were definite ideals of accurate scribal copying of manuscripts (a point often overlooked). One example from Egypt must here suffice. A funerary papyrus of about 1400 B.C. bears the colophon: "[The book] is completed from its beginning to its end, having been copied, revised, compared, and verified sign by sign." There is no reason to assume that the Hebrews would be less careful with their literary products, a further reason for the exercise of due caution in emending the consonantal Hebrew text.

Space permits only one direct comparison from Kitchen, although he makes many, between the Old Testament and corresponding Near East civil documents relating to ceremonials, festivals, laws, and customs. The one chosen is the Sinai covenant—because of its antiquity, its importance in history, and, because it has been most strongly singled out to be of far later origin than the period it addressed.

> At the heart of ancient Israelite religion stands the concept of the covenant, and, in particular, the covenant made between Israel and her God at Mount Sinai. Mendenhall has pointed out striking parallels in form between this covenant in Exodus 20 ff. (renewed in Joshua 24) and the international covenants or treaties

of the fourteenth/thirteenth centuries B.C. which have been recovered mainly from the Hittite archives at Boghazkoy. He also suggested that there was a significant difference in form between these late-second-millennium treaties and treaties of the first millennium B.C., and that the form of the Sinai covenant corresponded to that of the treaties of the second millennium but not to those of the first millennium B.C. This, if true, would suggest that the Sinai covenant (like its strictest parallels) really did originate in the thirteenth century B.C. at the latest (i.e., in the general period of Moses). However, because there are some elements common to the covenants of both the second and first millennia B.C., some scholars would claim that, in fact, there was no basic change in covenant-forms between the second and first millennia B.C. In this case, the parallel between the Sinai covenant and the second-millennium treaties would lose something of its chronological significance, but not its value for our general understanding of covenants. In view of this divergence of opinion, a brief re-examination of the forms of the Ancient Oriental and Sinai covenants is desirable.

(a) Covenants of the Late Second Millennium B.C.

These covenants show a remarkably consistent scheme, as established by Korosec and summarized by Mendenhall:

1. Preamble or title, identifying the author of the covenant.

2. Historical prologue or retrospect, mentioning previous relations between the two parties involved, past benefactions by the suzerain are a basis for the vassal's gratitude and future obedience.

3. Stipulations, basic and detailed, the obligations laid upon the vassal by the sovereign.

4. (a) Deposition of a copy of the covenant in the vassal's sanctuary, and (b) Periodic public reading of the covenant terms to the people.

5. Witnesses, a long list of gods invoked to witness the covenant.

6. (a) Curses, invoked upon the vassal if he breaks the covenant, and (b) Blessings, invoked upon the vassal if he keeps the covenant.

Nearly all the known treaties of the fourteenth/

thirteenth centuries B.C. follow this pattern closely. Sometimes some elements are omitted, but the order of them is almost invariable, whenever the original texts are sufficiently well preserved to be analyzed. This is, therefore, a stable form in the period concerned. Earlier than this, the pattern was apparently somewhat different. Besides these written elements, there were apparently also:

7. A formal oath of obedience.

8. An accompanying solemn ceremony.

9. A formal procedure for acting against rebellious vassals.

(b) Covenants of the First Millennium.

For the first millennium B.C., our material is at present much less extensive. It consists of some six Assyrian treaties of the ninth to seventh centuries B.C., and the Aramaic treaty or treaties of the eighth century B.C., of Bar-Ga'yah and Matiel. An analysis of even this limited material shows the following picture:

1. Preamble or title (where the beginning of the text exists).

2.
3. } then stipulations and curses, succeeded or preceded by the divine witnesses.
4.

While the second- and first-millennium covenants have a common core of Title, Stipulations, Witnesses and Curses, and also share some vocabulary and forms of expression, yet these are the banal, obvious things. One expects a title to any formal document, any covenant, must have stipulations or conditions; witnesses are necessary guarantors for many kinds of legal documents; the curse was an automatic sanction against disobedience, and some common terminology is only to be expected. Much more significant are the differences:

1. In the late-second-millennium covenants, so far as preserved, the divine witnesses almost always come between the stipulations and the curses, whereas in the first-millennium covenants, so far as known, they never do.

2. A historical prologue is typical of late-second-millennium covenants, but is unknown in our first-millennium examples.

3. In late-second-millennium covenants, the blessings are a regular, balancing pendant to the curses; in the first- millennium documents, the curses have no corresponding blessings.

4. The order of elements in late-second-millennium treaties shows great consistence, but the first-millennium ones show varying usage, stipulations and curses may occur in either order and be either preceded or succeeded by the witnesses.

Thus, on the evidence now available, there are clear and undeniable differences in form and content between covenant of the late second and the first millennia B.C.

(c) Analysis of the Sinai covenant.

The Sinai covenant is first preserved in Exodus 20 to 31; it was broken by the idolatry of the people *(Ex.* 32-33), and so had to be renewed immediately *(Ex.* 34). In the plains of Moab, this covenant was renewed with a new generation *(Dt.* 1-32:47) (recapitulated in 29-30), and again at Shechem *(Jos.* 24). In the analysis below, the three main (and one subsidiary) parallel sets of references are lettered A, B, C, D, for clarity. The following elements may be discerned:

1. Preamble: A. Exodus 20:1. B. Deuteronomy 1:1-5. C. Dt. 29:1. D. Joshua 24:2.

2. Historical prologue: A. Exodus 20:1. B. Deuteronomy 1:6-3:29. C. Dt. 29:2-8. D. Joshua 24:2-13.

3. Stipulations: A. Exodus 20:3-17, 22-26 (basic); Exodus 21-23, 25-31 (detailed), plus Leviticus 1-25. B. Deuteronomy 4, 5-11 (basic); 12-26 (detailed). C. Dt. 29:9-31:8. D. Joshua 24:14-15 (plus 16-25, the people's response, etc.).

4. (a) Deposition of Text: A. Exodus 25:16, Exodus 34:1, 28, 29; cf. Deuteronomy 10:1-5 (retrospect). B. Deuteronomy 31:9, 24-26. D. Cf. Joshua 24:26 (written in the book of the law).

(b) Public reading: B. Deuteronomy 31:10-13.

5. Witnesses: The gods of paganism were excluded, so the god-lists of the Ancient Oriental covenants are not found in the biblical ones. Instead, memorial-stones could be a witness (A. *Ex.* 24-4, cf. D. *Jos.* 24:27), or Moses' song (B. *Dt.* 31:16-30; *Dt.* 32:1-47), or the lawbook itself (B. *Dt.* 31:26), or even the people as participants (D. *Jos.* 24:22).

6. Curses and Blessings occur not in this order but reversed in the Old Testament, following the witness. A. Perhaps, cf. Leviticus 26:3-13 (blessings), 14-20 (curses, with more for repeated disobedience, 21-33). B. Deuteronomy 28:1-14 (blessings), 15-68 (curses). D. Implicit in Joshua 24:19-20.

Over and above this, one may see indications of items 7 and 8, the oath and solemn ceremony: A. Exodus 24:1-11. B. Deuteronomy 27 (fulfilled, *Jos.* 8:30-35). And finally, the Old Testament equivalent for the procedure for action against a faithless vassal or covenant-partner (9) is the so-called "controversy (Hebrew rib) pattern," in which (ultimately through the prophets) the God of Israel arraigns this people for breaking the covenant.

The relevant form taken by the "controversy pattern" in such cases directly reflects the covenant-form (historical retrospect), finds its starting-point in Deuteronomy 32, and has appropriate good parallels in the second millennium B.C.

Now, if we take the nature and order of nearly all the elements in the Old Testament Sinai covenant and its renewals as briefly listed above, and compare these with the patterns of the late second and the first millennium treaties already outlined, it is strikingly evident that the Sinai covenant and its renewals must be classed with the late-second-millennium covenant; it is entirely different in arrangement from the first-millennium covenants and shares with them only the indispensable common core (title, stipulations, witness and curses) and some terminology. In other words, on the total evidence now available, Mendenhall's original view is correct, that, in form, the Sinai covenant corresponds to the late-second-millennium treaties and not to those of the first millennium.

Accordingly, the obvious and only adequate explanation of this clear fact is that the Sinai covenant really was instituted and renewed in the thirteenth century B.C. (presumably under Moses at Sinai and in the plains of Moab, under Joshua at Shechem)—at precisely the period of the other late-second-millennium covenants (fourteenth to thirteenth centuries B.C.)—and is directly reflected in the frameworks and text of Exodus, Leviticus (chapter 26, at least), Deuteronomy and Joshua 24. This provided tangible, external ground for suggesting that considerable portions of these books (or, at least, of their contents), including almost the entire framework of Deuteronomy, originated in this same period.

If these works first took fixed literary forms only in the ninth to sixth centuries B.C. and onward, why and how should their writers (or redactors) so easily be able to reproduce covenant-forms that had fallen out of customary use 300 to 600 years earlier (i.e., after about 1200 B.C.), and entirely fail to reflect the first-millennium covenant forms that were commonly used in their own day? It is very improbable that Hebrew priests under the monarchy, or after the exile, would go excavating in Late Bronze Age ruins especially to seek for treaty-covenant forms that, in their day, would be merely exotic literary antiquities. So far, there is not a scrap of tangible evidence to show that the late-second-millennium pattern survived into the first millennium anywhere but in Israelite religious tradition—and the positive existence and wide use of new forms in the first millennium speak suggestively against the idea of any extensive survival of the older forms. It is surely entirely more rational to admit the plain explanation of a Sinai covenant actually made and renewed in the thirteenth century B.C. If this result, attained by a *Formgeschichte,* controlled by an external standard of measurement, perchance clashes, either in general, or in detail, with certain long-cherished theories of Hebrew religious evolution or of literary criticism, then (with all due respect) so much the worse for the theories in this field.

In his conclusion, pointing out that much additional work needs to be done in a cooperative way by Bible students and Near Eastern archaeologists to clarify the remaining points, Kitchen says:

All too obviously, this vast task [completion of cooperative studies] cannot be done at once. But it can be pursued bit by bit consciously, and sectional results used as they are gained. Needless to say, this is work for orientalists rather than theologians, but the material and results would have to be made available to the latter in suitable form. Prior theories about the Old Testament would have to be rigorously tested against the accumulated facts. The days of "primitive Israel," treated as though she had developed in isolation, are over and gone, obsolete beyond recall. If the Patriarchs had lived in 7000 or 6000 B.C., and the Exodus taken place in 5000, "primitive Hebrews" would have been conceivable—but, not so, very late in the culture and history of the Ancient Near East as the second and first millennia B.C.

On the other hand, it may perhaps be thought by some that run-of-the-mill Old Testament studies have come in for considerable incidental criticism. The criticisms that have been offered here are not, of course, directed at any such scholars personally. Some are very highly gifted men, and the writer has learnt much (and pleasurably) from their works. The criticisms made apply to facts and methods, and arise simply from the basic fact that the Ancient Orient provides means of external control upon our study of the Old Testament. The theories current in Old Testament studies, however brilliantly in a vacuum with little or no reference to the Ancient Near East, and, initially, too often in accordance with *a priori* philosophical and literary principles. It is solely because the data from the Ancient Near East coincided so much better with the existing observable structure of Old Testament history, literature and religion than with the theoretical reconstructions, that we are compelled—as happens in Ancient Oriental studies— to question, or even to abandon, such theories regardless of their popularity. Facts, not votes, determine the truth. We do not here merely advocate a return to "pre-critical" views and traditions (e.g., of authorship) merely for their own sake or for the sake of theological orthodoxy. Let it be clearly noted that no appeal whatsoever has been made to any theological starting-point in the body of this work, not to mention the miasma of late post-biblical Jewish or patristic (or later) Christian traditions. If some of the results reached here approximate to a traditional view or seem to agree with theological orthodoxy, then this is simply because the tradition in question or that orthodoxy are that much closer to the real facts than is commonly realized. While one must indeed never prefer mere orthodoxy to truth, it is also perverse to deny that orthodox views can be true.

The evidence for the historicity of the Old Testament is excellent and getting better with each passing year. In 1949, W. F. Albright, perhaps the premier archaeologist of Palestine in recent times, had noted in his *Archaeology of Palestine,* (Albright, 1949):

> Thanks to archaeological determination of the site of most biblical places, it is also possible to establish the age and historical significance of many lists of towns in the Bible. A good case in point is the list of Levitic cities in Josh. xxi and I Chron. vi, which Wellhausen, followed by most subsequent critics, considered an artificial product of some post-exilic scribe's imagination. Careful examination of this list, in the light of all known archaeological facts, makes it quite certain that the list is much more ancient, and that the only time when all the towns mentioned in it were in Israelite possession was under David and Solomon. Not a single town in the list can be shown to have been founded at a period subsequent to the middle of the tenth century B.C., though several cannot be much earlier than this date. A date between about 975 and about 950 B.C. may thus be fixed for the extant form of the list, which seems to have had a prehistory going back to the Conquest.
>
> Palestinian archaeology is much less helpful in throwing direct light on biblical personalities, mainly owing to the scarcity of inscriptions. Actually, more biblical personages are mentioned in inscriptions discovered outside of Palestine than in documents found in the country. Yet, there is a great deal of indirect light. It is far easier to appraise the careers of the Patriarchs, of Joshua, Gideon and Samson, of Samuel, Saul, David and Solomon, than it formerly was. The scanty light now shed on the building operations of Saul and David, and the rich new information bearing on the constructions of Solomon are most welcome aids to our understanding of the evolution of Israelite material culture under these rulers of United Israel, who thus become much more tangible figures

than they were. The events of the Omride Dynasty and the period of Jeroboam II also become much more sharply focused now that we know what the culture of Samaria was like in their day. The same is true of the times of Uzziah and Hezekiah in Judah. The end of the monarchy of Judah has been so brightly illuminated by the discoveries at Lachish, Tell Beit Mirsim, and other sites, that Jeremiah's life and times can no longer be drastically misinterpreted by competent scholars.

Archaeological field investigation studies conducted at Ebla in Northern Syria under Italian auspices since 1974 have revealed baked clay documents of the twenty-third century B.C., well before Abraham, which mention many biblical sites including Sodom and Gomorrah as then thriving communities.

A notable exception to the usual skepticism of Bible scholars of the past century is Meredith Kline, Professor of Old Testament at Gordon Conwell Theological seminary and Professor of Religion at the Massachusetts Institute of Technology, who subscribes completely to Kitchen's view though largely independently formulated. His book, *The Structure of Biblical Authority* (Kline, 1972), follows the same theme as Kitchen, also on the basis of comparative evidence in archaeology. In discussion of the formal origins of biblical canon, Kline says, "The theory or a process of canonization beginning in the post-exilic era, if not considerably later—whether a threefold process or otherwise, whether assuming a more extensive Alexandrian canon or following an approach like Sundberg's—is a grotesque distortion of the historical facts, a Wellhausenian anachronism on a millennial order of magnitude." Kline then concludes on this point:

> The origin of the Old Testament canon coincided with the founding of the kingdom of Israel, by covenant, at Sinai. The very treaty that formally established the Israelite theocracy was, itself, the beginning and the nucleus of the total covenantal cluster of writings which constitutes the Old Testament canon. While exposing the prevalent critical histories of the formation of the canon as the anachronistic fictions they are, orthodox Old Testament scholarship should also set to work on the biblical-theological task of delineating the real history of that process. When that

is done and the relevant historical realities of ancient covenant procedure are brought to bear, the formation of the Old Testament canon will be traced to its origins in the covenantal mission of Moses in the third quarter of the second millennium B.C., providentially, the classic age of treaty diplomacy in the Near East.

Our conclusion in a word, then, is that canon is inherent in covenant, covenant of the kind as attested in ancient international relations and the Mosaic covenants of the Bible. Hence it is to this covenant structure that theology should turn for its perspective and model in order to articulate its doctrine of canon in terms historically concrete and authentic. It is the covenant form that will explain the particular historical-legal traits of the divine authority that confronts us in the Scriptures.

As we have seen, the preponderance of recent *scientific* evidence supports the view that the Bible was written and, at least subjectively, related what was happening at the time it represents. The events of the Pentateuch and the other books of the Bible were recorded during, and shortly after, the things described took place. Historically, Moses has been considered the author of the Pentateuch in the sense of being the source of the information. There is now no reason not to believe so. The objective correspondence of that which is reported to that which happened, as in all reporting, might be reliable or it might not be. The question here goes to the credibility of the reporter and not of the historicity of the transmitting media which is, in the writer's opinion, well established. Our second point consists in establishing the thesis that the reporters were reliable, although perhaps given more to hyperbole and figurative speech than to scientifically descriptive data collection. In his excellent book, *The Religions of Man,* Huston Smith provides the motivation which caused the ancient Jews, to center on a unique course in history, that of reporters for their God. He says:

> In the beginning God. . . . From beginning to end the Jewish quest for meaning was rooted in their understanding of God.
> Whatever a man's philosophy, it must take account of the "other." There are two reasons for this. First, no man seriously supposes that he brought himself

into being; and as he did not, other men (being, like him, human) could not have brought themselves into being either. From this, it follows that mankind has issued from something other than itself. Second, every man at some point finds his power limited. It may be a rock too large for him to lift, a tidal wave that sweeps away his village because he cannot stem it. Added to the "other" from which he has issued, therefore, is the "other" by which he is confronted.

Faced by this inescapable "other," man wonders if it is meaningful. Four characteristics could keep it from being so: If it were prosaic, chaotic, amoral, or hostile. The triumph of Jewish thought lies in its refusal to surrender meaning for any of these alternatives.

The Jews resisted the prosaic in their thought of the "other" by personifying it. In this they were at one with their ancient contemporaries. The concept of the inanimate-senseless dead matter governed by blind, impersonal laws—is a late invention. For early man, the sun which could bless or scorch, the earth which gave of its fertility, the gentle rains and the terrible storms, the mystery of birth, and the reality of death, were not to be explained as clots of matter regulated by mechanical laws. They were parts of a world that was heavy with feeling and purpose to its very core.

It is easy to smile at the anthropomorphism of the early Jew who could imagine ultimate reality as a person walking in the Garden of Eden in the cool of the morning. But when we make our way through the poetic concreteness of his perspective to its underlying claim—that, in the final analysis, reality is more like a person, than like a machine, we must ask ourselves two questions. First, what is the evidence against this hypothesis? It seems to be so completely lacking that as knowledgeable a philosopher-scientist as Alfred North Whitehead could embrace it without reservation in our own generation. Second, is the concept intrinsically less exalted than its alternative? The Jews were reaching out for the most exalted concept of the "other" they could conceive, an "other" which embodied such inexhaustible worth that in all his history man would never begin to encompass its fullness. The Jews found a greater depth and mystery in persons than in any of the other wonders at hand. How could they be true to this conviction of the "other's" worth except by extending and deepening the category of the personal to include it?

Where the Jews differed from their neighbors was not in conceiving the "other" as personal but in focusing its personalism in a single, supreme, nature-transcending will. For Egyptians, Babylonians, Syrians, and the lesser Mediterranean peoples of the day each major power of nature was a distinct deity. The storm was the storm-god, the sun the sun-god, the rain the rain-god. When we turn to the Old Testament we find ourselves in a completely different atmosphere. Nature here is an expression of a single Lord of all being.

In the critical biblical studies characteristic of the mid-twentieth century, one of the main drives was to transfer the language to a twentieth century environment sometimes with hideous results. The sweeping grandeur of the older Old Testament translations which attempted to reflect the natural tonal rhythm of the Hebrew was lost. The intense, personal God-man dialogue which the language conveys reflecting a deep-set emotion, almost passion, does not come through in the language of "its." That this is not just a linguistic failure is clear when the commentaries, sometimes pages longer than the text, are analyzed. Many of the events are gratuitously labeled as "legends" or "stories" when, at the time the works were placed in the Canon, this was clearly not the view of the Fathers. Taken out of their natural context the events lose their meaning, whether literal or symbolic. Instead, the critic supplies, as fact, what he believes the motivations of the original writer were.

In the same vein, the skepticism concerning the historicity of the New Testament popular in the middle of the sixteenth century has been largely swept aside by archaeological finds in Palestine and Egypt. It is now generally accepted that virtually all of the canonical works of the New Testament were available in all the major Christian churches by the end of the first century. There was no gap relying on oral tradition alone. The idea that the Christian religion was a mixture of Mithraism or Judaic cults with Greek embellishments also has been largely superseded by closer and more realistic study of the various documents involved. There were living witnesses of the public life, Passion, death and Resurrection of Christ at the time the Epistles and Synoptic Gospels were written. There is no longer any reason for doubting that the author of the Gospel of John was in fact John the Beloved Disciple. The beginning of the Gospel of Luke, written about the year 60 A.D., about thirty years after the events related, begins: "Many have undertaken to compile a narrative of the events which have been fulfilled in our midst precisely as those events were transmitted to us by the original eye witnesses and ministers of the word. I, too, have carefully traced the whole sequence of events from the beginning and have decided to set it in writing for you. . . ." There were thus several (many) valid firsthand sources from which Luke and the other chroniclers of the time could glean the facts. The debate over "Mark" or "Aramaic Matthew" as the first "source" is largely academic. All of the evangelists would have had access to the primary sources of living witnesses.

Using evidence provided by the documents themselves, it appears that Luke wrote both his Gospel and the Acts of the Apostles shortly after he completed his journeyings with Paul at the beginning of Paul's imprisonment in Rome about the year 60. The "first person" writings of Luke in later chapters of the Acts give the impression of very fresh reminiscing. Since the Acts refer to the previous writing to Theophilus of the Gospel account, it appears the Gospel would have been written about that date. Mark and "Aramaic Matthew" would have been written before that time and would have been among the "sources" cited by Luke. The assured Epistles of Paul were clearly written in the last half of the fifth decade as evidenced by secular events concurrent with the writings of Paul—the games at Corinth for example.

It would appear that the first council at Jerusalem about the year 50 and the martyrdom of James would have been the events which would have brought home to the assembled disciples that the events should be committed to writing—that, as individuals, they were aging and fragile custodians of the word—that controversy could and would occur which required authoritative guidance and decision in the swiftly spreading Church. Thus about seventeen years after the death of Christ a more or less formal organizational structure would seem to have developed.

Chapter 12

THE BIBLE—WHAT IS TRUTH?

The strongest single theme that comes through in the Old Testament aside from its general expression of the quintessence of the personal in the God of Abraham, Isaac and Jacob and their descendants was that establishing the Hebrews as His chosen people in a way that no other were—or ever would be. The story of Exodus and the Sinai covenant was, and is, the skeletal structure on which all else depended. God the infinite suzerain had picked this peculiar people to be His special vassal—and with both blessings to be bestowed if they show their fealty in faithfulness and curses which would befall if they failed in loyalty. In a wryly humorous bit of midrash, the Jews say that God offered the same deal first to all other people but they were too smart and refused. But why, in all seriousness, should He select this insignificant people in this difficult place?

Two things need to be said about these Hebrew people and this geographic location which from purely human considerations would be important. First, they were a pastoral, nomadic people in basic culture. From the beginnings of history, they were a people of few material possessions completely dependent upon their flocks and the availability of forage and scarce water. The imagery of the shepherd, of the blessings of water and growing, living things pervades the texts of the Bible, both the Old and New Testaments. These people were dependent upon communal support in a way those more blessed with abundance were not. It was the personal relationships and not the material things which had greatest influence on their lives. They had to be clannish to survive and further they had time to think deeply as they followed their flocks in an unhurried, simple, existence—an existence which, in fact, could not be hurried by busyness or resort to complexity. The Hebrews had a passion for family and community, and God was an intimate part of that family and community. These were the stable things in a world of constant wandering and change. Family and community history must be passed down through the generations. The spoken word, the oral tradition must be faithful, almost sacredly true in transmitting this familiar and communal history.

The written word was even more sacred.

The second important thing, concerning the Hebrews, was the location of Israel at the land bridge linking Asia, Asia Minor, Europe and Africa. A look at the globe will disclose that it is close to the centroidal position of the total land mass of the world. From the standpoint of location with a view to later dissemination of peoples and/or their ideas it was a near optimum. Further, a review of history reveals the constant plowing by hostile armies which took place from remote antiquity as the tides of empire in the Ancient East ebbed and flowed. Palestine might not have been the target, or the prize, but it stood athwart the only viable passageway to those areas which were targets and prizes. Ravaged, conquered, carried off into slavery, and as a consequence dispersed throughout the world these people survived and they spread their cultural history worldwide. The mere survival of these people, as a people, and the maintenance of their culture took a solidarity of viewpoint and toughness of mind demanded of no other in history. Huston Smith in the book previously cited says in this regard:

> There is a striking point that runs through Jewish history as a whole. Western civilization was born in the Middle East, and the Jews were at its crossroads. In the heyday of Rome, the Jews were close to the Empire's center. When power shifted eastward, the Jewish center was in Babylon, when it skipped to Spain, there again were the Jews. When, in the Middle Ages, the center of civilization moved into central Europe, the Jews were waiting for it in Germany and Poland. The rise of the United States to the leading world power found Judaism focused there. And now, today, when the pendulum seems to be swinging back toward the old world and the East rises to renewed importance, there again are the Jews, in Israel. As the Star of David waves over their spiritual home for the first time in history and Israel stands again on its feet, the dominant thought in the minds of the Jews is: How wonderful to be alive today when all this is happening!

The survival of the Jewish nation is inexplicable by every sociologic principle. They not only would not have survived, they never would have been formed as a nation from a bunch of obstreperous, uncooperative slaves in Egypt, who had lived in bondage for a third of a millennium. Exodus tells how it happened. Having passed, we trust, the logic gate which says...anomalies can occur—that God can intervene—if and when He chooses—has there ever been a clearer case in point? The Jews, indeed, seem to have been a chosen people, as they claimed, from the beginning.

And now, if the historicity of the biblical narrative is granted, and there is no evidence that it should not be granted, to offset the clear evidence that it is a reliable history of a people, we can say that the prophets lived when they were reported to have lived, and not long afterwards as the critics had held, and the prophecies which were fulfilled were, in fact, actually fulfilled after the prophecy and not merely constructed after the event to establish a prophet in the past as the demythologizers would have it. The New Testament is filled with the allusion to old prophecies fulfilled and to future fulfillments.

One strong measure of the truth of evidence of a witness is its adversity to the witness's interests. Now, many, in fact, the vast majority of the prophecies were distasteful and uncomplimentary to the Jewish nation at the time they were made. It was only the profound respect for the "Word of God" that permeated the Jewish people which permitted such a record to be established and maintained with scrupulous care. Many of the prophecies were recorded and fulfilled in a distasteful manner. Some prophecies are still being fulfilled. A characteristic of prophecy is that it is susceptible to multifulfillment. God, in His sophisticated wisdom, projects the word so that it has application throughout the course of history. The prophecies are usually fulfilled once, in an identifiable literal absolute way, and then, at other times, either before or later in an allegorical way. The prophets, Isaiah, Jeremiah, Micah, and Zacariah have been outstanding in this particular mode, applying not only in Judaism, but also in Christianity. Over fifty references to Isaiah alone are contained in the New Testament in direct application to the role of Christ as the Messiah. A good example of the multiple interpretation of prophecy can be found in Chapter 53 of the Book of Isaiah which the Jews take as the personification of their own role as a nation in God's plan. On the other hand, the Christians, and by extension the Muslims, accept it as applying directly to Christ in person. This chapter is quoted to show the detail involved.

Who would believe what we have heard?
To whom has the arm of the Lord been revealed?

He grew up like a sapling before him, like a shoot from the parched earth;
There was in him no stately bearing to make us look at him, nor appearance that would attract us to him.
He was spurned and avoided by men, a man of suffering, accustomed to infirmity,
One of those from whom men hide their faces, spurned, and we held him in no esteem.
Yet it was our infirmities that he bore, our sufferings that he endured,
While we thought of him as stricken, as one smitten by God and afflicted.
But he was pierced for our offenses, crushed for our sins;
Upon him was the chastisement that makes us whole, by his stripes we were healed.
We had all gone astray like sheep, each following his own way;
But the Lord laid upon him the guilt of us all.
Though he was harshly treated, he submitted and opened not his mouth;
Like a lamb led to the slaughter or a sheep before the shearers, he was silent and opened not his mouth.
Oppressed and condemned, he was taken away, and who would have thought any more of his destiny?
When he was cut off from the land of the living, and smitten for the sin of his people,
A grave was assigned him among the wicked and a burial place with evil doers,
Though he had done no wrong nor spoken any falsehood. (but the Lord was pleased to crush him in infirmity.) If he gives his life as an offering for sin, he shall see his descendants in a long life, and the will of the Lord shall be accomplished through him.
Because of his affliction, he shall see the light in fullness of days;
Through his suffering, my servant shall justify many, and their guilt he shall bear.
Therefore I will give him his portion among the great, and he shall divide the spoils with the mighty, because he surrendered himself to death and was counted among the wicked; And he shall take away the sins of many, and win pardon for their offenses.

One of the key elements of prophecy, in fact, is that it should have value throughout history—that it have a universality in appeal—and not have application in only a very limited way. This aspect is manifestly true of the Old Testament, which for thousands of years has served to inspire and instruct peoples of such tremendous variety of cultural background and education. Much of the credit for this universality of relevance is that imagery is used because it does permit translation in terms of many peoples—ages and degrees of sophistication. Looking at an example from Genesis, had it depicted creation of the physical universe as the modern scientists do—as evidenced in the "Big Bang" or "continuous creation" mode it would have been completely incomprehensible to any people who lived before the twentieth century and many, now living, as well. There was no way to relate those theories to what man could possibly understand in a factual way and, further, the scientific views are only theories which a hundred years from now may be laughed at. But no one of any real sensitivity or sophistication laughs at Genesis, as Smith noted concerning Whitehead, himself, as we have seen, a great scientist as well as a philosopher. It is worthwhile to look at the first fifty or so words of the Bible.

"In the beginning, God created heaven and earth. And the earth was void and empty, and darkness was upon the face of the deep; and the spirit of God moved over the waters. And God said: 'Be light made.' And light was made. And God saw the light that it was good." The very first words spoken by God quoted in the Bible were "Be light made." When we realize that matter is increasingly coming to resemble a form of energy closely related to light, it may be that Genesis is very close to actual fact, as well as being beautifully allegorical, in naming light as the first thing called into existence, the first two sentences of Genesis being general preamble.

If the Bible is image in many cases, it is an imagery that conveys truth in a familiar, attractive way which, because of its familiarity and attractiveness, will be remembered and will be passed on substantially unchanged regardless of educational or linguistic difficulties. Deep theological and, more importantly, moral insights are conveyed by image of revelation. That is its sole purpose—not to educate in technology or the physical sciences. Yet, this is not to say that there is a two-level theory of truth, one theological and the other scientific. There is one truth but that truth is expressed in a different way—approached by different paths—to convey that truth.

If the mark of a statement's genuineness and intrinsic value is its survivability, through all times and circumstances, and its utility in assisting man to live an authentic life in those times and circumstances, no work has exceeded or even approached the Old Testament in this regard, particularly considering its foundation role for later revelation as well.

With that general background on the Bible as authentic history—and we will go further into the matter a bit later—let us review the concepts of some of the major theologians of the twentieth century. First, we will review that of one who follows the traditional Protestant theme, Geerhardus Vos. As a conditioning statement, it might be pertinent to note that the writer's review and comments are from the perspective of the "value" of the particular theologic viewpoint, and in the support of a viable social movement, in the Toynbee mode and centered on the idea of a brotherhood of man in a theistic orientation. The loftiest thoughts which would urge greater individual isolation from humanity, a new eremitic cult for instance, would not be considered a likely candidate for launching a public "back to God" movement, much less of a movement necessarily having strong sociologic, political, and economic implications. By the same token, a movement which would tear the fabric of well-established and emotionally bound tradition, which already has, within it, strong motivations, would also be unfavorable.

Geerhardus Vos is Professor Emeritus of Biblical Theology at Princeton University. In the writer's view, he represents earnest biblical scholarship at its best. Revelation, as the Word of God, must have its base in truth in the most fundamental manner. Stated simply, it is truth speaking truth. As such, there is no idle verbage thrown in to deliberately confuse even the most simple and particularly the most simple in the "good" sense of that word. That is the approach of Vos.

There is always a strong central theme in any revelation which appears—not on a casual reading—but as a consequence of an effort to understand. That theme is the main purpose of the revelation and contains the truth at its most basic. This is not to say that the subtleties of image, analogy, allegory and parable, which are extensively used, do not also express variations on the theme and that there are not harmonics in individual passages which bring out greater richness. Just as in any great work of music, but—and this would seem to be Vos' position— the variations and the harmonics do not constitute the theme. When biblical exegesis strains to interpret passages, only in terms of incidentals, it can and does present a distorted picture and a multitude of such works results in the tremendous dissonance being heard in Christianity in the middle and late twentieth century. Vos stands in sharp contrast in Protestant theology to Bultmann and Tillich, whom we will review next. Vos's view is quite like Karl Barth's, but he is not as fiercely disputatious as Barth nor does Vos despise the intellectual approach to God as Barth does.

Vos's work, *Biblical Theology*, in its eighth printing in 1973, is a good, solid, analytical review of the Bible as an expression of revelation that is rewarding reading whether one is, or is not, a Protestant. The brief selections have been chosen to address some of the deeper theologic problems which confront man today.

First Vos defines the field of biblical theology, stating:

Biblical theology deals with revelation as a divine activity, not as the finished product of that activity. Its nature and method of procedure will therefore naturally have to keep in close touch with, and so far as possible reproduce, the features of the divine work itself. The main features of the latter are the following:

(a) The historic progressiveness of the revelation-process; it has not completed itself in one exhaustive act, but unfolded itself in a long series of successive acts. In the abstract, it might conceivably have been otherwise. But, as a matter of fact this could not be, because revelation does not stand alone by itself, but is (so far as Special Revelation is concerned) insepara-bly attached to another activity of God, which we call Redemption. Now redemption could not be other-wise than historically successive because, it addresses itself to the generations of mankind coming into ex-istence in the course of history. Redemption is partly objective and central, partly subjective and individual. By the former, we designate those redeeming acts of God, which take place on behalf of, but outside of, the human person. By the latter, we designate those acts of God which enter into the human subject. We call the objective acts central because, happening in the center of the circle of redemption, they concern all alike, and are not in need of, or capable of, repe-tition. Such objective-central acts are the Incarnation, the atonement, the Resurrection of Christ. The acts in the subjective sphere are called individual, because they are repeated in each individual separately. Such subjective-individual acts are regeneration, justification, conversion, sanctification, glorification.

There lies only one epoch in the future when we may expect objective-central redemption to be resumed, viz., at the Second Coming of Christ. At that time, there will take place great redemptive acts concerning the world and the people of God collectively. These will add to the volume of truth which we now possess.

(b) The actual embodiment of revelation in history. The process of revelation is not only concomitant with history, but it becomes incarnate in history. The facts of history, themselves, acquire a revealing significance. The Crucifixion and Resurrection of Christ are examples of this.

The usual order is: first word, then the fact, then again the interpretative word. The Old Testament brings the predictive preparatory word, the Gospels record the redemptive-revelatory fact, the Epistles supply the subsequent, final interpretation.

(c) The organic nature of the historic process observable in revelation. Every increase is progressive, but not every progressive increase bears an organic character. The organic nature of the progression of revelation explains several things. It is sometimes contended that the assumption of progress in revelation excludes its absolute perfection at all stages. This would actually be so if the progress were non-organic. The organic progress is from seed-form to the attainment of full growth yet, we do not say that, in the qualitative sense, the seed is less perfect than the tree.

Some remarks are in place here in regard to a current misconstruction of this last-mentioned feature. It is urged that the discovery of so considerable an amount of variableness and differentiation in the Bible must be fatal to the belief in its absoluteness and infallibleness. If Paul has one point of view and Peter another, then each can be at best only approximately correct. This would actually follow, if the truth did not carry in itself a multi-formity of aspects. But infallibleness is not inseparable from dull uniformity. The truth is inherently rich and complex, because God is so Himself. The whole contention ultimately rests on a wrong view of God's nature and His relation to the world, a view at bottom Deistical. It conceives of God as standing outside of His own creation and therefore having to put up the instrumentation of His revealing speech with such imperfect forms and organs as it offers Him. The didactic, dialectic mentality of Paul would thus become a hindrance for the ideal communication of the message, no less than the simple, practical, untutored mind of Peter. From the standpoint of Theism, the matter shapes itself quite differently. The truth, having inherently many sides, and God having access to, and control of, all intended organs of revelation shaped each one of these for the precise purpose to be served.

(d) The fourth aspect of revelation determinative of the study of Biblical Theology consists in its practical adaptability. God's self-revelation to us was not made for a primarily intellectual purpose. It is not to be overlooked, of course, that the truly pious mind may, through an intellectual contemplation of the divine perfections, glorify God. This would be just as truly religious as the intensest occupation of the will in the service of God. But it would not be the full-orbed religion at which, as a whole, revelation aims. It is true the Gospel teaches that to know God is life eternal. But the concept of "knowledge" here is not to be understood in its Hellenic sense, but in the Semitic sense. According to the former, *"to know" means to mirror the reality of a thing in one's consciousness.* The Semitic, and Biblical idea, is to have the reality of something practically interwoven with the inner experience of life. Hence "to know" can stand in the Biblical idiom for "to love," "to single out in love." Because God desires to be known after this fashion, He has caused His revelation to take place in the milieu of the historical life of a people.

The circle of revelation is not a school, but a "covenant." To speak of revelation as an "education" of humanity, is a rationalistic and utterly un-scriptural way of speaking. All that God disclosed of Himself has come in response to the practical religious needs of His people, as these emerged in the course of history.

Unlike Barth, Vos sees a limited but real role for natural theology. He says:

Nature from within no longer functions normally in sinful man. Both his religious and his moral sense of God may have become blunted and blinded. And the finding of God in nature without has also been made subject to error and distortion. The innate sense of God, as lying closer to the inner being of man, is more seriously affected by this than his outward observation of the writing of God in nature. Hence, the exhortation addressed in Scripture to the heathen, that they shall correct their foolish pre-conceptions of the nature of God through attention to the works of creation, e.g. *Isa.* 40:25, 26; *Ps.* 94:5-11. The main correction, however, of the natural knowledge of God cannot come from within nature itself. It must be supplied by the supernaturalism of redemption. *Redemption in a supernatural way to restore, to fallen man also, the normalcy and efficiency of his cognition of God in the sphere of nature.* How true this is, may be seen from the fact that the best system of Theism i.e., Natural Theology has not been produced from the sphere of heathenism, however splendidly endowed in the cultivation of philosophy but from Christian sources. When we produce a system of natural knowledge of God, and, in doing so, profess to rely exclusively on the resources of reason, that is, of course, formally correct, but it remains an open question, whether we should have been able to produce such a thing with the degree of excellence we succeed in imparting to it, had not our minds, in the natural exercise of their faculties, stood under the correcting influence of redemptive grace.

Christ for Vos is both the eternal Logos, that is the second person of the Trinity and also fully human in the Incarnation.

A careful exegesis of the prologue (of John's Gospel) leads to the conclusion that the following stages are part of the Logos-work of which John is speaking. First the mediation of mankind of the knowledge of God conveyed through nature; this is a function which by no means ceased when Logos became flesh, but is going on alongside of His incarnate, redemptive, activity from the beginning onward till the end, as long as there shall be a world to need it. In the second place, there is the redemptive revelation given to the O.T. people of God. This had reference to redemption, although it was mediated by the as yet unincarnate Christ, so that, as to the state in which the Logos mediated it, there was as yet no difference between what He had been from the beginning of the world and what He was then. In the third place, the Logos-function reached its climax, when the Lord became flesh, and in this incarnate state, never to be laid aside again, issued the full interpretation of the redemptive work of God, either during His own earthly career in the state of humiliation, or during His exalted state, possessed since the resurrection and now brought to bear upon the redemptive revelation from heaven. On the one hand Jesus disclosed God through what He was; His nature, His character were God-revealing; ultimately this involved and postulates His being divine in His nature; His being God. On the other hand Jesus also revealed God through the speech He brought from God, through the words He spake. It goes without saying that these two modes were not sharply separated one from the other; the character-revelation was in no small part a disclosure of character, first the speaker, and next of one duplicated. It is, therefore, not so much the absence or the presence of the thought of word-revelation, but rather the prominence of the thought of character-duplication in one of the sources that distinguishes the two aspects.

Contrary to the view of many modern theologians, Christ always was conscious of His divinity and His mission.

Jesus had a true human nature, and human nature, as such, is subject to development, which however, is not equivalent to saying that it cannot exist, under any conditions, without development. The idea of evolution has taken such hold of the modern mind, and become so fascinating, that in many cases the existence of gradual acquisition of knowledge by the mind of Jesus is simply assumed without enquiring into the concrete evidence. As a matter of fact evidence for this assumption does not exist, so long as the faultless nature of the content of the teaching is maintained. There is no point in the life of Our Lord at which the inflow of a new substance or principle of thought can be traced.

There is no fancy footwork with Vos. The Revelation of God is not meant to convey fairy tales but the sheer, unvarnished truth.

Rudolf Bultmann was born on August 20, 1884, in Oldenburg, in northern Germany. He was sixteen when Nietzsche died and almost unavoidably was impressed by the rise of positivism even as Nietzsche was. His theology seems an odd forging of Kierkegaardian existentialism, crediting little ability of man to find objective truth and positivism—a positivism totally dedicated to the unchallengeability of scientific empiricism. The product seems held together only by a mechanical interlocking without any real cohesive forces. Bultmann was a thorough scholar of the Bible, far more so than Kierkegaard, to whose works he was greatly attracted, and from which, along with Heidegger's, he derived his existential total outlook. But as stated, he matured in a positivistic environment—Germany of the early twentieth century, when the "Vienna Circle" variety of positivism was being formulated. Bultmann was therefore also profoundly affected by that influence and his life efforts were devoted to bringing these two diverse elements into a forced wedlock. Bultmann's philosophy was basically the same as Nietzsche. However, instead of seeing a struggle to the death between these opposing theistic and atheistic or agnostic forces, he wished to reconcile them so that the family of man could have the maternal loving care of Christianity and the harsh but disciplining father's influence of a tough, technologic, world.

Two statements of Bultmann's illustrate these seemingly hopelessly opposed viewpoints. But first, we should look at his methodology which lay in "demythologizing" the Bible, but which resulted, in fact, in totally "mythologizing" it in the mode of Crombie quoted earlier. Bultman coupled this approach with an unquestioning acceptance of empiricism in his own theology and finally completed his masterpiece by throwing over the ungainly structure a cloak of mysticism to hide the points of impossible mismatch. While most of his work had application to the New Testament, it reflected back on the Old Testament as myth.

Bultmann's first theologic premise is, "Man's knowledge and mastery of the world have advanced to such an extent, through science and technology, that it is no *longer possible for anyone* seriously to hold the New Testament view of the world. In fact there is hardly anyone who does. He (Modern Man) also does not acknowledge miracles because they do not fit into the lawful order. When a strange, or marvellous, *accident* occurs, he does not rest until he has found a rational cause." (Emphasis this writer). Thus, science has ruled out the possibility of miracles. What this implies as to the power of God—whom he vigorously defends—he does not say, but his expression is of a positivistic view to the core.

Bultmann's next premise is this: "Thus the fact that God *cannot be seen* or *apprehended apart from faith* does not mean that He does not exist apart from faith. We must remember, however, that the affirmation of faith in its relation to its object, God, cannot be proved objectively—this is not a weakness of faith, it is its true strength." (Emphasis supplied). Bultmann states further that: "I have said that faith grows out of encounters which are the substance of our personal lives as historical lives. Its meaning is readily understood when we reflect upon the simple phenomena of our personal lives." This is existentialism's main thesis. We become authentic persons and grasp life's meaning only through our experienced encounters with others in life. Now here is a strange hybrid. We accept empiricism in everything technologic and scientific and reject it in all other aspects of our lives. It produces the two-tiered viewpoint of knowing going back to Siger of Brabant. Knowledge is purely objective as to science and technology, purely subjective as to our personal experiences including those relating to God.

In fact, when we review our own lives we realize that there are objective and subjective vectors in all aspects of knowledge. There is no such sharp cleavage as Bultmann suggests between one and the other. In any actual set of circumstances, our individual apprehension of reality, which is what we are trying to approach authentically, lies at a weighted position somewhere between the two modes. Any scientific theory, in its initial stages is largely subjective, in Bultmann's sense of being subjective. That is, a theory is something more intuited as representing reality than empirically established. That does not prevent the theory from having substantial objective basis as deduced from surrounding circumstances.

Bultmann, along with those of his age group in the behavioral sciences, insisted upon inductive empirical demonstration be-forehand. In that mode, objective knowledge is equated with empirical demonstration. It is the reef upon which positivism, as a philosophy, scuttled itself and sank. Positivism, which in its period of prominence had been supported, particularly in Germany, by a group of physical scientists, during Bultmann's maturity, was largely taken over by linguistics specialists who were bound up in word forms much more than in factual evidence.

The contrast between the two viewpoints of any entity by the phenomenologist and the positivist produces a paradox. In fact, the rigid positivist's viewpoint becomes almost totally subjective—biased by his very positivism. The phenomenologists say that any entity whatsoever must be looked at freed of any preconceived opinions as to the nature of the thing being reviewed. This approach includes the freedom to view the entity, event or process as it is presented to us by our senses and also as it appears to our mind's eye. Man is a good example. Man can be physically measured and, as a result, can be catalogued as to species of organism. But, is that what is conveyed by the idea of specific man or of mankind in general? How can a positivist distinguish between Karl Marx and T. S. Eliot in a way which sets forth the particular genius of the two men and yet retains both their generality and specificity? The descriptive adjectives needed are not in his vocabulary. Does that mean the difference is not meaningful? Is the purely physical measurement a better objective picture, in the real sense, than the total description?

Bultmann, by his blind acceptance of the idea of the *impossibility* of miracles because miracles are contrary to physical laws, thereby *subjectively* refuses to look at the possibility that the Author of the physical laws—whose existence he offers as real through faith—has the power to modify the very laws He enacted. Bultmann has a strongly preconceived notion as to what is "real." It leaves him in an untenable position, "to preach a faith" in the reality of an omnipotent God and His presence in the world through Christ, yet to hold resolutely to a very limited potency for Him and that limited potency is constricted into the bounds of the following limitations: God cannot even control His own creation, not even if His own Son is incarnate in the world at the time the events occur. Bultmann not only wants a "leap of faith," he wants to remove the jumping board from the approach to the chasm.

There are, to Bultmann, two kinds of apprehended reality

as applied to theology—the first one empirically based—limited to science—called "objective knowledge." The second reality is experiential and subjective in basic nature and is called "faith" and there is no legitimate linkage between them, only a chasm at which one must stop or somehow vault. Yet man has to live in this world divided between knowledge and faith, recognizing that he never makes a purely objective or purely subjective decision on any important matter—and on few unimportant ones. A theology, like a philosophy, should assist men, in general, in making an authentic way through life—and authenticity is not all that remote from reality. Why should religion strip itself of objective access to knowledge for no reason and contrary to available evidence? It appears counterproductive and certainly unanalytic to deliberately widen the gap of ignorance. By limiting oneself to objective scientific knowledge on one hand and faith on the other hand, substantial areas of uncertainty still remain, for the "leapers," which man must accept or reject on faith even after all rational avenues of thought have been explored.

Now, Bultmann asserts that this lack of objective basis is the strength and not the weakness of faith. What he has done is recast the emphasis of God's approach to the world. *The primary thing God wants, as Bultmann sees it, and in many ways as Kierkegaard sees it too, is for us to make the "leap of faith"—to cast away all cautions—all logic—all rationality—to the winds and humbly admit "I can't know You. It is absurd, but I believe."* Bultmann says, in fact, that belief in miracles, of the Old and more particularly of the New Testament, based on God's ability to perform them if He should so choose is a weakness, even sinfulness. God wants our faith and therefore He would not have so cluttered up the picture with all the reputed miraculous events if He had truly wanted man to do no more than believe in blind faith. Yet, somehow revelation, which records all those events, is to be relied upon, excluding the miraculous of course. It is a tough thesis to maintain and to use in argument to convince people, particularly on the eve of the twenty-first century when, to again requote Camus, "There is a passionate disbelief."

If the Exodus is fiction and the Resurrection fiction because miraculous, how can the presence of God, in Christ, be insisted upon? Yet, this is specifically Bultmann's theology. The weakness of Bultmann as compared to Kierkegaard is that Bultmann destroys the platform from which he would spring. *If fifty percent or more of the Bible is dismissed as pure fiction, how can one defend the remainder with any confidence?*

One of the interesting conclusions Bultmann comes to on this basis is related to the dual aspect of history. This concept had an important influence on the "demythologizing" of the biblical writings. History is not an empirical science in any strict sense. Its events are not repeatable for verification, and no two historians, in the presence of the best historical evidence, will agree exactly about the traditional questions of: who, what, how, or even when and where of the circumstantial realities of past events. Anyone who reads history will agree with that lack of empiricity. But Bultmann says history may be considered scientific and objective in the sense that historians are able to establish some standards or norms by which to frame the structure of specific events which then can be related internally to each other and externally to other events in space and time. Bultmann accepts this aspect of history as science. Answers to the topic questions beyond this frame are, in the main, interpretive and subjective and cannot be accepted as having a scientific relationship in objective reality. Thus, Bultmann accepted, as fact, the most likely erroneous conclusions of leading Old Testament biblical history scholars of his time, concerning the verification of dates when the books of the Bible were written. This is most important—to factually establish the dates of biblical writing and to corroborate those dates with dates of historical events already officially recorded! As we saw, this dating placed the writing, in most cases, long after the events they purported to describe. Also, as we have seen, the biblical skeptics of Bultmann's productive years held that both Old and New Testaments were late, largely mythological accounts of highly embroidered faith traditions that had little or no relationship to any actual events. If a theology is hung on a viewpoint which accepts that concept of the verity of revelation, there is literally no rational basis for accepting it at all! If the God of Revelation is so impotent and careless in His revelation of acts, He bears little resemblance to the God of Theism.

If Bultmann was making an *argumentum a fortiori,* stating in effect, that: *even if* we deny the miracles, God and the Incarnation are still acceptable on faith, it would be different. But Bultmann was explicit in his demand that the miracles must be denied because they could not be scientifically proven! Nevertheless, Bultmann's theology, as poorly hung together as it is, was important in shaping skeptical attitudes toward revelation during much of this century.

Having looked thus, perhaps over-critically because too briefly, at Bultmann's works, let us now look at some excerpts to let him speak for himself in his own defense. In his essay *"Christianity as a Religion East and West,"* Bultmann examines Christianity explainable as a basis of understanding life.

If Christianity—originally an oriental religion— became a religion of the West and, indeed, far more than that, a world religion, is the reason not that basic possibilities for the understanding of human existence are revealed in it, which we find everywhere and in every age the same, and so also in the West?

In suffering, man is brought to himself, while everything foreign, everything of the world in him, in which he mistakenly seeks his essential being, is removed from him, and the chains that bind him to the here and now are torn asunder; there takes place in him that process of withdrawal from the world, in the form of which the life of the believer should take its course. But in being brought to himself in this way, he does not become aware of his own strength, but becomes clearly aware of himself as the man who is not in control himself—as the man of no account. *In this way, however, abandoning all illusions of self-mastery, he is to recognize himself before God as the man who exists purely and simply in dependence of God's grace.* And in this very way he is pleasing to God, and so he is open to receive the grace of God, whose "strength is made perfect in weakness": for—as Paul says—"when I am weak, then am I strong" (*2 Cor.* 12:9 f). Out of suffering there develops for man an inner strength in which he is superior to every trick of fate: suffering to him is a source of strength. But in that rests the very inmost nature of the Christian religion: God is manifest in the Crucified One, whom He has made Lord as the risen one. "Though he was crucified through weakness, yet he liveth by the power of God" (*2 Cor.* 13:4). As the Gospel of John says, His Crucifixion is His exaltation, His glorification. The Cross then is the sign under which Christianity has set out on its victorious career into the Western World, and in the figure of the Crucified One an embodiment of the Deity was brought to the West, which contradicted all the views of the ancient world in the Occident: the Passion as the manifestation of divine strength and grace!

In *New Testament and Mythology* the following excerpts reveal some of Bultmann's critical viewpoints on the traditional approach to the Bible. He says man must make a decision—

> . . .the decision of faith: I here make a decision not for a responsible act, but for a new understanding of myself as a man who by God's grace is freed of himself and has received himself anew as a gift. I decide for a life by the Grace of God. . .so that all my decisions, all my responsible actions are grounded in love. Such a life, the life purely for others, is possible only to him who is free of himself. . . .The paradox of Christian existence is that he who believes is detached from the world—in a way lives an unworldly existence, and yet remains within the world, within his own historicity. Historical existence is existence from the future. First, because his faith and freedom can never be possessions; being eschatological events, they can never become facts that belong to the past, but have reality always as events only. Second, because the believer remains within history. In principle, the future always holds out to man the gift of his freedom. Christian faith means the power to accept that gift from instant to instant. Man's freedom of himself, the gift of divine grace, always becomes reality in the freedom of the historical decision.
>
> In this way the Resurrection is not a mythological event adduced in order to prove the saving efficacy of the Cross, but an article of faith just as much as the meaning of the Cross itself. Indeed, faith in the Resurrection is really the same thing as faith in the saving efficacy of the Cross, faith in the Cross as the Cross of Christ. Hence, you cannot first believe in Christ and then in the strength of that faith believe in the Cross. To believe in Christ means to believe in the Cross as the Cross of Christ. The saving efficacy of the Cross is not derived from the fact that it is the Cross of Christ: it is the Cross of Christ because it has this saving efficacy. Without that efficacy, it is the tragic end of a great man.

We are back again at the old question. How do we come to believe in the Cross as the Cross of Christ and as the eschatological event par excellence? How do we come to believe in the saving efficacy of the Cross? There is only one answer. This is the way in which the Cross is proclaimed. It is always proclaimed together with the Resurrection. Christ meets us in the preaching as one crucified and risen. He meets us in the world of preaching and nowhere else. The faith of Easter is just this—faith in the world of preaching.

. . .the Biblical doctrine that death is the punishment of sin is equally abhorrent to naturalism and idealism, since they both regard death as a simple and necessary process of nature.

And to attribute human mortality to the fall of Adam is sheer nonsense, for guilt implies personal responsibility, and the idea of original sin as an inherited infection is sub-ethical, irrational, and absurd.

The same objections apply to the doctrine of the atonement. How can the guilt of one man be expiated by the death of another who is sinless—if, indeed, one may speak of a sinless man at all? . . .what a primitive mythology it is, that a divine Being should become incarnate and atone for the sins of men through His own blood!

The man who wishes to believe in God as his God must realize that he has nothing in his hand on which to base his faith. He is suspended in mid-air, and cannot demand a proof of the word which addresses him. . . .Security can be found only by abandoning all security. . . .In fact, to desire security, that is, the security of evidence to make our belief rational, is sinful. The authentic life on the other hand, would be a life based on unseen intangible realities. Such a life means the abandonment of all self-contrived security. . . .The old quest for visible security, the hankering after tangible realities, and the clinging to transistory objects is sin. . .faith means turning our backs on self and abandoning all security.

The proclamation can call for the decision of faith only when it has shown that the confession of my sinfulness and the confession to God's grace in Christ are possibilities for my existence, which to reject is guilty unbelief. That, now, is exactly what existential interpretation does achieve, or to put it more humbly: that is what existential interpretation achieves in my opinion, to which I hold until somebody shows me a better heremeneutic method.

Paul Tillich was born in Germany in 1886, the son of a Lutheran pastor. His earlier philosophic leanings were thus influenced toward a Hegelian form of idealism characteristic of Lutheranism at that time. He was Professor of Theology at the University of Berlin following World War I. Then he went to Marburg, Dresden, and Leipzig. In 1929, he moved to Frankfurt where he succeeded phenomenologist philosopher Max Scheler in the chair of sociology and philosophy. His works have a strong sociologic flair to them and his philosophy seems to take a good deal from Scheler in his later period when, as it will be recalled, he veered from Catholicism to a "partnership" pantheism. Tillich seems to have retained some of the Hegelian influence even after he had switched to an existentialist position in philosophy. He was a contemporary of Bultmann and subject to the same pressures in his early life, but effects of positivism do not reveal themselves as strongly as with Bultmann, largely because Tillich's attack on traditionalism took a different approach.

When Hitler took over in Germany, Tillich was dismissed from his position in Frankfurt and, responding to an invitation from theologian Reinhold Niebuhr, came to the United States at Columbia University. He has lectured widely throughout the United States and his later works were published in English, which simplifies the problem considerably in interpretation of his view. He probably is the best known and most influential theologian in the United States.

As an overall comment on his works, this writer senses an intense strain in Tillich engendered by his change from Hegelian idealism to an existentialism largely in the mode of Heidegger. The strain reveals itself in his work in a continual oscillation between the traditional Lutheran view of Christianity, "justification in faith" and the existentialist emphasis on the experiential approach to God—a view in which God is seen as Being-in-Itself, the Ultimate Concern, the symbol for the outlet of man's religious sentiments.

Although Tillich had a sociologic approach in his theology and philosophy and stressed this appeal of religious symbology as a cohesive force in the Western culture, his own theology is so split that it offers no unifying symbol of its own about which people could rally. The brotherhood under the father-hood of man is impossible, given his purely intellectualized God. The concept lacks the down to earth grip of Luther which sparked the Reformation, for instance. Scheler's partnership pantheism was a stronger position, and yet, it has no strong appeal to the man on the street. A vague dedication to an ethereal non-being Ultimate Concern offers even less meaty emotional appeal—and emotional appeal, based on a strong integrated faith in which a cause stands, is a necessary ingredient in a durable social movement, as we shall see in Part VI. The following excerpts give a "feel" for Tillich's approach to theology. His view of the idea of justification by faith is far from that of Luther.

> The situation of doubt, even of doubt about God, need not separate us from God. There is faith in every serious doubt, namely, the faith in the truth as such, even if the only truth we can express is our lack of truth. But if this is experienced in its depth and as an ultimate concern, the divine is present; and he who doubts in such an attitude is "justified" in his thinking.

Of his theology he writes:

> If it is valid, no realm of life can exist without relation to something unconditional to an ultimate concern. Religion, like God, is omnipresent; its presence, like that of God, can be forgotten, neglected, denied. But it is always effective, giving inexhaustible depth to life and inexhaustible meaning to every cultural creation.
>
> History became the central problem of my theology and philosophy because of the historical reality as I found it when I returned from the First World War: a chaotic Germany and Europe; the end of the period of the victorious bourgeoisie and of the nineteenth-century way of life; the split between the Lutheran churches and the proletariat; the gap between the transcendent message of traditional Christianity and the imminent hopes of the revolutionary movements. The situation demanded interpretation as well as action. . . . My entrance into the religious-socialist movement meant for me the definite

break with philosophical idealism and theological transcendentalism.

"Kairos," the "fullness of time" according to the New Testament use of the word, describes the moment in which the eternal breaks into the temporal, and the temporal is prepared to receive it. What happened in the one unique kairos, the appearance of Jesus as the Christ, i.e., as the center of history, may happen in a derived form again and again in the process of time, creating centers of lesser importance on which the periodization of history is dependent. . . .

The interest of early Protestantism was, however, so much centered around individual justification that the idea of a "Gestalt of grace" in our historical existence could not develop. This development was also prevented by the fact that the Catholic Church considered itself as the body of objective grace, thus discrediting the idea of a "Gestalt of grace" for Protestant consciousness. It is obvious that the Protestant principle cannot admit any identification of grace with a visible reality, not even with the Church on its visible side. But the negation of a visible "Gestalt of grace" does not imply the negation of the concept as such. The Church in its spiritual quality, as an object of faith, is a "Gestalt of grace."

While the "Church" does not consist in a Gestalt—a structure of grace in its physical form—it does in the spiritual ideal. But that spiritual ideal must be adjustable to changing times.

Personal experience, the intimate observation of many individuals, the knowledge provided by psychotherapy, the trend of the younger generation in Europe toward the vital and prerational side of the individual and social life, the urgent desire for more community and authority and for powerful and dominating symbols—all these seemed to prove that the Protestant-humanist ideal of personality has been undermined and that the Protest cultus and its personal and social ethics have to undergo a far-reaching transformation. This impression was and is supported by the general development of Western civilization toward more collectivistic forms of political and economic life. The demand for a basic security in social, as well as in spiritual, respects has superseded (though not removed) the liberal demand for liberty. And this demand can no longer be suppressed, for it is rooted in the deepest levels of the men of today, of personalities and groups.... The question of whether Protestantism as a determining historical factor will survive is, above all, the question of whether it will be able to adapt itself to the new situation; it is the question of whether Protestantism, in the power of its principle, will be able to dissolve its amalgamation with bourgeois ideology and reality and create a synthesis, in criticism and acceptance, with the new forces that have arisen in the present stage of a revolutionary transformation of man and his world.

In his perceptive work, *Contemporary Philosophy and Religious Thought,* Malcolm Diamond, Professor of Religion at Princeton University (Diamond, 1974), says,

It would seem that Tillich's complex and many leveled analysis of the approach to ultimacy has left us without a reference for religious language. God as being-itself cannot properly be conceived as existing or as not existing, and there is nothing, literally no specific entity, that is ultimate. We may, therefore, ask, "What difference does the positing of being-itself make?" Tillich's answer, despite his difference with the Thomists, still has a cosmological ring. If being-itself were not then we would not be here to ask the question of being. There would be nothing, nothing at all: "... Everything finite participates in being-itself and its infinity (now understood as the unlimited which transcends the subject-object relation). Otherwise it would not have the power of being. It would be swallowed by non-being, or it would never have emerged out of non-being."

Tillich's vague, symbolic God compares with the end position of Scheler, who saw God as the Absolute Being in which all being is grounded. But Scheler, as a phenomenologist, did not totally disassociate this Absolute from "personality" as Tillich tends to. For Scheler, He is a "person" in partnership with man. For Tillich, He comes through as only the symbol of an ideal.

Diamond concludes his discussion of Tillich's thought with the statement:

> The application should be clear. Tillich manages to avoid most of the pitfalls of Christian thought, but he pays a high price for doing so. In the end his world seems indistinguishable from the secular world just as Mr. Sorley's (a character in a parable which Diamond gives) heaven would be indistinguishable from earth. If this is the case, there would seem to be little reason to talk Tillichese, for anything that he says in terms of Christian symbols could equally well be communicated in terms of the symbols of another faith, especially that of existentialistic humanism. It is not, therefore, altogether surprising that one of the movements most strongly influenced by Paul Tillich, a Christian thinker, called itself the "Death of God Theology."

We have previously reviewed Martin Buber, the existentialist philosopher, and have seen the depth that the "I—thou" dialogue penetrated all his thought, culminating in his viewing God as the Eternal and Absolute Thou. Let us study a few excerpts from Buber, the theologian of Judaism. First, he considers man as a spirit, the problem of evil and the source of ethics.

> Spirit is not a late bloom on the tree Man, but what constitutes man. The fact that man is a unit of substance which cannot be grasped if we regard it merely as a phenomenon of nature, the fact that there is a category of existence called Man, is based on the particular human consciousness. Spirit, then, is not just one human faculty among others. It is man's totality which comprises and integrates all his capacities, powers, qualities, and urges. When a man thinks he thinks with his entire body; spiritual man thinks even with his fingertips. Spiritual life is nothing but the existence of man insofar as he possesses that true human conscious totality, which is not the result of development; it goes back to the origin of mankind, though it may unfold differently in different individuals.
>
> The world is given to the human beings who perceive it and the life of man is itself a giving and

receiving. The events that occur to human beings are the great and small, untranslatable but unmistakable signs of their being addressed; what they do not fail to do can be an answer or a failure to answer. Thus the whole history of the world, the hidden, real world history, is a dialogue between God and His creature; a dialogue in which man is a true legitimate partner, who is entitled and empowered to speak his own independent word out of his own being.

I am far from wishing to contend that the conception and experience of the dialogical situation are confined to Judaism. But I am certain that no other community of human beings has entered with such strength and fervor into this experience as have the Jews.

What is presupposed when one is serious about the lived dialogue, regarding the moment as word and answer, is, of course that one is serious about the appointment of Man to the earth.

In the strongest contrast to the Iranian conception with all its later ramifications, the Jewish conception is that the happenings of this world takes [sic] place not in the sphere between two principles, light and darkness, or good and evil, but in the sphere between God and men, these mortal, brittle human beings who yet are able to face God and withstand His word.

The so-called evil is fully and as a primary element included in the power of God, who "forms the light, and creates darkness" (*Isa.* 45:7). The divine sway is not answered by anything which is evil in itself, but by the individual human beings, through who, alone, the so-called evil, the directionless power, can become real evil. Human choice is not a psychological phenomenon but utter reality, which is taken up into the mystery of the One who is. Man is truly free to choose God or to reject Him and to do so, not in a relationship of faith which is empty of the content of this world, but in one which contains the full content of the everyday. The "Fall" did not happen once and for all and become an inevitable fate, but it continually happens here and now in all its reality. In spite of all past history, in spite of all his inheritance, every man stands in the naked situation of Adam: to each man the decision is given. It is true that this does not imply that further events are deducible from that decision; it only implies that the human being's choice is that side of reality which concerns him as one called upon to act. . . .

The great question which is more and more deeply agitating our age is this: How can we act? Is our action valid in the sight of God or is its very foundation broken and unwarranted? The question is answered as far as Judaism is concerned by our being serious about the conception that man has been appointed to this world as an originator of events, as a real partner in the real dialogue with God.

This answer implies a refusal to have anything to do with all separate ethics, any concept of ethics as a separate sphere of life, a form of ethics which is all too familiar in the spiritual history of the West. Ethical life has entered into religious life, and cannot be extracted from it. There is no responsibility unless there is one to whom one is responsible, for there is no reply where there is no appeal. In the last resort, "religious life" means concreteness itself, the whole concreteness of life, without reduction, grasped dialogically, included in the dialogue.

For Buber, the ethical and moral life is inseparable from the concreteness of a life lived in a deeply personal dialogue with God. A God to whom man is responsible, to whom a debt of life well lived, in a religious sense, is owed and who can and will collect on that debt if there is a default.

In response to some theologians, like Tillich for instance, who avoided the term "God" because it has been rendered "useless" from overusage, Buber replies,

Yes, it is the most heavy-laden of all human words. None has become so soiled, so mutilated. Just for this reason, I may not abandon it. Generations of men have laid the burden of their anxious lives upon this word and weighed it to the ground; it lies in the dust and bears their whole Burden. The races of man with the religious factions have torn the word to pieces; they have killed for it and died for it, and it bears their fingermarks and their blood. Where might I find a word like it to describe the highest! If I took the purest, most sparkling concern from the inner treasure-chamber of the philosophers, I could only capture thereby an unbinding product of thought. I could not capture the presence of Him whom the generations of men have honored and degraded with their awesome living and dying. I do indeed mean Him whom the Hell tormented and Heaven storming generations of men mean. Certainly, they draw caricatures and write "God" underneath; they murder one another and say "in God's name." But when all madness and delusion fall to dust, when they stand over against Him in the loneliest darkness and no longer say "He, He" but rather sigh, "Thou," shout, "Thou," all of them the one word, and when they then add "God," is it not the real God whom they all implore, the One living God, the God of the children of man? Is it not He who hears them? And just for this reason is not the word "God," the word of appeal, the word which has become a name consecrated in all human tongues for all times?

As we saw earlier, the existentialist philosophy was centered in man as an existent—as a being in, and for, the world—which is really a transposition of the true emphasis—the world is an environment *for* man to be in and *for* his relationship. From Heidegger on to the present, man tends to become the *only* "existent" being. It is with difficulty that existentialists approach the idea of God since He must somehow be presented in a man-centered relationship. God is *for* man. It is thus very easy for them to slip off into the never-never-land of God as a subjective concept to provide man with a goal for which man may strive. Buber does not fall into the trap but both Bultmann and Tillich do. For Tillich, God is man's "Ultimate Concern," a symbol of that for which one lives, regardless of how defined. God is the ultimate concern *for* man. Bultmann sees Christ as essentially God in the world *for* man—a view which has much truth in it—if God is not limited to that perhaps totally symbolic function in which in Bultmann's case He is.

Regardless of how Tillich and Bultmann hedge, God emerges as a problematic "It" *for* man. In the case of Bultmann, God also emerges as an impotent faith object. Tillich perceives God as a numinous symbol having, perhaps, some unknowable form of reality, but not "existence." Buber, by visualizing God as the "Eternal Thou" to which the individual "I" relates in constant dialogue and who is never authentic if He is an "It," gives God the "personality" which the other two ignore, or deny. Buber's vision is magnificent.

Buber's theology gives tremendous effect to the idea of the communality of man, as the brotherhood of all men, under the fatherhood of God. He provides the motivation for a strong social movement based on that concept of the free individual, joined by mutual love, laterally and vertically in a community and not as a mechanical collectivity. Tillich and Bultmann both offer little motivation. There is nothing in either of their theologies to seize a man's imagination and provide the esprit for a sustained social movement. The idea of a brotherhood of man in the fatherhood of God is not there.

Somewhat paradoxically, the man-centeredness of most existential theology reduces the relevancy for man. Tillich changed his theologic viewpoint as he said, because of, among other things "the split between the Lutheran churches and the proletariat" yet his theology has little that the common man can grasp. Tillich's symbology is empty. The cross, the crescent, and the hammer and sickle were powerful symbols in social movements because of the driving force that lay behind the symbols which were conceived as sheer reality in people's minds.

Bultmann emphasizes faith, yet the sneaking impression is given that he, in fact, has none. His "leap of faith" is literally a last desperate lunge for "hope" that life has a meaning. In his own mind, he has destroyed any rational basis for faith, leaving only the irrational—and faith, without a credible basis, is mere wishfulness.

Faith does not require rigorous "proof" nor "sensual verification" to be credible. But, it must have a quality of "assurance" about it, a "goodness of fit" which gives confidence that the belief is true, that the statements to be accepted on faith are accurate and reliable. There must be something about the statement on religious faith which gives the "seal" of God's authorship. Any alleged "word of God," is not the word of God, unless it is reliable. If its reliability is impeached it gives no basis for confidence. One cannot base faith in God on a statement just because it asserts itself to be the word of the God in whom it seeks to have us believe. That is circularity of the argument at its most vicious. The "seal" of both the Old and New Testaments consists largely in the credibility of the events which are described at least as allegory and the unimpeachability of those who were their witnesses and acted as scribes. If the events described and presented as factual are fiction, the witnesses are not worthy of credibility. If it is recalled that all of the Apostles lived lives of great peril and discomfort and all except John were martyred for their faith in the reality of Christ's mission and for testifying to His life, for being witnesses of the things they had seen, and lived with, during His public life, it seems folly itself if they were not convinced of the truth of what they preached.

As we turn now to the Catholic theologians, Karl Rahner comes the closest among the well-established Catholic writers in the field to the existentialist viewpoint. There are others in the modern, "Post Vatican II" era who are somewhat more "advanced" in the "process" aspect—the Swiss theologian Hans Kung, for example. But, Kung does not represent any large following, not in the sense of Tillich or Bultmann in Protestant theology. Rahner would represent a broad theologic group among Catholics who have moved away from a strict scholastic stance.

Karl Rahner was born in Freiburg-im-Breisgau in 1904, entered the Jesuit order eighteen years later and was ordained in 1932. He was a student of Heidegger at Freiburg in 1934 and 1936 and was greatly influenced by that encounter with the existentialist ideas then moving into real prominence in Europe. Rahner's first major work, *Spirit in the World,* published in 1939, is an analytical study of the theology and philosophy of Thomas Aquinas in the light of some more recent philosophic developments. To some extent, Rahner's work was an attempt to arrive at a rapprochement between Aquinas and the Kantian rejection of the scholastic metaphysics. The writer feels that some of the introductory comments to the English edition (Rahner, 1968) by Francis Fiorenza, tell a good deal about Rahner's approach to theology. Fiorenza says,

> The significance of the differences between Rahner and Kant leads to the question of the positive aspects of his dialogue with Kant. How and where does Rahner assimilate Kant's philosophy? The fruitful reception of Kant is indicated by Rahner's assumption of Kant's basic question: How is metaphysics possible if all human knowledge is necessarily referred to a sensible intuition? Rahner's answer to this question departs from the traditional scholastic and philosophical positions and offers a transcendental understanding of being. Since he is aware that all human knowledge is related to sense intuitions, he rejects those philosophical positions which maintain

that a metaphysics of transcendence is possible because of a special innate idea or because of a specific
and immediate intuition of a metaphysical object, be
it an eternal truth or an objectively conceived absolute being. He denies explicitly that the absolute is
known as some object or that the human mind could
form an adequate objective concept of God.

Instead, he proposes a transcendental understanding of God, who is not known by man as an object
of reality but as the *principle* of *human knowledge
and reality.* This fundamental, non-objective, transcendental knowledge of God as the principle of
knowledge and reality is central to Rahner's whole
theology. It forms the background for his understanding of God's presence to man in grace and revelation, of the ontological and psychological unity of
Christ. Rahner's discussions on the development of
dogma, the anonymous Christian, the human knowledge of Christ, and on many other themes must be
seen within this context. This transcendental orientation of man to God is the unifying principle of Rahner's theology. It is the result of his fruitful and
serious dialogue with the philosopher par excellence
of modern times, Immanuel Kant. Still it is not the
end but only the beginning of a dialogue with modern philosophy.

Rahner has continued this dialogue insofar as he
has used the insights of modern existential philosophy to explain this transcendental orientation to God
in terms of a "supernatural existential." Man's relation to God is not an abstract or "natural" openness
to God, but is the result of God's historical calling
of man to Himself in Christ and thereby constituting
the historical nature of man. The fullness of human
nature therefore culminates not extrinsically, but intrinsically in Christ; Rahner's anthropology is thus
not a pure philosophical or transcendental anthropology, but is an anthropology only in relation to
God's revelation in Christ.

In an important, recently discovered manuscript
(1965) written by Kant at the end of his life, Kant
explains his ideas on the concept of philosophy and
reacts to some of the opinions of his students (especially Fichte). Kant emphasized that philosophy is not

a scientific or mystic subject, but a teaching of practice and wisdom. Rahner's theology is the synthesis
of these elements. Whereas Kant rejected the theoretical knowledge of God for a practical postulate
of God, Rahner has attempted to show the relevance
of a theoretical theology for the pastoral theology
and practical life of the Church. This synthesis is the
wisdom of Karl Rahner's theology and its source is
Spirit in the World.

Rahner, like Buber, does not fall into the existential trap in
his emphasis on man-centeredness, but he lurches around the
abyss. Rahner sees the relationship between God and man—not
as emotionally expressed as Buber's "I-Thou"—but similarly bi-
opolar. He remains, essentially a Thomist, but with a difference. He said, in 1966, in an address in Chicago,

As soon as man is understood as that being which
has absolute transcendence toward God (and it is
surely obvious that he is such), then anthropocentricity and theocentricity in theology are not con-
tradictories but strictly one and the same thing seen
from two different aspects, and each aspect is unintelligible without the other. That theology should be
anthropocentric does not contradict its being most
rigorously theocentric. Yet, this connection is opposed
to the view that man is merely one particular topic
in theology among others, for example, the angels
or the material world. It is contrary to the view that
it is possible to speak theologically about God without at the same time saying something about man,
and vice versa. Speech about God and speech about
man connect not only from the point of view of content, but also from the point of view of knowledge
itself.

Elsewhere, Rahner had shown the relationship of Christ to
this anthropocentricity in theocentricity. He had said,

Christology is the end and beginning of anthropology, and this anthropology in its radical realization,
namely, in Christology, is an external theology; it is
first of all that theology which God spoke in speaking His word as our flesh in the emptiness of the

ungodly and sinful. It is that theology which we, believing, pursue when we do not think that we could encounter God in bypassing the man Christ, and man, in general.

Rahner's particular revelance to this work is, as it relates to sociologic motivation, seen in his emphasis in the essential and unequivocal God-relatedness of Man. In an essay written in 1950 and entitled: *Concerning the Relationship Between Nature and Grace,* he had said,

God wishes to communicate Himself, to pour forth the love which He, Himself, is. That is the first and the last of His real plans and hence of His real world too. Everything else exists so that this one thing might be: the eternal miracle of infinite Love. And so God makes a creature whom He can love: He created man. He creates him in such a way that man can receive this love which is God Himself, and that he can and must at the same time accept it for what it is: the ever astounding wonder, the unexpected, unexacted gift. And let us not forget here that ultimately we only know what "unexacted" means when we know what personal love is, and vice versa; we do not understand what love is by knowing the meaning of "unexacted." Thus in this second respect God must so create man that love not only pours forth free and unexacted but, also, so that man as a real partner, as one who can accept or reject it, can experience and accept it as the unexacted event and wonder not owed to him, the real man. As unexacted, not only because he can also embrace it as unexacted when, already blessed in this love, he is allowed to forget that he was a sinner once.

From this point, Rahner sees men in the world as mutual partners with God in love. This is not the idealized "Partnership-Pantheism" of Scheler in which man assists God in coming to his consciousness—or even of Whitehead's God in his consequential nature as the comrade-in-arms against evil but in a relationship in which man has nothing to give but himself in love in response to love. All humanity is joined in this final testament of God's love represented by the Mystical Body of Christ. Rahner visualizes the present minority position of Christians throughout the world—extendable, in his logic, to all who seek to serve God—as a new diaspora placing those who have faith in God in a role much like that of the ancient Jews. The new mission, like the old, is to prepare the unbelieving, disillusioned world to receive the love of God in a total community of free individual human beings. In this age, it is to replace the materialistic slavery of mechanical collectives now being formed.

In his last years, Rahner seems to overemphasize the human pole of this theology, at times sounding as though the need of man for a loving God was like the need of a child for a teddy bear as a source of comfort in travail.

Under the impact of Modernism, the concept of Christian faith underwent radical devaluation in the minds of many theologians. The Brabant syndrome became popular—theologic truth and ontologic truth need not be the same. Indeed, we dare not approach ontologic truth beyond the sense world. Faith, alone, is all that can be relied upon in approach to theologic matters. Further, belief is the important thing—what you believe is secondary. There is no need for authoritative guidance— what Scripture means for the individual is what Scripture should mean for the individual.

Bultman added the final gutting of the victim; miracles are impossible, prophecy an illusion. The Old Testament does not foreshadow the New—rather the New "echos" the Old. The New Testament was "structured" to provide fulfillment of the Old. Faith must be limited to Scripture as seen in the human order without any supernatural overtones. The source of Scripture is cultic myth. When all these attitudes are combined and countenanced at the professional theologic level, the man in the street is left with little anchorage. He can certainly be excused if he gives the whole thing up as useless.

Now, the fact is and must be that there is only one complete truth with respect to any situational set. The truth is what it is as it is. Ontologic and theologic truth are one. Revelation, if from God, must present the ontologic truth though it be limited in expression to suit our human capability to comprehend. Our faith must conform to that truth or it is a false faith. Though human frailty subjects us to error as to morality and general knowledge of truth, our goal ought to be perfection to seek God in truth and not in falsity. David was not always heroic nor Solomon always wise. As to matters of truth their lives may be presented to us as object lessons which are harsh and hard to accept in our day, but they nevertheless convey how it in fact was in the understanding of those who wrote about them. If there are discrepencies in the statements of several witnesses, that fact tells us that there was uncertainty and confusion among the witnesses. That confusion may be precisely the point God wished to convey. The true situation in such problems may be determined in most instances by the composite of the stories or by later developments.

Chapter 13

THREE PROBLEMS

Three problems in Christian belief appear to be the chief stumbling blocks in modern times. These are the doctrines of man's primeval fall from Grace, the Trinity and that of the Incarnation of the Second Person of the Blessed Trinity as man. In the following analysis, the writer will attempt to stay close to what he considers to be a consensus among "traditional" theologians. Primarily, these will be drawn from Geerhardus Vos and Karl Rahner, presenting the Protestant and Catholic views respectively. On these three points, there is not a basic theologic confrontation between the main traditional branches of Christianity, the Protestant, Catholic, and the Eastern Orthodox, though there are many nuances of difference.

An analysis of the allegory of man's probation and fall is interesting. That the *Genesis* narrative was symbolic does not mean that it was not real. All the actors were real beings in the real historical event. Symbolism in the narrative was necessary because the lesson to be taught was for all generations—for all ages—the most primitive and the most sophisticated. The precise nature of the probation is beyond recapture, but it is not necessary that it be recaptured to understand it in principle. It has been clear from the beginning that God did not wish to be involved in a deeply personal and intense I-Thou relationship with a great multitude of automatons or will-less creatures who had no choice but to follow His demands explicitly and necessarily. All the purely material universe below man does that. But, all the purely material universe cannot respond in a personal, free way of love—or conversely, disdain or hate—if it should so choose.

As we have observed, the most logical purpose for the material universe was to produce creatures arising out of the material environment—intelligent, free, beings able to participate in God's glory. God wished man's love to be freely given, as was His own. Further, the individual creatures, themselves, needed the knowledge that they had indeed freely given themselves as a directly-willed, preferential act, and not in involuntary subservience. They needed this assurance if they were to retain

517

that personal individuality and that full human dignity in their relationship to God which He desired. He would settle for nothing less. A probation was necessary but, particularly for man's sake, to establish the relationship of mutual fidelity and trust. In most of our dealings here on earth we feel the need to test and prove ourselves to establish our authentic identity in a relationship. It is a human need. The solution is not unlike the idea of a "covenant" which we have previously examined. There was to be freely-entered contract of love between God and man. The alternatives of reward and punishment were entailed for man. This love, God wished, was not for the mere mouse of a person. It was for those who venture all without reserve—the quest for life and love everlasting, eternal, true, brilliant, burning, unquenchable. That love was the destiny God wished for man. Man was to be in God's image—that love was God and man must "image forth" that love.

The probation could either have been for the total species—a onetime test in the head of the species—or a test for each individual down through the ages. The comprehensive test for the whole species was first elected by God. Had man passed the probation, the entire species would have shared in the *covenant* God offered to Adam and Eve.

The doctrine of Original Sin arises from that covenant. In basic essentials, the covenant provided that the first pair of human beings which were ensouled—and regardless of how their bodies were brought into being, by an evolutionary process or direct creation, is of little import—God "breathed" into them their immortal rational souls. They were destined to live for a term in this world and then, without undergoing death, be assumed into the realm of the eternal blessed. But God desired these ratinal beings to love Him and to give themselves to Him freely and unequivocally. It is a characteristic for an individual to desire to be loved for himself and not for favors that that individual can bestow. The familiar little story of the prince and the peasant is a type of the "dilemma" which faces a being of obvious overwhelming status in being loved unselfishly by one of lower status. God wished to present His creature with all His favors but did not wish to overwhelm the creature with those favors so that his freedom to accept or reject God's freely given love was denied. If it be said that is anthropomorphic—it is. If we are images of God, it is He in whose image we are.

Therefore before our first parents were "confirmed" in their covenanted gifts, they were placed on probation and given the opportunity to choose between the love of God, represented in *Genesis* by the Tree of Life, and human pride in self-sufficiency and self-love, represented by the Tree of Knowledge of Good and Evil—the opposed attractions represent the insistent dialectic. God had said, "If you eat of the Tree of Knowledge of Good and Evil, you shall surely die." But the Tree of Life was there to select if they consented to live by the covenant God offered.

Fairly obviously, in the real probation we are not speaking of trees or fruit or likely of a garden in a natural sense. It is rather an intellectual moral and spiritual environment. From the beginning, the scene of probation for humanity has been a display of all the pathways man could take in pursuit of happiness. This is not unlike the direct temptations of Christ by Satan in the New Testament. Again, representing in His person, all humanity, as the "New Adam." In preference, Christ freely chose the route leading to the Crucifixion, for love of the Father, but that is part of another problem.

The test, as it was put to Adam, was largely moral. It was a question of obeying the command of God and accepting the covenant in His love, because it was the command of God, under the terms of the covenant. It included, as blessings, all the gifts of a supernatural life—immortality among them. The species man could have been given, as a free gift to man beyond the natural order, any privileges or prerogatives God wished. After all, everything that we have in the natural order is equally a free gift of God. The choice was clear. Adam could accept the terms of the covenant, with its benefits, and live a supernatural life because it was the command of God. He could accept the terms of the covenant without question, out of love and respect for God. The alternative was also open. Out of pride in being and independence from God, Adam could disobey the command, reject the covenant terms of life, and accept, as punishment of infidelity, the conditions of the natural order, which would always be hostile to him.

The test was not one designed to limit man's access to knowledge—only the methodology of that access. Man, if he was to be holy, must not know—in the Hebrew sense of "knowing" as "experience"—the difference between good and evil. He must not choose the evil and seek knowledge of evil, by experiencing the "condition of evil," which the very fact of disobedience to God's command would entail in its most essential form. Camus, if judged by his works, would have approved of Adam's choice. Sisyphus, defying the gods, though it brought him and all his offspring misery and death. Significantly, though

Adam blamed Eve for causing his fall, there is not the slightest hint of remorse in any of the passages of Genesis—only fear and shame—both derivations of evil as he felt them in his naked humanness.

It is plain, from Genesis, that the "Tree of Life" was freely open to Adam and Eve, standing, as it was, in the midst of the "Garden." They could have chosen to eat from that tree, and we have the same option. There is no evidence that the prototype man and woman, Adam and Eve, deliberated between the "Tree of Life" and the "Tree of the Knowledge of Good and Evil." All that is known is that the fruit of the latter was forbidden to them—that which was forbidden became the focal point. Eve is represented as the one who was tempted by the demonic exaggeration of the attractiveness of the forbidden fruit and of the "injustice" of its being forbidden. God was presented, by the "serpent," as an unjust, fundamentally impotent, deceitful, and selfish being who wished to keep the pleasures to himself.

But Adam acquiesed without any direct temptation by the intrinsic attractiveness of the worldly pleasures. His failure, therefore, had greater and controlling malice in following purely human advice in contravention of God's direct command to him. It was truly a flagrant, intellectual rejection of God's will. It was a direct rejection of the covenant God offered—indicating both lack of faith in God's word—"Thou shalt surely die" and, manifestly, a rejection of God's love as well. Adam freely willed to select the experiencing of moral evil in his direct act of disobedience to God, and he also freely willed to choose the path of self-will in all matters. It was a form of idolatry—Adam placing his own humanity above God.

The symbolism is still applicable to man generally, and that is the choice of reliance on one's own human resources of knowledge and a preference for material things ending in death or of reliance upon God's word, of trust in Him, and obedience to His laws for love of Him leading to eternal life. It was a probationary episode for Adam and Eve which, had they elected life, would have been passed on as a species—wide, free gift of God to all mankind. The alternative, freely chosen, passed on the natural consequences of man's material, biological origin with its spiritual blindness and orientation to the worldly.

God did not tempt man. He only established ground rules of his probation. All of the pleasures were attractive—as pleasures must be—but that pleasure of relying solely on one's own human resources in all life decisions was the most attractive.

It consisted then, as it does today, in an assertion of pride, as explicated by Camus' or Sartre's or Nietzsche's philosophies. The absurd—*L'Nausee* tells man that he should live his life as he sees it, freely and fully, but without hope—live existentially, experientially for today—call nothing or no person his superior.

The effect of Original Sin was, thus, not an arbitrary and unjust extension of punishment to us poor innocent offspring for Adam's failure. It was a withdrawal of free gifts which were in the covenant, offered conditionally to Adam and Eve and the species man and dependent upon Adam's and Eve's demonstration of love for God above self and all else. By the Fall, man was placed in the natural condition he would have been in in any case had not the preternatural gifts of innocence and grace been given him. We are in no position to blame Adam, Eve, or God unless we are prepared to live perfect lives in the Love of God—and, in that case, we would not do so. The guilt of Original Sin resulting from the Fall, in effect, is a total incapacity on our part to achieve those preternatural gifts that God freely gave to Adam and Eve which provided the natural innocence and permitted the ultimate ascent to God after the probation period on this earth. Depending on viewpoint, as a result, man is in either the state of total depravity as held by Luther, or of limited natural goodness and ability but with a predilection to follow in Adam's footsteps. This is the position of the Catholic Church. There are many variations between.

But God now indicates, in Genesis, two ways that He will give man another chance. He will exercise the second option, that of the individual testing. He says to Cain, who was disappointed that God had rejected his offering, "Why art thou angry? And why is thy countenance fallen? If thou do well, shalt thou not receive? But if thou do ill, shalt not sin forthwith be present at the door? But the lust thereof, shall be under thee and thou shalt have dominion over it." This statement indicated that God was trying to encourage Cain, as an evil-doer, to amend his ways. It was an indication that if Cain exercised his will he could overcome his temptations and faults and not give way to evil.

There was yet hope. Man could continue to seek God even though he was depraved (*Gen.* 4:7). A second chance was also indicated in the promise of a redeemer who was to come. This promise can be found in the words, "I will put enmities between thee (the serpent) and the woman, and thy seed and her seed: She shall crush your head, and thou shalt lie in wait for her heel." (*Gen.* 3:15). Why enmities, unless in the dialectic sense of a continuing contest which would eventually result in the defeat of the deceiver by the woman and her offspring? It could not apply to Eve who had already been defeated. Her offspring would likewise be Adam's without differentiation, so why would a distinction be made to the seed of the woman?

The Bible elsewhere characteristically traces genealogy through the male line and the "seed" is visualized as issuing from the "male." The above cited text seems to be a singular exception. What it seems to say, is, that the humanity—the human seed would come from the woman but that the fecundation is not of Adam or of any other man—that justifies the distinction. The excerpt is clarified if it is taken in context with two other closely related citations from Isaiah. The two passages seem to be conjoined with the Genesis passage in a continuing prophecy in more detail. Isaiah, Chapter 7, verse 14 reads: "Behold a virgin shall conceive and bear a son and his name shall be called Emmanuel" (God with us). Isaiah, Chapter 9, verse 6 also reads: "For a child is born to us, and a son is given to us, and the government is upon his shoulder and his name shall be called Wonderful, Counselor, God the Mighty, the Father of the world to come, the Prince of Peace." For Christian believers, these prophesies are fulfilled in Christ in the following words from the Gospel of Luke, Chapter 1, verse 35, addressed by the Angel Gabriel to the Virgin Mary, "The Holy Spirit shall come upon thee and the power of the Most High shall overshadow thee; and, therefore, the Holy One to be born of thee shall be called the Son of God." This past passage likewise implies the Trinity in specifically mentioning all three Persons as involved in the Incarnation.

There are several different wordings of these verses, but the meaning remains essentially unaltered. The clear implication of the first two texts cited is that now individual man must eke out his own life and, at least, attempt to live in accord with God's wishes. The contest between good and evil would not, however, be completed until the "Evil" was overcome by the "Good" which is represented by the women and the woman's offspring. The new Eve and the new Adam were necessary.

The doctrine of the Trinity, of course, is fundamentally unknowable by reason. Through analogy, however, there are certain symmetries which can be perceived. One, which goes back to Augustine through Bonaventure, is the need that a lover has for a fitting object of His love. Love must have an object. If God is infinite love, then there must, in symmetry, be an infinite object of His love. This is to say that there must be a loved object which is likewise God, for only God is infinite. The particular solution is seen in revelation: this object of love bears the relationship to God of an infinite, eternal offspring which is the Son—The Word of God who is God, Himself, in essence, though separate and distinct as "personality." The symmetry in symbolism continues with the concept that love is consummated only in its fruition. Here, the fruit again must be equal to the love whose consummation it represents. This is to say the fruition of consummated love must be infinite and must, therefore, be also God. This fruition is defined, by revelation, as the Holy Spirit, the Third Person of the Holy Trinity. The way in which the Holy Spirit proceeds as the fruition of this love has been a matter of crucial theological debate for centuries. It produced, at least, the theoretical theologic base for the schism between the Eastern and Western churches in the eleventh century. The Nicene Creed, in its present form, which also dates from the early eleventh century, presents it as "from the Father and the Son"; *Filioque.* The Holy Spirit is the fruition of the mutual love of Father and Son.

It will be recalled that Gabriel Marcel took the Trinity as the perfect model of intimate social interaction, found in love and affection, in which the membership participates in complete individual freedom for the common purpose.

The difficulty with the concept of the Trinity, like that of the "Fall," stems largely from its misconception or misinterpretation. Neither concept is irrational—nor are they derivable purely by reason. Yet, they do not contradict reason.

The third and crucial doctrine of the Incarnation hinges upon the previous two. The doctrine that the Second Person of the Trinity, the Son, the Word, became incarnate as man in the person of Christ to redeem mankind is, as it was prophesied to be, a stumbling block for many. Yet the difficulty, as always, goes back to man's ubiquitous underestimation of God. We say He is infinite and yet we do not really mean it. Because, if we do mean that God is infinite, the problem evaporates. Let us examine the case by a return to the "beginning." As a consequence of the free choice of Adam and Eve in rejecting the life of happiness under God's guidance, and in preference, choosing to follow their own path of experiencing good and evil in their natural powers only, there was, in effect, an inseparable gap opened by man, between God and man.

Man had no predilection for good after the Fall. He tended to be "Hobbesian." The fact that he had a free will meant that he could, and did, perform idolatrous acts, which only means placing things before God. God had desired that man be holy—but had let man freely make the choice. Man could not be neutral like a stone, since he was free. He had chosen to be unholy, and from that point he could not, of himself, alter that position of unholiness. Holiness is only from God the All Holy. Now, the chasm that man dug was, in fact, that of unholiness and the longer he continued in his own powers without divine assistance the wider and deeper the chasm became. Man was a hopeless case if left to his own powers.

Now, as we have seen, God does not make mistakes. Nor, can man forever thwart God's desires that He be freely adored and loved, for Himself, by this contrary creature, man. From all eternity, God had foreseen the freely chosen failure of Adam—and from all eternity, the Son had "programmed" Himself to reconcile this sad creature to the Father. Because the Son is infinite Love and Holiness, since He is infinite God, the solution must be the most sublime, the most exalted, the most complete, the most symbolic and the most compelling to man possible. The only solution meeting those criteria is the Incarnation. The chasm between the finite, unholy, human sinner and the infinite and Holy God could be bridged only by that humanity, in its totality, being raised to the infinite and the holy. The gap, the accumulating burden of human iniquity was man's and must be shouldered by man, but only a man who was infinite in his person could carry it—could make an adequate atonement for it. The solution—when the Son, the eternal Logos, the Word, was manifested in the form of man. "The Word became flesh and dwelt among us." The new Adam was conceived and took His humanity in the royal line of David of the chosen people from the woman, the new Eve, the Virgin Mary. He is the redeeming seed forecast from the beginning.

Christianity is meaningful only in this context. The teachings of Christ, His Crucifixion and death are hollow without this concept and His Resurrection, impossible, the magnificent vision of the Mystical Body of Christ of which all men, from Adam by anticipation, are members, at least in potential, flows from this idea. What a basis for a true community of men in love on this earth—even as Marcel saw in the Trinity!

To Christians, the Old Testament is pregnant with the prophetic burden of the Messiah realized in the person of Christ and the New Testament. The theme can be traced from the Pentateuch through Exodus through psalms and prophets. A few examples are cited here in illustration of this "goodness of fit" with the New Testament. They supplement those cited earlier.

In Chapter 14 of Genesis the meeting between Abraham (Abram) and Melchizedek, King of Salem is described: "Melchizedek, King of Salem, brought out bread and wine, and being a priest of God most high, blessed Abram with these words: Blessed be Abram by God most high, the creator of heaven and earth."

David, in Psalm 110, relates this passage to the Messiah when he says, "The Lord said to my lord (the Messiah) sit at my right hand/till I make your enemies your footstool'/The scepter of your power, the Lord will stretch forth from Zion/Rule in the midst of your enemies/Yours is a princely power in the day of your birth in holy splendor;/before the day star, like the dew, I have begotten you/The Lord has sworn and will not repent/You are a priest forever according to the order of Melchizedek." In the New Testament, the Gospel of Matthew, Chapter 22, Christ cites this text of David, affirming that it refers to the Messiah, and also that the Messiah is more than David's son, else why should David refer to him as "my Lord."

Paul, in Chapter 7 of the Book of Hebrews, develops the relationship of Christ's role as the eternal High Priest: "a priest forever in the order of Melchizedek." Paul further points out the symbology of Melchizedek's name which means "King of Justice"; he was also King of Salem, that is King of Peace. "Without father, mother or ancestry, without beginning of days or end of life, like the Son of God, he remains a priest forever." Unlike the Levitic priests of the Old Law, descendants of Aaron, this priesthood would not stem from geneology but from election of God most high and by choice, not by right. Henceforth, there was one high priest who once for all sacrificed himself in his humanity—a sacrifice of infinite duration and worth. In II Corinthians, Chapter 5, speaking of his own role as an Apostle, Paul says, "God, in Christ, has reconciled the world to himself, not counting man's transgressions, and he has entrusted the message of reconcilation to us [the Apostles]. This makes us ambassadors for Christ. God, as it were, appealing through us." The priesthood was to be one of pure intermediacy—of one standing in the place of—the eternal high priest Christ. Melchizedek becomes not only a prefigure of Christ, but, in his unique blessing of Abraham, imaged forth the blessings of the spiritual posterity of Melchizedek in the ministry of the Eucharist which is the ongoing and everlasting memorial of reconciliation.

In Abraham's incompleted sacrifice of Isaac, who by carrying his own sacrificial wood symbolized Christ, there is prefigured the offering up, by God, the Father, His only Son, in the sacrifice of Calvary. When Isaac asked: "Where is the sheep for the holocaust? Abraham answered, "Son, God himself will provide the sheep of the sacrifice" (Genesis, Chapter 22).

In Exodus, the Christians see in the sprinkling of the lintel and two door posts of the Hebrew houses with the blood of the paschal lamb to safeguard the first born from the avenging angel, a prefiguring of the Salvatory sacrifice of Christ. The rock in the desert bringing forth water is symbolic of the redemptive graces pouring forth from Christ. The manna, freely supplied nourishment for the Israelites, is seen as a prefiguring of the spiritual nourishment of the Eucharist. The bronze serpent, upraised on a staff, curing the people from the natural serpents wounds, is seen as a symbol of the rejected Christ, upraised on the Cross, restoring life to humanity from the wounds inflicted by the ancient serpent.

The psalms are full of reference to the Messiah which Christians see as fulfilled in Christ. In David's Psalm 22, there is a prophecy of the Passion: "But I am a worm and no man/The scorn of men, despised by the people/All who see me scoff at me/They mock me with parted lips/They wag their heads."/"He relied on the Lord: Let him deliver him"/"They have pierced my hands and my feet/They have numbered all my bones/They look on and gloat over me/They divide my garments among them/and for my vesture they cast lots."

In Psalm 72, attributed to Solomon, there is a different view of the Messiah.

> "The kings of Tarshish and the Isles shall offer gifts/The kings of Arabia and Seba shall bring tribute/All kings shall pay him homage/All nations shall serve him/For he shall rescue the poor man when he cries out/And the afflicted when he has no one to help him/He shall have pity for the lowly and the poor/The lives of the poor he shall save."

Turning now to the prophets in addition to Isaiah from which we have seen several excerpts: First, in Jeremiah, Chapter 31, we see a prophecy of the new covenant, "The days are coming, when I will make a new covenant with the house of Israel and the house of Juda. It will not be like the covenant I made with their fathers the day I took them by the hand to lead them forth from the land of Egypt. For they broke my covenant, and I had to show myself their master. But this is the covenant which

I shall make with the house of Israel in these days. I will place my law within them and write it upon their hearts! I will be their God and they shall be my people. No longer will they have need to teach their friends and kinsmen how to know the Lord. All, from least to greatest, shall know me. For I will forgive their evil doing and remember their sins no more."

In Chapter 5 of the Prophecy of Micah, Bethlehem is pronounced as the place of birth of the Messiah: "But you Bethlehem-Ephrathah/too small to be among the clans of Judah/From you shall come forth to me/one who is to be ruler in Israel/whose origin is of old,/from ancient times/ (Therefore the Lord will give them up until the time/she who is to give birth has borne/and the rest of his brethern shall return/to the children of Israel)/He shall stand firm and shepherd his flock/by the strength of the Lord/In the majestic name of the Lord, his God/And they shall remain, for now his greatness/shall reach to the ends of the earth/He shall be peace." For Christians, the reference to the woman is literally fulfilled in Mary and symbolically in the bringing forth of the Mystical Body of Christ through the Church, the total people of God.

In Zechariah 9, the Christians see the prophecy of the triumphal entry of Christ to the City of Jerusalem. "Rejoice heartily O daughter, Zion,/shout for joy O daughter, Jerusalem/see, your king shall come to you;' a just saviour is he,/meek, and riding on an ass, on a colt/the foal of an ass. . .and he shall proclaim peace to the nations/His dominion shall be from sea to sea,/and from the river to the ends of the earth."

The prophet Zechariah, in Chapter 12, also describes how it will be at some time after the restoration. "I will pour out on the house of David, and on the inhabitants of Jerusalem, a spirit of grace and petition and they shall look on him whom they have pierced and they shall mourn for him as one mourns for an only son and they shall grieve over him as one grieves over the death of the first born." Here again, particularly his mother following the Crucifixion, both immediately and eschatologically for the duration of the Christian era.

In order to show that the prophecy of the Messiah is not for the Jews alone, the Christian can cite the words of Malachi, Chapter 1: "For from the rising of the sun even to its setting/my name is great among the Gentiles/and everywhere they offer me a clean oblation/For great is my name among the nations/says the Lord of hosts."

There have been many interpretations through the centuries concerning Christ's position as God and man simultaneously—

many, of course, outright denials of His divinity. This procedure reduces the whole New Testament to a collection of admirable pious platitudes or pointless fairy tales. It becomes the sad saga of a sentimental fool and his misguided, and equally foolish, band of followers for 2,000 years—but it is an honest denial. A persistent modern version that stems from existentialist roots is that Christ was essentially only human and, if real, His divinity was vague and unassertive. Throughout His life He was uncertain of His divinity, if He was divine, perhaps not being fully aware until after His Resurrection. This schema, denied by Vos, was hinted at by Bultmann although he customarily denied the facticity of the physical resurrection. Tillich's writings seem to suggest that Christ is even less—perhaps only a symbol having no reality, as actual being, although the historicity of the human individual Christ is not denied.

This view saves a lot of nasty tangles in modern process exegesis in Christ's life and it provides a convenient Christ "becoming" to His divinity. But, unless all the reported miraculous events are discounted as "embroidery" a la Bultmann, this view of Christ creates many more problems than it solves. For example, in Luke, 1:39-43, we read: "Now in those days Mary arose and *went with haste* into the hill country, to a town of Juda. And she entered the house of Zachary and saluted Elizabeth. And it came to pass, when Elizabeth heard the greeting of Mary the babe in her womb leapt. And Elizabeth was filled with the Holy Spirit, and cried out with a loud voice, saying, 'Blessed art thou among women and blessed is the fruit of thy womb! And how have I deserved that the mother of my Lord should come to me? For behold, the moment that the sound of thy greeting came to my ears, the babe in my womb leapt for joy'."

After the Annunciation, the outcome for Christians of the previously cited prophecies in Genesis and Isaias, Mary "went with haste" to visit her cousin and the babe, John the Baptist, in Elizabeth's womb "leapt for joy" at six months of pregnancy, recognizing the divine personality of Christ in the fetus in Mary's womb. At what must have been only a few days pregnancy, the power went from Christ to John.

This does not mean that the fetus in Mary's womb had the developed brain through which the divine intuition flowed, but, rather that, the soul of the person of Christ, in hypostatic union with the divine essence, was present and that the person Christ, even at that stage, could act through His divine powers should He so will. Of the hypostatic union, a theologic concept, one writer has likened it to the intimacy of a drop of water added to a chalice of wine—once the drop has been added it is totally intermingled and cannot be separated. Undoubtedly Christ grew, learned, matured, and suffered as all humans. Yet there is no evidence He was ever unaware of His divine mission and Sonship.

Obviously, in accord with the Gospel written by St. Luke, the Gospel most intimately associated with the Incarnation and birth of Christ, from the instant of His conception the Incarnate Son of God was, and knew that He was, the Christ, the Son of God. Otherwise, throw away the whole book, it is a bunch of trash unfit to clutter modern brains unless one has a flair for image-filled, but pointless, myths. Either Christ was the Messiah completely, and absolutely, from His conception, or He was indeed a brief candle which has persisted overlong, the sooner extinguished and forgotten the better.

In this work the writer is not attempting to sell any particular religious belief—only a genuine religious attitude toward life—recognizing the obligation God places on man to love his neighbor. The writer happily admits his subjective bias to Christianity since he is a Christian and a Catholic priest. The reader, regardless of his views, can be aware of it and make whatever mental adjustments which seem necessary. The writer, by no means says, that there are no other authentic communications of God to man except those leading through Juadism to Christianity. In fact, he insists that there are other authentic communications—each suited to the conditions as eternally seen by God to whom time and space and circumstances are all creations to serve his purposeful acts. We must all seek the Holy— that which is God. We must aspire to perfection in truth, in love, and in virtue, which provides the ascent to God.

The writer believes God, down through the ages, has communicated with the most primitive and with the most sophisticated peoples—in ways most suitable. There can be little doubt that those who seek Him sincerely, will find Him, regardless of where, or when, or in what circumstances, they live. The writer equally insists, however, that, as given, communication has an intent, and that the intent is not properly manipulated to suit convenient ends. If one is fortunate enough to receive Christ's teachings, he should accept them in their totality as given, and honestly, if fumblingly, try to live by them.

In the next chapter, we will look more closely into the close relationship which must exist between a belief in God and moral principles. This present chapter was for the purpose of demonstrating one path through which God has revealed His desires to man in the moral order.

Chapter 14

IMMORTALITY KEY TO MORALITY

When Nietzsche said, in his characteristic black-white style: "People say virtue is necessary though they mean police are necessary," he placed, in cynical juxtaposition, the limits of behavioral control systems. As beings in the world, we are aware that our behavior, in any given situation, is a function of multiform pressures impinging from many sources, and we know all other persons are similarly affected.

The writer has been proceeding steadfastly down a road trying to establish a picture of God, as He relates to the universe, and to His intelligent creature, man, and what that picture and relationship imply as to the nature of man. The writer also has tried to define man as he, in fact, is by his nature and establish his position in the universe. We have, in short, attempted to establish the verity of the existence of God and the immortality of the human soul at high confidence levels. Here, in Chapter 14, and the remainder of Part V, we will change gears. We will continue to push those themes within the framework of the insistent dialectic, but will add a qualitative dimension so as to bring into prominence the place of values in all human relationships. Martin Buber's "I-Thou, I-It" dichotomy, while graphically delineating the qualitative extremes in relationship perhaps masks the "Thou-It" continuum, which, in fact, exists. There are gradations of one into the other and oscillations within the extremes in almost all actual relationships. The intent, in this portion of the book, is to examine, in some depth, the internetting of logic, emotion, instinct and intuition which motivates man in the moral sphere and constitutes his personal relationship with God and his fellowman. We will discuss concepts such as what "ought" to be the norms of morality in view of these personal relationships. How are these norms to be arrived at. What are the norms which do guide man?

The modern moral philosophers and psychologists such as Lawrence Kohlberg and Jean Piaget skirt the matter of motivation in moral behavior. Their main area of interest is the way moral concepts are internalized by the human organism and put into force. Morality, for them, is largely a matter of education in the culturally approved life-style. It is an updated Dewey concept. Kohlberg considers himself as a non-relativist because in the lofty "stage six" in his program of moral learning—a function of maturation—the individuals are ultimately guided by objective principles which are not changeable. Unfortunately most of us do not make it to stage six—most get no farther than "conventional mortality," at about stage four, which is purely relativistic to the current norms of the place and time.

Motivation, however, as we will see, is fundamental as to acceptance of standards, of living by the standards and, in the given culture, in formulation of the standards themselves. We do not contest the findings of the moral philosophies and educationists by any means—we merely say that they have stopped short of that which makes a voluntary behavioral system, a moral system work—its motivation. The motivation must be equal to the demands of responsibility.

In this chapter, I will try to establish the idea that a moral behavioral system begins with an intellectual concept, in a sensing of duty and responsibility arising out of justice and love. A moral system develops from a thought process in the abstract order. It is differentiated from a *de facto* behavioral system in the same way that Utopia is differentiated from New York City. *De facto* virtue and the police are both necessary!

The thought process, in the religious field, including the thought processes about morals, has been presented to the general public in a derated mode. It is, in fact, rather commonly held that thought processes concerning religion are somehow lacking the same acuity as the processes of scientific thought because thoughts or ideas about religion tend to be dominated by emotionalism. Religious questions are not, generally, value-free. As we have seen, some have questioned the competence of the human mind to speculate reliably on any matters beyond those related to direct sense perception.

If there is a validity to a moral behavioral system as a voluntary surrender of personal prerogatives out of love of God and fellowman, that validity is found in religious thought and religious thought processes extending from our perceived relationship with God. In Buber's language it is a behavioral system for a community of "Thou's." The validity of that thought process must first be established along with validation of what that thought process conveys.

There is a difference between morality as viewed from the aspect of religion and from the aspect of sociology. In the religious mode, morality and immorality equate to obedience or disobedience, respectively, to God's will, the will of God being directed to holiness for His intellectual creatures. Rightness or wrongness, good and evil, virtue and sinfulness would be the parameters of morality in any act. These parameters are rooted essentially in the individual intent and not only in the physical act stemming from the intent. The sin is committed when the human will gives assent to an act even if circumstances, the police, for instance, would circumvent the act. For Christians, the concept is expressed in the words of Jesus related in Matthew, Chapter 15. "From the mind stem evil designs—murder, adulterous conduct, fornication, stealing, false witness, blasphemy—These are the things that make a man impure." Virtue and morality, then, flow chiefly from a mental attitude—a determination, perhaps unconscious, to seek the good and avoid the evil, habitually.

Sociologically speaking, immorality begins with the initiating overt act. Behavior is either acceptable or unacceptable in terms of social customs, or normal and abnormal as judged in terms of human moral standards. Human behavior patterns reflect the total externally observable situation. Nevertheless, the motivation behind the observed conduct is of sociologic interest, whether religiously inspired or otherwise. The proportionality that the fear of reprisal by society, in the form of police action or peer group approval, bears to intellectually-supported morality arising from religious beliefs, in maintaining effective social order is of sociologic concern in the scientific order.

There is no question, however, but that the idea of morality in society stems from the sense of an obligation to behave in accordance with rational standards. Kant's posited categorical imperative, it will be recalled, was considered an *a priori* guide in man's conduct. Men innately, or virtually innately, had a sense of good and evil. Kant linked the categorical imperative to the sense of the immortality of man in all men and, of course, to the existence of God, which makes that immortality possible.

Without that sense of immortality and the concomitant idea of eternal reward or punishment dependent upon the individual's behavior in this life, the motivation for a moral behavioral control system is severely weakened in the early stages of development. Only after considerable moral maturity does the deep sense of obligation or of devoted love of the good for the sake of pleasing God become predominant. In this chapter, we will look at the intellectual basis of all those ideas. The anguish of modern times arises because of the apparent conflict between the answers provided the critical questions of life by scientific research and the various religious beliefs. The wide differences in organized religious belief are, in themselves, contributors to the problem. The world of science seems so positive in its findings—in stark contrast to the vague and often conflicting formulations of the religious sector. How can there be credibility in the individual dogmatic statements, when, taken as a whole, they appear in total disarray and disorder?

From the sixteenth century, in the West, there seems to have been no religious unity, and—worldwide—there has been no unity in recorded history. Meanwhile, in its orderly march, science developed to that point at which several prominent modern theologians have, in effect, said that religion must never attempt to contest the assertions of the scientific community as to man's origins, the pure materiality of his intellectual processes, or the emerging theory that a particular organism happens to be a man rather than a mouse solely because of the arrangement of a few atoms in the DNA-RNA chains of his ancestors. Given this picture of man in the universe, the three questions which are so universally asked by men seem childish indeed. Questions such as: "Who am I?" "Why am I here?" "What is to become of me?" are unaskable questions in that context.

The proliferation of articles in the popular literature preparing the young to accept aging and the terminally ill to accept their approaching death gracefully reflects the impact of scientific theories on questions which formerly have been answered primarily by religion. The death of God theology forces a restructuring of psychology in the death of man.

The naturalness of aging and dying seen in the context of pure organic process—which it is—strikes a sour note to a creature conditioned to pleasure and yet, which still sees itself as somehow different from the other animals. No other animal thinks about aging or death. No other animal has ambitions or plans for the future which can suddenly be changed by the prospects of aging and death. The intellect resents the intrusions of these dark images. It resents surrendering control to its biologic limitations. The human person looks about for acceptable answers in his biologism—answers which are not forthcoming. Camus' *Absurd* and Sartre's *L'Nausee* describe the hopelessness of the biologic theme. At this point, man looks to the spiritual side. This rationalizing trend of the finality of death has changed in more recent times. About 1970, there was a reassertion, in some of the popular publications, that, in fact, this life is not the end. A few examples are cited to illustrate this point.

A significant number of psychologists and medical doctors have described their experiences with patients who had effectively "died" and then been resuscitated. In one specific instance, Dr. Elizabeth Kubler-Ross stated, in an address at the Quaker Yokefellow Institute before the interdisciplinary Ministry on Death, Dying and Living, that she is now certain that the physical death of the human body is not the end. Her conclusions were based on research with the dying who were clinically dead and then who had come back to life through medical effort. These patients specifically relate experiencing three things almost constantly: first, a sensation of a floating out of the body and then being able to see, in an objective sense, and to perceive what is happening about them and to their body. Second, there is a feeling of peace and wholeness. Third, they often tell of meeting someone who is already dead, who had preceded them in death. Children frequently related experiences of being met by Jesus and Mary when revived from clinical death. She affirmed that none of the patients who ever had a death experience, and returned are ever afraid to "die" again.

Research being done at the University of Iowa by a psychiatrist, Dr. Russell Noyes, and a clinical psychologist, Roy Kletti, in 1975, found the same results. Their research conclusions were formed after interviewing approximately one hundred revived patients. One patient described it as though he were "sitting in the stands" watching himself and others about him in the activity. In virtually all cases, the experiences were described as pleasant rather than unpleasant.

In a book by Dr. Raymond Moody, an Augusta, Georgia, physician, entitled *Life After Life,* many cases are given. In one particular case, an elderly heart attack victim had said, "I felt almost as though I were a piece of paper that someone had blown up to the ceiling. I watched them reviving me from up there. . . . I heard one nurse say, 'Oh, my God! She's gone!' while I was looking at the back of her head while she did this. . . . As I saw them below beating on my chest and rubbing my arms and legs, I thought, 'Why are they going to so much trouble? I'm just fine now'." Philosopher-psychologist William James (1842-1910), whom we will encounter again, had written in 1909,

> In spite of rationalism's disdain for the particular, the personal, and the unwholesome, the drift of all the evidence we have seems to sweep us very strongly toward the belief in some form of superhuman life with which we may, unknown to ourselves, be co-conscious.

We may be in the universe as dogs and cats are in our libraries, seeing the books and hearing the conversation, but having no inkling of the meaning of it all. The intellectualist objections to this fall away when the authority of intellectualist logic is undermined by criticism, and then the positive empirical evidence remains. The analogies with ordinary psychology and with the facts of pathology, with those of psychical research, so called, and with those of religious experience, establish, when taken together, a decidedly formidable probability in favor of a general view of the world almost identical with Fechner's. The outlines of the superhuman consciousness thus made probable must remain, however, very vague, and the number of functionally distinct "selves" it comforts and carries has to be left entirely problematic.

As I have said earlier, in an approach from systems analysis, no areas of investigation from which the problem can be viewed are excluded simply because they are unorthodox—new or exotic. This area is not different, and this is not really a new subject—a similar case of a revivified soldier was mentioned by Plato.

Now opponents of the idea of an afterlife try to write off the recorded phenomena as a last bit of "wishful thinking" on the part of the dying person. He so wishes immortality that *in extrema* he hallucinates that condition. The "wishful thinking" for immortality itself is a difficult thing to defend in a purely biologic specimen. Looked at first from a theoretical position, given a solely material life-principle and using functional theory of biologic behavior, human psychological reactions, including longing for immortality and any residual fantasizing at onset of death symptoms ought to serve a purpose towards stimulation rather than diminution of the life urge.

Pleasant death-ameliorating fantasizing such as are recorded by Dr. Kubler-Ross and the others would have no place in such a scheme. They would be counter-productive to the controlling biologic drive for self-preservation. More practical, biologically, would be a terrifying scene to force a violent effort to continue life. In a godless universe there is no such thing as a kind "mother nature" which would seek to ease the anguish at the passing from life to death.

If there is in fact such fantasizing, its function must be sought elsewhere than in the biologic nature of man. There are two obvious possibilities and both require a personal and loving Caretaker of human creatures. (1) The fantasies are an analgesic charitably applied to ease death of a totally mortal, biologic, yet anxious organism, or (2) they are, in fact, precursorial events of non-biologic existence which follows death. In the first case, the fantasy is an admission that God could have done better and has to substitute an illusion for the real thing. It amounts to admission that the human being was an error in concept. In the second case, there is no such difficulty. The fantasizings are only transitional to the real things. Thus whether the experiences are "real" or only imaginary they point to the same conclusion—the immortality of the human soul.

On the experiential side, there are recorded instances that the recalled point of view of the stricken person was one impossible for him to take physically. There were observations of things which took place, and verified by others to have taken place, beyond his field of natural knowledge, in an adjoining room for instance. Fantasizing could not account for the knowledge the reporting individual had of circumstances and activities of others surrounding his "death." These instances support the view that the data supplied were acquired in an extracorporeal mode. Likely, there is a mix of fantasy and real experienced recall in the reported cases, but, as noted, both would suggest a solution stemming from nonbiologic sources.

Now, in addition to these experiences of people who have almost died and recovered, there are thousands of cases recorded of "communication from beyond the grave." Early research in this area which sincerely tried to be "scientifically impeccable" was recorded by the Society of Psychical Research based in London, which, from the mid-nineteenth century, has collected a tremendous volume of data. No doubt, some is spurious and quackery. Yet, equally as undoubtedly, some of it is genuine.

This type of experience has generated a good deal of thought outside of formal religious circles. It is thought of a speculative nature which seeks to find rational answers to phenomena beyond the scientific order as narrowly defined in modern times. It is certainly a valid area of inquiry, as James suggests. We will call such speculative thought, religious thought, to distinguish it from the philosophic-metaphysical analysis which was reviewed previously.

The scientific approach, the philosophical approach and the religious approach to the problems of life are all developed or evolve through thought processes. The thought processes are the same in all three cases. The only difference lies in the basic assumptions, varied treatment of the subject matter, and of the data acquisition process dictated by the subject matter.

The scientific researchers in the above recorded cases came to their conclusions through the same methodology that would have been used in any other investigative process. However, instead of the data concerning the phenomena being acquired directly, that data was acquired indirectly through testimony of witnesses they considered credible under force of circumstances. Virtually all scientific information is accepted in a similar way. Most of us are in no position to repeat the experiments. We accept, on faith, that the experiments were performed and the data was accurately recorded. The more times the same results have been recorded, the greater our confidence level in the truth of the information.

It is interesting, in connection with those clinical cases, that the individuals described were aware of their physical surroundings. The people and things—the sights, the sounds—were all perceived in their physical condition. Yet, at least in those cases where the events recorded were beyond the patient's observational field, there was no physical sensory mode by which that data could be acquired. We are back to Descartes' conclusion "It is the soul that sees."

Why is the religious thought process derated in the public mind? The generally perceived inferior position of religious thought vis-a-vis scientific thought in the intellectual world stems from the establishment of an arbitrary base line for investigations concerning man. That line, largely of Kantian definition, was drawn at the limit of sensory response to the phenomenal world. We speak of pushing back the frontiers of knowledge by scientific advance but, the advance is in a single plane. We limit, severely, the depth of penetration. Ever more powerful microscopes and telescopes are developed to identify structure, but there is no commitment to attempt to discover what supports the structure which is being investigated. We, indeed, attempt to do our research in isolation.

Kant, by defining the noumenon, acknowledged the existence of a "something" beyond phenomenon, but he denied our ability to investigate it in any significant way so as to advance our knowledge. Speculative metaphysics was an abomination. From that point on, "science" became coextensive in definition with analytical thought directly associated with sensory perception.

This definition involves accepting a material universe cut free from any primary causal consideration. The total environment in which the material universe must exist as but one unit in a tremendous free energy exchange situation is ignored. Rational man, whose free-ranging intellect seeks always to bring the unknown, wherever found, under scrutiny, is frustrated. He wants to ask the unaskable.

Until the past few decades, the mass of mankind was content to accept on faith that there was a real existence in a non-material order. Today, the validity of religious faith, as a reflection of reality, is denied at least as frequently as it is accepted. The question arises, what, if any, is the relationship between faith and knowledge? Looking at the question only from the viewpoint of the organization of matter and not from that of the organization of being, the presumptive answer comes back that only matter is the subject of knowledge, hence faith bears no relationship to knowledge. As we saw previously, sheer logic dictates that matter comprises only one and likely the least significant form of being. Yet the indefensible "Universe in Isolation" concept limits science to that narrow band of inquiry.

William James was the outstanding psychologist of the United States at the turn of the century—before the full Freudian invasion—and along with Whitehead and Dewey is considered one of the three great American philosophers. James was an empiricist and pragmatist in his approach to philosophy. Yet, speaking in the first decade of this century (Hibbert Lectures at Manchester College), he had said,

> The freedom to "believe what we will" you apply to the case of some patent superstition; and the faith you think of is the faith defined by the schoolboy when he said, faith is when you believe something that you know ain't true. I can only repeat that this is misapprehension. *In Concreto,* the freedom to believe can only cover living options which the intellect of the individual cannot, by itself, resolve, and living options never seem absurdities to him who has them to consider. When I look at the religious question as it really puts itself to concrete men, and when I think of all the possibilities which both practically and theoretically it involves, then this command that we shall put a stopper on our heart, instincts, and courage, and wait—acting of course meanwhile more or less as if religion were not true—till doomsday, or till such time as our intellect and senses working together may have raked in evidence enough—this

command, I say, seems to me the queerest idol ever manufactured in the philosophic cave. . . . Indeed we may wait if we will—I hope you do not think that I am denying that—but if we do, we do so at our peril as much as if we believed. In either case we act, taking our life in our hands. (Emphasis James').

James limits "living options" to things which, while not totally knowable, are not irrational and are worthy of belief. There must be a basis of faith. Faith or belief is the intellectual commitment to a thesis which has not been rigorously demonstrated—we might say a commitment on circumstantial evidence. It is a "considered opinion" of what is, in fact, the case.

Kant, on the other hand, tended to see faith or opinion as the antonym of knowledge or at least a thing of a different genre. But, as has been seen earlier, it should rather be considered, along with knowledge in the Kantian sense, as one of the degrees of apprehension of truth, or that which is reality. Both opinion and the "facts" of human knowledge are, to some degree, subjective because there is no humanly possible perfect apprehension of truth. Without accepting Kant's "thing in itself" as unknowable noumenon, we agree that there is inevitably something less than perfect knowledge, even of material things. Descartes' statement, "I think, therefore I am" still leaves questions as to the qualitative nature of the thinking subject as well as of the prediction of its existence. That does not mean that there is no aspect of truth in Descartes' statement. Quite the contrary, its basic truth is almost universally accepted. Descartes considered it knowledge in the most rigorous sense—certitude—but there are widely divergent opinions as to the content of that knowledge as truth.

We can now draw two parallel lines of human intellection leading to truth. The first would be from observed "fact," to knowledge of the "facts," from which truth can be projected. The second would be from the formation of opinion, or theories, from which truth, as a belief in what truth is, may be projected. For millenia, the phenomena of sunrise and sunset were factual evidence of the movement of the sun from east to west across the earth. Yet, Copernicus, and the Pythagoreans long before him, were of the opinion—they speculated, thought, believed—that the earth, in truth, rotated. Here the belief, initially unsubstantiated by competent observation, was closer to the truth than the widely held "knowledge" which was supported by a vast body of direct observation. Belief, therefore, does not occupy an intrinsically inferior position vis-a-vis empirically derived knowledge. In most scientific works, the two parallel lines become braided—some observed facts induce opinions which promote other observations and facts which induce more advanced opinions.

Our total "knowledge" of the physical universe is a highly intricate tapestry which is woven from such braided skeins. At the outer limits, in all areas, we are faced with opinions or theories or belief as to what the truth is. In spite of the relativism which occupies much space in our current literature, particularly in the moral sphere, the fact is, that the physical scientists as a group are dedicated to the principle that there is a singularity of truth which can be revealed, at least in part, by advancing research following intuitive projections or belief. Otherwise, research is disorganized and largely pointless.

As we looked at the philosophers of being—the metaphysicists in Part II—we noted how they, as a group, were dedicated to the pursuit of philosophy to first principles. They were not satisfied with considering the phenomena associated with matter, idea, life, existence or essence as complete in themselves. They wished to find out what it is that binds the whole package together—what comprises the ultimate truth. For the most part, these philosophers believed it was the philosopher's task as lovers of wisdom to attempt to elucidate that body of first principles and the complex of being in which these principles inhered. Principles do not exist *in vacuo,* or better *ex nihilo,* they define relationships of being.

There are degrees of credibility of opinion. One can assert, with high confidence, the opinion that every man now alive will die. Most people would not challenge the statement nor ask one why he believes so. It is based on a general and diffuse knowledge of the principle of man's existence. One can likewise assert, with a high confidence, the opinion that nothing which comes into existence does so without an agency in being which initiated its existence and caused it to be. Those challengers of the principle, Kant for instance, are forced to rely on the intrinsic unreliability of the human knowledge acquisition process.

We saw the epistemological difficulties that ensued for Kant. One can literally stop no place short of no knowledge at all and Camus' total epistemological pessimism is the end position. Yet Descartes, a true universalist in the knowledge of his time, who called his system of thought the Philosophy of Universal Doubt, did not arrive at any such similar conclusions. Descartes' approach was to question everything until he got to those things which were intellectually so unquestionable, concerning truth, that they could form the anchorage in ontology from which an epistemology could flow. Only after Descartes had satisfied his own stringent criteria and accepted the undeniable "fact" of his own existence as a thinking being did he approach the question of the existence of real being external to himself.

Descartes concluded that real being was the state of truth rather than non-being or solipsism which conclusion Aristotle, Thomas and Anselm before him had established. Descartes could then, and only then start to examine the things in the world about him. With Descartes, the universal principles were the only things that could be established without direct reference to sense data using the intellectual process and powers alone. His doubts began with the external physical world of the senses. He saw the analysis of t'-e world of phenomena and the senses as an outgrowth on the fundamental world of the intellect for its validity. Thought was his first concept.

It seems clear that if there are first principles, they, in fact, are "first" from which the rest of man's knowledge flows in boundary-less cascade. Thus, Descartes' concept was completely open-ended—divergent in scope; Kant's, close-ended and convergent in scope. If there are not first principles, then man's knowledge is indeed close-ended and a complete chaos in a narrow tomb. Such principles as are "established" only on an empirical basis are unsure and incomplete. If the idea of the causal sequence does not extend from first principles, how can the chain of knowledge be started?

If we take Descartes' starting point, we have no difficulty in moving into the world of things on a cause-effect sequence. On the other hand, starting from a great assortment of unrelated entities and events, Kant had to set up a wholly artificial set of *a priori* categories of knowledge into which the human judgment conveniently and automatically sorted things. *A priori* and universal only in the sense world, why? Why, indeed, unless there were behind the categories, principles that even the naive mind tends to observe as valid and which it subsequently utilizes to categorize observed events? And why should these *a priori* categories come to an impassable barrier at the boundary of sense perception which is demonstrably a very short band of the total spectrum even in the material universe? Wherever the band has been widened by science, the principles extend equally into the newly illuminated band.

With all due respect to Kant's genius, his hypothesis, (his belief is what it was), required constant emendation to meet new cases. As we saw, those advertised uncaused events in the physical sciences such as "spontaneous" fission turn out to be unexplained and not uncaused. We saw examples of unexplained phenomena in the area of religious experience. No one would suggest that they are uncaused. So we see that the world of human knowledge, limited as it is, is defined not by artificial barriers but by certain guidelines which continuously point toward directions of greater reliability or credibility. These are universal principles which, when violated in hypothesis, inevitably lead the searcher away from truth. Causality is one of these. Earlier, we looked at causality in the material world and affirmed its validity as a principle. Now we will look at it primarily in the world of the intellect and spirit, in the world of abstract thought.

When the cause-effect relationship involves rational agencies, material entities become secondary. For example, a book is produced—the author is cited specifically as the one who produced it, even though the publisher physically saw to its printing. The intellectual effect produced in the reader, Lenin, of the book, *Das Kapital,* was the product of an intellectual cause, the thought of Karl Marx, transferred by the printed word, a symbol an intellectual device. Now Kant would be forced, in his narrow epistemological view, to say that this analysis could not be made and has no validity. The sense perception by Lenin of the markings in the book bear no slightest cause-effect relationship to what Marx thought or what the printer produced or to anything else. Without Lenin's intellection of Marx's intellection, the relationships would be, in fact, unknowable. Kant's own statement that he was awakened from his "dogmatic slumbers" (an effect) by the thought of Hume (a cause) is hilarious in view of his stand on causal principles.

Concerning the nature of thought, in this relationship the eminent psychologist Carl G. Jung (d. 1961) wrote in his *Modern Man in Search of a Soul,*

> To this uncertainty about the localization of psychic functions another difficulty is added. Psychic contents in general are non-spatial except in the particular realm of sensation. What bulk can we ascribe to thoughts? Are they small, large, long, thin, heavy, fluid, straight, circular, or what? If we wished to form a vivid picture of a non-spatial being of the fourth

dimension, we should do well to take thought, as a being, for our model. (Jung, 1961).

A thought, a non-material entity, the product of one human being produced another thought, another immaterial entity, in another human being. And all of the statements of Hume about the mechanical formations of images in the brain and bundles of such images producing concepts cannot handle the transfer of thought by symbol, the spoken or written word, which bears no physical relationship to that which is symbolized. Nor can the mechanical mnemonic principles of thought suggested by Russell handle the difficulty. Symbol A, the word lion, produced image B, a conceptual physical lion in the brain. No one denies that the brain acts as a mnemonic device storing, in memory, a tremendous variety of data including symbols and relationship of symbols to the physical or mental reality. But the pulling together of all the various data bits and interrelating them and then extending the application to new situations in a problem-solving mode is not only mnemonic.

Modern computers are good mnemonic devices, yet no thoughts are produced. An intellect is required to interpret and to extend concepts but most of all to create ideas—thoughts which have had no previous formulation. That there are such new formulations is evident. Man otherwise would still be grubbing for roots along with the baboons and the great apes. These creatures' brains are also mnemonic devices. A recollected scent, when again received, raises an image of a thing previously encountered and stimulates emotions. However, it creates no questioning as to causality. The why and how modes are absent. These modes are not intrinsically time/space related. They arise from the ability to think. That ability is an intellectual capability.

Hume, Kant, and Russell, for one reason or another, arbitrarily, and not analytically, established a materialistic point of departure for their epistemology. Hume, arbitrarily—that is, without evidential support on a competent theoretical or empirical basis, equated material sense perception with personal being. Personality was the instantaneous condition of the collection of sense perception. If this perception is true, knowledge could be no more than that. Extrapolation from accumulated past data to permit formulation of a future plan of action for instance, a constant human activity—cannot even be approached under his epistemology. As we saw earlier in consideration of the "entropy" of communications, information improvement is negative "entropy." Only human beings are capable of ungrading information including making future predictions beyond the scope of stored data. With Russell, the concept of intellectual upgrading of data could not occur. There was no way to handle it. There could only be an association of sense perceptions current and past. When perception A was perceived then conclusion B followed—not by any speculative intellection of principle, but by comparison with stored reflex of prior empirical observation. Progress becomes impossible with this kind of thinking.

Kant's *a priori* categories were arbitrarily limited to those of sense perception—man automatically, by built-in programming, processed the sense data to formulate such complex relationships as causality. Man was preprogrammed to relate effect to cause not because the causal relationship was necessary, or true, but only because man was preprogrammed to handle the perceived "thing-in-itself." That is, he was preprogrammed to think in that way. The "cause" of the *a priori* preprogramming as an effect was not explained. Neither how, nor why, were considered. Kant's concept could not handle it: There could be no knowledge of such things even though, with Kant, the practical reason and judgment asserted they were "real."

Russell was equally arbitrary though, at least by association through memory, Hume's walking, talking bundle of perception stimuli accepted by Russell with the latter's memory bank could establish relationships. What the memory resided in, as personality, so as to possess associative powers, is not clear. Russell was totally arbitrary and dogmatic in asserting the materiality of thought. He could not even speak of the spirit of man in a rhetorical way. The thought for Russell—even such as involved in his complex work *Principia Mathematica,* could not be other than material. Even though thought is certainly real, and can be, and is, transmitted between human beings, it is not much like the physical world. With Russell, the thought transmitted is like computer to computer "cross talk." It is an energy transfer from memory unit to memory unit. Unit A thinks—unit B responds—cause and effect are empirical relationships—an observed "this" follows an observed "that" in time. A rock falls and crushes a tin can—two observations—that is sufficient in either case to explain the relationship.

Kant of course had no "real" world. It is sometimes overlooked in reviewing Kant, but his entire thesis is based on the premise that we cannot know anything about reality. The real is unknowable—only the unreal, the subjective interpretation of sense data input, is knowable. Knowledge is thus not by any means related to truth. The human person—in such an environment—is a pathetic figure. He is no more than a posturing madman wandering about in a nightmare world of studied misconceptions. There is no way of knowing who is having the nightmare! The actual grasp of the human mind is virtually zero in this environment of Kant.

Is there any evidence that these still popular viewpoints of the materially and unreliability of thought represented best by Kant, Hume, and Russell, even though not in accord with our observed life, actually represent the way that life, in fact, is? Kant obviously has no evidence since there is none that could be accepted as fact. Hume and Russell, while they might be willing to state that their mechanomen could recognize evidence, so severely limit what they would call evidence that it bears no relationship to what, in the life-as-lived, we could recognize as evidential. They insist on defining evidence in terms of that which could be recognized only if man, in fact, were specifically in the state which their hypothesis claims he is. It is thus circuitous.

There is no substantive evidence whatever that men are not the beings they seem to us to be—that is, individual human beings of varying levels of ability, physical and intellectual. People who are able to anticipate future problems and plan to meet them with greater or less success. People who act in accord with their understanding of a situation—who make mistakes of judgment and who are able to modify their decisions in the light of developing conditions. This picture does not describe the preprogrammed intellects of Kant, nor the robots without personality of Hume nor the walking memory banks of Russell.

The analysis of Merleau-Ponti and his emphasis on the unity of being in the behavior of all animal life forms, including man, is nowhere better shown than in the self-consciousness of human beings—realizing that they are, in fact, not mere bundles of sense perceptive acts, nor mnemonic devices, nor a mere collection of organs, or members, but a unique individual creation. The individual directs his total self to a problem which may include drawing sketches and, in intense sessions, even breaking out into a nervous sweat. It is not just a case of the brain, as a discrete part, cranking out answers in isolation. The brain functions as a center of organization. But the intending ego is the entire person engaged in any effort it undertakes.

In moments of introspection—soul searching—when we question our own motivation we ask, "Why did I lose my temper?" We feel ashamed of our lack of control of our own passions.

We are aware there is no one else to blame for our behavior but ourselves. We perceive that we could have acted differently. This sort of feedback does not make sense in any of the materialistic explanations. Why should a downstream bundle of perceptions look back on a recalcitrant upstream bundle? Freud's guilt complex would be a strange phenomenon indeed in such a "real" situation. In Russell's mnemonic device, while recall is provided, by what strange configuration would the memory look back on itself and develop painful associations with those memories which did not exist at the time the memories were implanted?

No real person, I am sure, has ever avoided such retrospective moments. At the time we did something, we felt as though we were behaving like heroes; when, in fact, in later events, we realize that we were total asses. None of the materialistic solutions look at the real world of human activity as it is lived. They are partial mechanical models which might have some use if they were not carried too far from proper application by their supporters.

Now, the fact that the categorical moral imperatives of Kant are universally recognized, yet are unexplicable, unless there is an infinite personal God to which they relate, does not necessarily say that God therefore exists. Unless one can also state categorically, that, in very fact, the concepts are or must be explicable.

How can this premise be approached? Kant seems to have been satisfied to stop with an intellectually persuasive argument. This argument would seem to say: "A human life must make sense. But, in view of the categorical imperative, belief in God is necessary for life to make sense. Therefore, belief in God is necessary. That is to say, the practical reason insists that life must be explicable. Therefore, God exists. Human life itself is inexplicable without the explicability of these categorical imperatives. Camus and Sartre would smile at this. In their world human life is, by definition, absurd, senseless, a useless passion and, in Camus' words, "The only ethical question is whether to commit suicide or not."

Though Kant denied the necessity of the causal relationship in the noumena, he is, in fact, forced, in this argument of persuasion, to proceed from the effects observed in man—the categorical imperatives—to the noumenal source of the imperative—God—or abandon the case. To be coercive, the argument needs support on an ontological footing. Epistemology itself falls short.

Had Kant not been so intent on trying to give the death blow to speculative metaphysics—that is, to the intellectual approach to God—he would have seen that literally no statement concerning being makes sense without the existence of God—not just a belief in God—but literally, no God, no Being. The statement "God is not" requires a definition of what God is. Regardless of whether we believe in God or not, this definition will yield, "God is the self-sufficient Being upon which all being depends." A direct denial also denies all being. If then, one says there is no self-sufficient Being and all being is dependent, upon what does it depend. Or, if one says all being is self-sufficient, one merely has to look about to see the denial. If some are self-sufficient, and some dependent on those, then there are multiple gods, or God is a multiplicity.

We return to Anselm's view, God exists necessarily or there would be no being whatsoever. The obvious existence of the many, the finite and imperfect beings, or imperfect qualities inherent in beings, demands the existence of the One. That Being must be the Being above which no greater being can be conceived—whose non-being is, in fact, inconceivable, whose non-being state would be a contradiction and denial of all other being. In this argument, the categorical imperative merely flows from, and reflects, the necessary nature of that Being.

Let us look a bit at the causal sequence implicit in the categorical imperative. Methodology implies purpose. When a specific set of means and ends activities, bracketed between situational sets, has been identified, two questions arise in critical analysis. The first is why was the end state considered sufficiently important to justify the initiating activity. The second question can be stated as follows: why was this set of activities selected out of those available to achieve the end state? Now, when these activities involve a moral judgment, i.e., an activity ought to be engaged in because duty demands it, an external agency is introduced. A relationship is recognized between the intending ego in the direct causal sequence the one who selects the activities and the entity or entities to whom the duty is owed. The bricklayer builds a wall so that he will be paid a wage so that he will be able to support his family so that his family can exist in society as a respected unit. This is a specific physical example of the above reasoning.

Society places an obligation on the head of a family in justice to provide for its needs. The bricklayer recognizes the obligation and builds the wall, though he might prefer to be off fishing. The obligation to society has a causal connection. It is the prime motivator. In the religious sphere, the moral judgments as to wrongness and rightness also have a prime motivator external to the direct causal chain and, nonetheless, but for its recognized presence, there would be no obligation and no judgment necessary. Picture a man completely alone on a deserted island. Does he have any conceivable moral obligation in the sense of Kant's categorical imperative? For him, his fellow man or society does not exist. Any obligations would be to himself, as a human being. As with Camus, ethics is reduced to the question of suicide, unless the man already recognizes that there is a God to whom he owes obedience, love and worship. If there is none such, the causal chain does not exist and, obviously, there would be no moral obligation. A debt owed strictly to oneself is, in fact, no debt. There is no sanction. One who says, "I owe it to myself to be honest and upright" or, "I couldn't live with myself if I did thus and so" is recognizing that his nature, as human, demands a certain minimum level of behavior. Not because, as an individual, he demands this behavior of himself, but because the categorical moral imperative does exist and there is an external causal source of the sense of obligation. While man is "preprogrammed" to see purpose in the universe and to extend purpose to his relationships, the "programming" stems not from an *"a priori"* innate trait but from man's human characteristics, as rational, relating individual observations to generalized conclusions.

One of the difficulties of the strict atheist evolutionist—who must deny fundamental purpose and causality or abandon his case—is, of course, the difficulty of explaining why man's thinking is thus "programmed" to see purpose and causality in the natural world around him if, in fact, the universe is causeless or purposeless. He must hold that the trait developed because it favored survival. But if, in fact, causality and purpose are pure fiction then pursuit of the illusion of causality is, in fact, a colossal waste of energy. Man's energy should be better applied elsewhere in a frantic random search for roots and grubs rather than rationalizing where he might logically find them on a cause and effect basis.

To further develop this trend of thought, if the causal relationship has intrinsic validity in any situation, it must then have intrinsic validity in every situation. That is a very broad statement. Let us take the case of God. God, by any cohesive definition, is the intrinsic reason or purpose or cause of His own existence. The "how" and "why" of God are one with His essence. God is, and has being. Now, if there is cause at all (that thing by which a being exists as a real thinking being) it is because the intrinsic capacity for one's existence resides in some being. It resides either in the individual person, as an intrinsic capacity, or in some other being as intrinsic capacity. But if one exists, the intrinsic capacity exists. If this is the case with the individual, one of a vast multiplicity of beings and with no apparent exceptions to be found, it seems clear that one is justified in universalizing the concept with a high confidence level of being correct.

With the establishment, it is hoped, of the high probablity that the creature man is able to form ideas having some relationship to reality beyond those which are totally sense related we can look at the place of opinion or belief in that context. The chain of development of knowledge can be shown to be endlessly iterative from opinion to principle thus:

1. An object of concern—being in its relationships with its environment, for instance, is examined physically and then intellectually.

2. An opinion (a hypothesis) is formed as to the nature of this object of concern.

3. Corroborative facts are collected or a test is conceived to try the opinion.

4. The opinion survives the examination or test, usually with certain modifications.

5. A tentative principle is formed leading us to extend the opinion to other objects of concern more or less related.

6. The tentative principle is examined; new corroborative evidence is gathered or new procedures derived to test the opinion extended to principle.

7. The opinion survives; a new principle is formed. Two things happen, the original opinion is strengthened by succeeding extension until it becomes an established principle with the boundaries of its application identified, and also the body of effective human knowledge is increased by each increment of valid opinion extending from the body of principles.

Obviously not all opinion is of equal validity. The degree of validity depends upon the "goodness of fit" between the opinion of hypothesis and the supporting evidence or corroborating facts. This evidence must be defined to respond to the six topical questions as applicable.

what—the constitutive identification
who—the personal identification
when—the temporal identification

where—spacial identification
how—methodological identification
and
why—purposive identification

When this identification has been completed for all surrounding circumstances, to the satisfaction of the intellect, the opinion can be said to have been validated for that intellect, and a "belief" justified.

Moving now into the realm of religious belief, we must ask ourselves the question: Are we forced to conclude that there are no guidelines and that one belief is as defensible or indefensible as any other in the course of rational inquiry? Is the root of monotheism, that is, a belief in a single personal God who is identically the loving father preached by Augustine, the Yahweh of the Hebrews, the Allah of Islam, the Great Spirit of many of the primitive cults, merely a fanciful bit of wishful thinking? The writer certainly thinks not. Rationality requires that evidence be collected from all sources, that the intellect evaluate the resultant body of facts and logical derivation of facts in their total interplay and then that the will gives assent. The will must judge that the case is convincing or unconvincing. The process is identical in basis to a properly conducted court case, in which the relative reasonableness of the adversary positions is determined.

If there is a rational basis for a decision in law, similarly, there is a rational basis for a decision in religious and moral matters, although the assembly of the body of evidence by the individual may be difficult and the natural tendency is to accept the word of those in whom one has "faith." We have seen those who insist that the only approach to religious belief is the irrational one—"the leap of faith"—which deliberately shuns the approach through an evaluation of evidence. Certainly those who are so privileged as to have such deep personal conviction need not dig any deeper, totally satisfied as they are in their precarious posture, perched "on the narrow ridge between abysses." Yet, it seems obvious one could as irrationally take the "leap of unfaith," as Sartre does. He says that there is no God. The two hopelessly opposed adversaries have no position in logic to discuss their positions quietly and calmly. They can only stand on that ridge and shout out their stark polar positions endlessly.

The writer thinks, however, that in the current milieu and given the violent winds and buffet that lofty moral summit, the views on the subject by Augustine and Anselm are not to be lightly tossed aside. Their approach *"credo ut intelligam,"* freely translated in its full context "I study, not that I may believe, but that I may understand what I believe and enhance and deepen my belief." One may still occupy that perch of faith, not "in fear and trembling" but rather serene with no fear that a sudden gust will sweep one into the abyss. Faith should be a thoughtful giving of assent.

A carefully reasoned faith, one whose basis is rational in its substantive aspects, is a tremendous source of reserve confidence in the essential meaning of life under all circumstances. Suicide in a rational man of faith does not appear as a question of theoretical ethics but as a cowardly betrayal of a trust equivalent to a soldier abandoning a difficult outpost under fire. With such a faith, no position ever becomes hopeless regardless of difficulty.

Thus, faith, in its true meaning, denotes the convinced giving of intellectual assent to the truth of a thesis. One ought to believe something only when he has been convinced through the intellectual examination of the evidence. This evidence includes the testimony of credible witnesses. It goes without saying that the key word here is "credibility." One believes a witness because he is worthy of belief. But there should not be a circuitry. Belief in a messiah, for instance, should not be based only on the reported testimony of that messiah in his own behalf. A claimant to a sum of money should not be believed only because he claims he is the legitimate claimant. Both become believable only when they present evidence to substantiate their claims—evidence that will establish their credibility. The better the class of evidence provided, the greater is the degree of credibility. Credibility rests on a thoughtful investigation of all the surrounding circumstances.

When someone says, "I believe in God or in Judaism or in Christianity because of the testimony of the Bible," there is, implicit in the statement, the fact that, for this individual, the credibility of the Bible rests upon the historical verification, literally or allegorically, of the events recorded in the Bible. In most cases, this, in turn, rests upon the credibility of witnesses to the events and, very importantly, to the cohesiveness of the totality of the witnesses provided by all of the canonical works. It is the harmonious dovetailing of the events recorded and of extraneous secular events over thousands of years which gives the high probability of superhuman guidance and provides the basis of intellectual assent. This is no irrational leap, but a studied appraisal and judgment. It is thoughtful and purposeful.

We have read, earlier in the book, that some of the modern theologians have tried to discredit the historical approach, thereby enhancing the awesomeness of their vault into the unknown. They have tried to reduce all of the recorded data to mere symbology, this being the reverse of the current irrationality of making the symbol real. In an already sufficiently confused world, this combination has compounded the difficulty of sorting out the real from the symbolic and the symbolic from the mere fantasy. The Bible is variform. Some of the recorded events are purely historic. Some events are prophetic and some symbolic and some symbolic and prophetic. The Bible is not fantasy, although imagery is used in highly impressionistic ways in the apocalyptic works, for instance. Again the solution is not an irrational surrender to an emotional urge but an analytical search for the evidence which supports the contending viewpoints. We can cite a few examples. Earlier, mention was made of the ancient prophecy in Genesis—"I will place enmity between thee and the woman—between her seed and your seed." In the previous citation, the prophecy was related by Christian believers to the incarnation of Christ. But, as in countless other prophetic statements or events in the Bible, the statements of events are both real and symbolic. The prophetic woman was literally fulfilled in Mary. The "woman" was also symbolic of the "Church" under both the Old and New Testaments, producing the community of the people of God, the Mystical Body of Christ which would overrun Satan. For Christians, Mary herself is both real and also symbolic of the universal motherhood of the Church. In their common motherhood, the roles of Mary and the "Church" are mutually supportive in symbology. "The ideas fit together."

Abraham, in ordering his only son, Isaac, to carry the wood for his sacrifice is symbolic of God the Father in that future event in which the sacrifice would be consummated. There are both real and symbolic messages conveyed and the duality of the function reinforces the authenticity of the long past events. The duality does not deny the reality nor give the events only symbolic meaning. Or, taking an example from the New Testament, the words of Christ on His way to Calvary (*Luke*, Chapter 23),

Daughters of Jerusalem do not weep for me, weep
for yourselves and for your children. The days are

coming when they shall say, "Happy are the sterile,
the wombs that never bore and the breasts that never
nursed!" Then they will begin saying to the mountains, "Fall on us" and to the hills "cover us." If they
do these things in the green wood what will happen
in the dry?

In the culture of the Jews at the time of Christ and long after,
it would have been unthinkable to praise the sterile. Sterility
was a curse. The words were intended to be prophetic—they
were not responsive in the immediate situation nor in the context of the times when pronounced and recorded. The contrasting periods "the green wood" and the "dry" symbolize
a time of the latter condition far in the future when the hearts
of men were hardened and dry to things of the spirit. Now,
in the premise, the conditions are becoming patently true. We
do say "Blessed be zero population growth." The conclusion
flowing from that premise is not attractive, and the high reliability of prophecies of the Bible through the ages gives no reason for comfort that it is only a symbolic statement of an
obsolete culture.

In the general world situation, it is the false symbolism, the
deliberate misrepresentation of reality through symbolism, which
is the real hazard of an age which has been super-conditioned
to the symbolic. Badly needed is a thorough, thoughtful questioning of the content of the symbology. Is there a reality behind the proposed symbol or is it only an artful construct
manipulated to suit a promoter's ends?

In the religious sphere, the problem is particularly difficult
because the best symbology must fall far short of expressing
the reality. The reach is too great to be spanned by the sensible
symbol. It is principally this difficulty which inspired the commonly expressed idea of the futility of the intellectual pursuit
of the reality of God and the need for the blind "leap of faith."
In other words, if there are no judgmental criteria in the religious area on which man can rely, then one must follow some
wild irrational impulse and say, "This I believe"—or, alterna-
tively "I don't believe."

During the past century—roughly, since the time of Kierkegaard, organized religion has been badly served by surrender
to this intellectually-weak position. While one may be intuitively attracted to a belief in a Supreme Being, as most people
are, one has little incentive to investigate a thesis which has
been authoritatively declared intellectually unsearchable—an

assumed dogmatic position by those so scrupulously denying dogma. Religion becomes an occasional wistful experience, which, come Monday morning, must be abandoned to the hard facts of the real world.

The human manipulation in symbolism is, in its essence, a continuous act of faith. We believe that the symbol—something which is only figurative—represents something else—something totally different—which is real. The letters d - o - g and corresponding sounds in English both represent a real animal in our minds and convey that meaning to others of the same culture. Further, that assembly of letters "dog" usually conveys the idea of a universal canine nature. We believe that the symbols are understood by others in the same way that they are accepted by us.

In its most developed form, symbolism is the means by which abstract concepts are communicated to others. The sybmol for the concept "peace," or the word "love," scrawled in graffiti around the world has invaded all modern Western cultures. But symbolism has its hazards. The symbol can be subverted, through propaganda, whereby it is used to promote something completely contrary to the original concept which it was meant to convey. Both the peace symbol and Churchill's "V" have been perversely used in support of all kinds of terrorism throughout the world. The clenched fist would have been far more appropriate but would have had far less general appeal. There is the danger that the symbol, instead of being a surrogate, becomes accepted as the principal. Those of the West, generally below the age of 45, have been nurtured on a fare of hedonistic symbolism in the graphic and vocal arts, while in the communist world colossal pictures of the leaders, current and historical symbols of the state, have gazed down benevolently from every direction for three or more generations. The symbol takes the place of the reality, "Big Brother" becomes a theologic entity and the normal religious sentiments are diverted to anti-religious ends.

Man takes no conscious action whatsoever without previously having made a conclusive judgment by which he acts one way or another. Call that judgmental conclusion what you will. It is an evaluation, by the intellect, of all data bits stored in the memory regardless of how those data bits were acquired. Man acts—if he acts rationally—on the basis of prior knowledge, and experientially-obtained data are as liable to judgmental error as any other. There is, in man, no perfect "knowledge." Rather there is a continuum of various levels or degrees of "reliability" of stored data. A unit of knowledge in these terms ought to be defined as a data bit in which the mental content agrees with that which, in fact, actually is. In man, this agreement possesses a greater or less reliability depending upon an infinite variety of variables. This is not to agree with Camus' statement, that "Nothing is certain but uncertainty." Because "absolute" certitude does not exist in man does not say that there is not an absolute certitude of which, man possesses, at best, only a flawed image. It is, in fact, arguable that the possession of a flawed image, recognized as flawed, is strongly evidential of the, at least theoretically, perfect original. How else do we judge it to be flawed? We do not throw away our telescopes or call them useless because they do not provide a perfect image. We try to improve our telescopes.

Let us look at the nature of thought in this context. It is real, but it has no extension. It utilizes energy, but it is not energy. Its human methodology is by means of the material brain, but it is not a product of the brain as "bile is of the liver." Thought can be transferred between rational individuals, yet those thoughts have little sensory registry beyond the symbol. It is an expression of the view of the human mind on a given subject, yet it is more than a mere data display. Thought, in short, reflects the results of a synthesizing process involving memory and a projective capability positing how any given subject in sheer reality stands in relation to its total environment. Thought relates subjects to predicates judgmentally. The thought process is not mechanical; it is illuminative beyond the sense order and it is obviously highly personal.

Just how are ideas provoked and images created in the mind with no sense stimulation whatever? The intellect is not an inert receptacle of ideas. It is intensely active. It does not wait for a sense stimulus. It can be stimulated as well by a conscious or unconscious reflection on the data previously stored. Thought is, in fact, the individual self manifesting itself as self under the various circumstances of life. Of all that is human, thought is the only valid expression of what one, in fact, is. The thought is the primary manifestation of one's being.

God has been defined as the "self-thinking thought"—that is to say, of all beings, God alone was not a consequence of another's thought. He is in eternal possession of all thought. He is the precedent thought without precedent from which all thought is subsequent. He is the perfect self-expression. It is this general concept, of course, which undergirds pantheism and pure idealism. If God possess all thought, how can there be independent thought? Neither school can comprehend a "solidified" thought in the sense of matter. The pantheists could not even conceive of an individualization discrete from the primeval thought. That problem, of course, stands at the other pole from the materialists who cannot conceive of being which is not solidified. For them, thought has to be somehow mere matter in motion.

With space/time rational beings thought, like all else, is temporal, sequential, but only because that environment is the condition of the thought. In a timeless environment, thought would be timeless and, under these conditions, the thinking being would be manifested by the summation of all its thought in a constant condition of presentness.

There is no conflict in the idea of a space/time configuration as one aspect in eternity. Our bodily configuration corresponds to that environment. It exists because God willed it to exist in that form. So likewise our sequential thought process is related to the infinite eternal thought. Sequential for us, constantly present to God. The intellect, source of thought, is the essential individual and is manifested in the display of the evaluational and judgmental activities performed through the brain upon the summation of all the data bits collected in material space/time. This is not only a material individual being displayed, it is a material manifestation of a being closely allied to the same "stuff" as thought, even as Carl Jung suggested.

What can we say about the relationship of our space/time universe and eternity? From the foregoing discussion we could conclude that eternity is the environment of all being. Space/time is that aspect of eternity which forms the environment of material being. It is a special case within a total which provides for all possible being. Under this concept adaptation of being to environment is only incidental. Primarily, the environment is that appropriate to the particular form of being. If a form of being is to develop along certain predetermined lines, then the environment would be such as would encourage development. Thus, the environment of earth has gone through a sequence of changes during geologic times, and at particular places, so as to place living forms in a tension of *elan vital*—drawing them—to change in a certain direction toward a condition of reduced tension.

It is apparently this directional sequencing which prompted Dyson to say,

> As we look out into the universe and identify the
> many accidents of physics and chemistry that have

worked together to our benefit, it almost seems as if the universe must in some sense have known that we were coming.

Indeed it did.

We live in an energy field of total "isness" but in a mode which is oriented to space and time. We cannot feel comfortable with an idea in which there is no "before" or "after"—only perpetual eternal now. Yet, perhaps the infinite is better appreciated by us who have a concept of the vastness of space and time than to those who had no such idea and to whom the "Infinite God" was yet still a rather "small scale" being by comparison with what we know must be the case. The incredibly subtle identification recorded in Exodus for the Absolute Being "I am," which expresses that unchangeable presence of being, has, or ought to have, far greater significance to our age than it has had at any time in the past three thousand years.

This concept of eternity as the environment of being explains the enigma of man. Alone, of all the creatures on earth, he is under constant, almost unbearable, tension. Earthbound, yet his imagination soars to the stars and beyond. Mortal, yet he yearns for immortality. Animal, yet he desperately seeks things of the spirit. But, if man, in fact, is destined for spirituality and immortality, this tension—this upward driving force—is the means by which the transition is accomplished. Man cannot remain satisfied with anything less. He must move forward and into that environment of being in which the tension will cease. He must move to the environment for which, in fact, he is destined as a being.

But with man, contrary to the other animal species, the urge is personal. It is *his,* the individual's transition that is the goal, not some advancement of the species. Indeed, as Herder suggested, man appears as the ultimate fruit of the development on earth and destined to leave it.

This concept also helps to explain the relationship between the many and the one. The one unchangeable, infinite, in which essence, being and existence, are not separable aspects of His unity. God is the One, intrinsically the One, who is also the environment of His own being. God exists in Himself, and of and for Himself comprehensively, as eternal Being. The many, the creatures, are existents in eternity as foci of specific being in aspects of eternity, relating to the eternity, which is of God, as the natures of the various beings permit. That is to say, there is but one eternity and that eternity is the total environment of being. The manner of our existence in that environment, as conditioned to our form of being, and the manner of God's intrinsic eternal existence, are totally different. The manner of the existence of each is analogous, perhaps, to the existence of a magnetic flux within the magnet itself and in magnetized particles more or less remote. There is the same environment by which a magnet is a magnet and the particles are magnetized. But the magnet is not intrinsically affected by the magnetism it induces in the particles, and the objects in the field are affected in relation to their individual capacity to be magnetized. The "magnetism" of being is inherent in the One and, indeed, in the many, by the One.

It must be appreciated that whatever we do along the lines of discussing the nature of God or of His intrinsic existence has to be done in the form of a model which satisfies the equations as we see then from the total evidence. Yet, as we have seen, this is far from agreeing with Kant that we can know nothing. We truly have to "look through a glass in a dark manner." But, just as we view molecular structures by forming beads in models in different arrays, so do we make models of God. We have already looked at a mathematical model. Now let us look at Him ontologically. No one denies that our knowledge of chemistry is enhanced by such models. Likewise, our ideas of God are enhanced by considering Him as the "self-thinking Thought" in a "total thought" environment which includes our environment. Yet, this is not the idealism of Plato or Kant. It is a model of Absolute Being.

In our model of God, change occurs only in the specific environment of the individual beings. What the many observe as change (for example, creatures coming into existence) would be to a Being of infinite presence, and presentness, no more a change than a blip on a radar screen moving to a different sector would be to us. Past and future are but aspects of the present. Yet, because of the infinite array of knowledge and presentness of God, the slightest detail is known to Him in an intensity of illumination completely beyond our comprehension. The facts of our individual lives as we live them, morally or immorally, in our environment are far more intimately known to God than they are to us.

The model also serves to soften the problem of physical evil in the world and provides a purpose. As we have noted, that problem devolves primarily from our inability to place events in perspective in the hierarchy of values. But if we relate the different environments in which man lives, and, in which God has His being, we observe that the "evils" stem from our human tensions in our unbalanced thought environment, not from a lack of love or omnipotence in God. We do not think of "evil" except in terms of man-related conditions. Moral evil begins in the mind. As we noted, the tension which the model recognizes serves the purpose of pushing man, compelling him, to be aware of the tenuousness of this life and the search for final answers elsewhere. The constant search of philosophy and religion, though often sidetracked, is to provide the lasting answers. The physical conditions we view as evil—poverty, disease, and misery in the world, the arrogance and cruelty of the proud and powerful, who seem to prosper in their malice—are but as the negative elements of a tensor matrix. When combined and contrasted with the other vectors, the heroism of struggle in the face of great odds, the bond of family love, and the thousands of lives lived selflessly devoted to mankind, the resulting force field in which each man must work out his existence in the insistent dialectic becomes clearer. Man can seek the resultant which will lead him to worldly power and position, or he can seek the moral resultant which will lead him toward God. The uncertainties of each day force him to make thousands of choices in a lifetime and thus to gravitate one way or the other on balance. It is this aspect which creates the excruciating testing ground this life is. No one who lives to adulthood escapes it.

Whitehead's "consequent nature of God" is eliminated in the model. God is as He must be in the environment—unchangeable. But we view God from our environment and we perceive Him in terms of that changeable mode. On the other hand, God also knows us and perceives us in our changeable mode while simultaneously He knows us and perceives us as we stand in His total eternal overview. The One and the many are thus juxtaposed in the true relationship they bear to each other as differentiated by their fundamental environments. The changeableness, the flow of time which we observe is real because that is the nature of our environment. But we stand over against God in our changeableness which to Him is a single panorama from horizon to horizon of eternity. God's love and His compassion shine constantly on that panoramic view, but we from time to time cast up, as it were, clouds of malice to hide it. We climb into intellectual caves so that we can escape it, thus its effect upon us is variable. The change is not in God, in His love, or His compassion, but in us, in our lives, in our world situation, which is greater or less receptive to God's initiatives to us from time to time.

Our time and space continuum is the specific environment of our material being. It is one "constituent" of the total eternal environmental manifold encompassing all being. Time and space are related in quantitative terms greater—lesser in distance and duration and possess no absolute values. Eternity as total environment is only presence of being in association of essences. The environment is what each essence demands in relation to its basic energy system. Distinction in being in eternity is in terms of relative essence. That which is, exists as discrete forms of being in relations of essence. Time and space appear to be related to eternity in an analogous sense that a constant term in mathematics is related to an indeterminate function. That is, a function which cannot be directly evaluated and can take on any value whatsoever, yet is no value. Still, the indeterminate function may yield a true value in a specific usage. Therefore, in eternity, energy forms can be manipulated so as to yield specific time/space/material configurations. Our universe is an example of such an instance.

We also think in terms of space and time in a directed sense as vectors, time as always moving forward, for instance, and of space as extending from here to there. One of the problems of eternity as a concept is that we habitually conceive of it as an infinite series in terms of time when it is in no wise a function of time. Time can be an aspect when related to specific beings. Infinity and eternity are correlate terms and, just as infinity is not expressible as a magnitude in number, eternity is not expressible as a value in time. It seems likely that eternity is, in fact, defined largely as a function of the essence of being involved. Instead of the space/time material environment conditioning, even driving, the being, in eternity, as it does in time, the specific presence of being conditions and dictates the environment of its existence.

Eternity is time/space indeterminate in the mathematical sense. Time and space exists as a bubble on the surface of a sea of eternity. The bubble forms at a "place" and lasts "for a time" then breaks and leaves no trace. In those cases in which a specific form of being requires a space/time environment, the parameters of that form of being determine the particular space/time configuration and the temporal interface with eternity. The nature of God uniquely determines eternity as a total environment and the will of God establishes the relationships between all other beings and His total "being."

The changes which occur in the "bubble" do not effect the changelessness of God. It should be noted that changelessness implies a steady state and not necessarily a static condition. The changelessness stems from God's own infinity—to which nothing can be added or subtracted. But, from an infinite source, there can be a constant outflow without diminution of the source. God's total being is of that nature. Creativity flows continuously from Him in endless formation of being and the concomitant of creativity—love—flows in the same way. The time/space "bubble" of our universe, perhaps only one of many, is not of the essence of God but a reflection of God's essence produced by His creativity and love. The "bubbles" could all disappear and God remain totally unchanged.

Those elements of being which are purely temporal vanish with their time, and as it were, leave no trace after the "bubble" bursts, their term and purpose of existence completely served. With man who also lives in the space/time bubble there is a difference. As we have seen he lives in constant personal tension with his environment unlike all the other physical creatures. And, traditionally, in his higher intellectual life, man perceives his primary purpose in the giving of honor and worship to God. This purpose is never completely served. It, in fact, serves a timeless function. These two realities combined, man's rejection of his mortality and his inclination to worship God, point in only one direction. Man is a transitional creature. The environment suited to his being form is not this one in which he lives his mortal life nor is it the sheer spirituality of the environment of God. There appears to be no reason why that, if God willed such a being, He would not have, in His perfection, willed also for the appropriate environment for that being when, and time is proper in this context, man has served the purpose of his mortal existence, a testing ground, and moves toward the spiritualized human life for which he was destined— toward which the *elan vital* drives him. This drive is in the intellectual/spiritual vector of man which demands an intellectual/spiritual environment. The insistent dialectic represents that tension between man and his earthly environment and is strongly suggestive of man's immortality. Man's preoccupation with time, the only creature in the world so afflicted, points to his frustration in being forced into a time-oriented environment. He wishes to be immortal above all else—his total essence demands it. Man tries to do the same thing in this world, to make this world conform to his demands, to force things to be, as he would have them be in that environment which would truly suit him as a total person.

Eternity, for God, would be far different than for any creature.

Infinitely so, God's presence includes the future as present, in the sense that His knowledge includes all future acts regardless of their sequelity. With creatures, the future remains anticipatory, even for creatures destined to be immortal. The future is not known to them unless God wills it. Man will exist in eternity in an environment suited for both his physical and spiritual needs. The non-physical vector in man transcends that time-oriented limit on its environment since it is non-physical. Man's environmental state in eternity after death will be determined by the essence of its being as it will then be in relationship to God. Individual man as the person he has become at the termination of this life will determine his own future environment in eternity. He will be largely what he has become, a creature of his own doing.

The self-conscious self, which is the human person constituting the essential being that is man in biologic existence before death, acts only through, and with, intimate participation of the body. That body, in fact, is the manifestation of the existence of the human being in space/time. At death that manifestation of being ceases but the being does not. That spiritual, living essence, that development of self during its temporal manifestation continues as the personality of the individual human being now manifested in a spiritual environment. Man remains a human selfness and continues to function in the intellectual and spiritual order, with clear and complete consciousness of his humanness. That non-material vector, the essentiality of humanity which distinguishes human life from all other material forms, is excluded by that spiritual definition from death and is unaffected. Yet a strong intuitive argument for the concept of the bodily resurrection can be given, in that a human being divested of his bodily form is incomplete. To be totally human, even in a modified non-space/time environment, the complete human being needs reconstitution in some form after death to restore its integrity as a total being form. It seems illogical that God would have provided a spiritual being with a material body and formed a "composite" material/spiritual person if that person, in its integrity, were not to be the entity uniquely to represent the "composite" material/spiritual form in glorifying him eternally.

An appropriate environment for such a being would appear to have two aspects, that of the time/space bubble and also that of the spacelessness/timelessness of God's own eternal environment. The bubble need not be opaque, as in this life it is. In the context of Christianity, at death the soul of man, his spiritual vector, lives on as pure spirit, perhaps also in this form undergoing purification so that in the fullness of time the soul rejoins and revivifies its body, of physical form but now immortalized. The space and time environment as we know it would be replaced by one vastly changed to suit lives directed solely to the love and glory of God. Yet, that love and glory being provided by means suited to our total humanity. We will be human beings loving and glorifying God and not pure spirits.

There are two aspects of self-awareness in human beings. The first aspect is purely physical. We share it with all other sensate. life forms. That is, the ability to differentiate the self from all others. It is instinctive and innate. The second aspect, limited to human beings, is intellectual and it is at least virtually innate. In many ways, it masks the instinctive self-awareness—taking over functions which in the nonhuman animals are largely automatically activated as the animal matures. The human individual knows itself as the "executive" at a very early age and seeks to direct itself and all else. Infantile tantrums (at any age) largely reflect the frustration of the innate executive self and are not merely a reflex response to the deprivation of some immediately perceived sensible "goal." One seeks to have his "own way" because he is conscious of his identity vis-a-vis all others. He resents submitting to other wills. This executive self is probably not explicit to the consciousness of the infant, but it is present in the sub-consciousness in full force from the beginning. A child which does not exhibit this symptom of "self will" at an early age is suspected of being of subnormal intelligence. What is the inference to be drawn? As with the instinctive traits of the non-human animal, in which the drive toward dominance observable in behavior is a reflection of the executive self-awareness but only a reflection. The innate self-awareness of the human is for the primary purposes of successful performance in its existential role. Man is to be self-aware and to feel personally responsible in his self-awareness because he is personally responsible to a self-awareness above him, although he may not be aware of the relationship. Man's own self-awareness points inevitably to another who is self-aware and to whom man responds in dialogue.

Man, the free social being, is such because he is self-aware and feels both free and responsible in his self-awareness. He recognizes his obligation to himself, to society, and somehow to the source of his awareness. In a manner of speaking, there is an innate awareness of God contained in our own innate self-awareness. If I am self-aware, it is because there has been a self-awareness primordially before me even as Descartes sensed in his disembodied man.

As there is an innate awareness of self, not intrinsically dependent on the experiential outside world, so there is a derived, corollary awareness of our own limitations in our self-awareness. We did not bring ourselves to self-awareness nor could all the experiential others have provided our self-awareness, though they serve to provide boundaries and as we mature to force us to recognize our limitations and our contingency.

What we, as adults, call self-awareness then is primarily our intellectual self-knowledge—a self appraisal of our motivations, our resources, our weaknesses, and an appraisal of our ability to direct ourselves to an objective, and also of our freedom to act or not to act. It includes our ability to reflect on the likely effects of our act in the light of the memory of our past acts and our aspirations for the future. It is the intending ego which directs the continuing self-appraisal and analyzes and interrelates all the "findings." It is also the intending ego which is the executive-self, the person, one, in fact, is. It is, of course, the very aspect whose existence Hume denied. Without it, there is no self-awareness except as the dog has. The executive-self has a fixed identity but a changeable character. Our "self-awareness" embraces both the fixed and the changeable. The person we are today is the result of our successes or failures in self-management, applied to our naive character. We, in our fixed identity, are aware that we are uniquely responsible. We are also aware that we can plan to change in the future if we so desire. We can direct ourselves to self-improvement however we visualize it.

Our view, of course, is profoundly influenced by the value system we have accepted. We are oriented to happiness—to our personal happiness as we measure it. For most people, happiness is a "mixed bag." It usually includes a significant amount of human respect. We want others to approve of us. Most people are unhappy if they are rejected by their close associates. It also includes a measure of self-respect. We cannot be happy if we dislike our self-image and we *know* who we are. Self-deception is not successful over any length of time. But we can modify our values to meet our performance and thus live with ourselves on the new basis. We equate the new values to happiness by rejecting the previously held values.

Throughout our lives our "executive" self projects images to the outside world, images of itself as it would have others view it. There may be several images, one for each role in which the individual is cast. There is a certain confusion within the self as to which is the "real me." The proliferation of "identities" most people must assume in modern cultures compounds the problem. The Jungian *Persona* is the montage of the projections, and the psyche is not satisfied until that montage and the real person are made congruent. But this presumes an "honest" psyche, one which does not desire to falsify appearances. The dramaturgical socialized and pragmatic behavioral models presume a level of motivation which has nothing to do with truthfulness. Expedience and convenience are the criteria.

Morality, as a behavioral control system is legitimatized—has validity—only in the perceived relationship between man, the dependent creature who will live forever and God, his source of being and life. Man perceives an obligation to organize his life in a way pleasing to God. Man perceives that God does know all of his thoughts and actions in greater detail than man himself knows them. He perceives that God will reward or punish him on the basis of his behavior. He perceives, in fact, that the primary reason of his existence here on earth is specifically to determine his future position in eternity, and that his own behavior will determine that future. Beyond all that, man perceives, in God, that which is infinite love and infinitely lovable, who by reason of that love created man. Man perceives that his highest destiny is in the love and service of God. He perceives an obligation to love and serve his fellowman because God loves him also. Man perceives that he and his thought are virtually one. Man is almost literally what his thought has made him.

All these perceptions arise in the thought processes of man. The legitimization of morality as a behavioral control system rests upon man's ability to think and to arrive at sound judgments in areas having few material interfaces. Yet through all history man has accepted that these thought patterns are correct and express reality in its highest form. The recent flurry of dissent is artificially contrived and is passing from the scene. In the future, as in the past, man will speculate on his relationship with God. He will develop a living faith in God as his loving father. He will see his fellowman as his brother. And, the moral vector developed in the environment of religious thought will again be the primary element in controlling man's behavior. Styles change but man, in his fundamental nature, does not change.

Chapter 15
THE MATRIX OF MORALITY

We have seen that the concept of morality, as a behavior control system, rests primarily upon a motivation in the religious order. Man surrenders some of the prerogatives of his freedom to act as an autonomous individual because he perceives an overriding obligation to serve God. Man perceives he will achieve happiness both in this world and the next through obedience to rules of behavior implicit in the service of God. Leading a moral life is linked to happiness. But happiness is many things. In the moral sense one who leads a "good" life is happy, but the concept "goodness" itself is a composite of many elements.

Morality, in the individual, is a complex concept comprising a personal evaluation of a great variety of influences. There are, however, dominant influencing elements which can be worked into an intellectual matrix. Each person, looking at his or her life, places each element in somewhat different perspective than someone else would. The solution of the matrix in a particular person is unique but would contain some appreciation for all of the elements. In this chapter, we will discuss what the writer believes are the principle elements in the concept of morality.

We will look first at the driving impulses in man and their acknowledged goal, a condition of happiness. As we examine what might be called the "parameters of felicity," the measures of levels of fulfillment in human existence, we can set up a series of companion expressions indicating a range of excellence in two dimensions. These would be, in descending order of intellectuality:

Happiness	—	Sadness
Joy	—	Sorrow
Delight	—	Disgust
Contentment	—	Anxiety
Pleasure	—	Pain

At least the bottom two are shared by most of the higher species of the animal world including man. They are primarily sensuous in energy relationship of stimulus and response. On the other hand, the upper three levels are characteristically induced by intellectual stimuli. Delight and disgust are characteristics of the aesthetic responses appreciated only at the human level. Joy and sorrow are emotional, but reflect the situational empathy of community in recognition of the drama of events and are characteristic of the human order alone.

The terms happiness and sadness are descriptive of an intellectual state produced by what could be called the "algebraic totality" of the other responses. All of the lower forms contribute to or detract from happiness. Properly speaking, it is an anthropomorphism to speak of a happy, joyful or delighted dog, though we often do, and it well expresses the response we observe when the master or mistress comes home after a long absence. It is more properly identified as a highly energetic response to memory stimulus in the sensual order of pleasure, though if described as happiness, as a measure of pleasure and contentment, such use would not be inappropriate.

Joy in particular has a spiritual connotation in the higher emotional response of man. A person can be joyous in time of hardship and even misery when the hardship is responsive to love in service performed for the beloved. Sorrow conversely reflects the deprivation of the beloved; both are concepts of man in an I—Thou context.

The nature of the joy/sorrow continuum is beautifully exemplified in St. John's account (Chapter 20) of the weeping Mary Magdalene at the tomb in deepest grief and sorrow. Not only was the beloved Master dead, but His body had been taken away. Then, in an instant, the one she had mistaken for the gardener called her by name and she recognized the risen Jesus. The transition from the depth of sorrow to the greatest joy occurred in microseconds!

Delight, although simply defined as a great joy or pleasure, connotes an intellectual/emotional response to an unanticipated pleasure—the intellectual aspect is essential. The fulfillment extends beyond expectation. It is the element of surprise, a prior intellectual assessment far exceeded, which is the critical ingredient of delight. At least in the natural order, it is limited to human beings. A child's Christmas, for instance, is characterized by delight. A dog has no corresponding response, though he savors a piece of candy at Christmas as much as a child. A human being is intellectually captivated by a delightful experience, whether it be coming upon a beautiful panorama, a breathtaking sunset, a gift of a flower from a loved one, or a sudden intellectual insight. The notion of delight is also ascribed to God. For example,

Psalm 149 expresses this aspect of His love for man: "For the Lord takes delight in His people. He crowns the poor with salvation. Let the Saints rejoice in their glory, shout for joy and take their rest." The antithesis of delight is dismay or disgust. Again, only human beings are subject to dismay or disgust.

If this analysis is acceptable, we must admit that the driving impulse in man, at his distinguishing level of activity, is of life form. Yet, it is essentially non-biologic. Experiments on the brain, through artificial stimuli, can induce sensations of pleasure and even euphoria and hallucinogenic drugs can likewise develop an exaggerated sense of real or pseudo-pleasurable awareness. Some have claimed this demonstrates the at-root, biochemical base, of man's intellectuality. What it demonstrates, in fact, is that the mechanism in the output stage of man's overall nervous system is biologic. No one would deny that. But the normal input stage, which has been preempted by the artificial stimuli, is not involved in the production. It would be analogous to claiming there was no open television transmission because closed circuit television is demonstrable. Man, in his normal operating state, responds to external stimuli by a judgmental process, unconsciously assigning various levels of "goodness of fit" of the stimuli to standards of the parameters of felicity, spiritual, intellectual, aesthetic, cultural, and biologic which he has developed internally during his life. This personal value appraisal, which guides the judgment, is intrinsic to the intending ego, the person one in fact, is. Its action is biologic at its interface with the material super-strate in man, but extends far beyond that interface in the intellectual and spiritual order which have no physical limitations to measure. These could be concepts of the mathematical, the symmetrical, the beautiful, and the good. But beyond this, the value appraisal points to the immateriality of man's most prized states! To be happy, joyous, delighted have only secondary relationship to our physical condition. It is our mental state which is most directly involved and measures our total felicity.

Along the same vein, man has, universally, a sense of the "holy." He has a sense of that which has transcendent value and is totally worthy of awe and worship. It certainly has always been present in all peoples and it is reflected naively in the animistic worship of the forces and forms of nature. The celestial bodies, the oceans, the forests and mountains, turbulent storms and the serenity of vast expanses evoke a sense of wonder well expressed earlier in the quotation of Einstein on the subject of religiousness and the scientist.

Again, this deeply sensed feeling is inexplicable except as it is universalized in that which is common to these phenomena, that which must undergird the manifestations and, of which, the manifestations are but faint and imperfect images. Deep inside all of us is a respect for proportionality of cause to effect. We sense that nothing can produce or give, in an effect, something which it does not itself possess in even greater degree than is exhibited in its emanation. If these natural phenomena are worthy of awe and wonder, how much more so must be that which produced them, which called them into being. Of what transcendent value, how holy, must be the Author of these things in themselves! How worthy of awe and wonder!

Three concepts are so intimately related in the mystery of being as to defy deep separate analysis. These three concepts are: life, love and holiness. The being of the created universe has its explanation only in the eternality of that supernal holiness which, in its exuberance of love and life, must, by its very essence, create, in endless proliferation, objects of its love, recipients of its life and reflections of its holiness and glory. And complete happiness, that goal of the rational creature, can find its attainment only in the rapturous possession of the holy and of giving itself totally to love and worship of the All Holy.

In a sense, all men seek God—the pleasure bent atheist as well as the mystic. That "Ultimate Concern" which Paul Tillich equates with God is an expression of man's inevitable choice of essential goals of his worldly existence. But that goal which each sees as of the greatest importance, of highest value, is a surrogate God which more or less approaches the reality of the True God, who is.

In a very real sense, the pagan idolatry, so continuously condemned in the Old Testament accounts, was symbolic of the more sophisticated, but no less actual, idolatry which would occupy man in the fullness of time. Each of us would place the pursuit of some limited, material end ahead of the infinite and the "All Holy." With Tillich, there appeared to be little difference—providing the pursuit was sincere. The point to be made here is not Tillich's, except in the oblique way that Tillich's thesis and conclusion pointed out the inevitability that there is the True God which we adorn with various masks and then worship falsely.

Putting aside for a moment the concept of life which we earlier examined in some detail, we should now consider "love," the other term in the trinity of characteristics which cannot be disassociated from the mystery of being or of analysis in that context separately from life and holiness. Love is the bond which unites life and holiness in being.

Life recognizes that which is holy and seeks to embrace it completely. Life seeks to encompass holiness within itself. The term "love," strictly speaking, should be reserved to that level of willed self-consciousness giving to the beloved in the I—Thou context of Martin Buber. When the lover is separated from the beloved there is a sense of loss, of unfulfilledness in its life until the bond has been reestablished. But even in the lowest form of life, the vegetal, there seems to be an inchoate seeking of the beloved—of attaining fruition as an expression of that compulsion of fulfillment which is closely akin to love itself. It is related to the categorical imperative of Kant, but at a more universal level than pure duty. In its universality, it is more passionate than intellectual. Love spans the entire spectrum of life. As with holiness and life, love must also have graduations implying a love greater than which, none can be conceived—a real, active, infinite, love which again must be the source of all love. The "Encompassing" of Karl Jaspers, expresses, symbolically, the idea of the outgoing, seeking, gathering, and fulfilling nature of the Deity. What He creates, He loves. And it is an unselfish love, a freely given love, an unexpecting, unexacting love. The Deity, the Infinite—the Totality of all being—lacks nothing. Yet, in His superabundance of love He eternally creates in love totally for love's sake. The return of love by His rational creatures can never approach the love which He bestows. His love can be and has been spurned. The potential maximum return might be that expressed by Simone Weil in *The Notebooks:*

> "It is not for me to love God. Let God love Himself through me as medium."

A channel must be built and a finite human bond established through which the energizing grace or love of God may flow. As we saw, in Christian theology Christ is that channel made necessary following the Fall which in this context was the deliberate destruction of the original channel by Adam's rejection. The channel found its new source on the human side of the abyss in Christ's humanity and was extended by Christ's Divinity to the Godhead itself. Each rational being forms an anchorage for the bond of love reflecting that being's own individuality and its own greatness or poverty of soul.

Love in the spiritual order is closely analogous to gravity in the material order. The strength of the attraction between beings varies inversely as the square of the "distance" between them and the sum of "quanta" of love possessed by each. The more intimate the association the greater the capacity for love and the stronger the bond of love between the beings. Religion in its true etymology is a tie-back from the creature to the Creator. If that tie is not love, if it is only fear-oriented, for instance, it is deficient and distorted.

The intimate relationship of being, life, love and holiness may be looked at in yet another way. As we consider these qualities in their highest possible state—that of infinite being, life, love, and holiness—all four would coalesce and become the single entity God. Thus we can say in strict reality God is Being, Life, Love and Holiness, the constant, essential Source of pure delight, paraphrasing Blake's definition of energy. The greater capacity that a created being has to attract and reflect this outpouring of divine energy, the more closely does that created form resemble the Source itself. If only a coarse and narrow band can be reflected, the creation has existence only as inert being. As broader and broader aspects are reflected, being plus life, being plus life plus love, being plus life plus love plus holiness that creature becomes more attracted to and attracted by the Source now cherished because more closely resembling that which it reflects. A stone, a tree, a worldly man, a grace-filled human soul would represent the comparable states. But here again there is to some extent a continuum within categories. Until a creature is able to relate love to that which is the holy and freely seeks the holy the attraction is not sufficient to assure ultimate union between that creature and the Source.

Similarly, as gravity is a form of energy inherent in all matter, love exhibited in the diffusion of God's grace is a form of energy inherent in all that possess life and is of the spirit. The love of God, synonomous and coessential with His creativeness may be likened to the gravitational field that exists everywhere in space and is the essential environment of matter. So love is the essential environment of life. The higher the life form, culminating in the purely spiritual, the more intense, the more personal, the more individualized, the more compelling this attractive energy bond becomes between individual created beings and between those beings and God Himself. Each rational being is a receptor of this energy-form able to convert it to a responsive, outgoing, reradiating impulse or perverting it to an inward, self-satisfying, love-diminishing force of opposite polarity. The rational will is the switch which determines the choice.

Beauty and goodness join with love, life, and the holy as

inseparable concepts. Beauty is defined here as that quality of a given situational set which provokes in the beholder a sense of delight at the harmony and appropriateness of the given set in the given situation. There is subjectivity indeed, but also, and importantly, an inherent objectivity to which the subject responds. The beautiful situational set has beauty in potential even though no one experiences it. Goodness here is used in the utilitarian sense of an internalized ethical attitude which seeks to know and follow positive norms of decency in all human behavior because that is man's duty as a human being. They are a "beauty" and a "goodness" that John Dewey would recognize. Yet Dewey and his like-thinking contemporaries believed and vociferously taught that there was no necessary connection between that quality and that attitude and the recognition of the holy. They sought to eliminate "the holy" from the vocabulary except in a purely poetic sense. For them, beauty and goodness had a reality in being which the holy did not possess.

We have said the concepts are inseparable. How can we demonstrate this? Both experienced beauty and goodness require an intelligence capable of differentiating the presence of these attributes from their absence and of arriving at graduations of each. Something is "more beautiful" than something else, a "better" than something else and there is a consensus among men in general terms of these graduations. Men experience awe at extreme levels of these qualities even in the natural order and they tend to blend together. One may say that at the extreme, delight becomes awe, goodness and beauty meet in the holy. Mahatma Gandhi was an example—while far from being physically prepossessing he was considered a good and beautiful person—beautiful because good by any human test. He was an object of love and reverence by his followers—a "holy man" though his arena was more political than religious. A collection of assorted molecules can be attractive to look at in many forms but becomes beautiful only when the intellect in its aesthetic grasp beholds the total composition and relationship of parts to whole, and judges that the object, whether it be a sunset or a human being, reflects a perfection and the intellect responds in delight or reverence.

If now we separate goodness and beauty to one side and deny that there is the holy, it becomes purely a matter of pragmatic appeal as to what they in fact are. Their very existence as legitimate concepts is suspect. Gandhi becomes a very foolish little old man. It is because Gandhi was recognized as a symbol of

the indominatable spirit of humanity in its highest expressions
and because he did seek out and freely follow those goals which
were his ultimate concern that he was revered. If beauty and
goodness are revered it is because they intimate and are symbolic of the holy which lies behind the beauty and goodness
we experience. Reverence is due only to that which is holy
at least in symbol.

One could contrast Gandhi and Karl Marx in this context.
For the Marx of *Das Kapital* there was nothing in the spirit
of man which impelled the individual to conquer the heights.
There was only the need and drive to advance and survive in
the economic environment. There is no delight, no beauty, no
love or goodness or reverence in the concept because the holy
is totally absent—in fact, it is a despicable myth. The good and
the beautiful perforce became a dream for children and the pre-
economic naive. Marx's life was pathetic, Gandhi's heroic in
a lexicon of man as a being designed to love the good and
the beautiful, in pursuit of that which is the holy. Marx was
heroic and Gandhi pathetic in the proper language of class struggle, where beauty and goodness and holiness are non-existent.
Yet, even in political and economic terms, Gandhi likely accomplished more for more people than Marx. The final confrontation of the philosophies represented by these two lies just
ahead. Again the conflict represents the insistent dialectic.

As we examine these concepts: beauty, felicity, love, goodness and holiness we become aware of their independent reality in spite of their abstractness. They are different from the
qualities redness or hardness or bigness which are similarly abstract concepts. But here in this latter group we are fully aware
that apart from material objects they have no existence, no independent reality—the concepts are all subject to physical definitions and norms. On the other hand the former concepts have
a spiritual quality about them. They are all concepts pleasing
to our intellect at its outermost power of comprehension. Love
and beauty have a passionate quality to them, beauty in an aesthetic, love in an emotional way. Yet even in the longing to possess the beloved and the beautiful which constitutes the passion
there is the intellectual recognition that the essence which constitutes the lovableness and the beautiful in our immediate object remains beyond our possession. We grasp a rose and admire
its beauty but we cannot analyze that which is beauty—we are
pleased by its configuration, its color, its fragrance, its texture
and all these things put together, yet the summation does not
equate to the intuition of beauty inherent in the rose we hold.

The human response to the intuition is what constitutes beauty or love. Here we have a condition reminiscent of Kant's thing-in-itself but at a different level. The human response is evoked by that which the intellect recognizes as possessing beauty—though the "things-in-themselves" evoking this response are of infinite variety. A crystal can be beautiful, an idea can be beautiful—in fact, one can say that for any object to become appreciated as beautiful it must become idealized. Yet there is "out there" that which the human being recognizes as possessing beauty. There is an objective concept "beauty" to which various intuitions are compared in judging beauty in a given case. As we noted earlier the response beauty is a constituent of the response love.

The concepts goodness and holiness are equally responses to intuitions, but completely beyond the material order where beauty and love have well recognized material components which however must be "dematerialized" through the intellect and compared with the ideal before acceptance. Holiness is the apotheosis of goodness. We ascribe identification of the quality "good" in the moral sense to the will, but as we saw there is no less a matter of judgment required in the concepts beauty and love, and the intellect must similarly intuit the presence of "good" in objects presented to it before judging. "Moral goodness" or perhaps better, the pursuit of ethical perfection, which is what people think of in terms of "being good," is only a particular expression of the Good.

The difference between the pair goodness and holiness and the pair beauty and love is that properly speaking there is no sense input whatsoever in developing the former terms. In nature the terms can only be applied to man—to man as a spiritual being. The terms have definitive meaning only in the context of the perceived condition of individuals before God. When we say of a young child "he is a good boy or girl" we mean that he or she behaves as a normal, unaffected child reasonably ought to behave. The possibility of evil in a child is repugnant; they are deemed innocent. We are usually more reserved in application of the term to adults; it is most used in the past tense. He or she was a good person—The cards have all been played, the chips cashed and that is the consensus. They tried to be "good" people during their lives. For the adult the evil is always a possibility. We are even more reserved in applying the term "holy" to an individual. This term implies goodness in a heroic, even supernatural degree. Still we have a definite intuition that in the world there are good people and even holy people in the sense used here. Even in an age which has denied sin, we recognize that there are evil persons in the world. These are well nigh universal judgments. They are not empty expressions. Goodness and holiness are qualities which have a real existence among people in the world in distinction from evil.

In the insistent dialectic it is this ubiquitous free choice facing men between the good and holy on the one hand and the evil on the other which provides the inescapable tension. The tension is real and the forces producing it are real; no sane man escapes them. Yet without the existence of a personal God they are absurd concepts and man folly incarnate for having inexplicably subjected himself to this crucifixion, a sacrificial victim for no cause. Sanity becomes the worst insanity.

Among the "human peculiar" characteristics which strongly influence moral concepts is the seeking after justice. The concept "justice" is normative in its application at a level which is almost totally intellectual. While goodness connotes an inherent attractiveness in that which is good, or apparently good, justice strikes a harsher note. Justice obliges a course of action which may be distasteful. A debt must be paid. In the natural order, only man is concerned with justice. While animals instinctively seek that which is physically good for them it is inconceivable that they seek justice in their behavior. Physical power to control a situation is the sole criterion in animal behavior and when a man resorts to that criterion it is recognized as brutal in the true sense of that word. Other men label the action tyrannical or cruel and unjust. Here, in justice, Kant's categorical imperative in morality stands out most clearly. An obligation in justice demands a response from pure duty, and is possible only in self-determining, rational beings.

What is the source of the sense of justice? The most primitive tribes now living have codes of justice and methods of deciding what is just. Some of the earliest written records concern action in pursuit of justice, simple bills of account for instance. We are inclined to say, perhaps, going to Locke's or Hobbes' form of the social contract, that survival in society demands justice. The concept, justice, goes straight to man's rationality and in its background that rationality sets up "the enforcer," the "being toward which man stands in awe," God implicit in Lock's contract, the government explicit in Hobbe's. Yet even in Hobbe's contract God is implicit. The mortal God, government, "The Leviathan" ultimately rested upon the "immortal God" in the chain of obligation.

Justice demands a supreme arbiter to whom all must submit,

one in whom justice is absolute, beyond whom there is no appeal. If there is justice at all, there is an absolute justice, the perfect norm, and a judge supremely competent to decide. It is in a denial of justice in any form that nihilism and its ugly offspring, tyranny and anarchy take their roots.

Justice was notably missing in the slogans of the French Revolutionaries and of modern Marxism as well. In the first instance the announced aim was "equality," in the second, economic sufficiency, which might or might not include justice. Equality under the law, the avowed American aim does reflect justice because "the law" implies "just law" and a lawgiver who seeks to be supremely just. An unjust lawgiver is, or ought to be, recognized as a tyrant. It is apparent that apart from an infinite personal God the concept of justice, qua justice, does not make sense. At the governmental level, the truncated Hobbesian contract, without God at the apex of the structure of obligation, the state is the supreme arbiter. At the very best, justice here is that of the benign establishment under a covenant between unequals. The individual members of society have "no rights" except as the establishment elects to abide by the covenant. The efficacy reverts to the animal level of ability to exercise power in a situation. The rationality extends only to the utilitarian, the pragmatic. What is good for the establishment becomes the norm; if that is "unjust" toward a particular class of citizens as the unborn, the old, the defective—those with no voice—so much the worse for them, but in any event there is no "evil" involved.

The problem of evil has no existence outside of the context of free will on the part of creatures over against God, yet it is everywhere acknowledged. Kant's moral imperative posited that since there is moral evil, there must be God. Much is made of the problem of evil by those who, like Camus, wish to avoid any acknowledgement of an infinite Supreme Being to whom an obligation of obedience is owed by man. Obviously if there is no God there is no evil nor good. Man has been described as the animal who can choose evil. We might better say in the positive direction, man is the creature who can choose God. Implicit in the idea of freedom is the absence of coercion to obey. Evil exists only because the creature elects to disobey, to assert itself in opposition, to be free from God's will. Since God is infinite Goodness the All-holy, anything contrary to His will has an opposite negative sense and, lacking good will, is by definition evil.

The coexistence of the infinite goodness of God and lack

of goodness among His earthly creatures is a manifestation of God's mercy as to the time and space condition of human creatures who lack the total decisiveness of intellectual action which would be characteristic of the pure intellect of spiritual beings. An angel which elects to use its freedom contrary to God's will is irrevocably dedicated forever to oppose God's will; time is not an element in its activity. Continued existence of such malevolent forms is a consequence of God's justice, also infinite. Each creature must bear the consequences of its free choice. It will in any event serve God's ends.

There is not a kingdom of evil as an entity opposed to the kingdom of Good. There is only a testing of a creatures' willingness, freely selected, to conform to his Creator or to refuse. To the extent that some choose evil, the creatures are permitted to operate as a part of that continued testing. They are confirmed in their malevolence as the good are confirmed in their benevolence—the one forever testifying to the other as to what would have been, had their choice been otherwise. The evil, lacking goodness, are only evidential of the imperfection of creatures and of God's willingness to provide a freedom of choice. Who would deny that to be given a free choice constitutes a superior status? A free condition for man is better than one of pure determinism. God can be truly loved only by a creature who is free and freely willing to surrender its prerogative of self-service for love. It is so even in the human order. Love implies a willingness to give oneself to the beloved without reserve. In symmetry, hate becomes the response of the evil. In the defiance of Sisyphus, as interpreted by Camus, is seen the pure hatred of those who rebel against the love of God and the self-surrender that love implies. They will to be free to hate without reserve. God does not condemn the evil ones, they condemn themselves freely from His love with full knowledge of their refusal of the intrinsic good God is. Contrary to Camus' conclusions, one cannot envision Sisyphus happy only arrogant, irrational, completely mad in his defiant hate.

Only that which is good can be truly loved; in fact love has been defined also as the response of a being to that which it observes to be good in another. The bond of love between two beings is the mutual response to the good each sees in the other. Good here includes all attributes of being which the judgment identifies as positive traits of being. Thus for example the beautiful as opposed to the ugly, virtue versus vice, order versus chaos, wisdom versus ignorance. The lover seeks to possess that which is loved and there is a tension of desire until that possession is complete. Now God is the totality and unification of all positive attributes of being. What the creature perceives as good in another creature is the reflection of the essence of God. That is, the attraction to any positive attribute in a created being results from a recognition in that being of a "God-like" quality and that quality is perforce an object of "love" which we must seek. A creature must seek what it perceives as the good, although its perception may be deceived or even perverted. In a rational creature the deliberate perversion of perception of a good constitutes moral evil because it is a form of idolatry. A substitute or illegitimate goal is made a god which, since other than the true God, its adoration is contrary to the creature's own fundamental nature.

God is as He is. It is not possible that He could be otherwise. His total infinitude envelops that which is possible. His being defines that which is possible. While at the human level we can conceive of God as being otherwise than as He is, in fact, we inevitably do so because of our own limitations; that does not imply that our conceptions in fact represent the God who is the only possible God. Anselm's definition "That being greater than which no being can be conceived" expresses the situation well. We are either in a case of shortfall though right as far as we go, as Amselm suggests, or we are erroneous *in toto*. Neither situation provides a "possible" God. God could be neither greater nor less than He is and be God. The God of modernism is a case in point which impacts on the moral concept. In modernism in its widest sense God is conceived of as a dynamic will to being, little more personal than Spinoza's loveless God where relations with man constitute mere encounters in being, a meeting of two "its" striving to become thou's to each other.

Under this popular concept both God and man receive enhancement through a becoming mode of actuality. God is akin to the groping deity of Hegel relying on his creature man to provide him his own realization of being. A dependent God, it reflects Scheler's "partnership pantheism." In none of these concepts, which find their roots in Kant's idealism, can we discern the compassionate, personal God who "so loved us that in the fullness of time He sent His only-begotten Son into the world . . ." As we have seen earlier, philosophically, the growing, groping "God in process" is a logical monstrosity, a necessarily infinite eternal being forced into a necessarily limited enclosure. The concept's attractiveness to modern man lies in its inference of limited power, even proneness to error. God somehow becomes a sharer in our own human weakness. There are no absolutes. This idea was also inherent in Whitehead's God in the concept of a "Consequential nature" as distinct from God's immutable "primordial nature"—God is somehow infinite in eternity yet developing in space/time.

These constructs are attempts to describe God not as He must be but as we would have Him, a comforting anodine to us in our stress-filled existence. God becomes, like us, a being in predicament. But what a strange and tortured as well as torturous path it is. We provide a deity in our own image because we do not wish to accept what God has told us of Himself through the world around us, through His revelations and through His interventionary acts in the world. We wish to stretch an existential philosophy into theology without admitting that we are doing so. This is far worse than what the medievals are accused of, combining philosophy and theology. The medievals were well aware of what they were doing; we appear not to be. This modern view asserts, God acts through process, therefore He must be process. It deprives God of His preeminence of being and it cannot explain the basic intellectual attraction man has toward the perfection which is God. We wish to substitute fellowship for filiation and companionship with God for dependency.

We have substituted for the being God is, the mechanism we conceive as His methodology. The concept of God, the very essence of all holiness and goodness and love and beauty, of infinite justice united in His ineffable infinity of omniscient being vanishes. The moral force vanishes at the same time.

The matrix of morality is, then, comprised of all these interrelated concepts plus many more of lower significance. Each person evaluates all of these in the context of his own life situation and directs his life accordingly. The individual "good will" of the person is reflected in the handling of his intellection as he chooses his individual way through life. He can will to dwell on the positive or negative on selected parts of the concepts. The probabilities are that if one habitually dwells on the negative side—thinks only of the animal satisfactions, never thinks of his relationship with God or with his fellowman in the context of justice and love, he will eventually reflect that thought in his overt behavior patterns. From the religious viewpoint such an individual by his thought processes would have been behaving immorally from the beginning. For the sociologist, the morality of the individual behavior patterns begins at the stage of action. Obviously the latter reflects the former, and in a society the average level of what is called morality reflects in large part the conditioned thinking of the individuals in that society on the total moral matrix. The "conscience, collectively, is the summation of the individual consciences." How finely tuned the individual's conscience is, reflects both his environment and his habitual attitude during life. The moral "climate" in which the conscience is formed is crucial. The trends in the current moral climate are discussed in the following chapter.

Chapter 16

CURRENT TRENDS IN THE
CONCEPT OF MORALITY

One of the things which is quite noticeable in the literature of current sociology, psychology, history, political science and other disciplines of the general liberal arts grouping is a blending together, almost a grafting of Marxist social theory on a base of logical positivism. The resulting world view—almost a consensus of the "liberal" intellectual community—reflects the current manifestation of the old secular humanism of Voltaire. It is a nameless philosophy. It surfaces as a philosophic attitude and not a formal movement and certainly not a school of thought. But, it permeates the various texts and collections of readings offered to students. The philosophy plays down the unpalatable aspects of the class conflict, the harsh materialism, and the valuelessness of human life of both the earlier schools. The blend is scarcely less materialistic than pure Marxism but it is more sophisticated in its urging of hedonistic convenience rather than dialectic economic struggle as the source of cultural change. Like its parent stocks, this hybrid materialism uses the passionate denial of a metaphysics based on a personal supreme being as an adhesive to keep the disparate parts together. Posing to be broadly rational, this hybrid is really just as narrow in its empirical epistemology as Marx, Proudon or Russell. Behind its sugary disguise it presents a dismal assessment of that strange creature man. This materialistic dogma is scarcely less pessimistic in end point than Camus' existentialism—and—it lacks Camus' honesty. If that is really all man's life amounts to, the only appropriate question can be, "How soon to end it?"

The president of the American Psychological Association, Donald T. Campbell takes a look at current psychological literature. He said in an address at a recent A.P.A. convention in Chicago:

> All the dominant modern psychologies are individualistically hedonistic, explaining all human behavior in terms of individual pleasure and pain, individual needs and drives. . . .They do not only describe people

as selfishly motivated, but they also either implicitly or explicitly imply that people ought to be so.

Campbell does not agree and he said, in effect, let us admit that our biological side provides a bias in favor of self-seeking, uninhibited behavior and then let us reinforce the ethical values "underlying the wisdom in the recipes for living that tradition has supplied us." As we have seen, that tradition responds to a demand of normal human nature. This demand is presently being studiously ignored.

This materialistically-inspired psychology is not new. Carl Jung wrote about it during the 1930's as follows:

> The spirit of the age cannot be compassed by the processes of human reason. It is an inclination, an emotional tendency that works upon weaker minds, through the unconscious, with an overwhelming force of suggestion that carries them along with it. To think otherwise than our contemporaries think is somehow illegitimate and disturbing. It is even indecent, morbid, or blasphemous, and therefore socially dangerous for the individual. He is stupidly swimming against the social current. Just as, formerly, the assumption was unquestionable that everything that exists takes its rise from the creative will of a God who is spirit, so the nineteeth century discovered the equally unquestionable truth that everything arises from material causes. Today, the psyche does not build itself a body, but, on the contrary, matter by chemical action, produces the psyche. This reversal of outlook would be ludicrous if it were not one of the outstanding features of the spirit of the age. It is the popular way of thinking and therefore it is decent, reasonable, scientific and normal. The mind must be thought to be an epiphenomenon of matter. The same conclusion is reached even if we say not "mind" but "psyche," and, in place of matter, speak of brain, hormones, instincts, or drives. To grant the substantiality of the soul or psyche is repugnant to the spirit of the age, for to do so would be heresy. . . .
>
> This being the state of affairs, we must ask ourselves how the spirit of the age attains such an uncanny power. It is without doubt a psychic phenomenon of the greatest importance—at all events,

a prejudice so deeply rooted that until we give it proper consideration we cannot even approach the problem of the psyche. . . .

If we were conscious of the spirit of the age, we should know why we are so inclined to account for everything on physical grounds; we should know that it is because, up till now, too much was accounted for in terms of the spirit. This realization would at once make us critical of our bias. We should say: most likely we are now making as serious an error on the other side. We delude ourselves with the thought that we know much more about matter than about a "metaphysical" mind, and so we overestimate physical causation and believe that it alone affords us a true explanation of life. But matter is just as inscrutable as mind. As to the ultimate, we can know nothing. Only when we admit this do we return to a state of equilibrium. . . .

The modern preference for physical grounds of explanation leads, as already remarked, to a "psychology without the psyche." I mean, it leads to the view that the psyche is nothing but a product of biochemical processes. As for a modern scientific psychology which starts from the mind, as such, there simply is none. No one today would venture to found a scientific psychology upon the postulate of an independent psyche that is not determined by the body. The idea of spirit in, and for itself, of a self-contained world-system of the spirit that is the only adequate postulate for the belief in autonomous, individual souls, is extremely unpopular with us, to say the least. . . .

If we keep this in mind, we can perhaps summon up the courage to consider the possibility of a "psychology with the psyche." That is, of a field of study based on the assumption of an autonomous psyche. We need not be alarmed at the unpopularity of such an undertaking, for to postulate mind is no more fantastic than to postulate matter. Since we have literally no idea of the way in which what is psychic can arise from physical elements, and yet cannot deny the reality of psychic events, we are free to frame our assumptions the other way about for once, and to hold that the psyche arises from a spiritual principle which is as inaccessible to our understanding as matter. To be sure, this will not be a modern psychology, for to be modern is to deny such a possibility. For better or worse, therefore, we must turn back to the teachings of our forefathers, for it was they who made such assumptions. The ancient view held that spirit was essentially the life of the body, the life-breath, or a kind of life-force which assumed spatial and corporeal form at birth or after conception, and left the dying body again after the final breath. . . .

It would all be so much simpler if we could only deny the existence of the psyche. But here we are with our immediate experiences of something that is—something that has taken root in the midst of our measurable, ponderable, three-dimensional reality, that differs bafflingly from this in every respect and in all its parts, and yet reflects it. The psyche may be regarded as a mathematical point and at the same time as a universe of fixed stars. It is small wonder, then, if, to the unsophisticated mind, such a paradoxical being borders on the divine. If it occupies no space, it has no body. Bodies die, but can something invisible and incorporeal disappear? What is more, life and psyche existed for me before I could say "I," and when this "I" disappears, as in sleep or unconsciousness, life and psyche still go on, as our observation of other people and our own dreams inform us. Why should the simple mind deny, in the face of such experiences, that the "soul" lives in a realm beyond the body? I must admit that I can see as little nonsense in this so-called superstition as in the findings of research regarding heredity or the basic instincts. (Jung, 1961).

An article in the *Scientific American*—April 1976 by Dorothy Nelkin under the title "The Science Textbook Controversy" illustrates the alleged problem of science-religious conflict. The article specifically treats of the rejection of a social systems curriculum: *Man: A Course of Study* (MACOS) funded by the National Science Foundation in large part. The program was begun in 1963 and generally introduced into the public school system in the late 1960's and early 1970's. Ms. Nelkin states that by 1974 the course had found its way into 1700 schools in 47 states. It then was successfully attacked by religious groups so that by 1975 the sales of MACOS had declined by 70 percent. The article is written in a tone sympathetic to the educators in the social sciences and yet it points out the dilemma faced by those educators in making the material palatable to the parents who object to the irreligious flavor of the works. The article citing examples of the material in MACOS demonstrates that the social science educators were, in fact, presenting a relativistic viewpoint of morals under the guise of science. Ms. Nelkin states:

> The development of the social-science curriculum, titled MAN: A COURSE OF STUDY (MACOS), was launched in 1963 when a group of scholars from the Education Development Center, Inc. (then Education Services, Inc.), of Cambridge, Mass., received a grant from the National Science Foundation to develop an integrated program of precollege social-science courses. Until MACOS was introduced the teaching of social science in the public schools had consisted mostly of descriptive presentations of American history. MACOS, designed for children in the fifth and sixth grades, asks three questions: What is human about human beings? How did they get that way? How can they become more so?
>
> The MACOS curriculum relies on studies of animal behavior and of the culture of the Netsilik Eskimos to explore questions about the nature of human beings, patterns of social interaction and child rearing, and the development of a culture's total view of the world. To the social scientists who worked on the MACOS curriculum the study of animal behavior provided a provocative metaphor to illuminate features of human behavior. The study of a traditional tribal culture showed how human beings as well as animals adapt to a particular environment; in order for the Netsilik to survive in an environment with limited food resources they practice infanticide and senilicide as means of controlling the population. MACOS *suggested* that in some societies such practices, disturbing as they would be in our own culture, *were functional, and that neither behavior, nor belief, have an absolute value apart from their social and physical context.* (Emphasis this writer).

The MACOS authors were flagrantly guilty of Whitehead's "fallacy of misplaced concreteness"—of drawing conclusions far beyond their data. The concluding statement that "neither behavior nor beliefs have an absolute value apart from their social and physical context" is not a scientific conclusion. It is, purely and simply, a moral judgment gratuitously thrown to the intended fifth and sixth grade pupils. Anyone with the slightest background in the history of ethics recognizes the means-ends justification in morality being proposed here. Murder is justified to limit population if the pressures are sufficient. Hitler used the same idea to eliminate the "inferior" race to obtain *lebensraum* for the "superior" race. And the concept does not end there. If murder is justified by circumstance, then obviously, given sufficient "pressure," embezzlement, larsony, rape or only cheating on examinations are clearly not to be absolutely condemned as immoral. The authors of the text were patently guilty of willfully making moral judgments well beyond the proper field of scientific education and projecting that judgment to a highly susceptible age group. Ms. Nelkin apologizes in a backhanded sort of way:

> Perhaps the most difficult concept for scientists to convey to those who are not scientists is the delicate balance between certainty and doubt that is so essential to the scientific spirit. Textbooks in particular tend to convey a message of certainty to the nonspecialist. In the process of simplifying concepts, findings may become explanations, explanations may become axioms and tentative judgments may become definitive conclusions. Few textbooks are careful to stress the distinction between fact and interpretation or to suggest that intuition and speculation actually guide the development of scientific concepts.

In the Nelkin article, the contrast was made sharply between the creationist religious viewpoint and the evolutionist scientific viewpoint as the central matter of the dispute. While the creationists were largely responsible for the decline of the MACOS projects, the fact is, that the texts should be highly objectionable to anyone interested in the preservation of morality as a human value. If environmental pressure and peer group acceptance establish moral criteria with no reference to normative basic levels of human behavior as human, morality ceases to have any meaning whatsoever. Ms. Nelkin continues:

Fundamentalist textbook critics are particularly dis-
tressed by the teaching of modern biology and social
science because of the *implication that moral values
are relative* and because of the *denial* that an omnipotent and omniscient force determines human development and behavior. They argue that emphasizing
the genetic similarities between human beings and
other animals may encourage animal-like and socially-
dangerous behavior. One creationist stated: "If man
is an evolved animal, then the morals of the barn-
yard or jungle are more natural. . .the artificially imposed restrictions of marital chastity and marital
fidelity—instead of monogamy, why not promiscuity
and polygamy?. . .Self-preservation is the first law of
nature; only the fittest will survive. Be the cock-of-
the-walk and the king-of-the-mountain. Eat, drink and
be merry for life is short and that's the end." (Emphasis this writer.).

The critics are correct in the assessment of the concepts
fostered by the texts and of the results, if taken at face value,
by the students. Again, this writer objects to the idea that only
the religious "fundamentalists" are concerned. The texts would
be contrary to any religious orientation except perhaps to a very
bland deism, in which case, there is no concern of God for
man's behavior. If there is a personal God who does judge man's
behavior then these criteria are unacceptable. If there is no personal God, then there are no criteria in behavior except man's
own desires of the moment, in which case the "scientists" have
not gone far enough. The problem here does not stem from
evolutionist theory—an infinite God could have selected that
route if He desired—but from a denial of man's responsibility
before God for his behavior.

There have been deliberate attempts to show that the religious viewpoint is unscientific. Part III of this work should have
dismissed that fallacy. The article by Ms. Nelkin tries to skirt
the issue and she says:

Nevertheless, it is not accurate to dismiss the critics
of science textbooks as being merely an antiscience
fringe group. Creationism is an unlikely combination
of religion and science in which theological beliefs
are conveyed in a context of research monographs
and scientific societies. And most of the people who

have been working against MACOS do not deny that
science is a useful activity. They object primarily to
an impersonal educational bureaucracy that fails to
represent their interests and that insults their personal
beliefs. They are not reacting against science so much
as resisting its image as an infallible source of truth
that denies their sense of place in the universe.

But then she adds:

In these reports, the textbook critics are part of
the romantic resistance to science that is reflected
in the popularity of astrology, mystical cults and the
imaginary cosmologies of Immanuel Velikovsky and
Erich Von Daniken. They are also part of a political
resistance to science that is reflected in increased social action against innovation and in the demands
for lay participation in scientific and technical decisions. As questions that are normally resolved by
professional consensus are brought into the political
arena, and as democratic values such as freedom of
choice, equality and fairness enter into science policy,
the consequences of such resistance to science may
be painful.

This statement is insulting, unintentionally, no doubt, but that
is no excuse. In the first place, what is being resisted is not
science by any stretch of the word. What is being resisted is
the unjustified insertion of unfounded moral judgments into
a scientific curriculum. The implication is that the scientists
are going to have to tolerate the intrusion of the lay mind in
scientific circles. The facts seem to be, rather, that if the scientific educationists wish to pass off moral judgments as scientific conclusions they had best consider carefully that zone where
their competence as scientists ends and their private ideas on
the desirable world order begins. The second area contains no
shelter of scientific privilege and it is there that most of the
controversy can be found.

It is not a romantic resistance to science which is involved
but a very down to earth recognition that there are, in the scientific community and particularly in the behavioral sciences, those
people who wish to promote a materialistic and secular humanistic view of life. They should not be given any forensic
privilege at public expense to promote these views under the

guise of teaching scientific curriculum. If they wish to promote their ideas in professional papers before professional groups very well, but in texts, whether publicly supplied or forced upon undergraduate students by the mandatory book lists, the subject matter should stick to the proper field of concern. If that includes speculation into the areas not yet well defined, all of the competing theoretical approaches should be covered and they should be covered very carefully indeed.

A little reflection will reveal the difficulty involved in drawing norms of human behavior from parallels in animal behavior. Animals are controlled by instinct. Normal animal behavior is established by repeated observations of how the animal behaves under various circumstances. A rather tight envelope can be drawn for their normality. A healthy animal is quite predictable in behavior. This is not true of human beings to any great extent. Here, instead of instinct, there is the individual will which judges and directs an act based on an intellectual evaluation of the circumstances.

Of course, the animal passions in man enter into the evaluation. The expression "good will" indicates that the individual so described has habitually placed the various aspects of the problem in perspective and acts as he "ought" to as a human being as judged by his contemporaries in the culture. Now, actual human behavior under *quite similar circumstances* can and does extend *through a tremendous range* from the most savage cruelty to the most sublime self-sacrifice. An envelope of behavior patterns is virtually useless.

But further, if we say that normal human behavior is determined by observation of actual behavior of human beings in their society, then in an "evil" society, the "evil" are behaving with "good will" as normal human beings and the "good" are abnormal. By moving from situation to situation, obviously any level can be established as normal—"good" and "evil" in these circumstances defined only by acceptability—yet we intuitively know that this is not so. The historic villains and evil tyrants are well recognized universally and so are the great "saints" of all cultures. The facts of universal recognition of levels of evil and heroism suggest strongly that the basic standards of human behavior are not established by peer group approval or environment but by absolute standards in terms of good and evil and not merely customary and deviant. The variability within environments, in fact, demands that the ultimate standards are not just a question of environment.

A true moral code is not reflected by analogy in animal

behavior. It is certainly true that force of circumstances will cause individuals and groups to behave in ways which would be under ordinary conditions recognized as immoral. The recent celebrated case of cannibalism by survivors of a plane crash high in the Andes is an instance. Specifically, in that case, the behavior toward which the world grimaced in disgust was very likely, in fact, not immoral. There was no violence done by the actors to themselves or to other human beings. There was only a case of cadavers being put to emergency beneficial use. Deep space travel would likely involve the same type of situation but in a more sophisticated way. There is no comparison in malice between those acts and deliberately taking innocent life. Murder, for convenience or for the sake of assuring adequate food supply, to the survivors in future months or years which MACOS smiled on approvingly, is a very different thing.

A popular teaching technique and a third generation product of John Dewey's philosophy of education is called "Value Clarification," or just V.C. The term was coined by Simon, Howe and Kirschenbaum in their book *Value Clarification, a Handbook of Practical Strategies for Teachers and Students,* (N.Y., Hart, 1972). V.C. offers this same idea that there are fundamentally "no right answers"—or, perhaps better, "no wrong answers"— only what is "right" or "wrong" for the individual under the given circumstances. Actions would be taken for peer group approval. This is the criteria for the "crowd" in Reisman's "Other Directed Man." The aim of the book is to spread that concept in the most effective way. Values have no other meaning. Along with other pet educational gimmicks such as: "Sensitivity Training," "Sociobiology," and "Situational Ethics," the emphasis is purely in the experimental biological level and degrading to the concept of man. It aims at destroying the tradition which Campbell praised.

All this is done in the face of clear, contrary directions provided by surveys of the parents' own desires. In a Gallup poll taken in January, 1976, the following question "Would you favor or oppose instruction in the schools that would deal with morals or moral behavior?" was presented to 1,538 adults, 18 years or older. The results were:

	National	No Children in School	Public School Parents	Parochial School Parents
Favor	79	76	84	85
Oppose	15	17	12	13
Don't Know	6	7	4	2

The reason is apparent in the results of another series of polls by Gallup. The last one was taken concurrently with the one above. The question, "Do you think people in general today lead as good lives honest and moral—as they used to?" The results were:

Year	Yes	No	No Opinion
1976	30	66	4
1965	39	52	9
1952	47	46	7

Jeffrey Hart in his syndicated column wrote in 1973:

> In its December edition, *The Libertarian Forum,* a journal of libertarian conservatism, comments on a debate in which I was involved concerning the legalization of marijuana. The Libertarian Forum takes the position that "every person" has the right "to order his own life in his own way," and it reasons from that assumption to the conclusion that not only marijuana but also other drugs such as heroin should be legalized too. . . .
>
> Is it satisfactory even as usually qualified: that every person has the right to order his life as he sees fit, as long as he does not directly injure someone else, and as long as he does not limit someone else's freedom to do the same?
>
> My objection is that it leaves out the entire dimension of community. Now a community is more than a collection of separate individuals each ordering his life as he sees fit. A community also has a collective existence, embodies a "way of life," a set of agreements on the way things should be done, and, by extension, a set of agreements on the way they should not be done.
>
> And I myself know of no ethical principle that enjoins the majority from attempting to protect its way of life, the quality of its collective existence, against the desires of the minority. I would in principle only require that the majority not be capricious: that its decisions, as the Constitution provides, be "deliberate."
>
> There can also be no doubt that the proliferation of pornography has affected the quality of community life both here and in Europe. You cannot walk through

Times Square or Piccadilly Circus without offense to the eye: and the stuff has penetrated to the newsstand in even the smaller cities and towns. Again, though there is a lot of legal shilly-shallying in the United States, it seems reasonable to me that a community or a nation ought to be able, should it so wish, to ban the stuff out of hand. And the same would apply to obvious pornography such as the movies "Deep Throat" and "Last Tango."

The problem is this has been created by the evolution of modern society. In an earlier day, custom and tradition would have applied all the restraint required. A news dealer or a theater operator dealing in the stuff would have been ostracized and driven out of business. Under modern conditions, because of mobility, anonymity, population size, and so on, these older sanctions have become ineffective. Yet I see no principled objection to having tough laws fill the gap. The framers of the First Amendment assuredly intended no such situation as now prevails, in which the balance has been tipped drastically in favor of individual license, and against community quality.

No, I do not myself think that an individual ought to be free to "order his life as he sees fit." Rather, the defense of community values is a legitimate function of government and law. Acting through its government, a community or a nation ought to be able to determine the modes according to which it wishes to live. The libertarian position simply omits the entire dimension of community from its fundamental axiom.

Hart is taking Hobbes' answer to the problem of how society exists and that is through strong government. But is strong government capable of performing what is asked of it if there is no moral sense in the body politic or in the mass of the people? The negative answer is increasingly apparent to the man in the street if not to those in the academic arena. The answer flows from what we have just seen. Man himself must control himself. Government can only take care of the exceptional case and cannot police all men in all societies. A governmentally-imposed "morality" is no morality. The essence of morality is its free acceptance. Yet, government control to bring about a climate conducive to morality is clearly within its powers.

All men to some extent experience the tension brought about by the internal conflict of what man would like to do biologically and what he knows he ought to do as a complete human being. Two conclusions seem derivable from the foregoing considerations. First, clearly if there is no God, there is little basis for morality or a moral law. There can be the state fiat and the policeman's club but there can be no obligation, in justice, toward our fellow man. No reason for man to behave in any way other than his current inclinations dispose him. Appeal to fairness, to equality, to fraternity, to economic solidarity fall short when opportunity and desire make their appearance on the scene. "I want to do it and I can get away with it, so why not. I am most certainly not my brother's keeper. There is no such thing as right and wrong. I owe only the duty to myself to get mine now." Moral law vanishes and coercive force takes over.

Second, it is a fact that there have been moral codes, throughout history. There has been a pervasive sense of justice and of right or wrong—even though many times violated. This fact is strongly supportive of a virtually innate recognition by man that there is a Supreme Arbiter—that there is a perfection in goodness and justice and that there will be certain retribution for evil acts and injustices, some time, some place.

It is popular in sociological circles to define deviancy in behavior as the effect of labeling process by the conforming dominant elite to the non-conforming minority or social subordinates. Ordinary conduct, or, what is acceptable conduct, is that which is agreeable to the dominant clique. In the essay *Misconceptions about the Human Mind* by Montague and Darling, an example of improper thinking is given: "To commit murder for instance, we say is abnormal—when, in reality, it is an extreme deviation from ordinary conduct." The term "abnormal" means deviant from a "norm" in some quantitative way. Murder as an "extreme deviation from ordinary conduct" is certainly also an abnormality except in a grossly abnormal society. The implication here is that if the dominant clique favored murder—genocide, for instance—so that it became ordinary conduct, those who did not favor that genocide would be deviant. But there would be no abnormality either way. These authors continue: ". . . Abnormal psychology is fully as absurd a term as abnormal physics." This is an example of where so called value-free behavioral science really leads. Montague and Darling have said in effect, all human activity is normal regardless of how deviant. While this writer does not believe all murder stems from an abnormal psyche, if all human intellectual or psychic activity is normal regardless of where it leads in behavior, then the jungle is a pleasant place compared to normal human society.

But are these statements scientifically correct, even if socially unfortunate. In physics, the subject matter is inert, the laws governing the observed actions and reactions are within the range of specific experiments, subject to mathematical analysis and prediction. A follows B inevitably. If a "deviance" is observed in physics, not the result of experimental error, a search is made for the cause of the deviance and, when found, correct equations are formulated, even though—as in the atomic world—these may be probablistic equations and a revised mathematical model is established. A report of "abnormal" behavior in physics is an admission of inability at that state of knowledge to formulate models or equations which correctly relate all of the parameters involved.

Psychology is significantly different and the difference is not solely or even largely our inability to study the objects of psychologic research in detail and in depth. The inert subject matter of physics is physically normative. Within very narrow bands the behavior of the objects in physics is exactly in accordance with the physical norms. A occurs, therefore B follows. On the other hand, the human subject of psychology has the freedom to choose his own behavior regardless of norms. He is a rational being.

A completely sane man—one who can make correct judgments as to ordinary norms of conduct—can elect to perform perverse human acts in the light of those norms, in spite of their recognized perversity. Murder is such an act. If, however, one wishes to propose the thesis that murder is conditionally normal, it is a convenient corollary that the human so acting, particularly habitually, has no psychic irregularity which deserves particular mention. Who wants to be called psychotic because of a few casual murders—unless, of course, it gets one off the hook?

The difficulty is that two quite different terms are being used by sociologists as synonymous, sometimes deliberately. These terms are "socially acceptable behavior" and "normal behavior." Murder can become socially acceptable in both large and small sectors of society. Hitler was no social outcast. Neither was the real life "Godfather" within his own culture. Both were murderers. Was their behavior humanly abnormal or only deviant from "ordinary" behavior? Was their behavior normal for a rational human being? The question goes back to the ideas of

Ockham and the later Nominalists who, it will be recalled, denied that there was a human nature. We noted the ridiculous and chaotic results which would flow from this idea if generally put to use. Abnormality reflects a condition contrary to that which the nature of the being establishes for the class being involved. The so-called "motiveless" mass murders of recent times are surely examples of "sick minds." An abnormal psychology would be one which studies cases of behavior attributable to the psyche that are contrary to what is considered naturally, normally, human. It is a valid field of psychological research and study—there are abnormal psyches. The question is not chiefly a matter of statistics but a judgment of what is and is not compatible with being fully human. The insistent dialectic, which constantly challenges man to be human or to deny his humanity, is at work here also. Man can deny his true nature and behave as an intelligent beast. He can make his techniques of murder highly efficient and he can propagandize his activities and cause them to seem of great social utility. But his denial does not change his nature. He is what he is, a human being acting *inhumanly*, that is to say abnormally. The question of when does a deviant act reveal an abnormal psyche is a matter of judgment but not one of impossible dimension. A "sick psyche" no longer possesses a valid scale of reference for its acts. It is no longer acting judgmentally as a human being. That is, it no longer places the facts it apprehends in perspective of its own humanity. With man there is a band of behavior which is classed as normal and social acceptability usually fits within that band, but the terms are not coextensive by any means. Man's nature determines normality or abnormality in behavior. Social custom determines social acceptability or deviance.

The search for our personal identity is the underlying drive of much of our activity. Who are we? The id, ego, superego psychological structure of the Freudian is an attempt to compartmentalize the activities of the human soul in its constant struggle to come to grips with total reality of which it is only one aspect but a highly complex aspect. It is one on which the individual is both subject and object of the search. The soul is oriented to knowledge and to love. It strives to know itself completely and to find in that knowledge an object of love. Real self-love is based on a conviction that, at root, that self is indeed worthy of love. Everyone cheats to some extent—pushing unpleasant discoveries concerning self into dark corners and throwing bright-colored draperies over them for better concealment. Yet, the self cannot forget them. Eventually, it must dig them out and expose them to the full concentrated view of the intellect. The self has only two alternatives when it looks intently at something within itself and concludes that what it sees is evil—a desire for revenge against someone for instance—an active hate—it can deliberately reject the evil or try to still the emotion or it can deliberately retain the evil and nurture it. The self knows which it does and is changed thereby. In thousands of decisions it eventually becomes habituated to the good or to the evil, as evil—knowing that it is evil and not only as an apparent good. Gradually, the self-concealment yields to self-revelation and the individual senses who he is. Only the good is worthy of love. The self can never love the evil as evil which it sees in itself, but it can accept itself as evil. It may, in fact come to admire its virtuosity in evil. It then hates the good and hates itself in hating the good. Hate is more than just the absence of love. One who hates is active in malevolence and not merely neutral. He wills evil to the object of his hate even to his own detriment. Such a person is mentally deranged but not necessarily insane. He knows what is good and what is evil and freely accepts the evil and may even delight in it. There are such persons. They are certainly the subject matter of abnormal psychology.

I find it striking that those individuals regarded with greatest affection throughout history have rarely been the great, the rich, the arrogant, or the powerful—but the humble, those poor in this world's goods—those placing service to humanity above themselves. He also believes this fact is evidential of what people deep in their hearts do feel that human nature ideally is and what each one of us ought to try to be. A person in possession of his intellectual powers knows when he is acting abnormally in terms of what a human being ought to be—it is a natural and a moral judgment.

Man is a normative being. He constantly sets standards in every sphere for himself and for others and for the world about him. He identifies normal behavior for insects and animals and likewise abnormal behavior, when it occurs, and tries then to identify the reasons for it. A code of ethics, always present where there is human society, is the most common example of this norm-seeking characteristic. Man has a sense of what is appropriate behavior in a given set of circumstances. These specific standards are greatly influenced by the prevailing culture, but the trait of normativeness is not a consequence of culture. Normativeness is, rather, the basis of culture. It makes a culture—any culture—possible. In fact, the trait makes some cultural form or other unavoidable. Uncommitted man will grope around until either he finds a milieu in which he can reasonably fit or he becomes, and remains, a permanent misfit, or an outcast, because he cannot satisfy his normative predilection, nor comply with others.

The question of anomie or normlessness was brought to prominence in the 1960's to describe the many disillusioned young people who rejected the standards of society and had no substitute of their own. It, more than likely, indicated that these young people, as products of an overly-permissive culture of ill-defined standards, sensed a void. One standard was as good as another. They wished to recognize no standards but their own which were egocentric and highly transitory with their changing moods. There was no permanent place they could fit. The permissive attitude is the outgrowth of an existentialist approach to life—Do your thing! But even in denial of the applicability of accepted social norms to the world scene as they perceived it, these young people were using self-established norms as a basis of judgment. The clear implication is, that man intuitively accepts the condition that there are certain behavioral obligations which apply to him as a human being as to no other creature on the earth because he does have a unique freedom of choice. He can comply with the cultural norms of his social environment or he can rebel and take the consequences. Camus saw this normativeness as the apex of the absurdity that is man. Man was responsible only to himself— having no superior to give him orders and no mandatory instinctive pattern to govern him. Man felt constrained to follow norms, feeling guilty if he did not conform to established standards. Utter absurdity incarnate! But the absurdity arises from the unsupported assumption that man has no obligation to a Supreme Being. The atheistic thesis is the factor which makes this thinking absurd.

To someone who looks at the universe as intelligible, indications are that the universe is capable of analysis according to laws which have wide application. In the atheistic mode, there is a strange unbalance here in the being, man. The behavioral equations do not, in fact, balance. Constraints, properly speaking, must be applied by some external agency. Yet, man consistently throughout history, has accepted constraints. As Camus saw it, it is ridiculous for man to dream up these constraints and make his life miserable like a dog pulling at his own tail. But does not this imply that it is not man's intellectual freedom which is absurd, but, rather, the omission by Camus, and other like thinkers, of the balancing moral constraint which is absurd. There is, indeed, an external agency which expects man to use his intellectual capacity as befits a free human being. The ubiquitous normativeness of man is evidential of the external agency. Man intuitively knows he is subject to intellectual responsibilities commensurate with his freedom. Man's responsibility is evidential of man's absurdity only to an individual who feels compelled to deny this rational solution.

Even in a relativistic world-view which states that truth varies in space/time circumstances—a notion which has only hypothetical, speculative significance—there would be, at every specific point of space and time, behavior which is worthy of being called human. Man would use his intellectual freedom in a manner consistent with being a fully-responsible human person. Murder, the deliberate taking of innocent human life, is an abnormal human act in those terms. If that abnormal act arises from a given state of mind, then that state of mind is perforce abnormal for human beings regardless of how the sociologists or psychologists would prefer to speak of it. The Nazi and Communist murderers of recent history were certainly not poor victims of labeling. They were vicious, perverted human beings, and grossly abnormal in behavior. They were not merely extreme deviants from ordinary conduct in their environment, because they were not that at all. The social acceptability of their acts is unescapable. They may have been heroes of their place and time, but their self-asserted norms were perverted. They were, in fact, abnormal in terms of humanity. Anything is considered normal only in terms of what that thing is. Normalcy, for man, has no meaning other than that relating man to his innate humanity. How does one measure up as a human being in terms of what a human being ought to be by his nature? First of all, man, in his freedom, ought to show human responsibility for the well-being of his fellows. Obviously, he ought not be a murderer though murder situationally may be socially acceptable as it has been at various times and places.

It is apparent from the foregoing discussion that morality involves far more than a system of quasi-legalistic behavioral guidelines. For one who believes in a personal, omniscient God, it has two distinct faces. There is the face of absolute morality founded in perfect love of God and of all members of the human species, including ourselves, for love of God. We love each other because He loves us and we should behave accordingly. Each of us forms his idea of what that morality consists of from the background of his own detailed life history and that is the second face, an imperfect reflection of the first.

The texture of morality is like a deep-piled Persian rug. The basic matrix is the inter-netting of perfect love in which all of our deeply held values developed from life experience are embedded. No two out of all of the human abstract apprehensions we have discussed: being, beauty, goodness, justice, love, happiness, joy, delight, the All-Holy, and an infinite variety of others are identical. But the relativity does not extend to the matrix. Only the patterns are relative and dependent on cultural differences and personal development. That which ties the whole thing tightly together is the first face, the warp and woof of the matrix—the nexus of God's love. For the convinced atheist, or indifferent non-believer, there is no such first face—no absolute morality. Surely, there is love for fellowman, each for his own sake, which provides some guidance. But the carpet is not tightly bound. Here, clearly, there is no idea of a permanent value or morality system. The situational context determines all.

Morality is not deprived of truth because of this controversy. The truth of morality extends to the truth and reality of the existence of God. For those who have passed that logic gate, there is an absolute morality and, here, the question of intent is all important. It is our good will—our intent—our determined effort, to live as God would have us live that gives the carpet its beauty in spite of its imperfection. It is indeed, the spirit of the law and not the wording of any moral code which is binding on man.

Again, the face morality presented to the atheist is different than the face seen by the theist. Each relates his responsibility to the community at large in providing for the safeguarding of what each regards as a healthy social environment. Both philosophies could be maintained if "responsible" citizens would agree on the need to minimize the crimes of violence against person and property and in maintaining some level of esthetic appeal in the world at large through standards of decent behavior. The atheist might even agree with the theist about the things Jeffrey Hart was complaining about as public outrages. But, at the next remove, the atheist does not care the least about matters which, by their very nature, directly effect the first two. They ignore, or oppose, education in a moral tradition which preserves the exterior "values" which they support. Most cannot see the difference between the solution via the policeman's club and via training of children and youth in moral discipline based on what man, in fact, is. Ms. Nelkin, atheist or not, does not perceive why the MACOS books are objectionable other than as a matter of "creationist" bias. She misses the whole point that, while men are not intelligent baboons, if you convince them from infancy that they are, they might insist on acting that way. Even atheist psychologist Sigmund Freud sensed this problem as the great threat to society.

Chapter 17

LIMITS OF A SECULAR MORALITY

We are now in a position to examine in some detail the moral law or simply "morality" as it exists in Western society today. It is a mixed morality reflecting a highly differentiated view of life, from that of the devout theist to the most hard-line-atheist. Morality is recognized as a legitimate concept by some, denied by others, and labeled as purely a cultural outgrowth by others. It is legitimized only to the extent that the cultural milieu extends recognition to it. In any form, it expresses an obligation to control our behavior. The chief sources of such obligation generally recognized are:

> family
> community
> state
> humanity
> nature (environmental)
> God

While our listing placed the religious moral obligations to God in the last place, it largely subsumes all of those listed above it. As we examined the development of morality in the Judeo-Christian tradition, as an example, we found a movement from purely covenantal formulation with appropriate blessings and curses for compliance or non-compliance and with emphasis on fear to one where love became the primary motivation. In the covenantal form, the moral obligations are quasi-contractual and have a contractual tone. The primary test described in *Genesis*—formulation of moral obligations to God, family, and society at large. They remained largely covenantal and were harsh in terminology. The Old Testament "wisdom literature" over the centuries softened the tone somewhat and introduced, in a prophetic way, the idea of a behavior structured on love rather than on command. The next series, in the New Testament, best exemplified in the Sermon on the Mount, went a step further from a basis in strict obligation under the word of the law. While blessings still accompanied those who

601

lived in accordance with these precepts, the emphasis was one of compliance through love or charity rather than through fear. We must love God and neighbor and conduct our lives on this spiritual plane as a voluntary giving of ourselves rather than as a coercive legalistic formal tit-for-tat compliance. The picture is a pastoral scene with the Good Shepherd, the free forgiveness of those who love much, God continuously seeking to bring His people to Himself. Emphasis is on love, humility, sincerity, and a life of patient bearing with human weakness in filial love of a beneficent and understanding father.

The Industrial Revolution, from its earliest beginnings, tended to upset the picture. Man, as labor, was increasingly viewed as a factor of production. Human relationships again tended to become contractual. Morality was now seen increasingly as a matter of law and order to foster a favorable climate for production. Max Weber's concept of the "Protestant work ethic" recognized the attempt to throw a mantle of religious piety over a harsh economic concept. The biblical concept of an obligation placed on the overseer, that the laborer was worthy of his hire, was rephrased to place the demand on the worker that he must indeed earn his way "by the sweat of his brow." There is, of course, truth both ways, but the latter is a harsher concept. It easily introduces coercion as a management tool and replaces a moral rationale by an economic demand.

The cleavage in man which surfaces in the insistent dialectic is at the interface between man's life as an intelligent animal and as a spiritual being, aware through his own consciousness that he rarely behaves in accordance with his highest aspirations. There may be people who have no aspiration above the animal level, even in moments of introspection, but they would be exceptional. Looking at historical characters, even at those who denied a true spiritual vector in man (John Dewey or Sigmund Freud, for example) there was a frequently expressed confidence that the human race would eventually rise above the crude selfishness and cruelty so generally exhibited. There is a species-typical longing to be something a bit more noble than we are. An individual desires to be loved and admired for what he, in fact, is and not for the facade he, perhaps, presents in his better moments.

There is a duality in humanity which the moral law enunciates everywhere in a demanding action opposed to the drives as intelligent animals. The source of the cleavage is referred to allegorically in *Genesis* in which God, having made man from the slime of the earth, "breathed into him a human soul." Man

was energized by the very "breath of God." The spiritual vitality which is the energy of God was infused into this creature,
man. Materiality and spirituality were brought together for the
first time in a single being. That breath cannot rest until it
produces its spiritual yield and returns to God, even though
as the prodigal son. The human spirit consciously or unconsciously, on the part of the individual, cries "Abba, Father"
throughout its mortal life in an unceasing quest by that soul
for satisfying union with God.

Fallen man must find his way via the trail of anguish and
tension. The cleavage in man results from the mismatch between the two vital elements which drive him in his single personality, the animal and spiritual vectors. The theme of the past
"golden age" of man is common to many cultures. Whether
one accepts the *Genesis* version of the Fall or not, the theme
points to the historical fact of the consistent yearning of man
for the condition of peace with himself.

We did not review Schopenhauer, the German pessimist
philosopher, but, in his works, he compared man to a bubble
under tension—unhappy, discontented—until the bubble bursts,
and the tension is released. Why such a creature should exist,
he did not explain. But the thought of a container for that which
could not be contained is present. The unbalance of forces,
the guilt complexes, the psychotic anxieties all point to the same
primary problem of human existence. Man is not the being he
ought to be. Morality, in a single word, wraps up the differential.

From this, we can say that a pluralistic society almost guarantees a pluralistic pattern of behavior and that much of the
behavior pattern has to do with matters of social acceptability,
and much is morally indifferent. The "crunch" comes when
social acceptability includes behavior patterns which are fundamentally contrary to moral behavior, which is to say humanly
abnormal, within the definitions given earlier. Examples are:
genocide, human sacrifice, abortion, infanticide, geronticide or
senilicide, torture, physical or mental, sexual abuse and deprivation of access by individuals to the necessities of life. These
are all acts which are "abnormal" when measured against
"human nature" viewed as the collective of functioning free
individuals in society for the common good of all.

Abnormality, in addition to its direct meaning of deviation
from a norm, is a term which conveys the idea of an organism
or system which is operating in a dysfunctional mode. A society is a system of organisms. An abnormality in society may
occur at either social or individual levels. As we have seen,

some behaviorists have held that no behavior is abnormal, either at the social or individual level, since examples of virtually all classes of behavior have been recorded. For them, behavior is rather usual or unusual in a normative sense. A moral nonconformist is merely a social deviant. One could as well say the same for an individual who is diseased. His condition is not abnormal, only unusual. In both cases, however, a subsystem is operating in a dysfunctional mode as to the total system.

It is at that point at which the human intelligence is used to pervert the natural functioning of the integral being, man, individually or collectively, that abnormality occurs. It is a subversion of the social means/ends structure. Society exists to facilitate individual human existence. When it functions to the detriment of the individuals in society it is an abnormal society. Social acts are carried out by individuals. Social acts which are abnormal, for the society as a whole, are likewise abnormal for the individual carrying them out. Similarly, private acts and attempts at such acts or incitement to such acts as murder, theft, rape, mayhem and suicide are similarly contrary to man's nature because the intellect is used to destroy, injure, or inhibit human life. Man's functions, integrally speaking, are used contrary to their intended use. His intellectual powers are opposed to his physical well-being, directly or indirectly. His rational control is being used in a self-destructive and, hence, abnormal manner.

Thus, we add one more definition of moral behavior to equate it to normal behavior of a properly functioning rational human being or of a properly functioning society. Just where the line is drawn is conjectural. Theists and atheists would disagree at the level at which the intellectual control becomes dysfunctional or abnormal. If there is no personal God to whom man is intellectually responsible, then expedience or convenience establishes the controlling criteria. Assuming an altruistic motivation as the ideal—there is no "evil," other than at the physical level—death, being the "ultimate" and pain, including mental suffering, are the general measure of evil. Under these criteria we come up with rather similar moral objectives to those of a theistic motivation. Our list of social abnormalities is somewhat the same. But, there are relationships now which modify the degree of "evil." Infanticide or geronticide in a famine stricken land become rational as a matter of expedience. If some must die, in any event, let it be those least productive. There is no absoluteness to the right of the individual to life if that continued life retards the continued progress of society as a whole.

At a less altruistic level, convenience may justify infanticide and geronticide on a rationale of "quality of life." At a still less altruistic level, genocide joins the list, and the means/ends structure becomes the intellectual arbiter of morality. The fallacy of that conclusion at the level of individual human nature is obvious. The existence of a real "human nature" must be denied. What has happened is that man's nature is defined in different terms. In the last stage, the intellect is viewed not as a guidance and control mechanism, even for biologic man, but purely as a sophisticated tool to assist in biologic gratification of the powerful.

Does all this imply that there is no moral law per se and that all morality is subjective? It does emphatically state that, in modern, technically-developed society, there is no unanimity concerning what constitutes the body of moral law. For theists, there is always, corresponding to a state of life, a level of moral perfection, est hlished by God, to which all men are called. This would be a life of perfect charity unattainable by men as are all absolutes. At the working level, man is expected to live in accordance with his understanding of his obligations and responsibilities. Further, he is expected to exercise reasonable diligence in determining what these obligations and responsibilities are, as a matter of conscience.

For atheists, or indifferentists, there can be no moral absolutes and no obligations binding in conscience. Morality can only be an individual acceptance of life standards for whatever reason the individual perceives. But as William James said, he accepts this position at his peril!

To repeat; the question, then, of the real existence of a moral law, or consistent standards of morality, goes squarely back to the question of the reality of God. If there is a God, there is a binding absolute moral law discoverable by reason, at least, in its broad outlines. If there is no God, there is no substantive moral law. In a way, in the latter case, we are saying that the intelligence of man, which is only an accident of biochemistry, if not an outright mistake, and which can, and does, override the usual instinctive controls governing biologic forms, is rather like a virus. It has invaded a genetic line of healthy organisms and is running wild and without any rules will destroy the host organism and itself as well in its greedy excesses. This picture does not make sense, but there is no "reason" why anything should make sense—given the atheistic premise.

It takes little investigation to identify both requirement and root characteristic in man's intellectual capacity. That capacity demands that human beings at least attempt to control their behavior as a continuous self-conscious activity. Man has the capacity to evaluate alternative courses of action in life situations and everywhere seeks the freedom to exercise that capacity. Human beings also characteristically seek to establish norms by which to judge the behavior both of themselves and other human beings. It is the constant human occupation of bringing together these two elements which establishes implicit behavioral codes recognized by members of a community. It is apparent that the code of human behavior extends in a continuum, from the most trivial matters of personal adornment and dress, to the most crucial matters of life and death and even of concepts of life beyond death. The zone which has been traditionally identified as "moral" is that considered essential to community survival. There is no question but that *de facto* morality is embedded in culture. In a very real sense, the two are coexistent and co-definitive.

It is in the normative root of the moral tree that the question of quality of a cultural regime arises. How are the standards established and by what means are they maintained? Obviously, the physical environment is a significant parameter. The rules of behavior, including the moral element, must be in consonance with the situation in which the people live. But the physical environment is not the determining parameter. The determining parameter is in the nature of man himself as a social being. On the one hand are the individual drives inherently anti-social towards attaining personal satisfaction with the least effort-drives toward pleasure, wealth and power by the most direct route exemplified by the pillaging warrior. On the other hand are the communal socially-oriented demands which counsel stability. These are directed toward relatively long-term gains, even though the same basic drives are at work in common effort at a lower level of intensity and under rational control. Ideally, the community would constitute a Weberian *gemeinschaft*.

As a consequence of these opposed aspects in every actual situation there arises the Hobbesian question of the rights of the individuals against the rights of the community. The community rights take the form of obligations placed on the individual to surrender certain personal freedom of behavior to the common good. Sanctions of one kind or another are imposed to enforce the rules. The incorrigible violator becomes an outcast. In primitive societies, past and present, that aspect largely controls the codes. In more advanced societies, or better stated perhaps, in more elaborate societies, the relationships of rights and obligations are less clearly traced. But the same concepts are valid. In both levels, primitive, or sophisticated, the intellectual motivation toward controlled behavior must be present. The rational mind must recognize the validity of the moral demands before assent to give up freedom is exchanged. Universally, these demands are referred back to an ultimate judicial authority from which there is no appeal. The judge refers to the codes which were accepted in that culture. Throughout history, the curses or blessings of the Deity were invoked on violators and observers of the law respectively, in addition to any purely secular sanctions. The offenses, and penalties therefor, against the Deity, against the king, against the person, against property and involving sexual deviance were the most severe since they reflected back most directly in disruption of the public peace and tranquility.

One could conclude that the desired effect was the father of the law and that religion as a basis of morality was the child of legalistic need. An ultimate authority is needed to assure compliance, therefore an ultimate authority is invented. This explanation is satisfactory at the level of pragmatism in a retrospective sense. Is it credible in terms of the oldest written evidence of "how it was" at the time of Moses for instance? Undoubtedly there were thousands of years of unwritten empiricism—This works—That does not. That behavior which was, in general, "morally required" was, in fact, that which was conducive to a tranquil existence. If a community, in fact, lived this way it was, in fact, blessed. If it did not, it was—in fact—cursed. This is nearly a universal judgment. Historically, in the Old Testament we have the examples of Sodom and Gomorrah, of Nineveh and of the various Kings of Judah and Israel. In these terms, idealistically, the moral law is a rational, freely accepted rule of behavior in recognition of the common brotherhood of man under the fatherhood of God. The rules find their sanctions *ad interim* in the penalties imposed by the local authorities and absolutely in the unfailing judgment of God.

Within this concept, there is an absolute code of morality at the level of the will of God independently of the human statutes. In the Judeo-Christian tradition, it is a code founded in the love of God and of fellowman because of God's love for him. To the extent that tradition lives on in the accepted moral codes of today there is an absolute, not relative, moral code. But in a pluralistic society, and particularly in today's environment, there is a substantial, perhaps a majority opinion in the West that would reduce the code to the level: "The moral code is a rational rule of behavior in recognition of the common interests of the human individual and human society as a collective of individuals." It is a morality founded in pragmatism, having no absolutes.

Thus, of concern in a sociology of morals in the late twentieth century is legislation, which is a formalizing of relationships of men in society and which increasingly finds polarization of viewpoints on this critical issue. Jeffrey Hart's comments addressed this point. The current political terminology "liberal" and "conservative," in large measure, expresses the polarization. The more that deeply religious issues are involved, the more deeply polarized are the political positions.

The conflict, personal, social, economic and political, represents the "insistent dialectic" in excruciating tension. The extreme liberal view takes the philosophy of hands off individual man's behavior unless it adversely affects the immediate collective position. Although it sounds sweetly humane, as noted earlier, it fails to recognize that a responsible adult does not suddenly appear fully developed in his proper place in the social structure. He is produced from infancy in a context of moral and secular value levels. He thinks and judges from the background of all the "data bits" his mind has assimilated. By the time he moves into action vis-a-vis the "immediate collective position" he is a preconditioned individual. His acts, following the permissive morality, may be totally and ruthlessly egocentric. His "value" orientation is guided only by what he perceives as his best immediate interest. There is no authority above him to which he must respond.

The extreme "conservative" view takes the position that man's freedom of action must be subordinated to the needs of the collective. It tends to excesses of control—even to religious choice—and including no religious choice, when the state becomes the authority of last appeal. It closely resembles the Hobbesian solution. In neither extreme position does the question of responsibility through love appear.

Man, the free, yet responsible creature under God, has no place in either camp except as a caricature where a particular viewpoint is served by stretching him one way or the other. It is obvious that somewhere between the extremes is the zone in which rational man must live. This conclusion does not agree with a random solution. It suggests system and deep rooted causality. Rational man was led to rational conclusions. It is unlike the instinctive community. The culture of the bee is a rational culture (i.e., intelligible to a rational being). But, it is not rational on the part of the bees. The ant culture is rational, but not on the part of the ants. The successful human culture is rational, because it is rational on the part of man. It appears that if a life form is capable of governing itself at the rational level, it will be permitted, even more, expected to do so controlled by appropriate rational sanctions. If man's sense of morality is evolutional in the sense of following a survival bias, it is because that bias, as all others we have looked at, was implanted in a purposeful, intentional, causal mode. The success of cultures having a well defined moral code is for the reason that such an outcome was the intended manner of human existence from the beginning. Man was, in the fullness of time, expected to live in fully developed relationship of harmony with his environment and his fellowman or accept the consequences of disorder and dissolution as a viable social form.

Morality, as a concept, invades every area of human activity in some way. From the white lie in social etiquette, to the awful decision to drop "the bomb," there is recognition somehow of an obligation to do what is "right and good" and not just be correct. Earlier, the writer made the statement: "Whereas, in the religious sphere, interest in morality began with the idea; in sociology, it begins with the act." This statement signifies that the sociologist is interested primarily in the behavior itself. But this writer further noted that the sociologist is also interested in the way that the morality level is maintained in a given society. It is of social concern whether the system of control is voluntary or involuntary. The moral behavioral control is voluntary. The restrained behavior by the individual is a result of free assent in the light of duty or love. The police systems are coercive through sanctions applied at the various societal levels. It is involuntary.

The motivation of a moral behavior system stems from devotion to the family, community, state, humanity, nature or to God from a sense of responsibility in a relationship which is recognized as valuable in itself. It is the perceived value of the relationship which prompts the forgoing of some personal freedom.

Aside from the idea of morality, we may have a sense of personal obligation to others, to parents, to benefactors, to the state, or even to the environment. But that obligation can be fulfilled in "immoral" ways. One can be an embezzler in order to be kind to his parents and benefactors. One can be an assassin to rid the state of enemies, and aside from an obligation owed to some still higher authority, why not?

It is popular to speak of "victimless crimes." These are acts in which only the question of morality in a religious sense is involved. Formerly, statutes were passed to control these occurrences under penalty of the law. Many of the statutes are still in force. There is pressure to have these statutes withdrawn on grounds of obsolescence. In this development, something noteworthy—the idea of public morals—has been lost—the idea of a debt owed to society to refrain from behaving in a certain way because it was defined as immoral. Again, what is the significance of the loss of this idea aside from the idea of a personal God to whom the obligation is owed to behave otherwise. If one wants to ignore the idea of public morals and no one complains, why not? Why should one be accountable to anyone else for his behavior in private matters?

The concept of a sociology of morals embraces many potential areas of study. A few of these areas would be: the accumulating of statistical data concerning the basic moral standards throughout the world; the following of trends in morality as specifically defined at different places under various circumstances—urban and rural trends for instance. Other areas of study might include the establishment of relationships between general levels of morality and levels of cultural stress in war and peace. For example, the correlating of levels of morality and educational systems. However—in order for such studies to be meaningful there should be an agreed-upon basic understanding of what "morality" consists of. If morality is only a transitory way of life accepted as normative by individuals, or in limited cultural groups without any reference to a universally recognized set of norms, what purpose is served by such studies? Unless there are standards which are generally recognized as constituting minimally human behavior in relation, first, to one's own self, and then, to all other human beings, as human, morality has no autonomous status and a sociology of morals is of little relevancy. A sociology of morals would be just another facet of ethnography in that set of circumstances. A sociology of morals has no basis unless the concepts "moral" and "immoral" are capable of clear definition. Even the keeping of statistics would be a useless exercise beyond studies in criminology, or for insurance reports.

The picture of the young, and not so young, American male and female in the late twentieth century painted by essayist, Tom Wolfe and other young contemporary writers is of a totally selfish, sexually obsessed generation. Wolfe labeled the 70's the "me decade." There is no sense conveyed of the joyousness associated with youth. Yet the undercurrent in most of these works, which surfaces occasionally, is the frantic, almost frenzied, seeking for what might be real underneath all the dramaturgical makeup. Many people, young and old, are trying to find out experientially what and who they are. They have lost the sense of beingness in the sullen, existential worlds of Camus and Sartre where there is no joy, only anguish, despair and the "tragic sense of life."

Joy, as we saw, has a spiritual connotation. It requires an inner confidence that the existent moment is of importance not just for itself but also for a future—a future which is likewise important and can be meaningful and joyous. Joy requires, in fact, a "joyous sense of life," to paraphrase the gloomy existentialists. A joyous sense of life does, however, require an ongoing self-consciousness that one is doing that which he ought to do even though that involves incidental pain and forgoing of personal pleasures. How does one decide what one ought to do?

Morality is a blending of many human concepts into a system of behavior criteria and controls and not a simple carefully bounded area that is labeled "standards of human behavior." However, the chief components can be identified and certain characteristics can be defined which assist in making the idea more manageable. First and foremost, morality provides a voluntary behavioral system. Therefore, it is an idea confined to free human beings. Central to the concept is the need of rational consideration of alternatives and the possibility of free choice. While the time and space circumstances under which the act occurs has an impact, that aspect is not the primary control. The environment is one aspect in the evaluation. It bears about the same relationship as terrain to strategy in military operations. It affects tactics in battle but not the total war plan. The environment strongly affects incidental maneuvers, but not the policy. The responsibility of the individual for his acts suggests that: (a) He can freely select a path of behavior among alternatives which then makes that behavior uniquely his act. (b) There is some entity to which the actor must answer for his act.

A moral obligation can be defined as a debt recognized by an individual as being owed to another individual or group by reason of a special relationship which exists between them. The best example of a moral obligation is the family in which the bonds between members carry certain responsibilities which are well recognized by each family member. Failures by members to carry out the responsibilities are normally not the subject of formal action outside the family circle. The sanctions which exert pressure on the member to perform are implicit. They lie in the danger of withdrawal of love and esteem by the other family members. The effectiveness of the moral obligation depends upon the value which the individual member places on the relationship.

We may make the statement, that: "Morality, as a concept in guiding behavior, stems from the moral obligation owed to God, to society in general, to the family in particular, and to the individual, at large, by individuals as rational beings capable of both recognizing those relationships involved and those duties and responsibilities which the relationships entail. Again, it is the value which the individual places on the relationships which determines the effectiveness. From this discussion, it may be deduced that of all of these relationships, only one extends through the entire fabric and has traditionally reinforced and undergirded the moral obligations which are owed at all other levels. The concept of an omniscient, omnipotent and all-just God imposes a separate and unavoidable sanction on the individual. Failure to accept and perform the duties and responsibilities owed the subordinate levels, carries with it not only the threat of loss of love and esteem by those individuals immediately concerned but also, unfailingly, at the divine level. In addition, while the emphasis is on obligation due to recognition of the love of God, the "fear of the Lord" is never far removed. If the existence of God is denied in any society, generally, the relationship between the individual and God loses all value and the concept of morality now drops to a level of competing demands and responsibilities. There is nothing wrong in stealing, as such, so stealing from the impersonal "society in general" or the stranger in the street does not irritate anyone very much except the victim. There is no intrinsic value attached to those "moral" concepts exerting pressure for compliance with duties or responsibilities as a citizen or member of the human race. Some rare individuals may possess that gleaming vision of the upward surge of humanity toward natural evolutionary perfection. But it will not likely be the average individual living in a competitive world. "What's in it for me?" is a much more pertinent proposition. Yet, a code of morals is not easily dismissed. The sense of a need for moral order is the next thing to being inherent in human nature. Nevertheless, if the concept of God is denied, there is very little leverage beyond brutal and detailed government involvement in personal lives to preserve order in human affairs. There is either Nietzsche's nihilistic anarchy or his dictatorship of the "supermen."

One who elects to delve into the sociology of morals has

got to accept some basis of morality. John Dewey was convinced, back in 1910, that when scientific psychology came of age all the philosophical claptrap on morality would wither away like Marx' government. When our psychic kinks had been sufficiently massaged by the practitioners of behavioral perfection, the idyllic age of natural bliss would have dawned. Our schools, freed of all the superstitious nonsense of God, would produce such naturally virtuous products that they would make Rousseau's natural man look like Bluebeard. For Dewey, morality was the response of a naturally healthy and scientifically-trained psyche, and immorality was the response of a sick or undeveloped psyche. Dewey's psyche, of course, having no connotation of soul, was nothing but activated matter. The educational process, including remedial therapy where necessary to provide happy, well-rounded personalities, would soon eliminate all the malice in the world. That stern concept of moral obligation, of a duty demanding fulfillment in spite of hardship, of sacrifice of wealth or position for the sake of a principle—the hard cases which must be faced with courage and resolution by all responsible adults in the world, do not enter into the curriculum. Yet, that is the real world where real people must live and morality survive or collapse.

There is an element of validity to Dewey's idea. Training is involved, but it is not the major factor at root level. The developed sense of morality, and it is developed, stems from a strong conviction that human life does have a meaning beyond one's own pleasure. If the values attached to those relationships, from which moral obligations arise, are neglected, then the individual's own life is the chief victim. If one has failed in the fullness of his own humanity, regardless of success, he cannot look at himself in moments of introspection and like what he sees. The comment, "I couldn't live with myself if I did such and such" well expresses the real personal bite of morality. In Freudian terms, it is the superego; it is the conscience of traditional religious literature; it also can be the self-conscious part of rational man responding to such questions as: Who am I? Why am I here? What is expected of me in my various relationships? If one believes that: I am a bundle of sense impressions; I am a chance occurrence; I am expected to do my thing and die, there is little motivation to be heroic, or to devote a lifetime to raise a family or care for the sick or face anything unpleasant just because it is of your own doing and your responsibility. Responsibility? By whose judgment? Responsibility to whom?

So long as an individual is placed or places himself in a given society, that society does, in fact, have an interest in his behavior, and can apply sanctions of one kind or other to enforce its rules. The individual develops a sense of responsibility largely through living in a family and community environment which stresses the importance of being a responsible member of the human family so that his intellectual evaluation of alternatives always includes the question of: "How should I act in view of the various obligations my state of life imposes?"

As to the individual then, we can only respond that the ingredients which determine probable levels of moral behavior are: (1) The level of development of a sense of the value of the various relationships. (2) The level of development of a sense of moral responsibility in those relationships. (3) The level of legitimacy which the individual ascribes to the sanctions exercised through the various relationships.

As individuals mature, the question of sanction should carry less weight in ordinary situations and decisions should be influenced more by the consciousness of responsibility in relationships. But in those hard cases where there is great pressure on the individual to act contrary to the demands of the relationships, the sanctions once more become very critical in importance. If family responsibilities are heavy and a clear chance comes to "unload" and "skip out," it becomes much more difficult to make the decision to stay with these responsibilities. This decision requires real moral stamina, sometimes at a near heroic level. The familial bonds may have collapsed under strain. The community at large is indifferent and perhaps, the only adhesive left is a sense of responsibility before God to keep going. Is it worth it to continue? If there is a clear sense that God knows one's problem better than he does, is keeping score, and will give one the strength if he tries, the chance that the crisis will be courageously faced and passed is far better than if that sense does not exist.

The concept of morality, then, cannot be disassociated from recognized standards of right and wrong or from recognized standards of responsibility in relationship with individuals, family, society at large, and, at the apex, God. There must be a deep personal sense of the value of these relationships to the individual and, finally, of recognition of, and appreciation for, sanctions which can be exercised at all these levels for violation of the behavior modes which the standards demand.

Further, if there is a breakdown in the moral system, at any level, the burden of enforcement at the other levels is increased. For example, if there is a breakdown in the community moral environment—a situation of general lawlessness—the family and larger society must move in to provide control. The worst situation is that one currently facing much of the world. Individuals, family, and communities are abandoning belief in God. This has the effect of placing the ultimate burden of behavior control upon the cities and states. These organizations can only exert their will through force—or a totally coercive system— through police methodology.

The importance of a sociology of morals, as a field of study, aside from the idea of a sociology of religion, is scarcely debatable. The basic motivation of all human relations is profoundly affected by the system of moral values which is dominant in any society. Further, there can be no doubt that if there is to be a sociology of morality or of morals, then the nature of morality—as a total concept—must be included in the field of study. The source of morality, the historical development, and the assessment of the basic human needs to which the moral system responds, are of critical importance to an understanding of the many social phenomena which reflect the moral system embedded in the various societal groupings.

The subject matter of religion interfaces with the subject matter of morality primarily at the methodological level. The theoretical bases are quite different. All religious systems promulgate codes of morality. Rules of behavior have historically been infused into social groupings through a program of religious teachings. Morality has always been related to a theistic theory—man in relationship with a deity system. Morality, as an autonomous subject, standing apart from a belief in God has been discussed in the West by various individuals from the time of the Renaissance, but the concept has never been generally accepted. The Eastern religions, Islam excepted, generally have a looser dogmatic texture and have always treated the idea of morality as one which flows from the nature of human life itself—life in which all things must be in balance with the divine urgings to perfection. The sense of the divine penetrated all activity.

In the West, the rise of agnostic skepticism and atheism has created a hiatus in moral theory. If God is a pure invention or at best is totally unknowable, moral theory can hardly use a historic base founded in theism. If there is no God, a comprehensive moral theory must find its base in some other concept. This concept must be one accepted by men universally as worthy of a binding commitment to surrender some elements of individual prerogatives for principle when faced with a choice. There are not many such concepts. As we saw earlier, philosophers generally have selected four, these being, God, humanity, nature, and society in the sense of the social contract. But a purely secular morality cannot sink its roots into, and gain nourishment from, man's relationship with God. All known social groups of any size do have established moral codes of some kind or other, this is a well-recognized fact. Most are either based on religious concepts or are residual of codes established on religious concepts. In most societies, responsibility implicit, or explicit of the individual, under some deity system was, and is, the keystone. If the keystone is loosened and then removed, it must be replaced by another or the structure will collapse. Morality, then, must stand squarely on its own feet if it is to stand at all. The question must remain—is it possible to build a viable moral theory on an overall atheistic philosophy?

There must be a defensible point of departure for the theory. The universal solidarity of humanity and the interdependence of individual men in various social structures is the strongest combination aside from a common belief in God. It is the base of modern secular humanism, a mixture of humanity, nature, society and the state. The structural-functional theory of society and politics leans heavily on that idea and presents the most likely possibility. The level of morality in any society will then be established by the functional requirements of that society. After its establishment, the social group will seek to preserve the existing structure within relatively close tolerances; shifts are evolutionary not revolutionary. Under the structural-functional theory, as a shift in moral structure is sensed by the society, the stability-seeking force will be exerted to try to preserve or restore the original position. In this case, the societal disapproval of deviant behavior would be stepped up with more rigorous enforcement of those appropriate laws, and community affairs programs would be stimulated, particularly among the youth, to increase their involvement in social improvement projects. But some shift eventually will be accepted. Moral codes cannot have absolute validity because God alone was the only absolute authority, and He has been pronounced dead for these people. The state represents society and can claim absolute moral powers, but no one believes it. It is absolute only to the extent of its ability to apprehend and punish violators. The rules must be allowed to relax to the level of credible enforcement.

The absolute notions of nature, society, and humanity, and the allegiance all men have, as natural human beings and members of society and the human race, carry a certain at least quasi-moral obligation to respect the other similarly situated being individually and collectively apart from the idea of God. As Duncan Williams said, there is a "certain sentimental attachment" which derives from the association "We're all in the same boat so let's make the best of it." This is still the insistent dialectic of earlier discussions in a modified form. The level of stress which is acceptable before the individual will reject the general obligation and go his own way is not high. There is no "clout" in the concept. The bland everyday activities pose no problem. But, in a "crunch," while the superego may wince a bit at an inhuman or anti-social or unnatural act, or at all three, if the personal appetite is satisfied, "What the hell, forget it." The new keystone does not fit well in the old slot. It is a "sloppy fit" and threatens to fall out entirely.

It appears there must be some stimulation above the purely pragmatic even with the idea of an enlightened self-interest approached as pragmatic. Otherwise, the level at which morality can be maintained, in the sense of a voluntary surrender of prerogatives to the public benefit, can be no higher than the threshold of actual "pain" to the individuals. The very first time that an individual feels a sense of deprivation or the slightest pinch, the voluntarism ceases. Look at a similar parallel and compare the idea of a United Fund to the federal income tax. The first is a case of voluntary altruistic giving from a sense of moral obligation—with some substantial public coercive pressure. The second is a case of coercive giving under severe penalty of law—with some slight overtones of duty. The vast difference in the annual "take" is significant. There can be little doubt, that if the coercive element in the tax system were removed the system would collapse.

The secular humanists contend that morality is only a question of training, of indoctrination of children and young adults with a sense of what is correct behavior in various circumstances—teaching them to be "sensitive" to the rights and feelings of others. Then, when they become adults, they will by force of habit continue to live their lives in this idyllic fashion. The moral order on a theistic basis was and is largely a result of training, who can deny it? But there is no such thing as right or wrong in this secular "morality"—only nice or mean, acceptable or unacceptable. All acts, in themselves, are neutral. They become acceptable or unacceptable, or remain indifferent, depending on the circumstance. It certainly appears that the individual's own appraisal of the fitness of the act to the circumstances is the only valid one. Why should any other view be superior to the one who is faced with the decision to act?

In a sense, every man becomes his own God. It is his life, and that is all. Why should he not be the total judge of his behavior?

On balance, what level of morality appears sustainable by a purely secular humanism. At the level of marriage and family, there is no way to maintain the traditional ideal of a permanent unit if either party can decide what is proper for him or her. There would likely result a series of temporary arrangements. The offspring, if any, would still be the object of affection at the animal level, and some degree of self-sacrifice on the part of parents could be expected. But the burden of children would be an awful drag in subsequent arrangements. State-operated child care and juvenile maturation institutions would be an appropriate solution. The idea of any deep mutual support by family members could be absolutely and irrevocably lost.

At the level of property rights, if there were a general surplus, there would probably be some security, at least to the point that the level of gain by stealing remained less than the level of difficulty in getting away with the theft. Some people would still steal for the sake of sport.

Violent acts against other persons are usually messy and get individuals into awkward circumstances with the established law enforcement group. Still, given suitable motivation one can put up with a little inconvenience if the personal rewards are great enough. Certainly the acceptability of murder, itself, is only a matter of environmental pressure suiting the murderer's convenience.

Probably the greatest difficulty with a purely secular humanistic moral system, from the structural-functional viewpoint, is that the pressure on the societal unit is always from the same direction and the homeostatic governor is a passive, inertial, device. Having yielded to modest demands toward the relaxation of traditional standards, there is no internal way to form a recovery of lost ground or to prevent continual erosion of the levels. If behavior should be appropriate to the surrounding circumstances and the environment of the acts, and if the conditions in the environment shift in the direction of social anarchy—a spiral of declining behavior patterns promoting declining public morality levels and permitting declining behavior patterns is unavoidable. This decline did not, and would not, occur under a theistic system. The basic standards are absolute. The culture might move away from the standards, but, periodically, when the situation had become sufficiently "raunchy" a spiritual revival would set in among the people to reassert the original standards and bring levels of behavior back into closer conformity. Here was a true structural-functional theory with an effective action control device built in.

The sustainable level of "morality" in any atheistic system is that of gross public abuse which law enforcement agencies can reasonably control. The controls on the law enforcement agencies of those in command of the situation simply do not exist. Anarchy would yield to a series of tyrannies with short interludes of anarchy. This type of social order demands a docile and not activist citizenry. A conflict mentality could not be tolerated. An analysis, under the conflict theory, with atheistic moral concepts throughout the culture, comes to the same end and probably with greater speed. The revised Marxist theory begins with tyranny and states what the moral behavior pattern will be for all concerned. The state determines what behavior is appropriate.

The final state for all atheistic systems is total surrender of all individual freedom in the general population and rigid control by the power elite backed up by severe punishment for violation. With the current means of psychological, surgical and medical behavior modification methods now available, that desirable level of docility may be possible. Man will have a Master. He cannot exist as his own God, among other equal gods, with his own sovereign and absolute freedom to act. If there are no behavior absolutes, there will be attempts at individual absolutism. Public order cannot exist in such a behavior climate. Standards will be set by some agency capable of enforcing them. If there are no moral laws binding on the individual conscience based on love and/or fear of God, there will be penal laws established by those in power with suitable enforcement methods.

Man exists in the tension between good and evil, the insistent dialectic. This is to say that man exists in a complex dialectic matrix operating between duty and irresponsibility, between care and carelessness, between hope and despair, love and hate, faith and faithlessness, and between generosity and greed. Throughout life, individuals are constantly made aware of the constant internal struggle involved in conforming actions to aspirations. They are constantly saying, "I do not that which I would do." No other creature in our world has this problem. They live in an instinctive balance. Our desire for animal satisfaction is augmented by the imaginative powers of the intellect urging us constantly toward excesses in animality, including the dominance of our fellow man. Freud developed his concept of the superego to accommodate this undoubted human problem. How can this problem of the tension between good and evil be explained in natural terms? Social pressures are only a superficial answer at the surface of the problem, because social pressures such as peer group approval stem from what the group as a collection of humans assess as the criteria for humanness. Social pressures create an ideal to be *sought*. But why should ideals in behavior be sought and rules formulated?

The "guilt complex," which psychiatrists find so widespread in civilized peoples, and which is alleged to stem chiefly from repressive religious teachings in childhood, is symptomatic of a "natural" intuition of man that he has acted contrary to his "conscience." The polygraph reveals that there is physically-measurable "shock" to the human person in stating something contrary to that which his intellect recognizes as truth. Few even hardened liars can avoid detection. If this is the case with a purely intellectual moral fault, it seems highly probable that faults which are both physical and intellectual in the sense of a giving of an intellectual assent to a violent act, like murder or rape would be grossly contrary to what the intellect comprehends is "right" and would also produce a great physical and mental shock resulting in obsessional guilt feelings, if religious teachings have influenced the subject and provided individuals or groups with the base of a sensitive conscience. It is then true that religious teachings are contributing to guilt complexes. But it is the intellectual assent to what the individual recognizes as evil, for whatever reason, that provides the sense of guilt. Many persons with little or no religious background admit to strong feelings of guilt and even a compulsion to confess their guilt to someone. What the conscience provides is not a dead picture of the past. Rather, the very situation is reduplicated. You are there. What did you do? What should you have done? What would you do now? The conscience is truly "a vehicle of truth against oneself."

The almost universal sense of right and wrong certainly provides a moral guide and some control over human behavior in society. But, at root, this corrective moral sense is not independent of the idea of God. An atheist who "follows his conscience" is consciously or unconsciously complying with a "higher rule" than his own biologic desires. He may ascribe his behavior to "socialization." Society has provided him with the norms. But, here again, there can be no infinite regression to the past. Society developed its norms on the basis of the common consensus of peoples that there is "right" and "wrong," relative to a way of life demanded at a level above them.

It is fundamentally human to establish norms of behavior—intellectual guidelines to operate beyond the instinctive zone. It is the procedural response to the sequential questions: "Who am I?" and "Why am I here?" and "How should I act in consequence of the rational answswer to those first two questions?" If one is intellectually satisfied with the answer that he is a "walking bag of seawater" or a "trousered ape" in response to the first question, the others have no significance whatsoever, and no tension should exist. It is the obvious fact that the vast majority of men are not satisfied with these answers. The psychiatric clinics testify to that. The tension does exist. It is real.

Man is incurably introspective, and it is the conflict and uncertainty he senses in his introspective moments that frustrate him. He does not like the person he sees himself to be because of his failures to live up to what he thinks of himself as being. He cannot forgive himself. He knows that intuitively, and yet he seeks forgiveness.

In past ages, man's faith sustained him. He was the child of a loving and forgiving Father. In spite of repeated failures, if one did the best he could, that was all that would be expected. Man must return to that idea or go collectively insane.

Chapter 18

THE INSISTENT DIALECTIC—
GROUNDS FOR A SOCIAL MOVEMENT

Let us review the insistent dialectic—man, the self-sufficient being versus man the dependent creature—in the perspective of all that we have looked on previously. As an approach to this review, one could select, subjectively, the names of those individuals who have most influenced man's thought and guided the trend in attitude and behavior in the world during the past century and a half. The writer has selected five in a rough temporal sequence, Comte, Marx, Darwin, Lenin and Freud. Then he has added five additional names of those in a similar position in the past fifty years. These are Russell, Dewey, Gandhi, Einstein and Mao. Individual lists might vary from these (This list has an "English-speaking bias"—Heidegger or Sartre might easily be substituted for Russell or Dewey.). The overall composition would not change much in attitude toward religion if the list is realistic. One common theme is that none of these people, in their last posture, were Christians. Except for Gandhi, they were not religious in any structured way. Except for Einstein, they were all materialists in basic orientation. The center of gravity of their thought would be far over toward the first term of our dialectic. The concept of God, except in its denial, would not have had any significant part in the direction that they urged—and, in some cases—coerced man to go. Such a definite, patterned trend strongly suggests a causal explanation.

Aside from Gandhi and Einstein, these individuals were not profound thinkers. They tended to be extensive rather than intensive in their coverage of any subject. None of them made any attempt to seek first principles. Most would have thought such a concept to be absurd. They all represent activity in many areas, covering the breadth of human affairs—except the religious. Their appeal appears to be in the package they are pushing, or better in the way they were packaging the product—and in the advertising. Religion on the other hand, and particularly Christianity, was non-competitive in the intellectual market place. The writer believes one could state with high confidence that the product offered by the religious orientation to man, that

is, life as free individuals in a community of mutual trust and
love under God, solving the problems of mankind by a dedicated common effort is far superior to life in a mechanical,
individual or collective slavery that was constantly seeking solutions to problems of human existence in the conquests of
the physical environment for material ends alone. That, stripped
of the fancy wrapping, is all the other package contains. Lenin
said repeatedly that: "It is the nature of communism to hate."
The idea that hate is a better basis for human relationship than
love is incredible.

The religious product was rejected not because of intrinsic
lack of value of content then, but because it lacked credibility
as it was offered. The second and third echelons in the intellectual leadership, those extending down to the educational level
for the bulk of humanity, rejected a religious orientation because they, as individuals, could not, in sheer actuality, believe
that man was the well-loved creature of an infinitely loving God
and Father. Had God changed so as to become less credible?
No. Had man in his intrinsic nature changed? No. Then if God
and man as existent are unchanged, the attitudinal change has
to be in the imaged beings and their relationships as man has
conceived them or as they are being "packaged" for education
and as they were being experienced in life as it was being lived
in the nineteenth and twentieth centuries. Now, let us consider
what appear to this writer to be the two most suspect areas
where the erroneous image was formulated. First, the theologians, or the "packagers," those who make the intellectual
journals, had gotten very fancy and finicky. God became so
"odd," so "depersonalized" that He was unbelievable. Those
theologians who wrestled and strained to twist God into a
"Hegelian" shape managed successfully to make God, if intellectually stimulating, thoroughly incredible as a "real" force. In
an age looking for the new and unique in everything, the good
old traditional God—so lovingly portrayed in the last quoted
excerpt from Buber—was pushed to the shelf to give space to
the newer and flashier, but much more fragile, Gestalt models.
Man was provided a God that has been formed from conceptual structures without personality or attractiveness to face the
real problems of life which are always personal. The grotesque
forms of modern art reflect this fabrication of reality, first hammered out and shaped at the forge of modern theology.

The second suspect area was touched on in the first. We live—
or, we have been living, in an age which finds attractiveness
almost solely in the novel and the sensational. The recent rush

to the antique shops and renewed interest in handcrafted things like old automobiles and the high prices demanded for old art work reveal the fact that there is a nostalgia or a seeking for something of permanent value and authenticity which the old and lovingly fabricated and maintained objects seem to convey. These old objects are beginning to have a "cash" value. They command a price which is a countervailing, and yet thoroughly modern, response to any felt need. The inchoate change remains in superficialities. But it is a significant movement from the valueless position.

Man has been, like God, wrestled into an unnatural shape and done so largely by force of circumstances. A makeshift metropolis, quickly assembled of, and from, heterogeneous migrants does not foster a spirit of communality. It is the opposite of the Weberian *"Gemeinshaft,"* which is a true community of people who are humanly personal in their relationships. Thus, since the Industrial Revolution, there has been increasingly developing a forced and unnatural relationship between an impersonal God and a mass of largely impersonalized human beings. Neither are recognizable as worthy of intimate trust and confidence, not even to mention love. That God is incredible to those men. There can only be purely "It" relationships between such beings—between mass men and whatever they wish to view as their ultimate concern—their God, in Tillichese.

Now, we are in a position to evaluate the sociologic implications of what we have seen in this Part V as those implications would relate to the Toynbee scenario. As we will see, in Part VI, the most fundamental ingredient in a social movement is a *generalized belief.* Without that, the movement cannot even be initiated. This is a strongly held central concept which serves as the rallying point for the forces which are to be mobilized. Generalized beliefs must have certain characteristics if they are to be effective. These are, chiefly, the following:

1. They must be convincing—have an intellectual appeal.
2. They must be persuasive—have an emotional appeal.
3. They must be simple in principle—easily understood.
4. They must be stable in form—not easily "fractionated."
5. They must have understandable ends—their goals must be explicable.
6. They must appear to have ends attainable in practice—not Utopian.
7. They must provide meaning to life—provide an ultimate concern.

8. They must promote enduring loyalty—be cohesive.

9. They must have sociologic ends—aim to establish a regime for society.

10. They must promise progress through change—provide a move to something better.

11. They must be "preachable"—expressible in appealing terms.

12. They must be balanced—have appeal to a wide sector.

13. They must be distinctive—stand out from the background.

Now, a mere mental rundown of this list will disclose that a generalized belief, having a religious basis, is at the very least conceivable within these terms. Both Christianity and Islam are historic examples. In fact, they remain viable movements which, while sociologically quiescent, still have considerable potential for reactivation in the interest of the betterment of the human condition. The sociologic end of a religiously-oriented movement ought to have just such an objective. That objective should be the establishment of a regime in justice for all men under the concept of a universal brotherhood of man under the fatherhood of God.

What are the blocking aspects that could serve to prevent or derail such a movement? Given the current state of malaise and cynicism, probably the idea of attainability of the ends is the weak link. It will be very difficult to initiate any sort of movement in the present atmosphere of near hopelessness prevalent among religious people. The extent of this attitude is reflected in a statement from a rather unexpected source. In an interview of evangelist Billy Graham, conducted in the spring of 1975, Kay Bartlett, Associated Press writer filed a report of which the following is an extract:

Graham, the patriot who views the Constitution as the second greatest document in the world, sees communism as a menace to the world.

> "They have a gigantic plan for the world and they may win temporarily," he says. "But Christ will win in the end."
> "I don't see any hope but the coming of Christ. I used to think the world really was going to turn to God. I don't believe that anymore."
> Graham feels the deterioration of moral values is a greater evil than communism.

"We will bury ourselves. It's our own affluence that will be our destruction."

Graham's basic fundamentalism, the belief that each man must be redeemed through Christ, has remained unchanged over the years. He sounds downright gloomy as he talks of the state of the world—the coming of Armageddon, the end of history, the Second Coming, terrorist organizations that could be building the bomb, and the quagmire America has found herself in since the assassination of President Kennedy.

This recently prompted Senator Warren Magnuson of Washington to ask if Graham considered himself an optimist or a pessimist.

"I told him I was an optimist because I have read the last page of the Bible."

Now with all due respect to Dr. Graham—and it is a great respect on the writer's part—that is a poor attitude. Christ's Second Coming might be this year or in 10,000 years, and "sitting on one's hands" in the interval is no solution. Not that Dr. Graham has been sitting on his hands by any means. As one very dear to me has said, "God expects us only to do the best we can with what we've got"—but that means, the best. It was exactly what theologian Karl Rahner had in mind with the idea of the new "Diaspora." There are people of all faiths worldwide and each individual has a few points of influence in his community. The first place a social movement must start is in the developing of confidence in the principles which the movement stands for and in stimulating interest in these principles in others.

Now, Dr. Graham mentioned communism as a menace. It is also an opportunity. One of the mottos of the communists, and a powerful one, is the expression "Power to the people." It seems to carry with it a simultaneous sense of urgency, of solidarity, of justice, of freedom and of potency. It has an appeal not only to the impoverished tenant farmer or the unskilled laborer, but to the liberal-minded of all levels (liberal here is defined in the sense descriptive of an attitude in support of the rights of all men as free individuals). The reality of communism is a far cry from fulfilling the motto's claim. But, that does not diminish the value of the motto as a motivating instrument and an existing one. In its raw form, it says little. The power lies in what the motto calls to mind or what it seems to symbolize that is important.

Let us compare two sets of values which can be subsumed under the motto. The first set of values is materialistic and the second is theistic. What power can materialism legitimately offer the people? Let us permit utopian, stateless Marxism to reign and assume all men can agree to control themselves and live in harmony. Still, at best, it offers the power to live the life of a contented animal—to let alone and to be let alone. Given everything that concept connotes or can connote, can man be satisfied? He is still going to age and die, and life does not rise courageously to its culmination, it fades whimperingly away. Life remains an absurdity, strive as he will, the end of man is the same. Sartre and Camus are right in that context.

Can we add any worthwhile conditioning statements—"Power to the people through Castro"; "Power to the people from birth to death"; "Power to the people through Castro from birth to death"; "Power to the people in joyous comradeship"? There is just not much one can do with the motto except shout it out as a rebel.

Take the same motto, "Power to the people" and add a second line "in and through God's love" and then add a third line "now and forever." That is a package which, given God and given man's immortal soul, makes an attractive proposition. That is a package which can be sold, at all levels, to all cultures, everywhere and in all political forms even to a reoriented communism.

Now we should look at the last set of logic gates we will encounter which can be simply stated without further explanation:

16. Given the existence of a personal loving God from previous logic gates, the ubiquitousness of man's strongly-held belief in the revelation of God to man is preponderantly evidential that such revelation does take place.

17. Supporting 16, and specifically demonstrated by the evidence, is that the Old Testament of the Bible is the historical record of God's dealing with a particular people in covenantal form.

18. The major religions universally convey, sometimes in general terms, but always definitively, a moral code which includes the concept that all men have an obligation to their fellowmen in justice, if not in love, as God's creatures.

19. Morality, as a rational behavioral system of free men, has no autonomy. It depends on the recognized existence of God as a personal being.

20. The Bible, both Old Testament and New, but particularly

the New, stress the concept of the brotherhood of all men under the fatherhood of God as a religious goal. This concept is implicable to all major religions.

21. There is strong motivating potential in the concept of the brotherhood of man under the fatherhood of God to spark a worldwide social movement which has both satisfying answers to life's meaning and social consequences promoting a productive and peaceful future for man. The motivation can be both emotionally and rationally supported.

22. There are, at least latent, traditions among all peoples available to support a movement such as formulated in 21. It is not a dream; not "pie in the sky," it can be real.

Theologian Paul Althaus expressed what ought to be the attitude of all God-seeking people in the current age, particularly to Christians, but also, by extension, to all religions. He said:

> We cannot wait for the new world and the new mankind, for the Kingdom and for eternal life, in any other way but "in practice." That is, by our quest in this our world, by deeply suffering its misery and doing battle with it. Christian hope is not a theory—it takes the whole man. To wait, is a whole stance of life. To wait means to suffer, to search, to labor, to live with eyes open through the conflict between Christ and world, to push on to the outermost limit, to knock on closed doors. If we do not forever in prayer, and in work, strain to escape from captivity into the endless freedom and splendor of the Kingdom of God, if we do not do battle against the misery and injustice on earth, if we do not struggle for sanctification, if we do not work to bring together and prepare the community of God—how will we know what it means to wait for the Lord! Hope is truly alive only in the act, daily renewed, of our soul and our whole life.

Part VI, An Extrapolation, which follows, is conceived as a worldwide model study in which the ideas of Nietzsche and Toynbee are contrasted in the rapidly changing last quarter of the twentieth century. The ideas we have explained will be tested in that model in the concepts of social movements. The theistic and atheistic moral theories will be viewed in that arena of action.

PART VI

AN EXTRAPOLATION

Chapter 19

AN OPENING TO LIGHT

Before an extrapolation can be made, it is necessary to summarize and thus consolidate the position which we have developed in the last four sections. We have seen in Part II that, in the twelfth century, man's concept of man in the West had reached a point of convergence on the Augustinian-Platonic philosophy which was a view of man primarily as a transcendental creature and the well-loved child of a benevolent, almighty and eternal God. It was an opening to light in philosopohy—a dynamic philosophy which had seen Christianity spread to all of Europe over the prostrate body of the pagan western Roman Empire, itself, a victim of its exhausted convergence on a theme of a materialistic world empire a thousand years earlier.

Christendom had expanded to include the Franks in the sixth century, Anglo-Saxons in the seventh, the Germans in the eighth, the Czechoslovaks in the ninth, the Poles in the tenth, the Magyars, Finns and Russians in the eleventh. But now in the twelfth century, it seemed as though the apostolic zeal which had spread this idea had become exhausted in the process, its tidal crest had been reached and the dynamism started to leave the system. In consolidating its position, the church had become much more political and the burgeoning feudal system with all of its bickering and conniving of each jealous little center of authority sapped what strength was left. Even the Crusades did not completely mobilize the forces. For, within those Christian armies, the political plotting continued and bled the organism.

One of the major counterforce elements which started the divergence was the new dynamism of Islam which brought about the introduction of Aristotelian and Eastern thought into the monolith. The split between the Platonic and Aristotelian schools was the first break, quickly followed by even more rapidly divergent views through the Renaissance, into the Age of Enlightenment in the late eighteenth century. That period marked the point of greatest divergence. The embattled scholastics and followers of Immanuel Kant were about the only holdouts emphasizing man as a being with a transcendental nature.

Then, gradually, the successive forces of rational scientism including early positivism, romanticism, logical positivism, and dialectic materialism became more polarized on the idea of the absolute material animality of man early in the twentieth century. The dominant theme in education, in the behavioral sciences, in the popular philosophies was man, the gifted animal, and God became a projective compensatory myth. There were still holdouts in the philosophical schools, but the mind of contemporary man, represented in the men directing the world thought at the working level, was materialistic. The individuals might display pious statements on occasion, but their driving force was pragmatic opportunism.

Again, though, the system having converged on this idea, began to lose energy and stagnate because it offered nothing in the way of satisfying answers to man, the rational animal. And, once again, thought began to diverge. Even the early successes of Marxism paradoxically were a result of this malaise. It was the revolt of the mass of people against the dominant forces in the established governments which paid lip service to humanity and laid ever heavier burdens upon the individuals. Marx provided some hope in the disenchanted world.

But, more hopefully, for the eventual reorientation of man, intellectualism began to move from its materialistic stagnation into new themes of man with some transcendental overtones. That is the position in which philosophy now stands. But the lag which always exists between the intellectual initiative and the world of present reality remains. The changed mood has not reached the people who control the power and who motivate and influence society.

In its end state, materialism is philosophically, sociologically and psychologically deficient. We saw how the idea of materialism utterly fails to provide any answers to the most compelling questions in the life of man. It cannot provide answers to the Hobbesian question of the existence of society in the very simplest terms. We saw that pure philosophic thought is strongly supportive of the concept of an intelligent Supreme Being.

We have seen in Part III that the evidence of physical science points overwhelmingly to the existence of an infinite, intelligent, purposeful Creator who does, providentially, guide the universe. Of the alternatives, only this would be acceptable in terms of modern cosmologic theory, or in terms of anthropology or extended thermodynamics. It alone would be in accord with the universe as a dynamic system or with the concepts of modern physics. The wonderous basic simplicity of the unfolding physical universe concomitant with its complex infrastructure pointed to an intellectual origin of the greatest sophistication.

We have seen that the evidence from physical science points strongly to the transcendental nature of man. It suggests that the logical ultimate purpose of the physical universe, as for all creation, is to provide the Creator external glory in His creative mode and intelligent objects of His infinite love. Only the freely-given response of materially-derived yet materially-independent beings assenting willingly to His loving guidance can supply those functions from the material universe. But man is free. The Creator does not impose His will over the will of man. Man is created a free being, and, to the maximum extent, in that mode, he is permitted to control his own destiny.

In Part IV, we have seen strong empirical physical evidence in the form of anomalous events that this Supreme Being is deeply and personally concerned in a beneficent way with man's life and the way he lives that life. That he does indeed act as the kind and loving Father that Augustine and his followers had preached throughout Europe, and which, though modified somewhat by Aquinas and his followers, remains a strong force into the present day. Further, it was noted that in several instances those anomalies could not have been established as valid exceptions to the physical laws without the scientific methodologies provided in this century. Those selected for this study were a tiny fraction of the total number of anomalous events which continue to occur each year.

In Part V, we found convincing evidence that God does reveal Himself to man, evidence that He has throughout history let man know that man was His special and well-loved creature in the world and that men were responsible to Him for their behavior toward each other because all were equally loved by Him. In a study in some detail, we explored the strong evidence that the Old Testament, as revelation, was an authentic historical expression of God's covenantal relationship with man. Some of the major theologic approaches were discussed and it was noted that those which were closer to orthodoxy also seemed to place most emphasis on the theme of the personal relationship of God to man in a dialogue of love. We pointed out that morality, as a free behavioral system, by its nature, cannot exist as a concept independent of that dialogue.

It appears unavoidable in a rational analysis, therefore, to accept at this point that there is a Creator of infinite intelligence and power, that this Creator is personal, beneficent, and intimately concerned with man and his individual life and that He has communicated His concern for man's welfare and established rules of conduct for man toward Him and toward his fellow man. It is also unavoidable to conclude that man has a transcendental nature and independent intelligence—a free intellect—which not only permits him, but obliges him, to reflect on his relationship with his Creator. This reflection should carry with it the intent to determine, to the extent possible, how the Creator would wish him to respond individually. The time has come for a new opening to light.

Chapter 20

THE STAGE SETTING

This brings us back to a point where we can start looking at the future probabilities in terms of the antithetical Nietzsche and Toynbee scenarios. As good a place to start as any is with a flashback review to the development of the current geopolitical situation in which the drama will be staged.

On March 15, 1917 as a result of reverses suffered by his armies in conflict with the Austro-German forces in World War I, Tsar Nicholas abdicated and permitted a provisional government to be set up under Prince Lvov. The latter decided to continue the war, a move which was opposed by the Socialist Revolutionaries. Shortly afterwards, Lvov resigned and Alexander Kerensky succeeded as provisional premier of a moderate Socialist Government confirmed by an open election. Lenin, however, refused to accept the results and started a revolt against Kerensky with his Bolshevist minority declaring, "It is naive to wait for a formal majority for the Bolshevists. No revolution does that." He forced the dissolution of the Constituent Assembly and by an armed intervention succeeded in gaining control in the Revolution of October 1917, (November 7, 1917 on the Gregorian calendar). Thereupon, he turned and crushed many of those who had supported him including the sailors at the Kronstadt Naval Base who were largely instrumental in bringing him to power. They made the mistake of demanding democratic freedom. The USSR was then organized in 1922 under Lenin's control. It is the well-established opening scene in the sequence which has since been played over and over throughout the world with minor variations.

In writing about this episode, Historian Adrienne Koch, in her book, *Philosophy for a Time of Crisis,* (Koch, 1959) says,

> In this Leninist phase many of the original Marxist theoretical notions about the origin and course of the Socialist Revolution were abandoned. For Marx held that the inexorable forces of the social relations of production themselves create a proper Socialist consciousness in the workers and lead them to

organize the revolt against capitalism; that capitalism
would be overthrown only at its highest point of development; and that the workers who are the overwhelming majority of the population would establish
workers' democracies to govern their own relations,
but a proletarian dictatorship was needed to defend
the revolution against the capitalist elements who
have been expropriated. . . .The Russian Communist
Party was not the architect but rather the scavenger
of a revolution against tsarism which had been carried out by others. It is sometimes forgotten that the
Russian workers formed less than 10 percent of the
population, and were generally not attracted to the
Russian Communist Party. Nor did the revolution take
place in a country with the economic preconditions
of capitalist maturity, such as Marx had designated
but one in which agriculture was predominant.

The "spectre" which Marx saw "haunting Europe" in the
opening lines of the *Manifesto* was not the one which finally
developed but the latter was and is a spectre nonetheless.

The scene now shifts to China in September 1949 where the
opening of the play remains the same. Mao Tse-tung who had
boycotted the National Assembly called in 1946 after the defeat
of Japan, declared himself head of the Chinese People's Republic and renewed the interrupted civil war in a country not yet
reorganized from the effects of World War II. He succeeded
by military means in ousting Chiang Kai-shek who had been
named the first constitutional president in 1948. In February
1950 the Soviet-Chinese pact was signed affirming the alliance
of the two communist powers.

With that as prologue let us now take a look at the geopolitical scene today, (1987), as the curtain rises on our test production. It is usual to talk about the "Non-communist World," the
"Communist World" and the "Third World" the latter being
chiefly the uncommitted and underdeveloped nations of Asia,
Africa and Central America which the communists and non-
communists constantly woo or exploit depending on the observer's point of view. But that is oversimplified and neglects
some highly important facts of life. There are inevitable over-
lappings and mixtures. Both the communist and non-communist
worlds are far from monolithic blocs in terms of their long
and short-term economic self-interest, and the "Third World"
is highly varied in culture and in specific economic interests

and even more importantly in cultural and ethnic background and values. Nevertheless, for discussion purposes, the division does have merit.

The "Communist World" can be broken into two principal groups, the USSR with its European satellites, Viet Nam and Cuba; and The People's Republic of China and its satellites— North Korea and elements in Southeast Asia. But, there are also the independent communist states such as Yugoslavia and Angola at this writing.

The "Non-communist World" comprises six principal blocs of nations, each zealously independent, but with many close cultural and economic interests in common. These blocs of nations are: (1) the United States and Canada; (2) The Euro-States and British Isles; (3) Central and South America (excluding Cuba); (4) Japan, Taiwan, South Korea and by a stretch Australia and the Philippine Islands, the latter more tied to the East now as the United States retreats from Southeast Asia; (5) If, as the writer foresees, there is the eventual recognition by both Arab Muslims and Jews of their common ethnic heritage and their common economic interests, there would be a Mideast bloc including both the Muslim Arab nations and the State of Israel. This writer sees both Islam and Judaism as fundamentally opposed to communism although this does not guarantee that there will not be some political takeovers in the Mideast along classic communist lines. The sixth group would be the far eastern Asian subcontinent nations—Pakistan, India and Bangladesh—which also have much in common in spite of the recent hostilities.

Now, obviously, these groupings include substantial elements of the Third World and there are nations omitted, South Africa for instance, which would normally fall into the non-communist camp but which has geographic and demographic situations peculiarly its own and are peculiary situated in internal policies.

The cleavage in the communist bloc between China and the Soviet Union is crucial in our two scenarios and must be examined fairly closely. The cleavage is one of increasing depth and breadth as the development of China progresses. In 1950, in the late Stalinist period, when communist China was consolidating its newly-established control on the mainland of Asia, there were sound reasons for believing that there would be a single dominant communist regime in the Euro-Asian land mass. It was a spectre of frightening magnitude to the non-communist world even in view of the clear military superiority and atomic monopoly possessed by the United States at that time. Many of the signals in the Korean conflict were called by Russia and played out by China.

The solidarity of communism was underscored by Kruschchev speaking as Secretary of the Communist Party at its Twentieth Congress in February 1956. He expanded on the great power which the friendly brotherhood of the USSR and The People's Republic of China now represented athwart of the Euro-Asian landmass and he said,

> The whole course of international relations in recent years shows that great popular forces have risen to fight for the preservation of peace. The ruling imperialist circles cannot ignore this. Their more far-sighted representatives are beginning to admit that the Position of Strength policy has failed.... (They) do not venture to state that capitalism will find its grave in another world—but are already obligated to admit that the socialist camp is invincible.... In those countries where capitalism is still strong, where it possesses a tremendous military and police machine, serious resistance by reactionary forces is inevitable. There the transition to socialism will take place under conditions of sharp class, revolutionary struggle.

And later in his famous comment on the futility of capitalist hopes that the communist stance would change, he suggested they would have to "...wait until a shrimp learns to whistle." The communist world would move forward under the Soviet banner to certain victory.

Krushchev apparently had not read Mao Tse-tung's work *On the Protracted War,* written many years earlier which emphasized the condition brought about by three centuries of European domination when he wrote, "This war (the Chinese civil war) is not only the banner of China's liberation, but is pregnant with significance for world revolution. We will lead the Chinese revolution to its completion and also exert a far-reaching influence in the East as well as in the whole world." This was not a silent partner writing. And Khrushchev, perhaps insensitively, turned his attention increasingly to the development of the Eastern Provinces in his "virgin lands program" and what had been an enormous buffer zone between the two massive communist powers began more and more to become one of competitive and conflicting interest.

China emerged from the Korean engagement as one end of

a Euro-Asian communist axis still subordinate to the Soviet Union, but increasingly independent in developing its own internal structure and foreign policy. The Soviet Union was too preoccupied with its program of developing military, naval and atomic superiority in its position vis-a-vis the United States to put a stop to this development. The "Great Leap" of the cultural revolution brought about by Mao in the 1960's was to rid the country of its pro-Soviet military clique and the capitalistic "revisionists." Mao also succeeded in bringing the local warlords into subservience to the central government. In spite of the tremendous upset to the nation's economy, that aspect of the program was largely successful. Some 39 million Chinese were killed in the course of the takeover according to an official U.S. Senate report on the subject.

More than a quarter of a century after the Korean conflict, Communist China is still the junior member of the axis but that axis is being subjected to enormous strain. There are counter "torques" at each end being introduced on more and more issues of mutual concern but opposite polarity. The entire idea of Marxism was that of arriving at "one world." No one seriously considers the Marxian theory of an eventual Utopia and of a withering away of the state in a single communist world order. What is developing is two communist worlds of greatly divergent interests. In terms of their basic ideology one must "eat the other" after they have digested the capitalist world—there cannot be two party bosses and sets of apparatus in the ultimate world. The time of peaceful rapprochement under a single leadership appears to have run out. The Soviet Union will not submit to China nor China to the Soviet Union short of a military imposition. The two ruling elites are ethnically, traditionally and culturally incompatible and a change does not appear likely. Both groups are independently power-oriented.

The non-communist world is even less a simple structure. There are differences in interests and culture—but neither the United States nor Western Europe nor Japan—the major elements—are, at this stage, or in the foreseeable future, set on establishing a world empire. World government, yes, but a single dictatorial super nation state or regime, no. These nations see unity in diversity and competition as desirable. The communists see unity in complete uniformity under total party "solidarity" and, necessarily, competition must go. It is one world in uniformity. It is a facet again of the ancient dialectic problem of the "One and the Many." This time, the argument is political. It is to the United States' everlasting credit, and forms the basic credibility in the idea of one world in diversity, that when it had the power of monopoly it did not exercise that power. To the contrary, the United States assisted in reestablishing competition everywhere in a prostrate world.

The position of the "Third World" is, of course, essentially that of supplier of raw material. As individual nations undergo their own industrialization, each will seek to get the best deal from the other groups in competition. This is a position which, in ideological terms, supports the capitalistic principles but one which also is susceptible to the communist propaganda pitch to the underprivileged contained in the Marxian motto, "To each in accord with his needs; from each in accord with his ability." Their needs far exceed their ability in terms of the industrialized world. But it is a trend of decreasing susceptibility with time as industrialization and economic independence is achieved, on the assumption of course that eventually it will be. The Arabian oil-producing states, for instance, are not particularly impressed with the Marxian pitch of need versus ability. Although, for political purposes vis-a-vis Israel, they may solicit communist help. A just, lasting peace in the Semitic internecine contest would obviously work to the benefit of the "Free World."

Obviously, there are many complex interrelationships in the geopolitical world today. However, at the current stage and for the next quarter century at least, the very complexity appears to work for no worldwide military confrontation so long as a credible level of military parity is maintained by the major groups. The rising industrial strength of China is, at this time, a factor working toward peace. Both China and Russia would fear to engage in an all-out war with a major third party. Even if they should win, the non-engaged member of the axis would seize and devour the wounded partner along with its prey. It is a truce of scorpions. Each knows the pragmatic level of the other's ethics.

Something more also can be said about the communist cleavage. There are both internal and external needs for each member of the axis to maintain a differentiation of posture. Each must present to its people and to the Third World the view that they alone represent the party continuity. The other has to be given a label as capitalistic revisionists or counter-revolutionists or reactionary traitors of the true Marxist/Leninist theory and practice. The greatest difficulty in this position lies with the Soviet Union. Their main strength is in their western provinces and is European in basic orientation. The Soviet Union is viewed throughout the world as European or Caucasian, regardless of how it would portray the image as the exclusive savior of the exploited colonial, non-European people. The use of Cuban troops is a device to project a "Third World image." In contrast, the Chinese are manifestly not tied pejoratively to a Western history and this has consistently been one of their main points. The Russian heritage is predominantly Byzantine Christian and those traditions and cultural traits are deep set in the people. As an ethnic group, they were really not good material for Marxism. It is as much an "accident of fate" as skilled planning that enabled an opportunistic Lenin to take over such a profoundly religious people. Seventy years of repression have not extinguished those traditions.

It is indeed a troubled world but the troubles do not lie entirely nor even primarily within the non-communist world. The leaders of the Soviet Union must soon commit themselves officially as nationalists for "Mother Russia" or internationalists for "one world of communism" and the latter position becomes tougher each year to maintain. It is the Soviet Red Army and Navy and space effort, largely European in top staff, and not the international communist brotherhood which the world recognizes. The international communist brotherhood cannot tolerate two "Big Brothers." One has to go.

For the next quarter century, we are facing a world of great tension and of shifting of interest as well as power. Tension implies that the opposite pulls are nearly balanced. That, in turn, means that the triggering agency itself which eventually upsets the balance and relieves the tension for better or worse may be a relatively small thing, an idea, for instance. In a closely matched tug-of-war, the simple act of adding a weak member to one side ends the struggle by overbalancing the other side.

The most critical aspect in my opinion is the tension between the mainland Chinese and the Soviet Union. This is not only because of the great resources, human and material, involved in this dispute but also because a real rapprochement on that axis would provide such strength in a central consolidated position as to overpower any other likely combination of forces. The ultimate denouement would merely be a question of working out from the center and then mopping up peripheral and outlying areas in conflict, including North and South America.

The effective coalition of Western Europe, the United States and Japan, though currently economically more powerful, is handicapped because so badly scattered geographically. This poses an enormous problem in carrying on a well-coordinated joint effort of containment, especially in view of strong "fifth columns" of communist ideologies in almost every country. Japan and Western Europe literally have no rear zone of communications in the military sense for positioning reserve strategic forces. And the United States is too remote from either to provide that function effectively, particularly as the United States forces are reduced in Europe and Asia. A rapid nuclear escalation would appear the only plausible military solution for the West. A successful containment using conventional forces would be almost out of the question.

A real and credible consolidated Euro-Asian land mass under a single aggressive communist leadership would probably end the tension on an international scale by eventual collapse of the nations of the West individually on an ultimatum basis similar to the Munich appeasement prior to World War II. A "better red than dead" philosophy would rule out a nuclear military solution given the dominant hedonistic and materialist attitude of the West. There are few Patrick Henrys currently on the political scene or, likely, in the streets either.

The existence of a strong difference between the Soviet and Chinese official positions in who is going to be the source of authority is thus a crucial triggering mechanism. How strong is that difference? Oddly enough, the political question of the ideological dedication to international communism by the Soviet Union is the difference. China needs agricultural land area and the only large contiguous areas are in, and immediately adjacent to, Soviet Union territory. The land in question is in the Upper Lena, Ob, and Yenisky River basins and adjacent to the Aral Sea and Lake Balkhash east of the Urals and generally north and west of Mongolia. China cannot acquire the land by appeal to the Russians as fellow communists and they know it. The Russians know the Chinese covet those lands and they have no intention of giving them up.

The Italians relate a story about the depth of true communist sentiment in Italy which is to the point. A candidate for party membership was being examined for fitness by the local party boss, so the boss asked, "If you had five farms and the regime needed assistance what would you do?" The candidate responded instantly, "I'd give four to the party and keep one for myself." The question is asked next, "And if you had five tractors?" The ready reply was, "The same." Then came the question, "And if you had five chickens?" There was a pause, then the candidate expostulated, "But I have five chickens!" The "parent" country's generosity largely applies only to the property of "others." They remain strangely human.

That apparently is the crux of the matter. The Soviet Union has the most available chickens, which they are not anxious to share. If that thesis is acceptable, the political trigger is a highly resistant mechanism. The Soviet Union and China will in probability remain competitive. But where does that leave the Soviet Union? Each year the military potential of China increases. Yet, an interdictive war to prevent a future military expansion is singularly unattractive from any viewpoint—given the sheer numbers of the Chinese forces and an unsympathetic West. Further, a major military engagement for the Soviet Union in the West is suicidal in terms of the Asiatic question. That leaves them as alternatives, an early political, ideologic takeover of the West or a restructuring of its own ideology to permit real Soviet-Western compatibility and not a phony detente. Either of the alternatives provides at least a temporary solution. If the first alternative is preferable, it is also much less certain. It hinges on an economic collapse and general social disorder of the West so that leftist "coalitions" can gain control. Prosperous conditions are not conducive to communism—again on the "five chicken theory," only to those whose "needs" far exceed "abilities" is it attractive. The Soviet Union's position is both crucial and pivotal. A true commitment of the Soviet Union either way to the East or to the West is determinative for many years, but their long term survival seems to lie in alignment with the West rather than the East.

Hypothetically, what are the chances of a real rapprochement of the Soviet Union with the West? Their dominant and traditional cultural ties are to the European West. What is required is a philosophic change in policy, which also implies an ideological change as well. The philosophic roots of Marxism are at best moribund. The situation on this point is well made by philosopher Abraham Kaplan in his work, *The New World of Philosophy*, published in 1961 (Kaplan, 1961). He writes,

> Of course, there is an official communist philosophy in the standard nineteenth century European sense, called as you know dialectical materialism. I must tell you at once I will have very little to say on that subject, narrowly conceived. As a metaphysic, I think it is largely anachronistic irrelevancy even from the standpoint of communism itself. The materialism has been pretty well outdated by the developments in the physical sciences in the twentieth century and the dialectic outdated by the development in logic and mathematics.

The communists seek to ignore those facts—and in one way they are unimportant—the impoverished communist recruit is not much interested in philosophic coherence. But a communist subject, who is also an intellectual, very well may be interested and concerned.

In the Soviet Union, a communist subject may be also well aware of the box in which his nation, as his nation, is placed by continued adherence to the outmoded philosophy and its ideology even though he may feel quite legitimately that the nation has been made stronger by its past adherence to those policies. Only a fool clings to outmoded methodology when its continued use guarantees disaster—though on that basis there have been many fools in history as C. P. Snow, cited earlier, pointed out. Involved for the Russians is the change of attitude, is an open and real abandonment of the Marxist internationalist ambitions and willingness to become a member of the family of nations as one in a community of freedom. That action would leave communist China alone as leader in that world of subversive policies, but China alone is not the global threat the combination is.

Strangely enough, the posture of China as the leader of an international revolutionary and conspiratorial movement is contrary to the traditional Chinese pride in their position as the "Middle Kingdom"—the real representative of the highest in intellectual and cultural values on earth. This is a viewpoint with an integral abhorrence of the "extreme" in any form. Communism has made strange bedfellows in its procrustean bed!

The Western rapprochement policy for the Soviets also implies an opening up of the Soviet Union on its economic, commercial and cultural relationships with all other Western nations. Eventually, it involves return to a non-dictatorial regime and restoration of individual freedom. In this writer's view that is a very fruitful alternative for all concerned.

In every "strategic" contest it is of course essential to "preserve the options" as long as possible so as to keep the opponent "in the dark" and thus force him to spread his forces to provide for all the alternatives. In a condition of global tension, however, there is always the risk of inducing a preemptive action by one of the opponents if he senses that his position is weakening by attempts to cover all the options. A strategy based on that of the "counter-puncher" has no realistic chance in this business. That has essentially been the West's position vis-a-vis both China and the USSR. The West was economically able to assume that stance, but that situation also is coming to an end.

That process, in itself, is economically debilitating. Sooner or later, commitments must be made and some options forgone, or a preemptive nuclear strike becomes a real possibility. In fact, all three of the major power blocs will soon have to make up their minds. There are not too many cards left to be dealt in this poker game. The nations of the world have been in a position of political and sociological strain for several decades and the strain is intensifying and will continue to intensify until something triggers a release.

While the writer foresees a major worldwide conflict as improbable in the next two decades, yet the strain internationally will be at times at intolerable levels. For the first time in history for all practical purposes there are no "virgin" isolated lands to be exploited—no place to accommodate either the increasing population or to which the "disenchanted" can migrate to live their own way. As far back as 1955, scientist-philosopher John von Neumann had written,

> ..."the great globe itself" is in a rapidly maturing crisis—a crisis attributable to the fact that the environment in which technological progress must occur has become both undersized and underorganized.
>
> In the first half of this century, the accelerating industrial revolution encountered an absolute limitation—not on technological progress as such, but on an essential safety factor. This safety factor...a matter of geographical and political *Lebensraum*...
>
> Now this safety factor mechanism is being sharply inhibited; literally and figuratively, we are running out of room. At long last, we begin to feel the effects of the finite, actual size of the earth in a critical way. (*Fortune* Magazine, June, 1955).

There is today (1975) about 25 percent less *lebensraum* per capita than there was in 1955 and this situation plus the ubiquitousness of world affairs through modern communications literally leave no "quiet corners" on earth untouched by the world's emotion-filled events. Societal tension and strain are inevitable and both will be of increasing intensity for the rest of this century at least.

The chief source of anxiety and strain, demographic at root, comes from perceived differentials in availability and accessibility of life, resources and nations see themselves as relatively advantaged and disadvantaged—society is divided between the "haves" and "have nots." The deeply disadvantaged as individuals and as collectives are well aware that the chances of self-betterment are poor and getting poorer. The visions of a bright new world tomorrow which in prior times most people had—if not for themselves at least for their children—have shrunk with the shrinking globe. And the percentage of the disadvantaged increases with the population and hence with time. The anxiety has a broad base. The lists of the items of disadvantage are endless ranging from sufficient food at one end to the luxury of time to relax and think at the other.

The current population in 1987 is just over five billion. By the year 2000 most estimates place the population at something in excess of six billion—about 50 percent more than 1975, so that von Neumann's critical safety factor continues to shrink and the tensions and differentials and strains will continue apace.

The critical increases will occur in those nations labeled as the "Third World." Two-thirds of the population live in the poorest countries, including China and India. Sociologic studies demonstrate that when nations become economically stable, the population expansion comes under tolerable limits—children are not looked upon as potential social security—we will view a reverse implication of that fact a little later. The United Nations identifies (1975) 33 nations that have serious food shortages. Yet, moderate estimates of the potential production of land areas, not including production from sea resources, indicate that a population of about 20 billion could be sustained at adequate nutritional levels by a worldwide effort of moderate extent—a financial effort favorably comparable to the total annual military budgets over a period of about ten years, in fact. The objective can be achieved through increased production on existing lands and by more efficient methods in reclamation of lands, principally in the tropical areas which have never been cultivated. These latter areas also are in, or adjacent to, the regions which have the greatest population pressures.

Development of the potential requires the best in technology and a full commitment by the "have" nations to assist the "have nots." The response in the past has been one of widespread apathy or even hostility. This aspect of the problem, recognized by intellectuals worldwide, is viewed by the disadvantaged as the clinching evidence of capitalism's policy of self-perpetuation in insatiable greed, and by the advantaged as justifiable and prudent self-protection. The polarity of views is a potent source of social revolution if an evolutionary policy of "one-worldness" does not develop realistically within the next two or three decades. The fact of the polarity seems to be studiously ignored by the leaders and by most of the citizens of the West who make noises of commitments to humanitarian principles but look the other way in the hard cases.

What difference does man's concept of man make in the context of today's problems? The difference is literally life and death in the current arena of destructive potential. Both the communist world and the noncommunist world, despite other differences are centering on the biological concept of man—the "gifted animal." Individually man has no more intrinsic value than a cow or a sheep—perhaps less—because the latter two have a recognized economic value, which man, as such, in a world seen as overpopulated does not have. Man in that sense is seen as an economic liability. In a world of scarcity, unless one can produce more "goods" than he consumes, he should be destroyed much as a chicken which ceases to lay eggs. We need look no further than Belsen or any of the other Nazi death camps for our model mass execution equipment. It has already been designed and test-proven.

In an article prepared for the *National Geographic Magazine* (July, 1975), by Thomas Y. Canby, the subject of prospects of meeting the world food problem is addressed: "Among some, this pessimism (of inability) has led even further, into the realm of how the 'have' nations should react when massive famine strikes the 'have nots.' One such scenario is called the 'lifeboat ethic.' It prescribes that the self-sufficient nations must, at some point, refuse help to those who are stricken, lest the added burden swamp the survivors' lifeboat, dragging all to the bottom."

Numerous philosophers have pointed out, and we have seen in a brief way, that there are only four universal ideas which have sufficient appeal to provide man the motivation for a complete, personal commitment. These are the concepts of God, society, nature, and man. Philosopher Ferrater Mora in his work, *Man at the Crossroads,* wrote:

> Let us confine ourselves, then, to assuming that belief or faith must always be intimately connected with truth. Consequently, it is impossible to accept a very common contention: That since man needs a faith, any faith will do, because faith does nothing but fill the void of man's existence. Faith, of course, usually appears as a psychological attitude. But it is not sufficient for faith to be a psychological attitude;

what is asserted in an act of faith is also an essential ingredient of faith. We do not imply that affirmations of faith must have a very specific content. It will suffice here if we point out that there are contents that are capable of providing the "objective" basis for a faith, and others that are not. Among the former, we count four: God, man, society, and nature. None of them excludes the others, possibly each implies the others. . . . But let us leave this for later. What is important now is that the following three points be made perfectly clear. First, that, in fact, men cannot live without faith. Second, that faith cannot be "any affirmation whatever." Third, that it cannot be reduced to a merely psychological attitude. (Mora, 1957).

Mora essentially equated faith to a commitment to one of these four concepts. They are not by any means concepts of equal "weight." If one were to take the last three and place them in the form of an inverted equilateral triangle with man at the bottom and society and nature above him at the angle points to either side, there would be two-way arrows connecting all three points indicating that man, society, and nature mutually interact. But man as an individual is scarcely competitive in a contest with the other two. He is literally Sartre's "useless passion" or Camus' "absurd," powerless against hopeless odds. That is the "total" picture for modern man, the biologic specimen. It is scarcely a matter of wonder that he should feel anxious, alienated and overcome with a sense of "anomie." He has no appeal from his plight. Belsen and the "lifeboat ethic" apply here with an appalling reality.

Now if one completes the diamond and, at the apex above and between society and directly above man, positions God and then places one-way arrows from God toward nature and society, but a two-way arrow between God and man one has the theist picture. Nature and society do not act on God, He acts on them. But between God and man, the individual, every man, regardless of how weak or powerful in society, there is an intimate dialogue. There is the freely-willed, "I-Thou," relationship so beautifully drawn by Martin Buber. Now the scales are brought into balance and man stands in the legitimate dignity and strength he has as a beloved child of God. And there is an ultimate appeal regardless of where or how the accounts are settled.

There is no chance of a society, having these values at heart, giving in to Belsen or the "lifeboat ethic." Every man is a member of a true brotherhood of man under the fatherhood of God and every man will be evaluated and judged on his response in that context. It is only in such a milieu that the problems facing the world can be solved and the human race survive as human. Man, without God, is selfishly Hobbesian and solutions on that basis can only yield anarchy or dictatorship in today's shrinking world. Given Nietzche's atheism, his scenario will eventuate.

Unless a forward-looking policy is achieved which sees a free community of nations with all cooperating in their mutual problems, unless "we" are willing to make present sacrifices for the ultimate improvement of the life of our fellowman, civilization will not survive. This solution can only come about if there is a deep sensing that we are, all, one family under the fatherhood of God, the same all-loving omnipotent Being which our analysis has shown Him to be. He is patient with our weakness and at the same time not unconcerned in our well-being.

It seems reasonable that any social movements in the religious order must originate within the religious "Diaspora" throughout the world. The presence in all cultures and nations of enclaves of religious peoples of all beliefs constitute cadre's in-being for insemination of these ideas in the surrounding peoples when the disillusionment and anxiety become sufficiently deep, as it most certainly will within the next few decades. There is no way of predicting what the precipitating event will be which will stimulate the change. The more dramatic and broadly-based the appeal to all peoples, the more rapid the change in values will be. While God does not interfere with man's freely-willed choice of behavior, He is not indifferent, nor is He powerless to force the change by many separate paths, some punitive and some rewarding. He remains the Master of History.

Chapter 21

THE WORLD OF SOCIAL MOVEMENTS

In the introduction, I had said that the last phase of the contest between the Nietzsche and Toynbee scenarios will see the emergence of major social movements. It is in the framework of the geopolitical world we have just reviewed that we must place the potential large scale social movements which certainly will emerge in the severely strained conditions of the next twenty or thirty years.

The evolution of the Nietzschean theme depends upon the continued trend toward the destruction of cultural values and norms and thus upon the absence of new invigorating movements in support of such values or norms. It will be recalled that his final emergence of a "superman elite" culture and value system springs from a base of anarchic nihilism. In his prediction that movement comes later, but as we will see it may well come ahead of his prediction, depending on the path events take in the period immediately ahead.

On the other hand, the Toynbee scenario requires strong social movements to develop or re-establish cultural values and norms having religious connotations. In these movements, the values and norms must be recognized by the public at large as valid in providing lasting solutions to the strain and tension in the world. They thus must establish in the bulk of the people the sense of primacy of a religious ordering of things in a community of all people. This religiously-oriented sense of community requires a non-Hobbesian concept of man and presupposes the existence of a Supreme Being who, in fact, is the final judge of human acts and stands above any secular authority.

It is quite possible in the period ahead that there will be outbursts of radical anarchism. The level of tension almost guarantees it. But these periods of anarchy are scarcely the social movements in the sense of this discussion. They could either contribute to further decline in the value system or, by reaction, induce strength in countervailing forces. Such outbursts could be directly stimulated by organized social movements in the Marxian mold to cause further dislocations and failure in legitimate governments already under severe strain.

This writer approaches the problem of social movements of the scale here concerned using what amounts to a composite of three sociological viewpoints: (a) The structural-functionalist approach is represented by the value-added concept developed by Neil J. Smelser chiefly in his work, *Theory of Collective Behavior,* (Smelser, 1971); (b) The functional-conflict theory represented by Lewis Coser contained in his numerous works on this subject, particularly, *Continuities in the Study of Social Conflict* (Coser, 1967), and (c) The dialectical conflict theories represented by Rolf Dahrendorf contained chiefly in his *Essays in the Theory of Society* (Dahrendorf, 1967), and also in his numerous articles in various sociological technical journals. The three represent what might be called "rightist," "centrist," and "leftist" viewpoints on the nature of social change and hence of the very essence of social movements. The writer's theoretical grouping is not a matter of proposing an eclectic composite in an averaging-out sense, but of recognizing that this subject is difficult to analyze in any single theoretical setting. The subject does present various faces which are susceptible to different interpretation and all have some validity. Each of the authors cited tends to emphasize some facets more than others.

For the definition of a large-scale social movement, the writer has opted for a paraphrase of Neil Smelser's which would yield that it is a collective attempt to restore, protect, modify or create societal values or norms in the name of a generalized belief. The definition implies that there is a "strain" between the sets of values and norms being promulgated by the "establishment" and those to which the movement is committed. It implies that success of a social movement is closely related to a widely held generalized belief in the efficacy and legitimacy of the espoused values and norms. The definition does not fit the anarchistic rampages.

Whether the movement be revolutionary as the Marxist/Leninist takeover in Russia and China, or evolutionary as the Christianizing of the Roman Empire in the first four centuries A.D., it seeks a transfer of power. It proposes the substitution of one ordering of affairs for another at some level. The success of the movement depends upon establishing the generalized belief in a substantial and active part of the population not only that the existing conditions are intolerable, but also that the solution offered by the particular movement does, in fact, have the answers to correct the condition. It also depends upon establishing in the minds of the people the conviction that the movement has the capability of bringing those answers into realization in the general milieu. The feeling of ability to change the status quo is essential. There must be a sense of being possessed of the power to gain control of the particular situation. For example, there have undoubtedly been many within the Soviet Union since the beginning, individuals and even groups, which considered the situation intolerable. But, under the tight social control exercised, there was no hope of a successful movement to change it.

From the foregoing, certain prerequisites—actually the conjunction of certain favorable conditions—are necessary for a successful outcome:

1. There must be either a condition of apathy or positive dissatisfaction in the general population with circumstances as they presently exist. The time must be "ripe" for change.

2. The generalized belief must have a wide potential appeal—a philosophical base that can attract the intellectuals and a practical down-to-earth application which meets the mood of the general population.

3. There must be a means of mobilizing and consolidating the adherents to the movement. There must also be some kind of an organizational structure and communications network to coordinate the activity and a propaganda arm to recruit and indoctrinate new adherents and also to keep older members energized.

4. The objective of 3, above, must be to instill in the members a sense of the "cosmic" invincibility, the fatedness of a success of the movement. There must be therefore a building of intensity of feeling and enthusiasm which must, however, not be premature. The "pitch" must be carefully timed.

5. There must be a weakness in the "establishment" and the establishment must be penetrated and "subverted" by the new ideas. If the establishment is militarily strong, the armed forces must be intruded so as to be unwilling or ineffective in carrying out the demands of the executives to crush the movement.

6. There must be clearly identifiable concrete targets and objectives. Emphasis and actions must be concentrated on these targets which are seen as milestones on the way to success. "Culprits" must be personally identified with the malice of the *status quo*.

7. There must, in the past, have been lack of response to the individual or small group requests for relief using channels in the existing establishment. These failures in response must be emphasized and those agencies associated with the lack of response identified. This determines the level of power to which the movement must address itself. Striking unnecessarily high or low in the "establishment" may be either fatal or futile and likely both. The higher the level at which the blame for the "intolerable" conditions is placed, the broader based the movement must be in appeal, in numerical strength and in geographical distribution.

The overthrow of the Marcos regime in the Philippines is a recent example of a successful movement. The history of early Christianity may be taken as a model of a religiously-oriented social movement. Earlier, in Part II, it was noted that the intellectuals of the Roman Empire no longer believed in the "official gods." As a consequence, the monotheistic philosophy of neo-Platonism and the pantheistic ideas of Stoicism had moved strongly into the scene and the oracular religions symbolized by the Sibyls had widespread devotees among the intellectuals. There was a widespread curiosity about things religious throughout the Roman world, as the New Testament writings indicate. The people, themselves, were dissatisfied with the pagan culture and values. In short, the time was ripe for change. The Christian community had a well-organized hierarchical structure throughout the empire. They met frequently, and they were active in preaching and in demonstration in gaining recruits. They had a centuries-old cadre of the Jews in Diaspora which formed the early nuclei of the Christian communities. These Hebrew communities were used to perseverance in hardship and persecution. They were "patience" personified. The Roman Empire itself provided the communications network.

The Christians penetrated the army and the political apparatus, as a review of the early martyrologies testifies; and the martyrs were by no means confined to the lower class. The appeal was made from the highest to the lowest class of people, to patricians and to slaves. The end itself came with the conversion of Constantine when he saw the cross in the sky with the words "In this sign, conquer" before the battle in the Milvan Bridge in 312 A.D. This was quickly followed in

313 A.D. by the Treaty of Milan. This treaty granted freedom of religion to the Christians and culminated in Constantine's movement of the capital of the empire to Constantinople in 330 A.D. Constantinople was a city dedicated, by the emperor, to the Blessed Virgin. Christianity soon thereafter, became the "official" religion of the empire. The movement was an evolutionary success within the structure of the "establishment" and it happened without a revolution.

The Russian/Marxist/Leninist takeover could be similarly modeled as an example of an ideological revolutionary movement assuming power following internal collapse. The well-organized communist machine applied the *coup-de-grace* to a government in the state of dissolution following the disastrous military defeat by Germany. There was no well-entrenched establishment. The Kerensky government had not yet established control. There was organizational chaos, widespread unemployment, and even starvation. It could scarcely have been made easier.

Whether a movement proceeds on an evolutionary or revolutionary course, there is usually a precipitating event which crystallizes the movement's position and makes the transfer of power possible. In the case of Christianity, it was the victory of Constantine following the omen. In the Marxist/Leninist revolutionary movement, the precipitating event was associated with the collapse of the inept Kerensky government. The communist minority-forced dismissal of the Constituent Assembly, followed by the revolt of the sailors at Kronstadt, were the overt precipitating events.

In accordance with our definition, and as we have seen from the examples, the motivating force in any large-scale social movement must be an intensely held generalized belief in the efficacy of certain cultural values or norms which are in conflict with those values that the "establishment" represents. This belief must be such that the members of the movement withdraw "legitimacy" upon the established values or norms and confer "legitimacy" upon those of the movement.

It is not necessary that legitimacy be withdrawn from the political regime completely, but only from that sector, or those officials, who represent promulgation of the unsatisfactory norms and values or who oppose introduction of the proposed replacements. For example, the United States Constitution may well be considered an adequate frame of government to provide for the values of freedom for the individual, and an adequate protecting social order. However, at the same time, office holders and makers of official policy (i.e., the Supreme Court, the Congress, or the Executive bureaucracy) may be considered to be acting contrary to the plain intent of the Constitution. Legitimacy would be withdrawn from those individuals or agencies identified as promulgating the erroneous and illegitimate values and norms. In the past, certain Populist and States Rights movements typified this attitude.

On the other hand, Marxist movements target in on the government itself if "capitalistic" or just plain "non-communist." In their view, the values and norms flow from the government structure itself and are thus inherently contrary to Marxist/Leninist principles. A reversal from communism to a true constitutional republic would likewise be at that same top value level. The frames of government are incompatible.

On the world scene today we may distinguish a few social movements in being, or in various stages of development, which can affect the outcome in our two scenarios. First of all, communism is growing old as an ideological movement. Yet it is still active and aggressive in underdeveloped nations, and obstructive in the industrialized and capitalistic nations. It seems to be losing impetus in the developed nations. Its fresh aspect of a revolutionary idea and any intellectual appeal are nearly gone. The trend in the Soviet Union and China appears to be nationalistic rather than internationalistic, although either the Soviet Union or China will move very quickly to fill any existing vacuum in the international scene. They remain as opportunistic as always. They will continue to apply ideologic pressure on the Western "capitalistic" nations. But the *elan* and crusading esprit of the early and mid-century era are increasingly meeting with cynicism. Seventy years have produced no Marxian Utopias anywhere.

The radical-left movement characteristic of the 1960's in the West has largely lost novelty. It is no longer chic to be a wild-eyed anarchist. A totally permissive society is too yielding a medium to support any enthusiastic leaps toward further liberalization much less to stimulate a dedicated organization in that direction. The "Ecological Groups" display continuing disillusionment with the scientific and technologic potential to provide a better quality of life in the developed countries of the West. They illustrate a deepening of the already deep cynicism directed toward "middle-class" economic and cultural values. Yet, here too, the milieu is too spongy and plastic to generate much activism. "If you don't like the way it is, go do your own thing but don't bother me" is the usual reaction. "Why be uncomfortable if you're not getting any attention?'' The impact of this cluster of groups could be important chiefly as a "moral" deterrent to continued industrial development and thus to a weakening of the position of the West vis-a-vis the Communist World, and through contagion of cynicism in the "middle-class" value system hasten the demise of what little remains of any value system. On the other hand, their espousal of "nature projects" reveals that there are other than purely selfish materialistic values which must be recognized.

The current Christian-Socialist movement in the underdeveloped nations, particularly in South and Central America, is quasi-religious in ends and social in primary means. It targets on existing badly unbalanced social conditions—which are more feudal than bourgeoisie—particularly in the rural situation. They thus may offer competition to the atheistic Marxism. The movement says, in effect, that "this worldliness" and "other worldliness" are not incompatible, but mutually supportive in many areas. It has been a powerful social movement even if religiously controversial. Its early successes portend future similar movements elsewhere in an evolutionary rather than revolutionary context. Its hazards lie in its being penetrated and sabotaged by Marxist agencies for Marxist ends and hence away from those religious values which were the original motivating elements. To the extent that the existentialist "man-centeredness of God for man" attitude dominates the thinking, the Christian-Socialist movement is highly susceptible to such diversion. Its philosophical position is weak.

The Pentecostal movement among various religious sects is almost totally religious in orientation, directed by religious means to religious rather than social ends, though it may impact on social ends. Its potential in the two scenarios lies in its capability to generate an "evangelistic" spirit in the sects which could stimulate the development of a generalized belief in the overall efficacy of religious values and norms as a solution to social problems. It is still too scattered for an appraisal of its likely course in the next quarter century.

In addition to these identifiable movements, there are trends which can be identified extending from the past which likely will continue in the future either in their present form or somewhat modified. These are:

> 1. For the next decade the philosophic trend will continue away from the materialistic side but also probably away from the analytic and rationalistic and

toward the existential viewpoint. Perhaps a new philosophic system, blending aspects of the phenomenological, the analytic, and the metaphysical will emerge to compete with the existential thought and to provide rebirth in reason. Survival, in view of the demographic problems of the world scene, does require a rational rather than irrational approach. If philosophy is to fulfill its prophetic role as well as its role of reflecting the current intellectual world view, it seems as though this trend to rationality is unavoidable. That solid defender of extended reason, Jaques Maritain, had said in his work, *The Range of Reason*, published in 1952:

> A historical reckoning such as the one we are undergoing does not take place in one day. Time is necessary to stir up from the depths of human bewilderment, the moral and spiritual revolution that is incomparably more needed than any other revolution. . . .The renewal of civilization that we hope for, the age of integral humanism, the time when science and wisdom are to be reconciled, the advent of a fraternal commonwealth and of true human emancipation—all this we do not await on the morrow. But we await them on the day after the morrow, on the day which St. Paul announced will be after the worst darkness, like a springtime of splendor and renovation of the world.

Maritain was writing more than a quarter century ago; must the darkness become much deeper?

2. The traditional drives toward what could be called an integrated sense of community among peoples within individual nations, except for the very newest, will continue to diminish as they have for the past fifty years—indeed, as they have since the onset of the industrial revolution. Such community ideals as national patriotism, defense of ethnic, moral, religious or territorial views and such personal ideals as the value of hard work, thrift, heroism or even honesty and loyalty will meet with increasing cynicism and be viewed as incredibly naive. Yet, as Marcus

Aurelias had said in his *Meditations,* "Such as are
your constant thoughts, such will be the character
of your mind; for the soul is colored by the thoughts."
An individual, culture or nation will rise no higher
than its ideals. If the thought is cynical so will be
the culture. The residual religiously oriented vector
of the population will everywhere be in the minority approximating theologian Karl Rahner's "new
Diaspora" but there will continue to be such religious enclaves of one system or another everywhere.
Rahner sees it as a good portent for a future
regeneration.

3. Yet, amid the intellectual decay there will be
a sense of dissatisfaction of increasing depth and intensity among the bulk of the people with the shal-
lowness of the hedonistic values. There will be a
developing sense of urgency amid the deteriorating
norms and values to find a satisfying meaning of life
in all of the confusion. This sense of urgency has
developed first in the industrialized world with an
existentialist, relativistic tinge to it. Life is lived authentically in the particular environment in which
the individual finds himself. The human being becomes self in the world by the fully-lived experiential moment. This answer still does not have much
staying power nor breadth of appeal. As moments
continue to pass into years, the experiential spice loses
its savor not only for individuals but also for society
in general. For the poor, none of this makes any sense.
It was in this relationship that Rahner saw the regener-
ative aspect of the new Diaspora. The new leaven
was in place and the now inert dough will become
responsive to it. Quite likely, in this connection, the
"religious spirit" which survives in the communist-
controlled nations will have greater strength and dedication than that in the "free world." The tempering
of years of hard persecution and privation provides
a toughness of spirit in contrast to the debilitation
of resolve produced by a mushy permissiveness and
indifference.

In his work, *The Revolt of the Masses,* Jose Ortega y Gasset
commenting on the situation in the 1960's wrote:

No one knows toward what center human things
are going to gravitate in the near future, and hence
the life of the world has become scandalously provisional. Everything that today is done in public and
in private—even in one's inner conscience—is provisional, the only exception being certain portions of
certain sciences. He will be a wise man who puts
no trust in all that is proclaimed, upheld, essayed
and lauded at the present day. All that will disappear
as quickly as it came. All of it, from the mania for
physical sports (the mania, not the sports themselves)
to political violence; from "new art" to sunbaths at
idiotic fashionable watering-places. Nothing of all that
has any roots; it is all pure invention, in the bad sense
of the word, which makes it equivalent to fickle ca-
price. It is not a creation based on the solid substra-
tum of life; it is not a genuine impulse or need. In
a word, from the point of view of life it is false. We
are in presence of the contradiction of a style of living which cultivates sincerity and is at the same time
a fraud. There is truth only in an existence which
feels its acts as irrevocably necessary. There exists
today no politician who feels the inevitableness of
his policy, and the more extreme his attitudes, the
more frivolous, the less inspired by destiny they are.
The only life with its roots fixed in earth, the only
autochthonous life, is that which is made up of inevitable acts. All the rest, all that it is in our power
to take or to leave or to exchange for something else,
is mere falsification of life. Life today is the fruit of
an interregnum, of an empty space between two organizations of historical rule—that which was and
that which is to be.

Every large-scale social movement, religious or ideological,
needs a philosophic central core. While it is customary to say
that Christianity had no philosophy until it was wedded to the
Platonic-Aristotelian system, the statement is not even remotely
true. The philosophy of Christianity was and remains the brotherhood of man under the fatherhood of God. Platonism was the
conveyance first styled to fit that chassis, Aristotelism followed.
It was and remains an aggressive, activist philosophy whereas
the Hellenic philosophy was not. Christianity recognizes the
mandate to bring all men into the brotherhood. Christianity starts

at the other dialectic position from Marxism in the modified primordial confrontation of man, the collectively self-sufficient, versus the free-willed creature responsible to God; dependent, and yet, individually self-reliant. Society for man, not man for society.

Marxism, the cornerstone of the communist world, aggressive and activist in its dialectic, remains as hostile as ever to religion. It must remain so. Like, but in opposition to, Christianity it sees its destiny one of converting all mankind to its image—the apotheosized state. It cannot be satisfied with a passive intellectual role. It cannot achieve its end in passivity any more than Christianity can. It must move out, engage, overpower and use the industrializing material world. It promises man the full fruits of his productivity here and now. It was, and continues to be, utopian but provides only a limited utopia. Man is to achieve happiness as an economic mechanism. Communism holds out no lift to man's spirit. Man lives by bread alone. He must look no higher than the soil he works or the machine he manages. But he will be fed and clothed and housed and even given some of the luxuries of this life for the price of his soul. A cheap price in any event, since, not material, it does not exist. It is not an unattractive proposition for the underfed, under-clothed, under-housed, under-cared for majority of the peoples of the world.

The challenge to religion, particularly to Christianity and Islam, which has a similar "evangelizing philosophy," is to "put up or shut up" in the world of social movements. Man does not live by bread alone, but he needs bread to live. In the shrinking world of today the "brotherhood of man" takes on its true familial meaning. There are three alternatives. A fatherhood of God, of the state or of a fatherless orphanism—everyone for himself unrestrainedly, a valueless, normless existence—nihilism. And Nietzsche saw it with the "Death of God." The first alternative would cease to exist, and would bring about the second, which would inevitably yield to the third.

The solution in the Toynbee scenario demands, then, that the credibility of the fatherhood of God be established not only by philosophic or rational argument (which the writer considers a fact which is inescapable as traced through these pages) but by demonstration in an actualization of the brotherhood of man in the world in the religious context.

What other philosophic positions are there that exhibit motivation for a social movement? The existentialists have no end of concepts for social change. Except for those who sprang from phenomenological roots and then retained that methodology, the existentialists tend to be irrational. They are, above all, individualistic. Their main appeal is to an intellectual sophisticate. In spite of Sartre's espousing the value of working and of "salvation through action," his writings were directed to the intellectuals and not to the man at the machine or in the field. Even when they turned to physical work, as Simone Weil did, it was to provide a personal sense of solidarity with the masses and personal gratification in vicarious participation with the less privileged. This is not to say it was not an honest attempt "to do something." It was the same response which saw many of the middle and upper class young people in the United States miming the condition of the poor in dress, speech and behavior, seeing in this action something authentic. They do not comprehend that the bite of real poverty is the raw realization that there is no escape whenever the individual chooses. The existentialist's dramatic participation was, for the most part, a reaction to a surfeit of affluence and not a response in the Franciscan spirit of poverty as the poorest of the poor for assistance to the poor. It does not seem likely that the worldly existentialist can develop and support a generalized belief of the necessary depth and breadth. Even with the exalted views of Marcel, Jasper and Buber, it remains philosophically individualistic.

The British empiricism historically was also not aggressive, nor even progressive. It could not be. Advance could only be made as sense perception provided verification. Most of the great problems facing man could not be addressed in terms of this philosophy. It offers no stimulus beyond the rigidly observable.

Positivism was scarcely more promising toward motivation even in the sociological sphere in which it had its origins. Man is far more than a simple biologic specimen which, placed in society, yields to cold analysis. The sociology of collective behavior itself shows how volatile man can be in explosive situations and how deliberately, deeply, and steadfastly motivated he can be in others.

The analytical philosophers suffer from their genetic background both in empiricism and positivism. They have developed powerful methodologies but have no adequate broad, theoretical base in which to employ them. The phenomenologists too, seem to rest at the level of methodology. Husserl's dream of having arrived at the ultimate system is dead. Certain aspects of the perennial problems of man can be attacked effectively piecemeal by the phenomenological approach but no final synthesis ever seems to evolve. It truly seems that, in the final analysis, there still remains the ancient many-faceted problem of the One and the Many, the powerful and the weak, the changeless and the changing, the necessary and the contingent, the eternal and the temporal, and any other philosophic system of broad appeal that is sufficient to support a social movement must respond to this problem. That is, the basic problem of the One and the Many because it occurs in some form to all men, rich and poor, in all things and in all environments, and it demands a satisfying answer. This philosophical problem demands an answer which is valid in actuality as well as in theory, and the answer must appeal to the man daily facing the problems of living in the world as well as to the academic intellectual.

Here in the last quarter of the twentieth century, as philosophies, both Marxism and Christianity are in a condition of change. The materialistic and theoretical base of Marxism has been largely invalidated by philosophic and scientific advances. How the Marxist theorists will handle the problem is not clear. Currently, the philosophy is in a state of limbo. It may move toward an existential fatalism similar to Sartre's or Camus', "Make the best out of the absurdity of life by dedication and revolt, as comrades in arms."

Christianity, for several centuries, has been to a large extent detached from scholasticism. The Christian principle has been used to support various systems such as existentialism, phenomenology, Hegelian idealism, and even modified forms of Marxism and Analyticism. Its primitive philosophy remains the same, including all humanity in a brotherhood under the fatherhood of God. However, since the fascist and communist military emergence, a definite move has been made to emphasize the fact that man is indeed his brother's keeper. The Christian socialist movement, and the idea of social justice generally, is a reflection of this love. Islam also, in spite of Iran, is undergoing a process of invigoration in a social sense. It is currently one of the more active religious groups in the "evangelizing" of Africa. The differences between Christianity and Islam are, at root, theological rather than philosophical.

The other great religions of the world, as we have noted, are different in that they are not expansionist in basic philosophy. Even where international as Zionism, for instance, their sociological stance is centripetal rather than centrifugal. A large scale international social movement toward a religious orientation from these bases is unlikely. Their existence in being, however, is tremendously supportive of such a movement in opposition to a hardline atheistic Marxism. This writer's viewpoint is to some degree at variance with the Toynbee scenario because the latter saw the solution to the Western materialism coming primarily from an "Easternizing" of the West in the sense of a penetration of Western culture by Eastern mysticism at the intellectual level. From this level, the values would permeate the mass of men. That would be a long process indeed, and it does not seem to address the pressing demographic problems at all.

Today, the battle for the minds of men has moved to the area of fundamental values. What is, or ought to be, of ultimate concern to man at all levels? To this, there is added the further question, "How does that ultimate concern relate to the problem of the sociological tension and strain in the world at large?"

The answers will vary with the individual and with his situation, but they will all contain certain physical ingredients in common, such as, economic security, personal security, individual freedom, opportunity for cultural development, and a healthful physical environment. But, given all of these, would the individual have achieved Aristotle's greatest good, that of happiness? If the answer is no, which it must be after a time in which all these physical things are taken for granted, as they are among the truly affluent, what is it that is lacking? The theoretical hedonist would say unlimited pleasure. The existentialist would say living an authentic life to its utmost. The true Nietzschean would say power—power over others. The Marxists ought to say service to the collective. The theist ought to say service to God and fellowman. Now those non-physical added values are, or ought to be, the real ultimate concern for the type-cases involved, the physical ingredients being less than ultimate. Any social movement, to have broad appeal, must include promise of a substantial share of the physical ingredients plus that which forms the true ultimate concern of the society concerned. Organization of a movement must show that the other "ultimate concern," including the physical ingredients in legitimate degree, are subsumed in the movement's own ultimate concern. They must show that, in fact, the movement's ultimate concern, if wholeheartedly pursued, will bring the others in due course. Social movements avowedly aim at improvement of the total way of life. All of the non-physical items mentioned, a seeking for happiness in pleasure, in power, in authenticity, in service to the collective society, in service to God and fellowmen are ideas which are present in any significant group and one could almost say, to some extent, in any individual. The list is not comprehensive; there are other values, but these are believed to be the main concepts.

All of these "ultimate concerns," except the last two, can be pursued under a materialist philosophy, one without any belief in God. The religious mode, then, must succeed or fail on the premise that the one necessary ingredient for true happiness is achievable only in that which goes beyond the materialistic scope in service to God and fellowmen for the love of God. If the drift toward materialism and eventual nihilism is to be countered, it must be countered by an emphasis on what is different in the religious mode.

At some risk of oversimplification, the world philosophic outlook can be divided into the anthropocentric—agnostic, a hedonistic humanism; sociocentric—atheistic, a dialectic materialism; and theocentric-theistic, an integrative humanism. We can even suggest philosophers which could approximately represent those views. Bertrand Russell and John Dewey would represent the anthropocentric. Karl Marx and Mao Tse-tung would represent the sociocentrist and Jaques Maritain and Mahatma Gandhi would represent the theo-integrative. Gandhi, particularly, represents the latter group. Although he was educated in England as a lawyer, he returned to India and lived a life in accord with the Hindu ethic. While his mode of operation was passive resistance in accord with Hindu philosophic stance, he was, paradoxically, an activist in his passiveness. The resistance was real and effective. He frequently superimposed Christian and Islamic teachings into his works. He preached the unity of man under one God and the unalienability of those human rights which devolve from that relationship. His activity in the social movement which saw the eventual independence of India is too well-known to require discussion here. Pope Leo XIII in the late 19th century in his great social encyclical *Rerum Noverum* pointed out a Christian path to a just society work by Pius XI and John Paul II in the same vein expounded on Pope Leo X's theme. Social justice and Christianity are compatible.

The anthropocentrists represent a broad band of thought in the West and of the upper and upper-middle class elsewhere in the world. Their attitude, by imitation, could be said to permeate the Anglo-American culture and, unfortunately, typifies the image of the United States which is held in the Third World. It is humanitarian in a coldly aloof, scientistic, pragmatic sense. Russell's statement contained in his work, *New Hope for a Changing World* (Russell, 1951) illustrates the theme of the Western viewpoint. "In the West, we see man's greatness in the individual life. A great society for us is one which is composed of individuals who, as far as humanly possible, are happy, free and creative." No one could object to that statement. It suggests coverage of all of our physical requirements plus a soupcon of that unattainable one—happiness—but it conveys no sense of real passionate dedication to humanity in predicament. It is a view taken from an easy chair with pipe in hand, not from some vermin-infested hut in the jungle. The picture is viewed thus: "If the peasants would quit breeding, we wouldn't have these demographic problems." It is not the kind of attitude which is likely to "stir men's souls" in a large-scale social movement. It is not the correct view of the West, and particularly the United States, but a distortion which much of our own propaganda contributes to. The copious mass of propaganda which the communist world generates about the decadent capitalists is scarcely necessary.

The sociocentrist position dominates the communist world and also much of the thought in socialist movements in the rest of the world as well. It has, and predictably will continue, to command the energy of a great many in the Third World.

From an analytical viewpoint, these three basic philosophic stances are in competition worldwide for the minds of men and not just in the Third World. In fact, the outcome within the Third World depends, in large measure, on the outcome of the intellectual and political struggles within the communist and non-communist worlds.

The anthropocentric viewpoint has little chance to take hold in the communist world so that there the contest is principally between the sociocentric and a submerged theo-integrative viewpoint. The established culture and norms, while residual from the previous religious orientation, have been modified to fit the superimposed collectivist theme. In China, this change has apparently been more radical than in Russia and its satellites. There, the regime has attempted to completely uproot the millenia-old, strong, familial integration and force the country into the larger collectivist pattern. But, in every case, the sociocentric view seeks to concentrate all loyalties in the state, representing society. It is possible to paraphrase Russell's statement above, "In the communist world, we see man's greatness in the collectivist life. A great society for us is one composed of the proletariat collective which is as far as possible productive, creative, and collectively secure under the state regime." Happiness does not really appear in the vocabulary. They could not make Durkheim's leap to a collective happiness, nor does the idea of individual freedom appear, since it is antithetical to the solidarity of the collective.

The theo-integrative opposition in communist-dominated countries appears largely only as a semi-clandestine clinging to the old cultural ways and likely is more active in smaller communities and in ethnic islands in the larger cities. The establishment has everywhere exerted strong social controls over dissidents. Deviates are not looked upon with any tolerance. They are crushed whenever their operations are discovered, and the system is thorough in its internal intelligence apparatus. A change is not going to come about easily. If men's minds have not been captivated, they have been imprisoned. Nevertheless people still think of happiness as a goal that is somewhere and somehow possible.

In the non-communist world, there is the three-way struggle. But it takes place in a sort of eutectic mixture—at the lowest temperature. The "welfare state" concept which has become an accepted role of government generally among the industrialized non-communist nations includes many of the sociocentric ideas. The security of the collective is sought without the undue sacrifice of individual freedom. The seeking of happiness in material and biological exploitation is at least the most publicized, if not the most prevalent, aspect of life. It is just as materialistic an outlook as the dogmatic Marxian dialectical form—and far more attractive. For many, among the comfortably situated, the search for happiness ends on this level. Dogmatic atheism, like dogmatic materialism, has a harsh and repressive sound. Because of this, an enlightened agnosticism is used to serve the same purpose, which is that of inhibiting diversion of loyalties from the central theme of man's biological totality—an essential tenet of both the sociocentric and anthropocentric positions.

The third element, the theo-integrative, seems to form an incompatible lump in the mixture. Although the theistic integral viewpoint supports most of the above aspects of the non-communist world scene in seeking collective security and pleasure in life and thus blends in up to a point, it insists on dragging in the idea that these happy materialistic people are not really happy. They are not even temporarily satisfied. Instead of dwelling contentedly in their idyllic bliss like cows or sheep in a pleasant pasture, they are more neurotic, more anxious, more restless and far more guilt-ridden and unhappy than their severely disadvantaged brothers and sisters in the Third World. That, as "happy as biologically possible," of Bertrand Russell does not seem to be happiness at all. Dewey's as "happy as biologically possible," which would be roughly the same in Russell's logic does not respond to the totally human at all. It is therein that the eutectic mix seems to curdle and the blending temperature rises. Dewey, Russell and their like-minded colleagues in the first half of this century, strove manfully to get rid of the lumps through the educational process. The effect has been one of an increasing frustration as the lumps continue to form.

It appears desirable to review the concept of morality. We saw that a moral obligation is one springing from a sense of duty. One ought to do something because of something else. There is the inference of a causal relationship.

It will be recalled that John Dewey scoffed at the idea of any need of a separate "moral law." A code of "ethics" would automatically emerge based on sheer scientific maturity as people outgrew the superstitious nonsense of religion. Now, a code of ethics is also something arising out of a sense of duty. Pragmatically, quite aside from laws—moral or otherwise—one ought to conduct one's business affairs honestly because it is good for business in the long run. It just makes good business sense. It is therefore, a "duty" of a good businessman to be honest, i.e. practical. That is a position fairly low on the scale of "values," but it is rational.

What we are faced with, then, in morality or ethics is a logical statement which requires a turning of a judgmental corner. A statement of "what is"—a fact—requires an action, an imperative, in terms of duty in a judgment. Some have questioned whether an indicative can ever yield an imperative, but all law is based on that concept. The moral law, as seen by theists, would take the following approximate form: "God exists and is infinitely wise and good. Therefore, one *ought* to do that which pleases Him or that which he has revealed as pleasing to Him. Granted the premise, the conclusion of duty follows more or less coercively. The threat of potential punishment is secondary, but it is there.

Let us look again at some other bases of morality or ethics, such as: "I am rational, therefore, I ought to behave rationally." This can be truly said, but what is rational behavior for a trousered ape or "a featherless biped capable of speech," as Plato expressed it. What are the norms? How are they established? How are they enforced and how are they sanctioned? A second approach might be, "Moral behavior in accord with the Golden Rule is in the best interest of society. Therefore,

I ought to conduct myself in accord with that principle." In the face of an actual moral decision, the question will arise, "Why should I? What has society done for me?" A third approach might be, "The state and community cannot survive in a state of moral anarchy. Therefore, citizens ought to conduct themselves in accordance with moral principles established by the state." Hobbes agreed with this precept and then raised the question, "How can this be enforced?" His answer, as we saw, was strict government and the iron fist behind it. This devolves into a challenge to the citizenry and can be effectively enforced only by the strictest surveillance and punishment. This philosophy characterizes the classic police state. Somewhere, there must be a sufficient reason why one *ought freely* to choose to behave one way or another.

Like all such questions, the correct answers must come by analysis of man's nature. Man as a free, intending ego can, and does, reflect purposively on all his past activities and makes his future decisions purposively based on a judgment of the new set of conditions in the light of all his "stored data." His moral judgments are made exactly the same way. His "sense of duty" derives from the summation of his past exposure as conditioned by those intellectual and emotional traits peculiar to his personality. His behavior is largely a product of his cultural environment, his inherited characteristics and his motivational background. It is the latter aspect which is crucial in moral considerations. The motivational background is largely subsumed in the first two considerations, but not entirely so. There is an important vector which depends upon how the individual as an independent, reflexive, intending ego in his own free-willingness disposes himself and evaluates himself in relationship to all else. His human nature drives him to a continuous self-examination. He can and does study his own motivations and decides for himself whether his actions are in accord with what he can visualize as "good will." He does make individual value judgments.

A moral judgment is made when one makes a decision between two alternative courses of actions and says this is better (in a moral sense) than that, because of such and such, therefore I ought to choose it. A person must, consciously or not, explain to himself why one course is better than the other and why he *ought* to choose it. A pure code of ethics, as a code of ethics, does not carry an answer to first principles. It leaves the "Why?"

The Ten Commandments, as a code of ethics, have no at-root

validity apart from the concept of the God who dictated them and who *ought* to be obeyed. The "natural law" has no validity apart from the God of nature for the same reason. No other laws or ethical codes have any primary validity, in themselves, apart from the authority and sanctioning power which established them.

Morality or ethics, apart from a belief in God, are of necessity baseless, artificial, and temporary. They become a mere statement of a situational ethic of expediency and one that is a great deal less justifiable than Machiavelli's. The relativism which the educational system in the West projected to the students of the middle decades of the twentieth century left no basis for critical evaluation of norms among the generatioin now coming into leadership throughout the non-communist world. A code of situational ethics is productive of disharmony and distrust in private life. Yet, it is to be accepted as normal. However, in public life, by escalation of opportunity, it suddenly seems to become intolerable and the subject of proper outrage. Even Machiavelli would blush at such hypocrisy. Oddly, in contrast, it will be recalled, he called for honor and integrity in private affairs and a "situational ethic" in conduct of high-level political matters. Nevertheless, the public situation has caused some reflection concerning the adequacy of such flexible norms of conduct, private or public.

It is totally hypocritical for private "cheaters" to point accusing fingers at those who happen to get caught in public. It is also difficult to provide a rational basis to support the following statement, "While there are no normative absolutes in behavior of individuals, absolute norms do exist in position of 'trust' at the societal and public administrative levels." But what is "trust" except a recognized obligation to act honestly in behalf of the beneficiary which is the "public," in this case. If the obligation is moral, from what does it flow? Why is the public any more precious than a wife, or husband, or child, or business associate? If the sanction of such norms is placed in the penal codes, then it is only the ineptness of the individual, not his malice, which is to be condemned and for which he is subjected to punishment. Many people expressed just this sense of the matter over the recent Watergate and Iraq scandals, saying: "Nobody that stupid should be in a position of high responsibility."

But the public outcry, generally, over the lack of "morality" in politics should certainly not provoke surprise. Somehow, people know that there is a right and a wrong mode of conduct.

A dishonorable act is called dishonorable because its perpetration reduces the human being to the status of an intelligent animal only and no longer trustworthy. It is humanity which is dishonored. If man is only an intelligent animal by his nature, there could be no such term as trustworthy or dishonorable, only stupid or inept rather than crafty or adroit.

No, the eutectic mix is getting more lumpy as the basic incompatibility between the purely materialistic view and human nature is revealed under the stress of modern age or better, perhaps, post-modern age problems. The moment of truth is rapidly approaching for all three philosophic outlooks. That brief candle of truth at the deeper spiritual level will once again be given the chance to awaken the sleeping humanity.

From the geopolitical standpoint, a reawakened non-communist world has the clear potential to bring the Third World into the technological age with its humanity intact and to provide the best of the sociocentric and anthropocentric viewpoints without their dehumanizing aspects. It requires the honest application of the Gandhi ideal of the unity of all men as brothers and sisters under the one God. If that candle only flickers, and is then extinguished, the darkness of the new age will be nearly impenetrable.

If any large scale social movements are to emerge, they will have to find motivation in generalized beliefs in opposition to the established values and norms. We have seen a strange contrast between the established norms and values in the communist and non-communist worlds. There are, in fact, two sets of forces which, initially, in the early twentieth century, were in strong confrontation in the economic arena. These forces are private enterprise versus state control and individualism versus collectivism. There is a gradual rapprochement as the welfare state concept *de facto* introduces many aspects of collectivism and state control to the non-communist world, and the introduction of internal competitive ideas to improve production has brought about some ideas of private enterprise to the communist world. The ideologic confrontation on the issue of individual freedom remains potent and pervasive, however.

In the communist world, which is based on collectivism and state control, the image projected—and it agrees with the declared goal—is that of an atheistic civilization directed by a unitary political party and administrative apparatus maintained in total control by a rigid discipline within the party and the populace. It projects a regimented life-style, including a state enforced code of morality. Any opposition social movement set upon restoring individual values and norms has to be completely clandestine, at all stages, awaiting patiently for some disastrous event in the establishment to give it an opportunity. A premature move would result in a brutal and complete destruction of the movement. The outcome of the Hungarian uprising and the Czech suppression is sufficient example of the fate to be expected by participants. It is not an attractive setting for the Toynbee scenario in the foreseeable future.

The Nietzsche scenario does little better. The apparatus-applied social control is coercive of the party norms and values. Yet, should the party succeed over a long term in stripping all sense of individual responsibility and, then, should the party collapse from some disaster, a populace accustomed to being directed in all things would find itself literally normless and valueless. It thus approaches nihilism involuntarily. The people lose any normative and value sense without any participation in the fundamental process. They are brainwashed into personal nihilism. Outcomes following either the Toynbee or the Nietzsche scenarios hinge on a party disaster. The Toynbee scenario requires that personal values and norms persist until the disaster. The Nietzsche scenario requires that the disaster be deferred until the personal norms and values have been completely eroded. Both must wait until the "shrimp learns to whistle."

The second set of forces representing individualism (those in the non-communist world) project an image of a totally permissive culture indifferent to religion and moral standards. It approaches nihilism voluntarily. Individuals care less and less about more and more until they care absolutely nothing about everything. Any social movement here in opposition would have to begin in the public forum in the open. It must succeed by its "cash value in the marketplace," to steal an expression from Justice O. W. Holmes. This is, indeed, all any social movement, religiously oriented or otherwise, should ask for. The very permissiveness of such a society, however, to some extent, slows down the energy building process by providing no resistance to work against. To a theist, an easygoing agnostic is a far tougher intellectual foe than a dedicated atheist. The agnostic view that "not only can I not know, but it doesn't make any difference in any event," is far more difficult to handle from a theistic position than the Marxist dogma, "There is no God and that is what does make the difference." It is the difference between trying to pick up a large, plastic sack half full of water as compared to a set of barbells. In the former case, there is no good way to approach the lift.

A generalized belief that the anthropocentric viewpoint has failed to pay off in the marketplace does seem to be in its incipient stage in the United States. As quoted in *Time* magazine (July 25, 1977), the late Geo-analyst Herman Kahn, then director of the Hudson Institute, said, concerning the looting in New York during the "Blackout of 1977," "They have no idea of what moral standards are. This 'suppressed rage' idea is crap. This kind of reasoning will make the same thing happen all over again." Having heard him speak several times, the writer recognizes that Kahn is not a man who uses language loosely. This somewhat violent statement indicates a fairly deep conviction that the moral situation is chaotic. An attitude of lawlessness has brought about widespread crime and disorder in high places as well as in the urban ghetto. The response to this condition does not have to be one of theistic orientation, however. The disorder can stimulate a dictatorial law and order movement having either a fascistic or communistic smell to it—a rigid sociocentric response.

Let us review what theoretical steps a large scale organized movement must go through in the non-communist world:

1. Frustration and anxiety develop in the general population over their powerlessness under the existing conditions to achieve a life situation offering personal and economic security.

2. Attempts to have the establishment bring about satisfactory conditions under existing policies through normal channels meet with repeated failures.

3. Emotional intensity increases as the situation deteriorates and no correction in the unsatisfactory condition has been achieved by recourse to the normal procedures. The conditions are seen as "intolerable."

4. It is concluded, by a substantial number of people, that there are no channels in the existing establishment through which the "intolerable" conditions can be corrected. Legitimacy is withdrawn from the establishment.

5. Various alternative ways to obtain relief are considered by various "subgroups" and their likelihood of success at the established levels of social control is evaluated. The chief "culprit" or "culprits" responsible are identified.

6. A general consensus develops within subgroups

THE WORLD OF SOCIAL MOVEMENTS

that a solution can be achieved by a certain set of organized actions.

7. A coalition of like-minded activists is formed and a more or less formal structure is established.

8. Support for the embryonic movement is solicited among all groups having closely allied grievances and plans of action.

9. A tentative platform is prepared identifying the principal targets of attack and goals to be achieved and the methodology of attainment is worked out. A fundamental philosophic position is evolved from this combination. The trend is from a collection of specific grievances and methodologies to a statement of principles which the movement stands for (i.e., "States' Rights," "Prohibition," or "Integrative Humanism").

10. The platform is revised, showing flow from principles to correction of abuse and a generalized belief develops that following these principles and methodologies will solve the problem.

11. The movement organizational structure is established, leaders designated and channels of communication developed for recruitment and propagandization as well as for internal coordination of activities.

12. The movement is underway. Enthusiasm develops at all levels in a feeling of invincibility in the finally developed philosophy of the generalized belief.

I developed this theoretical set of steps using the chain of events leading to the U.S. Revolution but stopping just short of that war. The model was deliberately selected for application in the non-communist world because, the writer believes, in fact, that the "platform" provided by the causes set forth in the Declaration of Independence of the United States and, ultimately, its Constitution is still completely valid for a social movement designed to restore the principles for which that movement stood. There remains the need to extend the principles, but not the details, to all men. It is the forced interpretations of the "platform" documents in the past half century by all three branches of government in the United States which have led to the erosion of the principles of freedom and likewise of justice and responsibility, personal and societal, for which that platform and that movement stood.

In the United States therefore, and in the non-communist world generally, the structural strain which has developed is primarily at the normative level. The principles of government, as legitimately established, adequately provide a statement of values. It is thus not a question of withdrawing legitimacy at the basic governmental level, but from the "culprits" at the next level down who would be seen as usurping to themselves powers not conferred either expressly or inferentially in the various constitutions. The establishment in power thus would be seen as *de facto* rather than *de jure* in control, and the condition becomes correctable within the existing institutions by a reversal of public policy.

Obviously, while the voluntaristic trend toward nihilism may be the result of normative deterioration, the value system does not go unscathed. The structural-functional theory of society postulates a "homeostatic variable" in the system which seeks to restore balance in a social system undergoing assault. The theory states that there is a societal "governor" which, through an automatic feedback in the population, seeks to repress change. But like any inertial governor it must sense a change before it can respond. There is a lag. In the case of society, the lag follows a cyclic pattern as the public attitude swings from periods of conservatism to liberalism. To avoid the confusion those terms have been forced to bear, they might better be designated periods of relative "closedness" to change, a seeking of stability alternating with periods of "openness" to change. The governor is further of the pure inertial type, the gyroscopic, which yields slowly to constant pressure, from any direction, though resisting sudden change.

In the West, generally, since the thirteenth century and the "openness" which the newly emerging city universities fostered in the intellectual element, the trend, the constant pressure, has been unidirectional in the openness to change. The slope of the trend had certainly not been uniform; there have been localized reversals. But the change, and it has been in the main beneficial, has been toward greater latitude in man's individual sphere of action and less to his responsibility toward society. Values as well as norms have shifted with the trend. The situation, long continued, would obviously approach true anarchy as an asymptote. "Openness" to change ought not to be defined in unidirectional terms. The openness ought to extend to changes which show promise of a betterment of the totally human condition even and, perhaps currently, especially if they promote a sense of community responsibility. The "reactionary" label which is habitually applied to any appeal to responsibility of the individual in society is "closed" to change at the second differential level, that is, opposition to change in direction of change. In the West, generally there is a sense that this 800-year trend has produced its best fruits for man's betterment and that the latest crops have been increasingly bitter.

Therefore, it seems inevitable that if the tensions in the world are to be relieved, man's view of man both in the communist world and in the non-communist world needs to undergo a substantial change. The biologic concept has led to the extremes of repression and of permissiveness in the two sets of forces. It is perhaps inevitable that the tyrannical and anarchistic would result if biologic man represents the highest court of appeal. Between these limits no rationally defensible control can be placed on biologic man's individual instincts. The very terms, societal norm or value are completely artificial in the context of biologic man. What is normative or of value to the individual in or out of society is the whim of the existential moment. It is the Hobbesian world and demands Hobbesian-imposed controls if there is to be any order in society. Possession of power is its own source of legitimation for any acts performed and terror becomes the most potent, almost the only, weapon of enforcement. Even Rousseau, with his concept of the "General Will," having arrived at the conclusion that natural man has been spoiled by civilization, was of the opinion that surrender of individual rights was necessary for the common good. This was no sweetly democratic surrender. The general will was not a consensus but rather that governmental rule, which the people would have selected, had they known enough and had they been wise enough to choose. It presumed an "enlightened" attitude for government. The consent of the governed was assumed in the general will itself.

The bulk of this book has been devoted to an analytic assessment of man's nature and what that nature demands of him, for him and for others in the social relationships. Given that nature which the study reveals as by far the most likely; that is, not limited to the material, selfish, and hedonistic embedment, not animalistic in man's higher intuitive aspirations and man is not forever going to be pounded or pampered into the distortions now caricatured in the two dominant systems. A reaction will appear, first, as a general anxiety with man's condition, an anxiety generated from man's dissatisfaction and frustration with the meaning of his life as it is being lived.

Man seeks happiness, and he cannot find it in anything less

than that which is in harmony with his total nature. Neither of the systems as constituted respond to that nature. In the noncommunist world, man can change the picture within the establishment at any time he becomes sufficiently motivated. In the communist world, the establishment itself must be changed and that would not be easily done almost regardless of the intensity of the individual motivation. In both situations, barring some sensational and world shattering development, the time does not appear "ripe." The bottom has not yet been reached—the darkness is not dense enough to reveal the candle marking the ascent from the pit. When will the bottom be reached?

Within the United States there has been a historic tendency for a cyclic variation between conservatism and liberalism having a period of about fifteen years. This trend was noted by historian of the American scene, A. M. Schlesinger, and reported in his article *Tides of American Politics,* published in 1940. This periodicity appears to coincide with the 15-year, functional, generational span proposed by philosopher Ortega y Gassett referred to earlier. It is at least appropriate to conjecture that there is a relationship between these two—that as a succeeding challenging generation arrives on the scene it seeks to assert its own identity in contrast to its predecessor. Both cycles would be skewed somewhat as a result of the more dramatic events which influenced the different periods of history. The Great Depression and World War II as well as the more recent Korean and Viet Nam incidents and their political ramifications would have affected differently the three generations involved.

The point has been made that openness to change is not a linear function in which the directional sense is either forward "progressive" or backward "reactionary," using some pet propaganda labels. Openness to change is characterized by a critical attitude in appraising "where we are," "how we got here" and more importantly, "what do the answers to those questions suggest as to the direction we should take in the future?" What new goals should we seek and how do we get there? The homeostatic variable in the structural-functional theory for society, and, in political science as well, is perhaps, more properly considered as a rational response to individual inquiry in this vein than as a gyroscope which seeks to stabilize society by inhibiting any changes at all in social or political policy. The questioning automatically introduces a modicum of conflict into the structural-functional monolith.

While it is true that the cited article by Schlesinger did have reference to "liberal" in the sense of relaxing social and political constraints, it is also true that in the period of American history which Schlesinger reviewed (prior to 1940), "liberal" policy was one which extended the concept of individual freedom under the law to more and more people. It was not one of relieving individuals at large of responsibility as members of society. The basic values and norms were left largely unchanged, but they were applied with greater equity. The value concept expressed by "equal protection under the law" was to be something besides a high-sounding, but empty, phrase. It was not, however, to become "freedom from law."

If we were to apply the combined hypotheses of Schlesinger and Ortega y Gassett to the current and projected United States societal and political scene, we should begin with the period since 1960. This is a period of fifteen years after the conclusion of World War II when the major readjustments from that catastrophe had been made. The three 15-year generational groups involved in the Ortega y Gassett hypothesis would have median ages of 22, 37, and 52 respectively in 1960. The youngest group, the rising generation, would have escaped direct involvement in World War II almost completely—but most would have remembered it hatefully as a piece of stupid and disruptive insanity. The older members would have been involved in the limited Korean War. The middle group, the challenging generation, would have carried the major burden in combat and suffered the greatest social dislocation from both World War II and Korea. The oldest group, the establishment in 1960, would have been, for the most part, too old for direct involvement in War II or Korea but would have largely managed the effort. Originally, many of this older group would have been of the young "Roosevelt Liberals" who would have been the challengers to the Coolidge and Hoover conservatives.

Both of the older groups would have been quite conservative in 1960 however. The post-war period was one of rebuilding a devastated world, and that would have been a sufficiently challenging enterprise. The civil rights problem would have been the dominant social issue in the United States. That issue was started strongly in the 1930's by the Roosevelt intellectuals. The war itself was a great leveler of differences by causing both an explosion in population mobility and a recognition of the great commonality of man. The two older groups would have been subjected to, and would have responded to, strong emotional appeal to national unity, patriotism, discipline and the values of family life. They would have been "law and order" oriented. The youngest group according to the Schlesinger hypothesis, would have been strongly liberal in reaction to the two older groups. They would be the "rebels," the "disenchanted," and the "alienated" of the 1960's.

By 1975, those liberals would be of average age 37; they would be the challengers. The previous challengers in 1960, the World War II young conservatives, are the establishment and a new rising generation more "conservative" in tone, would be of average age 22—they would also be the largest element of the population, products of the post-war "baby boom." They would have heard nothing but war and confusion and international and national turmoil all their lives. As children they would have seen the greatest blossoming and as young adults the fading of the promise of the technologic age. They would be looking for answers to the turmoil through some stabilizing agency. This writer has been looking for several years for a change in the downward trend of religious attitude among the young—the first he has seen is from a poll conducted by the publishers of *Who's Who Among American High School Students.* In 1975, 82 percent of those prominent young Americans felt that religion was relevant to contemporary life compared with 77 per cent in 1974.

By 1990, then, these last will be the challengers, still the largest population component and largely conservative. The establishment will be liberal and there will be a rising generation of liberals. If our geopolitical projection for the scenarios has been not too far afield, the period between 1975 and 1990 will have been one of uneasy peace but with no major confrontation. The trend to the welfare state will have reached some very considerable economic barriers with an aging population in most areas outside the "Third World." It will be a time when major reassessments will be urgently required. The "muddle through" policy in the non-communist world which seeks to avoid issues by backing off and letting nature take its course, a reenactment of the pre-World War II attitude in the West, will be under tremendous strain. The demographic problems will not have disappeared. They will have intensified.

In the universities—and the pattern will be reflected among the non-academic intellectuals—the philosophic orientation at the top staff levels will be the liberals and the product of the current existentialist phase. The analyticists will no longer be "big" in the universities. The establishment will be "open to change," perhaps even somewhat disenchanted with their own living for the existential moments. The naturalist-pragmatist followers of John Dewey will have ground out in the preceding generation. The bulk of the teaching staff, the challengers, will be conservative and looking for stability in philosophic thought. They will be acutely aware of the demographic problems, having grown up in the period after World War II when it was first fully recognized. For them the burden of the aging population and the welfare state must be faced realistically. The succeeding generations will become progressively numerically less able to support the "overhead." Their generation may be the first victims of the trend—those who "get dropped" in the chain-letter philosophy.

The rising generation, the students, will be liberal, will be open to change. They will also be well aware of the implications of the aging population. They will become the first to pay the full price of a top-heavy "womb to tomb" social security system. They will have to benefit less and pay more per capita than preceding generations. They will realize firsthand that, in fact, as the extended farm families always knew, the rising generations are the social security for the aging. Both the "unproductive" young and old—those generally under 15 and over 60—are dependent upon the productivity—and indirectly on the good will and generosity—of those in the active, middle years. The administrative bureaucracy may manage to conceal those facts, but they are there. Everything consumed has to be produced by someone, the more reserved for the young and old, the less available for those between who are producing. What a test for situational ethics! For those liberal students, unless technologic advance can offset the numerical deficit, or there is a change in moral climate, their outlook in old age is not good. They will indeed be open to change and looking for answers. Worldwide, it will not be an aging population; the Third World takes care of that. The "lifeboat ethic" now becomes ridiculous from two aspects. There is no one to pull the oars for the affluent lifeboat, even if it could be kept afloat in a sea of drowning humanity. A more attractive ethic to this age group would likely be one which says, "Do not abandon ship but repair the damage which centuries of neglect have caused."

This situation, which it can be conjectured will occur toward the end of this century, is one made to order for a new philosophic viewpoint, one more stability-seeking in outlook in the general population than the individualistic momentariousness of existentialism and more compatible with the idea of the total community of man. It will be an atmosphere conducive to a large-scale social movement to heal wounds and regenerate the true spirit of man both as an individual and as a responsible member of society. While what has been said applies in particular to the United States, there is no reason to believe similar cyclic conditions and forces do not apply throughout the non-communist world, and likely in the communist world as well.

Trends in the communist world are so controlled by the party political policies that the underlying sociologic forces active among the people themselves are largely masked, if they are not eradicated. The more tightly the social control is maintained, the more dangerous to the regime any relaxation becomes. The less that grievances can be relieved through establishment channels, the greater the dormant pressures and hostility which develop. A sudden, though moderate, relaxation can be disastrous as the French and Russian communist revolutions well demonstrated. And, of course, any open schism within the communist party also could change the situation dramatically. Both sides could easily lose control to a middle ground.

There is some evidence that such an outcome is at least a possibility. Russian writer and exile Alexander Solzhenitsyn, in his various appearances throughout the United States, in the summer of 1975, pictured two aspects of change in the attitude of the people of the Soviet Union. The first aspect of change is philosophical. In an address to the AFL-CIO delegates in Washington, D.C., Mr. Solzhenitsyn said, "Marxism has fallen so low it is simply an object of contempt." The second aspect of change is sociological. At the same meeting, he said, "There is a new generation growing up behind the iron curtain that is unwilling to accept tyranny." This might indicate something quite similar to the "generation gap," the rejection of the older values in the United States a decade past. In a strongly polarized situation such as exists in the Soviet Union, it could be explosive.

There is, perhaps, a weakening of these statements because Solzhenitsyn is a "hostile witness" against the U.S.S.R. However, a third fact is obvious—Solzhenitsyn's presence in the United States would not have occurred during the Stalin regime. Even if his writings had "leaked out," that would be all that would have been known of Solzhenitsyn. There are political implications here of a relaxation of social control, and if the first two statements of Solzhenitsyn have any validity, a change in total orientation is far more than just a happy dream. The "shrimp might learn to whistle" sooner than Khrushchev thought. Solzhenitsyn also provided some warnings about over-optimism on this score, however, saying in effect, "Never turn your back on the bear when he seems friendly, he is at his most dangerous when he senses weakness."

Along this vein in April 1975, an interview was given by the late Anthony Eden, Earl of Avon, former prime minister for Great Britain, looking to the occasion of the thirtieth anniversary of "V-E Day." Colin Frost, Associated Press writer reported the interview in part, as follows:

> Lord Avon was asked if he thought that the West had any share of blame for the Cold War.
>
> "No," he said, "the breaches of the letter and spirit of wartime treaties came from across the Iron Curtain.
>
> "But it could be effectively argued that we ought to have been firmer with the presentation of Western points of view at an earlier stage."
>
> He cited President Franklin D. Roosevelt's reluctance to press the Polish issue at the Tehran Conference of 1943. Britain was urging Russia's Stalin to come to terms with the Polish government in exile in London.
>
> But Roosevelt was looking toward the presidential elections of 1944 and, Lord Avon recalled, told Stalin privately that for electoral reasons he could not discuss the Polish issue for another year.
>
> "This," said Lord Avon, "was hardly calculated to restrain Stalin. He would think that time was on his side and act accordingly.
>
> "The president for whatever reason, was always convinced that he could handle Stalin as no one else could."
>
> Lord Avon is, at 77, the only survivor of the Western leadership at the meetings with Stalin which shaped postwar Europe.
>
> Now, speaking amid a succession of Communist victories in Southeast Asia, he warned against appeasement of Stalin's successors. The North Atlantic Alliance, he said, is more than ever important.
>
> "If Western Europe were ever lost to the free world," he said, "the balance of resources and manufacturing capacity and therefore of political power would be dangerously tilted against the American continent and the remaining free countries of the Pacific.

"That must not be allowed to happen. Above all, no appeasement, which means no yielding to obtain a little present ease at the cost of the future."

He closed the interview with this warning: "We can afford no illusions: The margin of survival for the free nations is now dangerously low."

Lest we forget Eden's strong position as the foreign minister in Neville Chamberlain's cabinet during the "time of appeasement" just prior to World War II, the following excerpt from Winston Churchill's work, *The Gathering Storm* (Churchill, 1948) is appropriate:

Late in the night of February 20, a telephone message reached me as I sat in my old room at Chartwell (as I often sit now) that Eden had resigned. I must confess that my heart sank, and for a while the dark waters of despair overwhelmed me. In a long life I have had many ups and downs. During all the war soon to come and in its darkest times I never had any trouble in sleeping. In the crisis of 1940, when so much responsibility lay upon me, and also at many very anxious, awkward moments in the following five years, I could always flop into bed and go to sleep after the day's work was done—subject, of course, to any emergency call. I slept sound and awoke refreshed, and had no feelings except appetite to grapple with whatever the morning's boxes might bring. But now, on this night of February 20, 1938, and on this occasion only, sleep deserted me. From midnight till dawn I lay in my bed consumed by emotions of sorrow and fear. There seemed one strong young figure standing up against long, dismal, drawling tides of drift and surrender, of wrong measurements and feeble impulses. My conduct of affairs would have been different from his in various ways; but he seemed to me at this moment to embody the life-hope of the British nation, the grand old British race that had done so much for men, and had yet some more to give. Now he was gone. I watched the daylight slowly creep in through the windows, and saw before me in mental gaze the vision of Death.

From what we have seen, it can be projected that the tension within the communist world should be very intense by the end of this century, particularly if China continues to develop its military and industrial potential, as it gives every sign of doing. Both China and Russia will be straining resources to the limit to maintain supremacy. For both, their pragmatic efforts in the underdeveloped world may lose appeal if there are no economic rewards forthcoming to them for all their expenditures. It will be recalled, Marxism was originally based on the economic theory that the communist takeover would coincide with the peak of bourgeoisie industrial development in each country. It did not envision a policy of moving into underdeveloped nations and putting them on their feet. It will be a severe test of the real "humanitarian" depths of the communist movement. The moment of truth for the entire world, then, appears to be close at hand, within the next quarter century.

The path which the world takes will be decisive for a long period ahead. The path following approximately the Toynbee scenario which will lead to a free community of nations each with its own cultural, social and political viewpoint but dedicated to the unity of mankind in a cooperative venture in a world of limited but adequate resources appears the only rational solution. And it also appears to be the most likely by a good margin. The materialistic, pragmatic climate—whether individualistic or collectivist—will give way to the dignity of man conceived as a free being responsible to God for his brother's well-being and for his own well-being and moral behavior as well.

Any time one attempts to project the course of history he is departing from the realm of "observables" and his conclusions are open to challenge on many counts. Still, the conclusion that the presently maturing crisis will be resolved along the general lines of a genuine religious rebirth is not mere wishful thinking by any means. Despite the vastly larger scale of the demographic problems facing humanity today, the world situation is remarkably similar to that which saw the emergence of Christianity from the materialistic convergence in the Roman Empire in the early centuries of this era. Then the ancient pagan religious beliefs were being abandoned and the anxious and discontented populace was being soothed by a superficial "bread and circus" program.

The political solutions which are being attempted today are likewise largely *ad hoc* emergency measures applied to symptoms which do not address the underlying malady—the stress and tension producing philosophical position—at all. Marxism made a serious effort to attack the organic difficulties arising from the Industrial Revolution through a philosophic reorientation of the materialistic disease. It came to grips with the problem as it was somewhat differently diagnosed by Marx, Lenin and Mao, but it was treating the illness by methods which, while offering temporary local relief, could do nothing but aggravate the condition which produced the tension and stress. Materialism was treated by applying a new form of materialism more aggressive and more virulent. The powerful social movement which Marxism was and is merely shows how great are the forces of discontent and anxiety which are just below the surface in all present political regimes.

Man is and remains a "discontented animal" as long as that animality is the only view he has of himself. He cannot long remain in that attitude. Sooner or later—and the later the more dramatic and possibly violent the sociological reaction will be—the stress will be relieved. That stress can only be relieved by a change in the prevailing materialistic values and norms which are its source. Large scale social movements of religious orientation do appear to be inevitable, given the present world conditions. The demographic problems are of human origin and they must be resolved by solutions which are applied to mankind in its total humanity. As we have seen, the only philosophies which can offer such solutions are those stemming from a theistic background where man is indeed his brother's keeper under God.

While this is to some extent an anticlimatic thought one may object that, in this happy conclusion, the writer has equated the concepts of atheism with materialism, and ask are there not other alternatives, a non-materialistic atheism for example, just as there is an atheistic existentialism? Are there other likely alternatives? There was an atheistic idealist, or if you will, a non-materialistic atheist, John McTaggart (1866-1925), who held that there was no God and no matter—only individual immaterial sources of ideas which gave us the illusion of materiality; reality consisted in a system of ideational selves, but McTaggart was more of a curiosity than a philosopher who could be taken seriously. His position had too many obvious difficulties, not the least of which was that of materialism itself: What was the source? Did the ideational selves bring themselves into being across the boundary from nothingness, or has my ideational self existed forever?

The two positions of materialism and atheism, while perhaps not motivated in the same way, are forced into a common end position. If there is no God, there is nothing spiritual—there is only matter subsistent from eternity or self-creating in time. One can scarcely say that there are three forms of independently existent "stuff"—material, ideational and spiritual. The materialists would say that all is material, there is no spiritual and that the ideational subsists in matter in some Humean way. The true idealists, with the main exception indicated, believe that the ideational is a reflection of the spiritual source and there is no matter as distinct from idea. The theist-realists would say the ideational subsists in the spiritual and the material is real as God wills it to be real and has its root source in and is dependent upon the spiritual. There is no apparent room for compromise. The agnostic who says he does not know but generally opts for the hedonistic, materialistic lifestyle is not uncommitted. If he thinks about it, as William James pointed out, he has made his act of faith. There is no middle solution as to the existence of God.

Chapter 22

TOWARD A MORAL SOCIETY

I believe that we have established and brought together two sets of premises in logic leading to two conclusions: First, that the world and, most crucially, man in the world are under the dominion of an infinite, loving and personal God who is concerned in man's behavior, and, second, that man in the world stands at a point in crisis in the insistent dialectic much as that first historic man and woman. There is the Tree of Life with its promise of a climactic ascent to a future for us and our children of the greatest happiness in a free community of the people of God. And there is the Tree of Knowledge of Good and Evil inviting us to continue our decline into the pit in a defiant and egotist self-sufficiency as Hobbesian men and women in a Hobbesian world.

We have seen that the geopolitical setting for our crisis scene for the next few decades is one that offers the opportunity to select the way of light but also that portends disaster ahead if the opportunity is not accepted promptly. If there is no move made to solve the pressing demographic problems in a community of free men, these same problems will carry us relentlessly into anarchy and brutal slavery worse than Hitler and his bestial staff ever dreamed of. These conclusions bring us then, to a moral decision point that cannot be put off with an agnostic hopelessness of finding answers. The answers are available, we have seen them, and the means of putting these answers to effective use are available and we have seen these too. As in all moral questions the decision depends upon man's "good will" and upon his recognizing and accepting the duty which the moral decision always carries with it—to do what one ought to do.

Very well, what ought one do? As always the answer to that depends upon one's position in the world. At the risk of sounding sweetly sanctimonious, all of us can very well pray that God will grant us the guidance and assistance we need. In addition, most of us can do something more than that. People can try to reinvigorate the essential sense of morality in a world which has gotten lazy and indifferent and perhaps, even openly hostile to morality in its pursuit of the soft life. Unless human beings can find the strength of character to face the hard cases that lie ahead with courage and be willing to sacrifice, people are doomed to undergo defeat and eventual loss of everything worthy of being called human. For background, let us first review briefly, how we got to the impoverished situation regarding the moral attitude as it stands today. Let us also view honestly where the moral attitude does stand today. Let us then suggest what needs to be done to remedy the situation, if indeed it needs a remedy.

Up until the beginning of the twentieth century, man, in the West, generally accepted the idea of a moral law of some sort. This attitude of accepting the inherent rightness and wrongness involved in moral decisions has been on the decline, and under increasing attack, since the late seventeenth century by rational humanists, materialists, positivists, and other intellectuals. In the novelty of scientific discoveries, these specialists saw the "emancipation of man" from the "slavery" of the theologic dominance of a divinely established moral concept. At first, this attack was carried out under a deistic concept. That is, that there was a Creator but once He had completed His creative act, He permitted the natural laws to govern and had no personal interest in individual man, much less his behavior. Man was a splendid creature, richly endowed with all of those faculties which would permit him to develop and use the resources of the world scientifically, hence wisely, and to govern himself rationally without the meddling interference of his Maker who, in any event, was indifferent.

From this attitude, a number of fictitious constructs came into being. These were: the natural man of Rousseau, the various economic men of the classical economists, the exploited man of Marx. God, no longer important, was gradually replaced by the concept of "Mother Nature." Individual man became part of a collective largely uncounted as the atoms are uncounted, and was, in turn, morally unaccountable. His very anonymity placed him beyond any idea of individual responsibility.

This situation brought about two countervailing, but oddly convergent, currents. In the positive direction, but with deepplunging implications, was the sense of man's freedom, the sense of the possibility of unlimited achievement. All man needed to do was to follow his most cherished ambitions even at the expense of less diligent and resourceful individuals who, in any event, were doomed by the evolutionary forces of survival of the most adaptive. Man was accountable only to himself, hence *laissez faire* was the keynote in all things. There was, from the beginning, a sense of anomie, an awareness of a normlessness and hence meaninglessness to human existence. If man was free, his very freedom threatened him, because his freedom was now that of an insignificant being, floating in a space of unknown dimensions. Man had no anchorage. He was a drifter, having no purpose but to pass as painlessly as possible between two states of nothingness.

As the trend developed into the present, the dignity of man, as a creature whose life had a transcendental purpose, was lost. This loss has invaded deeper and deeper into man's consciousness as he moves farther and farther away from any sense of belonging. The fiction of "Mother Nature" died slowly, but by the end of the nineteenth century, it was largely dead. In some ways, the poetry of the nineteenth century reflects its demise. As Duncan Williams (Williams, 1973) so well pointed out, the literature of a period is a good reflection of its character. And if we use, in that context, the words of William Cullen Bryant's *Thanatopsis,* in which he called for man to reconcile himself to his fate, to die in harmony with nature, and hence to become again as one with the elements. It was a beautiful but purely futile attempt to rationalize meaning into an otherwise meaningless existence.

> ...Thou shalt lie down
> With patriarchs of the infant world—with kings,
> The powerful of the earth—The wise, the good,
> Fair forms and hoary seers of ages past
> All in one mighty sepulchre!...

It was the best a philosophy, reflected in his poetry, had to offer. It was replaced a hundred years later typically by Carl Sandberg's powerful *Chicago Poems* in 1916, in which nature, if thought about at all, was no longer a kind and tender mother whose embrace was sought in time of trouble, but something more resembling a "woman of pleasure" to be used with zest but seldom loved. In between the early Bryant and the early Sandburg, the Industrial Revolution had come into full bloom and in our own country brought forth strange fruit indeed.

The ravaging of "Mother Nature" in this century need not be recounted here again, but its reality, as our expression of man's new contempt for all life which developed from a growing contempt of his own, is clear. Life became a can of beer to be savored, drained, and at end flung crushed into the growing heap of debris even without hope of recycling. There was now no sanctioned moral law. Law without sanction is only a gesture. There was also no "Mother Nature." There was nothing, except man's ability to gratify his own desire to exercise power—power over the material world, power over other men. Where power was, there was legitimation, there was authority. When sheer exercise of power is the only norm, the only basis of morality, the result can again go two opposite and yet, ultimately conjoined directions, one to anarchy, and the other to resentful mechanical slavery. Inevitably, the one abuse leads to the other, there is a built-up energy of frustration and an undampened oscillation develops. Each swing becomes more wild than the last until the system destroys itself. This century has seen examples of this phenonemon in the excesses of dictatorial regimes. But these were only limited samples of what a fully developed amoral culture would develop. There is no responsible homeostatic governor such as Parsons saw to control and bring sense out of chaos.

This age is living on the residual sense of morality which had been internalized in the culture from centuries of moral tradition. Though a religious sense still exists among the bulk of man, it is, for many, almost reduced to habit, and habits depend on exercise for continued proficiency. Unless habits are reinforced by constant, determined usage they atrophy and, in addition, moral habits must be carefully fostered and nourished in each new generation.

The basic educational and other socializing communications media outside the family in this age are amoral and becoming, in many ways, immoral in tone. In this way, they counter the continuing cultural trait which has been one of solid morality. There has been a diminished role of the family and of the community as a community and hence as a socializing agency vis-a-vis the rise of the mass media and its strong propagandizing influence. The gravest peril to Western civilization lies in the conjunction of these trends in the socializing process. The remedy does not lie in attempts to restore the individual socializing agencies to their former rank order of importance because that manifestly is working against the course of technological advancement and that is a self-defeating course. The remedy lies in supplying moral nutrient to both the family and mass media as socializing agencies which should be mutually supportive rather than competitive.

The task of developing a deep sense of morality is not one of short term effort. The required nutrient itself must first be grown and brought to harvest. Society has not arrived at its current state suddenly and it will not extricate itself suddenly. The new trends in philosophy away from materialism have not yet started to make themselves felt except in a vague dissatisfaction among the people with the old impoverished themes. Even the most dedicated enthusiast of the erotic must agree that the materialistic wave has spent its energy. He can find little left to titillate or titivate his jaded senses. Duncan Williams saw, in the degraded literature of the period, a "barely concealed cultural, social, and individual death wish." This writer sees it only as a guttering out in banal obscenities of an invalid philosophy. But the sense of dissatisfaction in the general public has to be brought into full maturity as a resolute searching for alternatives. This is a program calling for years of reassessment and reeducation in new values and requiring at least one full generation of adults raised in that environment before being brought to full fruition. But the effort has to be begun and begun quickly; delay only increases the size and difficulty of the task.

As we have followed the trend in development of the concept of man through the centuries it became apparent that at every significant change in direction some new rising organizational form appeared to promote the intellectual change. There were the city universities of the thirteenth and fourteenth centuries and from them developed the royal academies of the eighteenth century which saw the Enlightenment come into full bloom. Even the Marxist cells of the nineteenth and twentieth centuries were of this intellectual nature. In the modern bureaucratic world, it is hard to visualize a new and independent intellectually-oriented structure of that type. Probably some of the student underground organizations constituted such an attempt. But it appears that, this time, any significant change must be brought about from within the existing highly efficient forms.

Examining the earlier organizations we can note several things in common. Prominently, there was an intensive and extensive exchange of information, horizontally and vertically, within individual organizations and between like organizations. There was little compartmentalizing by the separate disciplines, even among the Marxists, although, with Marxism, the ideology set the frame of reference. There was a strong sense of common purpose which spurred and gave vitality to the efforts and there was a rapport between the organizations and the people, a feeling that all shared in the common goals even for those not directly participating. They were all part of a surge to a better way. Today the problem is one of getting that same esprit and effective use of communications which was displayed by the earlier organizations into existing institutions. If that is achieved, the organizational form is unimportant.

The first objective that appears here is for masses of the people to be brought strongly into the picture once again and not just left as an inert background. The general population is, of itself, far better educated, far more knowledgeable of world affairs than any past group inside or outside of the earlier intellectual structures. If the general sense of the mass of the people is one of dissatisfaction, as it appears to be, they are the ones who are in the best position to do something about it in the West. They, rather than a prince, prelate, or commissar, control the patronage both in education and the media. They are the ones who should demand that the alternatives be brought into the open and critically examined so that they, as well as the students and leaders in scholarship, have a free and intelligent choice. Such a choice does not exist in much of scholarship today. Materialism and positivism have been moribund for almost half a century and yet these hackneyed philosophies still control much of the thinking in the behavioral fields.

The educators seem as bored with the biologic theme as anyone else, but appear uncertain as to how to change. The writer is convinced that they would welcome a more open scholarship. But there is a certain security in conformity and uniformity. There is a fear of being labeled unscientific for advocating a scientific openness to questioning. But when the people, and the people include the educators, become sufficiently dissatisfied with degenerating conditions that they are willing to call for corrective action, they will find a great deal of support in academic circles. Similarly when the people are sufficiently disgusted with the media, the media will change. The media's business is providing what the public demands and when the public, by its demonstrated tastes, demands a reasonable restraint they will find a ready response in the media whose primary motivation is financial, not moral or intellectual.

The question then, of restoration of a moral tone to life is up to the masses of individual people, as the public collectively. This time there appears to be little likelihood that an organizational form will arise to take over the intellectual role of sponsor as it has in the past. Nor is there any clear need for one to do so. The public is far from powerless. It is an intelligent, well-educated, well-informed public with ready access to by far the most efficient communication system in history. All that is lacking, which the older organizations had, is the sense of common purpose and the will.

Those ingredients must be found in a convinced and sturdy belief in the infinite personal God and in the transcendent meaning of individual human life. For, today, the strength of purpose and will leading to a sound moral life cannot be developed without an intellectual acceptance of those truths. As we have seen, in the purely biologic order morality is meaningless. Because of the severe erosion which has taken place in the traditional deep religious faith, there is a great need for intellectual insight to restore it. In these days, Riesman's "other-directed man," is a very realistic model. No one wants to feel he is the queer eccentric moving against the trend. There must be a strong conviction that "different" viewpoints are far better-based and much more forward-looking than those of the prevailing countercurrents before people will stand up for these viewpoints. Because the need is for a well-developed, intellectual base, action, when it comes, must begin with the educational system, in all its forms and at all its levels. The basic intellectual nutrient in the present age comes from the educational system whether it is productive of good public policy or not.

In the world of education today, academic recognition of the spiritual capacity of man is lacking at all levels. The emphasis is almost completely biologic, and is in direct opposition to what the vast majority of adults feel should be done. To some extent, in the United States at least, this is the result of narrow interpretation of the public law. But to a far wider extent, it is the result of a process of attrition at an accelerated rate, as each succeeding generation of educators passed along the accrued results of its own learning process.

When, in the mathematical expression c^x, a substantive teaching effort ("x") in any educational component "c," is less than unity, an amount holding that expression on exactly even terms with its fellow disciplines. The application of that discipline would decline at an accelerated rate in the succeeding curricula. As can be shown from biologic analogy, such a process will produce an extinction point.

When stripped to the stark essentials, what are the rational outcomes of pursuing a purely biologic orientation in morality? There is a two-part answer. First, for the individual, there is no sense of innate wrongdoing in any action. Wrongness is only a label attached by others in society with different viewpoints. The indvidual is freed from any personal responsibility to any norms. Just do not get caught. Second, for society, there is no legitimate limit to its power over the individual. Society may resort to any action it chooses, since, as the source of all ethics or morality, it is the only and final arbiter. The first of these answers is the philosophic base of anarchy. The second of these answers is the philosophic basis of totalitarianism. Here are the ingredients of a true dialectic confrontation but one without a synthesis! The one idea breeds the other at the opposite pole. It is Heraclitus' *Oppositorum*. It is a confrontation with no happy outcome.

What good things does the viewpoint offer man? The writer can think of none. The hackneyed alleged freedom of the individual from superstitious theologic control is a true myth. Freedom is not the product. Slavery, abject and total, is the product. The joyous, experiential, pure biologic life held out by the proponents is quickly submerged in the mires of brutalized self-gratification. It is the way of the mythical and uncontrolled savage categorized by Hobbes as a condition of "constant fear and danger of violent death and the life of man solitary, poor, nasty, brutish and short."

It is the writer's conclusion that, in the "Western world," and particularly in the United States, the levels of learning relative to spiritual content and value in the educational system, and through it, in the generations of citizens has reached the extinction point. In large measure it was planned that way, its side effects being unforeseen. No improvement in public or private ethics or moral attitudes will develop as long as the educational system which is the source of intellectual nourishment, continues its exclusive biologism.

As is probably natural, since they were the most heavily indoctrinated by the positivistic ideas, those disciplines most closely tied to the nature of man have been the last to shift or to sense the shift away from positivism and materialism. Even the splintered concepts of man's nature which present anthropologists, sociologists, and psychologists have developed are not yet generally recognized for what they are, the tatters from an exhausted idea which has no reality at base.

The revolt of the young sociologists in the 1960's against all theorizing referred to by Gouldner (Gouldner, 1970) should have registered as a signal that new winds are blowing even in academic circles. The young, sophisticated student fortunately has been taught to think, whatever shortcomings the educational system has in tone. Courageous and thoughtful intelligence leads eventually to the truth, though if unguided or guided falsely, its progress is tentative, painful and slow.

The most hopeful sign today is that the young people are less materialistic. They are far less concerned with immediate economic problems than the older generation. Perhaps it is because, looking at our errors, they have determined that these problems are of secondary importance. They do not yet appear to have decided what is of primary importance. However, it is in this new outlook of the youth, revealed currently in a concern for nature and what we, as mankind, are doing to it that the real potential energy lies. It is up to the educators at all levels in universities, schools, churches, synagogues and, most of all in our homes, to try to provide moral guidance for the rising generation so that those energies are directed toward what is of primary importance. This is the generation which must rise to the main challenge and provide leadership in those social movements which are almost certain to arise near the close of this century. They will need all the resources of courage and moral stamina that they can muster from all sources. Mostly, they will have to find those resources within themselves.

The advance in technology which the young tend to deprecate has been good. What is needed is a process of reeducation to permit direction of the available high technology with wisdom and confidence for the benefit of man now and in the future. The advances in the physical sciences have shown man the way to solve the demographic problems in their physical dimensions. The physical sciences cannot reveal how to solve the problems in their human dimensions. What is needed is to bring the humanities, including the philosophy of morals, into focus, as they were for centuries, in the forefront of man's development. Instead of aping the detailed procedures and methodology of the physical sciences, the shallow empiricism in the social sciences should be replaced by honest study of the complete human being in all his richness and depth of consciousness. Empirical methodology should be used within its fields of application but not contrived in its interpretation as the full measure of man. Finally, man should be viewed not as a laboratory specimen, but as a singular being with roots in the "here and now" material world and, more importantly, with a spiritual vector which is destined for eternity.

Sociology comprises two complimentary fields of interest. First is the study of individual human beings in groups and groups in society in all aspects of their interrelationships; their attitudes, motivations, processes and achievements. Second, is the study of society as the structure in which the individuals and groups interact. The structure can be as light and airy as a trapeze

array in a circus tent, and as hazardous, or it can be as heavy
and sullen as a dungeon. The sociologist is neither the architect
nor the builder of the structure, but he is the architectural critic
and building inspector. His recognized presence in the intellectual world of human studies places him squarely in the role
of criteria formulation and criticism in matters affecting society
and virtually all aspects of human life.

The three principal social theories, the Parsonsian structural-
functional, Marxian dialect and conflict approaches to society
do not provide any recognition of the non-biologic aspects of
man. Yet, clearly, society, which represents man's attempts to
structure his total environment to meet his endless needs, is
more than biological. By Parsons' own analysis, religion, in its
broadest context, is one—even the primary one—of the four
essential requirements of any society. Religion in any context
is not a biologically derived element. It derives from man's intuitive perception of his dependence upon extra-biological
resources. As we have seen, it is a sound perception no less
true today than in antiquity. In a sense, biologically induced
social entropy must be offset by a spiritual replenishment or
the society dies.

The insistent dialectic would have long ceased to exist had
not the impinging spiritual element of man been continuously
reinforced to offset the ever present individual attractiveness
of pure egoism. That the insistent dialectic remains in force
is evidential of man's indefatigable spirituality, along with his
earthiness, and of the constant spiritual urge which makes the
spirituality possible.

Society, which presents a very complex subject matter, requires, in its explication, a model, which while not equally complex at least permits recognition of the major elements which
are at work. The author would identify five such elements.

The basic element is purely inertial—the sheer mass of traditional habit and custom opposes sudden changes in society at
all levels. The remaining elements are dynamic influences which
tend to move society each in its own direction. These are:

> 1. *Individual dynamism.* Man is egocentric by na-
> ture. He is ambitious. Most of his time and effort is
> directed to advancing his personal interests. This ele-
> ment is easily recognized as the "poker" syndrome.
> 2. *Collective dynamism.* Man is oriented to organi-
> zation, to collective security and action. Yet, the
> "herd instinct" can work either toward stability or

against it. A stampede can result as well as quiet "pasturage" in common.

3. *Technologic dynamism.* Man's technologic capacity advances through time and forces unidirectional change in society toward complexity in organization and yet, also toward specialization and isolation in specialization.

4. *Moral dynamism.* Man is religious. This element derives from the pervasive motivating sense of love and duty. It is frequently masked—often attenuated in effect—by the other more aggressive dynamisms. Yet, it is this one chiefly which bends society into a cohesive whole and renders its existence credible—even as Durkheim saw. In any given situation, these elements may be either competitive or reinforcing. It is the relative weight which is given each in combination with the basic inertial "mass" which gives any society its particular character and stability and also which determines the rate and direction of future change.

The thermostat-actuated furnace is frequently used as a "model" for the structural-functional theory. The thermostat senses changes in temperature ΔT and modulates the furnace output ΔH so as to maintain the preset temperature level. Similarly the "feedback" from society provokes changes in emphasis to maintain the societal status quo. The model would work as well for a society of ants. Expressed as an equation

$$T = T_0 \pm \Delta T \mp \Delta H = K, \text{ a constant.}$$

A similar analogy would be a battery-powered automobile equipped with a "cruise control" device which, regardless of the profile of the road, uphill or down, maintains a constant velocity. On the ascent, energy is drawn from the battery and on descent energy is returned. Expressed as an equation, the formula would be as follows:

$$V = V_0 \pm \Delta V \mp \Delta E = K, \text{ a constant.}$$

In this case, the battery represents the stabilizing "mass" of custom, tradition and habit. If we provide a human "override" to our "cruise control," the velocity can be changed at will—subject to the condition of the battery of course, and the ride is under rational control with a good deal of automatic direction. The new equation would be:

$$V = V_0 \pm \Delta V \mp \Delta E + \Delta R = f(R), \text{ a function of reason.}$$

The new model could no longer be applied to a non-human

society. The characteristics of the rational control would depend upon the weight given all of our elements at any given time; it would always be positive in its correction.

The rational "override" in our modified structural-functional model which permits society to change in accord with the several dynamisms must include all essential elements in reasonable proportions or a badly warped society will result. The three aggressive dynamisms—individual, collective and technological have dominated recent sociologic thought. A sociology which shows human values as not scientifically real cannot help but contribute to its demise and the decline of the moral dynamism in society.

Sociology, which should play the leading role in the study of modern man in society does not yet appear ready to take the integrative approach to man. Yet, the total educational structure, and that is the key to the future, needs a foundation in a realistic sociology as well as philosophy. In Part II, while discussing current sociology, the writer cited the viewpoint of the late Pitirim Sorokin as the one clear prestigious voice in sociology that has advocated the integral viewpoint of man. In the controversy, Sorokin certainly represented a small minority among the more vocal sociologists.

The sociologists, up to the present, seem reluctant to accept the burden of inquiry into the question of morals in relation to society. It will be recalled that Alvin Gouldner was puzzled at the lack of a "sociology of morals," suggesting that sociologists feared to find that morals or morality would lose its position of autonomy by such an inquiry. As we saw, such fears were soundly based. There is no universally binding morality possible apart from the concept of God. It is not an autonomous subject. It is also crystal clear that a discipline must be sufficiently broad to comprehend all essential aspects of its subject matter. If the question of morality is of sociologic importance, it should be included.

There is a manifest difference between a sociology of morals and a moral sociology. Our first task was to define what would be the "universe" of a sociology of morals. It became apparent quickly that the problem was, in fact, to establish the place of "human values" in sociology. A sociology of values has a closely equivalent statement of scope; the two concepts are inseparable.

Sociology seeks to discover and understand the laws which govern social processes just as physics seeks to discover and understand the laws which govern physical processes. As we have seen, other then in broad statistical terms, man, the unit of sociology, is not as predictable as the atom or quantum and they are not completely predictable except in statistically significant numbers. Man the individual is a free-intending ego who can make a decision, then change his mind and proceed in many ways contrary to expectations. The things which influence man's mind and govern final decisions, are *motivations*.

The laws of social process, in turn, are broadly reflective of the motivations which are effective in society. Marx saw the motivation as primarily economic; Parsons saw it as group security in social stability. Conflict theorists generally see it in terms of power seeking—a competition for dominance. We saw other motivation, peer group approval, public recognition, and in quasi-economic terms, in the dynamism of reciprocity in exchange. At root, these motivations are closely related, one grading into another. All are motivations which would appeal to man the gifted animal. Within limits all are valid and morally indifferent.

It is perhaps safe to say that in the normal course of daily events these motivations control the way we behave. In "non-crisis" sociology, they are explanatory of much social process. Newtonian physics is adequate to explain most day-to-day physical processes as well. Both the sociologist and the physicist must be aware of the limits within which they can safely ignore the more subtle aspects of their science which can drastically affect the processes beyond those limits.

Morality consists in a blend of justice and love. Justice connotes what is strictly owed. Love connotes what is freely given. A code of ethics should be based on justice. A truly human morality should go beyond. One cannot live as an "it" to all others. The "rage" projected in the looting mob in the "blackout" of July 13, 1977 in New York was real. Yet Herman Kahn's final comment was still true. The looters had "no moral standards." The two facts are not unrelated. The people of the ghettos feel as though they are "its" to all others and even to each other. The complaint of one looter mentioned in the article by *Time* magazine when another looter "stole" her loot was: "That's just not right—They shouldn't have done that." That statement reflects the "unlovedness" that is endemic in these "isolation wards." "They shouldn't have done that," the girl said; she believed there was a "duty" at least to respect each other. It is a totally different situation than in the historic Jewish ghettos where the familial and communal bonds of love held the people together. There likely was a keen sense of the injustice of their predicament—the more so, because it was a forced isolation. But, there was no burning rage against humanity because they knew that in each other's eyes and in God's eyes, they were beloved "Thous." Moral standards cannot coexist with an atmosphere of hate or rage. Revenge, envy, jealousy, lust are the immoral emotional responses of an unloved "it." When there are thousands of such "its" collected together, all that is needed is the opportunity to release these pent-up emotions with relative immunity to bring about a disastrous riot.

This is not to say that the looters were justified by any means, merely that the summation of all the "data bits" stored in their memories contained no morality-forming base to offset natural greed and the hatefulness of their environment. The looters are a perfect example of biologic man in predicament—there is no love beyond the animal level and no real hope of escaping the jungle they are committed to. Had the same individuals been taught from childhood that there is a loving God who is their Father and that no situation is hopeless, that they are loved by their fellowmen, that they are important in God's plan, that rage would not have developed. This moral socializing process is not begun at age 25, however. The fact that the situation now exists is the result of a long-standing effort to reduce man's schooling to his biologic lowest denominator on the pretext that by so doing he is freed of repressive inhibitions and guilt feelings and thus may develop into a completely "natural" person. Well, the effort succeeded. Now, what?

Man is motivated by the desire to be free. He seeks to throw off constraint of any sort. But he is motivated also by love in its highest sense as well as in the biologic order. He, as a species, is in love with love itself. He seeks that which is worthy of his love. He aspires to be happy in the possession of that love even while he cannot define it. He literally thirsts for beauty and goodness and holiness. He despises ugliness and evil. Man is motivated by the desire for knowledge and for answers to the deep set questions of life that he asks. As Ortiz says, "Man cannot live without answers." In fact, man cannot live without freedom, at least intellectual freedom or without love, or without beauty and goodness as well as without answers to the questions of life. These then are the motivations from the spiritual side of man's nature which are interwoven with the others, the more material. Man is neither pure animal nor angel.

Sociology sets itself the task of investigating and identifying scientific principles by which men interact in various social groupings. It presumes that such principles may be found. The key to the motivation in the various physical models we looked at was self-interest. With biologic man that is the case. Man's self-interest here lies in a narrow band of material gratification of the physical appetites. Although religious motivations and groupings are recognized and studied, they are studied in the context of satisfaction of a felt-need by a biologic organism. Whether the felt-need reflects an actual relationship between God and man in society is beyond the scope of current sociology.

In the crisis social mood characteristic of much of the world in the late twentieth century, sociology must be a "crisis" sociology able to come to grips with these less material motivations or cease claiming to be a valid science. As in physics, there is a "microphysics" which explores the nature of the atom so there must be a "micro-sociology" which explores the nature of man—the greater and more important part of man.

People and people-solving problems in the social environment is the subject matter of micro-sociology. Is there something fundamentally unscientific in sociology about looking at people and people's problems as people, in fact, looking at them and solving them or failing to solve them? If so, sociology is a strange science indeed for it neglects the behavior of its basic element. The data are available on the "micro-sociological" basis even though in a less convenient form and one less manageable by statistical routines and formulas than on a "micro-sociological" basis.

Social theory would find that the "homeostatic variable" in society was still there, but its action would be by a far more subtle feedback system than the model's picture. The triggering mechanism in a specific race riot which terminates a long period of tension building, may be some very prosaic incident, a power failure, for instance. Both the tension and the trigger are tied acutely to human values and emotions not measurable in generalized approaches. Only a detailed advance knowledge of the situation in particular cases can enable responsible civil authorities to bleed off the tension and reduce the threat of a precipitating incident before the disaster occurs. Attempts to cover this exposed flank of sociology have been made by the social psychologists. Unfortunately, they too look only at man, the biologic organism.

The general social theory can well be established by broad studies but a useful sociology today must be applicable in specific critical situations and there a sociology must be prepared to study the problems in detail in terms of human values, fears and frustration, motivations and aspirations. That is the approach which must be undertaken if Gouldner's crisis is to be passed and a strong, dynamic period of sociology is to emerge. I believe that is what Gouldner suggests.

Such a change in sociology will require a corresponding change in the basic philosophies of sociology. Max Weber early pointed out the difficulty involved in taking a purely impersonal approach both as to the researcher and the object of research. Merleau-Ponty pointed out in behavior analysis that the environment was an essential part of the pattern. Animate beings are not units that can be isolated in behavior. This combination of circumstances suggests that society cannot be studied adequately when divorced from the inherent nature of man, nor can man be studied adequately when divorced from the society of which he is a part. Sociology ought to be broad enough to accept this total scope—that is, the study of society as it constitutes the environment for integral man, or man as he is. In this view, society is not an independent entity to be studied for its own sake. It is a man-related or man-dependent society.

As we have seen, for the foreseeable future, any sociology of morals in the West must be somewhat bifurcated. For theists, there is an absolute standard of morality and for atheists, or indifferentists, there is a totally relative morality (i.e., no absolute standards can be set). Sociology must comprehend both viewpoints. A theistic absolutism cannot be forced upon an atheist nor can atheistic relativism be forced upon a theist. These are the ingredients of a dialectic situation. However, since, in the West generally, there are habitual working moral standards residual from a theistic orientation which is Kant's categorical imperative, if you will, the disagreements currently are generally not in severe strain. At heart, the atheist, or indifferentist, does not want a Hobbesian world, nor does he want tyrannical controls to maintain some level of order which a true amoral "society" would require. While the motivation of the atheist is different than that of the theist, there is a broad area of general agreement on human values held for whatever reason. The anarchist is an exception in any culture, although most anarchists are made and not born.

The point to be made is that sociology ought to be looking at the nature of man as Dennis Wrong suggested so that sociology is relevant to people, to their values and their needs. Atheists, or indifferentists, do not agree with theists as to the transcendental nature of man and to goodness and holiness as values, but they do agree, in general, as to the importance as values of the concepts freedom, beauty, love and happiness and seek to enhance these aspects of life which, to the theist, are correlatives of the former two. There is, thus, a substantial band of common ground from which to start a common edifice of what could be called a moral sociology. Hopefully, from a theist's viewpoint, such efforts will ultimately reveal the source from which all moral concepts must flow, the incarnate consciousness—the soul of man, as he is. We have seen that there is no source in biologic man as such.

Sociology, in its current state, neglects the higher intellectual drives of man in its devotion to biologic man and to empiricism as the only guide. It is hard to gather empirical data on values, particularly as to levels of specific values. The social psychologists have, in the past and currently, attempted to reduce man's motivations to the biologic responses to glandular activity or to sense stimuli, to the Freudian contrasted with the Jungian viewpoint. Yet the study of large scale social movements has revealed the tremendous weight which values have as motivations of human beings. It is the "idea" embodied in the movement which must capture the imagination of thousands or millions of individuals, as individuals of all classes, in a society, which makes such enterprises possible. And the ideas are value-laden and largely non-biologic in formulation.

It is a sardonic twist, that for 100 years, sociologists have been using biologic man as a standard unit of society though society was generally theistic and basing behavior on theistic standards. Now, sociologists are faced with a society which begins to reflect their model and finds the actual situation theoretically unmanageable. Condorcet's, Comte's, and Dewey's idealized biologic human did not eventuate. An irresponsible, self-centered, anarchistic bunch of Hobbesian individuals emerged instead. Society, rather than becoming stable, became critically unstable. It is no coincidence that conflict theory is a late arrival on the sociologic scene.

For the time being, the reality of the relationship between God, man and society can be left alone. Nonetheless, if there is to be a definitive sociology of morals, and a moral sociology, it should be clear by now that the *reality* of that relationship must eventually be established in the same sense that the reality of the relationship of man with his fellowman and with his environment are established. Sociology, as a science, is faced with the same level of change in basic posture that physics faced ninety years ago. Gouldner's crisis in sociology reflects the precurser wave of that approaching shock front. Never was a realistic, down-to-earth, yet, up-to heaven, sociology more needed than in our own crisis-ridden times.

The flaw in basic logic in the mechanistic theme is the presumption that man could be taught that he, in fact, is responsible to no one but himself and then be expected to live in society as responsible to that society for his behavior in an attitude of enlightened self-interest. As we have seen, human action reflects motivation. Hence, if an act is to be responsive at a level above the animal, motivation must stem from above the level of the animal. Even an intelligent, rational animal, if such a pure animal form could exist, would be little motivated to sacrifice a present pleasure for a principle of betterment not directly related to its own life situation. It is difficult for us to place ourselves in that situation of normlessness since we do have norms. A situation in which all acts are strictly indifferent, except as they relate narrowly to the present instant in our life passage between points of nothingness, is not easy to conceive since even the most dedicated atheist does not think that way. It will be recalled that atheist existentialist Paul Sartre wrote of the "forlornness" of man without God. A pure animal organism no matter how intelligent, would not put it that way. The attitude of "forlornness" reflects, at least the *possibility* of God. It talks of a case which *could have been.* Barring a miracle, the development of the actuality of God as a primary influence in sociology likely must remain somewhat in the future after the first hurdle of man's integral humanness has been passed. If man (in his total humanity) is recognized, then that upon which the humanness depends, cannot remain unrecognized.

The sociologist, when he recognizes man as something other than a gifted animal must reassess his basic stance as a scientist. First, he needs to abandon the positivistic idea of knowledge. This need was Sorokin's main point in the work cited. There are other sources of knowledge than sheer empiricism. When the subject of study is man, the difference becomes severe. Values are as real as physical appetites and, in the long term, far more essential to man's fulfillment as an integral human being. Love is not a mere biologic sensation, beauty and goodness are expressions of man's innermost needs, and religion is more than Freud's "universal obessional neurosis of humanity." Deprived of these recognized values, the human organism wilts and dies and society wilts and dies with him.

Whereas sociologists have certainly been well aware of these truths, the structure of sociological research, education and what might be called application would not accept the concepts as equal parameters with the more physical aspects of man in society. Positivism died as a philosophy because it could not come to grips with problems of real human relevancy. Sociology must likewise face the problems of society as human problems or atrophy.

A moral sociology needs a moral social theoretical base. If social theory is to be based on integral man as a basic model, certain changes have to be made in approach to the phenomena of social interaction as it relates to morality. In the structural-functional theory, for example, the various aspects of the homeostatic variable would become more finely tuned. In the case of integral man in society, the control mechanism can be either active (driving toward change) or passive, as before, depending entirely on the adequacy of the given society to meet man's total needs. Society truly becomes for man. In this mode, that which the "governor" seeks is not the status quo but an evolutionary forcing of humanly "better" society. That ought to be the aim of every society. The governor is provided a "moral" bias to foster moral ends. When the status quo reflects an ordered moral society, control can be homeostatic and perform its usual function of resisting change toward immoral forms through educational and religious channels.

On the other hand, in an immoral, tyrannical, or overly permissive society, that segment reflecting integral man would take unusually stringent actions to change the status quo toward humanly acceptable levels. It may seem the writer has described an aspect of conflict theory and, in some situations, this may be the case. Where the inhuman aspects are severe in an existing society, that society becomes the arena for active social movements. Generally speaking, in an established society, these tendencies toward integral humanism would be encouraged and those tendencies toward inhuman aspects would be resisted by political means without deep conflict. In the United States, we have seen a situation in which the political and societal "governor" was biased toward "liberalism" over many years. Although there were moderate conservative swings, that has been the direction. Inevitably societies will change. An integral humanism would seek that change which is better for the total man. The question of "better" is, of course, one of great difficulty in a pluralistic society.

Still, if this hurdle can be passed even on a compromise basis on shared values, societies would be seen as more stable yet more progressive in personal freedom within the framework of social responsibility rather than in the frame of pragmatism.

Globally, the encouragement of support to developing nations would be with less emphasis on military strategy and commercial possibilities or on the power position in ideologic struggles and with more emphasis on the moral obligations to assist other people toward their own self-fulfillment.

If, as would seem likely, the sociologists will be willing, as the physicists were, to broaden their theoretical base and methodologies, then the internal structural and theoretical changes to fit the emerging expanded discipline should be begun and begun quickly. The sociologists will probably find, as did the physicists before them, that this is not the end of the world for their science, but, rather, the beginning of a new and fascinating phase.

In Part III, I suggested in cybernetics terminology, that the crucial difference between man and the lower animals is that the latter are "preprogrammed" in their activities to follow built-in instinctive guides. Man possessed his own programming essence and through operations of his intellect and will, guides his own destiny. With this concept as a model the idea of man as a truly free agent can be expanded and incorporated into a social theory along Sorokin's lines enunciated in Part II.

Without suggesting any compartmentalization of the human personality or the "ghost in the machine," if the brain is taken as an organic computer through which a programming essence, the human individual, operates, we can conceive of information being fed to the computer from many sources and conveying many levels of inference. During the individual's lifetime, from infancy, data banks or memory storage units record and catalogue the information, so that, at maturity, the individual is equipped to assess the incoming data from all sources, compare them with stored data from all sources and decide on future courses of action. It is through the operation of the human programmer's intellect and will, the evaluation of current input data, and the complete comparisons with stored data that the individual determines the future course of action in every changed situation. Such decisions have two vectors. One stems from the biologic demands and the other stems from the non-biologic or spiritual demands. Both vectors would have been subjected simultaneously to the intellectual processes of the programming essence. The decision the individual makes, in any specific case, reflects the motivations which are also largely the result of the processing of the data supplied through life to that point, plus the factor of personal disposition and the crucial moral imponderable.

This is the unit element of which the proposed model of society becomes the aggregate. In this analogy, man is not a being with two natures, he is a singular being acted upon and reacting to stimuli of different types. Society should be perceived in this same way. Society reflects the summation of the individuals in all their diversity of background, personality, and motivation. Society is man, in the aggregate, responding to new situations in the light of past experience, making decisions in relation to the mores, customs, and traditions which form his culture. The evolving social environment is conditioned by the past, the pressing present, and the anticipated future. Social decisions are moral and secular. Both have spiritual and biological vectors. In the secular sphere, any of the current sociologic, theoretical systems and models apply but they are conditioned by moral values impinging from the moral sources. In the great majority of secular cases, the moral vector is neutral and, hence, of no concern. In many cases, the moral vector is reinforcing to the secular in which case the resultant direction likewise is largely unaffected. But in the crucial cases, where the moral vector is in opposition, the moral value system becomes controlling and value judgments and decisions on these judgments are necessary. They will reflect the motivations prevalent in the given society. A society will be that which the mature citizens have learned to be, have chosen to be. If the educational process is balanced so that man sees himself as he truly is, it will be a moral society.

Sociologists must ask two questions. First, is some code of ethics or morality essential to a stable society? Second, what are the elements of a viable code of ethics or morality in the late twentieth century? The writer believes the answer to the first question has to be an unequivocal yes. The answer to the second would be somewhat variable with the society, but the writer can find no support for the proposition that either a naturalistic or materialistic code will survive in the absence of a morality residual from theistic origins. If the residual theistic based morality collapses, so will the total edifice of secular moral or ethical codes.

The evaluation of moral codes in relation to society implies value judgments, at least to the extent that a stable society is judged *better* than an unstable one; that freedom is *superior* to slavery, that a degree of organization is *superior* to total disorganization, that freedom from fear is *superior* to terrorism. Where the value judgments stop is a question of the level of pluralism in a given society. In a highly pluralistic society with a certain commonality of culture, the latitude between what is acceptable without being considered "immoral" is fairly wide. Yet, social acceptability does not equate with morality, though, as we saw, the two ideas are not unrelated, by any means. The range between the two concepts is an inverse measure of the cohesiveness of the society. In line with Durkheim's ideas of religion as a social cohesive in amelioration of anomie, religion serves to mediate between the moral and the socially acceptable. Religion attempts, in fact, to draw them together.

The question immediately arises, "Who, or what, is the arbiter of moral behavior?" How would a sociologist approach the problem when norms of morality have been so widely disputed throughout the history of human existence? The biological approach is far more tractable on a general basis—so was the Newtonian physics.

The evaluation of the moral vector must always remain, to some extent, subjective. The biologic vector is also not always crystal clear and objective, and the range of subjectivity in the moral sphere is not gross. Norms of decent human behavior are not as elusive as some of the "label theorists" in the sociology of deviance would have students believe. Over the centuries, the range of acceptable moral behavior has swung between extremes. The central trend has, however, remained consistent and closer to what are more likely the asymptotic "ultimate norms" of behavior than any of the wide variations from the trend.

One of the tasks of a new approach would be to trace such trends through an historical sociology. Sorokin suggests, "integral cognition means that we learn about the total reality not only from empirical scientists, logicians and mathematicians, but also from great religious and ethical leaders like Buddha, Lao-tse, Jesus, and from creative geniuses like Beethoven and Mozart, Phidias and Michelangelo, Homer and Shakespeare." (Sorokin, 1966, page 256). It is probable that a continuum of behavior norms flowing from all sources of information from the basic biologic pole to the highest spiritual pole would result.

Sorokin's approach presents many problems to sociologists trained in positivistic social theory and strict empirical methodology. The sociology of transcendental man would be more demanding than that of biologic man. At the same time, the combination would also be far more rewarding to the sociologist and to society.

What is required is not a mass replacement of social theories, or of basic methodologies, but the emergence of a set of complementary theories and methodologies; a change much like that which has already occurred in physics—a change which reflects growth in the discipline and an openness to change itself. Most of all, then, it requires a fresh outlook and attitude and a reappraisal of what constitutes reality and scope within the field of sociology. Such fresh outlooks have already been noted in philosophy in the strong swing from materialism and positivism and in psychology, at least, in the Jungian wing.

In all the troubled, even violent, outpourings of frustration we see in the world about us so characteristic of this time, and probably every time, of change in spiritual tides, we can dimly perceive in the diverging and converging streams, the beginning currents of what will be the following surge of history. While the direction it will take is not yet clear, the "Toynbee scenario" is a far more probable outcome. It is the only path which, this time, can prevent disaster and even the catastrophic destruction of civilization. The writer has attempted to show that the Toynbee scenario, if it is to become more than just a historian's concept, must be brought to reality by large scale social movements having strong religious orientation. These must be movements of deep intellectual energy and spiritual renewal, renewal pervading men's thoughts and extending to all walks of life. Initially, these movements must appeal, above all, to those having philosophical, sociological, religious, and educational motivations where the intellectual strength must rise. In its most fundamental sense it must involve the creation of an attitude among the people. This must be an attitude which no longer avoids or demeans spiritual values, but rather seizes upon them for what they are, the deepest and most real facts of life. The fantasy lies in materialism, whose advocates must be seen and shown for what they are: misguided, irrational, and outdated.

Toynbee seemed to be under the impression that the flame had gone from the philosophies and culture of the West. He felt they were snuffed out in the technologic revolution. In the present world situation, with much of the Eastern source-land of philosophy in chains, it appears the main drive must still come from the deep spiritual energies of the "free world" which, for the most part, represent the Western tradition. While we are free, we can work in that freedom. No revolutions are required, only courage and rededication to principles long since established in our individual national heritages.

The political scientists of the West, among the educators and in government, can do a great deal to promote pride in those same heritages which in the middle decades of this century were held up to cynical ridicule. The smirkers and scoffers merely reveal their own crude and colossal ignorance.

The days of the rationalistic and yet irrational materialistic collective man are numbered, one way or another. For those who believe in the providence of God, a way will be made in spite of man's recalcitrance. Man, individually and collectively, can make the passage facile or difficult. That option is up to him. If the path of biologic materialism is followed, only disaster lies ahead for mankind. Most people today seem to sense that, but their response is confused. Technology, with all its wonders, or production, is beginning to stutter and stumble. It has so far outstripped the capabilities of dehumanized man to control its power that it threatens as a monstrous, misbegotten offspring, to destroy him in its blind death agonies. Only when man recognizes that he is not the ruler of the earth and its resources, but its custodian under God, will he find the will and the self-discipline to manage these resources to mankind's best interest. So long as power, human power, reflected in technology, is perceived as a private right, with no external higher control than that of the individual or state which happens to exercise it, so long will man be on the threshold of outright annihilation or descent into precivilized anarchy. Nietzsche is in the ascendancy in that context. It is only in the surrender of this stolen prerogative in accord with the Toynbee scenario, man recognizing that he is a custodian under God, that man has hope of survival.

Chapter 23

THE PLACE OF THE INDIVIDUAL

After roughly two centuries of continuous emphasis on man, the animal, as the appropriate mode to bring about the good life, society finds itself in a position much like that of a spinning top. Its stability is dependent on the residual inertia which millenia of a religiously-oriented culture and moral order have provided it. Western civilization now stands at the critical balance point where, like the top, it begins to wobble uncertainly, its energy almost gone. The socializing milieu of the religiously-oriented community and family, the source of the moral attitude, is of diminished strength, and the countervailing force of impressed, amoral materialistic attitude in the mass media is being emphasized. We have seen there is no answer to the Hobbesian question in the materialistic view of man or society. If society remains under the de-energizing influence much longer, it will topple. The crisis will have turned to disaster.

But is the solution we seek one which can be applied at the gross social level? The answer appears to be negative. While Durkheim thought of society almost exclusively as an entity in itself, and much of sociology has followed that thought, the attitude which represents society can be nothing less than the summation of individual attitudes. The totality of the system energy which maintains stability is formed by that same summation. The only way to increase the total social moral energy level is by raising the individual levels. Thus, the answer to the Hobbesian question goes back to the matter of individual motivation. Given the adequate motivation, the question vanishes.

A society based on the integral viewpoint of man would be one in which the Hobbesian question would not occur because its answer arises first in the definition of society. Society is all men working together for their common heritage as the well-loved children of God. This is no Utopia, it is the way man in the West lived for centuries. There were scoundrels and there was bloodshed and violence, but the bulk of the men and women who made up the society were secure and confident within themselves as to their dignity and place in God's universe.

That, in turn, goes back to the series of questions raised in the introduction and repeated here in the same way. "It is all very well to talk about mankind in general and immortality of the species, the upward thrust of civilization through time, the unconquerability of the spirit of liberty, but how about me, my life, my liberty. What happens to me? What does my life mean?"

This entire work boils down to providing the keys to those questions. How have we answered them? The writer has attempted to show that the answers are of crystalline clarity, simplicity and beauty. Man is the highest and the ultimate creature in God's plan for the earth. The individual's goal is not the biologic evolutionary improvement of the species. One's goal is a life of loving, free and dedicated service to God and also to man because one's fellowman is like oneself, a well-loved creature of God. One can be as actively heroic or as quietly productive as he wishes within the framework. But the way one lives his life in this world means everything to him, not only here, but far more importantly, forever. A life of prayerful dependence upon God *always* produces happiness, the ultimate goal of all life.

Yet, this is not sacrificing this life to the next, far from it. The biologic viewpoint, at most, gives a selfish promise of earthly pleasures for pitifully few years, and even then with that spector of declining capacity and final disillusionment and disintegration. It is an anxiety-ridden, frustration-laden life passage. The transcendental viewpoint provides the same pleasures but deepens their value in a selfless sharing with one's intimates and all mankind in a common, joyous, dynamic striving toward God, the Source of all happiness and perfection. And rather than a declining capacity with time, it is a constant crescendo toward that final union with Him.

If high adventure is facing the unknown with intrepid *elan,* then this choice is its epitome, for exploring eternity, and the mysterious infinity of the very essence of God, will remain a perpetual adventure. This life provides but a brief conditioning for that ultimate ascent toward those unscalable and yet always beckoning and fulfilling heights, in God's love.

I believe the evidence is overwhelmingly suggestive of these answers to the point of certitude. This evidence is not for some sentimental emotional or intuitive "never-never land," but from the hardest kind of evidence there is in the physical universe, as well as in the best-reasoned theses in philosophy. And what a wonderfully satisfying set of answers they are. What have we to lose by attempting to live that way? Even if one were prone to apply the pragmatic logic of game theory to the problem and to select that course of action leading to the maximizing, or optimization of the results, one might say to playing it "cozily" safe, the answer would be the same.

Long ago Pascal formed his "wager"—almost as famous as the *"cogito"* of Descartes. Briefly restated, he says man has two ways he can approach life: As the one who believes his soul survives, or the one who believes it does not. A man must opt for one or the other; the compromise, as will be seen, is a certain loser. Likewise, there are only two possible answers in objective reality: man has an immortal soul, or he has not. Take first the response of the one who believes he has a soul, and so directs his life. He is happy in this life, regardless of its vicissitudes in the sure faith of the eternal joys. If he is right in his assumption, then he is also supremely happy for eternity. If he is wrong, he never finds out.

Now the other response, the one who believes he has no soul and lives his life on that basis. He still has the same unavoidable vicissitudes, which he fights with mounting frustration as his life fades away. If he was right in his belief, he never finds out. If he was wrong. . . .The doubter, of course, who lives by his doubts loses both ways. He compounds the problems of his earthly life with constant anxiety. He does not enjoy his misdeeds, nor does he enjoy his good deeds, and he carries his uncertainty to the grave.

Thus clearly, if the odds were exactly even, which, in the absence of any substantive evidence to support the purely biologic viewpoint they are not, man should believe and live confidently in accordance with the assumption that he is a transcendental being. "The contrary is the choice of fools." In view of the scale of the wager, what is at stake, the odds can never reach equality even if the evidence were balanced. Those who insist on playing against the odds in the belief that it shows an independent and daring insouciance are truly to be pitied.

If, as individuals, we have little control over the route society will take in the future, we have control over our own lives as completely as we wish to make it. Man is free to choose his way of life, and for the individual that is, or ought to be, the point of chief concern. Each must work out his own destiny. Society at large may follow the hopeful signs emerging in the world of philosophy and rise to new heights of moral and material well-being. This is an outcome greatly to be sought and struggled for. But if, instead, it is too late to restore the balance, if society and Western civilization does topple and fall, the individual who lives his life as a complete human being, even in a collapsing society, will not despair. He will remain secure in his knowledge that his own life does have value, that God is intimately aware of his striving in the face of mounting trials and that, regardless of a world in flames, he himself can live a life of complete fulfillment.

As we have viewed the two antithetical scenarios in the stage of the world as it seems to be emerging, the prospects are that Toynbee had the clearer vision of the evolving drama. His vision stemmed from his conviction that man, man the ordinary individual, does have deep-running spiritual resources which in periods of crisis enable him to rise above his habitual embedment in the surrounding environment. Toynbee believed that these resources will lead man back to a way of life in the twenty-first century founded in his relationship with God.

Nietzsche despised the "common" man and trusted only in the "elite." But, historically, it is always the common man who survives the crises. It is the common man with his hard, good sense, patience, courage and loyalty to his beliefs who fills the breach when the fainthearted would surrender. It is this "passively industrious mass of humanity," as Toynbee termed the "drowsy sleepers" who need to be awakened and, if this writer has analyzed the prospects correctly, who will be awakened in the years immediately ahead by those brief candles which the theistic Diaspora represents.

One must admit the twentieth century so far has offered a "sporty course." And the next few decades leading into the twenty-first will likely offer the greatest challenge that man has faced in all of history. It is the challenge, however, that can be met and produce, in the twenty-first century for man, at last, the true age of an integrated humanity. The action and outcome rest with each of us as individuals and as members of society. That others are indifferent is no excuse. Indifference is but a mask of uncertainty, of lack of knowledge or of will. Life has a meaning, or it has not. The question must be asked and must be answered. A man has but one life. He is given one opportunity to find the answer and the meaning, or fail. For him, his individual response is all that matters.

The time has come to leave Plato's cave and seek the light and answers in that light. If we fail to go, but remain instead chained in the darkness, our life becomes the Absurdity of Camus, L'Nausee of Sartre, the tragedy expressed by the beseiged and doomed Macbeth:

Out, out, brief candle!
Life's but a walking shadow, a poor player
That struts and frets his hour upon the stage
And then is heard no more; it is a tale
Told by an idiot, full of sound and fury,
Signifying nothing.

Act V, Scene V.

BIBLIOGRAPHY

Prefatory Comment

Because, in this work, I have borrowed so heavily from the efforts of others, I consider it fitting to make special mention of that indebtedness here rather than to limit the bibliography to a mere recitation of sources.

First, as a backdrop against which to display the developing concept of man, the work of the eminent American historian and statesman, Carlton J. H. Hayes, has been extensively quoted and otherwise incorporated in the text in general references. Hayes's *Political and Cultural History of Modern Europe* accompanied the writer throughout the Pacific Theater during the seemingly endless years and months of World War II. During some of these years, Hayes was the U.S. Ambassador to Spain and is credited with contributing, in a major way, to keeping that nation neutral in the conflict. It was natural that this writer use Hayes' work as the basic historical text of the major period under study. It has all the comfortable familiarity of an old friend. The thorough scholarship and fast-flowing literary style of Hayes' writing make the study of history pure enjoyment. And of course, the central historical thread of this work has been developed from Arnold J. Toynbee, the preeminent figure in what may be called a philosophy of history.

The clear, incisive works of Alvin Gouldner were also prime sources in the field of sociology. Gouldner's statement of the myriad problems and issues facing sociology, and clearly implied by society itself, did much to stimulate this writer's own approach to the problem. Gouldner's viewpoints, while not necessarily agreeable with this writer's, are forthright, lucid, and always thought-provoking. His is sociologic commentary at its best.

Freeman Dyson's article on "Energy in the Universe" is a brilliant combination of the not too technical and yet comprehensive delineation of the mystery of the unfolding universe. It was, seemingly, made to order to the writer's requirements for a work which could carry to the non-technical, but scientifically literate reader, the awe-inspiring evidence of the creative purposefulness and intelligence which must lie behind it. He expressed clearly the deep appreciation for that intelligence which most physical scientists seem to feel.

The essay by H. Margenau and J. E. Smith on the "Philosophy of Physical Science in the Twentieth Century" likewise furnished a lucid picture of the status of the philosophical approaches evolving in the physical sciences and, simultaneously, a good picture of the emerging thought in the world of microphysics.

The masterful philosophic works constituting an in-depth survey of recent and current philosophic thought by I. M. Bochenski and James Collins were invaluable in the writer's attempts to project the direction of the now emerging trends in philosophy. For the overall history of philosophy, the writer leaned heavily on the massive work in that area by Frederick Copleston, S.J.

Those authors have provided this writer with the main benchmarks and baselines from which his own surveys could start. Many, many others contributed substantially in the overall development. Chief among these were Bertrand Russell, Alfred N. Whitehead, John Dewey, Maurice Merleau-Ponty, Albert Camus, Dennis Wrong, Neil Smelser, Pitirim Sorokin, Duncan Williams, Lewis Coser, Talcott Parsons, Rolf Dahrendorf, Frank Kapp, Philipp Frank, John Haffert, Alexis Carrel, Pierre Auger, Adrienne Koch, Abraham Kaplan, Ferrater Mora, Jose Ortega y Gassett, Brand Blanshard, M. D. Chenu, F. J. Sheed, Donald H. Mensel, Romano Guardini, Bruno Sammaciccia, Walter Kaufmann, K. A. Kitchen, Martin Buber, Paul Tillich, Rudolph Bultmann, Malcolm Diamond, Geerhardus Vos, Karl Rahner, Meredith Kline, Huston Smith, Carl Jung and Sigmund Freud.

BIBLIOGRAPHY

Albright, W. F.
    1949, The Archaeology of Palestine, Baltimore: Penguin Books, Inc.
Ali Abdullah Yusut
    1965, The Holy Quran, Beirut: Printing Production. (copyright Khalil Al-Rawaf).
Allport, Gordon W.
    1963, Pattern and Growth in Personality, New York: Holt, Rinehard and Winston.
Aradi, Zsolt
    1954, Shrines to Our Lady Around the World, New York: Farrar, Straus and Young.
Aristotle (Translation by John H. MacMahon) 1943, On Man in the Universe, Roslyn, New York: Walter J. Black, Inc.

Ashton, Beryl G.
1967, Genes, Chromosomes and Evolution, Boston: Houghton Mifflin Company.

Auger, Pierre
1963, Structure and Complexity in the Universe (In the Evolution of Science, Metraux, 1963, Ed.).

Behrens, Helen
1964, The Virgin of Guadalupe, Mexico D.F.: Editorial Progresso S.A.

Benz, Ernst (Translation, Richard and Clara Winston) 1963, The Eastern Orthodox Church, New York: Doubleday and Co.

Blanshard, Brand
1966, A Verdict on Epiphenomenalism in Current Philosophic Issues, edited by Frederick Dummeyer, Springfield, Ill: Charles C. Thomas Publishers.

Bochenski, I. M. (Translation by Donald Nicholl and Karl Aschenbrenner)
1956, Contemporary European Philosophy, Berkeley: University of California Press.

Boller, Paul F. Jr.
1971, American Thought in Transition. The Impact of Evolutionary Naturalism (1865-1900), Chicago: Rand McNally Co., Inc.

Bourke, Vernon J.
1968, History of Ethics, Garden City, New York: Doubleday.

Buber, Martin
1970, I and Thou (Walter Kaufmann, translator and editor), New York: Scribner Co.

Bultmann, Rudolf
1953, The New Testament and Mythology (Kerygma and Myth), H. A. Bortsch, ed., New York: McMillan Co.

Carrel, Anne (Alexis, Posthumously)
1950, Voyage to Lourdes, New York: Harper and Row Publisher, Inc.

Carty, Charles Mortimer
1971, Padre Pio, The Stigmatist, Rockford, Ill.: TAN Books and Publishers, Inc.

Casali, Giuseppe
1965, Santa Zita, Lucca: Edizioni Regnum Christi.

Caserta, Aldo and Gastone Lambertini
1972, Storia Science de Fronte al Miracolo di S. Gennaro, Naples: D'Auria.

Cassagnard, Chanoine J. M.
1971, Carrel et Zola Devant Le Miracle a Lourdes, Lourdes: Editions de la Grotte.

Chesterton, G. K.
1956, St. Thomas Aquinas, The Dumb Ox, Garden City, N.Y.: Doubleday Inc.

Chenu, M. D. (Translation by Albert M. Landry and Dominic Hughes)
1964, Toward Understanding St. Thomas, Chicago: The Henry Regnery Co.

Chevrot, Georges
1961, On the Third Day, Dublin: Scepter Publishers Ltd.
Churchill, Winston S.
1948, The Gathering Storm, Cambridge, Mass: The Riverside Press.
Collingwood, R. G.
1942, The New Leviathan, Oxford: Clarendon Press.
Collins, James
1969, Crossroads in Philosophy, Chicago: The Henry Regnery Co., (Gateway Edition).
Copleston, Frederick, S.J.
1967, A History of Philosophy (in 8 volumes), Garden City, New York: Image Books.
Coser, Lewis A. (Ed.).
1967, Continuities in the Study of Social Conflict, New York: Free Press.
1956, The Functions of Social Conflict, New York: Free Press.
Crisogono, P.
1971, Vida de Santa Teresa, Madrid: Editorial de Espiritualidad.
Dahrendorf, Rolf
1967, Essays in the Theory of Society, Stanford, California: Stanford University Press.
Daniel-Rops, Henri (Translation, Patrick O'Brian).
1962, Daily Life in the Time of Jesus, New York: Hawthorn Books, Inc.
1960, (Translation, Alastair Guinan) The Book of Mary, New York: Hawthorn Books, Inc.
Davies, C.S.L.
1977, Peace, Print and Protestantism, London: Hart Davis McGibbon Ltd.
De Cayeux, Andre (Translation, Joyce E. Clemow).
1969, Three Billion Years of Life, New York: Stein and Day, Publishers.
De Rosa, Peter
1967, Christ and Original Sin, Milwaukee: The Bruce Publishing Co.
Dewey, John
1965, The Influence of Darwin on Philosophy, Bloomington, Ill.: Indiana University Press.
Diamond, Malcolm L.
1974, Contemporary Philosophy and Religious Thought, New York: McGraw Hill Book Co.
Dunaway, Philip and George de Key
1958, Turning Point, New York: Random House.
Durkin, Joseph T.
1965, Hope for Our Time, New York: Harper and Row Publishers.
Dyson, Freeman J.
1971, Energy in the Universe in Scientific American, September 1971.
Eldon, G. R.
1963, Reformation Europe 1517-1558, Glasgow: William Collins Sons and Co. Ltd.

Erasmus, Desiderius
  1942, The Praise of Folly, (Translation by John Wilson, 1627). Foreword by Hendrik Van Loon, Roslyn, N.Y.: Walker J. Black, Inc.
Fiedler, Leslie A.
  1964, Waiting for the End, New York: Stein and Day.
Frank, Philipp (Translation by George Rosen).
  1963, Einstein, His Life and Times, New York: Alfred A. Knopf.
Freud, Sigmund (Translation by James Strachey).
  1963, The Standard Edition of the Complete Psychological Works of Sigmund Freud, Vol. XV (Introductory Lectures on Psycho Analysis), London: The Hogarth Press.
  1933, New Introductory Lectures on Psycho Analysis (Translation, W. J. H. Sprott), New York: W. W. Norton and Company, Inc.
Gouldner, Alvin W.
  1970, The Coming Crisis of Western Sociology, New York: Basic Books, Inc.
Guardini, Romano (Translation, Joseph Theman and Herbert Burke).
  1968, The End of the Modern World, Chicago: Henry Regnery Co.
  1961, Power and Responsibility, (Translation, Elinor C. Briefs), Chicago: Henry Regnery Co.
  1960, The Conversion of St. Augustine, (Translation, Elinor C. Briefs), Chicago: Henry Regnery Co.
  1952, The Faith and Modern Man, (Translation, Charlotte E. Forsyth), Chicago: Henry Regnery Co.
Haffert, John M.
  1967, The World's Greatest Secret, Washington, N.J.: AMI Press.
Hardman, James B.
  1967, Philosophy of Recent Times, New York: McGraw-Hill.
Hayes, Carlton, J. H.
  1932, A Political and Cultural History of Modern Europe, New York: The Macmillan Co.
Heidegger, Martin (Translation by Ralph Manheim).
  1961, Introduction to Metaphysics, New Haven, Conn.: Yale University Press.
Heilbroner, Robert L.
  1964, The Worldly Philosophers, New York: Simon and Schuster, Inc.
Herberg, Will
  1956, The Writings of Martin Buber, New York: Meridian Books.
Hobbes, Thomas
  1962, Leviathan, London: Aldine House.
Hodges, H. A. in Reformation Old and New, F. W. Camfield Ed. 1947, The Crisis of Philosophy, London:
Hughes, Philip
  1970, A Short History of the Catholic Church, London: Search Press Ltd.
Imperato, Giuseppe
  1956, Ravello and Its Beauties, Salerno: de Luca.

Jeans, James H.
1961, Astronomy and Cosmogony, New York: Dover Publications, Inc.
1958, The Growth of Physical Science, Greenwich, Conn.:
Fawcett Publications, Inc.

Joad, E.E.M., Ed.
1960, Classics in Philosophy and Ethics, New York:
Philosophical Library Inc.

Jones, W. T.
1969, A History of Western Philosophy, New York: Harcourt, Bruce
and World, Inc.

Jongen, H. (Translation by Francis M. White).
1959, Look—The Madonna is Weeping, Bay Shore, New York:
Monfort Publications.

Joniaux—Dufresnoy, Fabien
1969, Dieu Existe Et il T'Aime Toi, Paris: Editions Ligel.

Jung, Carl G.
1972, Four Archetypes, (Translation, R. F. G. Hall), London: Routledge and Kegan Paul Ltd.
1971, Psychological Reflection, (Jolande Jacobi Ed.), London:
Routledge and Kegan Paul Ltd.
1961, Modern Man in Search of a Soul, (Translation, Carl F. Baynes),
London: Routledge and Kegan Paul Ltd.

Kaplan, Abraham
1961, The New World of Philosophy, New York: Random House.

Kapp, Reginald O.
1960, Toward a Unified Cosmology, New York: Basic Books Inc.

Kaufman, Gorden D.
1960, Relativism, Knowledge and Faith, Chicago: The University of
Chicago Press.

Kaufmann, Walter
1956, Existentialism, New York: The New American Library, Inc.

Kenniston, Kenneth
1965, The Uncommitted, New York: Dell Publishing Co.

Kierkegaard, Soren
1970, The Sickness Unto Death, Princeton, N.J.: Princeton Press.

Kitchen, K. A.
1966, Ancient Orient and Old Testament, Chicago: Inter Varsity Press.

Kline, Meredith G.
1968, By Oath Consigned, Grand Rapids: William B. Ferdman's
Publishing Co.

Koch, Adrienne
1959, Philosophy for a Time of Crisis, New York: E. P. Dutton and
Co., Inc.

Kristeller, Paul Oskar
1972, Renaissance Concepts of Man, New York: Harper and Row
Publishers.

Lamirande, Emilien, OMI, (Translation A. Manson).
1963, The Communion of Saints, New York: Hawthorn Books Publishers.

La Tourelle, Rene
1967, Theology of Revelation, Staten Island: Alba House.

Lercaro, Cardinal, Bologna, (Translation, T. F. Lindsay)
1957, Methods of Mental Prayer, Westminster, Maryland: The Newman Press.

Lienhardt, Godfrey
1964, Social Anthropology, New York: Oxford University Press.

Loewe, Michael
1968, Everyday Life in Early Imperial China, New York: G. P. Putnam's Sons.

Lonergan, Bernard J. F.
1958, Insight, New York: Harper and Row, Publishers.

Lortz, Joseph
1968, The Reformation in Germany, New York: Herder and Herder.

Machiavelli, Niccolo, (John Plamenatz, Ed.).
1972, Machiavelli, The Prince, Selections from the Discourses and Other Writings, London: Wm. Collins Sons, Ltd.

Marcel, Gabriel
1967, *Foi Et Realite,* Aubier: Editions Montaigne.

Marcuse, Herbert
1968, Negations, Boston: Beacon Press.

Margenau, H. and J. E. Smith
1963, Philosophy of Physical Science in the Twentieth Century (in The Evolution of Science, Metraux, 1963 Ed.).

Maritain, Jacques
1954, Man and The State, London: Charles Birchall and Sons, Ltd.
1952, Human Knowledge and Metaphysics, New York: Scribner and Co.
1952, The Range of Reason, New York: Scribner and Co.

Mascall E. L.
1957, Christian Theology and Natural Science, London: Longmans Green and Co. Ltd.

McDonagh, Enda
1972, Invitation and Response, New York: Sheed and Ward.

Mensel, Donald H., Fred L. Whipple and Gerard de Vaucouleurs
1970, Survey of the Universe, Englewood Cliffs, N.J.. Prentice Hall, Inc.

Merleau-Ponty, Maurice, (Alden L. Fisher, Translator)
1963, The Structure of Behavior, Boston: Beacon Press.
1962, Phenomonology of Perception, (Colin Smith, Translator), New York: Humanities Press.

Metraux, Guy S. and Francois Crouzet
1963, The Evolution of Science, New York: New American Library of World Literature, Inc.

Miller, S. M.
1963, Max Weber, New York: Thomas Y. Crowell Co.
Montagu, Ashley
1969, Man His First Two Million Years, New York:
Columbia University Press.
Montaigne, Michael de, (Translation by Donald M. Frame) 1943, Selected
Essays, Rosyln, N.Y.: Walter J. Black, Inc.
Mora, Jose Ferrater
1957, Man at the Crossroads, Boston: Beacon Press.
Musumeci, Ottavio, (Translation, Rosario Musumeci Tringoli).
1954, The Madonna Wept in Syracuse: Syracuse: Marchese.
Nelkin, Dorothy
1976, "Man, a Course of Study" in Scientific American, April 1976.
Novak, Michael
1965, Belief and Unbelief, New York: Macmillan Co.
O'Brien, John A.
1942, God: Can We Find Him? Glenrock, N.Y.: Paulist Press.
Oliveira, Joseph Galambra de, (Translation by Humberto S. Madeiros
and William F. Hill).
1972, Jacinta—The Flower of Fatima, Washington, N.J.:
AMI International Press.
Olivieri, Alfonso
1972, Avvengono Ancora Miracoli a Lourdes, Rome: Essi-Gi-Essi.
Ong, Walter J.
1968, Knowledge and the Future of Man, New York: Simon and
Schuster.
Ortega y Gasset, Jose, (Translation, Toby Talbot).
1967, The Origin of Philosophy, New York: W. W. Norton Company, Inc.
Ortiz, Alfonso
1969, The Tewa World, Chicago: The University of Chicago Press.
Padovano, Anthony T.
1966, The Estranged God, New York: Sheed and Ward.
Parsons, Talcott
1964, Evolutionary Universals in Society in American Sociological
Review, Vol. 29.
Peschke, C. Henry
1977, Christian Ethics, Dublin: C. Goodliffe Neale.
Plato, (Translation by B. Jowett).
1942, Plato—Five Great Dialogues, Roslyn, N.Y.: Walter J. Black, Inc.
Rahner, Karl, (Translation, Hilda Graef).
1969, Grace in Freedom, New York: Herder and Herder.
1968, Spirit in the World, New York: Herder and Herder.
1964, The Eternal Year, (Translated by John Shea), Baltimore:
Helicon Press, Inc.
1963, Mary Mother of the Lord, (Translation, W. J. O'Hara),
New York: Herder and Herder Co.
1963, The Christian Commitment, (Translation, Cecily Hastings),
New York: Sheed and Ward.

Ravier, Andre
1973, The Body of Saint Bernadette, Beseancon, IME.
Regan, George M.
1971, New Trends in Moral Theology, New York: Newman Press.
Rinaldi, Peter M.
1973, It Is The Lord, New York: Warner Paperback Library.
Runes, Dagobert D.
1972, Dictionary of Philosophy, Totawa, N.J.: Littlefield Adams and Co.
St. Augustine, (Translation by F. J. Sheed).
1943, The Confessions of St. Augustine, New York: Sheed and Ward, Inc.
Sammaciccia, Bruno
1973, Il Miracolo Eucaristico di Lanciano, Lanciano:
Sanctuario del Miracolo.
San Jose, R. P. Fabian de
1961, Padre Balbino Del Carmelo, Madrid: Imprenta-Colegiata.
Scheler, Max
1972, On The Eternal Man, (Translation, Bernard Noble).
Hamden, Connecticut: The Shoe String Press, Inc.
Schrader, George Alfred Jr. (Ed.).
1967, Existential Philosophers: Kierkegaard to Merleau-Ponty,
New York: McGraw Hill Inc.
Schuster, Idelfonso, Cardinal
1954, Profilo Storico del B. Placido Riccardi O.S.B.,
Milan: Edizione S.T.E.M.
Simpson, George
1963, Emile Durkheim, New York: Thomas Y. Crowell, Co.
Sisters of Charity
1968, La Sainte Du Silence, Paris: Sisters of Charity of St. Vincent
de Paul, Rue de Bac, Paris.
Smelser, Neil J.
1962, Theory of Collective Behavior, New York: The Free Press.
Smith, Huston
1958, The Religions of Man, New York: Harper and Bros.
Sorokin, Pitirim A.
1966, Sociological Theories of Today, New York: Harper and Row
Publishers.
Sorokin, Pitirim A. and Walter A. Lunden
1959, Power and Morality, Boston: Porter Sargent Publisher.
Teilhard de Chardin, Pierre, (Translation by Norman Denny).
1959, The Future of Man, New York: Harper and Row Publishers.
Thurston, Herbert, S.J. (J. H. Crehan S.J. Ed. Posth).
1952, The Physical Phenomena of Mysticism, Chicago:
Henry Regnery Company.
Tillich, Paul
1957, Dynamics of Faith, New York: Harper Co.
Trouncer, Margaret
1959, Saint Jean Marie Vianney: Curé of Ars, New York:
Sheed and Ward.

Unamuno, Miguel de, (Translation, J. E. Crawford Flitch).
1954, Tragic Sense of Life, New York: Dover Publishers, Inc.
vanKaam, Adrian
1969, Existential Foundations of Psychology, Garden City, New York:
Image Books.
Van Til, Cornelius
1972, Common Grace and the Gospel, Philadelphia:
Presbyterian and Reformed Publishing Co.
Vos, Geerhardus
1948, Biblical Theology, Grand Rapids: Wm. B. Eerdmans Publishing Co.
Wahlig, C. J.
1973, Juan Diego, Mexico D.F.: Editorial Progresso, S.A.
Williams, Duncan
1971, Trousered Apes, New Rochelle, New York:
Dell Publishing Co., Inc.
Wittgenstein, Ludwig
1951, Tractatus Logico Philosophicus, London:
Routledge and Kegal Paul Ltd.
Wrong, Dennis
1961, The Oversocialized Conception of Man, (American Sociological Review, XXVI pp. 185-193).

ABOUT THE AUTHOR

Father John Coony was born in Santa Monica, California in July, 1916. He became a priest late in life, being ordained at the age of 64. As a young man John Coony studied engineering at Loyola University in Los Angeles and at the University of Southern California, receiving the B.S.C.E. degree from U.S.C. in June of 1938. He joined the U.S. Army Corps of Engineers as a civilian on August 15, 1938 and worked in Water Resources Planning with the Los Angeles and Sacramento Districts until June of 1942, when he was commissioned an officer with the Corps. He served three years in the Solomon Islands, the Philippines and Japan and then returned to work as a civilian with the Corps' Los Angeles District in June of 1946.

Just before World War II, In September of 1941, John Coony married Frances Wilson of Alamosa, Colorado. The first wedding anniversary the couple was able to spend together was five years later.

In subsequent years they lived at many locations in the United States and around the world—thirteen to be exact—on assignment with the Corps of Engineers. In 1963 the future Father Coony was selected as the Chief of Design for the Canaveral

District of the Corps, responsible for the design and construction of the facilities for the U.S. Space Program, including those for the Apollo lunar landings and explorations. He was then assigned as Chief Engineer of the Mediterranean Division of the Corps for construction in Europe and Asia, from Italy to Burma, and in Africa, from Libya to Somalia. His last assignment was Chief of the Sytems Engineering Division of the Huntsville Division for the Sentinel-Safeguard Anti-Ballistic Missile (A.B.M.) Program. He has been a registered professional engineer in California since September of 1947.

John Coony retired in July of 1971, when the A.B.M. program was curtailed by the United States' SALT Agreement with the U.S.S.R. He received a master's degree in sociology from the University of Texas at El Paso in December of 1973. He is a member of the Southern Sociological Society.

John Coony's wife, Frances, died on Christmas Day, 1972. During the subsequent years the thought of studying for the priesthood often came to him; the idea became increasingly urgent—but, in view of his age, increasingly unlikely, as well.

Then in 1976, while engaged in short-term engineering work in Athens, Greece, the future Father Coony happened to meet Father Royce Hughes at St. Dionysius Cathedral in Athens. Father Hughes, who is the Director of the International Studies Program for delayed vocations, invited him to join the program, which he did in the fall semester of 1977. Both priests believe their meeting was providential. Father Coony received the S.T.B. degree from the *Angelicum* in Rome in June of 1980 and was ordained priest on January 18, 1981 for ministry of the pious union, *Pro Fratribus,* under the direction of Bishop Paul Hnilica S.J., a Czechoslovakian refugee. The work of the Pious Union consists of providing spiritual assistance to those behind the "Iron Curtain," both the persecutors and the persecuted.

Through the gracious hospitality of Archbishop Robert Sanchez, Father Coony established the Pious Union in the United States in 1980 with headquarters in the Diocese of Santa Fe, New Mexico. There are now about 14,000 members of *Pro Fratribus* in the United States. The spirituality of the Pious Union is Trinitarian and Eucharistic, with emphasis on the approach to the Godhead through the intercessory powers of the Blessed Virgin Mary.

Father Coony is convinced that the malaise of secular humanism infecting the world will be overcome by an avalanche of grace. Man will return to God, but we must do our part through steadfast prayer and sacrifice.

NOTES

NOTES

NOTES

NOTES